SpringerBriefs in Finance

SpringerBriefs present concise summaries of cutting-edge research and practical applications across a wide spectrum of fields. Featuring compact volumes of 50 to 125 pages, the series covers a range of content from professional to academic. Typical topics might include: a timely report of state-of-the art analytical techniques, a bridge between new research results, as published in journal articles, and a contextual literature review, a snapshot of a hot or emerging topic, an in-depth case study or clinical example, and a presentation of core concepts that students must understand in order to make independent contributions. SpringerBriefs in Finance showcase emerging theory, empirical research, and practical application in corporate finance, banking, financial management, behavioral finance, financial markets, social and entrepreneurial finance, microfinance, and related fields, from a global author community. Briefs are characterized by fast, global electronic dissemination, standard publishing contracts, standardized manuscript preparation and formatting guidelines, and expedited production schedules.

More information about this series at http://www.springer.com/series/10282

Yonghyup Oh

Sustainability Valuation of Business

Springer

Yonghyup Oh
University of Antwerp
Antwerpen, Belgium

ISSN 2193-1720 ISSN 2193-1739 (electronic)
SpringerBriefs in Finance
ISBN 978-3-030-18647-0 ISBN 978-3-030-18648-7 (eBook)
https://doi.org/10.1007/978-3-030-18648-7

This Springer imprint is published by the registered company Springer Nature Switzerland AG
The registered company address is: Gewerbestrasse 11, 6330 Cham, Switzerland

To my parents,

Preface

The word "sustainability" throughout this book follows its most commonly used definition that spans environmental, economic, and noneconomic human right-related social sustainability. Our method is a conceptual framework in which the value of a business is determined by the values of sustainability businesses contribute to the sustainability of society. This is the main departure from conventional valuation methods. Our method finds a win-win situation between businesses and the sustainability of society, as the value of the business would increase only if the business improves the sustainability of society. While it serves as a basis for valuation for virtually all businesses, the actual implementation will require a certain degree of empirical adaption.

Antwerpen, Belgium Yonghyup Oh

Acknowledgements

I would like to thank the participants of the workshops I gave at the Club of Rome—EU Chapter in Brussels where my first thought on this monograph was born. My special thanks are due to Daniel Abts, Jesus Alqueszar-Sabadie, Seung Kwan Baek, Ian Channing, Matthew Rendall, and Georges de Ménil. Their help at various stages was essential to complete this book. I thank seminar participants at the 3rd Corporate Social Responsibility conference in Köln, at the 22nd ISDRS conference in Lisbon, at the 5th EcoSummit in Montpellier, and at the 8th World Health Summit in Berlin, this last for which I gratefully acknowledge financial aid from the headquarter of the Club of Rome. I thank the reviewers to whom I am gratefully indebted for the improvement of the original manuscript. I thank Judith Kripp, Femina Joshi Arul Thas, and in particular Barbara Fess, at Springer for their help throughout the process.

Contents

List of Figures

List of Tables

List of Boxes

Chapter 1
Structure of Sustainability Valuation

Climate is res communis (common property) that belongs to mankind and as such can never be private property. Emperor Justinianus (Eastern Roman Empire, 534AD)

1.1 Win-Win Between Business and Sustainable Development of Society

Would businesses acting more environmentally friendly or more socially conscious receive a higher value in the market than those less so, other things being equal? Sustainability valuation of business aspires to do precisely what would be necessary to make this happen.

Sustainability of society is considered accruing on three pillars as environmental, economic, and social. While economic sustainability is completely payable, values creating environmental and social sustainability are not as payable. In the context of business, businesses produce economic sustainability by producing goods and services and are paid for what they sell. In this production process, businesses also produce environmental or social sustainability, positive or negative, which tends to be easier to be ignored. As a result, those not payable are not included in the value of business. Increasing business values may detriment sustainability of society that business wins and society loses.

The role of sustainability valuation is to find undiscovered cash values that are linked to sustainability that business produces. It builds on the philosophy that it facilitates win-win situation between the value of business and the level of sustainability of society.[1] Sustainability values produced by business are reflected in the value of business because they affect sustainability of society. This kind of win-win situation

[1]There are various contexts of win-win situation. One of the canonical examples may include one in the context of economic development and climate change engagement given in Appendix A.

Y. Oh, *Sustainability Valuation of Business*,
SpringerBriefs in Finance,
https://doi.org/10.1007/978-3-030-18648-7_1

is particularly important in the era in which sustainable development is the ultimate goal of society as now.

Inclusion of such values in the actual value of business can appear naturally if more people recognize such values and are willing to pay the prices attached to them. It can also appear institutionally if policymakers find it useful to enforce in order to progress sustainability goals further. Once certain sustainability values are cashed, they are automatically included in the market value of business as this implies that they enter into the official accounting system of business. Once this practice spreads, it is certain that businesses will function in the way that they improve sustainability of society. In such case, sustainability values whose origins are non-economic become integrated into economic sustainability.

The scope of valuation of business is complex in the case of sustainability valuation. In particular, the success of sustainability valuation lies in discerning businesses acting sustainability conscious from those less so and working toward granting higher values to those businesses. This is a reason why active engagement of the public sector is assumed, as policymakers are in the position to recognize non-cashable sustainability values as cashable.

1.2 *De Jure* and *De Facto* Sustainability Values

An individual consumes goods and services, private or public. These goods and services produce economic sustainability as they are payable. We may broaden the perspective of goods and services to that of sustainability in a holistic way. Goods and services would include not only conventional economic goods and services but also the ecosystem and the ecosystem services, and other services that are not remunerated. The qualities of these goods and services and their quantities would determine the level of sustainability in the right formula of the holistic calculation of sustainability. We do not have quantifiable holistic measures of sustainability.[2] While such measures may give more precision in decision making, we can proceed without them and build a conceptual framework of sustainability valuation.

Figure 1.1 is a capture of how sustainability is compiled at the society level into its three pillars. All goods and services of sustainability create sustainability values that contribute to improving the three pillars of sustainability and may be entitled to have prices. Sustainability of society is the sum of sustainability values that are generated in the society that can be attributed to one of three pillars of sustainability. The subjects that produce sustainability and possess values (sustainability values) are sustainability elements.

[2] A related issue is the critique on the gross domestic product (GDP) as a measure of sustainability. A brief discussion on this is given in Appendix B.

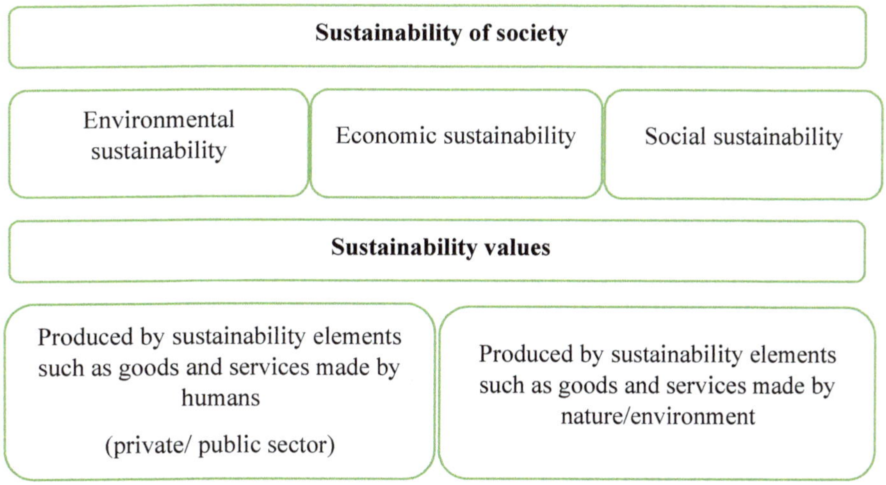

Fig. 1.1 Sustainability of society

de jure and *de facto* sustainability

Sustainability values may be further decomposed into (1) those that are already being remunerated (*de facto* sustainability), (2) those that are entitled to be remunerated but not yet remunerated (*de jure* sustainability), and (3) those that are granted for free (*sacris* sustainability). The sizes and the elements of the three components are varying over time and can be very heterogeneous across different geographical areas.

The determination of *de jure* sustainability is granted by the judgment if anyone is taking advantage of the situation taking profits that harms sustainability, or not receiving benefits for the good that the person is doing on sustainability of society. Emergence of elements that used to produce *sacris* sustainability turning into producing *de jure* sustainability implies that sustainability of society is likely to be deteriorating. In other words, there is sustainability justice to be resolved. Transferring *de jure* sustainability into *de facto* sustainability on the other hand improves sustainability of society. Sustainability justice is done if such correction is made.

It is straightforward to extend the notion of production from one associated with the goods and services in the conventional sense to the one associated with sustainability: Production of sustainability would refer to production of three elements of sustainability, namely environmental, economic, and social. The ideology of business in search of profits may conflict with the ideology of sustainability of society. This conflict may persist, but there seems to be ample room to reduce it, possibly in a harmonious way.

Does economic sustainability, one of the three pillars of sustainability, entail *sacris* sustainability and *de jure* sustainability? The answer is yes *sacris* economic sustainability implies that there will always be an area which will be discovered and turned into *de jure* economic sustainability whether cashable or not *de jure* sustainability implies that a project may have economic value, but not all elements may have cashable prospect.

Businesses search opportunities in which *de jure* sustainability values can be transferable to *de facto* sustainability, as this means earning money. Businesses would exploit all the opportunities to realize *de facto* sustainability that may exist in the market for their goods and services and transfer *de jure* sustainability into *de facto* sustainability. But the set of *de jure* sustainability is determined by members of society. Transferring it to *de facto* sustainability should resolve contradictory interests and different opinions, which may involve political process.

1.3 Structure of Sustainability Valuation

1.3.1 Sequence of Sustainability Valuation

In the context of business, *de jure* sustainability refers to the values that should be reflected in the value of business *de facto* sustainability is already reflected in business values. Sustainability valuation is to reduce the gap between *de jure* and *de facto* sustainability produced by business. This requires a process in which one needs to know how sustainability of a society is built and progresses and how policymaking directs them, how businesses are contributing to the sustainability of society, as well as identify *de jure* sustainability of business in the society, how money values that businesses earn are in line with sustainability of society, review the facilities to transfer it to *de facto* sustainability, and reflect the transfer from *de jure* sustainability into *de facto* sustainability in the calculation of future cashflows. In addition, one needs to estimate the cost of capital of business, in other words discount rates. Once future cashflows and their cost of capital are obtained, it is straightforward to calculate the discounted future cashflows which is in effect the value of business of today.

Figure 1.2 summarizes the sequence of sustainability valuation.

The framework of sustainability valuation connects the macrolevel sustainability to microlevel firm value. This connection is mediated by the public sector. Being the facilitator to help create and preserve sustainability of society, the public sector[3] interacts with businesses and induces them to become more engaged in the production of sustainability. In this process, one identifies sustainability values produced by a business beyond the values related to economic sustainability, actively searching for new *de jure* sustainability and opportunities to transfer it into *de facto* sustainability.

This process is sufficiently adaptive that it would allow the public sector to learn from the private sector and jointly establish a system of sustainability for the society. This system of sustainability allows sustainability values of each business to be identified in all three dimensions of sustainability. The public sector modifies its means (taxes, incentives, regulations, and so forth) to facilitate this process.

---

[3]Civil societies can be considered a part of the public sector in this regard.

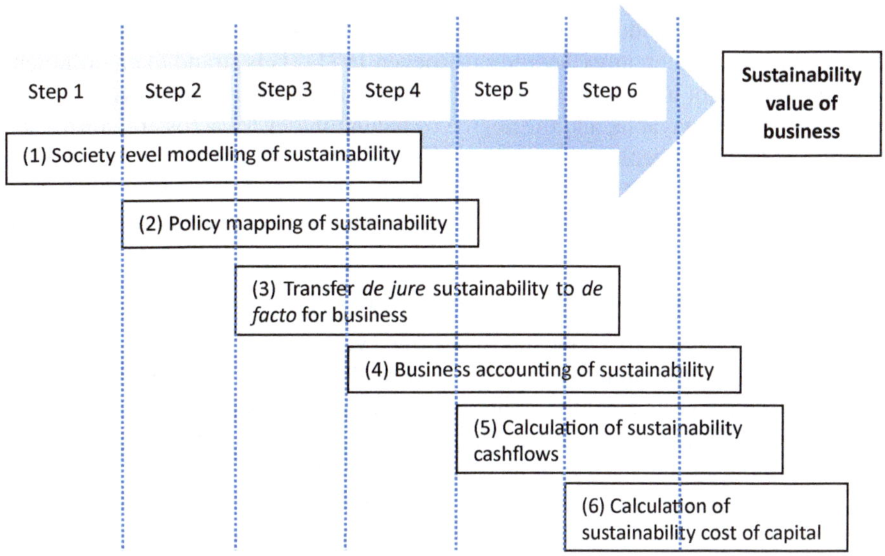

Fig. 1.2 Sequence of sustainability valuation

The job of the valuator doing sustainability valuation necessitates a good idea of the level of sustainability of the society and its ideal state. It understands how this gap can be narrowed via policymaking.

1.3.2 Distinguished Features of Sustainability Valuation

(A) ***Comparison with conventional valuation of business***

Conventional valuation refers to the family of the valuation method whose framework is completed in Copeland et al. (1990) and its later version (Koller et al. 2005). Miller and Modigliani (1961) is an influential work to bring this method to the market. It calculates in steps future cashflows and future capital structure. The present value of a business is the estimated future cashflows discounted at the business-specific cost of capital applicable. As the comparison between sustainability valuation and conventional valuation is made throughout this book, just one notable remark may merit here. Sustainability valuation is identical to conventional valuation once there is no more *de jure* sustainability of business in the future. This is not a likely scenario in practice.

(B) ***Comparison with environmental valuation or valuations of ecosystem and ecosystem services***

The valuation of resources uses energy as a numeraire to denominate the value of resources (Odum and Odum 1976; Randall 1987). Such approach typically follows thermodynamic laws to identify energy and material flows to value the natural ecosystem and the human economy (Georgescu-Roegen 1971). This strand of environmental valuation cannot use cashflows as a unit of measure. Much of the environmental values may not be payable, and the degree of paying may vary across regions.

In the literature of ecological economics (Daly 1968; Roepke 2004; Ayres 1984; Pierce 1987; Christensen 1987; Costanza et al. 1997), cashflows play little role. Values in these exercises are not grounded in transactions because much of them are not traded.

(C) ***Comparison with practices of sustainability valuation in the industry***

This is an area where financial industry offers yet a primitive level of services. Two points are worth mentioning in this regard. First it may not be surprising to see consulting firms (financial, accounting, or auditing firms) among others selling packages of valuation with sustainability implied.[4] We need to be certain that the increase of the value of business in such exercises may turn out to harm sustainability at the society level and see how holistic such approaches are. The underpinning of sustainability valuation that this book prescribes lies in its emphasis on the role of business in improving the sustainability of a society. This is a stark difference from most of other methods that may lack the direct link to the societal sustainability.

Second, we need to be cautious if practices tend to focus on future values of *de facto* sustainability values, cash-earning prospects related to sustainability that are already existing. What would be as important in the valuation of business is to predict the transformation of *de jure* sustainability values into *de facto* values.

(D) ***Comparison with corporate social responsibility (CSR), public–private partnership (PPP), and circular economy (CE)***

There are facilities that help create sustainability values other than sustainability valuation. They include the corporate social responsibility (CSR), the public–private partnership (PPP), and the circular economy (CE).

The corporate social responsibility (CSR) (Caroll 1979; Dahlsrud 2008) according to the European Commission is defined as "*the responsibility of enterprises for their impacts on society.*" And it further states that "*to fully meet their corporate social responsibility, enterprises should have in place a process to integrate social, environmental, ethical and human rights concerns into their business operations and core strategy in close collaboration with their stakeholders*" (EC COM 2011).

The corporate social responsibility refers to the acts of businesses that work toward the fundamental values of sustainability. A slight gap from the sustainability concept of this book is that sustainability endorses growth, while the concept of the CSR concerns the non-growth part of business. Such gap is natural, as the primary activities of businesses center on growth, and the CSR enlightens the ethical duty of business that may not be in line with growth-oriented business interests. This is a reason why there can be tension between the CSR and business. Firms exercising CSR principles

[4]For example, see PwC (https://www.environmentalleader.com/2012/05/pwc-report-how-companies-can-put-a-dollar-value-on-sustainability/).

may perform better in the conventional valuation. Better doing businesses may tend to be more easily engaged in CSR principles. Engaging in CSR principles may send positive signals to the market and customers which may bring new opportunities to business.

Businesses giving donations are acting on corporate social responsibility. These acts are reflected in the value of the business. The public sector may reward them by additional benefits, which will have implications to business values. Sustainability valuation would foresee this possibility and take it into account in valuation.

The public–private partnership (PPP) refers to the practices in which private money is invested to finance public projects. Public projects preserve environmental and social sustainability. In return, the private sector receives the right to develop profit-making model in the project. For example, it can own the right to receive the payout for a fixed period of time in return to their initial investment.

Valuation is a key to the success of such projects. Sustainability concerns may significantly alter the economic profile of such project. Certain sustainability values may not be adequately included in valuation to attract private investment. The PPP was born in the era when sustainability issues were less prominent. It is facing challenges in terms of criteria setting where the PPP can be implemented, and its valuation scheme.

The circular economy (CE) refers to an economy in which wastes are minimized and recycled in the life cycle of a product. Its ultimate goal is zero waste for the whole society.

A completely circular economy would predict that raw materials enter production with the use of only recyclable energy. Waste produced from production and all other operations of the business (e.g. management of offices and sites and logistics) is completely recycled with no residual waste[5] (McDonough 2002).

The circular economy can be a useful concept as a measure of sustainability (Korhonen 2018). It has a direct impact on environmental sustainability. It also helps growth as resources are recycled, saving costs. This alters the way raw materials are procured and processed for production, and the way the entire business is organized and managed. Its primary challenge lies in the supposition that such a principle can be embedded in a business as a veritable business model for all. We will need to make sufficient technological progress to back up the idea of no waste without harming business prospects. We will need regulatory supports to encourage businesses to make transformation to a circular economy model. We will need to resolve all the measurement and accounting issues of the CE for business. Much of these challenges are shared with sustainability valuation.

---

[5]Residual waste is the waste that cannot be processed and erased through waste management. They remain in the ecosystem.

Cited Works

Ayres, R. U. (1984). Theormodynamics and economics. *Physics Today, 37,* 63–68.
Caroll, A. B. (1979). A three-dimensional conceptual model of social performance. *The Academy of Management Review, 4*(4), 497–505.
Christensen, P. (1987). Classical roots for a modern material-energy analysis. *Ecological Modelling, 38,* 75–89.
Copeland, T., Koller, T., & Murrin, J. (1990). Valuation: Measuring and managing the value of companies. Wiley.
Costanza, R., D'Arge, R., De Groot, R., Farber, S., Grasso, M., Hannon, B., et al. (1997). The value of the world's ecosystem services and natural capital. *Nature, 387,* 253–260.
Dahlsrud, A. (2008). How corporate social responsibility is defined: an analysis of 37 definitions. *Corporate Social Responsibility and Environmental Management, 15*(1), 1–13.
Daly, H. E. (1968). On economics as a life science. *Journal of Political Economics, 76,* 392–406.
European Commission. (2011). A renewed EU strategy 2011–14 for corporate social responsibility. *EC COM,* 681. https://ec.europa.eu/growth/industry/corporate-social-responsibility_en.
Georgescu-Roegen, N. (1971). *The entropy law and the economic process.* Cambridge M. A.: Harvard University Press.
Koller, T., Goedhart, M., & Wessels, D. (2010). *Valuation: measuring and managing the value of companies* (4th ed.). Wiley.
Korhonen, J. H. (2018). Circular economy: The concept and its limitations. *Ecological Economics, 143,* 37–46.
McDonough, W. (2002). *Cradle to cradle: Remaking the way we make things.* New York: North Point Press.
Miller, M. H., & Modigliani, F. (1961). Dividend policy, growth, and the valuation of shares. *The Journal of Business, 34*(4), 411–433.
Odum, H. T., & Odum, E. (1976). *Energy: Basis for man and nature.* New York: McGraw-Hill.
Pierce, D. W. (1987). Foundations of ecological economics. *Ecological Modelling, 38,* 9–18.
Randall, A. (1987). *Resource economics: An economic approach to natural resource and environmental policy* (2nd ed.). New York: Wiley.
Roepke, I. (2004). The early history of modern ecological economics. *Ecological Economics, 50,* 293–314.

Further Readings

Albareda, L., Lozano, J. M., & Ysa, T. (2007). Public policies on corporate social responsibility: The role of governments in Europe. *Journal of Business Ethics, 74,* 391–407.
Azzone, G., & Manzini, R. (1994). Measuring strategic environmental performance. *Business Strategy and the Environment, 3*(1), 1–14.
Bénabou, R., & Tirole, J. (2010). Individual and corporate social responsibility. *Economica, 77,* 1–19.
Cheung, S. N. S. (1983). The contractual nature of the firm. *Journal of Law and Economics, 26,* 1–21.
Daly, H. E. (1991). *Steady state economics* (2nd ed.). Washington, D. C: Island Press.
Davis, L., & Hopkins, M. (2011). The institutional foundations of inequity and growth. *Journal of Development Studies, 47*(7), 977–997.
Escrig-Olmedo, E., Muñoz-Torres, M. J., Fernández-Izqierdo, M. Á., & Rivera-Lirio, J. M. (2017). Measuring corporate environmental performance: a methodology for sustainable development. *Business Strategy and the Environment, 26*(2), 142–162.

Gowdy, J. (1997). The value of bio-diversity: Markets, society, and ecosystems. *Land Economics, 73,* 25–41.
Jackson, T., & Victor, P. (2016). Does slow growth lead to rising inequality? Some theoretical reflections and numerical simulations. *Ecological Economics, 121,* 206–219.
Lietaer, B., Arnsperger, C., Goerner, S., & Brunnhuber, S. (2012). Money and Sustainability: The Missing Link. A report from the Club of Rome. EU Chapter to Finance Watch and the World Business Academy, Triarchy Press.
Lee, Norman, & Kirkpatrick, Colin. (2001). Methodologies for sustainability impact assessments of proposals for new trade agreements. *Journal of Environmental Assessment Policy and Management, 3*(3), 395–412.
Levin-Waldman, O. M. (2005). Welfare reform and models of public policy: Why policy sciences are required. *Review of Policy Research, 22*(4), 519–539.
Liang, H., & Renneboog, L. (2017). On the foundations of corporate social responsibility. *Journal of Finance, 72*(2), 853–910.
Lowi, T. J. (2015). *Arenas of power: Reflections on politics and policy*. New York: Routeledge.
Max-Neef, M. (2016). Philosophy of ecological economics. *International Journal of Management and Science, 5,* 366.
Naeem, S., O'Neill, R. V., Paruelo, J., Raskin, R. G., Sutton, P., & van der Belt, M. (1997). The Value of the World's ecosystem services and natural capital. *Nature, 387,* 253–260.
Oh, Y. (2019). Corporate social responsibility and the value of a firm. In R. Schmidpeter (Ed.), *International dimensions of sustainable management, CSR, sustainability, ethics & governance*. Switzerland: Springer Nature.
Windolph, E. S., Schaltegger, S., & Herzig, C. (2014). Implementing corporate sustainability: What drives the application of sustainability management tools in Germany? *Sustainability Accounting, Management and Policy Journal, 5*(4), 378–404.

Chapter 2
Sustainability Channels of Business

Out of own interests, people have authority to delegate making and forcing laws to the state. They keep certain rights that can never be given to the state. These constitutional rights, e.g. right of health and healthy climate, must always be able to be brought to court in case government fails. (Locke, 17th century)

2.1 Sustainability Modeling of Society

Each area of the world owns its own set of sustainability needs and objectives. So do different levels of governance—local, regional, national, international, and global. Ideally, the different levels of governance should fit into the system of sustainability in a holistic way such that flows going through them do neither block nor distort the overarching goals of the highest governance, namely the governance of the earth. Sustainability modeling of society refers to an idea or a picture how sustainability in its three pillars are constructed and how they move for a society. It can be conceptual, intuitive, or quantitative.[1] There is no preference such that such model should be of a certain form or character. What matters in this modeling is the quality of the picture of sustainability of society and the ability to let it advance.

Figure 2.1 indicates how descaling of sustainability can be made. It can be applied to a society at all levels of governance. Theoretical development is integrated in this picture. For instance, it would be adequate to include as elements of environmental sustainability environmental degradation and the degree of substitutability, the latter indicating the degree of technological progress that substitutes natural capital by human-made capital (Neumayer 2013; Dedeurwaerdere 2014).

The tree of sustainability in Fig. 2.1 shows how the most overarching ones can be decomposed to the bottom of the tree. The top layer in the system of sustainability is the three pillars of sustainability, the ultimate sustainability goals. These constitute the overarching goals of sustainability. Under these come sustainability elements in

[1] Appendix D is an example of a macromodeling of sustainability at the earth level.

Y. Oh, *Sustainability Valuation of Business*,
SpringerBriefs in Finance,
https://doi.org/10.1007/978-3-030-18648-7_2

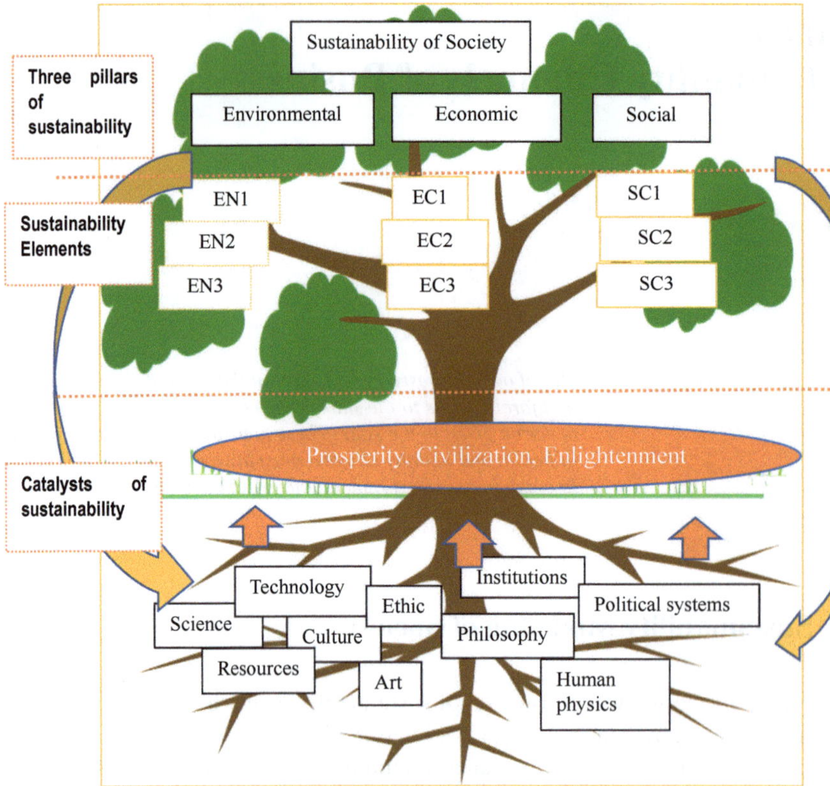

Fig. 2.1 Descaling sustainability of society. *Notes* EN, EC, and SC denote environmental, economic, and social sustainability elements, respectively

each level that constitute an element of a level higher. Each layer may have a few elements. EN1, for instance, is a set of two variables, environmental degradation and the degree of substitutability. The subcategory of first rank is the elements that are directly under each of the three pillars. Climate changes could be one under environmental degradation. Greenhouse gas emissions can be one element under climate changes. Under greenhouse gas emissions comes, for instance, industrial use of fossil fuels and so on.

The part under the tree indicates catalysts that nourish sustainability of society. They lay the basis for soiling the development of a society. They are distinguished from sustainability elements, as the impacts are broader and actors providing them may be located over multiple societies.

The picture of sustainability such as Fig. 2.1 clearly shows direct link to policymaking. The concerned society is the body of governance that influences any element above the ground level most, while catalysts, elements under the ground, may be influenced by various governance bodies inclusive of the concerned society itself.

Every region has peculiarities to fill up own sustainability elements as well as catalysts, in the tree of sustainability. The local public sector should have a good idea of it. It should have a good idea how to establish channels to communicate effectively with other levels of governance.

Conceptual modeling like Fig. 2.1 is effectively a policy model of sustainability applicable to any level of governance. Not all governments have the same ideology about sustainability even within a nation. They also differ in the intensity of commitments. In the next section, we give a practical, yet abstract, account of policymaking of sustainability.

2.2 Political Regimes of Sustainability

We continue with visual conceptualization to understand the process of policymaking of sustainability.

As policy measures of sustainability aim to improve each one of all three pillars of sustainability, a measure is classified as belonging to one of the three categories.

- Environmental measures (k_{EN})
- Economic measures (k_{EC})
- Social measures (k_{SC})

Environmental measures (k_{EN}), economic measures (k_{EC}), and social measures (k_{SC}) refer to those having a distinguished character biased toward environments, growth, and equity, respectively.

The following diagram shows that policy is displayed in the environmental–economic–social space. We can give a weight to each measure that implies its relative importance, for example, by the budget it receives. Once all measures are spotted in the diagram with its importance, we can see the sustainability regime of the society at a glance. It will show how the society is tilted toward one pillar against others, and how balanced policy measures are across the three pillars of sustainability.

K_{EN}, an environmental measure, is located on the 45° line. It is neutral with respect to social or economic sustainability and may correspond to a varying degree of them. Moving away from the origin to the outer direction implies all three types of sustainability improve. The further away a measure is from O along one axis, the stronger the measure becomes. There are limits to growth in all three dimensions as the curve indicates.

Policy measures collectively determine the political stance on sustainability, political regime of sustainability, of a society. K_{SC}'s, socially oriented policy measures, lie on the right side of the 45° line. K_{EC}'s, economy-oriented policy measures, are found on the left side of the line. If we mark all policy measures that are adopted in the (EC, EN, SC) plane, a society that is economy-oriented should have spots dominantly in the upper left of k_{EN} line. An environmental regime would see its mass of measures around the 45° line.

Governments do their own accounting on the policy it implements. They select policy, give a priority level, and allocate resources. They do the accounting along their sustainability goals, if the latter is their overarching goals.

It may be worth mentioning that carefully designed and implemented foresight studies can be useful in adopting new policy as well as revaluating existing policy. Box 2.1 below is a summary of a new approach that is increasing considered in policymaking, namely foresight methods.

Box 2.1 Foresight Methods for Policymaking

Foresight exercises, or studies about the future, may be considered an ambitious attempt to become a scientific discipline. It may nevertheless add a valuable input in various fields, one of them being policymaking. The Book of Changes (周易, *I-Ching* pronounced in Chinese, Wilhelm 2011) is an ancient classic that has made a big influence in the politics of the east. There is potential to improve present decisions if we are conscious of the end. The approaches using foresight methods in policymaking place an accent on ethical aspects and try to minimize bad outcomes, while increasing the chance to obtain good outcomes. This strand of literature (Inayatullah 1993; Bell 2009; Hines and Bishop 2006; Slaughter 1999) offers basic foresight technics, but the number of foresight technics is rapidly increasing. They include benchmarking, bibliometrics, brainstorming, citizens panels, conferences/workshops, essays/scenario writing, expert panels, forecasting, genius forecasting, indicators, interviews, literature review, modeling, simulation gaming, strength–weaknesses–opportunities–threats analysis, surveys, time series analysis, trend and impact analysis, backcasting, cross-impact/structural analysis, Delphi, science fictioning, scenarios and scanning, wild cards and weak signals, key/critical technologies, and so on (Georghiou et al. 2008).

Foresight methods on policymaking should take a holistic approach, as they try to take into account all relevant factors and their potential impacts. They typically involve the following two stages.

1. Forecasting
2. Backcasting

Forecasting is about identifying potential scenarios that may occur from now to the future. Backcasting is about identifying what need to be done now to increase the chance for certain scenarios to be realized.

The adoption of public policy is a political process that is a central subject in political science (Moran et al. 2006). Political ideologies of people who participate in the decision-making process may clash, and political power behind them may determine if a measure is adopted. This is the process of democratic decision making.[2]

[2]We develop a model how political economic regimes naturally arise in Appendix E.

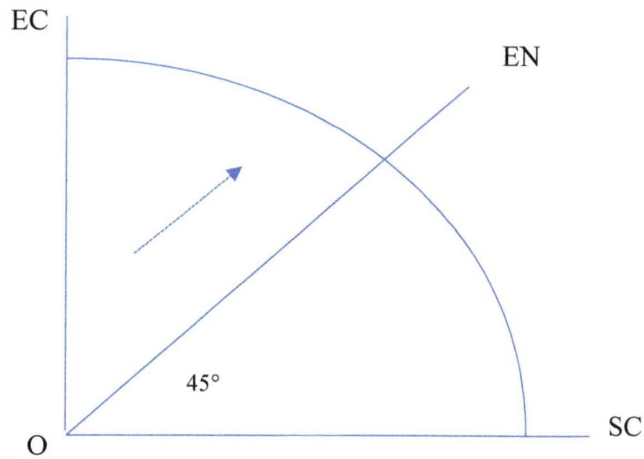

Fig. 2.2 Regimes of sustainability. *Notes* EC, SC, and EN denote economic, environmental, and social sustainability, respectively. They refer to the degree of policy orientation accordingly

There usually is a pre-selection process before the actual adoption of public policy. This process filters proposed measures if they are qualified to become actual measures. Criteria used to evaluate a measure in the pre-selection process may be summarized into the following four criteria: performance, ethics, completeness, and efficiency. The performance criteria would indicate how much (EC, EN, SC) would improve by adoption of a measure in the way policymakers want. Suppose the society finds itself on the left side of the 45° line in Fig. 2.2 shown in the previous section. It wants to move toward the direction indicated by the arrow. The measures that bring a higher value in (EC, EN, SC) are qualified.

The ethical criteria would indicate how ethical a measure is. Such measures are pre-selected with their adequacy toward social values such as human rights. Invading in another country might promise a huge growth opportunity for economy but is inappropriate on an ethical ground. The completeness criteria would indicate if there is no gray area in the reach of policy. The efficiency criteria verifies if there is no overlapping of policy measures, that is whether the measure would not be overshadowed by existing measures.

As measures may represent different sustainability values, different political views will clash and determine the actual adoption of policy. Each policy can be labeled with its budgeting need when proposed; actual budgeting can take place once a policy is adopted.

2.3 Sustainability Channels of Business

As the role of the public sector is to improve sustainability of society, the public sector would try place sustainability ethics on business practices all the time. This may imply increasing intervention on business which may modify the cash earning capacity of business. Transfer of *de jure* sustainability that business produces into

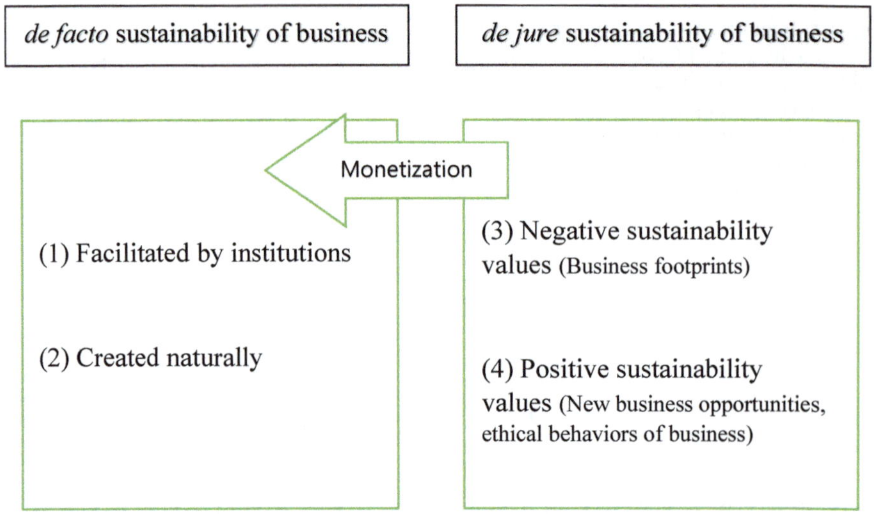

Fig. 2.3 Sustainability channels of business

de facto sustainability is the key facility of the public sector to let businesses engage in sustainability principles. But neither may all *de jure* sustainability be transferred into de facto sustainability, nor may the transfer be homogeneous across societies.

The actual transfer is done via *sustainability channels*. They are established jointly by businesses and the public sector to improve the sustainability of society. They are society specific, although there may be common features that one can envisage for all societies like basic human rights.

Figure 2.3 indicates four categories of sustainability that business produces (we call it sometimes sustainability of business, or business sustainability). They are (1) the de facto business sustainability facilitated by public institutions, (2) the de facto business sustainability created naturally, (3) the negative *de jure* sustainability (*de jure* business footprints), and (4) the positive *de jure* sustainability values.

Businesses create positive and negative sustainability. Positive sustainability is obtained by (1) production and sales (positive economic sustainability), (2) improved social or environmental sustainability, or (3) corporate social responsibility (positive environmental and social sustainability). Negative environmental or social sustainability can be produced by (1), while negative economic sustainability can be produced by (2) and (3). Business footprints refer to the negative sustainability produced by businesses on environmental and social sustainability.[3] They can be produced in the procurement of resources if this implies a depletion of natural resources, or the use of less environmentally friendly raw materials. They may be produced in the process of production if the process involves pollution, or the use of less environmentally friendly processes, among others. They may also occur in the final products.

[3]We would not call it business footprints if economic sustainability of business is hurt by focusing on other two types of sustainability disproportionately.

Any footprints produced for marketing, or general management of the business not directly related to production, would fall under this category. Examples would include the use of non-recyclable packaging materials to wrap products, the use of less environmentally friendly materials in promoting booklets. Business footprints may also take place on social sustainability. Examples would include inequality, discrimination, violation of human rights in workplaces, or other working conditions including wage gaps or employment protection, and so on.

Businesses are free to choose their business practices, so long as the scope and practices of the businesses satisfy legal constraints. Legal enforcement is an effective way to fill the gap between *de jure* and de facto sustainability. This can happen when businesses make negative impact on social or environmental sustainability in the course of pursuing sustainability of growth, tolerated by legal institutions. It can also happen to allow new business to be exploited, thus pursuing economic sustainability further. When cannabis plantation was legalized in Canada, cigarette companies have popped to seize the opportunity to create a new market. Cannabis plantation is illegal in most of other nations and stays as *de jure* sustainability of the fourth category. Examples of the second category are abundant in the history of business. It refers to an invent of new industry, a recent example including Internet-based businesses in the twenty-first century.

The third category refers to the business footprints that are not paid by the businesses who produce them. The range of the scale of them would vary to a large extent across nations. The fourth category refers to the positive sustainability businesses produces but not rewarded in cash term. Note that the overall size of sustainability is positive. This category of business sustainability may incur actual cash payment by the business that produces it, which is negative sustainability in the economic pillar of sustainability. An example is the corporate social responsibility (CSR). Businesses engaging in it may pay cash for it, in which case the cash profile of the business is harmed. But it stays as de jure sustainability until such acts are rewarded and transferred into de facto sustainability.

The sustainability channels identify business sustainability that are either positively or negatively associated with the production of environmental, economic, and social sustainability. They identify the means to transfer the *de jure* sustainability to the de facto sustainability. This transfer process is monetizing *de jure* sustainability such that de facto sustainability is the outcome of monetization of *de jure* sustainability.

These channels include public sector facilities, but the societal atmosphere in which these channels are established and function would also be critical in the determination of sustainability transferred. The sustainability regime of the society may come to the forefront to define the channels. The need of pushing one ideology against another along different pillars of sustainability may vary to a large extent across regions and countries. Such channels are not stagnant and may constantly evolve. It is a process which entails broad interactions between businesses and the public sector. It would be difficult to define a one-size-fits-all model of monetizing *de jure* sustainability values into de facto sustainability values.

Nations have different priorities, means, and the set of challenges to pursue their sustainability goals. Sustainability is a concept to which humans are central and as such is fundamentally a local concept. Local administrations may hold a primary responsibility to monitor and manage the sustainability values of people it administers. They communicate with the national government, to make sure local needs are well understood. The public sector needs to find how to trigger business involvement into sustainable development. The process of transferring *de jure* sustainability to de facto sustainability would be one of the main duties of the public sector to this end.

Cited Works

Bell, W. (2009). *Foundations of futures studies: Human science for a new era (Vol. 1 and 2)*. Transaction Publishers.

Dedeurwaerdere, T. (2014). *Sustainability science for strong sustainability*. Cheltenham, UK; Northampton, USA: Edward Elgar.

Georghiou, L., Cassingena Harper, J., Keenan, M., Miles, I., & Popper, R. (Eds.). (2008). *The handbook of technology Foresight—concepts and practice*. Cheltenham, UK: Edward Elgar Publishing Limited.

Hines, A., & Bishop, P. (Eds.). (2006). *Thinking about the future: guidelines for strategic Foresight*. Social Technologies LLC: Washington D.C.

Inayatullah, S. (1993). From 'who am I?' to 'when am I?'. *Futures, 3,* 235–253.

Moran, M., Rein, & M.Goodin, R. E., (Eds). (2006). *The Oxford handbook of public policy* (Vol. 6). Oxford Handbooks of Political.

Neumayer, E. (2013). *Weak versus strong sustainability: Exploring the limits of two opposing paradigms* (4th ed.). Cheltenham, UK; Northampton, USA: Edward Elgar.

Slaughter, R. (1999). Professional standards in futures work. *Futures, 31*(8), 835–851.

Wilhelm, H. (Ed.). (2011). *The I Ching or book of changes*.

Further Readings

Adelle, C., & Weiland, S. (2012). Policy assessment: The state of the art. *Impact Assessment and Project Appraisal, 30*(1), 25–33.

Albert, M., & Hahnel, R. (1990). *A quiet revolution in welfare economics*. Princeton, N. J.: Princeton University Press.

Alston, J. L., Eggertsson, T., & North, D. C. (1996). *Empirical studies in institutional change*. Cambridge: Cambridge University Press.

Bergh, C., & Gowdy, J. (2003). The microfoundations of macroeconomics: an evolutionary perspective. *Cambridge Journal of Economics, 27,* 65–84.

Cabezas, H. P. (2005). Sustainable systems theory: Ecological and other aspects. *Journal of Cleaner Production, 13*(5), 455–467.

Cabezas, H., Whitmore, H., Pawlowski, C., & Mayer, A. (2007). On the sustainability of an integrated model system with industrial, ecological, and macroeconomic components. *Resources, Conservation and Recycling, 50*(2), 122–129.

Campante, F. R. (2011). Redistribution in a model of voting and campaign contributions. *Journal of Public Economics, 95*(7–8), 646–656.

Campiglio, E. (2016). Beyond carbon pricing: The role of banking and monetary policy in financing the transition to a low-carbon economy. *Ecological Economics, 121,* 220–230.

Castaño, M. S., Méndez, M. T., & Galindo, M. A. (2016). The effect of public policies on entrepreneurial activity and economic growth. *Journal of Business Research, 69,* 5280–5285.

Corneo, G., & Grüner, H. P. (2002). Individual preferences for political redistribution. *Journal of Public Economics, 83*(1), 83–107.

Cosme, I., Santos, R., & O'Neill, D. W. (2017). Assessing the degrowth discourse: A review and analysis of academic degrowth policy proposals. *Journal of Cleaner Production, 149,* 321–334.

Dafermos, Y., Nikolaidi, D., & Galanis, G. (2017). A Stock-flow-fund ecological macroeconomic model. *Ecological Economics, 131,* 191–207.

Fankhauser, S., Smith, J. B., & Tol, R. S. J. (1999). Weathering climate change: Some simple rules to guide adaptation decisions. *Ecological Economics, 30*(1), 67–78.

Fuerth, L. S. (2009). Foresight and anticipatory governance. *Foresight, 11*(4), 14–32.

Germain, M. (2017). Optimal versus sustainable degrowth policies. *Ecological Economics, 136,* 266–281.

Giaoutzi, M., & Sapio, B. (2013). *Recent developments in foresight methodologies*. New York: Springer.

Graves, P. E. (2017). Global climate policy will have net benefits larger than anyone thinks (and welfare gains, strangely, are likely to be much larger yet). *Ecological Economics, 136,* 73–76.

Greening, L., Green, D., & Difiglio, C. (2000). Energy efficiency and consumption—the rebound effect—a survey. *Energy Policy, 28,* 389–401.

Grindle, M. S. (2011). Governance reform: The new analytics of next steps. *Governance: An International Journal of Policy, Administration, and Institutions*, *24*(3), 415–418.

Haegeman, K., Marinelli, E., Scapolo, F., Ricci, A., & Sokolov, A. (2013). Quantitative and qualitative approaches in future-oriented technology analysis (FTA): From combination to integration? *Technological Forecasting and Social Change, 80*(3), 386–397.

Harms, P., & Zink, S. (2003). Limits to redistribution in a democracy: A survey. *European Journal of Political Economy, 19*(4), 651–668.

Hertwich, E. (2005).Consumption and the rebound effect: An industrial ecology perspective. *Journal of Industrial Ecology*, *9*(1–2), 85–98.

Hicks, J. R. (1939). The foundations of welfare economics. *The Economic Journal*, 696–712.

Hines, A. (2006). *Thinking about the future: Guidelines for strategic Foresight.* New York: Social Technologies.

Hines, A., & Gold, J. (2013). Professionalizing foresight: Why do it, where it stands, and what needs to be done. *Journal of Futures Studies, 17*(4), 35–54.

Israel, J. I. (2001). *Radical enlightenment: Philosophy and the making of modernity 1650-Mc1750.* New York: Oxford University Press.

Jackson, Tim, & Victor, P. A. (2016). Does slow growth lead to rising inequality? Some theoretical reflections and numerical simulations. *Ecological Economics, 121,* 206–219.

Jonas, H. (1984). *The imperative of responsibility*. Chicago: The University of Chicago press.

Martin, B. R. (2010). The origins of the concept of 'foresight' in science and technology: An insider's perspective. *Technological Forecasting and Social Change, 77*(9), 1438–1447.

Nikolova, B. (2014). The rise and promise of participatory foresight. *European Journal of Futures Research, 2*(33), 2–33.

Nordhaus, W. D., & Tobin, J. (1972). Is Growth Obsolete? In W. D. Nordhaus & J. Tobin (Eds.), *Economic research: Retrospect and prospect* (Vol. 5). NBER: Cambridge, Massachusettes.

Olson, M. (1965). *The logic of collective action*. Cambridge, Massachusettes: Harvard University Press.

Ostrom, E. (1990). *Governing the commons: The evolution of institutions for collective actions.* Cambridge: Cambridge University Press.

Pierce, D. W. (1987). Foundations of ecological economics. *Ecological Modelling, 38,* 9–18.

Popper, R. (2008). Foresight methodology. In L. Georghiou, J. Cassingena, M. Keenan, I. Miles, & R. Popper (Eds.), *The handbook of technology foresight—concepts and practice*. Cheltenham, UK: Edward Elgar Publishing Limited.

Radaelli, C. M. (2005). Diffusion without convergence: How political context shapes the adoption of regulatory impact assessment. *Journal of European Public Policy, 12,* 924–943.

Ravetz, J. (1997). The science of what-if? *Futures, 29*(6), 533–539.

Rijkens-Klomp, N. (2012). Barriers and levers to future exploration in practice experiences in policy-making. *Futures, 44*(5), 431–439.

Smith, K. B. (2002). Typologies, Taxonomies, and the benefits of policy classification. *Policy Studies Journal, 30*(3), 379–395.

Stiglitz, J. E., Sen, A., & Fitoussi, J. P. (2009). *Mismeasuring our lives: Why GDP doesn't add up*. Report by the Commission on the Measurement of Economic Performance and Social Progress. (http://ec.europa.eu/eurostat/documents/118025/118123/Fitoussi+Commission+report).

Taylor, C. (1989). *Sources of the self: The making of the modern identity*. Cambridge, MA.: Harvard University Press.

Werlin, H. H. (2003). Poor nations, rich nations: A Theory of governance. *Public Administration Review, 63*(3), 329–342.

Zerbe, R. O., Jr. (1980). The Problem of social cost in retrospect. *Research in Law and Economics, 2,* 83–102.

Zhang, C., Chen, W., Liu, G., & Zhu, D. (2017). Economic growth and the evolution of material cycles: An analytical framework integrating material flow and stock indicators. *Ecological Economics, 140,* 265–274.

Chapter 3
Sustainability Cashflows

3.1 Sustainability Accounting

Anthropologists could trace the presence of accounting practices in written forms back to ancient Mesopotamia, ancient Egypt and Babylonians, and the Roman governance. The birth of modern accounting or bookkeeping is believed to be around thirteenth century when the idea of double-entry bookkeeping (debits and credits) started to appear and coincided with the newly spreading use of money and banking of loans. The region of northern Italy and southern France was a forerunner, and the printed work of Luca Pacioli of Venice (1494) is believed to be the first who laid out the foundation of modern bookkeeping. The profession of accountants as we see now was established much later in Scotland in the early nineteenth century. By this time, the accounting system was well developed with its rigorous and meticulous methods that could match today's standards and served for management purposes and for taxation purposes for authorities. Professional accountants were active both internally and externally with a firm and monitored by third-party auditors, who are themselves accountants, just like today.

The system of accounting is continuously evolving. There is an increasing awareness about the need to account for the environmental impact of business. Reports on corporate sustainability, and methods such as environmental management accounting, sustainability accounting, and social and environmental accounting (SEA) have been proposed, among others. Organizations like the International Financial Reporting Standards (IFRS) are progressively recognizing the need for reflecting the environmental impact of business in the accounting system. But it is not evident if impact values from these studies can be used to value a business, when they do not imply prices that businesses have to pay.

Looking into the present system of business accounting, we see that it does not discern values along the sustainability pillars. All *de facto* sustainability values are aggregated along with the items selected by the present accounting system, but not by the three pillars of sustainability in any way. As a consequence, it is difficult to match the business to the sustainability of society. For example, business footprints are not

Y. Oh, *Sustainability Valuation of Business*,
SpringerBriefs in Finance,
https://doi.org/10.1007/978-3-030-18648-7_3

declared and their origins on sustainability are veiled in the business accounting system.

Sustainability values that are transferred from *de jure* to *de facto* values through sustainability channels are identifiable by their origins and characters linked to the pillars of sustainability. A label of sustainability can be attached to each entry, which helps to see their link to the sustainability of society. They can be entered automatically in the accounting system of the business. This would imply that it would be possible for any item in the present business accounting system to have a label indicating its sustainability values, once the sustainability channels are activated.

This would imply a significant deepening of the system of business reporting. It would be best if institutions are the driving force of it. But even without official production of such reports, industry can offer such services by establishing its own system of sustainability valuation.[1]

We can see how to formulate such change using the following framework.

Denote *the price of a unit of final products* as P such that

$$P = P_r + P_p + P_m \tag{3.1}$$

with

P: the price of a unit of final products
P_r: the price of the resources used (r) to produce a unit of final products
P_p: the price of the process used (p) to produce a unit of final products
P_m: the markup in the final price of a unit of final products

and

$$r + p + m = 1$$

r, p, and m denote the proportions in terms of quantity, of the resources, the process and the markup in per unit of the final products. Products go through a lifecycle of three stages as resource procurement (resources), process of production (processes), and sales (sales).[2] Denote the quantity of the final products sold as Q. Q is decomposed into rQ, pQ, and mQ. The total value of the final products sold is P*Q.

The value of business sustainability, BS, is the sum of *de jure* and *de facto* sustainability and decomposed to

$$BS = BS_r + BS_p + BS_m \tag{3.2}$$

where BS_r, BS_p, and BS_m refer to business sustainability produced in the stages of resource procurement, of the production process, and of sales, respectively. BS can refer either to *de jure* sustainability or to *de facto* sustainability. They can be

[1] In fact, the similar situation is true for conventional valuation. Future cash flows are never published by official documents of business, and it is the valuers' service to provide their own estimates.

[2] Activities after the production stage until sold.

Table 3.1 *de facto* business sustainability (BS^{df}) by sources and sustainability impacts

BS^{df}	$BS_{EN}{}^{df}$ (Environmental)	BS_{EC} (Economic)	BS_{SC} (Social)
$BS_r{}^{df}$ (Resources)	$BS_{r,EN}{}^{df} = \alpha_{1EN}P_r rQ$	$BS_{r,EC}{}^{df} = \alpha_{1EC}P_r rQ$	$BS_{r,SC}{}^{df} = \alpha_{1SC}P_r rQ$
$BS_p{}^{df}$ (Processes)	$BS_{p,EN}{}^{df} = \alpha_{2EN}P_p pQ$	$BS_{p,EC}{}^{df} = \alpha_{2EC}P_p pQ$	$BS_{p,SC}{}^{df} = \alpha_{2SC}P_p pQ$
$BS_m{}^{df}$ (Sales)	$BS_{m,EN}{}^{df} = \alpha_{3EN}P_m mQ$	$BS_{m,EC}{}^{df} = \alpha_{3EC}P_m mQ$	$BS_{m,SC}{}^{df} = \alpha_{3SC}P_m mQ$

Notes BS, P, and *Q* refer to business sustainability, the unit price, and the quantity of the products sold, respectively. *m* is a markup in the final price. Subscripts, *r*, *p*, and *m* refer to the stages of resource procurement, production processes, and sales, respectively. Subscripts *EN*, *EC*, and *SC* refer to environmental, economic, and social sustainability

further decomposed to indicate which one of the three pillars of sustainability can be attributed to them. This is indicated in Table 3.1.

The first column indicates the sources of business sustainability: resources, processes, and sales. Business sustainability is further decomposed by its impact on sustainability: environmental, economic, and social sustainability (EN, EC, SC).

$\alpha_{1,EN}$ to $\alpha_{3,EN}$ indicate the proportions of business sustainability produced in the procurement of resources. Their sum equals to 1 as they are expressed as a proportion within this category. Analogously, $\alpha_{1,EC}$ to $\alpha_{3,EC}$ apply for the stage of processes and $\alpha_{1,SC}$ to $\alpha_{3,SC}$ for sales. This way enables business sustainability to be expressed firmly embedded in cash values of the goods sold.

Using resources that are eco-friendly improves sustainability and thus reduces footprints. Adoption of more eco-friendly technology reduces footprints in the process. Using recyclable materials reduces footprints. Engaging in a circular economy would reduce business footprints in the process. Note that business sustainability would not be volatile, as in the way business is run. αs would not change drastically, a positive factor in the estimation of business sustainability.

Once business sustainability is recorded as in Table 3.1, it is straightforward to unveil the contribution of business to the sustainability of society. This is indicated in Table 3.2. *de facto* as well as *de jure* sustainability of the business sector in a society can be shown along with both their origins and sustainability impacts.

The information to draw Tables 3.1 and 3.2 is not fully available at the moment. But it is on the way. The present accounting system does not compile business information that can build Table 3.1. We do not have a clear guideline of how a product can be decomposed as indicated in Table 3.1. We argue that this should be

Table 3.2 Business sustainability to societal sustainability

	de jure business sustainability (BS^{dj})			*de facto* business sustainability (BS^{df})		
	Environmental	Economic	Social	Environmental	Economic	Social
Resources						
Processes						
Sales						

done without much difficulty: a conservative consensus on them with institutional recognition would do. It may take time for such decomposition to be realized in the official statements of businesses. But such information is valuable and valuers can take the task to propose their appraisal of sustainability values of the business.

The decomposition of business sustainability would offer a useful tool to the public sector in communication with businesses to improve the sustainability of society. The public sector has its own sustainability policy with clear priority areas in mind. The public sector can see where business footprints are generated. It may induce businesses to modify the profile of their footprints that would adjust to the sustainability goals of society. Governmental facilities such as incentives, tax benefits, and regulatory changes, through sustainability channels as seen in the previous section, can be mobilized to facilitate this process.[3]

Identification of the *de jure* business sustainability is essential for businesses to receive incentives, tax advantages, or other public facilities, as much as it is essential for the public sector in their policy planning. Businesses may be invited to claim de jure sustainability (BS^{dj}) and ask for the transfer to *de facto* sustainability (BS^{df}). BS^{dj}s are gradually to be eradicated and transformed into BS^{df}s.

Businesses are in the best position to measure their own footprints. They have all the information and knowledge to keep track of the footprints they produce. They may not be fully inclined to disclose them. The public sector maintains to monitor and provide guidelines of how business sustainability may be defined and classified along with the categories of its sustainability policy. Again, this can also be a task of valuers to estimate the true business footprints.

The public sector may take a main role in establishing sustainability channels. The public sector would constantly search for the ways to rebalance its policy to improve the sustainability of society. The facilities of the public sector function as a catalyst to change the cashflow profile of businesses and reduce business footprints. Imagine, for instance, governments take a measure to reward businesses that produce smaller footprints than the industrial average and penalize businesses that produce larger footprints than the industrial average. This is one of the possible facilities that can be adopted in sustainability channels. The process of policymaking for sustainable development and the identification of business footprints have the potential to make profound changes in the way businesspeople do their business. The job of valuers will have to face a major additional dimension: the foresight of the transfer from *de jure* sustainability into *de facto* sustainability, or the characteristics and the progress in sustainability channels.

[3]There may be policy failures, or certain sustainability regimes may find it difficult to recognize certain *de jure* sustainability values. Transfer to *de facto* sustainability will be delayed in such cases.

3.2 Sustainability Cashflows

As what counts are future cashflows, predicting the progress of transferring *de jure* sustainability values into *de facto* values in the future becomes a central task of sustainability valuation. Sustainability cashflows are the *de facto* sustainability values expressed as,

$$BS_{df} = P \times Q - C - T \tag{3.3}$$

P, Q, C, and T refer to the price of the product, the quantity sold of the product, the cost to produce the product sold, and corporate taxes, respectively. The cash value of the sustainability that a business produces (BS_{df}) can be inferred from the sales of goods and services sold, minus the costs (operational and financial) to produce them, and the taxes paid. Equation 3.3 is the way in which cashflows are calculated in conventional valuation methods.[4] But as active sustainability channels would modify all four elements in the right-hand side of Eq. 3.3, sustainability cashflows inferred from the *de facto* sustainability can be very different from cashflows without such channels.

Once the prediction of sustainability cashflows is completed, it is straightforward to calculate future cashflows, as is indicated in Table 3.3. Note that not only may the profile of future cashflows be modified, but we have a rich array of information at hand about the sources of them by the three pillars of sustainability. We may see the prospect of business, if they will grow or decline and the details, and its impact on the sustainability of society. We may also see the impact of the business sector to the sustainability of society once we have enough number of valuations.

Note that only the future *de facto* sustainability values are included in the valuation. Not only the foresight of the existing *de facto* sustainability but of the new ones that will be transferred from *de jure* sustainability will count. They enter into the accounting system of business, and the calculation of future cashflows is straightforward. We can use the technic developed in conventional valuation.

To recapitulate how future cashflows are estimated, it is useful to know that there are four elements to determine the cashflow of a business: (1) Total cash inflows, (2) Operating costs, (3) Interest payments, and (4) Corporate tax payment. Cashflow calculation is done by establishing the future income statements of a business. The basic scheme of cashflow calculation for a manufacturing firm is as follows.

The cash remaining in the firm, the difference between cash inflows—(1) above—and cash outflows—the sum of (2), (3) and (4) above—determines the value attributed for investors, debt and equity holders. This amount is to be discounted using the appropriate discount rates (the topic of the next chapter) to get the present value of the business.

There exists the cashflow statement as part of the financial statements of a firm, but this is about the past cashflows. What counts for calculating the value of a business is

[4] Table 3.3 elaborates the cashflow calculation.

Table 3.3 Calculation of cashflows

Sales turnover
− Operating costs
= Operating profits (Earnings Before Interests and Taxes)
− Interest payment
− Corporate tax
= Net profit
+ Interest payment
+ Depreciation
+ Gross investment (decrease in inventory, increase in accounts payable, capital expenditures)
+ After-tax non-operating income
+ Decrease in equity investments
= Net cashflows

Notes See for the detail, Koller et al. (2005), in particular P. 165

the future ones, and it is the job of valuers to come up with good estimates. Foresight of future cashflows on main items of business accounting may yield very different results. But one assuring point is that the proportions of the four elements of cashflows are stable with respect to the total sales turnover and with respect to each other over a reasonably foreseeable period of time. In calculating future cashflows, valuers can use such relationship.

Cited Works

Koller, T., Goedhart, M., & Wessels, D. (2005). *Valuation: Measuring and managing the value of companies* (4th ed.). Wiley.

Further Readings

Amir, E. (1993). The market valuation of accounting information: The case of postretirement benefits other than pensions. *The Accounting Review, 68,* 703–724.

Arnold, P. J. (2009). Global financial crisis: The challenge to accounting research. *Accounting, Organizations and Society, 34*(6), 803–809.

Baldvinsdottir, G., Mitchell, F., & Nørreklt, H. (2010). Issues in the relationship between theory and practice in management accounting. *Management Accounting Research, 21*(2), 79–82.

Balint, T., Lamperti, F., Mandel, A., Napoletano, M., Roventitni, A., & Sapio, A. (2017). Complexity and the economics of climate change: A survey and a look forward. *Ecological Economics, 138,* 252–265.

Bezemer, D. J. (2010). Understanding financial crisis through accounting models. *Accounting, Organizations and Society, 35*(7), 676–688.

Bhattacharya, S., & Constantinides, G. M. (Eds.). (1988). *Theory of valuation: Frontiers for modern financial theory* (Vol. 1). Rowman and Littlefield Publishers.
Bishop, R. C. (1993). Economic efficiency, sustainability, and biodiversity. *Ambio, 22*(2–3), 69–73.
Brealey, R., & Myers, S. (2003). *Principles of corporate finance*. New York, NY: McGrow-Hill.
Brown, J. (2006). Approaches and perspectives in social and environmental accounting: An overview of the conceptual landscape. *Business Strategy and the Environment, 15*(2), 103–117.
Burritt, R. L., & Schaltegger, S. (2010). Sustainability accounting and reporting: Fad or trend? *Accounting, Auditing and Accountability Journal, 23*(7), 829–846.
Camilleri, M. A. (2017). Corporate citizenship and social responsibility policies in the United States of America. *Sustainability Accounting, Management and Policy Journal, 8*(1), 77–93.
Christensen, P. P. (2005). Recovering and extending classical and Marshallian foundations for post-Keynesian environmental economics. *International Journal of Environment, Workplace and Employment, 1*(2), 155–173.
Costanza, R., & Patten, B. (1995). Defining and predicting sustainability. *Ecological Economics, 15*(3), 193–196.
Daly, H. E., & J. Farley. (2004). *Ecological economics: Principles and applications*. Island Press.
Demeritt, D., & Rothman, D. (1999). Figuring the costs of climate change: An assessment and critique. *Environment and Planning A: Economy and Space, 31*(3), 389–408.
Dou, X. (2015). The essence, feature and role of low carbon economy. *Environment, Development and Sustainability, 17*(1), 123–136.
Ekins, P. (1999). European environmental taxes and charges: Recent experience, issues and trends. *Ecological Economics, 31*, 39–62.
Freeman, A. M., III. (2014). *The measurement of environmental and resource values*. New York: Taylor and Francis.
Glavič, P., & Lukman, R. (2007). Review of sustainability terms and their definitions. *Journal of Cleaner Production, 15*(18), 1875–1885.
Global Footprints Network, The Ecological Wealth of Nations. (2010).
Goodland, R., & Daly, H. (1996). Environmental sustainability: Universal and non-negotiable. *Ecological Applications, 6*(4), 1002–1017.
Givoly, D., & Hayn, C. (2000). The changing time-series properties of earnings, cash flows and accruals: Has financial reporting become more conservative? *Journal of Accounting and Economics, 29*, 287–320.
Gray, R., Kouhy, R., & Lavers, S. (1995). Corporate social and environmental reporting a review of the literature and a longitudinal study of UK disclosure. *Accounting, Auditing and Accountability Journal, 8*(2), 47–77.
Hall, C., Lindenberger, D., Kummel, R., Kroeger, T., & Eichhorn, W. (2001). The need to reintegrate the natural sciences with economics. *BioScience, 51*(8), 663–673.
Heyes, A. G., & Liston-Heyes, Catherine. (1995). Sustainable resource use: The search for meaning. *Energy Policy, 23*(1), 1–3.
Huang, C., & Litzenberger, R. H. (1988). *Foundations for financial economics*. New York: Prentice-Hall.
Kydland, F. E., & Prescott, E. C. (1982). Time to build and aggregate fluctuations. *Econometrica, 50*, 1345–1370.
Maas, K., Schaltegger, S., & Crutzen, N. (2016). Integrating corporate sustainability assessment, management accounting, control, and reporting. *Journal of Cleaner Production, 136*, 237–248.
Magano, T. (2013). A model for managing corporate sustainability. *Business and Society Review, 118*(20), 223–252.
Ohlsen, J. A. (1995). Earnings, book values, and dividends in equity valuation. *Contemporary Accounting Research, II*(2), 661–687.
Osteryoung, J., Derek, L., & Davies, L. (1997). *Small firm finance: An entrepreneurial analysis*. Forth Worth, TX: Dryden Press.
Russel, D. (2014). Corporate sustainability: Accounting standards vs tax by design. *Social Responsibility Journal, 10*(3), 386–398.

Sachs, J., Schimidt-Traub, G., Kroll, C., Durand-Delacre, D., & Teksoz, K. (2017). *SDG index and dashboards report.* New York: Bertelsmann Stiftung and Sustainable Development Solutions network (SDSN).

Savitz, A. (2006). *The triple bottom line: How today's best-run companies are achieving economic, social and environmental success—and how you can too.* Jossey-Bass.

Schmidheiny, S. (1992). *Change of course: Global business prospects for development and the environment.* Boston: MIT Press.

Schaltegger, S., Gibassier, D., & Zvezdov, D. (2013). Is environmental management accounting a discipline? A bibliometric literature review. *Meditari Accountancy Research, 21*(1), 4–31.

Söderholm, P. (2011). Taxing virgin natural resources: Lessons from aggregates taxation in Europe. *Resources, Conservation and Recycling, 55*(11), 911–922.

Stacchezzini, R., Melloni, G., & Lai, A. (2016). Sustainability management and reporting: The role of integrated reporting for communicating corporate sustainability management. *Journal of Cleaner Production, 136*(A), 102–110.

Taticchi, P., Carbone, P., & Albino, V. (Eds.). (2013). *Corporate sustainability.* Berlin Heidelberg: Springer.

Verbooma, J., Alkemadeb, R., Klijna, J., Metzgerc, M. J., & Reijnena, R. (2006). Combining biodiversity modeling with political and economic development scenarios for 25 EU countries. *Ecological Economics, 62*(2), 267–276.

Chapter 4
Sustainability Discount Rates

4.1 Sustainability Capital

The process of sustainability valuation of business involves a new set of policy in accordance with the three pillars of sustainability and the establishment of sustainability channels, as well as the new accounting of business that accommodates the transfer. The last, and equally important if not more important than all of these, is to find the corresponding business-specific discount rates. The discount rates to discount the future sustainability cashflows of a business (cashflows earned on sustainability values) would complete the valuation. In this chapter, we discuss how the holistic concept of sustainability could alter the determination of the discount rates on business valuation.

Discount rates are the rates that equalize the future values of an asset to its present value. It is the rate of return on capital. Capital has several faces and typically is classified into fixed income capital, or debt capital, that pays out fixed amounts following a predetermined schedule, and equity capital whose payouts depend on the performance it finances. There are many derivatives rooted in these two types of capital. An asset may be composed of multiple types of capital. The share of each type of capital in the total defines the capital structure of the asset. The rate of return on business, i.e., the discount rate of business, is the composite rate of return on different types of capital that comprise the capital structure of the business.

Sustainability capital would refer literally to capital used to produce sustainability, like production of sustainability, which refers to the production of one or more of the three pillars of sustainability by the business. Capital in the conventional sense would refer to capital used to produce economic sustainability, regardless of its characters whether it is of *sacris*, *de jure,* or de facto economic sustainability. The return on this capital is determined by de facto sustainability over the capital invested. In the context of sustainability valuation, capital invested in business produces sustainability in a holistic manner, not only economic sustainability, but environmental and social

Y. Oh, *Sustainability Valuation of Business*,
SpringerBriefs in Finance,
https://doi.org/10.1007/978-3-030-18648-7_4

sustainability. But it is indeed only de facto sustainability of the future that will be counted as contributing to the value of the business.

The de facto business sustainability produced in the future would be the sum of the de facto sustainability. It is possible that investors once more conscious of the impact on the sustainability of their investment may be able to direct where their capital to be spent (by influencing management). This is a complex process, especially because this would have implications in the way sustainability channels are established and run. Sustainability capital would modify the discount rates as indicated in the next section.

4.2 Sustainability Discount Rates

Would sustainability capital affect the way discount rates are determined? The answer would be yes. Sustainability cashflows would alter the cashflow profile of a business, which will eventually result in the alteration of the discount rates of business.

There are at least three perspectives to determine the discount rates of sustainability capital. First, the discount rates of consumption, *consumption-based discount rates*, are the rates equalizing the future consumption to the present one in the expected utility of consumption of an individual, an essential element in the classical economics literature. It concerns how much more (units of) consumption at a certain time in the future would be required to compensate for the delay of today's (one unit of) consumption. The higher this rate, the less patient people are in holding back their consumption needs. Second, the discount rates of capital prevailing in the financial assets and *financial discount rates* concern how much interest to ask for lending money for a given period of time. The higher the rates, the higher the interest capital holders demand. Third, the *discounting-the-future rates* are the rates that would justify the size of today's expenditure on projects that will prevent future risky events from happening, or at least minimize the impact of future events if they happen. The events may include natural calamities or environmental degradation such as climate changes as well as building a dam or a bridge. The lower the rate, the riskier the future hazard is believed to be.[1]

These three rates of return are interconnected. But we only observe the discount rates of the second type, financial discount rates. The discount rates of the first type, sometimes called *social discount rates*, are not observable, though they can be estimated, typically used in the cost-benefit studies of social projects (Lopez 2008). There is little consensus on discounting-the-future rates,[2] though more studies tend to use the rates close to financial discount rates.

The rates of return of the debt capital are straightforward to attain, because its risk is limited. The rates of return of the equity capital are not straightforward, because it is a risky asset. The future discount rates of equity capital are the intrinsic rates of

[1]Appendix F illustrates how greatly perception of future risk may modify the discount rates.

[2]The Stern report (2007) uses a low 0.1%. Most others and Nordhaus (1994) use rates close to market rates that are higher.

return, or the expected rates of return, of the capital, which can be estimated with the means and the variances over a reasonably long period of time. The capital asset pricing model (CAPM) is one of the most popularly used approaches to calculate the discount rates of equity capital.

Box 4.1 CAPM for Sustainability Capital

The capital asset pricing model (CAPM) is one of the most popular models used to find the discount rates, or the rates of return, of an asset. It assesses the risk and the return prospects of the asset.

A typical CAPM equation is written as

$$r_i = r_f + \beta_i (r_m - r_f)$$

r_i, r_f, and r_m are the rate of return on asset i, the rate of return on the risk-free asset, and the rate of return on the market portfolio, respectively. β_i represents the risk of the asset *relative* to the risk of the market portfolio in which the asset is traded. A standard formula to calculate β_i is the covariances of the rates of return on asset i and the rates of return on the market portfolio, r_m, divided by the variance of the rates of return on the market portfolio.

The expected rates of return can be estimated in practice on the share prices over a substantially long period of time. Sustainability cashflows would alter the cashflow profile of a business. This will eventually result in the alteration of the rates of return, the discount rates, of business, after a while.

If the values of all businesses move in the same direction and with similar magnitude with sustainability valuation, then there will be little change in the discount rates. The return-risk prospects with respect to the market portfolio would alter little, as the rates of return of the market (a composite of all businesses) adjust as much as the discount rates of individual businesses. But this is not likely. Businesses will exhibit different performances as sustainability channels are activated. Those acting more sustainability conscious will receive more benefits than those less so. The market will soon start to see how consistent this would be and adjust their expectations on the rates of return of each business accordingly. This would bring a fundamental alteration to the risk-return profile of the market portfolio.

The way to calculate the discount rates is illustrated in Copeland et al. (1990). We will briefly describe the process below. The valuer estimates the capital structure of a business which shows the present values of the different types of capital the business uses. Each one of them may have a different discount rate. The discount rates of the debt securities can be obtained as their term structures are known. The discount rates of equities can be estimated using a CAPM. The market values of all different types of capital can be obtained and the capital structure of the business is identified.

Once we have all of these figures, the business-specific discount rates, i.e., the discount rates for the sustainability cashflows of a business, can be obtained in a straightforward manner. They are the weighted averages of the rates of return of capital (debts and equities) of the business, with the weight derived from the market value of each capital in the total capital of the business.

It can be written as,

$$r_t = \sum_{d,t} w_{dt} \times r_{dt} + \sum_{e,t} w_{et} \times r_{et} \tag{4.1}$$

r_t: the period discount rate for sustainability cashflows earned by business
w_{dt}: the weight of the market value of debt d in the market value of the total capital of business
r_{dt}: the period discount rate of debt d of business
w_{et}: the weight of the market value of equity e in the market value of the total capital of business
r_{et}: the period discount rate of equity e of business.

The discount rate for a period-sustainability cashflow of a business is the weighted average of the discount rates of all securities outstanding in the period that business uses, where the weight of each type of capital is estimated using the market price of the capital. The discount rate of each capital is calculated independently from each other. In practice, the risk-free rates of the market used are typically short-term public rates (e.g., one-year treasury bill rates for the USA). The rates of the market portfolio are typically the rates of return of the market index in which the equities are traded.

The market values of capital are the present values of capital outstanding. The value of a debt security d (V_{dt}) is calculated with its predetermined contracts. The market value of equity e (V_{et}) is more difficult to get, but can be approximated by the market value of the equities outstanding in the stock markets if the business is listed. Comparable stock prices may be used as a benchmark to calculate the market value, if the business is not listed in the stock exchanges. Then the weight of individual capital is,

$$w_{dt} = V_{dt} \Big/ \sum_{d,e} (V_{dt} + V_{et}) \text{ for debt security d}$$

$$w_{et} = V_{et} \Big/ \sum_{d,e} (V_{dt} + V_{et}) \text{ for equity security e}$$

Each group of capital, being debt or equity related, has its specific rate of return. The capital structure of business does not change as much as the firm's business performance. It may not be necessary to try finding the capital structure and the discount rates in the same frequency as cashflows that are estimated in higher frequencies.

Cited Works

Copeland, T., Koller, T., & Murrin, J. (1990). *Valuation: Measuring and managing the value of companies*. Wiley.

Lopez, H. (2008). The social discount rate: Estimates for nine Latin American countries. *The World Bank Policy Research Working Paper*. 4639.

Nordhaus, W. D. (1994). *Managing the global commons: The economics of climate change*. Cambridge MA: The MIT Press.

Stern, N. (2007). *The economics of climate change: The stern review*. Cambridge University Press.

Further Readings

Arrow, K. (1959). Towards a theory of price adjustment. In M. Abramovitz (Ed.), *Allocation of economic resources: Essays in Hornor of Bernard Francis Haley* (pp. 41–51). Stanford: Stanford University Press.

Arrow, K. J., Cropper, M., Gollier, C., Groom, B., Heal, G., Newell, R., ... Weitzman, M. (2012). How should benefits and costs be discounted in an intergenerational context? The views of an expert panel. *RFF Discussion Paper, 12*(53).

Figge, F., & Hahn, T. (2005). The cost of sustainability capital and the creation of sustainable value by companies. *Journal of Industrial Ecology, 9*(4), 47–58.

Garnaut, R. (2008). *The garnaut climate change review*. Melbourne: The Cambridge University Press.

Chapter 5
Completion and Further Issues

5.1 Completion of Sustainability Valuation

With the cashflows and the discount rates, the value of a business is calculated.

In equation,

$$SV_i = \sum_t CF_{it} \div \left(1 + r_{it}\right)^t \tag{5.1}$$

SV_i refers to the present value of business i. CF_{it} and r_{it} are the future periodic net cashflows (inflows minus outflows) and the periodic discount rates of business *i*, respectively. Equation 4.1 says that the present value of a business is the future net cashflows discounted with their appropriate discount rates. It is the net present value (NPV) of the business. This framework is exactly the same as conventional valuation.

In practice, the valuation is done for two periods: the period for which a detailed foresight of future is possible and the residual period for which such foresight is not feasible. In the latter case, a reasonable extrapolation may be used with only a very limited number of items to estimate anew.

Suppose a detailed foresight can be done to period T. The value of business i is,

$$SV_i = \sum_{t=0,T} (\text{periodic discounted cashflow } s_t) + 1 \big/ (1 + r_T) \times SV_{Ti} \tag{5.2}$$

SV_{Ti} is the terminal value of business i. It is the value of business i valued at time T, with r_T, its corresponding discount rate. The business is assumed to continue. The first part is the sum of the periodic sustainability cashflows discounted for today over the periods for which a meaningful foresight is possible. The cashflows beyond this period are summed in the second part.

From the business value obtained, it is straightforward to draw the value of equity of the business. The total equity value of the business is the difference between the

Y. Oh, *Sustainability Valuation of Business*,
SpringerBriefs in Finance,
https://doi.org/10.1007/978-3-030-18648-7_5

business value and the market value of the debts outstanding. The per share value of equities, the value of an equity, is calculated as the total equity value of the business divided by the number of the equity shares outstanding. This estimated per share value would serve as a reference to equity traders: it would be a signal to buy the shares if this value is higher than the present share price and vice versa.

The sustainability valuation may yield very different values from those without sustainability concerns. But it is hard to say if there would be any normality in the change of business values. The profile of the future cashflows may change as well as the risk-return profile of the business. This will, in turn, have implications to the capital structure of the firm.

The principles of sustainability valuation would apply to any business including individual projects. The value of a project is equal to the sum of all discounted future net cashflows the project generates. It may be easier to think of the discount rates as the required rates of return that capital would demand to participate in the project.

5.2 Impacts of Employing Sustainability Valuation

Sustainability valuation connects the value of a business to the sustainability of society. The shift promoting sustainability valuation would imply a fundamental change in the system of public budgeting, pricing in financial markets, particularly stock exchanges, and in the benchmark values of some macroeconomic parameters such as economic sustainability, or sustainability, among others. Ultimately, it would change the way the sustainability of society evolves, in a good way.

The process operating in sustainability channels would induce changes in the way the public sector manages its budgeting. The public sector will assess the society's sustainability and review its policy portfolio to see if the society is heading to a desirable direction of sustainable development. It identifies areas where policy rebalancing is needed and carefully examines its system of policy to adjust. This policy adjustment can alter business values systematically to eventually make a positive impact on the sustainability of society.

Once sustainability principles are incorporated into resources, production technologies, or sales process of final products, it would help diminish potential trade-offs between the interests of investors and the other parties involved in business.[1] This would mean a reduction of social footprints. Financial markets would immediately react to the sustainability values that create cash. As business values would alter with sustainability values, the profile of the returns and the risks of business would adjust and so would equity prices of business. The processes in sustainability channels would be the driver in the change of business values.

When management wants a short-term increase of shareholder values, they may be tempted to suppress items in the part of the costs wherever legal: Wages, raw materials, welfare expenses, and so on. This type of acts may harm sustainability

[1]Managers, employees, consumers, and the public sectors.

and as a result harms the value of business and shareholder values.[2] Suppression of the costs in favor of creating shareholder values that harms sustainability would no longer be an interesting option.

5.3 Further Issues

This monograph enlightens a way how businesses can contribute to the sustainable development of society. It suggests how a win-win situation can be achieved among business, nature and environment, and humans through the change of the valuation mechanism of businesses. But the actual implementation of this type of valuation will take place gradually until it achieves its goal. Its progress will also depend on institutional supports.

5.3.1 Valuation of Small Businesses

Valuation of small businesses is an interesting topic, especially with respect to the sustainable development of society. Little attention has been paid on small businesses such as restaurants, grocery shops, barbers and hairdressers, bakeries, butcher shops, and independent professions such as doctors, accountants, lawyers, and so on. While such businesses have limited tradability, they constitute a large part of the economy. Their resilience is one of the key factors for sustainable development of society.

The oldest firm in the world that keeps its business today is known to be Nishiyama Onsen Keiunkan, a Japanese hotel founded in 705 A.D. This company never tried to open numerous branches, nor build a hotel chain. Not only has the same family run the hotel for 52 generations, but there are families among the staff who have held the same post for generations. There is believed to exist a spirit of service as the way to earn wages and protect the hotel business.

There seem to be more than five thousand companies in the world that are older than 200 years. More than half of them are Japanese, followed by Germany, Netherlands, and France. Most of them are employing fewer than 300 people. The average lifespan of companies listed in the S&P 500 of the USA is believed to be a surprisingly low 15 years. Making growth a priority may be anathema to long-term survival. Small companies have a good chance to survive.

The value of this type of business would include the value of the intangible asset that the business has acquired such as reputation or locational advantage.[3] The discount rates to calculate the business value of this type may not be evident. But there would be no other way. One could still find comparable businesses and assess deviations in the profile of risk and return, to estimate the discount rates of the business.

[2]It is possible to enhance this mechanism through sustainability channels.

[3]Examples include the “bail à céder”(in france) and “gwon-li-gum,” in Korea.

If the actual trade of small businesses is easier than now, it would help the economic sustainability of society. Valuation of such businesses should follow. The public sector may ponder on the ways to create infrastructure and improve tradability of small businesses.

5.3.2 How Can We Apply in Practice the Framework Presented in This Book?

Valuation as illustrated in this book proposes a complete holistic framework. The most suitable way to implement this valuation would be to start at a local community level that is run by a local municipality. The local administration knows business people by face, and policy of the local administration is easy to monitor and its impact is fast sensed by people in the region.

Sustainability valuation and what it requires may have the potential to provoke a big wave. Transfer from non-cashed sustainability into one having money value might provoke serious adverse and irreversible effects. An immense sense of responsibility is called for. If you are a policymaker in charge of the policymaking such process, it is advised that you follow your conceptual, and often intuitive, the way that is firmly grounded to the required level of ethics, in parallel with the advice what you receive from theoreticians and practitioners. The gap between what needs to be done can be shortened in small steps, and the gap can be closed remarkably quickly.

The methodological framework presented in this book would allow freedom for a person to conduct a seemingly enormous task of sustainability valuation. Note that there is plenty of room for one to go deeper into the framework. Valuation can be enriched with deepened insights on political philosophy, policymaking, discount rates, business ethics, and corporate social responsibility. Valuation will go smooth once we have reliable measurement of sustainability, institutional hurdles are lifted, and the system of business accounting accommodates the changes. While the framework presented in this book serves as a basis for valuation for virtually all businesses, the actual implementation will require a certain degree of empirical adaption.

Further Readings

Dukes, J. (2001). Where do we stand on closely-held firm valuation. *Journal of Entrepreneurial Finance., 6*(1), 129–155.

Liesen, A., Figge, F., & Hahn, T. (2013). Net present sustainable value: A new approach to sustainable investment appraisal. *Strategic Change: Briefings in Entrepreneurial Finance, 22*(3–4), 175–189.

Lloret, A. (2016). Modelling corporate sustainability strategy. *Journal of Business Research, 69*(2), 418–425.

Minna, Y., & Roland, Z. (2015). Sustainability and firm valuation: An international investigation. *International Journal of Accounting and Information Management, 23*(3), 289–307.
Morgan, J. (2017). Piketty and the Growth dilemma revisited in the context of ecological economics. *Ecological Economics, 136,* 169–177.
Weston, J., Chung, K., & Juan, S. (1998). *Takeovers, restructuring and corporate finance*. London: Prentice Hall.

Appendix A
An Example of Win–Win: Economic Development Versus Commitment Against Climate Changes

Environmental sustainability can be compromised in exchange of the development of economy in global diplomatic stages. A lucid example is found in the commitment countries made on the reduction of CO_2 emission following the Paris Declaration (Box A.1).

Box A.1 Paris Declaration (2015)

The Paris Declaration is a global agreement on actions against climate changes. It was the outcome of the United Nations convention held in Paris during the 30th of November and the 13th of December, 2015. The agreement entered into force on 4 November 2016.

The Agreement aims, by the end of the twenty-first century, to limit the global temperature increase under 1.5 °C and well below 2 °C above the pre-industrial levels. Participating nations have declared their commitments on the reduction of national greenhouse gas emissions by 2030.

Intended nationally determined contributions (INDC)

The Paris Declaration requires all participating nations to put forward their own "nationally determined contributions" (NDCs). This is a bottom up approach. Assessment is to be done every 5 years on the collective progress and the results are to be circulated among the participating nations to eventually guide further individual actions.

Figure A.1 below shows the commitments on the reduction of greenhouse gas (GHG) emissions of top seven GHG emitters in the world following the Paris Declaration. It lists the commitments as reported in the Intended Nationally Determined Contributions (INDC), an official document of the United Nations. They are China, the United States, the European Union, India, Russia, Japan, and Brazil.

Y. Oh, *Sustainability Valuation of Business*,
SpringerBriefs in Finance,
https://doi.org/10.1007/978-3-030-18648-7

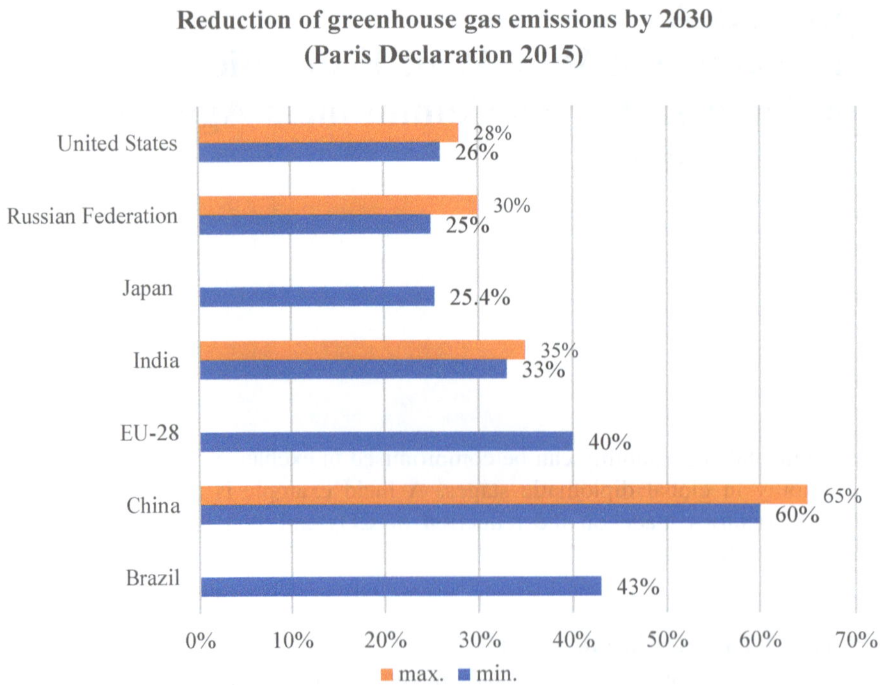

Fig. A.1 Announced commitment of the reduction of greenhouse gas emissions. *Notes* The figures are the Intended Nationally Determined Contributions (INDC) to be achieved by year 2030 following the Paris declaration (2015)

Nations have discretion in deciding their commitments. Note that the figures in Fig. A.1 are copied from the announcement from the UN. Unfortunately, they are not directly comparable across nations as benchmark years and ways to calculate the reduction are not homogeneous across nations. Thus Fig. A.1 needs to be interpreted carefully. For example, the benchmark year is 1990 for the EU and the Russian Federation, whereas it is 2005 for other countries. Among the largest emitters of the GHG, the EU turns out to be a leader. The GHG emissions of the EU has been decreasing since 1990, and its actual emission level of 2005 was 6% lower than that of 1990, and the commitment of 40% cut is against the level of 1990. For China and India, the reduction of the GHG is committed on the intensity to produce GHG in a unit of GDP—carbon intensity—China's commitment of 60% reduction in carbon emission would imply that China's GHG emission would *increase* by almost 72% above the level of 2005, assuming an annual GDP growth of 6 percent. In effect Brazil's commitment is stronger than China. The United States withdrew its membership of the Paris Declaration in June 2017.

The spirit of the Paris Declaration lie in the fact that it is a down to top approach. Substantial discretion is granted in nations' commitments, particularly with a link to the level of economic development. There is consensus that It is tolerated that developing countries would need to make compromise between economic growth and environmental sustainability. Rich countries may afford to taking more progressive measures than poor countries.

Sustainability is a holistic concept and economic development is one of its core elements. It is central to economic sustainability, one of the three pillars of sustainability. CO_2 emissions cannot be avoided in economic development. Allowing it at the expense of environmental degradation may be considered a win-win game among the three pillars of sustainability as well as between the rich and poor nations in the process of balanced sustainable growth.

The Paris Declaration also poses challenges on data collection and reporting of GHG reductions at all governance levels. This would involve central collection of data with a system that prevents moral hazard in the measurements and reporting. Credible scientific data is the essential basis on which comprehensive research can be made to develop the right policy. These data will clarify many aspects regarding what the core drivers of climate changes are and what impact they create, as well as how earth would evolve in reacting to climate changes. In due course it should be revealed how climate changes would modify human living conditions, and how policy can be formulated with corresponding impact analysis and a varying degree of interventions. A refined accounting system may also be needed to record the national level reductions of GHG emission more systematically, with disaggregated data of its businesses, humans, and nature. This accounting system should be compatible across nations.

Appendix B
The Beyond—GDP Debacle

The impact of human activities on nature and the environments is now widely recognized, particularly in the context of the climate changes (Koch 2019). A report of the Intergovernmental Panel on Climate Change of the United Nations (IPCC 2014) shows that economic and population growths continue to be the most important drivers of the CO_2 emissions. The impact of economic growth on CO_2 emissions has risen sharply between 2000 and 2010 from the previous three decades, while the impact of population growth on the increase of CO_2 emissions remained roughly identical.

It is now widely accepted that the GDP is a measure of economic activity but with limited welfare implications. No tractable measures of economic welfare (MEW) appeared until as early as Nordhuis and Tobin (1972). They proposed a sustainable measure of economic welfare (SMEW) for the United States which was adjusted from the GNP (Gross National Products). In terms of sustainability, the GDP is considered a measure of economic sustainability, but has no link to the other pillars of sustainability, namely environmental and social sustainability.

These two aspects would constitute the main arguments in the beyond—GDP debacle (Fleurbaey and Blanchet 2013; Heun et al. 2015). The Stiglitz-Sen-Fitoussi report (2009) reviews the literature and proposes practical yet conceptual recommendations to overcome the limitations of the GDP. There are basically two strands of literature associated with this topic. One is the literature that departs the GDP framework. They would include independent environmental impact studies, survey-based measures, measures on social development, and so on. The other strand either modifies the GDP framework (Jones and Klenow 2016) or extends it (Bullard and Herendeen 1975; Feld and Schneider 2010).

The following table summarizes a non-exhaustive list of beyond—GDP measures (Table B.1).

Y. Oh, *Sustainability Valuation of Business*,
SpringerBriefs in Finance,
https://doi.org/10.1007/978-3-030-18648-7

Table B.1 Beyond—GDP measures

Beyond—GDP framework	Types	Measures
Departing the GDP framework	Dashboards	Variety of quantitative indices Survey based measures: Subjective well-being (SWB) and Stated preference (SP) Equitable and sustainable well-being (BES) Capability approach (CA)
	Alternative welfare measures	Index of Sustainable Economic Welfare (ISEW) Genuine Progress Indicator (GPI) SEEA (System of Environmental Economic Accounting) Environmentally Adjusted GDP (Green GDP) National Welfare Index (NWI) Regional Welfare Index (RWI) IEWB (Index of economic well-being) Ecological Footprints
Staying in the GDP framework	Extensions/modifications	Sustainable measure of economic welfare (SMEW) Net Domestic Capital (NDP) Energy Input-output Adjusted net savings (ANS) Black markets

Notes Adjusted from Stiglitz-Sen-Fitoussi (2009)

Cited Works

Bullard III, C. W., & Herendeen, R. A. (1975, December). The energy cost of goods and services. *Energy Policy, 3*(4), 268–278.

Feld, L. P., & Schneider, F. (2010). Survey on the shadow economy and undeclared earnings in OECD countries. *German Economic Review, 11*(2), 109–149.

Fleurbaey, M., & Blanchet, D. (2013). *Beyond GDP: Measuring welfare and assessing sustainability*. Oxford University Press.

Heun, M. K., Carbajales-Dale, M., & Haney, B. R. (2015). *Beyond GDP: National accounting in the age of resource depletion*. Springer.

Intergovernmental Panel on Climate Change (IPCC). (2014). *Climate Change 2014: Mitigation of Climate Change*. Contribution of Working Group III to the Fifth Assessment Report of the Intergovernmental Panel on Climate Change.

Jones, C. I., & Klenow, P. J. (2016). Beyond GDP? Welfare across countries and time. *American Economic Review, 106*(9), 2426–2457.

Nordhaus, W. D., & Tobin, J. (1972). Is growth obsolete? In W. D. Nordhaus and J. Tobin (Eds.), *Economic Research: Retrospect and prospect, Volume 5, Economic Growth* (pp. 1–80). National Bureau of Economic Research.

Stiglitz-Sen-Fitoussi Report. (2009). *On the measurement of economic performance and social progress*. European Commission. (http://ec.europa.eu/eurostat/documents/118025/118123/Fitoussi+Commission+report).

Appendix C
A Brief History of Sustainability

Around the 1970s doomsday scenarios surfaced on the future of earth. Notable ones would include Boulding (1966) and Meadows et al. (1972). The first one alerts the realization that earth being a closed single spaceship has limited reservoirs of resources for extraction and against pollution. It enlightens the very nature of the interaction between humans and nature in the process of industrial production and economic growth. The second one develops their own quantitative model. They demonstrate how economic growth could be detrimental to the life of earth as human population, industrial production, use of land, depletion of nonrenewable resources, and pollution grow exponentially. They suggest to deliberately limit growth by (1) keeping the industrial capital and the population constant in size, (2) keeping all input and output rates—births, deaths, investment, and depreciation—to a minimum, and (3) keeping the levels of capital and population and the ratio between the two in accordance with the values of society.

Critiques to the second one include one that raises the lack of consideration of technological progress in the model which might have potential to solve the problem (Cole et al. 1973), or one pointing out the ignorance of social dimensions (Hirsch 1976). But there has also been recognition that the model predictions are after all not incorrect examining their points years after (Turner 2008; Kool 2013). The very authors re-examined their model later in their new books and stated: "The possible paths into the future do not include continuous growth. The choices are to bring the burden of human activities upon earth down to a sustainable level through human choice, human technology and human organization, or to let nature force the reduction through lack of food, energy or materials, or an increasingly unsound environment" (Meadows et al. 1992, p. 12).

Wackernagel and Rees (1996) reconfirm this view by stating "a rough assessment… shows that current appropriations of natural resources and services already exceed the earth's long-term carrying capacity".

Y. Oh, *Sustainability Valuation of Business*,
SpringerBriefs in Finance,
https://doi.org/10.1007/978-3-030-18648-7

When the original Club of Rome book was published, the word sustainability was not present in the meaning we are familiar with today. The concept of sustainability may refer to the state of the carrying capacity of earth where humans live. The paradox between growth and the physical limitations that earth poses has been the rationale for steady state economy (Daly 1991). One of the debated themes is whether technical progress would be sufficient to overcome restraints on resources: the debate on the weak versus strong sustainability (Neumayer 2013). The former says that technology cannot fully replicate resources, and the limit to growth is needed even with technological progress. The latter advocates that technology can replicate all the resources and suggests that the danger to humans can be avoided with positive growth (Pearce et al. 1989, Dedeurwaerdere 2014).

Evolution in the real world seems to have pointed to strong sustainability. One example is the clear decoupling of economic growth and energy intensity observed during the 1970s and 1980s. Energy intensity (the amount of energy used per unit of GDP) diminished by 25% in the US during 1973–1986. It fell by 20% in the OECD countries during 1973–1985. During these periods, energy use grew only by 5% while the GDP grew by 32% in countries belonging to the International Energy Agency.[1]

Despite this, greater awareness of environmental threats spread throughout the 1990s. The definition of sustainable development appeared for the first time in the UN report "Our Common Future" (The WCED 1987),[2] named the Brundtland Report. It defines sustainable development as socially and environmentally sustainable growth. "*sustainable* development is development that meets the needs of the present without compromising the ability of future generations to meet their own needs." This definition is widely accepted around the world.

The Rio summit (1992), the UN Conference on Environment and Development held in Rio de Janeiro, Brazil, also known as the Earth Summit, drew the first global agreement for sustainable development at the global level. Some key areas, notably businesses, culture, and education, were recognized for the first time as the priority areas to improve sustainability of society. There was also an increasing awareness on the win-win situation between environmental sustainability and economic growth. "Taking a long-term perspective, it follows then that economic growth, trade expansion and environmental protection are goals that can only be reached in conjunction" (p. 70, Schmidheiny 1992). "In the longer run, the surest way to improve your environment is to become rich" (p. 491, Beckerman 1992).

The possibility of win-win between economic development and environmental protection gained more supports. The World Bank Report (1992) recognizes that "there may be trade-offs between income growth and environmental protection" (p. 1)". But it also asserts that "Some problems are associated with the lack of

[1]29 member countries in the world as of 2017.

[2]The World Commission on the Environment and Development of the United Nations.

economic development; inadequate sanitation and clean water, indoor air pollution from biomass burning, and many types of land degradation in developing countries have poverty as their root cause. Here the challenge is to accelerate equitable income growth" (p. 7).

The term 'Sustainable' can have different meanings depending on the context as it simply means durable or resilient. Sustainable business for instance may not imply business contributing to environmental sustainability, but rather resilient business that lasts long without any environmental implication.

There was attempts to value the ecosystem and its services. Costanza et al. (1997) estimate the value of the entire biosphere of earth to be in the range of US $16–54 trillion. The climate change models of Stern (2007) and Nordhaus (1994), the global model of the Club of Rome (1972), and the eco-system valuation model of Costanza et al. (1997) are examples of global models of sustainability. They are some of the grand efforts to bring a holistic approach into a modelling of sustainable earth. These models and other smaller scale models are built on different underlying assumptions which could lead different policy suggestions. For instance, the Stern report supports strong and immediate action to mitigate greenhouse gas emissions, while Nordhaus takes a position for more gradual action.

We would need more modelling efforts that incorporate a holistic concept (Demeritt and Rothman 1999). Drechsler et al. (2007) shows that none was successful at maintaining a holistic perspective among 60 models they studied. Proops and Safonov (2004) compare eight modelling methodologies in ecological economy, (1) evolutionary models, (2) input-output models, (3) Neo-Austrian models, (4) entropy models in ecological economics, (5) thermodynamic models, (6) multi-criteria evaluations, (7) agent-based models, and (8) the environmental Kutznets curve. They are very different from each other in several main aspects, and none of them seems to satisfy the holistic criteria. We may try to relate the global models cited above to these modelling approaches. The model of Stern seems to have connection to the environmental Kutznets curve approach in part, the Nordhaus model to the evolutionary models based on the growth theory, and the model in Costanza et al. (1997) to the Input-Output approach in part. The Club of Rome model may be difficult to connect to one or more of these modelling approaches, though evolutionary models share a conceptual feature.

The most notable global initiatives on sustainable development would include without doubt the eight Millennium Development Goals (MDG 2000–2015) and seventeen Sustainable Development Goals (SDG 2015–2030) of the United Nations. The seventeen SDGs identify the focus areas of global sustainable development. They are, (1) no poverty, (2) zero hunger, (3) good health and wellbeing, (4) quality education, (5) gender equality, (6) clean water and sanitation, (7) affordable and clean energy, (8) decent work and economic growth, (9) industry, innovation and infrastructure, (10) reduced inequalities, (11) sustainable cities and communities, (12) responsible consumption and production, (13) climate action, (14) life below water, (15) life on land, (16) peace, justice and strong institutions, and (17) partnerships. For each goal, specific targets are stipulated to be achieved by 2030. Their progresses are monitored each year.[3]

The precursor of the SGDs is the eight Millennium Development Goals (MDGs). Agreed by 189 nations, they are (1) to eradicate extreme poverty and hunger, (2) to achieve universal primary education, (3) to promote gender equality and empower women, (4) to reduce child mortality, (5) to improve maternal health, (6) to combat HIV/AIDS, malaria and other diseases, (7) to ensure environmental sustainability, and (8) to develop global partnership for development. The progress towards these goals were appraised in 2015, which show mixed signs of progress.

Another notable global initiative on sustainable development is actions against climate changes culminated in the Paris declaration (2015). In less than two decades since the first appearance of the term of sustainable development climate changes have become one of the most captivating issues in the discussion of environmental sustainability. Inducing a smoother transition to lower carbon society has become one of the central topics, in parallel with economic development of lower income economies.

Literature on sustainability uses other terms to indicate the key features of sustainability. They are inter-generational equity and intra-generational equity (Neumayer 2013). Inter-generational equity insures future generations will enjoy at least the same level of environmental, economic and social quality as today. The intra-generational equity refers to the gaps being narrow among people within a generation in all three pillars of sustainability.

Lastly it is worth mentioning another initiative on the scientific front, namely the study on Planetary boundaries (Steffen et al. 2015). This provides us with a direct picture on the physical conditions of earth. With an international team of 18 researchers, the study compiles nine areas where physical conditions of earth are represented. Four of the nine planetary boundaries are direct result of human activity: (1) climate changes, (2) loss of biosphere integrity, (3) land-system change, and (4) altered biogeochemical cycles (phosphorus and nitrogen). Two of these, climate changes and loss of biosphere integrity, are what the scientists would call "core boundaries". Significantly altering either of these "core boundaries" would "drive the Earth System into a new state". Transgression of the planetary boundaries creates substantial risk of destabilizing the state of the eco system of earth. This framework offers a useful tool to understand sustainability of earth and for global policy making, in conjunction with frameworks that are socially or economically oriented.

In short, sustainability has become, to many nations, an ultimate goal. The goal is to keep living conditions better, not worse, over generations. Sustainability is a transdisciplinary concept (Kuhlman and Farrington 2010) encompassing environmental protection, economic performance and social equity. It is a holistic concept that links nature, ecological systems, humans, and human-made society to the system of earth.

[3]http://www.un.org/sustainabledevelopment/sustainable-development-goals/.

Cited Works

Beckerman, W. (1992). Economic growth and the environment: Whose growth? Whose environment? *World Development, 20*(4), 481–496.

Boulding, K. E. (1966). The Economics of the Coming Spaceship Earth. In H. Jarett (Ed.), *Environmental Quality in a growing economy.* Washington, D. C.: Johns Hopkins University Press.

Cole, H. S. D., Freeman, C., Jahoda, M. & Pavitt, K. L. R. (Eds). (1973). *Thinking about the future: a critique of the limits to growth.* Chatto and Windus for Sussex University Press.

Costanza, R., d'Arge, R., De Groot, R., Farber, S., Grasso, M., Hannon, B., … & Raskin, R. G. (1997). The value of the world's ecosystem services and natural capital. *Nature, 387*(6630), 253.

Daly, H. E. (1991). *Steady-State Economics* (2nd, ed.). Washington, D. C.: Island Press.

Dedeurwaerdere (2014). *Sustainability science for strong sustainability.* Cheltenham, UK; Northampton, USA: Edward Elgar.

Demeritt, D., & Rothman, D. (1999). Figuring the costs of climate change: an assessment and critique. *Environment and Planning A: Economy and Space, 31*(3), 389–408.

Drechsler, M., Grimm, V., Mysiak, J., & Wätzold, F. (2007). Differences and similarities between ecological and economic models for biodiversity conservation. *Ecological Economics, 62*(2), 232–241.

Elkington, J. (1997). *Cannibals with folks: The triple bottom line of 21st century business.* Oxford: New Society Publishers.

Hirsch, F. (1976). *Social limits to growth.* Cambridge, MA: Harvard University Press.

Intergovernmental Panel on Climate Change (IPCC). (2014). *Group III contribution to The Fifth Assessment Report of the Intergovernmental Panel on Climate Change.*

Kool, R. (2013). Limits to Growth, environmental science and the nature of modern prophecy. *Ecological Economics, 85,* 1–5.

Kuhlman, T., & Farrington, J. (2010). What is sustainability? *Sustainability, 2*(11), 3436–3448.

Meadows, D. H., Meadows, D. H., Randers, J., & Behrens III, W. W. (1972). *The limits to growth: A report to the club of Rome.* Universe Books.

Meadows, D. H., Meadows, D. L., & Randers, J. (1992). *Beyond the limits: Confronting global collapse, envisioning a sustainable future.* Vermont: Chelsea Green Publishing.

Neumayer, E. (2013). *Weak versus strong sustainability: Exploring the limits of two opposing paradigms* (4th ed.). Edward Elgar.

Nordhaus, W. D. (1994). *Managing the global commons: The economics of climate change.* Cambridge, MA: The MIT Press.

Pearce, D., Markandya, A., & Barbier, E. B. (1989). *Blueprint for a Green Economy.* London: Earthscan.

Proops, J., & Safonov, P. (Eds.). 2004. *Modelling in ecological economics.* Edward Elgar.

Schmidheiny, S. (1992). *Change of course: Global business prospects for development and the environment.* Boston: MIT Press.

Steffen, W., Richardson, K., Rockström, J., Cornell, S. E., Fetzer, I., Bennett, E. M., … & Folke, C. (2015). Planetary boundaries: Guiding human development on a changing planet. *Science, 347*(6223), 736–736.

Stern, N. (2007). *The economics of climate change: The Stern review.* Cambridge University Press.

Turner, M. G. (2008). A comparison of the limits to growth with 30 years of reality. *Global Environmental Change, 18*(3), 397–411.

Wackernagel, M., & Rees, W. E. (1996). *Our Ecological foot-print: Reducing human impact on the Earth.* B.C.: New Society Publishing.

The WCED. (1987). *Our common future.* Oxford University Press.

Willard, B. (2002). *The sustainability advantage: Seven business case benefits of a triple bottom line.* Canada: New Society Publishers.
The World Bank. (1992). *World Development Report.*

Further Readings

Ekins, P. (1993). Limits to growth and sustainable development: Grappling with ecological realities. *Ecological Economics, 8*, 269–288.
Evans, M. R., Grimm, V., Johst, K., Knuuttila, T., de Langhe, R., Lessells, C. M., et al. (2001). The need to reintegrate the natural sciences with economics. *BioScience, 51*(8), 663–673.
Heyes, A. G., & Liston-Heyes, G. (1995). Sustainable resource use: The search for meaning. *Energy Policy*, 23(1), 1–3.
Lovelock, J. (2006). *The revenge of Gaia: Why the earth is fighting back and how we can still save humanity*. London: Penguin Books.
Nordhaus, W. D. (2007). *A review of the Stern review on the economics of climate change. Journal of Economic Literature, 45*(3), 686–702.
O'Malley, M. A., Orzack, S. H., Weisberg, M., Wilkinson, D. J., Wolkenhauer, O., & Benton, T. G. (2013). Do simple models lead to generality in ecology? *Trends in Ecology and Evolution, 28*(10), 578–583.
Randers, J. (2012). *2052: A Global forecast for the next forth years.* Vermont: Chelsea Green Publishing.
Rhoten, D. (2004). Interdisciplinary research: trend or transition? *Items and Issues, 5*, 6–11.
Savitz, A. W.,& Weber, K. (2006). *The triple bottom line: How today's best-run companies are achieving economic, social and environmental success—and how you can too.* Jossey-Bass.
Skonhoft, A. (1998). Resource utilization, property rights and welfare—wildlife and the local people. Ecological Economics, *26*, 67–80.
Stern, N. (2014). Ethics, equity and the economics of climate change paper 1: Science and philosophy. *Economics and Philosophy, 30(3)*, 397–444.
Sverdrup, H., & Ragnarsdóttir, K. V. *40 years after limits to growth: The World 3 system dynamics model and it's impacts.* SIMRESS Project.
Sverdrup, H., & Ragnarsdóttir, K. V. (2004). Natural resources in a planetary perspective. *Geopolitical Perspectives, 3*(2), 129–341.
Turner, G., & Alexander, C. (2014, September 2). Limits to growth was right. New research shows we're nearing collapse. *The Guardian.*
von Weizsäcker, E. U. & Khosla, A. (2011). *Decoupling natural resource use and environmental impacts from economic growth.* UNEP.

Appendix D
A Macro Model of Sustainability

Understanding how sustainability is created or destroyed would be incomplete without a global perspective on earth. This understanding is particularly important as it would inform each public administration whether local, municipal or national of a big picture of global sustainability goals. Each administration may comprehend how it can contribute to the global sustainability goals. This would imply adjustments of the use of resources or priority policy areas at each level of governance.

Our objective in this appendix is to shed light on key parameters and concepts that would help establishing a model of sustainability at the earth level. Modelling of sustainability may be named a macro model of sustainability, if it concerns sustainability in a holistic sense: All principal actors, nature and environments, humans, human made institutions and artifacts are taken in this framework, and the ways that they evolve and interact would determine the future state of society. We will see that such modelling would culminate in sustainability indicators that would have valid policy implications.

Features of a macro model of sustainability would,

- Have a minimalistic feature with a manageably small number of variables
- Be a holistic model that does not distort the functioning of earth by the structure of the model
- Address boundary conditions
- Clarify ultimate objectives of the society
- Suggest policy
- Treat equitably parameters across environmental, economic, and social activities
- Be extendable vertically by decomposition and descaling.

In the modelling of earth, the following two properties should be attained. First, the model describes well how the earth functions. Second, the model should yield indicators of the three pillars of sustainability. This is the transcendent feature of modelling, which signifies such indicators of sustainability arise naturally in the model.

Y. Oh, *Sustainability Valuation of Business*,
SpringerBriefs in Finance,
https://doi.org/10.1007/978-3-030-18648-7

In the model we describe below, we use human consumption as the main driver of the model. It represents the needs and wants of humans. Humans interact with nature directly or indirectly through industrial production.

The functioning of earth may be described as follows.

Figure D.1 shows a conceptual picture of the earth system. It shows that earth may be seen in an unbiased way through actors and objects, both having physical presence, and the environments in which they co-live. Principal actors are humans and non-human creatures like animals and plants. Non-human creatures belong to nature and so do mountains and seas. Natural resources are objects in nature. The environmental components include air, water and land. Nature, humans, and the environment are mutually exclusive in this framework.

How earth is evolving is portrayed in the following manner. There are entries and exits into and from the system of earth, indicated by In's and Out's. The objects in nature (N) and human made artefacts (A), and population (P) as well as objects in the environments are subject to 'In' and 'Out'. New entries in nature would include not only natural breeding, but those created by humans, which would in turn include those depleted by humans but substituted, and those polluted by humans but recovered. 'Substituted' implies replaced by human made substitutes, and 'recovered' implies revived or recycled. Exits from nature would include wastes which may take time to perish and those depleted by humans neither recovered nor substituted. Classifying this way would make it easier to identify where actions could be taken. Entries and exits of humans are reflected in human population (P). Note that man-made artefacts (A) enter and exit the earth as well.

Humans produce to consume and interact with nature and the environments when they are engaged in consumption or production. Production includes goods and services that humans create in both the private and the public sector. Energy

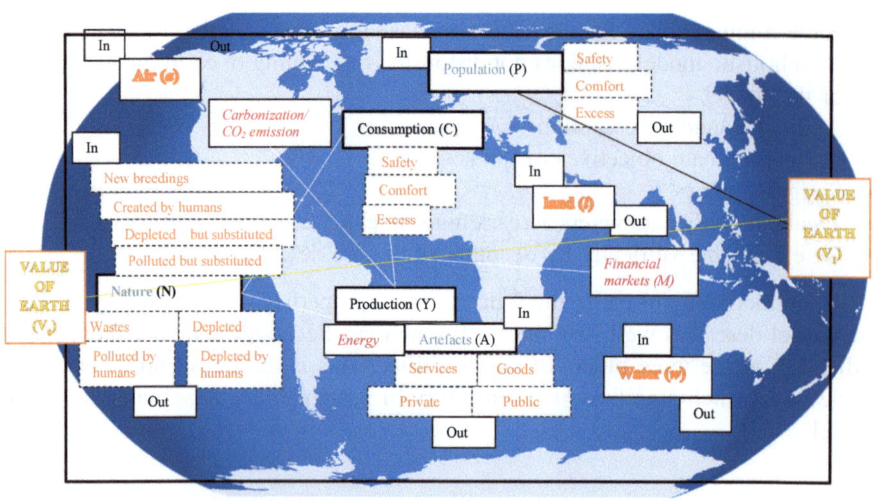

Fig. D.1 A macro model of sustainability

can be consumed directly from nature and the environment, or produced by humans. Humans tend to proliferate, but population may diminish in certain areas. Financial markets act as intermediating the gaps between consumption and production by mediating borrowing and lending.

Consumption of sustainability (C)

People consume the goods and services that humans, nature or the environment produce. People consume sustainability goods and services, in short somewhat loosely sustainability.

Table D.1 shows our classification of consumption of sustainability.

People consume goods and services which are provided through human production or directly by nature. Securities, freedom, and protection of rights are examples of public services that people consume. People pay for these services as they pay taxes to the public sector. All the categories of consumption are mutually exclusive.

Consumption falls under one of the following categories. The first one is *safety consumption* (sc) that satisfies basic needs of humans to survive and live in safety. This is the consumption assuring a basic level of housing, health, food, and security. This category of consumption should include minimum level of sanitation, access to water, and education, as well as protection from crime, war, and so on.

The second category is *comfort consumption* (cc). It refers to consumption beyond satisfying basic needs. Consumption in this category upgrades living quality as it provides comfort beyond safety. Comfort consumption may take a form of higher quality or of a larger quantity in the same goods and services as in basic consumption or refer to the goods and services that basic consumption does not offer. Having a quality home of a decent size would be an example.

Table D.1. Classification of consumption of sustainability

Criteria of consumption				
		Safety level	Comfort level	Excess level
Goods	Manmade goods	1. Eat		
	Nature's goods	2. Drink		
Services	Private sector services	3. Wear		
	Public sector services	4. Dwell		
	Nature's services	5. Have access to education		
		6. Have access to health care		
		7. Be mobile		
		8. Have access to leisure		
		9. Have security		
		10. Have rights		
		11. Enjoy environmental quality		

Note There is no double accounting

The third category is *excess consumption* (ec). Excess consumption refers to consumption that is higher than the level of comfort consumption most people would agree being excessive. Excess consumption may be of higher quality and in larger quantity either in the same goods and services as in comfort consumption, or refer to the goods and services that comfort consumption does not offer.

An individual satisfies first safety consumption, then comfort consumption, and then excess consumption. This set-up would help tackle the equality problems and possibly exploitation related issues.

We will maintain that excess consumption does not improve sustainability of society. The only exception would be environmental quality. Comfort level consumption of environmental quality would not improve sustainability, because environmental quality is assured at the safety level consumption for all humans.

Population (P)

The human population (P) is divided in three groups according to their consumption pattern. A human can be located on the continuous linear line of safety consumption, comfort consumption, and excess consumption.

Nature (N) and the environment (*a*, *l*, *w*)

Nature (N) evolves and interacts with humans as it is recycled, depleted, or polluted by humans. When depleted materials are substituted by human capital, it is said to be substituted (if it is substituted by nature, it is called recycled). Same applies for polluted materials. Air (a), water (w), and land (l) are the three components to comprise the environmental goods and services. They can be estimated on both quality and quantity.

Financial markets (M)

Financial markets moderate the gap between consumption and production of sustainability. The role of financial markets is to ensure smooth consumption of sustainability along the production cycles.

Production of sustainability (Y)

Production refers to production of sustainability by humans. Whilst it is based on the production of the goods and services by humans, and the by-products that are related to sustainability in the process, such as environmental or social footprints.

The goods and services that humans make are man-made artefacts that satisfy human consumption. New artefacts are produced, and they decay or are destroyed. Energy is an object of production. Societies may have different paths of civilization, which would bring heterogeneity in the system of man-made institutions. Public sector services can be further divided into government driven and non-government driven, namely by civil societies or non-governmental organizations (NGO's).

Result 1: The value of earth

The value of earth is derived from an anthroposophical perspective that what matters to humans count in the value of earth. We argue that it is equal to the sum of safety consumption and comfort consumption of humans except for environmental quality for which only safety consumption is counted. We consider the excess consumption not countable in sustainability, particularly because it is detrimental to the sustainability of equity and an undesirable level of resource use is associated with them. The value of earth defined this way is equal to the value of sustainability of earth.

Result 2: Three pillars of sustainability

It is possible to infer the state of three pillars of sustainability. Environmental sustainability can be inferred primarily from (1) the entries and exits into and from earth as the continuation of species are concerned, and (2) the environmental qualities. Economic sustainability can be inferred from production or consumption in relation with the growth in population. Social sustainability can be inferred by observing when and how much the population of the comfort group increases and the population of the safety group diminishes.

The sustainability indicators like these can be monitored over time to see if they do not deteriorate over time (inter-generational equity), and if the disparity among people shrinks (intra-generational equity).

Result 3: A policy modelling

Policy modelling of sustainability can be derived from the framework illustrated above.

(1) The total sustainability (S) of the earth equals to the value of earth, which is the sum of safety consumption (sc) and comfort consumption (cc) except for environmental quality for which only safety consumption counts

$$S = sc + cc \text{ except for environmental quality}$$

and

$$S = sc \text{ for environmental quality}$$

S should not diminish over time.

(2) The condition in favor of sustainability would require (1) three pillars of sustainability (EN, EC, SC) being above their minimum levels, and (2) not getting worse over generations.

$$\begin{aligned} &(1)\ EN\text{-} \leq EN_0 \leq EN_1 \ldots \\ &(2)\ EC\text{-} \leq EC_0 \leq EC_1 \ldots \\ &(3)\ SC\text{-} \leq SC_0 \leq SC_1 \ldots \end{aligned} \quad (D.1)$$

where (EN-, EC-, SC-) are the minimum levels of (EN, EC, SC) respectively. Attaining these points is a valid policy objective with a high degree of priority. One may even put an extra constraint that satisfying the minimum levels be the absolute priority. Such policy would justify policy of an underdeveloped economy whose economic growth may need to be reconciled with environmental sustainability.

(3) Denote EN, EC and SC as the actual levels and E^*, D^* and Q^* their desired levels.

$$
\begin{aligned}
g_{EN} &= (EN^* - EN) \\
g_{EC} &= (EC^* - EC) \\
g_{SC} &= (SC^* - SC)
\end{aligned}
\tag{D.2}
$$

g_{EN}, g_{EC}, and g_{SC} refer to the gaps between the actual and the desired levels of sustainability. They imply the levels of alarm in each category: The further away they are from their desired levels, the worse the situation is. Policy should aim to diminish these gaps.

It may be argued that it should be permitted for growing economy to pursue economic growth at the expense of environmental sustainability. Suppose that the population of a nation falls in the category of safety population, and that the environmental sustainability of the area will have consequences. Then a transfer of wealth from comfort population to safety population, for example in the form of the official development aids (ODA), may be justified to compensate for preserving environmental quality at the cost of slower economic growth for those economies.

Appendix E
Political Economic Regimes

This appendix develops a simple model in which different regimes of political economy emerge over a long period of time. Economic gains are the sole criteria of decision making both at the individual and collective levels. In such a set-up, the most ancient type is the growth-oriented regime, which can surface before politics is created. Politics starts to form and exert power to creation of wealth. Growth is moderated and equity starts to take its weight. Politics may take different forms, of which a democratic regime may be the most advanced one, but economic implications of direct (direct voting system) and indirect (voting via political parties) political systems differ on the prospects of growth and equity.

I. ***A growth-oriented regime***

People form a society and institutions are created. Denote the collective total cost to adopt and implement a policy measure k, as C_k. a_{ij} is the proportion of this cost that incurs for individual i such that the actual cost for individual i is $a_i C_k$. Individual and collective decision rule of policy making are as follows. A measure k may be growth-oriented, equity-oriented or neutral. The measure is decided at the society level. C_k, the cost of policy k, is the public sector expenditure paid ultimately by people.

People will be inclined to support the measure as long as they perceive that their economic situation improves with it. That is when,

$$E(\Delta I_{ik} - a_{ik} C_k) > 0 \tag{E.1}$$

I_i is the wealth of individual i. $E(\Delta I_{ik})$ is the expected value discounted for today of the gross gains for individual i from the adoption of k.

In a growth-oriented society, the society adopts a policy if $E(\Delta W_k)$ is positive.

Y. Oh, *Sustainability Valuation of Business*,
SpringerBriefs in Finance,
https://doi.org/10.1007/978-3-030-18648-7

$$E(\Delta W_k) = \sum_{i=1,\ldots N} E(\Delta I_{ik} - a_{ik}C_k) > 0$$
$$\text{with} \sum_{i=1,\ldots N} (a_{ik}) = 1 \tag{E.2}$$

W is the sum of the wealth of all individuals. ΔW_k is the increase of wealth of the society with the adoption of k. N is the number of the economically active people in the society. This is the most primitive state. People have no saying on the choice of policy even if it goes against their interest.

II. *The politics-moderated growth regime*

Polity arises naturally in the society. Some may want to have more power than others (for instance for their economic interests to be better ensured). Or those who are excluded from gaining by policy measures may not stay silent. People have different degrees of power to exert in the collective selection process of policy measures.

Denote such power as $P_i \in [0, 1]$, such that $\sum_{i=1,\ldots N}(P_i) = 1$. This includes extreme cases where some people have no power, or a single person has all the power. When the power is equally distributed in the society, P_i equals to 1/N. Individual decision-making rule does not change, but the collective rule does.

The society accepts a policy measure if

$$\sum_i P_{ik}[E(\Delta I_{ik}) - a_{ik}C_k)] > 0 \tag{E.3}$$

The politics-moderated growth regime is born with the introduction of politics in the society. This rule is biased in favour of the individuals with higher power.

(Result 1) Adverse selection can occur with the politics-moderated regime. Suppose that two measures, $k1$ and $k2$, are competitive. $k1$ is preferred to $k2$ if

$$\sum_i [E(\Delta I_{ik1}) - a_{ik1}C_{k1})] > \sum_i [E(\Delta I_{ik2}) - a_{ik2}C_{k2})]$$

But $k2$ is adopted if

$$\sum_i P_{ik1}[E(\Delta I_{ik1}) - a_{ik1}C_{k1})] < \sum_i P_{ik2}[E(\Delta I_{ik2}) - a_{ik2}C_{k2})]$$

The politics moderated rule may not be sustainable. The growth-oriented regime and the politics-moderated regime lead to different decisions.

III. *The equal-vote regime*

The equal-vote regime refers to one in which $P_i = 1/N$ in the politics-moderated regime. People are granted the same voting power. Then the decision-making rule leads to the same results as the growth-oriented rule. As before, a policy measure can be adopted, from which a majority is not benefited, thus still non-democratic.

The society accepts a policy measure if

$$\sum_{i} (1/N) * [E(I_{ik}) - a_{ik}C_k] > 0 \tag{E.4}$$

(Result 2) The governance rule of the equal-vote regime, $\sum_i (1/N) * [E(I_{ik}) - a_{ik}C_k] > 0$, yields the same result as that of the growth regime, $\sum_i [E(I_{ik}) - a_{ik}C_k)] > 0$.

The problem that the number of people who lose may outnumber those who gain is not resolved.

IV. ***The democratic regime***

The democratic regime is the one that chooses a measure that maximizes the number of people who gain regardless of the size of the gains or losses at the society level. Generally, the society establishes a certain agreed number for the voting such that

$$n/N \geq \alpha$$

If α is ½, this is in effect a majority rule.

V. ***The economically democratic regime***

The economically democratic rule is the one that combines the economic rule and the democratic rule.

It accepts a policy measure if

$$\sum_{i} [E(I_{ik}) - a_{ik}C_k] > 0 \text{ and } n/N \geq \alpha,$$

where n is the number of individuals who gain by adopting the measure.

The economically democratic regime yields the same gain as the growth rule only when the growth rule coincides with $n/N \geq \alpha$. When $n/N < \alpha$, the growth-oriented regime yields the larger gain at the society level than the *economically democratic* rule.

The economically democratic regime balances a purely growth-oriented regime and a purely equity-oriented regime.

VI. ***Does the system of political parties ensure social equity better than the system of direct voting?***

As the model described above suggests, politics naturally occur to infuse equity into the society where growth is an underlying driver in the economy.

We may see the degree of equity in wealth of a society (EQ). Denote the gain of the society on equity by an adoption of policy k, as ΔEQ_k. It is measured on two factors: the increase in number of people engaged in economic activities due to the adoption of policy k, denoted n(k)/N, where N is the total number of people engaged in economic activities before policy k. n(k) is the increase of the number of people engaged in economic activities after policy k. ΔGAPW(k) is the increase in the gap in wealth across people due to the adoption of policy k. These two parameters would have little importance in growth-oriented societies.

$$\Delta EQ_k = \{n(k)/N\} / \Delta GAPW(k) \quad (E.5)$$

Would a more elaborate system of politics improve equity? Suppose that there are political parties, and the society has established an indirect political system replacing the direct voting system.

An individual i can participate to exert their power through the parties they belong to such that

$$P_{ik} = Pd(i)k \quad (E.6)$$

d(i) refers to the political party to which individual i supports. Pd(i)k is the power of the political party that individual i belongs to with respect to the adoption of policy k.

Suppose a case where (1, n) people, i.e. from the first person to the n-th person in the total population of N, voted for d(1) with n/N larger than ½. Therefore d(1) is a majority party.

We allow that individuals in the same party may have different preference on k's. That is, d(1) chooses k, despite the people in d(1) who do not benefit from k. When a party has the voting power, not the people themselves, the majority party can vote against the majority of the population. This would not happen in the case of direct democracy. Equity is not necessarily better ensured with a political system that runs with political parties than with direct democracy.

Public policy in favour of equity may take different faces. If equity is the priority, one way to ensure this is to have as little disparity as possible across different political parties concerning their political agenda toward equity in employment, job creations or new business creation.

The clash point of policy

Lastly, it may be useful to conceptualize the clash point of a public policy. The clash point indicates the degree of difficulty with which the adoption of the policy in question faces. One may conceptualize it with the following equation.

The clash point regarding the adoption of a public measure k, CP(k), can be found with

$$CP(k) = CP(f_d, f_s, PT \mid f_e, k) \quad (E.7)$$

f_d, f_s and f_e are the demand side force, the supply side force, and the external force respectively. PT refers to politics. k is the policy in question. The demand side force refers to the relative force that is exerted by people who need this measure and those who support them against those who do not. The supply side force comes from reigning institutions who make policy. Suppose that a majority of the population would like a change in a certain political agenda that goes against the political stance of the reigning government. Then f_d is larger than ½, whereas *fs* is much smaller than ½. Politics (PT) would smoothen the conflicts between f_d and f_s. If it smoothens perfectly the conflicts (PT = 1), then CP is null. If it does not smooth at all (PT = 0), then it does not make any difference to the clash point. f_e refers to the governance outside of the internal governance, such as international communities toward the national government. The conflict between f_d and f_s for instance can be lessened by f_e, if f_e is in favor of the policy in question. This implies that Eq. E.6 can be written as for given k,

$$CP(k) = |f_d - f_s| * (1 - \mathrm{PT}) - f_e \tag{E.8}$$

CP cannot be negative. It is 0 for unanimity for passing.

For k to be adopted as a measure, CP(k) should be smaller than a certain level. Denote this level as α. Where a majority rule persists, α is ½, or this level may be pre-agreed at other values. Suppose a direct democracy where each person can vote directly at a forum (examples include Ancient Greek, or cantons in Switzerland of today). CP(k) is directly observable by n/N with n the number of people voting for the measure and N the total population.

Appendix F
Crisis Prevention Discount Rates

Discount rates can be defined and calculated in diverse ways. What matters should be the underlying risk profile that would demand compensation for a given period of time. One of the typical ways to think of this is to use the concept of insurance. It would not be a bad idea if one wants to learn about the discount rates of a certain product, just to ask an insurance firm to do the job by asking for insurance of the product.

What an insurance company would do is to foresee a range of possibilities, assigning probabilities to each one of them, estimating the costs of the damages in each case and the insurance payments that would accompany when the damage occurs. The insurance company will make its own business model that there will be no possibility of loss on its side.

Action on sustainability principles would reduce possibilities of crisis, particularly large-scale calamities that could affect large areas of the globe concomitantly. It can be natural calamities, but it may also be a financial or political crisis. The latter kind have already been witnessed a few times in recent decades.

Reducing the possibility of a crisis can be achieved with much lower costs (C) than the size of the actual damages (D) when such events happen.

Denote the probability of a crisis of type 'a' at time t: $\left(\mathrm{Pb}_t^a\right)$

Costs to prevent it now: $\left(\mathrm{C}_{0,t}^a\right)$

Damages when a crisis 'a' actually happens: $\mathrm{D}^a_{>=t}$

$_{0,\,t}$ and $_{>=t}$ refer to 'from now before time t' and 'at any time after t' respectively. $\left(\mathrm{C}_{0,t}^a\right)$ is estimated at time 0 (now).

Gains are calculated with the difference between the present value of the damages and the costs as,

$$\text{Gains} = \Delta_{0,t} * \mathrm{D}^a_{>=t} - \mathrm{C}_{0,t}^a \tag{F.1}$$

Y. Oh, *Sustainability Valuation of Business*,
SpringerBriefs in Finance,
https://doi.org/10.1007/978-3-030-18648-7

$\Delta_{0,t}$ is the discount rate between now and t. * is the sign of multiplication. Equation 17 says that the initial investment can prevent the event of calamity at the cost below the present value of the damages caused by the calamity. The lower this cost, the more gain we receive.

$\Delta_{0,t}(0)$ is one that makes the gains equal to zero. We call this discount rate 'Crisis Prevention Discount Rate (CPDR)', the most conservative one among the discount rates. The investment needed in this case is,

$$C^{a}_{0,t} = \Delta_{0,t} * D^{a}_{>=t} \tag{F.2}$$

This is the theoretical discount rates of the pessimists who would like to take actions immediately and in full force.

The more reasonable estimate of investment would be based on,

$$\left(C^{a}_{0,t}\right) = \Delta'_{0,t} * \text{Prob.}\,(D) * D^{a}_{>=t} \tag{F.3}$$

with Prob.(D) being the probability of D taking place at time t.

The market rates of discounts are likely to take Prob.(D) being smaller than 1. Markets may demand investment closer to (3) rather than (2).

MIX
Papier aus verantwortungsvollen Quellen
Paper from responsible sources
FSC® C105338

If you have any concerns about our products,
you can contact us on
ProductSafety@springernature.com

In case Publisher is established outside the EU,
the EU authorized representative is:
Springer Nature Customer Service Center GmbH
Europaplatz 3, 69115 Heidelberg, Germany

Printed by Libri Plureos GmbH
in Hamburg, Germany

Functional Materials in Biomedical Applications

Functional Materials in Biomedical Applications

edited by
Costas Demetzos, Natassa Pippa, and Nikolaos Naziris

JENNY STANFORD
PUBLISHING

Published by

Jenny Stanford Publishing Pte. Ltd.
101 Thomson Road
#06-01, United Square
Singapore 307591

Email: editorial@jennystanford.com
Web: www.jennystanford.com

British Library Cataloguing-in-Publication Data
A catalogue record for this book is available from the British Library.

Functional Materials in Biomedical Applications

ISBN 978-981-4968-65-2 (Hardcover)
ISBN 978-1-003-41146-8 (eBook)

Contents

Preface

Drug delivery is the multidisciplinary scientific field of engineered technologies for the targeted delivery and/or controlled release of active pharmaceutical ingredients (APIs). The technology of drug delivery has evolved dramatically in the past few decades and even greater changes are anticipated in the near future. Biomedical engineers have contributed substantially to our understanding of the physiological barriers to efficient drug delivery, such as transport in the circulatory system and drug movement through cells, tissues and barriers; they have also contributed to the development of several new modes of drug delivery that have entered clinical practice. In parallel, formulation scientists have begun to reformulate APIs in a tailored manner, so that they may be more safely used in specific pathological conditions. This multi-authored book presents some recent trends and research achievements in the field of drug delivery systems. The routes of administration, special techniques, the advanced materials and their characteristics *in vitro* and *in vivo* are discussed in depth.

In **Chapter 1**, chitosan bio-based materials, which are a class of natural polysaccharides, are presented and discussed, with respect to their design, biological properties, and applications. Methods of preparation and material reinforcement techniques are described first, followed by food packaging and biomedical applications. Chitosan can be combined with various types of nanoparticles, in order to develop functional hybrid films with enhanced properties.

Cyclodextrins as functional pharmaceutical excipients are discussed in **Chapter 2**. The chapter introduces us to a historical background of these nanomaterials and their utilization in biomedical applications, followed by a brief presentation of their structure and properties. A mechanistic explanation of complex formation with drug molecules is given, as well as some pharmacokinetic and toxicological aspects. The main part of the chapter comprises the available cyclodextrin-related applications in pharmaceutics and medicine, with reference to advanced technologies, such as nanosponges and complexes with metal-organic frameworks.

Polymers, proteins, and peptides are key blocks for building drug delivery systems and other technological platforms for biomedical purposes. **Chapter 3** is dedicated to mixed/hybrid nanosystems of these two classes, aiming to highlight their wide range of applications. The structural and physicochemical properties of the polymer- and protein/peptide-based biomaterials are presented, while the potential nanosystems that emerge from their combination are discussed in detail. Several examples of the application of these hybrids in nanomedicine and other fields are finally presented.

Chapter 4 aims to familiarize the reader with the innovative concept of stimuli-responsive polymers in theranostics. The term "theranostic" was introduced to describe any nanomaterial that combines the therapeutic and diagnostic/imaging modalities. These nanomaterials are classified based on their nature, giving rise to polymer theranostics, hybrid material theranostics and small, organic molecule theranostic systems. External or internal stimuli, including pH, light irradiation, and others, can be utilized to trigger the functionality of these biomaterials, facilitating the concurrent diagnosis, through optical imaging, magnetic resonance imaging and ultrasounds, and therapy, such as chemotherapy, photodynamic, photothermal, and sonodynamic therapy. Future perspectives and clinical investigation are also included in the chapter.

Inorganic nanoparticles have been systematically studied as diagnostic agents and therapeutics. However, their toxicity is a major obstacle in their clinical translation and market approval. Proteins and peptides are utilized to functionalize inorganic nanoparticles, which leads to hybrids with improved biocompatibility and pharmacokinetics. Quality theranostic formulations can be developed by integrating proteins of natural origin, short peptides, or engineered amino acid sequences with inorganic nanoparticles. These technologies, their properties, functionality, advantages, and applicability in biomedicine are thoroughly discussed in **Chapter 5**.

In **Chapter 6**, an elaborate presentation of conjugated polymeric nanoparticles and their applications in cancer theranostics is given. First, the chemistry and properties of conjugated polymeric nanoparticles are presented. Then, several imaging modalities of this class of nanoparticles are discussed, including fluorescence imaging, photoacoustic imaging, and Raman imaging, followed by their therapeutic potential, through photothermal or photodynamic therapy. Finally, the multifunctionality of conjugated polymeric nanoparticles is discussed, which combines concurrent imaging, phototherapy, and drug delivery.

Another innovative technological platform for drug delivery is presented in the next chapter, that of functionalized carbon nanohorns. **Chapter 7** classifies these nanosystems in two categories, those with covalently grafted drugs or biomolecules and those with non-covalent interactions between the nanohorns and the molecules. The functionalization of carbon nanohorns with specific groups can also lead to improved biocompatibility and hydrophilicity, while their properties render them appropriate as intelligent drug carriers for the delivery of bioactive molecules *in vitro* and *in vivo*.

Chapter 8 presents some of the available technologies for dermal and transdermal delivery of drug molecules, with emphasis on nanodispersions. Fundamental elements of the skin, as well as the interaction between the skin and nanocarriers, are explained. Thereafter, microemulsions, nanoemulsions, and nanodispersions are discussed as colloidal nanosystems, while emulsification methods are also provided. For emulsions, the ratio of water, oil, and surfactants determines their physicochemical properties, biocompatibility, and penetration efficacy. Several important applications of nanodispersions in skin drug delivery are finally presented.

Another approach on skin disorders utilizes functional peptides, which have been studied for their effect and modulation of various biological processes that take place in the skin. **Chapter 9** offers a presentation of a plethora of such peptides, with respect to their properties, interactions with the skin, and effect on various pathological mechanisms. The possible applications of these molecules in skin disorders and diseases, followed by strategies for peptide stability and skin permeability enhancement, are provided.

The final chapter concerns the utilization of small angle neutron scattering (SANS) as a powerful and versatile technique for the investigation of soft matter structures, including the aforementioned polymers, proteins, and biological materials. **Chapter 10** provides the theoretical background of SANS, the experiment preparation and functions in each case of nanosystem, while application in various classes of nanoparticles is presented. SANS allows us to study the morphology complexity of nanomaterials at length scales between 1 nm and 1000 nm, offering quantification of their multi-scale and hierarchical organization.

We thank all the authors for sharing with us their valuable expertise and knowledge in the field of drug delivery. This work will guide young scientists in their future studies and research, while it is also a guide for experienced scientists on recent advances in the area of functional biomaterials for applications in formulation and drug delivery.

Prof. Costas Demetzos
Assist. Prof. Natassa Pippa
Dr Nikolaos Naziris

Chapter 1

Functional Bio-Based Chitosan Films: From Material Design to Biological Properties

Abdelkrim El Kadib,[a] Natalia Wrońska,[b] Katarzyna Lisowska,[b] Aicha Anouar,[a] Nadia Katir,[a] Katarzyna Miłowska,[c] Beata Bielska,[c] and Maria Bryszewska[c]

[a]*Euromed Research Center, Engineering Division (Center Is Part of the Division), Euro-Med University of Fes (UEMF), Route de Meknes, Rond-Point de Bensouda, Fès 30070, Morocco*
[b]*Department of Industrial Microbiology and Biotechnology, University of Lodz, 12/16 Banacha St. Lodz, 90-236, Poland*
[c]*Department of General Biophysics, University of Lodz, 141/143 Pomorska St. Lodz, 90-236, Poland*

a.elkadib@ueuromed.org

Petroleum-based plastics are used in many different daily-life commodities, including food packaging and agrochemicals, disposable catering supplies, medical devices, and flexible electronics. Unfortunately, conventional plastics generate annually a substantial amount of waste with a negative and extremely alarming impact on our environment and public health. Consequently, there is heightened interest in searching for bio-based materials to find sustainable alternatives. The use of renewable resources, their transformation and processing through

Functional Materials in Biomedical Applications
Edited by Costas Demetzos, Natassa Pippa, and Nikolaos Naziris

ISBN 978-981-4968-65-2 (Hardcover), 978-1-003-41146-8 (eBook)
www.jennystanford.com

straightforward, and clean and energy-efficient procedures are making significant breakthroughs in the realm of the bio-based packaging industry.

Natural polysaccharides constitute an interesting class of polymers that can be used for this purpose. Among those of interest is chitosan, extracted from marine waste, which has, many advantages including its abundance (the second most abundant polysaccharide on the earth after cellulose), the presence of amino groups on its skeletal structure, and its flexibility, handling, and possible chemical modification. Due to its physical and chemical properties and biological activity, it is of great interest, since it is a biodegradable, bioactive, non-toxic, bacteriostatic, biocompatible compound with film-forming and fiber-forming properties, characterized by high absorption capacity. It can be molded as thin or thick films with controlled transparency, which is why, it is widely used in industries and medicines.

We, herein, describe the preparation of chitosan films. A large panel of hybrid films can be obtained by mixing chitosan solution with preformed nanoparticles or other nano-objects to further modify or enrich their structure. This includes the use of graphene, clay nanoparticles, cellulose nanocrystals, hydroxyapatite, and other fillers. The introduction of these particulates improved the thermal stability and mechanical resistance of the shaped films, but most importantly, these additives improve their surface-biological response, including their antibacterial and hemolytic activity.

1.1 Introduction

Petrochemical-based plastics have undeniably improved modern life; they have been made indispensable in our daily life, with dependency on their use constantly increasing for decades. Plastics are used in food packaging, kitchen utensils, computers, and bathtubs for a huge range of purposes. Despite the many advantages they offer, plastic waste (dominated by packaging) disposal is causing major environmental threats because these materials take many years to decompose, their perishing releases toxic substances and their combustion releases toxic substances into the air, causing pollution [1]. Accordingly, CO_2 emissions from the plastic life cycle released into the atmosphere reached 860 million tons in 2019 [2], decreasing the carbon footprint of plastics is thus an urgent and pressing matter. Replacing conventional plastics with bio-based synthetic polymers is one way to mitigate the environmental challenges. Polymers from renewable resources, such as polylactic acid (PLA), are currently widely used, as their overall CO_2 emission is lower compared with conventional plastics [3]. Moreover, sustainable sources of materials offer the advantage of biodegradability and in some cases biocompatibility. A more generalized use of PLA is, however, conditioned by its synthesis since it is generally prepared by ring-opening polymerization of lactide [4], making the design of sustainable and high-performing bioplastics or films starting from biopolymers of great interest. Among the materials readily available, seaweed-derived polysaccharides offer sustainable alternatives to petroleum-based plastics [5].

Chitin, next to cellulose, is a very abundant naturally occurring linear amino polysaccharide generally found in the shells of arthropods. It consists of a repetition of N-acetyl-D-glucosamine monomers linked by a $\beta(1\rightarrow4)$ glycosidic bond. Natural chitin in the form of crystalline microfibers is a component of the outer shells of crustaceans, as also in the cuticle of arthropods and cell walls of fungi [6].

Every year, about 10^{10}–10^{12} tons of chitin are biosynthesized. The great interest in this polysaccharide stems from its properties, including its strength, biocompatibility, biodegradability, and bioactivity. Many studies have shown that chitin is non-toxic, a physiologically inert compound with antibacterial properties that has an affinity for proteins. The usefulness of chitin, however, is strictly limited, due to its poor solubility, which explains the ongoing interest in its derivative, chitosan [7].

Chitosan is a polysaccharide obtained by deacetylation of chitin in an alkaline medium; being an amino-polysaccharide whose structure is essentially composed of D-glucosamine units, with the structural difference being determined by the degree of acetylation. Indeed, the level of acetylation in chitin is >50%, whereas the ideal structure is characterized by a fairly low degree of acetylation. The main advantage of chitosan is its solubility in aqueous acetic acid, this being due to the protonation of amino groups in an acidic medium. The number of D-glucosamine groups present dictates its interactions in aqueous solutions; therefore, gauging the amount of deacetylation accurately is of paramount importance, as it dictates its intrinsic viscosity and ability to form aggregates.

The presence of hydroxyl and amino groups in chitosan allows its chemical modification. Furthermore, it can be produced in different forms, such as fibers, films, membranes, or microspheres, thus offering a variety of catalytic supports with modifiable properties [8]. Chitosan is a versatile substance used in many industries. This is due to its unique properties, such as biodegradability, antibacterial and antifungal activity, and non-toxicity. Easy processing and the possibility of combining it with other substances may lead to the discovery of new uses for chitosan that should make everyday life easier.

One of the most important fields of application of chitosan is in the food industry. Research on the use of chitosan as an active ingredient in packaging intended for food storage has proved that it is a suitable material for the protection of food products, due to its antibacterial and antioxidant properties [9]. Chitosan is in the form of films or coatings in packaging. The use of active packaging ensures that the food maintains high quality, safety, and organoleptic properties. Compared to traditional packaging, active packaging extends the shelf-life of food [10].

1.2 Preparation of Chitosan Films

Chitosan is insoluble in water and the most common organic solvent. In acidic media ($pH<6$), the amino groups are protonated and thus chitosan becomes polycationic, characterized by a high positive charge [11]. Films are prepared by pouring acidic solutions of chitosan into casting dishes or flat surfaces, followed by subsequent evaporation of the solvent. After evaporation of the solvent, transparent films are obtained; depending on the molecular weight, the films have a slight yellowish coloration [12]. Numerous factors such as the degree of deacetylation

(DD), the molecular weight, or the drying method used greatly affect the quality of the resulting films [13]. Films prepared from high-molecular-weight chitosan usually have high tensile strength and bigger elongation at breaks than low-molecular-weight films probably due to the chain entanglement of the network during film formation. The DD not only affects the solubility of chitosan, but also conditions the mechanical properties of chitosan films. Nunthanid et al. [12] found that for a DD of 100%, the molecular weight determines the final mechanical properties of the resulting films. Accordingly, chitosan films with high molecular weights (600,000–800,000) have denser packing of the biopolymer chains than those made from low-molecular-weight chitosan that does not have sufficient chain entanglement to form films [12]. The DD indicates the extent to which N-acetyl glucosamine units have become glucosamine units. It can be determined by spectroscopic characterization techniques, such as Fourier-transform infrared spectroscopy (FTIR) and nuclear magnetic resonance (NMR) spectroscopy [14]. As DD is a parameter that influences the solubility and the performance of chitosan films in a wide range of applications, the use of FTIR, a readily available analytical technique, is generally preferred. The FTIR spectrum of chitosan is generally recorded in the middle infrared (4000–400 cm^{-1}) range and is characterized by a series of absorption bands corresponding to the vibrations of the different atoms of the polysaccharide chains. In the 3,600–3,200 cm^{-1} range, the absorption bands generally correspond to –OH stretching vibrations. The broad absorption band at approximately 3,440 cm^{-1} corresponds to the overlapping of amino and hydroxyl groups [15–17]. In the 1680–1400 cm^{-1} range, –C=O (amide I), NH (amide II), and NH–CO (amide III) stretching vibrations are observed [16]. For the DD determination, two absorption bands are taken into consideration, a characteristic band that is greatly affected by the DD (or acetylation) units, and a reference band representing unaffected by DD. ^{1}H-NMR is a powerful technique used to estimate the amount of D-glucosamine and N-acetyl-D-glucosamine by using the areas under the curve of the signals. Prior solubilization in CD_3COOD or DCl in D_2O is required [14, 18].

The thickness of chitosan films depends on the method used to cast the solutions onto a flat surface. For instance, by spin-coating chitosan solutions on silicon chips, an average thickness of 30 nm was measured by an ellipsometer [19]. Thicker films are generally obtained by simple evaporation of the solvent. Their thicknesses range from 20 μm to 150 μm, and depend on the volume cast on the dish and the concentration of chitosan in the acidic solutions. When 3 ml 2 wt% chitosan solution is cast on a 5.5 × 5.5 cm^2 Petri dish, the average thickness is ~26 μm [15].

Chitosan films are hydrophilic in nature and have poor barrier properties to moisture, limiting for instance their use in food packaging, where moisture control is mandatory. Independently of the molecular weight and deacetylation degree, chitosan films readily dissolve in acid solutions and normal saline, whereas dissolution in distilled water is slower [12]. Films have to maintain their excellent properties throughout their useful life. Unfortunately, native chitosan films are characterized by their rigidity and brittleness, which limits their widespread use. Several strategies have been proposed to circumvent these limitations and improve chitosan film properties. The mechanical properties of chitosan films can be enhanced by improving their structural integrity by forming crosslinks between the amine groups of chitosan and other groups, such as phosphate and aldehydes [20–23]. Covalent crosslinking of chitosan forms stable covalent bonds between the crosslinking agent and the polysaccharide chains. Despite its toxicity, glutaraldehyde is generally used, the crosslinking occurs by chitosan primary amine nucleophilic addition to the carbonyl of the aldehyde, forming a Schiff's base [22]. A compromise between the amount of glutaraldehyde used must be generally met because high concentrations increase the viscosity, making the casting of the film difficult [23]. While chitosan films completely dissolve in water after 24 h, films containing glutaraldehyde swell to a lesser extent in water; the higher the concentration of glutaraldehyde, the lesser the degree of swelling. Any decrease in film swelling is attributed to the fact that the crosslinking reaction promotes interconnections between the chains of chitosan and reduces the amount of free amino groups, thereby decreasing the ability of the biopolymer to form hydrogen bonds with water molecules that would otherwise increase the degree of swelling. Moreover, adding as little as 0.5 wt% of glutaraldehyde in the formulation is enough to reduce the mobility of the polymeric chains and decrease the film's elongation at a breaking point by 50%, leading to more rigid films [23]. Although chitosan crosslinking with ionic agents improve the hardness of the films, they are usually more brittle than those that are not crosslinked [20]. Other means are generally used to enhance the elasticity and mechanical properties of these films, e.g., heat treatment of the film-forming solution or using plasticizers (glycerol) [24]. Due to growing environmental concerns, greener approaches are normally sought for improving the mechanical, barrier, and antibacterial properties of chitosan films; crosslinking agents, such as cinnamaldehyde and sorbitol, have been used [15, 17]. More recently, a deep eutectic solvent based on choline chloride with malonic acid has been proposed as a potential plasticizer of chitosan [16].

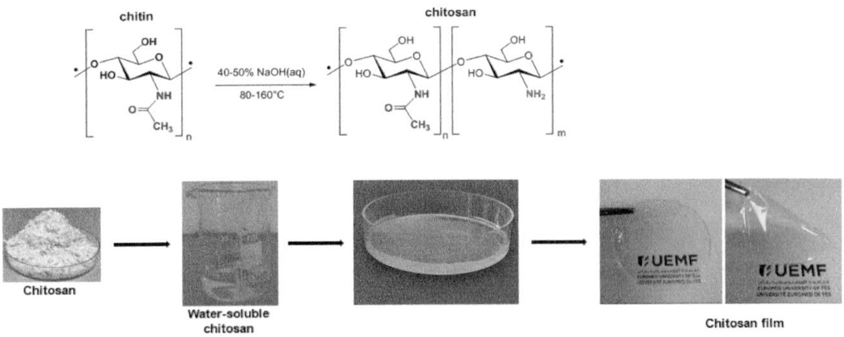

Figure 1.1 Chemical structure of chitin and chitosan and preparation steps of chitosan films (dissolution, casting, evaporation of solvent, and peeling of the film from the casting dish). Adapted from reference 56.

1.3 Chitosan Reinforced with Lamellar Particulates

To make biopolymers attractive and competitive with petroleum-based plastics, their mechanical and thermal properties need to be improved. Among the proposed strategies is the elaboration of bio-nanocomposites by adding small amounts of nanofillers, such as clay, carbon nanotubes, or graphene, to the biopolymer matrix [25–27]. Effectively since the pioneering work performed by Toyota Motor Corporation [28], polymer-clay nanocomposites have received considerable interest, as they usually have superior mechanical properties [29]. In general, modification of the clay filler is necessary to make it compatible with polymeric matrices. When mixing clays with polymers, preventing tactoids and favoring intercalation and exfoliation of the clay layers are the best procedures, which generally lead to nanocomposites with improved properties [30, 31]. Due to the polycationic nature of chitosan, the layers of montmorillonite (MMT, layered phyllosilicate) are first intercalated by the polysaccharides positively charged chains leading to an expansion of the interlayers distance; depending on the chitosan content, exfoliation of the clay layers into individual ones occurs. One of the first works reported on the reinforcement of chitosan films with MMT showed that bio-nanocomposites containing only 1 wt% of MMT have higher tensile strength than the pristine chitosan films and that increasing the amount of MMT to 3 wt% improves the tensile strength by 62%. The enhanced properties have been ascribed to the formation of an exfoliated state and uniform dispersion of the clay within the chitosan matrix. Furthermore, not only the mechanical properties improved, but also the thermal ones as the onset temperature of thermal degradation and melting temperature increased after the addition of a low loading of the clay nanofiller [32]. When preparing the film-forming solution containing clay, a decrease in its viscosity generally occurs, due to the lubricating effect of clay. This decrease is ascribed to the intrusion of clay lamellas between chitosan chains breaking the inter- and intra-molecular interactions of the polysaccharide network [33]. Furthermore, as MMT has negative zeta potential values (around –50 mV) at pH 5, electrostatic interactions might take place between the cationic ammonium groups of chitosan and negatively charged silanols on the clay surface [34]. A molecular dynamic simulation study showed that, under acidic conditions, chitosan binds strongly to MMT with an adhesion energy of 32.7 kcal mol^{-1} [35]. X-rays diffraction (XRD) patterns of chitosan films containing 5% of MMT are shifted toward lower angles compared to native sodium exchanged MMT, indicating accommodation of the biopolymer within the galleries of layered MMT and ensuring the cationic exchange of sodium with the polycationic chitosan. Adding clay (MMT, sepiolite, or halloysite) to chitosan films decreases the contact angles compared to chitosan films, implying increased hydrophilicity of the films [33]. Mechanical properties have been further assessed for films with varying clay content and up to 10%, with Young's modulus increasing independently of the clay topology. Beyond 10%, the mechanical properties are lost, probably because of clay agglomerating within the polymer matrix. With fibrous clays, such as sepiolite, improved mechanical properties have been obtained for reinforced chitosan films, due to the elastic modulus of the fillers and their high external surface area made available for interactions [36]. Studies on chemical uptake and release using chitosan thin films as sustained-release systems are useful in biological applications. Studies of these properties provide, for instance, a means to simulate food preservation conditions. In general, an antimicrobial agent can be successfully added during film formation, as long as the added compound is not volatile during its assembly. One means to add an antimicrobial agent, such as cinnamaldehyde, to chitosan is through Schiff base formation. The aldehyde is generally added to the solid-state film, favoring imine bond formation and to some extent inducing its hydrophobization. Early studies attempting to simulate food preservation conditions have shown that the imine bond formed through covalent immobilization of cinnamaldehyde on chitosan films undergoes hydrolysis depending on the pH and temperature of the milieu. Thermal treatment of the films at 95 °C for 10 min led to a higher release of cinnamaldehyde in pasteurized milk samples. Although the milk took on a cinnamon aroma, the antimicrobial activity was at its highest since it inhibited the growth of *L. monocytogenes* for 12 days under refrigeration conditions, extending the microbiological shelf-life of dairy products [37]. Recently, MMT has been added to covalently aromatic aldehyde immobilized on chitosan films to assess its role in increasing or decreasing the kinetics of the release of aromatic aldehydes from chitosan films. Depending on the aromatic substituent position with respect to the aldehyde group, the release could be either fastened or slowed down by adding clay particles. With salicylaldehyde bearing the hydroxy at the ortho position, its release from chitosan films reinforced with MMT was faster as the clay particulates disturbed the intramolecular hydrogen bonding occurring between nitrogen and phenolic hydrogen imine [38]. While clay lamellas give bio-nanocomposites with mechanical, thermal, and barrier properties [39–41], their stability is generally compromised by temperature and pH [42]. Furthermore, a complete dissolution of MMT is generally attained in hyperalkaline pH [43]. In this regard, a good balance between chemical stability and layered morphology is highly desired. Substituting lamellar clay minerals with chemically stable graphene or graphene derivatives for the elaboration of nanocomposites becomes very attractive [44, 45].

Graphene, a two-dimensional (2D) material has fascinated researchers since its exfoliation from graphite. Effectively, the discovery of the flat 2D crystal contradicted Landau–Peierls–Mermin–Wagner arguments stating that these flat crystals are unstable [46]. Since then, graphene has become a research focus concerning 2D materials. Graphene-based materials are single- or few-layer platelets that can be produced by different methods. While physical methods like chemical vapor deposition led to high-quality defect-free graphene, the need for sophisticated equipment, high-working temperature and pressure, and metal catalysts, hinders their use in the production of nanocomposites, where bulk quantities are generally needed [47]. Chemical methods based on exfoliation and reduction of graphite oxide [48] lead to high yields of graphene-based materials that can be used as nanofillers for the production of high-performing nanocomposites [45]. One of the early studies dealing with the preparation of graphene reinforced chitosan films used N-doped graphene that had been obtained by direct-current arc-discharge. While the graphene obtained was characterized by a few defects (characterized by a low ID/IG ratio from the Raman spectrum), the zeta potential of the dispersion of graphene in chitosan solution was <30 mV, suggesting a metastable suspension. Accordingly, due to the lack of functional groups on the surface of the graphene, a good dispersion within the matrix is difficult and could lead to the formation of tactoids during evaporation-induced assembly of the film [49]. The use of graphene oxide (GO) instead of graphene is an attractive way of overcoming localized dispersion of the nanofillers, due to the high level of dispersion of GO in water [50]. Chitosan films reinforced with different loadings of GO (ranging from 0.25 to

3 wt%) have higher tensile strengths compared to native chitosan films [51, 52]. Generally, the higher the amount of GO, the higher the tensile strength. The strong dependence of tensile strength on the GO content has been ascribed to molecule-level dispersion of GO and the strong H-bonding between chitosan and the oxygenated surface of GO [51]. While small amounts of GO improve to some extent the thermal stability of chitosan films [53], contents of up to 20 wt% of GO are detrimental to the thermal stability of chitosan films at temperatures <350 °C, due to the thermal decomposition of the oxygenated groups decorating the surface of GO, as well as the catalytic oxidative action of GO cleaving the pyranosic C-O-C bond [54]. To impart GO with high thermal stability, functionalization with flame-retarding elements proved quite effective [55]. Accordingly, phosphorylation of GO with phosphoryl oxychloride not only improves its thermo-oxidative stability by shifting the temperature of half-weight decomposition by 379 °C compared to unmodified GO, but also by retaining its colloidal stability in most polar solvents [56]. When processing phosphorylated graphene oxide (PGO) with chitosan solutions to prepare films reinforced with PGO, transparent films are obtained in comparison with those reinforced by the same amount of GO, suggesting enhanced interfacial interactions between nitrogen-containing groups of chitosan and phosphonic acid groups grafted on the surface of PGO. The thermal stability of chitosan films can be enhanced by adding 3 wt% PGO, since the general catalytic oxidative ability of GO at 365 °C is delayed by 80 °C [56]. Reinforcing with PGO improves chitosan film mechanical properties. Although the films reinforced with the same amount of GO have a higher tensile strength, they were stiffer, ruling out their use in packaging applications where a degree of stretchability is generally desired [57]. Functionalization of chitosan with aromatic aldehydes followed by the addition of GO enhances the thermal stability of chitosan films. The fast thermal degradation normally occurring between 100 °C and 200 °C for neat chitosan films can be delayed in ternary reinforced chitosan-aromatic aldehyde-GO films, attributed to reduced moisture uptake resulting from the conjugation of the aromatic moieties within the carbohydrate backbone [38].

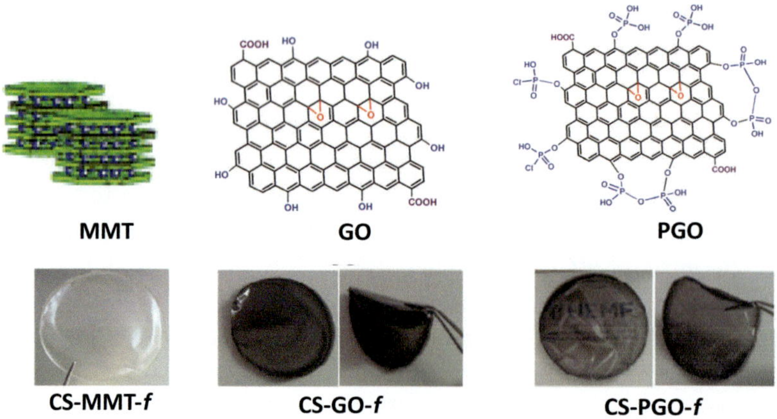

Figure 1.2 Layered nanofillers and corresponding nanocomposite films. Adapted from reference 56.

1.4 Chitosan Reinforced with Cellulose Nanocrystals

Due to alarming environmental issues, a need for greener nanofillers for the improvement of nanocomposite properties is an urgent matter, as the extraction, synthesis, and modification of conventional nanofillers involve huge amounts of corrosive products [58]. The trend in the design of fully sustainable bioplastics nowadays consists of the use of both nanofillers and polymers derived from abundant bio-renewables, and synthetic approaches that produce minimal waste [59–61]. Bio-nanocomposites meet the demand for green technology because both the matrix and reinforcement are biodegradable, providing environmental benefits in their ultimate disposability [62]. Early attempts to synthesize sustainable bioplastics generally reinforced oxidized cellulose with different amounts of chitosan. Due to the insoluble nature of cellulose in water, effectively, prior modification is needed for film processing. Oxidation of cellulose by ozone was usually carried out to increase the amount of carbonyl groups in modified cellulose since their presence increases the crosslinks in the composite film. A comparison of the acids used to prepare the blended films was also assessed; those prepared using acetic acid had the highest wet tensile strength and were biodegraded within 24 days, whereas those prepared using lactic acid were biodegraded within 13 days [63]. Later studies using trifluoroacetic acid to dissolve both chitosan and cellulose have shown that the mechanical properties of blend films of cellulose-containing 30 wt% chitosan had higher tensile strength, due to the improved plasticity derived from interactions between cellulose chitosan and water molecules as the blend films usually have high water uptake and high swelling degrees [64]. Due to the need for stretchability and flexibility in food packaging applications, the tendency of reinforcing cellulose with chitosan was switched; nowadays chitosan-based films reinforced by cellulose micro- or nano-crystals are increasingly used in packaging as edible films or coatings [65]. The size of microcrystalline cellulose (MCC) ranges from a few to hundreds of microns. It is available in abundance and has a low cost. MCC's high mechanical strength makes it a potential contender for reinforcing polymer materials. Unfortunately, its large particle size and its insolubility in water limits its reinforcing effect. To overcome this problem, surface modification of MCC is of key importance in enhancing the dispersion within the polymeric, as also its strengthening effect. Surface modification of MCC with urea improves its dispersion in chitosan solution. Effectively, while MCC precipitation from 2 wt% chitosan solution occurred after 48 h standing, urea-modified MCC had greater colloidal stability. Upon casting, improved mechanical properties were observed by reinforcing chitosan films with 7 wt% modified MCC [66]. Cellulose nanocrystals obtained from acid hydrolysis of cellulose have recently gathered a lot of attention due to their high modulus, lateral dimensions ranging between 50 nm and 300 nm, and enriched surface prone to chemical modification [67]. Outstanding reinforcing effects have been seen upon the addition of cellulose nanocrystals to chitosan films, an improvement thought to be due to the high modulus of cellulose nanocrystals and their orientation within the composite film [68]. Increasing the amount of cellulose nanocrystal up to 52 wt% in chitosan films gave rise to thicker lightweight films [69]. Mechanical properties, such as elongation at break and tensile strength, were however compromised. Adding small amounts of phosphorylated nanocellulose improved the mechanical properties of chitosan films. Depending on the phosphorus derivative used, tensile strength and thermal stability both increased in comparison with non-reinforced chitosan films [70].

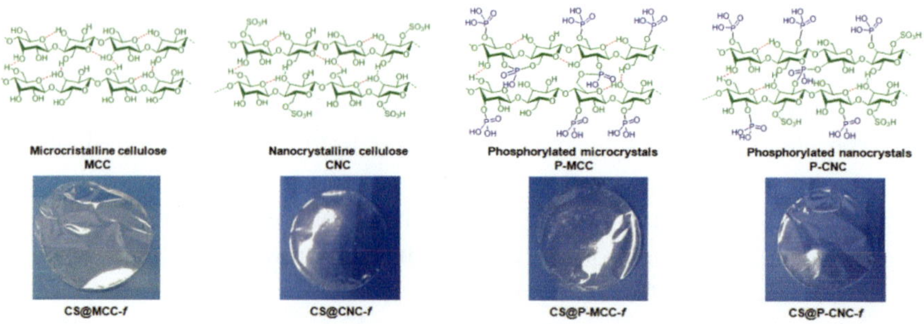

Figure 1.3 Sustainable chitosan films reinforced with unmodified and phosphorylated cellulose in the form of micro or nanocrystals. Adapted from reference 70.

1.5 Biological Response of Chitosan-Based Films

1.5.1 Chitosan-Based Antimicrobial Films for Food Packaging Applications

Chitosan and its derivatives have been used in the food, textile (antibacterial fibers), and biomedicine (wound healing, drug delivery, vaccine delivery, tissue regeneration) industries, due to their antimicrobial properties. One line of research is the use of a biopolymer as a component of food packaging. Increasing consumer demand for safe unprocessed foods and prolonged storage time are mobilizing the food industry to introduce antimicrobial food packaging. Commonly used metal, plastic, or glass packaging remains a serious environmental problem. Moreover, they are often enriched with toxic compounds (polyethylene, polypropylene, and other petroleum compounds) that have a negative impact on human health. It has been estimated that the annual production of plastics in the world reaches >350 million tons [71]. The ideal package, besides a protective function against environmental factors, should also improve the quality and safety of the product. Films made from chitosan composites offer an excellent alternative to traditional packaging.

Moreover, advances in the search for new materials capable of extending the shelf-life of food products may significantly reduce the current worldwide problem of food waste, which is one of the causes of the inefficiency of the global food system, and contributes to environmental pollution.

Food contamination, whose source can be, e.g., packaging, posed a serious threat to human health. Pathogens developing in poorly stored food may cause food poisoning or even debilitating infective diseases, such as meningitis. Microorganisms that spoil food include bacteria, including *Listeria monocytogenes, Staphylococcus aureus, Bacillus cereus, Escherichia coli, Salmonella typhimurium, Campylobacter,* and *Yersinia,* and filamentous fungi of the genera *Aspergillus, Penicillium,* and *Fusarium.* Ensuring the safety of foods, while retaining their properties (organoleptic and nutritional), is presently a high priority.

Chitosan has valuable biological properties, e.g., biocompatibility, biodegradability, antimicrobial activity, and non-toxicity; and it also has antioxidant properties [72]. Due to the amino and hydroxyl groups on the chitosan backbone, it can be easily modified by both enzymatic and chemical methods [73]. The presence of amino groups in the chitosan backbone gives it a catalytic activity [74], metal chelating ability [75], and biological efficiency [76]. Based on literature data, chitosan has both antibacterial [76–78] and antifungal [79–82] activities. Moreover, it has been confirmed and generally recognized as safe (GRAS) by the US Food and Drug Administration (FDA).

The antimicrobial activity of these polymers depends on the molecular weight of chitosan, chitin deacetylation degree, pH, ionic strength, chelating capacity, and concentration [83]. Chitosan below pH 6 is positively charged [84] and can interact with negatively charged components of bacteria. This action leads to the disruption of the bacterial cell, thereby altering membrane permeability, followed by attachment to DNA, inhibiting DNA replication, which leads to cell death [85]. Several mechanisms of food protection have been proposed for chitosan films: they can act as a physical barrier by preventing microorganisms from accessing food; they can block the access of oxygen and nutrients to microorganisms; nutrients can be chelated by chitosan chains; and electrostatic interactions can lead to disruption of the outer cellular membrane of microorganisms. The antibacterial activity of chitosan may also involve damage to the cell membrane of microorganisms and consequently cause leakage of intracellular substances. On the other hand, diffusion of chitosan chains inside the cell can chelate the nutrients and essential metal ions. Moreover, they can bind the DNA and inhibit the replication process [86].

The excellent film-forming ability of chitosan has opened up great opportunities for bio-based packaging materials [87]. However, its poor mechanical strength and high sensitivity to humidity constitute a serious impediment to this specific application, including food packaging and biomedicine. The addition of a small amount of nanosized fillers, e.g., MMT [33], GO [55], hydroxyapatite [88–90], carbon nanotubes [35], and zinc oxide nanoparticle [91], offers a way to tune chitosan's mechanical properties, thermal stability, and antimicrobial activity. Moreover, the film-forming properties of chitosan have led to the development of film packaging materials, in combination with other natural compounds, such as pectin, cellulose, gelatin, and essential oils and extracts from plants. Films and coatings synthesized on a chitosan base are now being used as "Active Food Packaging" (Fig. 1.4). Addition of the active substances in packaging materials increased their antimicrobial and antioxidant activity. It is one of the most dynamic developing solutions used to improve the quality, safety, and sensory properties of food products.

Chitosan can be used as an edible film [92–97]. Different types of food can be coated by chitosan films, e.g., eggs, strawberries, bananas, tomatoes, fish, etc. These films prevent the growth of bacteria and prolong the shelf-life of food products. Chitosan-based emulsions as edible coatings have been described as an innovative approach to improving food quality. Torrico et al. [98] tested a mineral oil-chitosan emulsion as a coating material on eggs, and found it extended their shelf-life during storage; a similar effect was noted for a soybean oil-chitosan coating on eggs [99]. In the case of strawberries, the coating method prolonged their freshness [100]. The use of active components in the chitosan-based films is very important for strengthening the effect (e.g., antimicrobial) of coatings. Nanoparticles, plant extracts, and oils have been incorporated into chitosan films [94, 101–103]. Among the group of nanoparticles, those based on silicon compounds are often combined with chitosan [82]. See the chapter on "Antimicrobial Activity of Plant-Based Chitosan Films" for more information.

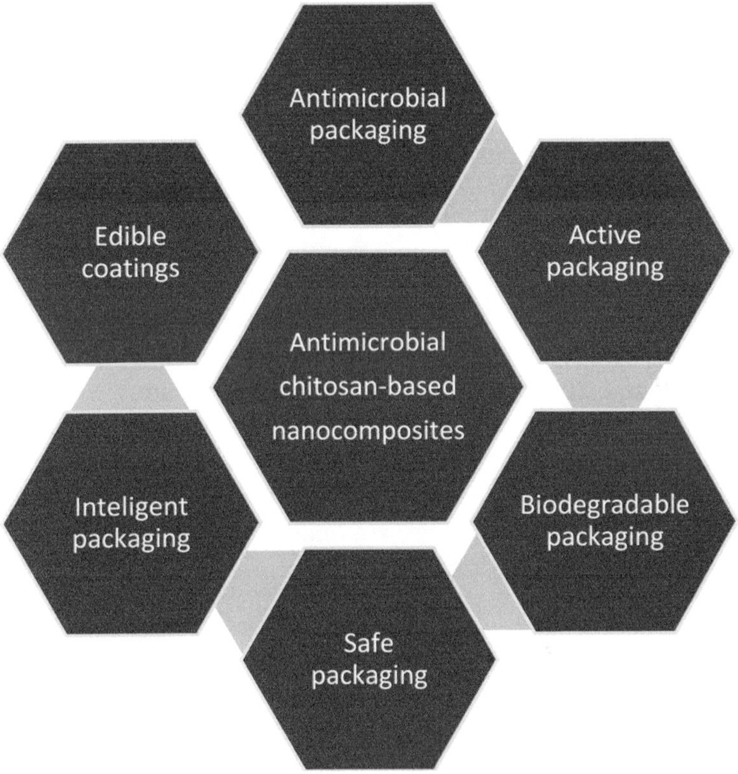

Figure 1.4 Antimicrobial activities of chitosan-based nanocomposites for food packaging application.

Chitosan-based biomaterials are also used to immobilize enzymes. This process protects the enzymes from environmental changes and allows them to be reused. Chitosan-based supports have been found to be stable and cost-effective, and were therefore used in the biomedicine and food industries. Immobilized *Trichoderma reesei* cellulase retained about 80% of its activity after 15 cycles of carboxyl methylcellulose hydrolysis [104]. Nguyen et al. [101] confirmed that immobilized β-galactosidase on chitosan-coated magnetic nanoparticles can be applied in the production of prebiotic galactooligosaccharides.

1.5.1.1 Antimicrobial activity of graphene-CS and metal (oxide)-CS nanocomposites

Increasing interest is seen in graphene derivatives for manufacturing advanced functional nanocomposites. Graphene brings additional properties (electronic mobility, conductivity, path tortuosity, catalytic and adsorptive ability, and sensing and biological activity) that open up new avenues in biomedicine and wearable electronics. Previous reports have disclosed the synthesis of chitosan-graphene nanocomposites [102, 105], with special emphasis on their thermal, mechanical, and biological properties [49, 106, 107], and thereby clearly substantiate the pivotal role of graphene in these bio-based materials.

The addition of a small amount of GO leads to stable chitosan nanocomposites with excellent mechanical properties, thermal stability, and antimicrobial activity against *S. aureus, E. coli, L. monocytogenes,* and *C. jejuni* [108]. Marked inhibition of S. *aureus* and *E. coli* has also been recorded by chitosan-graphene oxide-polyhexamethylene guanidine hydrochloride composites, providing 92% and 95% growth inhibition, respectively [109]. Mazaheri et al. [110] reported on the antimicrobial activity of chitosan-graphene nanocomposites against the gram-positive strain *S. aureus.* Strong antibacterial activity toward methicillin-resistant *S. aureus* and *E. coli* was seen with chitosan-iron oxide-coated graphene hydrogel films [111]. *B. subtilis* and *A. niger* are often responsible for food spoilage, in particular fresh fruits and vegetables. Xu et al. [32] described high antimicrobial activity (against *B. subtilis* and *A. niger*) of self-assembled film of GO and chitosan with titanium oxide nanoparticles. Moreover, these coatings had no cytotoxicity against mammalian somatic cells. Synergistic antibacterial activity of graphene-magnetite-chitosan nanocomposites (Gr/CS/Fe_3O_4 NCs) has been described by Maruthupandy et al. [112]; these nanocomposites were active against *P. aeruginosa* and *K. pneumonia.*

The mechanisms of action of graphene-based chitosan coatings have only partially been described in the literature. Most likely the antimicrobial mechanism of graphene-based chitosan nanocomposites is caused by direct contact and interaction of the graphene sharp nanosheets with the bacterial cell membranes, resulting in altered membrane permeability. These changes lead to cellular deformation and surface perforation [113, 114].

Metal agents, such as zinc oxide, titanium dioxide, and silver, have antimicrobial potential, but their properties depend on the size, morphology, and distribution of nanoparticles [115, 116]. Recently, metal oxides have attracted attention in food applications because they are stable under high pressure and temperature. Moreover, these may occur under difficult food-processing conditions, and they are also regarded as safe for humans relative to organic substances [117, 118]. They are used as nano-filler in the chitosan matrix to improve its mechanical and antimicrobial properties. Al-Naamani et al. [119] tested the antimicrobial properties of chitosan and chitosan-zinc oxide coatings on polyethylene; these coatings completely inactivated and prevented the growth of *S. aureus, E. coli,* and *S. enterica* after 24 h incubation. This environmentally friendly active packaging material could be a chitosan-zinc oxide nanoparticle composite loaded with gallic-acid films. Significant antibacterial potential and antioxidant properties were found compared to pure chitosan film [120]. Silver and zinc oxide nanoparticles affect bacterial membranes [69]; the antimicrobial mechanism of action of Zn nanoparticles is based on their ability to induce oxidative stress in bacterial cells [121]. Zinc ions may interact with the thiol group of bacterial respiratory enzymes, stimulating the production of reactive oxygen species (ROS). As a consequence, bacterial cell membranes, DNA, and mitochondria are damaged, leading to cell death [122–124]. Silver nanoparticles are effective as antibacterial agents at low concentrations [125], and they interact with cell membrane proteins and bacterial DNA, which contain phosphorus and sulfur complexes with a high attraction to Ag nanoparticles [126]. Silver nanoparticles are effective against a wide range of Gram-negative and Gram-positive bacteria [127] and fungi [128]. Ediyilyam et al. [129] synthesized chitosan-gelatin-silver nanoparticle composite films that had all the desired features of packaging materials. Moreover, these films have antimicrobial activity against *S. mutans, S. aureus, P. aeruginosa, E. coli,* and *C. albicans.*

Active coatings based on titanium dioxide have also been developed by Siripatrawan et al. [130], whose results showed that chitosan film containing 1% TiO_2 had antimicrobial activity toward Gram-negative (*E. coli, S. typhimurium, P. aeruginosa*), Gram-positive (*S. aureus*) bacteria, and fungi (*Aspergillus, Penicillium*) [130]. The antimicrobial activity of chitosan was enhanced by the incorporation of titanium dioxide into a polymeric matrix [131–133]. Li et al. [134] found that chitosan-TiO_2 coatings had better antimicrobial activity toward *X. oryzae pv. Oryzae* than the two compounds applied separately under dark and light conditions. Others have shown that CS-TiO_2 coatings have no antibacterial activity toward *E. coli* and *K. pneumoniae* and medium activity against *S. aureus* [135]. Research into the mechanisms of action of CS-TiO_2 composites shows that the films can destabilize bacterial membranes, leading to deformation and changes in the cell wall, and to its disruption [136].

Applications of the antimicrobial activity of graphene-chitosan and metal-chitosan nanocomposites for active packaging are shown in Table 1.1.

Table 1.1 Commonly used graphene-chitosan and metal-chitosan nanocomposites for active packaging

Nanomaterial	Antimicrobial activity	Properties/mechanism of action
CS/GIO*	Methicillin-resistant *S. aureus, S. aureus, E. coli, C. albicans*	Rupture of the bacterial membrane resulting the release of intracellular materials [111]
CS/PVA*/GO	*B. cereus, S. aureus, E. coli, Salmonella spp*	Direct contact of GO and the bacterial cell membrane [137]
CS/GO; CS/rGO*; CS/PGO*	*S. aureus, E. coli*	Direct contact and interaction of the graphene sharp nanosheets with the bacterial cell membranes [57]
CS/GO; CS/rGO; CS/GO/Ag, CS/PGO/Ag	*C. jejuni, L. monocytogenes*	Cell fluid leakage due to cell destruction [108]
CS/GO	*S. aureus*	Significant antimicrobial activity [110]
(GO)(GO-CS-PHGC*)	*S. aureus, E. coli*	PHGC caused the destruction of the bacterial membrane. Guanidine polymer inhibits bacterial growth by attacking them through electrostatic attraction between the

Nanomaterial	Antimicrobial activity	Properties/mechanism of action
		cationic guanidino groups and anionic groups on the cell surface of bacteria. This action induces bacterial membrane collapse, and the intracellular components leak thereafter [138]
CS/GO/TiO_2	*B. subtilis, A. niger*	Adhesion of the nanoparticles to the bacteria resulted in the destruction of the cell membranes, accompanied by cell deformation and structural changes [139]
(CS)/Fe_3O_4, (Gr*)/CS/ Fe_3O_4	*P. aeruginosa, K. pneumoniae*	Antimicrobial activity [112]
CS/ZnO NPs CS/Ag NPs	*B. cereus, S. aureus, E. coli, L. monocytogenes, S. typhimurium*	Antimicrobial activity [140]
CS/ZnO	*S. aureus, E. coli, S. enterica*	ZnO nanoparticles improved the antimicrobial activity of CS [119]
CS/ZnO/GAL*	*B. subtilis, E. coli,*	Antimicrobial activity [120]
CS/ZnO	*S. aureus, E. coli*	Release of ROS damage bacterial cell walls [141]
CS/ZnO	*S. aureus*	Improved the quality of pork meat during cold storage as observed [142]
CS/GEL*/Ag NPs	*S. mutans, S. aureus, P. aeruginosa, E. coli, C. albicans*	Antimicrobial activity [129]
CS/Ag NPs	*E. coli, S. typhimurium A. niger, P. citrinum*	Antimicrobial activity. Surface charge on chitosan influences adsorption of Ag NPs [143]
CS/Ag NPs	*S. aureus, E. coli, B. cereus, P. aeruginosa, C. albicans*	Distortion of the cell wall, protein denaturation, and, as a consequence, cell death [144]
CS/LAP*/Ag NPs	*E. coli, S. aureus, A. niger, P. citrinum*	Significant antimicrobial activity [145]

(*Continued*)

Table 1.1 (*Continued*)

Nanomaterial	Antimicrobial activity	Properties/mechanism of action
CS/TiO_2 NPs	*E. coli, S. typhimurium, P. aeruginosa, S. aureus, Aspergillus, Penicillium*	Exposed to UV light, showed higher antimicrobial activity [130]
CS/TiO_2 NPs	*E. coli, S. aureus, Salmonella, and L. monocytogenes*	Antimicrobial, antioxidant, and ethylene scavenging properties [146]
CS/TiO_2 NPs	*X. oryzae pv. Oryzae*	Good antimicrobial activity under dark and light conditions [134]
CS/TiO_2 NPs	*E. coli, S. aureus, C. albicans, A. niger*	Higher antibacterial activity toward Gram-negative strain [133]

*GAL, gallic-acid; CS, chitosan; GEL, gelatin; GIO, iron oxide coated graphene oxide; Gr, graphene; LAP, laponite; PGO, phosphorylated graphene oxide; PHGC, polyhexamethylene guanidine hydrochloride; PVA, poly(vinyl alcohol); rGO, reduced graphene oxide.

1.5.1.2 Antimicrobial activity of plant-based chitosan films

The most commonly used plant-based antimicrobials include essential oils and extract from plants. They have antioxidant and antimicrobial activities used in the food packaging industry [95]. The oils used to enhance the antibacterial effect are cinnamon, rosemary, lemon, and bergamot [102, 103, 147–150]. The main active compounds in essential oils are terpenes, terpenoids, and phenylpropenes. Feyzioglu and Tornuk [151] examined the antimicrobial activity of summer savory essential oil-loaded chitosan nanoparticles against three different foodborne bacteria (*E. coli, L. monocytogenes,* and *S. aureus*), and showed promising application in food packaging materials. Chitosan supplementation with essential oils from cinnamon, eucalyptus, clave, or oregano increased its antimicrobial properties in active food packaging applications [140]. Moreover, essential oils and extracts from *Cuminum cyminum L., Eugenia caryohyllata,* and *Inula helenium,* tested as antimicrobial compounds in chitosan films, showed antibacterial properties against *E. coli, S. typhimurium, B. cereus, S. aureus,* and *L. monocytogenes*. Khalifa et al. [100] found an increase in antifungal activities (against *P. expansum* and *R. stolonifer*) after the addition of olive oil residue extracts to chitosan films. Others have shown that coating of chitosan with bergamot oil inhibits the growth of *Penicillium italicum* [150]. Plant extract-based-chitosan edible films (green tea extract) had strong antibacterial activities against *E. coli* and *L. innocua*. Phenolic compounds in blueberry fruit and leaf extract (BLE 44) showed good antimicrobial activity against *S. aureus, L. monocytogenes, S. typhimurium,* and *E. coli*, and also against fungi isolated from rotting blueberry fruit [152]. The results suggest that chitosan-BLE extract coating can be used to extend shelf-life and maintain the nutritional value of blueberries. Ramirez-Guerra et al. [153] determined the antimicrobial effect of a tomato extract incorporated into an edible chitosan coating on the quality and shelf-life of sierra fish fillet, and concluded that, alone or in combination with chitosan, the latter was extended.

In summary, chitosan-based packaging materials lengthen the shelf-life of many products, e.g., vegetables [129, 130], fruit [100, 102, 154], and fish [153, 155], while reducing synthetic plastics and promoting a safer and more pleasant environment.

1.5.2 Antimicrobial Activities of Chitosan-Based Films for Biomedical Application (Antibacterial Agent, Drug Delivery, Wound Healing, Tissue Engineering)

As a result of intensive technical development, the demand for natural materials with unique physicochemical and biological properties is increasing. Special attention is being devoted to materials that are completely biodegradable, non-toxic, and do not pose a threat to human life. Considerable interest is now being shown among researchers regarding the unique properties of chitosan films, such as biodegradability [156], biocompatibility [157], and antimicrobial activity, which can be used in medicines. Moreover, films can be prepared in different forms, such as nanoparticles, fibers, gels, membranes, and sponges. Due to these properties, chitosan has become an attractive material for biomedical applications (Fig. 1.5), e.g., in wound dressing [158, 159], drug delivery [160], tissue engineering [161, 162], and skin regeneration [131, 163]. Moreover, chitosan-based coatings can be easily loaded with other antimicrobials [147]. The latest research shows three main strategies for the development of antimicrobial coatings: antibacterial agent release, contact-killing, and adhesion resistance/bacteria-repelling [164].

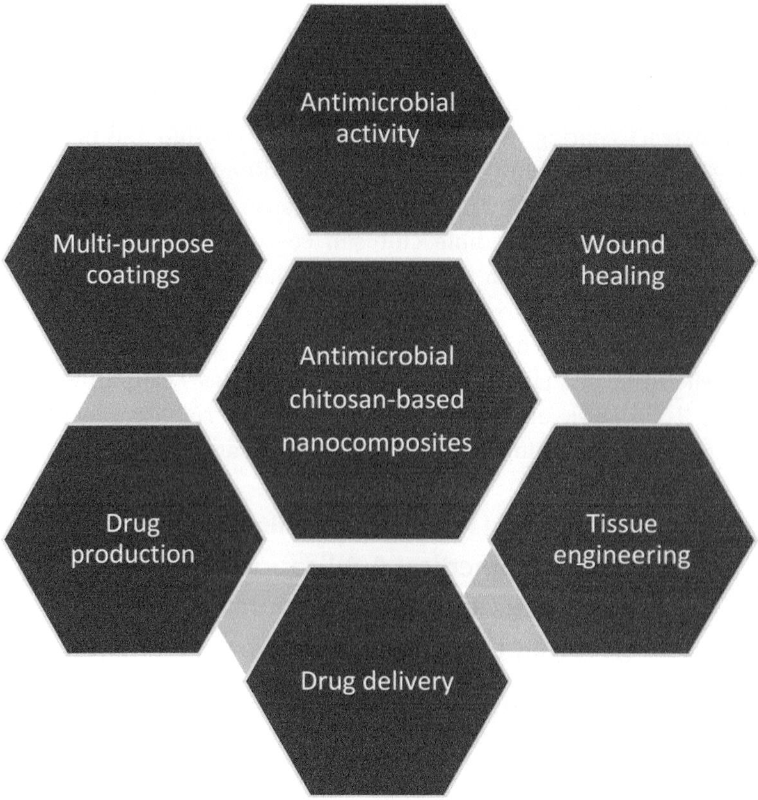

Figure 1.5 Antimicrobial activities of chitosan-based nanocomposites for biomedical application.

The chitosan has shown excellent action in healing wounds, being preferred in particular for the treatment of burns, due to its easy film formation, biocompatibility, and water absorption capacity. Furthermore, it is naturally degraded by body enzymes [165]. Wound healing is a spontaneous process, but may be disrupted if the wounds are large or difficult to heal, complications that make it impossible to use an autologous skin graft. In this case, chitosan polymers can be used, which will stimulate and initiate the process of proper healing of damaged skin and epidermis [166].

The basis of wound treatment is to cover it quickly with a dressing. The use of chitosan in therapeutic preparations as a dressing for wounds aids their healing, as it has quite strong hemostatic activity independent of the classic coagulation cascade. Chitosan causes blood cells to aggregate immediately, producing clotting and activating, and the homeostasis process. This leads to adhesion, the formation of an aggregate of platelets, and their activation. Later stages of wound healing are accelerated [166].

Modification of the chitosan surface to obtain biofunctionality and appropriate mass properties makes it useful as a dressing for wounds or in other clinical materials. The antimicrobial properties of chitosan due to its cationic nature prevent wound infection by killing or inhibiting microbial growth. This is particularly important as bacterial infection can delay wound healing, and complications such as sepsis could occur [53].

Active antibacterial dressings based on chitosan are available on the world market, e.g., ChitoFlex®, Tromboguard®, HemCon®, and Chitodine®. Chitosan is an excellent antimicrobial barrier and improves tissue regeneration, while allowing high gas exchange [167]. Moreover, it has been proven that chitosan promotes the activity of macrophages, leukocytes, and fibroblasts, thus enhancing extracellular matrix deposition, which, in turn, aids scar formation [168]. Chitosan-based films are used in hospitals. This polysaccharide was grafted on acid-activated non-woven polypropylene, which is useful to produce hospital fabrics that have antibacterial activity toward *P. aeruginosa* [169]. Ferreira et al. [170] investigated chitosan-Rose Bengal (CHRB) coatings; composites that reduce the risk of infection during surgery were active against *S. aureus*. In other research, medical silicone surfaces were modified with dopamine and carboxymethyl chitosan. A reduction was noted in the adhesion of *E. coli* and *P. mirabilis*. Moreover, the coatings were not cytotoxic for fibroblasts [171]. Kouchak et al. [172] measured the activity of chitosan-based dressings with the addition of polyvinyl alcohol and nitrofurazone; these coatings showed strong antibacterial activity against *S. aureus* and *E. coli*.

Chitosan hydrogels are also promising for wound dressing. Hydrogels consist of crosslinked polymer chains brought together by crosslinking components, thus forming 3D networks. This crosslinking improves the performance of chitosan because it has a fairly high degree of similarity to the extracellular matrix, and provides a number of useful physical properties. This similarity to the matrix, combined with the appropriate properties, helps cell proliferation and diffusion.

Chitosan-containing hydrogels have antimicrobial properties. Strains coated with a chitosan-containing hydrogel crosslinked by irradiation with ultraviolet light showed resistance to *E. coli* both in vitro and in vivo. Chitosan hydrogels can also provide small molecule drugs, growth factors, and other ingredients that accelerate cell growth and differentiation, and thus the wound healing process. They are also easy to remove without damaging the newly regenerated tissue [53].

It has also been proven that hydrogels based on chitosan and silver nanoparticles regenerate epithelial and collagen deposition, effectively accelerating wound healing. In this case, the silver nanoparticles act as both fillers to improve the mechanical properties of the hydrogel and the antimicrobial agent. The mechanism of the bactericidal action was based on the combination of disruption of the cell membrane and DNA binding, preventing bacterial replication. In summary, modified or unmodified chitosan-based hydrogels (bactericides, growth factors, etc.) play an important role in wounds by direct action at several stages of the healing process [173].

Many scientists are developing innovative dressings based on chitosan films. Chitosan films hydrolyzed to chitooligomers stimulate the proper deposition, folding, and orientation of collagen fibers, which is important in scarring [174]. Moreover, histological results indicate that chitosan films stimulate the migration of inflammatory cells and determine cellular organization during healing [175].

Clinical data show that chitosan films adhere uniformly to freshly injured skin surfaces, a basic property that a dressing material should fulfill. If adhesion is incomplete, air-filled voids are created in which the exudative fluid accumulates and bacteria can multiply, causing infection. Chitosan nanocomposites have hemostatic activity, influencing cascade clotting reactions, and a blood clot is formed between the chitosan film and the regenerating epithelial tissue [176]. The composites reduce itching and any pain then may accompany wounds, and will also accelerate scarring. Chitosan films allow wounds to heal after a few days; the area is kept clean and healthy compared to commonly used tulle bandages [177, 178]. Histological examination confirmed that epithelization was accelerated and collagen deposition in the dermis covered the wound area [179].

Chitosan-based hydrogels, due to their high water content, porosity, biocompatibility, and ability to promote cell adhesion and proliferation, can be used as scaffolds for tissue engineering [25], skin [180], bone, cartilage [181], and nerves [182] regeneration.

Chitosan and its derivatives have found many uses as pharmaceutical products, e.g., in the production of medications. Chitosan can extend the period of action of the drugs, thus improving their therapeutic efficiency and reducing side effects related to high peak doses [183].

Chitosan is also of interest in tissue engineering. Initially, it was used unmodified. The growing interest in this polymer resulted in the introduction of numerous modifications that increased the possibility of their being used. These modifications are based on increasing the solubility of chitosan and changing the required properties, as well as adding different types of side-chains to its molecule. These changes affected some properties, but the basic properties of chitosan, such as its biodegradability, biocompatibility, antibacterial activity, muco-adhesiveness, and acceleration of the wound healing process, were all retained [184].

Studies have been carried out with this polymer in the production of scaffolds for tissue culture [25]. It may also be used in the production of implants and artificial organs in the future [185]. Stevanović et al. [162] determined the biological properties of graphene-based hydroxyapatite chitosan coating with gentamycin for potential application in bone tissue engineering. Antibacterial assays confirmed the activity of this composite toward *S. aureus* and *E. coli*.

Biodegradable chitosan is also used in bone tissue engineering as a substitute inserted in the form of a temporary skeleton to replace skeletal damage or lost bone areas. This action is aimed at supporting and stimulating bone tissue to regenerate; at the same time, the substitute is gradually degraded and replaced by fresh bone tissue. The chitin derivative promotes the growth and deposition of a mineral-rich matrix by osteoblasts. Additionally, the biocompatibility of chitosan minimizes any local inflammation. This chitin derivative is easily biodegradable and can be formed into porous structures that assist osteoconduction. Composites based on chitosan and calcium phosphate make a suitable material for bone tissue repair and regeneration because their chemical composition is similar to inorganic components of bone tissue [184, 186, 187].

The use of chitosan as a carrier of active substances is designed to deliver them to target sites. The choice of chitosan is associated with its low toxicity as well as its biodegradability and biocompatibility, which affect the expected release of the drug, as also the simple removal of carriers after the drug administration stage [188, 189].

The 3D structure of chitosan allows for drug encapsulation, but it can also control the drug release mechanism in relation to needs. By using chitosan, it is possible to influence the pharmacokinetics of an active substance, which will minimize side effects and improve the efficiency of the entire system [190]. The use of chitosan as a carrier for the oral delivery of drugs may improve the transport of the active agent to the desired site, so that local and systemic absorption would increase their efficiency and at the same time minimize early degradation of the therapeutic agent [191]. Premature degradation of an active agent is due to secretions produced in the gastrointestinal tract, e.g., enzymes, as well as the specific nature of the environment in which pH conditions may change. Absorption of orally administered drugs can also be inhibited by other physiological factors, such as transit time, blood supply, and the presence of food [192]. An example of an enzyme encapsulated in chitosan nanoparticles is L-asparaginase used in anti-cancer therapy, e.g., treatment of acute lymphoblastic leukemia. L-asparaginase encapsulated in chitosan nanoparticles had a longer half-life in vitro compared to the free enzyme [192].

Chitosan is also used in anti-inflammatory drugs and may have an analgesic effect. Chitosan directly applied to a wound can alleviate pain and provide a soothing effect [53].

Bacterial contaminations in medical environments can pose a serious issue. Therefore, the development of antibacterial coatings for biomedical applications is being moved forward. Surfaces would prevent bacterial adhesion, proliferation, and biofilm formation, thus reducing the risk of infections associated with biomedical devices. It should be added that chitosan, apart from its antimicrobial activity, has a series of properties for applications in biomedicine, namely, high biocompatibility, low immunogenicity, and allergenicity. It is also inexpensive material, which can easily be modified and processed in different forms, e.g., membranes, films, and gels. Despite numerous reports on chitosan, there is little information on the performance of chitosan antibacterial coatings in vivo. The positive results of the activity of chitosan-based films nevertheless encourage the future implementation of these coatings in wider areas of medicine.

1.5.2.1 Biological properties of graphene-CS, cellulose-CS, and metal-CS nanocomposites films

The synthesis or creation of new substances and composites that can potentially be used in the medical industry or medicine requires examining their biological properties, especially their toxicity. Therefore, the hemolytic and cytotoxic properties of the chitosan films had to be tested. All chitosan-reinforced graphene nanocomposite films induced hemolysis at a low level, with a maximum of 7.5% after 24 h incubation. However, hemolysis did not depend on the incubation time, which prompted the authors to check whether hemoglobin released during hemolysis was not adsorbed on the surface of the tested films. After 3 h incubation of the hemolysate with graphene composites, the adsorption of hemoglobin was negligible. However, after 24 h, it had reached up to 30% depending on the wettability and hydrophobic nature of the tested film. This means that released hemoglobin was adsorbed on the surface of the film, contributing to a decrease in the hemoglobin content of the solution; the results did not reflect the actual hemolytic activity of the films [108]. The authors suggest that chitosan-graphene films, regardless of surface modification, affect the erythrocyte membrane, possibly by deforming it, leading to the damage and release of hemoglobin. The proteins present on the surface of red blood cells can also be adsorbed onto the surface of chitosan-graphene composites, which can also significantly reduce their viability [193].

A similar situation occurred for modified cellulose-chitosan films. After 3 h incubation, all cellulose-chitosan films induced hemolysis up to 8%; and after 24 h, hemolysis increased to 10–16%. However, these results, as for graphene-chitosan films, do not reflect real hemolysis, because adsorption of hemoglobin on the surface of cellulose-filled chitosan materials also occurred [70]. Any increase in the degree of hemolysis after incubation with chitosan-cellulose films could be the result of many factors, which may be due to the presence of glucose at high concentrations generating free radicals in its autooxidation, resulting in an increase in cell lipid peroxidation and membrane damage. Protein adsorption on the surface of the films is also possible, and a decrease in the ionic strength of the external solution can occur, leading to the expansion of the membrane and the formation of small pores, which then leads to the release of hemoglobin [70].

When the ability of cells or the organism to degrade ROS is impaired, their toxicity leads to a range of undesirable cell changes or health complications in the body. Therefore, it has been important to assess the effect of chitosan-based films on hemoglobin and the activity of intracellular catalase. All graphene and cellulose-chitosan composites caused oxidation of hemoglobin after 24 h of incubation. This oxidation is inversely correlated with catalase activity [194], and this enzyme became less active.

Catalase is one of the important antioxidant enzymes necessary for the body's defense against a buildup of ROS, and variation in its activity can be used to reflect the oxidation-reduction balance in cells. GO affects the secondary structure of proteins and reduces catalase activity [195, 196]. Chitosan-graphene films initially and significantly increase catalase activity in erythrocytes compared with controls. After 24 h incubation, the catalase activity decreased compared to the 3 h incubation, but it was still higher than the activity of untreated films. The opposite occurred with cellulose-chitosan nanocomposites. After 3 h incubation with them, erythrocyte catalase activity decreased significantly compared to the control. After 24 h incubation, activity increased compared to the 3 h incubation, but only for the native form of CS@-f activity was increased compared to the control. These results suggest that the inclusion of cellulose reduces catalase activity, leading to an oxidative imbalance [57].

The growing interest in nanomaterials and the increasing possibilities of their application mean that skin cells can be exposed to them. Therefore, the toxicity level of all the new composites to human skin cells must be taken extremely seriously. The effect of chitosan-metal oxide and chitosan-graphene on the viability of human skin fibroblasts BJ and keratinocytes KERTr was measured by the MTT test. The unmodified chitosan film was non-toxic. Cell viability only slightly decreased to 85% for BJ cells and 77% for KERTr. Modification of chitosan films with zinc oxide proved crucial to the toxicity of the films; they caused a concentration-dependent effect on the skin cells. In films with a low ZnO content, the decrease in cell viability was minimal; whereas, at higher concentrations of oxide, the viability was markedly drastically. This is probably due to the influence of zinc oxide on the cell membrane and the production of ROS [108].

A concentration-dependent cytotoxic effect of iron (III) oxide films was found with KERTr cells. Nanocomposites, including iron oxide like chitosan-zinc oxide, cause changes due to the production of ROS and damage to cell membranes. Titanium dioxide-containing chitosan films do not cause significant changes in the toxicity of fibroblasts, but CS-TiO_2 decreased keratinocytes viability. Therefore, keratinocytes were more sensitive than fibroblasts to the action of films containing either oxide [108].

Chitosan-graphene composites had slightly lower cytotoxicity to KERTr cells compared to unmodified chitosan films. It follows that the presence of GO and its derivatives in chitosan films makes them less toxic to skin cells, which is advantageous from the point of view of their practical application. Cell viability decreased significantly after adding chitosan-graphene composites with silver (GO-Ag and PGO-Ag). BJ cells are more sensitive than KERTr cells, which means that the toxicity of different composites also depends on cell type and their individual sensitivities. In contrast, chitosan-silver composites (without graphene) were less toxic to KERTr cells compared to chitosan alone or chitosan-graphene-silver films. Silver ions, probably released from chitosan-graphene-silver nanocomposites, are toxic to cells. In chitosan nanocomposite without graphene, silver is more strongly bound to the chitosan structure and is not released or released less, making it non-toxic to KERTr cells and less toxic to BJ cells than chitosan-graphene-silver films [108].

1.6 Conclusion and Perspective

The field of bio-based nanocomposites is developing rapidly, driven by both energetic and environmental factors aiming at reducing the dependency on petroleum-based chemistry and synthetic materials, while preserving the quality of the environment and helping to avoid toxic chemicals and materials. One of the outstanding fields facing such a trend lies in the replacement of petroleum-based plastics with natural and biocompatible ones, referred to as bioplastics. Chitosan as a functional, amino-containing carbohydrate is one of the most acceptable structures, owing to its straightforward casting into nano- or micro-scale thick films. Benefitting from the advances made in classical nanocomposites, chitosan can be reinforced with an unlimited array of nanofillers to improve its thermal and mechanical properties. The compatibility of chitosan with nanofillers and even its role in dispersing them have triggered the design of many polymer-filler bioplastics. Furthermore, conjugations of different types allow for the insertion of biologically-relevant functional groups within the bioplastics, which is less common for conventional plastics. This rational design has resulted in bioactive films with different applications in biology and material science. Despite these achievements, far more remains to be achieved with chitosan chemistry and polysaccharides, in general, to fully replace conventional plastics and prevent their alarmingly detrimental effects on human health and the environment.

Acknowledgments

This work was partially financed by the National Science Centre (NCN) Poland, grant No. 2017/25/B/NZ9/02900.

AEK thanks UEMF for research facilities. NK thanks PHC Toubkal CNRST-CNRS (19/87) for funding. Financial support from Académie Hassan II des Sciences et Technique (project Nano-Bio-Mat) is warmly acknowledged.

References

1. Rodrigues, M. O.; Abrantes, N.; Gonçalves, F. J. M.; Nogueira, H.; Marques, J. C.; and Gonçalves, A. M. M. (2019). Impacts of plastic products used in daily life on the environment and human health: What is known? *Environ. Toxicol. Pharmacol.,* **72**, pp. 103239.
2. Hamilton, L. A. and Feit, S. (2019). Plastic & climate: The hidden costs of a plastic planet. https://www.ciel.org/plasticandclimate/.
3. Bishop, G.; Styles, D.; and Lens, P. N. L. (2021). Environmental performance comparison of bioplastics and petrochemical plastics: A review of life cycle assessment (LCA) methodological decisions, *Resour. Conserv. Recy.*, **168**, pp. 105451.
4. Masutani, K. and Kimura, Y. (2015). *Poly(lactic acid) Science and Technology: Processing, Properties, Additives and Applications,* Jiménez, A.; Peltzer, M.; and Ruseckaite R. (eds.), Chapter 1 "PLA synthesis: From the monomer to the polymer," The Royal Society of Chemistry, pp. 1–36.
5. Abdul Khalil, H. P. S.; Saurabh, C. K.; Tye, Y. Y.; Lai, T. K.; Easa, A. M.; Rosamah, E.; Fazita, M. R. N.; Syakir, M. I.; Adnan, A. S.; Fizree, H. M.; Aprilia, N. A. S.; and Banerjee, A. (2015). Seaweed based sustainable films and composites for food and pharmaceutical applications: A review, *Renew. Sustain. Energy Rev.,* **77**, pp. 353–362.
6. Younes, I. and Rinaudo, M. (2015). Chitin and chitosan preparation from marine sources: Structure, properties, and applications, *Mar. Drugs,* **13**, pp. 1133–1174.
7. Joseph, S. M.; Krishnamoorthy, S.; Paranthaman, R.; Moses, J. A.; and Anandharamakrishnan, C. (2021). A review on source-specific chemistry, functionality, and applications of chitin and chitosan, *Carbohydr. Polym. Technol. Applications,* **2**, pp. 100036.

8. Dang, N. T. T.; Chau, T. T. L.; Duong, H. V.; Le, H. T.; Tran, T. T. V.; Le, T. Q.; Vu, T. P.; Nguyen, C. D.; Nguyen, L. V.; and Nguyen, T.-D. (2017). Water-soluble chitosan-derived sustainable materials: Towards filaments, aerogels, microspheres, and plastics, *Soft Matter*, **13**, pp. 7292–7299.

9. Ansorena, M. R.; Marcovich, N. E.; and Pereda, M. (2019). *Handbook of Ecomaterials*, Martínez, L. M. T.; Kharissova, O. V.; and Kharisov, B. I. (eds.), "Food Biopackaging Based on Chitosan," Springer International Publishing, Cham., pp. 2057–2083.

10. Muxika, A.; Etxabide, A.; Uranga, J.; Guerrero, P.; and de la Caba, K. (2017). Chitosan as a bioactive polymer: Processing, properties and applications, *Int. J. Biol. Macromol.*, **105**, pp. 1358–1368.

11. Ilium, L. (1998). Chitosan and its use as a pharmaceutical excipient, *Pharm. Res.*, **15**, pp. 1326–1331.

12. Nunthanid, J.; Puttipipatkhachorn, S.; Yamamoto, K.; and Peck, G. E. (2001). Physical properties and molecular behavior of chitosan films, *Drug Dev. Ind. Pharm.*, **27**, pp. 143–157.

13. Blair, H. S.; Guthrie, J.; Law, T.-K.; and Turkington, P. (1987). Chitosan and modified chitosan membranes I. Preparation and characterization, *J. Appl. Polym. Sci.*, **33**, pp. 641–656.

14. Kumirska, J.; Czerwicka, M.; Kaczyński, Z.; Bychowska, A.; Brzozowski, K.; Thöming, J.; and Stepnowski, P. (2010). Application of spectroscopic methods for structural analysis of chitin and chitosan, *Mar. Drugs*, **8**, pp. 1567–1636.

15. Chen, H.; Hu, X.; Chen, E.; Wu, S.; McClements, D. J.; Liu, S.; Li, B.; and Li, Y. (2016). Preparation, characterization, and properties of chitosan films with cinnamaldehyde nanoemulsions, *Food Hydrocoll.*, **61**, pp. 662–671.

16. Jakubowska, E.; Gierszewska, M.; Nowaczyk, J.; and Olewnik-Kruszkowska, E. (2020). Physicochemical and storage properties of chitosan-based films plasticized with deep eutectic solvent, *Food Hydrocoll.*, **108**, pp. 106007.

17. Liu, M.; Zhou, Y.; Zhang, Y.; Yu, C.; and Cao, S. (2013). Preparation and structural analysis of chitosan films with and without sorbitol, *Food Hydrocoll.*, **33**, pp. 186–191.

18. Dimzon, I. K. D. and Knepper, T. P. (2015). Degree of deacetylation of chitosan by infrared spectroscopy and partial least squares, *Int. J. Biol. Macromol.*, **72**, pp. 939–945.

19. Ligler, F. S.; Lingerfelt, B. M.; Price, R. P.; and Schoen, P. E. (2001). Development of uniform chitosan thin-film layers on silicon chips, *Langmuir,* **17**, pp. 5082–5084.

20. Aryaei, A.; Jayatissa, A. H.; and Jayasuriya, A. C. (2012). Nano and micro mechanical properties of uncross-linked and cross-linked chitosan films. *J. Mech. Behav. Biomed.*, **5**, pp. 82–89.

21. Jóźwiak, T.; Filipkowska, U.; Szymczyk, P.; Rodziewicz, J.; and Mielcarek, A. (2017). Effect of ionic and covalent crosslinking agents on properties of chitosan beads and sorption effectiveness of reactive black 5 dye, *React. Funct. Polym.,* **114**, pp. 58–74.

22. Monteiro, O. A. C. and Airoldi, C. (1999). Some studies of crosslinking chitosan–glutaraldehyde interaction in a homogeneous system, *Int. J. Biol. Macromol.,* **26**, pp. 119–128.

23. Pavoni, J. M. F.; dos Santos, N. Z.; May, I. C.; Pollo, L. D.; and Tessaro, I. C. (2021). Impact of acid type and glutaraldehyde crosslinking in the physicochemical and mechanical properties and biodegradability of chitosan films, *Polym. Bull.*, **78**, pp. 981–1000.

24. Thakhiew, W.; Champahom, M.; Devahastin, S.; and Soponronnarit, S. (2015). Improvement of mechanical properties of chitosan-based films via physical treatment of film-forming solution, *J. Food Eng.*, **158**, pp. 66–72.

25. Croisier, F. and Jérôme, C. (2013). Chitosan-based biomaterials for tissue engineering, *Eur. Polym. J.*, **4**, pp. 780–792.

26. Lu, L. and Chen, W. (2011). Supramolecular self-assembly of biopolymers with carbon nanotubes for biomimetic and bio-inspired sensing and actuation, *Nanoscale*, **3**, pp. 2412–2420.

27. Sharma, B.; Malik, P.; and Jain, P. (2018). Biopolymer reinforced nanocomposites: A comprehensive review, *Mater. Today Commun.*, **16**, pp. 353–363.

28. Usuki, A.; Kojima, Y.; Kawasumi, M.; Okada, A.; Fukushima, Y.; Kurauchi, T.; and Kamigaito, O. (1993). Synthesis of nylon 6-clay hybrid, *J. Mater. Res.*, **8**, pp. 1179–1184.

29. Galimberti, M.; Cipolletti, V. R.; and Coombs, M. (2013). *Developments in Clay Science* **5**, Bergaya, F. and Lagaly, G. (eds.), Chapter 4.4 "Applications of Clay–Polymer Nanocomposites," Elsevier, pp. 539–586.

30. Bousmina, M. (2006). Study of intercalation and exfoliation processes in polymer nanocomposites, *Macromolecules*, **39**, pp. 4259–4263.

31. Sinha Ray, S. and Bousmina, M. (2005). Biodegradable polymers and their layered silicate nanocomposites: In greening the 21st century materials world, *Prog. Mater. Sci.*, **50**, pp. 962–1079.

32. Xu, Y.; Ren, X.; and Hanna, M. A. (2006). Chitosan/clay nanocomposite film preparation and characterization, *J. Appl. Polym. Sci.*, **99**, pp. 1684–1691.

33. Frindy, S.; Primo, A.; Qaiss, A. E. K.; Bouhfid, R.; Lahcini, M.; Garcia, H.; Bousmina, M.; and El Kadib, A. (2016). Insightful understanding of the role of clay topology on the stability of biomimetic hybrid chitosan-clay thin films and CO_2-dried porous aerogel microspheres, *Carbohydr. Polym.*, **146**, pp. 353–361.

34. Bate, B. and Burns, S. E. (2010). Effect of total organic carbon content and structure on the electrokinetic behavior of organoclay suspensions, *J. Colloid Interface Sci.*, **343**, pp. 58–64.

35. Wang, S. F.; Shen, L.; Zhang, W. D.; and Tong, Y. J. (2005). Preparation and mechanical properties of chitosan/carbon nanotubes composites, *Biomacromolecules*, **6**, pp. 3067–3072.

36. Fernandes, F. M.; Vázquez, L.; Ruiz-Hitzky, E.; Carnicero, A.; and Castro, M. (2014). Elastic properties of natural single nanofibers, *RSC Adv.*, **4**, pp. 11225–11231.

37. Higueras, L.; López-Carballo, G.; Gavara, R.; and Hernández-Muñoz, P. (2015). Reversible covalent immobilization of cinnamaldehyde on chitosan films via Schiff base formation and their application in active food packaging, *Food Bioproc. Tech.*, **8**, pp. 526–538.

38. Chabbi, J.; Aqil, A.; Katir, N.; Vertruyen, B.; Jerôme, C.; Lahcini, M.; and El Kadib, A. (2020). Aldehyde-conjugated chitosan-graphene oxide glucodynamers: Ternary cooperative assembly and controlled chemical release, *Carbohydr. Polym.*, **230**, pp. 115634.

39. Darder, M.; Aranda, P.; and Ruiz-Hitzky, E. (2007). Bionanocomposites: A new concept of ecological, bioinspired, and functional hybrid materials, *Adv. Mater.*, **19**, pp. 1309–1319.

40. Ruiz-Hitzky, E.; Darder, M.; and Aranda, P. (2005). Functional biopolymer nanocomposites based on layered solids, *J. Mater. Chem.*, **15**, pp. 3650–3662.

41. Yao, H.-B.; Tan, Z.-H.; Fang, H.-Y.; and Yu, S.-H. (2010). Artificial nacre-like bionanocomposite films from the self-assembly of chitosan–montmorillonite hybrid building blocks, *Angew. Chem. Int. Ed.*, **49**, pp. 10127–10131.

42. Lahann, R. W. and Roberson, H. E. (1980). Dissolution of silica from montmorillonite: Effect of solution chemistry, *Geochim. Cosmochim. Acta*, **44**, pp. 1937–1943.

43. Satoh, H.; Ishii, T.; and Owada, H. (2018). Dissolution of compacted montmorillonite at hyperalkaline pH and 70°C: In situ VSI and ex situ AFM measurements, *Clay Miner.*, **48**, pp. 285–294.

44. Potts, J. R.; Dreyer, D. R.; Bielawski, C. W.; and Ruoff, R. S. (2011). Graphene-based polymer nanocomposites, *Polymer*, **52**, pp. 5–25.

45. Stankovich, S.; Dikin, D. A.; Dommett, G. H. B.; Kohlhaas, K. M.; Zimney, E. J.; Stach, E. A.; Piner, R. D.; Nguyen, S. T.; and Ruoff, R. S. (2006). Graphene-based composite materials, *Nature*, **442**, pp. 282–286.

46. O'Hare, A.; Kusmartsev, F. V.; and Kugel, K. I. (2012). A stable "flat" form of two-dimensional crystals: Could graphene, silicene, germanene be minigap semiconductors? *Nano Lett.*, **12**, pp. 1045–1052.

47. Zhang, Y.; Zhang, L.; and Zhou, C. (2013). Review of chemical vapor deposition of graphene and related applications, *Acc. Chem. Res.*, **46**, pp. 2329–2339.

48. Hummers, W. S. and Offeman, R. E. (1958). Preparation of graphitic oxide, *J. Am. Chem. Soc.*, **80**, pp. 1339–1339.

49. Fan, H.; Wang, L.; Zhao, K.; Li, N.; Shi, Z.; Ge, Z.; and Jin, Z. (2010). Fabrication, mechanical properties, and biocompatibility of graphene-reinforced chitosan composites, *Biomacromolecules*, **11**, pp. 2345–2351.

50. Paredes, J. I.; Villar-Rodil, S.; Martínez-Alonso, A.; and Tascón, J. M. D. (2008). Graphene oxide dispersions in organic solvents, *Langmuir*, **24**, pp. 10560–10564.

51. Han, D.; Yan, L.; Chen, W.; and Li, W. (2011). Preparation of chitosan/graphene oxide composite film with enhanced mechanical strength in the wet state, *Carbohydr. Polym.*, **83**, pp. 653–658.

52. Pan, Y.; Wu, T.; Bao, H.; and Li, L. (2011). Green fabrication of chitosan films reinforced with parallel aligned graphene oxide, *Carbohydr. Polym.*, **83**, pp. 1908–1915.

53. Ahmed, J.; Mulla, M.; Arfat, Y. A.; and Thai T. L. A. (2017). Mechanical, thermal, structural and barrier properties of crab shell chitosan/graphene oxide composite films, *Food Hydrocoll.*, **71**, pp. 141–148.

54. Frindy, S.; Primo, A.; Ennajih, H.; el kacem Qaiss, A.; Bouhfid, R.; Lahcini, M.; Essassi, E. M.; Garcia, H.; and El Kadib, A. (2017). Chitosan-graphene oxide films and CO_2-dried porous aerogel microspheres: Interfacial interplay and stability, *Carbohydr. Polym.*, **167**, pp. 297–305.

55. Georgakilas, V.; Otyepka, M.; Bourlinos, A. B.; Chandra, V.; Kim, N.; Kemp, K. C.; Hobza, P.; Zboril, R.; and Kim, K. S. (2012). Functionalization

of graphene: Covalent and non-covalent approaches, derivatives and applications, *Chem. Rev.*, **112**, pp. 6156–6214.

56. Anouar, A.; Katir, N.; Mamede, A.-S.; Aboulaich, A.; Draoui, K.; Royer, S.; and El Kadib, A. (2019). Synthesis and multifaceted use of phosphorylated graphene oxide: Growth of titanium dioxide clusters, interplay with gold nanoparticles and exfoliated sheets in bioplastics, *Mater. Chem. Front.*, **3**, pp. 242–250.

57. Wrońska, N.; Anouar, A.; El Achaby, M.; Zawadzka, K.; Kędzierska, M.; Miłowska, K.; Katir, N.; Draoui, K.; Różalska, S.; Piwoński, I.; Bryszewska, M.; El Kadib, A.; and Lisowska, K. (2020). Chitosan-functionalized graphene nanocomposite films: Interfacial interplay and biological activity, *Materials,* **13**, pp. 998.

58. Pourchez, J.; Chivas-Joly, C.; Longuet, C.; Leclerc, L.; Sarry, G.; and Lopez-Cuesta, J. M. (2018). End-of-life incineration of nano-composites: New insights into nanofiller partitioning into by-products and biological outcomes of airborne emission and residual ash, *Environ. Sci. Nano*, **5**, pp. 1951–1964.

59. Huang, J.; Chang, P. R.; Chen, Y.; Gao, S.; and Liao, J. (2017). *Handbook of Nanocellulose and Cellulose Nanocomposites,* Kargarzadeh, H.; Ahmad, I.; Thomas, S.; and Dufresne, A. (eds.), Chapter 9 "Fully Green Cellulose Nanocomposites," Wiley-VCH Weinheim, pp. 301–334.

60. Mohan, T. P. and Kanny, K. (2020). *Green nanomaterials: Processing, properties, and applications,* Ahmed, S. and Ali, W. (eds.), "Green Nanofillers for Polymeric Materials," Springer Singapore, Singapore, pp. 99–138.

61. Tedeschi, G.; Guzman-Puyol, S.; Ceseracciu, L.; Paul, U. C.; Picone, P.; Di Carlo, M.; Athanassiou, A.; and Heredia-Guerrero, J. A. (2020). Multifunctional bioplastics inspired by wood composition: Effect of hydrolyzed lignin addition to xylan–cellulose matrices, *Biomacromolecules*, **21**, pp. 910–920.

62. Azizi Samir, M. A. S.; Alloin, F.; and Dufresne, A. (2005). Review of recent research into cellulosic whiskers, their properties and their application in nanocomposite field, *Biomacromolecules*, **6**, pp. 612–626.

63. Hosokawa, J.; Nishiyama, M.; Yoshihara, K.; Kubo, T.; and Terabe, A. (1991). Reaction between chitosan and cellulose on biodegradable composite film formation, *Ind. Eng. Chem. Res.*, **30**, pp. 788–792.

64. Hasegawa, M.; Isogai, A.; Onabe, F.; Usuda, M.; and Atalla, R. H. (1992). Characterization of cellulose–chitosan blend films, *J. Appl. Polym. Sci.*, **45**, pp. 1873–1879.

65. Costa, S. M.; Ferreira, D. P.; Teixeira, P.; Ballesteros, L. F.; Teixeira, J. A.; and Fangueiro, R. (2021). Active natural-based films for food packaging applications: The combined effect of chitosan and nanocellulose, *Int. J. Biol. Macromol.*, **177**, 241–251.

66. Huang, X.; Xie, F.; and Xiong, X. (2018). Surface-modified microcrystalline cellulose for reinforcement of chitosan film, *Carbohydr. Polym.*, **201**, pp. 367–373.

67. Habibi, Y.; Lucia, L. A.; and Rojas, O. J. (2010). Cellulose nanocrystals: Chemistry, self-assembly, and applications, *Chem. Rev.*, **110**, pp. 3479–3500.

68. Celebi, H. and Kurt, A. (2015). Effects of processing on the properties of chitosan/cellulose nanocrystal films, *Carbohydr. Polym.*, **133**, pp. 284–293.

69. Gajjar, P.; Pettee, B.; Britt, D. W.; Huang, W.; Johnson, W. P.; and Anderson, A. J. (2009). Antimicrobial activities of commercial nanoparticles against an environmental soil microbe, Pseudomonas putida KT2440, *J. Biol. Eng.*, **3**, pp. 1–13.

70. Billid, S.; Kędzierska, M.; Miłowska, K.; Wrońska, N.; El Achaby, M.; Katir, N.; Belamie, E.; Alonso, B.; Lisowska, K.; Lahcini, M.; Bryszewska, M.; and El Kadib, A. (2020). Phosphorylated micro- and nanocellulose-filled chitosan nanocomposites as fully sustainable, biologically active bioplastics, *ACS Sustainable Chem. Eng.*, **8**, 50, pp. 18354–18365.

71. Corbari, L.; Maltese, A.; Capodici, F.; Mangano, M. C.; Sará, G.; and Ciraolo G. (2020). Indoor spectroradiometric characterization of plastic litters commonly polluting the Mediterranean Sea: Toward the application of multispectral imagery, *Sci. Rep.*, **10**, pp. 1–12.

72. Shariatinia, Z. (2019). Pharmaceutical applications of chitosan, *Adv. Colloid Interface Sci.*, **263**, pp. 131–194.

73. Pighinelli, L. and Kucharska, M. (2013). Chitosan-hydroxyapatite composites, *Carbohydr. Polym.*, **93**, pp. 256–262.

74. El Kadib, A. (2015). Chitosan as a sustainable organocatalyst: A concise overview, *ChemSusChem.*, **8**, pp. 1–29.

75. Varma, A. J.; Deshpande, S. V.; and Kennedy, J. F. (2004). Metal complexation by chitosan and its derivatives: A review, *Carbohydr. Polym.*, **55**, pp. 77–93.

76. Ignatowa, M.; Manolova, N.; and Rashkov, I. (2013). Electrospun Antibacterial Chitosan-Based Fibers, *Macromol. Biosci.*, **13**, pp. 860–872.

77. Ke, C-L.; Deng, F-S.; Chuang, C-Y.; and Lin, C-H. (2021). Antimicrobial actions and applications of chitosan, *Polymers*, **13**, pp. 1–21.

78. Kumar, S.; Mukherjee, A.; and Dutta, J. (2020). Chitosan based nanocomposite films and coatings: Emerging antimicrobial food packaging alternatives, *Trends Food Sci. Technol.*, **97**, pp. 196–209.

79. Huang, X.; You, Z.; Luo, Y.; Yang, C.; Ren, J.; Liu, Y.; Wei, G.; Dong, P.; and Ren, M. (2021). Antifungal activity of chitosan against Phytophthora infestans, the pathogen of potato late blight, *Int. J. Biol. Macromol.*, **166**, pp. 1365–1376.

80. Qin, Y.; Li, P.; and Guo, Z. (2020). Cationic chitosan derivatives as potential antifungals: A review of structural optimization and applications, *Carbohydr. Polym.*, **236**, pp. 116002.

81. Shih, P. Y.; Liao, Y. T.; Tseng, Y. K.; Deng, F. S.; and Lin, C. H. (2019). A potential antifungal effect of chitosan against *Candida albicans* is mediated via the inhibition of SAGA complex component expression and the subsequent alteration of cell surface integrity, *Front. Microbiol.*, **10**, pp. 602–616.

82. Sun, T.; Wu, C. L.; Hao, H.; Dai, Y.; and Li, J. R. (2016). Preparation and preservation properties of the chitosan coatings modified with the in situ synthesized nano SiOx, *Food Hydrocol.*, **54**, pp. 130–138.

83. Kong. M.; Chen, X. G.; Xing, K.; and Park, H. J. (2010). Antimicrobial properties of chitosan and mode of action: A state of the art review, *Int. J Food Microbiol.*, **144**, pp. 51–63.

84. Lim, S. H. and Hudson, S. M. (2004). Synthesis and antimicrobial activity of a water-soluble chitosan derivative with a fiber-reactive group, *Carbohydr. Res.*, **339**, pp. 313–319.

85. Nagy, A.; Harrison, A.; Sabbani, S.; Munson, R. S. Jr; Dutta, P. K.; and Waldman, W. J. (2011). Silver nanoparticles embedded in zeolite membranes: Release of silver ions and mechanism of antibacterial action, *Int. J Nanomedicine*, **6**, pp. 1833–1852.

86. Wang, H.; Qian, J.; and Ding, F. (2018). Emerging chitosan-based films for food packaging applications, *J. Agric. Food Chem.*, **66**, pp. 359–413.

87. Lou, M. M.; Zhu, B.; Muhammad, I.; Li, B.; Xie, G. L.; Wang, Y. L.; Li, H. Y.; and Sun, G. C. (2011). Antibacterial activity and mechanism of action of chitosan solutions against apricot fruit rot pathogen *Burkholderia seminalis*, *Carbohydr. Res.*, **346**, pp. 1294–1301.

88. Nazeer, M. A.; Yilgör, E.; and Yilgör, I. (2017). Intercalated chitosan/hydroxyapatite nanocomposites: Promising materials for bone tissue engineering applications, *Carbohydr. Polym.*, **175**, pp. 38–46.

89. Adamski, R. and Siuta, D. (2021). Mechanical, structural and biological properties of chitosan/hydroxyapatite/silica composites for bone tissue engineering, *Molecules*, **26**, pp. 1976–1991.

90. Pistone, A.; Iannazzo, D.; Celesti, C.; Piperopoulos, E.; Ashok, D.; Cembran, A.; Tricoli, A.; and Nisbet, D. (2019). Engineering of chitosan-hydroxyapatite-magnetite hierarchical scaffolds for guided bone growth, *Materials*, **12**, pp. 2321–2334.

91. Zabihi, E.; Babaei, A.; Shahrampour, D.; Arab-Bafrani, Z.; Mirshahidi, K. S.; and Joz Majidi, H. (2019). Facile and rapid in-situ synthesis of chitosan-ZnO nano-hybrids applicable in medical purposes: A novel combination of morphology-conducting agent, *Int. J. Biol. Macromol.*, **131**, pp. 107–116.

92. Abral, H.; Pratama, A. B.; Handayani, D.; Mahardika, M.; Aminah, I.; Sandrawati, N.; Sugiarti, E.; Muslimin, A. N.; Sapuan, S. M.; and Ilyas, R. (2021). Antimicrobial edible film prepared from bacterial cellulose nanofibers/starch/chitosan for a food packaging alternative, *Int. J. Polym. Sci.*, pp. 1–11.

93. Anis, A.; Pal, K.; and Al-Zahrani, S. M. (2021). Essential oil-containing polysaccharide-based edible films and coatings for food security applications, *Polym.*, **13**, pp. 575–607.

94. Elsabee, M. Z. and Abdou, E. S. (2013). Chitosan based edible films and coatings: A review, *Mater. Sci. Eng. C*, **33**, pp. 1819–1841.

95. Kocira, A.; Kozłowicz, K.; Panasiewicz, K.; Staniak, M.; Szpunar-Krok, E.; and Hortyńska, P. (2021). Polysaccharides as edible films and coatings: Characteristics and influence on fruit and vegetable quality—A review, *Agronomy*, **11**, pp. 813–851.

96. Pavinatto, A.; de Almeida Mattos, A. V.; Granato Malpass, A. C.; Okura, M. H.; Balogh, D. T.; and Safelice, R. C. (2020). Coating with chitosan-based edible films for mechanical/biological protection of strawberries, *Int. Biol. Macromol.*, **151**, pp. 1004–1011.

97. Wang, H.; Ding, F.; Ma, L.; and Zhang Y. (2021). Edible films from chitosan-gelatin: Physical properties and food packaging application, *Food Biosci.*, **40**, pp. 100871.

98. Torrico, D. D.; No, H. K.; Prinyawiwatkul, W.; Janes, M.; Corredor, J. A. H.; and Osorio, L. F. (2011). Mineral oil–chitosan emulsion coatings affect quality and shelf-life of coated eggs during refrigerated and room temperature storage, *J. Food Sci.*, **76**, pp. 262–268.

99. Wardy, W.; Torrico, D. D.; Jirangrat, W.; No, H. K.; Saalia, F. K.; and Prinyawiwatkul, W. (2011). Chitosan-soybean oil emulsion coating

affects physico-functional and sensory quality of eggs during storage, *LWT-Food Sci. Technol.*, **44**, pp. 23749–2355.

100. Khalifa, I.; Barakat, H.; El-Mansy, A. H.; and Soliman, S. A. (2016). Improving the shelf-life stability of apple and strawberry fruits applying chitosan-incorporated olive oil processing residues coating, *Food Packag. Shelf Life*, 9, pp. 10–19.

101. Nguyen, V. D.; Styevkó, G.; Madaras, E.; Haktanirlar, G.; Tran, A. T. M.; Bujna, E.; Dam, M. S.; and Nguyen, Q. D. (2019). Immobilization of β-galactosidase on chitosan-coated magnetic nanoparticles and its application for synthesis of lactulose-based galactooligosaccharides, *Bioprocess Biochem.*, **84**, pp. 30–38.

102. Perdones, A.; Sánchez-González, L.; Chiralt, A.; and Vargas, M. (2012). Effect of chitosan-lemon essential oil coatings on storage-keeping quality of strawberry, *Postharvest Biol. Tec.*, **70**, pp. 32–41.

103. Xing, Y.; Li, X.; Xu, Q.; Yun, J.; Lu, Y.; and Tang, Y. (2011). Effects of chitosan coating enriched with cinnamon oil on qualitative properties of sweet pepper (Capsicum annuum L.), *Food Chem.*, **124**, pp. 1443–1450.

104. Sánchez-Ramírez, J.; Martínez-Hernández, J.; Segura-Ceniceros, P.; López, G.; Saade, H.; Medina-Morales, H.; Ramos-González, R.; Aguilar, C. N.; and Ilyina, A. (2017). Cellulases immobilization on chitosan-coated magnetic nanoparticles: Application far Agave Atrovirens lignocellulosic biomass hydrolysis, *Bioprocess Biosyst. Eng.*, **40**, pp. 9–22.

105. Kim, D. S.; Dhand, V.; Rhee, K. Y.; and Park S.-J. (2015). Study on the effect of silanization and improvement in the tensile behavior of graphene-chitosan-composite, *Polymers*, **7**, pp. 527–551.

106. Kosowska, K.; Domalik-Pyzik, P.; Krok-Borkowicz, M.; and Chłopek, J. (2019). Synthesis and characterization of chitosan/reduced graphene oxide hybrid composites, *Materials*, **12**, pp. 1–13.

107. Valencia Zapata, M. E.; Mina Hernandez, J. H.; Grande Tovar, C. D.; Valencia Llano, C. H.; Diaz Escobar, J. A.; Vázquez-Lasa, B.; San Román, J.; and Rojo, L. (2019). Novel bioactive and antibacterial acrylic bone cement nanocomposites modified with graphene oxide and chitosan, *Int. J. Mol. Sci.*, **20**, pp. 2938–2956.

108. Wrońska, N.; Katir, N.; Miłowska, K.; Hammi, N.; Nowak, M.; Kędzierska, M.; Anoouar, A.; Zawadzka, K.; Bryszewska, M.; El Kadib, A.; and Lisowska, K. (2021). Antimicrobial effect of chitosan films on food spoilage bacteria, *Int. J. Mol. Sci.*, **22**, pp. 5839.

109. De Kwaadstenied, M.; Botes, M.; and Cloete, T. E. (2011). Application of nanotechnology in antimicrobial coatings in the water industry, *Nano*, **6**, pp. 395–407.

110. Mazaheri, M.; Akhavan, O.; and Simchi, A. (2014). Flexible bactericidal graphene oxide-chitosan layers for stem cell proliferation, *Appl. Surf. Sci.*, **301**, pp. 456–462.

111. Konwar, A.; Kalita, S.; Kotoky, J.; and Chowdhury, D. (2016). Chitosan–iron oxide coated graphene oxide nanocomposite hydrogel: A robust and soft antimicrobial biofilm, *ACS Appl. Mat. Int.*, **8**, pp. 20625–2634.

112. Maruthupandy, M.; Rajivgandhi, G.; Muneeswaran, T.; Anand, M.; and Quero, F. (2021). Highly efficient antibacterial activity of graphene/chitosan/magnetite nanocomposites against ESBL-producing Pseudomonas aeruginosa and Klebsiella pneumoniae, *Colloids and Surfaces B: Biointerfaces*, **202**, pp. 111690.

113. Kumar, P.; Huo, P.; Zhang, R.; and Liu, B. (2019). Antibacterial properties of graphene-based nanomaterials, *Nanomaterials*, **9**, pp. 737–769.

114. Li, J.; Wang, G.; Zhu, H.; Zhang, M.; Zheng, X.; Di, Z.; Liu, X.; and Wang, X. (2014). Antibacterial activity of large-area monolayer graphene film manipulated by charge transfer, *Sci. Rep.*, **4**, pp. 4359–4367.

115. Duncan, T. V. (2011). Applications of nanotechnology in food packaging and food safety: Barrier materials, antimicrobials and sensors, *J. Colloid Interface Sci.*, **363**, pp. 1–24.

116. Król, A.; Pomastowski, P.; Rafińska, K.; Railean-Plugaru, V.; and Buszewski, B. (2017). Zinc oxide nanoparticles: Synthesis, antiseptic activity and toxicity mechanism, *Adv. Colloid Interface Sci.*, **249**, pp. 37–52.

117. Fu, G.; Vary, P. S.; and Lin C. T. (2005). Anatase TiO_2 nanocomposites for antimicrobial coatings, *J. Phys. Chem.*, **109**, pp. 8889–8898.

118. Yamamoto, O.; Komatsu, M.; Sawai, J.; and Nakagawa, Z. E. (2004). Effect of lattice constant of zinc oxide on antibacterial characteristics, *J. Mater. Sci. Mater. Med.*, **15**, pp. 847–851.

119. Al-Naamani, L.; Dobretsov, S.; and Dutta J. (2016). Chitosan-zinc oxide nanoparticle composite coating for active food packaging applications, *IFSET*, **38**, pp. 231–237.

120. Yadav, S.; Mehrotra, G.; and Dutta P. K. (2020). Chitosan based ZnO nanoparticles loaded gallic-acid films for active food packaging, *Food Chem.*, **334**, pp. 127605.

121. Dwivedi, S.; Wahab, R.; Khan, F.; Mishra, Y. K.; Musarrat J.; and Al-Khedhairy, A. (2014). A reactive oxygen species mediated bacterial biofilm inhibition via zinc oxide nanoparticles and their statistical determination, *PLoS ONE*, **9**, pp. 1–9.

122. Bishop, G. M.; Dringen, R.; and Robinson, S. R. (2007). Zinc stimulates the production of toxic reactive oxygen species (ROS) and inhibits glutathione reductase in astrocytes, *Free Radic. Biol. Med.*, **42**, pp. 1222–1230.

123. Kumar, R.; Umar, A.; Kumar, G.; and Nalwa, H. S. (2017). Antimicrobial properties of ZnO nanomaterials: A review, *Ceram. Int.*, **43**, pp. 3940–3961.

124. Mishra, P. K.; Mishra, H.; Ekielski, A.; Talegaonkar, S.; and Vaidya, B. (2017). Zinc oxide nanoparticles: A promising nanomaterial for biomedical applications, *Drug Discov. Today*, **22**, pp. 1825–1834.

125. Krajewski, S.; Prucek, R.; Panacek, A.; Avci-Adali, M.; Nolte, A.; Straub, A.; Zboril, R.; Wendel, H. P.; and Kvitek, L. (2013). Hemocompatibility evaluation of different silver nanoparticle concentrations employing a modified chandler-loop in vitro assay on human blood, *Acta Biomater.*, **9**, pp. 7460–7468.

126. Arokiyaraj, S.; Arasu, M. V.; Vincent, S.; Prakash, N. U.; Choi, S. H.; Oh, Y.-K.; Choi, K. C.; and Kim, K. H. (2014). Rapid green synthesis of silver nanoparticles from Chrysanthemum indicum L and its antibacterial and cytotoxic effects: An in vitro study, *Int. J. Nanomed.*, **9**, pp. 379–388.

127. Franci, G.; Falanga, A.; Galdiero, S.; Palomba, L.; Rai, M.; Morelli, G.; and Galdiero, M. (2015). Silver nanoparticles as potential antibacterial agents, *Molecules*, **20**, pp. 8856–8874.

128. Venkateshaiah, A.; Havlíček, K.; Timmins, R. L.; Röhrl, M.; Wacławek, S.; Nguyen, N. H. A.; Černík, M.; Padil, V. V. T.; and Agarwal. S. (2021). Alkenyl succinic anhydride modified tree-gum kondagogu: A bio-based material with potential for food packaging, *Carbohydr. Polym.*, **266**, pp. 118–126.

129. Ediyilyam, S.; George, B.; Shankar, S. S.; Dennis, T. T.; Wacławek, S.; Černík, M.; and Padil, V. V. T. (2021). Chitosan/gelatin/silver nanoparticles composites films for biodegradable food packaging application, Polymers, **13**, pp. 1680–1698.

130. Siripatrawan, U. and Kaewklin P. (2018). Fabrication and characterization of chitosan-titanium dioxide nanocomposite film as ethylene scavenging and antimicrobial active food packaging, *Food Hydrocoll.*, **84**, pp. 125–134.

131. Behera, S S.; Das, U.; Kumar, A.; Bissoyi, A.; and Singh, A. K. (2017). Chitosan/TiO_2 composite membrane improves pro-life ration and survival of L929 fibroblast cells: Application in wound dressing and skin regeneration, *Int. J. Biol. Macromol.*, **98**, pp. 329–340.

132. Haldorai, Y.; Shim and J. J. (2014). Novel chitosan-TiO_2 nanohybrid: Preparation, characterization, antibacterial, and photocatalytic properties, *Polym. Compos.*, **35**, pp. 327–333.

133. Zhang, X.; Xiao, G.; Wang, Y.; Zhao, Y.; Su, H.; and Tan T. (2017). Preparation of chitosan-TiO_2 composite film with efficient antimicrobial activities under visible light for food packaging applications, *Carbohydr. Polym.*, **169**, pp. 101–107.

134. Li, B.; Yang, Z.; Yang, Y.; Wen, Q.; Wang, X.; Liu, B.; Wang, Y.; and Sun, G. (2016). Synthesis, characterization, and antibacterial activity of chitosan/ TiO_2 nanocomposite against Xanthomonas oryzae pv. oryzae. *Carbohydr. Polym.*, **152**, PP. 825–831.

135. Kavitha, K.; Sutha, S.; Prabhu, M.; Rajendran, V.; and Jayakumar, T. (2013). In situ synthesized novel biocompatible titania–chitosan nanocomposites with high surface area and antibacterial activity, *Carbohydr. Polym.*, **93**, pp. 731–739.

136. Anaya-Esparza, L. M.; Montalvo-González, E.; González-Silva, N.; Méndez-Robles, M. D.; Romero-Toledo, R.; Yahia, E. M.; and Pérez-Larios, A. (2019). Synthesis and characterization of TiO_2-ZnO-MgO mixed oxide and their antibacterial activity, *Materials*, **12**, pp. 698–710.

137. Ruiz, S.; Tamayo, J. A.; Ospina, J. D.; and Grande Tovar, C. D. (2019). Antimicrobial films based on nanocomposites of chitosan/poly(vinyl alcohol)/graphene oxide for biomedical applications, *Biomolecules*, **9**, pp. 109–126.

138. Li, P.; Gao, Y.; Sun, Z.; Chang, D.; Gao, G.; and Dong A. (2016). Synthesis, characterization, and bactericidal evaluation of chitosan/ guanidine functionalized graphene oxide composites, *Molecules*, **22**, 12– 27.

139. Xu, W.; Xie, W.; Huang, X.; Chen, X.; Huang, N.; Wang, X.; and Liu, J. (2016). The graphene oxide and chitosan biopolymer load TiO_2 for antibacterial and preservative research, *Food Chem.*, **221**, pp. 267–277.

140. Yuan, G. F.; Chen, X.; and Li, D. (2016). Chitosan films and coatings containing essential oils: The antioxidant and antimicrobial activity, and application in food systems, *Food Research. Int.*, **89**, pp. 117–128.

141. Rahman, P. M.; Mujeeb, V. M. A.; and Muraleedharan K. (2017). Flexible chitosan-nano ZnO antimicrobial pouches as a new material for extending the shelf life of raw meat, *Int. J. Biol. Macromol.*, **97**, pp. 382–391.

142. Suo, B.; Li, H.; Wang, Y.; Li, Z.; Pan, Z.; and Ai Z. (2017). Effects of ZnO nanoparticle-coated packaging film on pork meat quality during cold storage, *J. Sci. Food Agricult.*, **97**, pp. 2023–2029.

143. Hajji, S.; Salem, R. B. S.-B.; Hamdi, M.; Jellouli, K.; Ayadi, W.; Nasri, M.; and Boufi, S. (2017). Nanocomposite films based on chitosan–poly(vinyl alcohol) and silver nanoparticles with high antibacterial and antioxidant activities, *Process Saf Environ.*, **111**, pp. 112–121.

144. Salari, M.; Sowti Khiabani, M.; Rezaei Mokarram, R.; Ghanbarzadeh, B.; and Samadi Kafil, H. (2018). Development and evaluation of chitosan based active nanocomposite films containing bacterial cellulose nanocrystals and silver nanoparticles, *Food Hydrocol.*, **84**, pp. 414–423.

145. Wu, Z.; Huang, X.; Li, Y. C.; Xiao, H.; and Wang X. (2018). Novel chitosan films with laponite immobilized Ag nanoparticles for active food packaging, *Carbohydr. Polym.*, **199**, pp. 210–218.

146. Zhang, X.; Liu, Y.; Yong, H., Qin, Y.; Liu, J.; and Liu J. (2019). Development of multifunctional food packaging films based on chitosan, TiO_2 nanoparticles and anthocyanin-rich black plum peel extract, *Food Hydrocol.*, **94**, pp. 80–92.

147. Abdollahi, M.; Rezaei, M.; and Farzi, G. (2012). A novel active bionanocomposite film incorporating rosemary essential oil and nanoclay into chitosan, *J. Food Eng.*, **111**, pp. 343–350.

148. Ali, A.; Noh, N. M.; and Mustafa, M. A. (2015). Antimicrobial activity of chitosan enriched with lemongrass oil against anthracnose of bell pepper, *Food Packag. Shelf Life*, **3**, pp. 56–61.

149. Mohammadi, A.; Hashemi, M.; and Hosseini, S. M. (2015). Chitosan nanoparticles loaded with *Cinnamomum zeylanicum* essential oil enhance the shelf life of cucumber during cold storage, *Postharvest Biol. Tec.*, **110**, pp. 203–213.

150. Sánchez-González, L.; Pastor, C.; Vargas, M.; Chiralt, A.; González-Martínez, C.; and Cháfer, M. (2011). Effect of hydroxypropyl-methylcellulose and chitosan coatings with and without bergamot essential oil on quality and safety of cold-stored grapes, *Postharvest Biol. Tec.*, **60**, pp. 57–63.

151. Feyzioglu, C. C. and Tornuk, F. (2016). Development of chitosan nanoparticles loaded with summer savory (Satureja hortensis L.)

essential oil for antimicrobial and antioxidant delivery applications, *Food Sci. Tec.*, **70**, pp. 104–110.

152. Yang, G.; Yue, J.; Gong, X.; Qian, B.; Wang, H.; Deng, Y.; and Zhao, Y. (2014). quality of fresh blueberries, *Postharvest Biology and Technology*, **92**, pp. 46–53.

153. Ramírez-Guerra, H. E.; Castillo-Yañez, F. J.; Montaño-Cota, E. A.; Ruíz-Cruz, S.; Márquez-Ríos, E; Canizales-Rodríguez, D. F.; Torres-Arreola, W.; Montoya-Camacho, N.; and Ocaño-Higuera, W. M. (2018). Protective effect of an edible tomato plant extract/chitosan coating on the quality and shelf life of sierra fish fillets, *J. Chem.*, **1**, pp. 1–6.

154. Kumar, S.; Shukla, A.; Baul, P. P.; Mitra, A.; and Halder, D. (2018). Biodegradable hybrid nanocomposites of chitosan/gelatin and silver nanoparticles for active food packaging applications, *Food Packag. Shelf Life*, **16**, pp. 178–184.

155. Previdi, M. P.; Franceschini, B.; Umita, E.; Zurlini, C.; Bovis, N.; Montanari, A.; and Brutti, A. (2018). Effect of chitosan film and coating on microbiological characteristics of fresh fish and fish burger during storage at refrigerated condition, *Int. J. Appl. Sci. Tec.*, **9**, pp. 1–6.

156. Ordikhani, I. F. and Simchi, A. (2014). Long-term antibiotic delivery by chitosan-based composite coatings with bone regenerative potential, *Appl. Surf.*, **317**, pp. 56–66.

157. Li, W. W.; Wang, H. Y.; and Zhang Y. Q. (2017). A novel chitosan hydrogel membrane by an improved electrophoretic deposition and its characteristics in vitro and in vivo, *Mater Sci. Eng. C Mater. Biol. Appl.*, **74**, pp. 287–297.

158. Anitha, A.; Sowmya, S.; Kumar, P. T. S.; Deepthi, S.; Chennazhi, K. P.; Ehrlich, H.; Tsurkan, M.; and Jayakumar, R. (2014). Chitin and chitosan in selected biomedical applications, *Prog. Polym. Sci.*, **39**, pp. 1644–1667.

159. Deepthi, S.; Venkatesan, J.; Kim, S.-K.; Bumgardner, J. D.; and Jayakumar, R. (2016). An overview of chitin or chitosan/nanoceramic composite scaffolds for bone tissue engineering, *Int. J. Biol. Macromol.*, **93**, pp. 1338–1353.

160. Khor, E. and Lim, L. Y. (2003). Implantable applications of chitin and chitosan, *Biomaterials*, **24**, pp. 2339–2349.

161. Grolik, M.; Szczubialka, K.; Wowra, B.; Dobrowolski, D.; Orzechowska-Wylegala, B.; Wylęgała, E.; and Nowakowska, M. (2012). Hydrogel membranes based on genipin-cross-linked chitosan blends for

corneal epithelium tissue engineering, *J. Mater. Sci. Mater. Med.*, **23**, pp. 1991–2000.

162. Stevanović M.; Djošić, M.; Janković, A.; Kojić, V.; Vukašinović-Sekulić, M.; Stojanović, J.; Odović, J.; Sakač, M.; and Mišković-Stanković, V. (2020). Antibacterial graphene-based hydroxyapatite/chitosan coating with gentamicin for potential applications in bone tissue engineering, *J. Biomed. Mater. Res. A.*, **108**, pp. 2175–2189.

163. Feng, P.; Luo, Y.; Ke, C.; Qiu, H.; Wang, W.; Zhu, Y.; Hou, R.; Xu, L.; and Wu, S. (2021). Chitosan-based functional materials for skin wound repair: Mechanisms and applications, *Front. Bioeng. Biotechnol.*, **9**, pp. 1–15.

164. Vaz, J. M.; Pezzoli, D.; Chevallier, P.; Campelo, C. S.; Candiani, G.; and Mantovani, D. (2018). Antibacterial coatings based on chitosan for pharmaceutical and biomedical applications, *Curr. Pharm Des.*, **24**, pp. 866–885.

165. Mohandas, A.; Deepthi, S.; Biswas, R.; and Jayakumar, R. (2018). Chitosan based metallic nanocomposite scaffolds as antimicrobial wound dressings, *Bioact. Mater.*, **3**, pp. 267–277.

166. Patrulea, V.; Ostafe, V.; Borchard, G.; and Jordan, O. (2015). Chitosan as a starting material for wound healing applications, *Eur. J. Pharm. Biopharm.*, **97**, pp. 417–426.

167. Ahmed, S. and Ikram, S. (2016). Chitosan based scaffolds and their applications in wound healing, *Achiev. Life Sci.*, **10**, pp. 27–37.

168. Dai, T.; Tanaka, M.; Huang, Y.-Y.; and Hamblin, M. R. (2011). Chitosan preparations for wounds and burns: Antimicrobial and wound-healing effects, *Expert Rev. Anti. Infect. Ther.*, **9**, pp. 857–879.

169. Yang, J. M.; Lin, H. T.; Wu, T. H.; and Chen C. C. (2003). Wettability and antibacterial assessment of chitosan containing radiation-induced graft non-woven fabric of polypropylene-g-acrylic acid, *J. Appl. Polym. Sci.*, **90**, pp. 1331–1336.

170. Ferreira, A. M.; Carmagnola, I.; Chiono, V.; Gentile, P.; Fracchia, L.; Ceresa, C.; Georgiev, G.; and Ciardelli, G. (2013). Surface modification of poly(dimethylsiloxane) by two-step plasma treatment for further grafting with chitosan-Rose Bengal photosensitizer, *Surf. Coat. Tech.*, **223**, pp. 92–97.

171. Wang, R.; Neoh, K. G.; Shi, Z.; Kang, E. T.; Tambyah, P. A.; and Chiong, E. (2012). Inhibition of *Escherichia coli* and *Proteus mirabilis* adhesion and biofilm formation on medical grade silicone surface, *Biotechnol. Bioeng.*, **109**, pp. 336–345.

172. Kouchak, M.; Ameri, A.; Naseri, B.; and Kargar Boldaji, S. (2014). Chitosan and polyvinyl alcohol composite films containing nitrofurazone: Reparation and evaluation, *Iran. J. Basic Med. Sci.*, **17**, pp. 14–20.

173. Lee, D. W.; Lim, H.; Chong, H. N.; and Shim, W. S. (2009). Advances in chitosan material and its hybrid derivatives: A review, *Open Biomater J.*, **1**, pp. 10–20.

174. Lee, Y. M.; Kim, S. S.; Park, M. H.; Song, K. W.; Sung, Y. K.; and Kang, I. K. (2000). Beta-chitin-based wound dressing containing silver sulfurdiazine, *J. Mater. Sci. Mater. Med.*, **11**, pp. 817–823.

175. Boucard, N.; Viton, C.; Agay, D.; Mari, E.; Roger, T.; and Chancerelle. (2007). The use of physical hydrogels of chitosan for skin regeneration following third-degree burns, *Biomaterials*, **28**, pp. 3478–88.

176. Wu, T.; Zivanovic, S.; Draughon, F. A.; Conway, W. S.; and Sams, C. E. (2005). Physicochemical properties and bioactivity of fungal chitin and chitosan, *J. Agric. Food Chem.*, **53**, pp. 3888–3894.

177. Biagini, G.; Muzzarelli, R. A. A.; Giardiono, R.; and Castaldini, C. (1992). *Advances in chitin and chitosan,* Brine, C. J., Sanford, P. A.; and Zikakis, J. P. (eds.), "Biological material for wound healing," Elsevier, London, pp. 16 –23.

178. Ishihara, M.; Nakanishi, K.; Ono, K.; Sato, M.; Kikuchi, M.; and Saito, Y. (2002). Photocrosslinkable chitosan as a dressing for wound occlusion and accelerator in healing process, *Biomaterials*, **23**, pp. 833–840.

179. Rai, M.; Yadav, A.; and Gade, A. (2009). Silver nanoparticles as a new generation of antimicrobials, *Biotechnol. Adv.*, **27**, pp. 76–83.

180. Ng, W. L.; Yeong, W. Y.; and Naing, M. W. (2016). Development of polyelectrolyte chitosan-gelatin hydrogels for skin bioprinting, *Procedia CIRP*, **49**, pp. 105–112.

181. Choi, B.; Kim, S.; Lin, B.; Wu, B. M.; and Lee M. (2014). Cartilaginous extracellular matrix-modified chitosan hydrogels for cartilage tissue engineering, *ACS Appl. Mater. Interfaces*, **6**, pp. 20110–20121.

182. Gnavi, S.; Barwig, C.; Freier, T.; Haastert-Talini, K.; Grothe, C.; and Geuna S. (2013). The use of chitosan-based scaffolds to enhance regeneration in the nervous system, *Int. Rev. Neurobiol.*, **109**, pp. 1–62.

183. Lichtenfels, E.; Frankini, A. D.; Cardozo, M. A.; and D'Azevedo, P. A. (2011), Stent graft infection, *J. Vasc. Bras.*, **10**, pp. 50–54.

184. Kim, I.; Seo, S.; Moon, H.; Yoo, M.; Park, I.; Kim, B.; and Cho, C. (2008). Chitosan and its derivatives for tissue engineering applications, *Biotechnol. Adv.*, **26**, pp. 1–21.

185. Islam, M. M.; Shahruzzaman, M.; Biswas, S.; Sakib, M. N.; and Rashid, T. U. (2020). Chitosan based bioactive materials in tissue engineering applications: A review, *Bioact. Mater.*, **5**, pp. 164–183.

186. Kim, C.; Park, S. J.; Yang, D. H.; and Chun, H. J. (2018). Chitosan for tissue engineering, *Adv. Exp. Med. Biol.*, **1077**, pp. 475–485.

187. Martino, A.; Sittinger, M.; and Risbud, M, V. (2005). Chitosan: A versatile biopolymer for orthopaedic tissue-engineering, *Biomaterials*, **26**, pp. 5983–5990.

188. Dass, C. R. and Choong, P. (2008). The use of chitosan formulations in cancer therapy, *J. Microencapsul.*, **25**, pp. 275–279.

189. Prabaharan, M. (2008). Review paper: Chitosan derivatives as promising materials for controlled drug delivery, *J. Biomater. Appl.*, **23**, pp. 5–36.

190. Riva, R.; Ragelle, H.; Des Rieux, A.; Duhem, N. J.; Jèrôme, C.; and Prèat, V. (2011). Chitosan and chitosan derivatives in drug delivery and tissue engineering, *Adv. Polym. Sci.*, **244**, pp. 19–44.

191. Singh, B. N. and Kim, K. H. (2000). Floating drug delivery systems: An approach to oral controlled drug delivery via gastric retention, *J. Control. Release*, **63**, pp. 235–259.

192. Parhi, R. (2020). Drug delivery applications of chitin and chitosan: A review, *Environ. Chem. Lett.*, **18**, pp. 577–594.

193. Yildirim, A.; Ozgur, E.; and Bayindir, M. (2013). Impact of mesoporous silica nanoparticle surface functionality on hemolytic activity, thrombogenicity and non-specific protein adsorption, *J. Mater. Chem. B*, **1**, pp. 1909–1920.

194. Maćczak, A.; Cyrkler, M.; Bukowska, B.; and Michałowicz, J. (2017). Bisphenol A, Bisphenol S, bisphenol F, and bisphenol AF induce different oxidative stress and damage in human red bloods cells (in vitro study), *Toxicol. In Vitro*, **41**, pp. 143–149.

195. Scibior, D. and Czeczot, H. (2006). Catalase: Structure, properties, functions, *Postepy Hig. Med. Dosw.*, **60**, pp. 170–180.

196. Wei, X. L. and Ge, Z. Q. (2013). Effect of graphene oxide on conformation and activity of catalase, *Carbon*, **60**, pp. 401–409.

Chapter 2

Cyclodextrins in Drug Development: Challenging Multifunctional Excipients

Paraskevi Papakyriakopoulou, Konstantina Manta, and Eirini Christodoulou

Section of Pharmaceutical Technology, Department of Pharmacy, School of Health Sciences, National and Kapodistrian University of Athens, Greece

e_christod@pharm.uoa.gr

Cyclodextrins (CDs) are cyclic oligosaccharides with a hydrophilic outer surface and a lipophilic inner cavity. These molecules began to occupy the interest of the scientific community in the 19th century when they were first discovered. Natural CDs and their derivatives have been widely used as pharmaceutical excipients, in order to increase the aqueous solubility of poorly soluble drugs and enhance the drug permeability through biological membranes. The ability to trap lipophilic substances or lipophilic fragments of drug molecules in their cavity leads to the formation of water-soluble complexes. The understanding of the way in which complexes are formed is of particular interest, as it will enable the future use of CDs, not only as excipients, but as multifunctional systems, as well.

Recently, compositions of metal-organic frameworks (MOFs) with CDs made feasible the preparation and use of non-toxic MOFs in drug delivery. Especially the structure of γ-CD enables the binding

Functional Materials in Biomedical Applications
Edited by Costas Demetzos, Natassa Pippa, and Nikolaos Naziris

ISBN 978-981-4968-65-2 (Hardcover), 978-1-003-41146-8 (eBook)
www.jennystanford.com

with alkali and alkaline earth metal ions forming amphiphilic nanopores. The high porosity of CD-MOFs results in higher loading capacities than CDs, retaining the benefits of CD-drug complexes (solubilization, stability, taste masking, etc.) and ensuring the delivery of higher doses in certain biological targets.

In nanotechnology, crosslinked CDs have been employed to produce CD-based nanosponges (NSs). NSs are non-toxic and highly stable colloidal structures, able to encapsulate several drug substances in their nanocavities. CD-based NSs combine the already established advantages of CDs with the tailored release of guest substances, in a controlled and predictable manner. The fine-tuning of the three components constituting the NSs can lead to effective drug delivery in specific pharmacological targets.

Overall, the long-term use of CDs in pharmaceutical applications has led to a profound inquiry of their interactions either with the guest molecules in the internal hydrophobic cavity or with ligands on the external hydrophilic surface. In the future, the approach of precision medicine will engage current CD applications, encouraging the development of CDs-based NSs and CD-MOFs drug carriers, which are able to meet the needs of personalized treatment.

2.1 Introduction

Since their discovery and for more than 100 years, CDs have been the subject of many scientific publications. It is mentioned that in 2021, CDs were the subject of more than 2400 research articles published in scientific journals. In addition, they are contained in over 2300 patents, many of which relate to pharmaceutical applications [1].

Many scientists have separated the development of CDs into three stages: discovery, exploratory, and utilization.

1. Discovery (1891–1935)

   The first publication describing CDs was by Antoine Villiers, who discovered crystalline dextrins (cellulosines) obtained by enzymatic digestion of potato starch by *Bacillus amylobacter* [1]. In the early 20th century (1903), Franz Schardinger, an Austrian microbiologist, after extensive research on these derivatives managed to separate and purify them. Schardinger recommended that "crystalline dextrins" was an improved name for these derivatives. In 1911, it was found that CDs are cyclic oligosaccharides and later these compounds started to be called CDs or cyclomaltodextrins [2]. Schardinger had dealt with two CD derivatives, i.e., of α- and β-CD. In 1935, Freudenberg and Cramer discovered the γ-CD derivative. Until then, the only known fact about these macromolecules was that they were oligosaccharides.

2. Exploratory (1935–1970)

   In the following decades, the researchers who further studied CDs were able to identify key elements related to their structure. In 1936, CD cyclic structure was uncovered, and in the 1940s, Cramer mentioned the idea that CDs may have the ability to form inclusion complexes with other molecules. In this decade (1942–1948), W. Borchert managed to identify the structures of α-, β-, and γ-CD with X-ray diffraction [3]. After this discovery, researchers considered that CDs could form inclusion complexes with other compounds [4].

   At the beginning of the 1950s, two groups of scientists led by French and Cramer started to explore the physicochemical properties of CDs, focusing on their complexation properties. The milestone year in CDs research was 1953, when the first patent for CDs was issued. More precisely, Freudenberg, Plieninger, and Cramer described the utilization of CDs in drug formulations. The main applications described were the improvement of solubility of insoluble molecules and the protection of sensitive substances from atmospheric oxygen.

   In 1967, Cramer tried to explain the mechanisms that govern inclusion complexes using fluorometric methods. He reported the basic points of an inclusion complex formation between a CD and a substrate [5].

   The first attempt to study the toxicity of these molecules took place by the French a few years later. He reported that when Schardinger purified β- dextrins, he had used them as part of the rats' diet. At this point, it is worth mentioning that rats can identify toxic substances and avoid their consumption. It was observed that the rats recruited in the study consumed very small lusts of their food and by the end of the week almost all of them had died. Researchers could not determine the cause of death. Two possible explanations were reported, the first concerning the high dose of purified dextrin, and the second the possible impurities of organic solvents. This period was crucial for determining all the physicochemical properties of dextrins and elucidating all the aspects of their toxicity. However, the main question that occurred by these experimental observations was how dextrins could affect the human body [6].

3. Utilization (1970–today)

   After the extensive study of their properties for more than four decades, the scale-up of their production and their possible industrial application was the next challenge. The development of genetic engineering led to the use of new enzymes and to the production of highly purified CDs in much larger quantities, which paved the way for their widespread use as excipients in various industries [2]. The enzymatic digestion of starch by *Bacillus macerans* gave a crude mixture of α-CD (approx. 60%), β-CD (approx. 20%), and γ-CD (approx. 20%) and fragments of CDs with glucose units [2]. This bacillus produces an enzyme called cyclomaltodextrin glucanotranferase that is responsible for the digestion of starch [3].

2.2 Structure and Physicochemical Properties of CDs

CDs are cyclic oligosaccharides with a hydrophilic outer surface and a lipophilic inner cavity. They consist of a-D-glycopyranose monomers, which are linked by a-[1,4]-glycoside bonds. The most common natural CDs are α-, β-, and γ-CDs with six, seven, and eight D-glycopyranose units, respectively [1]. The special formation of the glucopyranose units results in the truncated cone shape of CDs. The primary hydroxyl groups that extend from the narrow end of the CD and the secondary hydroxyl groups that extend from the lower end of the cone are responsible for the formation of the hydrophilic outer surface and hydrophobic inner cavity of the CD molecule [7].

CDs are large molecules with molecular weight varying from 1000 to 2000 Da [8]. The main properties of the three natural CDs, described by Martin Del Valle [4], are presented in Table 2.1.

Table 2.1 Physicochemical properties of natural CDs

Properties	α-CD	β-CD	γ-CD
Number of glycopyranoze units	6	7	8
Molecular weight (g/mol)	972	1135	1297
Solubility in water at 25 °C (% w/v)	14.5	1.85	23.2
Outer diameter (A)	14.6	15.4	17.5
Cavity diameter (A)	4.7–5.3	6.0–6.5	7.5–8.3
Height of torus (A)	7.9	7.9	7.9
Cavity volume (A^3)	174	262	427

Many of the physicochemical and biological properties of CDs are common to those of the linear structural analogs, although some differences have been identified. For example, β-CD and its linear analog maltoheptaose were tested, and it was found that they have similar molar mass (1135 g/mol for β-CD and 1153 g/mol for maltoheptaose), logP (about 14), and almost the same array of H-donors and H-receptors. Their main differences were the water solubility at room temperature, 18.5 mg/mL for the β-CD, while for the linear analog is equal to 50 mg/mL [4].

The low water solubility of β-CD is attributed to its structure. The formation of intramolecular hydrogen bonds reduces the hydration of β-CD and consequently, its solubility [3]. Overall, the main advantage of CDs compared to linear dextrins is the conical shape of CDs, their resistance to enzymatic degradation, and their improved complexation and solubilization capabilities [1].

2.3 CDs Derivatives

As mentioned before, CDs have very low water solubility, which is attributed to the presence of strong hydrogen bonds in their crystal lattice. This fact, combined with the evidence of the toxicity of natural CDs when administered parenterally, has increased the scientific interest in CD derivatives [8].

The hydroxypropyl derivatives of β- and γ-CD (HP-β-CD and HP-γ-CD, respectively), the randomly methylated-β-cyclodextrin (Me-β-CD), and the sulfobutylether-β-cyclodextrin (SBE-β-CD) are the main derivatives used as pharmaceutical excipients [9] and their main physicochemical characteristics, described by Loftsson et al. [2], are shown in Table 2.2.

Table 2.2 Physicochemical properties of modified β-CD derivatives

Cyclodextrin	Subst.*	MW (Da)	Solubility in water (mg/ml), 25 °C
HP-β-CD	0.65	1400	>600
RMe-β-CD	1.8	1312	>500
SBE-β-CD	0.9	2163	>500
HP-γ-CD	0.6	1576	>500

*Substitution: Average number of substituents per glucopyranose unit.

It has been observed that substitution of any hydroxyl group of the CD molecules, even with hydrophobic groups such as methoxy groups, resulted in a significant increase in their water solubility, as shown in Table 2.2. Regarding alkyl derivatives (HP-β-CD, HP-γ-CD), they are characterized by greater aqueous solubility mainly attributed to the substitution of hydroxyl groups of β-CD, with hydroxypropyl groups. Thus, the intermolecular network of hydrogen bonds is disturbed, favoring the interaction with the water molecules and therefore the increase of the molecules' solubility [10].

2.4 Complex Formation

CDs are able to trap lipophilic molecules or lipophilic moieties in their inner cavity, when found in the aqueous environment. Hence, they form the so-called "inclusion complexes".

Regarding the complex formation, no covalent bonds are even formed or broken during the formation of the complex. The phenomenon of complexation and the physicochemical laws governing these interactions are characterized by high complexity. Specifically, the driving forces behind the complexation may be electrostatic or hydrophobic interactions, the development of Van der Waals forces, the formation of hydrogen bonds, and the release of "high-energy" water (with high enthalpy) molecules from the cavity [7, 8]. Moreover, the drug molecules in the complex are in quick equilibrium with the free molecules in the aqueous solution [7], and not every molecule will be trapped in each of the available cyclodextrin molecules. In fact, the whole process is characterized by a dynamic equilibrium in which drug/cyclodextrin complexes are constantly formed and decomposed. This equilibrium is described by a complex formation constant (K_s) which takes values from 2 to 4000 M^{-1} [11]. The formation of an inclusion complex is described by Eq. 2.1, where drug molecules $m\ D$ interact with $n\ CD$ molecules to form the complex Dm/CDn.

$$m \cdot D + n \cdot CD \leftrightarrows Dm/CDn \tag{2.1}$$

The $K_{m:n}$ is the stability constant (K_s) of the complex, whose the most common type of complex is 1:1 D/CD ($m = 1, n = 1$) [12].

As mentioned above, Cramer was one of the first to describe the formation of complexes [5, 13, 14]. Many of the principles described by him are scientifically accepted to date. Among those, four basic points are given below:

1. When the substrate/drug approaches the CD molecule, water molecules escape from the CD cavity, and this phenomenon results in a new energy state for CD. Van der Waals interactions and the number of hydrogen bonds decrease, while the degrees of freedom of released water molecules increase.
2. Respectively, as the two molecules approach each other, the water molecules, surrounding the substrate, spread and reorganize, enabling it to be in a new energy state.
3. This new energy state considers to be a "perfect gas state" for the substrate forcing it to enter the CD cavity. The formed complex is stabilized by Van der Waals forces and

hydrogen bonds. Between the ejected water molecules new hydrogen bonds are formed.

4. Around the part of the substrate that remains in contact with the solvent and around the CD molecule, the structure of the water layer is restored [13, 14].

2.5 Pharmacokinetic Approach

The oral bioavailability of CDs is very low in animals and humans (0.1–3%). Due to their high molecular weight and the hydrophilic outer surface, insignificant amounts of CDs are absorbed from the gastrointestinal tract through passive diffusion. More precisely, α-CD is absorbed at a rate of 2–3% after *per os* administration in mice. It is not metabolized in the upper intestinal tract, but is only broken down by the intestinal microflora of the colon. Its excretion is 60% in the form of CO_2 and 7–14% as metabolites in feces and urine. Concerning β-CD, after *per os* administration, only 1–2% is absorbed in the upper intestinal tract. However, it is not metabolized in it but by the microflora of the colon, as α-CD. Similarly, γ-CD shows low absorption after *per os* administration and is metabolized into glucose in the upper intestinal tract by intestinal enzymes. However, it is not metabolized after intravenous administration [4].

2.6 Toxicological Approach

Many studies have shown that CDs are characterized by low toxicity at low concentrations, but this may be differentiated at higher doses or after administration through alternative routes.

Per os administration is less possible to cause toxicity issues, because of the direct metabolism of CDs by bacteria in the upper and lower gastrointestinal tract, which also reduces their absorption. In contrast, intravenous administration can cause kidney damage. Also, microcrystals formed from the interaction of CDs with cholesterol, eventually cause nephrotic syndrome [15]. Furthermore, α- and β-CDs are suitable for intravenous drug administration, because of the possible cause of renal toxicity [16]. Kidney damage can also be caused by modified CDs, in a concentration-dependent manner.

2.7 Basic Applications

Since the structure of CDs had been extensively studied and identified by the early 70s', thousands of applications have been noted, especially in the fields of drug, food, and agriculture. Concerning pharmaceutical products, the beginning of CD applications can be associated with the arrival of NMR analysis. NMR studies confirmed the initial hypotheses about the complex formation and this technique remains the fundamental tool for CD complexes characterization to date. It is worth mentioning that in 1971, Thakkar and Demarco were the first to publish their work based on the formation of inclusion complexes of β-CD with four barbiturates [17]. The change of physicochemical properties of drug substances when complexed with CDs results in the extended use of these macromolecules as pharmaceutical excipients. Global CDs in the pharma market are expected to account for USD 134,474.40 thousand by 2027 [18].

Most of CDs' applications in pharmaceutical science are linked to their ability to increase the solubility of poorly water-soluble drugs. The amphiphile structure of CDs has solved the problem of poor solubility capturing less polar parts of molecules in the internal lipophilic cavity and interacting with water molecules due to their external hydrophilic surface. The solubilizing effect of CDs has been applied in various cases such as those of nonsteroidal anti-inflammatory drugs [19], acidic drugs and salts [20], anticancer drugs [21], natural products [22–24], antifungal and antibiotics [25, 26], estrogens [27], antiandrogens [28], etc. The greater solubility of the formed complexes allowed the attainment of *per os* administration of drugs classified in BCS classes II and IV. Furthermore, the introduction of more hydrophilic CD derivatives like HP-β-CD, led to higher solubility values, in cases where the natural CDs do not provide a sufficient solubilizing effect.

In literature, several attempts have been made to ensure the stability enhancement of the captured substances by producing drug-CD complexes. Specifically, the inclusion of the unstable and volatile parts of a molecule in CDs' inner cavity reduces the possibility of drug degradation when exposed to thermal, oxidative, or ultra-violet light conditions [29]. Also, in certain conditions, drug-CD complexes can protect the guest molecule against the hydrolysis effect of certain enzymes such as b-lactam [30] and esterase [31]. Popielec and Loftsson [30] in their review about the "effects of cyclodextrins on the chemical stability of drugs", cite 104 cases of studies about the effect of CDs on stability issues. In most cases, the effect is positive and leads to ameliorated shelf-life of the pharmaceutical product. However, they mention 32 drugs, whose complexation with CD accelerated their degradation in aqueous solutions [32]. Concerning the liquid formulations, the likelihood of hydrolysis can, significantly, decrease when the drug is complexed with a CD. A recent study about the development of latanoprost-loaded CD microaggregates suspension depicts the stability improvement of the prepared suspension, compared to commercial pharmaceutical products. Eye drops suspension containing aggregates of latanoprost-γ-CD has a better stability profile even at thermal (60 °C) or light exposure [33].

The inclusion of moieties in the inner cavity of CDs is widely used for the masking bad taste or odor. Regarding taste masking, the key point lies in the capturing of the molecule's parts that are responsible for the bitterness or the unpleasant taste of the drug. Apart from some exceptions, this effect of drug-CD interaction can be correlated with the value of the binding constant (K) of the complex [34]. Consequently, the lipophilicity of the drug influences the effectiveness of masking, taking into consideration that more lipophilic drugs can be bound more readily in the CD cavity. Furthermore, between α-CD and β-CD, the greater diameter of the toroid cone of β-CD leads to better taste suppression, because of the more effective inclusion of the guest molecule [35]. Lee et al., in their study using two different methods, aimed to prepare a cetirizine-β-CD complex to suppress the bitter taste of the drug. The prepared complexes by the freeze-dryer and supercritical antisolvent (SAS) methods were evaluated by 15 volunteers who rate the taste of formulations from 3+ to 0, as very strong bitter or no bitter, respectively. All the volunteers rated from 0 to 1, the taste of the complex prepared by the SAS method; and from 0 to 2.5, for the one prepared by the freeze-dryer [36]. Moreover, Alopaeus et al. [37] prepared freeze-dried complexes of two poorly soluble drugs, indomethacin, and furosemide, to increase their solubility, and at the same time, improve the unpleasant taste of the drug substances. The evaluation of palatability was performed with the use of an electronic tongue. The study proves the improvement of taste after the inclusion of drugs in the HP-β-CD cavity, when compared to the free drug solution [37].

The contribution of CDs to the elimination or decrease of drug toxicity and/or of the adverse effects accompanying their administration to patients is of great interest to scientists. This feature can be successfully applied in the case of anticancer agents, which are usually characterized by high levels of cytotoxicity even against healthy cells. A recent study about the inclusion complex of doxorubicin with a galactosamine derivative of β-CD demonstrated the encapsulation of the drug in the modified CD resulted in the elimination of cardiotoxic effects [38].

2.8 Advanced Applications

2.8.1 Nanosponges

NSs are porous colloidal structures consisting of hyper-crosslinked polymers forming particles with nanosized cavities. These cavities can encapsulate small-sized drug molecules with a molecular weight of less than 500 Da [39, 40]. NSs release guest molecules, when found in the body, in a controlled and predictable manner [41], governed by the binding constant between the nanosystem and the drug molecule. They are non-toxic, highly stable, and can effectively deliver peptides, proteins, and various active moieties which, otherwise, would be directly metabolized. The encapsulated molecules can be either hydrophilic or lipophilic. Furthermore, NSs improve the aqueous solubility of lipophilic drugs and make feasible their rapid dissolution and absorption after oral administration [42]. Generally, NSs consist of three components: the polymer, the crosslinker, and the drug. Concerning the polymer, NSs could be divided into five main categories:

1. CD-based
2. Hyper-crosslinked polystyrene-based
3. Carbon-coated metallic-based
4. Titanium-based
5. Silicone-based

The biocompatibility of CDs and their extended use as pharmaceutical excipients render CD-based NSs the most advantageous. Especially, β-CD is more frequently used, due to the special features of its structure, such as:

1. High complexing potential with crosslinking agents
2. High drug-loading capacity in nano-sized cavities
3. Cost-effective nature of this substance, due to the long-term experience in β-CD formulation development [43, 44].

2.8.1.1 CD-based NSs

CD-based NSs are mostly used and applicable in pharmaceutical sciences. CDs are extensively studied macromolecules with a lipophilic inner cavity and a hydrophile outer surface, able to be crosslinked with several agents. Crosslinking of CDs creates a network (Fig. 2.1) of connected cavities with a high-inclusion capacity. Namely, these nanoporous systems favor the interactions with both hydrophobic and hydrophilic molecules by the inclusion and non-inclusion complexations, even in the intermediate spaces between the components of the system. The time of entrapment can be prolonged or modulated, depending on the case, adding functional groups in the polymeric structure. Natural CDs (mainly α- and β-CD) and their derivatives, like alkyloxycarbonyl CD, Me-β-CD, and HP-β-CD, have been used for the formation of NSs water disinfectants, or as drug delivery nanocarriers. The already established safety profile of CDs as pharmaceutical excipients and their numerous applications in solubility and stability improvement, taste and smell masking, and permeation enhancement, render them the more commonly used polymer for NSs development.

2.8.1.2 Possible crosslinkers

Crosslinkers act as the connecting agents of the polymeric system called NS. In the case of CD-based NSs, these parts are responsible for the binding between the CD molecules to form the nanoporous network. Epichlorohydrin, dialdehydes, diacyl chlorides, and epoxides were firstly described as possible crosslinkers for NSs. Epichlorohydrin is preferably used to prepare hydrophilic NSs via careful polycondensation [45]. In addition to epichlorohydrin, for hydrophobic NSs, various crosslinkers such as diphenyl carbonate (DPC), diaryl carbonates, diisocyanates, pyromellitic anhydride, carbonyldiimidazoles (CDI), carboxylic acid dianhydrides, 2,2-bis (acrylamido) acetic acid, dichloromethane (DCM), and polyamidoamine have been described as generally used crosslinkers for the synthesis of NSs [46].

Figure 2.1 CD-based NS network.

2.8.1.3 Preparation methods

NSs preparation has been described in literature following various methods. The most cited are the solvent evaporation method and the melting method. Also, the emulsion solvent diffusion method and ultrasound-assisted or microwave-assisted synthesis have been reported.

- Solvent evaporation technique

  In this method, solvents like dimethylsulfoxide (DMSO) and dimethylformamide (DMF) are used as solubilizing agents of the crosslinkers. The polymer is dispersed in a polar aprotic solvent. The resulting polymer solution, after being mixed with the crosslinker solution, is left to be refluxed for 1–48 h. The system's temperature could range from 10 °C to the reflux temperature of the solvent, to ensure the appropriate conditions for the reaction. Subsequently, in order to obtain the crosslinked polymer, the solution should be added to a large amount of cold distilled water. Then, the final product is collected after filtration and it is purified by prolonged Soxhlet extraction. The resulted NSs consist of spherical and solid nanosized particles, characterized by high water solubility. The size of the particles can be further reduced with a high-pressure homogenization technique. This solvent evaporation method is preferred because fusion or melting steps are avoided [46, 47].

- Melting method

  In the melting method, the polymer (mainly CD) is allowed to melt with the crosslinker and the mixture is stirred and heated at 100 °C for 5 h. Thereafter, the solution is left to reach room temperature, and crystallization and purification steps follow as described in the evaporation method [48].

- Emulsion solvent diffusion method

  For the preparation of NSs with the emulsion solvent diffusion method, different proportions of ethyl cellulose and polyvinyl alcohol can be used. More precisely, ethyl cellulose and the chosen drug should be dissolved in DCM, whereas polyvinyl alcohol in an aqueous phase. DCM dispersed phase is slowly added in the aqueous continuous phase and the mixture should be stirred for 2–4 h at 1000 rpm. The prepared NSs are obtained by filtration and the final product is, then, collected after drying in an oven at 40 °C for 24 h [49].

- Ultrasound-assisted synthesis

  Ultrasound-assisted synthesis is a method based on the reaction of the polymer and the crosslinking agent, without any solvent, in an ultrasound bath pre-filled with water, at 90 °C, followed by 5 h of sonication. Subsequently, the mixture is allowed to reach room temperature and then, the purification method is applied, using excess amounts of water. The final product is obtained after drying under vacuum and prolonged Soxhlet extraction. This method is characterized by a fast rate of formation of spherical NSs with uniform size, smaller than 5 μm. For this procedure, DPC or pyromellitic anhydride crosslinkers are considered the most appropriate [49, 50].

- Microwave-assisted synthesis

  This method is characterized as the simplest. More precisely, NSs are prepared by microwave irradiation, which increases the reaction velocity, forming NS with uniformity in particle size distribution and crystallinity. Furthermore, their degree of crystallinity is significantly higher, in comparison with the products of the other methods [51].

2.8.1.4 Loading of drugs into NSs

NSs crystal structure strongly affects their loading capacity. More precisely, they could be either paracrystalline or in a crystalline form. The comparison of the two forms reveals the higher loading capacity of crystalline NSs [52, 53]. Also, the crystallization either of the active substance that aims to be trapped NSs, or of the NSs that play an important role in their complexation. Furthermore, the crosslinked NS network is characterized by high porosity and has numerous interaction sites to achieve the inclusion or binding of drug molecules. More precisely, as the hydrophobic channels of CDs are crosslinked, hydrophile nanocavities are created between them, because of their external hydrophilic surface. This architecture enables the capturing of guest molecules of a wide range of lipophilicity and size [54]. CD-based NSs offer a higher solubilizing and protective effect on the drug guests, compared to the simple CD-drug inclusion complexes.

However, the ratio of CD to crosslinker significantly affects the solubilization, reducing it when takes values greater than 1:4. This phenomenon is explained by the creation of a denser network of nanocavities, which is less accessible by the drug molecules that cannot interact freely with the NSs matrix [55, 56].

Briefly, the drug loading in the NSs consists of the following main steps (Fig. 2.2):

1. Dispersion of the drug in an aqueous suspension of NSs
2. Continuous stirring to achieve the complexation between the drug moiety and the NSs
3. Freeze-drying

An initial pretreatment of NSs to reduce the particle size at values lower than 500 nm, will ensure better entrapment of the guest in the nanocavities [57, 58]. Moreover, in the case of water-insoluble drugs, the solvent evaporation method would be more appropriate for drug loading into NSs. Namely, an organic solvent can be used to dissolve the drug. Thereafter, the NSs are added to the drug solution and the resulted suspension is triturated till the evaporation of the solvent [59–62].

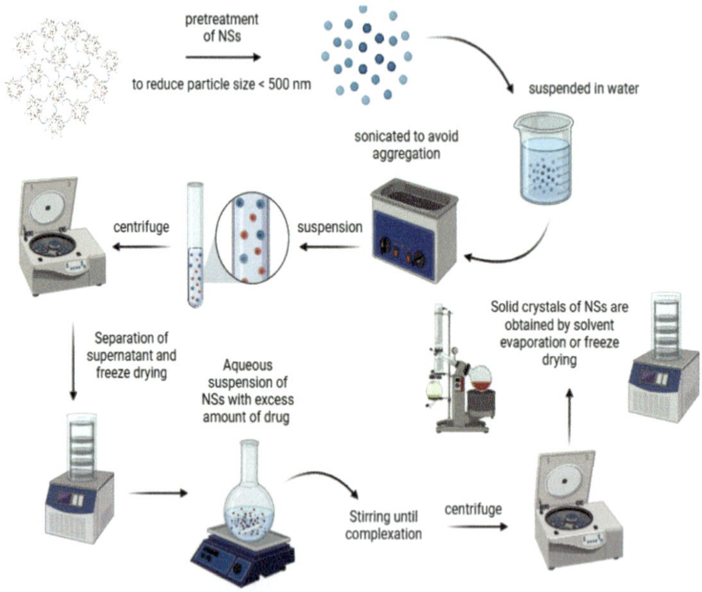

Figure 2.2 Drug loading into NSs.

2.8.1.5 Main pharmaceutical applications of CD-based NSs

- Drug carriers

  CD-based NSs have been extensively studied as multifunctional drug carriers combining the advantages of CD-formulated drugs and the nanoporous nature of NSs. Hence, they are suitable for the solubility enhancement of BCS class II and class IV drugs and the increase of stability, as well as for taste and odor masking. In recent studies, they have been applied in the development either of topical or oral formulations [63, 64]. Namely, for *per os* administered dosage forms, the inclusion and non-inclusion complexes of NSs with the encapsulated molecules, enables the bioavailability enhancement, due to the solubility and stability enhancement. In the case of transdermal delivery, CD-NS formulated moieties present higher permeation across the skin barrier [63].

- NSs for enhancing drug and protein stability

  As mentioned before, CD-based NSs can improve the stability of the trapped drugs, preventing degradation caused by enzymes, hydrolysis, oxidation, radiation, etc. [57]. Especially, in the case of natural products, NSs make feasible the administration and delivery of photosensitive and easily oxidized molecules like quercetin, resveratrol, and γ-oryzanol [65, 67]. Consequently, the bioavailability of the molecules increases, and the need for repeated doses is reduced as well. It is worth mentioning the application of NSs in protein delivery, preventing their enzymatic degradation and the possible denaturation or aggregation. More specifically, Appleton et al. presented in their study, the development of a novel pH-sensitive CD-NS, suitable for oral delivery of insulin. The developed formulation promotes the intestinal absorption of insulin and it could be the onset of a more extended application of NSs in proteins, peptides, antibodies, and enzymes delivery [68].

- NSs for solubility enhancement

  The administration of several poorly soluble drugs became feasible with the introduction of CDs in drug delivery.

Drugs classified as BCS class II and class IV molecules can be encapsulated into CDs, resulting in solubility, and therefore, absorption and enhancement. The introduction of CD-based NSs in this field offered a new alternative with a possible greater solubilizing effect on the captured substances in the nanocavities. Recently, the contribution of carbonate NSs to the solubility enhancement of dexibuprofen has been shown. Namely, the loss of drug crystallinity due to the entrapment of the drug into the NSs led to a 6.3-fold increase in dexibuprofen aqueous solubility [19]. Also, carbonate NSs have enhanced telmisartan's bioavailability, as follows by the 54.4% increase of AUC in the case of the ternary NS complex of the drug [69]. Furthermore, a high increase in bioavailability is noted in the case of lapatinid, an anticancer drug approved for breast cancer. More precisely, C_{max} of lapatinid loaded in NSs was 3 times higher than that of the pure substance [70].

- NSs as drug release modulators

  The stability and solubility enhancement achieved with CD-based NSs are also combined with a tailored drug release. These systems are characterized as drug release modulators. Depending on the hydrophilicity of NS, the release would be either immediate or sustained. Specifically, for water-soluble drugs, hydrophobic NSs can be used for controlled release, while hydrophilic NSs can release the loaded drug rapidly [62].

- NSs and SARS-CoV-2

  The outbreak of coronavirus 2 (SARS-CoV-2) disease (COVID-19) made necessary the development of new therapeutic strategies against severe respiratory syndrome caused by the virus. Zhang et al. presented a novel approach based on the idea of cellular NSs. The findings about the mechanism of action of SARS-CoV-2 indicate that its infectivity is expressed via its binding on angiotensin-converting enzyme 2 (ACE 2) receptors or other unidentified ones, placed on the surface of many human cells [71]. Hence, the development of cellular NSs displaying the same protein receptors can act as neutralization agents against the virus, blocking cells' infection. In this study, two types of cellular NSs were fabricated, epithelial-NSs and macrophage NSs, and then, were evaluated for their acute toxicity and their neutralization ability, after in vivo administration to mice. The results of the study show that both types of cellular NSs can neutralize SARS-CoV-2 in a concentration-dependent manner, and namely, macrophage NSs manage to reduce the viral load even in the early or late stages of the disease [72].

In Table 2.3, a list of the published works about β-CD-NSs-formulated drugs is presented (2006–2021).

Table 2.3 Publications of drugs formulated as β-CD-NSs and their pharmaceutical application in the period of 2006–2021, listed from the most recent to the oldest

Drug	Indication	Study	Refs.
Econazole	Antifungal	In vitro evaluation and in vivo pharmacodynamic study	[73]
Clobetasol propionate	Psoriasis	Antipsoriatic potential and biochemical estimation	[74]
Flutamide	Prostate cancer	Cytotoxicity study in cell lines	[75]
Dexibuprofen	NSAID for moderate and severe pain	Acute oral toxicity studies in rats	[19]
Insulin	Diabetes	Cytotoxicity study, in vivo pharmacokinetic study and efficacy study in mice	[68]
Imiquimod	Genital warts, superficial basal cell carcinoma, and actinic keratosis	In vitro release, in vitro permeation, and biological studies	[76]
Norfloxacin	Antibiotic	In vitro release, antimicrobial in vivo study	[77]
Atorvastatin calcium	Hyperlipidemia	In vitro release and in vivo pharmacokinetic study in rats	[78]
Rosuvastatin	Hyperlipidemia	In vitro release, short-term stability, and in vivo pharmacokinetic study in rats	[79]
Rilpivirine	HIV	In vitro dissolution and in vivo pharmacokinetic study in rats	[80]

(Continued)

Table 2.3 (*Continued*)

Drug	Indication	Study	Refs.
Celecoxib	NSAID for rheumatoid arthritis, osteoarthritis, inflammation of joints, acute pain, and pre-/post-surgical pain	In vivo pharmacokinetic study in rats	[81]
Efavirenz	HIV	In vitro dissolution and in vivo pharmacokinetic study in rats	[82]
Nifedipine	Angina pectoris and hypertension	In vivo pharmacokinetic study in rats	[83]
Erlotinib	Pancreatic cancer	Cytotoxicity study, in vivo pharmacokinetic study in rats	[84]
Doxorubicin	Breast cancer, bladder cancer, Kaposi's sarcoma, lymphoma, and acute lymphocytic leukemia	Cytotoxicity study, in vivo pharmacokinetic study in rats, and efficacy study in cancer cells	[85]
Lansoprazole	Peptic ulcer disease, gastroesophageal reflux disease, and Zollinger–Ellison syndrome	In vitro release study	[86]
Levodopa	Parkinson's disease	In vitro release study	[87]
Meloxicam	NSAID for rheumatoid arthritis, osteoarthritis	In vitro release and stability studies	[88]
Repaglinide	Diabetes	Phase-solubility studies	[89]
Calcium	Hyperphosphatemia	In vitro release study, accelerated stability study	[90]
Tamoxifen	Early and advanced estrogen receptor-positive breast cancer in pre- and post-menopausal women	In vitro release studies, cytotoxicity studies, in vivo pharmacokinetic study	[91]
Telmisartan	Hypertension	In vitro dissolution studies, in vivo pharmacokinetic study	[92]
Acyclovir	Herpes simplex virus infections	In vitro release, cytotoxicity studies	[93]
Acetylsalicylic acid	Pain, fever, or inflammation	In vitro release study, accelerated stability study, in vivo evaluation in rats for acute toxicity and analgesic activity	[94]
Paclitaxel	Ovarian cancer, esophageal cancer, breast	In vivo pharmacokinetic study	[96]

Drug	Indication	Study	Refs.
	cancer, lung cancer, Kaposi sarcoma, cervical cancer, and pancreatic cancer		[95]
Itraconazole	Antifungal	In vitro dissolution studies, phase solubility studies	[96]
Dexamethasone	Inflammation	In vitro release study	[97]
Flurbiprofen	Inflammation	In vitro release study	[97]

To conclude, NS, namely CD-based NS, is a non-expensive, biocompatible, and biodegradable alternative to prepare formulations with improved solubility, stability, and toxicity features. Their nanoporous network permits the encapsulation of a higher number of drug molecules than the conventional drug-CD complexes. This fact renders them as promising drug carriers, able to be applied in several scientific fields such as pharmaceutical, cosmetics, biomedicine, and agro chemistry. Concerning, the drug substances, CD-based NSs may be carriers of either hydrophilic or lipophilic drugs and they can be administered topically or parentally. Also, NSs made feasible the development of formulations with the tailored release for delivery of drugs in a predictable manner ensuring higher efficacy and fewer side effects for the patients. The adaptation of the drug release rate to the needs of each clinical case enables more effective and focused treatment even in complex diseases. Hence, the application of NSs in the development of pharmaceutical products opens new perspectives in the field of precision medicine.

2.8.2 Cyclodextrin-Metal-Organic Framework (CD-MOF)

Based on the unique structural features of CD molecules, comprising a hydrophobic central cavity and a hydrophilic outer surface, they possess the ability to coordinate with alkaline earth metals leading to the formation of CD-MOFs [98].

These can be prepared by crystallization of CDs with cations. CD-MOFs possess the main structure of a CD and also have the ability to incorporate the drug not only in the CD cavity but in the formed pores as well. This extra advantage makes

CD-MOFs even more popular drug delivery systems than CDs alone [98, 99].

2.8.2.1 Preparation methods

The main synthetic strategies for the preparation of CD-MOFs are listed below [98, 99]:

1. *Vapor diffusion method*: This is the basic method involving ambient conditions (temperature and pressure) and is characterized as a "green" way for the preparation of CD-MOFs [100].
2. *Hydrothermal/solvothermal method*: Typically, this method involves heating a solution of γ-CD and metal salts under high-pressure conditions. In common with classical synthetic protocols involving this method, reaction times, temperatures, stoichiometries, dilutions, pH, and additives all play crucial roles [101–103].
3. *Microwave-assisted and conventional method*: This method is fast and leads to a high yield of CD-MOFs. In a typical reaction, γ-CD-MOF is prepared from 1 equivalent of γ-CD and 2 equivalents of potassium hydroxide dissolved in water, followed by: (i) addition of methanol, (ii) heating at 10–100 °C with microwave irradiation for 1–120 min, and (iii) addition of PEG 20000 to induce crystallization of the micrometer-sized CD-MOF-1 crystals.

   Reaction times, temperatures, and solvent ratios can be adjusted in order to obtain micro- or nanometer-sized crystals [104].
4. *Post-synthetic modification method*: This method is a combination of the above and aims at the purification of the obtained CD-MOF after its synthesis.

2.8.2.2 CD-MOF stability and solubility characteristics

CD-MOFs possess certain stability and solubility characteristics, due to their hydrophobic internal cavity and hydrophilic external surface in aqueous media. Also, the size of CD-MOFs seems to affect their stability as micro- and nano-sized CD-MOFs, which seem to be more stable than other CD-MOF forms. Finally, the incorporation of extra functional groups or materials on the surface of CD-MOFs improves their stability and inertness in water or physiological fluids.

Generally, the stability of CD-MOFs in water has been improved through chemical modification to enhance their drug-loading and -release capabilities [105]. Smaller CD-MOF crystals have been produced by the modified [104] vapor diffusion method. Homogeneous and monodisperse crystals of nano- and micrometer-sized γ-CD-MOFs have been prepared [106] by introducing cetyl-trimethylammonium bromide (CTAB) and methanol into an aqueous solution of γ-CD and potassium hydroxide. These chemical modifications have improved the stability of CD-MOFs in water, in combination with: (i) the incorporation [107] of hydrophobic C-60 molecules into CD-MOF matrices, (ii) the surface modification [108] with cholesterol, and (iii) the post-synthetic treatment with H_2S [109]. 3,4-Ethylenedioxythiophene has also been adsorbed and polymerized [110] inside the hydrophilic nanochannels of a CD-MOF in order to reduce its water solubility and achieve thermal stability [111].

2.8.2.3 CDs-modified MOFs

One more up-to-date technique is the preparation of CDs-modified MOFs that can combine diverse functions for the application in biomedicines such as the improvement of biocompatibility and solubility of delivery systems, introducing particular functional groups for recognizing specific-targeting receptors, escaping the immune system, delivering various drugs and drug models, and releasing drugs according to external stimuli as well as delaying the release for different requirements of medical treatments [111–113].

2.8.2.4 Main pharmaceutical applications of CD-MOFs

CD-MOFs gradually become more and more popular in many aspects and their applications are significantly broadened. They are useful as catalysis and detection materials, in gas absorption and sensing, in separations and purifications (e.g., separation of chiral molecules) and, of course, in drug release and delivery.

The applications in drug delivery are numerous and some examples from the literature are provided hereunder. CD-MOFs can accommodate different drug molecules within their extended framework. Drug molecules are loaded onto the CD-MOFs with the principle of host-guest molecular inclusion (the main methods of inclusion are absorption, grinding, and co-crystallization). CD-MOFs with controlled sizes have shown their usefulness to incorporate molecules [100, 106, 114, 115] such as anti-inflammatory drugs (e.g., furbiprofen, fenbufen, ketoprofen, and piroxicam), angiotensin-converting enzyme inhibitors (e.g., captopril), food additives (e.g., curcumin and sucralose), dyes (e.g., 4-phenylazophenol and rodamine B), and various pharmaceutical ingredients (e.g., salicylic acid, ferulic acid, and pseudolaric acid B) [102, 116].

Example 1

Ibuprofen is an insoluble in water and unstable molecule that can be trapped [117, 118] in pharmaceutically relevant quantities in nanometer-sized CD-MOFs by co-crystallization. Bioavailability studies conducted in mice after an oral administration of loaded with ibuprofen CD-MOF-1 nanocrystals revealed a rapid appearance of the drug substance in the plasma sector with concentration levels comparable to the salt of the drug substance when administered alone. The use of co-crystals leads to a 100% elevated half-life of ibuprofen in blood plasma and higher ibuprofen plasma levels 10–20 min after administration, compared to the pure salt of ibuprofen. This observation is very useful for the future development of NSAIDs encapsulated in the pores of CD-MOFs.

Example 2

Curcumin was encapsulated by Zhou et al. [119] in order to achieve pulmonary delivery. Curcumin is a kind of poorly soluble [120] polyphenol extracted from the roots of turmeric [121], possessing anti-inflammatory [122, 123], antitumor [124], antioxidant [125], and antimicrobial properties [121, 126].

In the present case [119], Cur-CD-MOFs were successfully synthesized by an in-site vapor diffusion method. The complex formed had a cubic shape and uniform porous structure with a large surface area. Cur-CD-MOFs showed excellent aerodynamic behavior when administered and an ameliorated dissolution rate of curcumin, due to the improved wettability and the molecular distribution of curcumin in the porous interior of CD-MOFs [127].

Example 3

Also, Abuçafy et al. [128] incorporated diclofenac sodium (an anti-inflammatory agent) in γ-CD-MOF coordinated with cations (K^+, Na^+, Fe^{3+}) in order to achieve effective delivery of the drug substance. In vivo experiments, the inflammation mouse model showed the applicability of these materials and the efficacious administration. The most promising results were provided after administration of the complex with iron (Fe^{3+}) [128].

Example 4

β-CDs-modified Fe-MIL-88B-NH_2 [113, 129] could encapsulate alendronate into the pores of MOFs and the cavities of loaded β-CDs. The amount of drug loaded is therefore significantly increased, after the incorporation of alendronate. Golmohamadpour et al. [129] showed that hydroxyapatite can be combined in the drug delivery system and modify the drug release rate in order to achieve an optimum pharmacological effect, as it can simulate the release rate from bones as a physiological condition.

Example 5

External stimuli-responsive molecules such as azobenzene can be introduced into the hybrid materials, e.g., Zr-MOF, then it acts as the switch tool to associate/disassociate with coated-CDs [113, 130]. Also, β-CDs can be applied as a release tool of drugs inside the UiO-68-azo-bearing Zr-MOFs after encapsulating, e.g., amantadine in their hydrophobic cavity. As a result, this kind of β-CDs-coated Zr-MOFs might be used as a platform for on-command drug delivery systems.

Example 6

Lajevardi et al. [131] developed a drug release model for the antibiotic cephalexin. The organic–inorganic hybrid material, β-CDs/Fe_3O_4@SiO_2@MIL-100 (Fe) was used as a pH-responsive drug delivery system, due to the possession of pH-sensitive β-CDs. This kind of CD is easily hydrolyzed at lower pH values.

When cephalexin is incorporated into such a delivery system, the release is slower after administration and happens in a controlled manner. It was also shown that the difference in temperature (and more specifically an increase in temperature) enhances the drug release percentage.

As shown from the above studies performed, a large number of perspectives are opened, and a lot of work is yet to be done in order to obtain effective drug delivery systems. Different-sized CDs could be used for the preparation of novel CDs-modified/coated MOFs (e.g., β-CDs) [132]. Also, functional groups with N-donors [133] should be considered for modifying CDs that will lead to stronger interactions with MOFs and to materials with ameliorated stability properties. Furthermore, magnetic materials [131] should be fully characterized and evaluated in order to be properly used in such delivery systems. Moreover, CDs-based amphiphiles are an unexplored area and their possible use as surfactants should be investigated [134]. As an extra research field, the different pore sizes between MOFs and CDs should be explored in CDs-modified/coated MOFs [135].

Focusing should be made on the incorporation of drug molecules into the CD-MOFs pores for the development of new pharmaceutical formulations. Besides in vitro studies, computational research is a pre-requisite [136] to create opportunities in the field and suggests solutions for insoluble and low-bioavailability drug substances. CD-MOF-based technologies are sustainable, inexpensive, and easy-to-apply, and have the potential for commercialization in a large number of fields and especially in the pharmaceutical industry.

2.9 General Conclusions

The amphiphile character of CDs and their ability to form inclusion complexes with drugs, already known since the 19th century, have been a field of extensive study and continuous applications of these molecules in the development of pharmaceutical products. Their contribution to solubility and stability enhancement, as well as in taste and odor masking has been described in several works in literature, and in

2013, EMA published the first guideline approving CDs as pharmaceutical excipients [16]. Data analysis of the global CD market states that in the following six years, it will be noted a constant increase in demand for CD-formulated products across the world. In this context, new compositions, employing CDs, gain ground constantly, improving the already established applications of CDs or expanding the agenda, proving the multi-functionality of the CD excipients. MOFs and CD-based NSs are two categories of new biocompatible systems, showing an improved encapsulation technology, and being more effective drug delivery systems than conventional CD-drug complexes. Also, these systems can be designed to release drugs in a controllable and predictable manner, paving the way for the development of custom formulations and meeting the needs for personalized treatments.

References

1. Jansook, P., Ogawa, N., and Loftsson, T. (2018) Cyclodextrins: structure, physicochemical properties and pharmaceutical applications. *Int. J. Pharm.*, **535**, pp. 272–284.
2. Loftsson, T. and Duchene, D. (2007) Cyclodextrins and their pharmaceutical applications. *Int. J. Pharm.*, **329**, pp. 1–11.
3. Kurkov, S.V., Madden, D.E., Carr, D., and Loftsson, T. (2012) The effect of parenterally administered cyclodextrins on the pharmacokinetics of coadministered drugs. *J. Pharm. Sci.*, **101**, pp. 4402–4408 b.
4. Martin Del Valle, E.M. (2004) Cyclodextrins and their uses: A review. *Process Biochem.*, **39**, pp. 1033–1046.
5. Cramer, F. and Hettler, H. (1967) Inclusion compounds of cyclodextrins. *J. Pharm. Sci.*, **54(24)**, pp. 625–632.
6. Szejtli, J. (2004) Past, present and future of cyclodextrin research. *Pure Appl. Chem*, **10**, pp. 1825–1845.
7. Loftsson, T., Jarho, P., Masson, M., and Jarvinen, T. (2005) Cyclodextrins in drug delivery. *Expert Opin. Drug Deliv.* **2,** pp. 335–351.
8. Jambhekar, S.S. and Breen, P. (2016) Cyclodextrins in pharmaceutical formulations I: Structure and physicochemical properties, formation of complexes, and types of complex. *Drug Discov.*, **21**, Number 2.

9. Tiwari, G., Tiwari, R., and Rai., A.K. (2010) Cyclodextrins in delivery systems: Applications. *J. Pharm. Bioallied. Sci.*, **2(2)**, pp. 72–79.
10. Wenz G. (2012) Influence of intramolecular hydrogen bonds on the binding potential of methylated β-cyclodextrins derivatives. *Beilstein J. Org. Chem.*, **8**, pp. 1890–1895.
11. Kurkov, S.V. and Loftsson, T. (2013) Cyclodextrins. *Int. J. Pharm.*, **30(453)**, pp. 167–80.
12. Loftsson T. (2020) Cyclodextrins in parenteral formulations. *J. Pharm. Sci.*, **110(2)**, pp. 654–664.
13. Cramer, F. (1981) Cyclodextrin: A paradigmatic model. *In Proceedings of the First International Symposium on Cyclodextrins*, **1**, pp. 3–14.
14. Cramer, F. (1988) Introductory remarks. *Proceedings of the Fourth International Symposium on Cyclodextrins. In Advances in Inclusion Science*, **5**, p. 1.
15. Crumling, M.A., King, K.A., and Duncan, R.K. (2017) Cyclodextrins and iatrogenic hearing loss: New drugs with significant risk. *Front. Cell. Neurosci.*, **11**, p. 355.
16. Background review for cyclodextrins used as excipients EMA/CHMP/333892/2013 (CPMP/463/00 Rev. 1).
17. Thakkar, A.L. and Demarco, P.V. (1971) Cycloheptaamylose inclusion complexes of barbiturates: Correlation between proton magnetic resonance and solubility studies. *J. Pharm. Sci.*, **60(4)**, pp. 652–653. https://www.databridgemarketresearch.com/news/global-cyclodextrins-in-pharma-market.
18. Khalid, Q., Ahmad, M., Minhas, M. U., Batool, F., Malik, N. S., and Rehman, M. (2021) Novel β-cyclodextrin nanosponges by chain growth condensation for solubility enhancement of dexibuprofen: Characterization and acute oral toxicity studies. *J. Drug Deliv. Sci. Technol.*, **61**.
19. Redenti, E., Szente, L., and Szejtli, J. (2001) Cyclodextrin complexes of salts of acidic drugs: Thermodynamic properties, structural features, and pharmaceutical applications. *J. Pharm. Sci.*, **90(8)**, pp. 979–986.
20. Szabó, Z.I., Orbán, G., Borbás, E., Csicsák, D., Kádár, S., Fiser, B., Dobó, M., Horváth, P., Kiss, E., Budai, L., Dobos, J., Pálla, T., Őrfi, L., Völgyi, G., and Tóth, G. (2021) Inclusion complexation of the anticancer drug pomalidomide with cyclodextrins: Fast dissolution and improved solubility. *Heliyon*, **7**.

21. Loron, A., Gardrat, C., Tabary, N., Martel, B., and Coma, V. (2021) Tetrahydrocurcumin encapsulation in cyclodextrins for water solubility improvement: Synthesis, characterization and antifungal activity as a new biofungicide. *Carbohydr. Polym Tech Appl.*, **2**.

22. Li, H., Chang, S-L., Chang, T-R., You, Y., Wang, X-D., Wang, L-W, Yuan, X-F., Tan, M-X., Wang, P-D., Xu, P-W., Gao, W-B., Zhao, Q-S., and Zhao, B. (2021) Inclusion complexes of cannabidiol with β-cyclodextrin and its derivative: Physicochemical properties, water solubility, and antioxidant activity. *J. Mol. Liq.*, **334**.

23. Manta, K., Papakyriakopoulou, P., Chountoulesi, M., Diamantis, D., Spaneas, D., Vakali, V., Naziris, N., Chatziathanasiadou, M.V., Andreadelis, I., Moschovou, K., Athanasiadou, I., Dallas, P., Rekkas, D.M, Demetzos, C., Colombo, G. Banella, S., Javornik, U., lavec, J., Mavromoustakos, T., Tzakos, A.G., and Valsami, G. (2020) Preparation and biophysical characterization of Quercetin inclusion complexes with β-cyclodextrin derivatives for the preparation of possible nose-to-brain Quercetin delivery systems. *Mol. Pharm.*, **17(11)**, pp. 4241–4255.

24. Loh, G. O. K., Tan, Y. T. F., and Peh, K.-K. (2016) Enhancement of norfloxacin solubility via inclusion complexation with β-cyclodextrin and its derivative hydroxypropyl-β-cyclodextrin. *Asian J. Pharm. Sci.*, **11**(**4**), pp. 536–546.

25. Silva, I.R., Kronenberger, T., Gomes, E.C.L., César, I.C., Oliveira, R.B., and Maltarollo, V.G. (2020) Improving the solubility of an antifungal thiazolyl hydrazone derivative by cyclodextrin complexation. *Eur. J. Pharm. Sci.*, **156**.

26. Celia, C., Scala, A., Stancanelli, R., Surdo, E., Paolino, D., Grattoni, A., Micale, N., Crupi, V., Majolino, D., Fresta, M., Tommasini, S., Venuti, V., and Ventura, C.-A. (2017) Physicochemical properties of inclusion complexes of highly soluble β-cyclodextrins with highly hydrophobic testosterone propionate. *Int. J. Pharm.*, **534**(**1–2**), pp. 316–324.

27. Volkova, T.V., Drozd, K.V., and Surov, A.O. (2020) Effect of polymers and cyclodextrins on solubility, permeability and distribution of enzalutamide and apalutamide antiandrogens. *J. Mol. Liq.*, **322**, p. 15.

28. Challa, R., Ahuja, A., Ali, J., and Khar, R.K. (2005) Cyclodextrins in drug delivery: An updated review. *AAPS Pharm Sci Tech.*, **6**, pp. 329–357.

29. Popielec, A., Fenyvesi, É., Yannakopoulou, K., and Loftsson, T. (2016) Effect of cyclodextrins on the degradation rate of benzylpenicillin. *Die Pharm. – Int. J. Pharm. Sci.*, **71**, pp. 68–75.

30. Monteiro, J.B., Chiaradia, L.D., Brandao, T.A.S., Dal Magro, J., and Yunes, R.A. (2003) Enzymatic hydrolysis of diloxanide furoate in the presence of b-cyclodextrin and its methylated derivatives. *Int. J. Pharm.*, **267**, pp. 93–100.

31. Popielec, A. and Loftsson, T. (2017) Effects of cyclodextrins on the chemical stability of drugs. *Int. J. Pharm.*, **531**(2), pp. 532–542.

32. Zhou, X., Li, X., Xu, J., Cheng, Y., and Cao, F. (2021) Latanoprost-loaded cyclodextrin microaggregate suspension eye drops for enhanced bioavailability and stability. *Eur. J. Pharm. Sci.*, **1,** p. 160.

33. Guo, Z., Wu, F., Singh, V., Guo, T., Ren, X., Yin, X., Shao, Q., York, P., Patterson, L.H., and Zhang, J. (2017) Host-guest kinetic interactions between HP-β-cyclodextrin and drugs for prediction of bitter taste masking. *J. Pharm. Biomed. Anal.*, **140**, pp. 232–238.

34. Astray, G., Mejuto, J.C., Morales, J., Rial-Otero, R., and Simal-Gandara, J. (2010) Factors controlling flavors binding constants to cyclodextrins and their applications in foods. *Food Res. Int.*, **43**, pp. 1212–1218.

35. Lee, C.-W., Kim, S.-J., Youn, Y.-S., Widjojokusumo, E., Lee, Y.-H., Kim, J., Lee, Y.W., and Tjandrawinata, R. R. (2010). Preparation of bitter taste masked cetirizine dihydrochloride/β-cyclodextrin inclusion complex by supercritical antisolvent (SAS) process. *J. Supercrit Fluids*, **55(1)**, 348–357.

36. Alopaeus, J. F., Göbel, A., Breitkreutz, J., Sande, S. A., and Tho, I. (2021) Investigation of hydroxypropyl-β-cyclodextrin inclusion complexation of two poorly soluble model drugs and their taste-sensation: Effect of electrolytes, freeze-drying and incorporation into oral film formulations. *J. Drug Deliv. Sci. Technol.*, **61**.

37. Swiech, O., Krzak, A., Majdecki, M., Trębińska-Stryjewska, A., Wakuła, M., Garbacz, P., Gasiorowska, W., and Bilewicz, R. (2020) Water-soluble galactosamine derivative of β-cyclodextrin as protective ligand and targeted carrier for delivery of toxic anthracycline drug. *Int. J. Pharm.*, **589**.

38. Osmani, R.A., Kulkarni, P., Manjunatha, S., Vaghela, R., and Bhosale, R. (2018) Cyclodextrin nanosponge-based systems in drug delivery and nanotherapeutics: Current progress and future prospects. *Organic Materials as Smart Nanocarriers for Drug Delivery*, **16,** pp. 659–717.

39. Pawar, S., Shende, P., and Trotta, F. (2019) Diversity of β-cyclodextrin-based nanosponges for transformation of actives. *Int.J. Pharm.*, **565**, pp. 333–350.

40. Singh, D., Soni, G.C., and Prajapati, S.K. (2016) Recent advances in nanosponges as drug delivery system: A review article. *Eur. J. Pharm. Med. Res.*, **3 (10)**, pp. 364–371.

41. Subramanian, S., Singireddy, A., Krishnamoorthy, K., and Rajappan, M. (2012) Nanosponges: A novel class of drug delivery system—Review. *J. Pharm. Pharm.*, **15(1)**, pp. 103.

42. Vyas, A., Saraf, S., and Saraf, S. (2008) Cyclodextrin-based novel drug delivery systems. *J. Incl. Phenom. Macrocycl. Chem.*, **62(1)**, pp. 23–42.

43. Trotta, F., Tumiatti, V., and Cavalli, R. (2009) Cyclodextrin-based nanosponges as a vehicle for antitumoral drugs. World Patent 2009003656.

44. Renard, E., Dearatani, A., Vozet, G., and Sebille, B. (1997) Preparation and characterization of water soluble high molecular weight. *Eur.*, **33**, pp. 49–57.

45. Rahi, N. and Kumar, K. (2017) Nanosponges: A new era of versatile drug delivery system. *Univ. J. Pharm. Res.* **2(3)**, pp. 31–35.

46. Trotta, F. and Tumiatti, W. (2005) Cross-linked polymers based on cyclodextrins for removing polluting agents. United States patent application US 10/510,792.

47. Tejashri, G., Amrita, B., and Darshana, J. (2013) Cyclodextrin based nanosponges for pharmaceutical use: A review. *Acta Pharmaceutica. AP.*, **63(3)**, pp. 335–358.

48. Osmani, R.A., Thirumaleshwar, S., Bhosale, R.R., and Kulkarni, P.K. (2014) Nanosponges: The spanking accession in drug delivery—An updated comprehensive review. *Der. Pharmacia Sinica.*, **5(6)**, pp. 7–21.

49. Trotta, F., Cavalli, R., Tumiatti, W., Zerbinati, O., Rogero, C., and Vallero, R. (2007) Ultrasound-assisted synthesis of Cyclodextrin-based nanosponges. EP. 1 786 841 B1.

50. Singireddy, A. and Subramanian, S. (2016) Cyclodextrin nanosponges to enhance the dissolution profile of quercetin by inclusion complex formation. *Particulate Science and Technology*, **34(3)**, pp. 341–346.

51. Swaminathan, S., Pastero, L., Serpe, L., Trotta, F., Vavia, P., Aquilano, D., Trotta, M., Zara, G., and Cavalli, R. (2010) Cyclodextrin-based

nanosponges encapsulating camptothecin: Physicochemical characterization, stability and cytotoxicity. *Eur. J. Pharm. Biopharm.*, **74(2)**, pp. 193–201.

52. Jain, A., Prajapati, S. K., Kumari, A., Mody, N., and Bajpai, M. (2020). Engineered nanosponges as versatile biodegradable carriers: An insight. *J. Drug Deliv. Sci. Techno.*, **57**.
53. Trotta, F., Zanetti, M., and Cavalli, R. (2012). Cyclodextrin-based nanosponges as drug carriers. *Beilstein J Org Chem.*, **8**, pp. 2091–2099.
54. Anandam, S., and Selvamuthukumar, S. (2014). Fabrication of cyclodextrin nanosponges for quercetin delivery: Physicochemical characterization, photostability, and antioxidant effects. *J Mater Sci.*, **49**, pp. 8140–8153.
55. Taghi, H.S., Rasool, A.A., and Khalil, Y.I. (2016). Enhancement of tenoxicam solubility by HP-betacyclodextrin based nanosponge. *World J Pharm Pharm Sci.*, **5(4)**, pp. 525–534.
56. Kumar, S., Dalal, P., and Rao, R. (2020) Cyclodextrin nanosponges: A Promising approach for modulating drug delivery. *Colloid Sc. Pharm. Nanotechnol.*
57. Sherje, A.P., Dravyakar, B.R., Kadam, D., and Jadhav, M. (2017) Cyclodextrin-based nanosponges: A critical review. *Carbohydr Polym.*, **173**, pp. 37–49.
58. Tejashri, G., Amrita, B., and Darshana, J. (2013) Cyclodextrin-based nanosponges for pharmaceutical use: A review. *Acta Pharmaceutica.*, **63(3)**, pp. 335–358.
59. Richhariya, N., Prajapati, S.K., and Sharma, U.K. (2015) Nanosponges: An innovative drug delivery system. *World J. Pharm. Pharm. Sci.*, **4(7)**, pp. 1747–1759.
60. Rahi, N. and Kumar, K. (2017) Nanosponges: A new era of versatile drug delivery system. *Univ. J. Pharm. Res.*, **2(3)**, pp. 31–35.
61. Panda, S., Vijayalakshmi, S., Pattnaik, S., and Swain, R.P. (2015) Nanosponge: A novel carrier for targeted drug delivery. *Int. J. Chemtech. Res.*, **8(7)**, pp. 213–224.
62. Pushpalatha, R., Selvamuthukumar, S., and Kilimozhi, D. (2019) Cyclodextrin nanosponge based hydrogel for the transdermal co-delivery of curcumin and resveratrol: Development, optimization, in vitro and ex vivo evaluation. *J. Drug Deliv. Sci. Technol.*, **52**, pp. 55–64.

63. Omar, S. M., Ibrahim, F., and Ismail, A. (2020) Formulation and evaluation of cyclodextrin-based nanosponges of griseofulvin as pediatric oral liquid dosage form for enhancing bioavailability and masking bitter taste. *Saudi Pharm. J.*

64. Ansari, K.A., Vavia, P.R., Trotta, F., and Cavalli, R. (2011) Cyclodextrin based nanosponges for delivery of resveratrol: In vitro characterisation, stability, cytotoxicity and permeation study. *AAPS Pharm. Sci. Tech.*, **12(1)**, pp. 279–286.

65. Singireddy, A. and Subramanian, S. (2016) Cyclodextrin nanosponges to enhance the dissolution profile of quercetin by inclusion complex formation. *Part. Sci. Technol.*, **34(3)**, pp. 341–346.

66. Sapino, S., Carlotti, M.E., Cavalli, R. Ugazio, E., Berlier, G., Gastaldi, L., and Morel, S. (2013) Photochemical and antioxidant properties of gamma-oryzanol in beta-cyclodextrin-based nanosponges. *J. Incl. Phenom. Macrocycl. Chem.*, **75**, pp. 69–76.

67. Appleton, S. L., Tannous, M., Argenziano, M., Muntoni, E., Rosa, A. C., Rossi, D., Caldera, F. Scomparin, A., Trotta, F., and Cavalli, R. (2020) Nanosponges as protein delivery systems: Insulin, a case study. *Int. J. Pharm.*, **590**.

68. Rao, M., Bajaj, A., Khole, I., Munjapara, G., and Trotta, F. (2013) In vitro and in vivo evaluation of beta-cyclodextrin-based nanosponges of telmisartan. *J. Incl. Phenom. Macrocycl. Chem.*, **77**.

69. Prabhu, P. P., Prathvi, Gujaran, T. V., Mehta, C. H., Suresh, A., Koteshwara, K. B., Pai, K.G., and Nayak, U. Y. (2021) Development of lapatinib nanosponges for enhancing bioavailability. *J. Drug Deliv. Sci. Technol.*, **65**.

70. Boopathi, S., Poma, A.B., and Kolandaivel, P. (2021). Novel 2019 coronavirus structure, mechanism of action, antiviral drug promises and rule out against its treatment. *J. Biomol. Struct. Dyn.*, **39(9)**, pp. 3409–3418.

71. Zhang, Q., Honko, A., Zhou, J., Gong, H., Downs, S.N., Vasquez, J.H., Fang, R.H., Gao, W., Griffiths, A., and Zhang, L. (2020) Surface glycan modification of cellular nanosponges to promote SARS-CoV-2 inhibition. *Nano. Lett.*, **20(7)**, pp. 5570–5574.

72. Srivastava, S., Mahor, A., Singh, G., Bansal, K., Singh, P. P., Gupta, R., Dutt, R., Alanazie, A.M., Khan, A.A., and Kesharwani, P. (2021) Formulation development, in vitro and in vivo evaluation of topical hydrogel formulation of econazole nitrate-loaded β-cyclodextrin nanosponges. *J. Pharm. Sci.*, **110 (11)**, pp. 3702–3714.

73. Kumar, S., Prasad, M., and Rao, R. (2021) Topical delivery of clobetasol propionate loaded nanosponge hydrogel for effective treatment of psoriasis: Formulation, physicochemical characterization, antipsoriatic potential and biochemical estimation. *Mater. Sci. Eng. C-Mater. Biol. Appl.*

74. Allahyariab, S., Esmailnezhada, N., Valizadehc, H., Ghorbanid, M., Jelvehgaria, M., Ghazid, F., and Zakeri-Milanie, P. (2021) In-vitro characterization and cytotoxicity study of flutamide loaded cyclodextrin nanosponge. *J. Drug Deliv. Sci. and Technol.*

75. Argenziano, M., Haimhoffer, A., Bastiancich, C., Jicsinszky, L., Caldera, F., Trotta, F., Scutera, S., Alotto, D., Fumagalli, M., Musso, T., Castagnoli, C., and Cavalli, R. (2019) In vitro enhanced skin permeation and retention of imiquimod loaded in β-cyclodextrin nanosponge hydrogel. *Pharmaceutics*, **11(3)**, pp. 138.

76. Mendes, C., Meirelles, G. C., Barp, C. G., Assreuy, J., Silva, M. A. S., and Ponchel, G. (2018) Cyclodextrin based nanosponge of norfloxacin: Intestinal permeation enhancement and improved antibacterial activity. *Carbohydr. Polym.*, **195**, pp. 586–592.

77. Zidan, M.F., Ibrahim, H.M., Afouna, M.I., and Ibrahim, E.A. (2018) In vitro and in vivo evaluation of cyclodextrin-based nanosponges for enhancing oral bioavailability of atorvastatin calcium. *Drug Dev. Ind. Pharm.*, **44(8)**, pp. 1243–1253.

78. Gabr, M.M., Mortada, S.M., and Sallam, M.A. (2018) Carboxylate cross-linked cyclodextrin: A nanoporous scaffold for enhancement of rosuvastatin oral bioavailability. *Eur. J. Pharm. Sci.*, **111**, pp. 1–12.

79. Rao, M.R., Chaudhari, J., Trotta, F., and Caldera, F. (2018) Investigation of cyclodextrin-based nanosponges for solubility and bioavailability enhancement of rilpivirine. *AAPS Pharm. Sci. Tech.*, **19(5)**, pp. 2358–2369.

80. Gangadharappa, H. V., Chandra Prasad, S. M., and Singh, R. P. (2017) Formulation, in vitro and in vivo evaluation of celecoxib nanosponge hydrogels for topical application. *J. Drug Deliv. Sci. and Technol.*, **41**, pp. 488–501.

81. Rao, M.R.P. and Shirsath, C. (2017) Enhancement of bioavailability of non-nucleoside reverse transciptase inhibitor using nanosponges. *AAPS Pharm. Sci. Tech.*, **18(5)**, pp. 1728–1738.

82. Shringirishi, M., Mahor, A., Gupta, R., Prajapati, S. K., Bansal, K., and Kesharwani, P. (2017) Fabrication and characterization of nifedipine loaded β-cyclodextrin nanosponges: An in vitro and in vivo evaluation. *J. Drug Deliv. Sci. and Technol.*, **41**, pp. 344–350.

83. Dora, C. P., Trotta, F., Kushwah, V., Devasari, N., Singh, C., Suresh, S., and Jain, S. (2016) Potential of erlotinib cyclodextrin nanosponge complex to enhance solubility, dissolution rate, in vitro cytotoxicity and oral bioavailability. *Carbohydr. Polym*, **137**, pp. 339–349.

84. Daga, M., Ulllio, C., Argenziano, M., Dianzani, C., Cavalli, R., Trotta, F., Ferretti, C., Zara, G.P., Gigliotti, C.L., Ciamporcero, E.S., Pettazzoni, P., Corti, D., Pizzimenti, S., and Barrera, G. (2016) GSH-targeted nanosponges increase doxorubicin-induced toxicity "in vitro" and "in vivo" in cancer cells with high antioxidant defenses, *Free Radic. Biol. Med.*, **97**, pp. 24–37.

85. Penjuri, S.C., Ravouru, N., Damineni, S., and Bns, S. (2016) Formulation PSR: Evaluation of lansoprazole loaded nanosponges. *Turkish J. Pharm. Sci.*, **13(3)**, pp. 304–310.

86. Trotta, F., Caldera, F., Cavalli, R., Soster, M., Riedo, C., Biasizzo, M., Uccello Barretta, G., Balzano, F., and Brunella, V. (2016) Molecularly imprinted cyclodextrin nanosponges for the controlled delivery of L-DOPA: Perspectives for the treatment of Parkinson's disease. *Expert Opin. Drug Deliv.*, **13(12)**, pp. 1671–1680.

87. Shende, P. K., Gaud, R. S., Bakal, R., and Patil, D. (2015) Effect of inclusion complexation of meloxicam with β-cyclodextrin- and β-cyclodextrin-based nanosponges on solubility, in vitro release and stability studies. *Colloids and Surf. B: Biointerfaces*, **136**, pp. 105–110.

88. Olteanu, A.A., Aramă, C.C., Radu, C., Mihăescu, C., and Monciu, C.M. (2014) Effect of β-cyclodextrins based nanosponges on the solubility of lipophilic pharmacological active substances (repaglinide). *J. Incl. Phenom. Macrocycl. Chem.*, **80(1–2)**, pp. 17–24.

89. Shende, P., Deshmukh, K., Trotta, F., and Caldera, F. (2013 Novel cyclodextrin nanosponges for delivery of calcium in hyperphosphatemia. *Int. J. Pharm.*, **456(1)**, pp. 95–100.

90. Torne, S., Darandale, S., Vavia, P., Trotta, F., and Cavalli, R. (2013) Cyclodextrin-based nanosponges: Effective nanocarrier for Tamoxifen delivery. *Pharm. Dev. Technol.*, **18(3)**, pp. 619–625.

91. Rao, M., Bajaj, A., Khole, I., Munjapara, G., and Trotta, F. (2013) In vitro and in vivo evaluation of β-cyclodextrin-based nanosponges of telmisartan. *J. Incl. Phenom. Macrocycl. Chem.*, **77(1–4)**, pp. 135–145.

92. Lembo, D., Swaminathan, S., Donalisio, M., Civra, A., Pastero, L., Aquilano, D., Vaviac, P., Trotta, F., and Cavalli, R. (2013)

Encapsulation of Acyclovir in new carboxylated cyclodextrin-based nanosponges improves the agent's antiviral efficacy. *Int. J. Pharm,* **443(1–2)**, pp. 262–272.

93. Shende, P.K., Trotta, F., Gaud, R.S., Deshmukh, K., Cavalli, R., and Biasizzo, M. (2012) Influence of different techniques on formulation and comparative characterization of inclusion complexes of ASA with β-cyclodextrin and inclusion complexes of ASA with PMDA cross-linked β-cyclodextrin nanosponges. *J. Incl. Phenom Macrocycl. Chem.*, **74(1–4)**, pp. 447–454.

94. Torne, S. J., Ansari, K. A., Vavia, P. R., Trotta, F., and Cavalli, R. (2010) Enhanced oral paclitaxel bioavailability after administration of paclitaxel-loaded nanosponges. *Drug Deliv.*, **17(6)**, pp. 419–425.

95. Swaminathan, S., Vavia, P.R., Trotta, F., and Torne S. (2007) Formulation of betacyclodextrin based nanosponges of itraconazole. *J. Incl. Phenom. Macrocycl. Chem.*, **57(1–4)**, pp. 89–94.

96. Cavalli, R., Trotta, F., and Tumiatti W. (2006) Cyclodextrin-based nanosponges for drug delivery. *J. Incl. Phenom. Macrocycl. Chem.*, **56(1–2)**, pp. 209–213.

97. Han, Y., Liu, W., Huang, J., Qiu, S., Zhong, H., Liu, D., and Liu, J. (2018) Cyclodextrin-based metal-organic frameworks (CD-MOFs) in pharmaceutics and biomedicine. *Pharmaceutics*, **10(4)**, p. 271.

98. Kritskiy, I., Volkova, T., and Terekhova, I. (2019) γ-Cyclodextrin-metal organic frameworks as efficient microcontainers for encapsulation of leflunomide and acceleration of its transformation into teriflunomide. *Carbohydr. Polym.*, **216**, pp. 224–230.

99. Smaldone, R.A., Forgan, R.S., Furukawa, H., Gassensmith, J.J., Slawin, A.M.Z., Yaghi, O.M., and Stoddart, J.F. (2010) Metal-organic frameworks from edible natural products. *Angew Chem, Int. Ed.*, **49**, pp. 8630–8634.

100. Eddaoudi, M., Moler, D.B., Li, H., Chen, B., Reineke, T.M., O'Keeffe, M., and Yaghi, O.M. (2001) Modular chemistry: Secondary building units as a basis for the design of highly porous and robust metal-organic carboxylate frameworks. *Acc. Chem. Res.*, **34**, pp. 319–330.

101. Li, X., Guo, T., Lachmanski, L., Manoli, F., Menendez-Miranda, M., Manet, I., Guo, Z., Wu, L., Zhang, J., and Gref, R. (2017) Cyclodextrin-based metal-organic frameworks particles as efficient carriers for lansoprazole: Study of morphology and chemical composition of individual particles. *Int. J. Pharm.*, **531(2)**, pp. 424–432.

102. Liu, J., Bao, T.Y., Yang, X.Y., Zhu, P.P., Wu, L.H., Sha, J.Q., Zhang, L., Dong, L.Z., Cao, X.L., and Lan, Y.Q. (2017) Controllable porosity conversion

of metal-organic frameworks composed of natural ingredients for drug delivery. *Chem. Commun.*, **53**, pp. 7804–7807.

103. Liu, B., Li, H., Xu, X., Li, X., Lv, N., Singh, V., Stoddart, J.F., York, P., Xu, X., Gref, R., and Zhang, Z. (2016) Optimized synthesis and crystalline stability of α-cyclodextrin metal-organic frameworks for drug adsorption. *Int. J. Pharm.*, **514**, pp. 212–219.

104. Roy, I., Stoddart, F.J. (2021) Cyclodextrin metal–organic frameworks and their applications. *Acc. Chem. Res.*, **54**, pp. 1440–1453.

105. Furukawa, Y., Ishiwata, T., Sugikawa, K., Kokado, K., and Sada, K. (2012) Nano- and microsized cubic gel particles from cyclodextrin metal-organic frameworks. *Angew Chem, Int. Ed.*, **51**, pp. 10566–10569.

106. Li, H., Hill, M.R., Huang, R., Doblin, C., Lim, S., Hill, A.J., Babarao, R., and Falcaro, P. (2016) Facile stabilization of cyclodextrin metal-organic frameworks under aqueous conditions via the incorporation of C60 in their matrices. *Chem. Commun.*, **52**, pp. 5973–5976.

107. Singh, V., Guo, T., Xu, H., Wu, L., Gu, J., Wu, C., Gref, R., and Zhang, J. (2017) Moisture resistant and biofriendly CD-MOF nanoparticles obtained via cholesterol shielding. *Chem. Commun.*, **53**, pp. 9246–9249.

108. Ke, D., Feng, J.F., Wu, D., Hou, J.B., Zhang, X.Q., Li, B.J., and Zhang, S. (2019) Facile stabilization of a cyclodextrin metal-organic framework under humid environment via hydrogen sulfide treatment. *RSC Adv.*, **9**, pp. 18271–18276.

109. Michida, W., Nagai. A, Sakuragi. M., and Kusakabe, K. (2018) Discrete polymerization of 3,4-ethylenedioxythiophene in cyclodextrin-based metal-organic framework. *Cryst. Res. Technol.*, **53**.

110. Roy, I. and Stoddart, F.J. (2021) Cyclodextrin metal–organic frameworks and their applications. *Acc. Chem. Res.*, **54**, pp. 1440–1453.

111. Agostoni, V., Horcajada, P., Noiray, M., Malanga, M., Aykaç, A., Jicsinszky, L., Vargas-Berenguel, A., Semiramoth, N., Daoud-Mahammed, S., Nicolas, V., Martineau, C., Taulelle, F., Vigneron, J., Etcheberry, A., Serre, C., and Gref, R. (2015) A "green" strategy to construct non-covalent, stable and bioactive coatings on porous MOF nanoparticles. *Sci. Rep.*, **5**.

112. Zhang, H., Liu, Z., and Shen, J. (2020) Cyclodextrins modified/coated metal–organic frameworks. *Materials*, **13**, pp. 1273.

113. Michida, W., Ezaki, M., Sakuragi, M., Guan, G., and Kusakabe, K. (2015) Crystal growth of cyclodextrin-based metal-organic framework with inclusion of ferulic acid. *Cryst. Res. Technol.*, **50**, pp. 556–559.

114. Moussa, Z., Hmadeh, M., Abiad, M.G., Dib, O.H., and Patra, D. (2016) Encapsulation of curcumin in cyclodextrin-metal organic frameworks:

Dissociation of loaded CD-MOFs enhances stability of curcumin. *Food Chem.*, **212**, pp. 485–494.

115. Li, Z., Mao, Z., Zhou, W., and Chen, Z. (2020) γ-Cyclodextrin metal-organic framework supported by polydopamine as stationary phases for electrochromatographic enantioseparation. *Talanta*, **218**.

116. Li, H., Lv, N., Li, X., Liu, B., Feng, J., Ren, X., Guo, T., Chen, D., Stoddart, J.F., Gref, R., and Zhang J. (2017) Composite CD-MOF nanocrystals-containing microspheres for sustained drug delivery. *Nanoscale*, **9**, pp. 7454–7463.

117. Hartlieb, K.J., Ferris, D.P., Holcroft, J.M., Kandela, I., Stern, C.L., Nassar, M.S., Botros, Y.Y., and Stoddart, J.F. (2017) Encapsulation of ibuprofen in CD-MOF and related bioavailability studies. *Mol. Pharmaceutics*, **14**, pp. 1831–1839.

118. Zhou, Y., Zhao, Y., Niu, B., Luo, Q., Zhang, Y., Quan, G., Pan, X., and Wu, C. (2020) Cyclodextrin-based metal-organic frameworks for pulmonary delivery of curcumin with improved solubility and fine aerodynamic performance. *Int. J. Pharm.*, **588**.

119. Homayouni, A., Amini, M., Sohrabi, M., Varshosaz, J., and Nokhodchi, A. (2019) Curcumin nanoparticles containing poloxamer or soluplus tailored by high pressure homogenization using antisolvent crystallization. *Int. J. Pharm.*, **562**, pp. 124–134.

120. Wu, C.H., Zhu, Y., Wu, T.T., Wang, L., Yuan, Y., Chen, J.C., Hu, Y.Q., and Pang, J. (2019) Enhanced functional properties of biopolymer film incorporated with curcurmin-loaded mesoporous silica nanoparticles for food packaging. *Food Chem.*, **288**, pp. 139–145.

121. Crivelli, B., Bari, E., Perteghella, S., Catenacci, L., Sorrenti, M., Mocchi, M., Farago, S., Tripodo, G., Prina-Mello, A., and Torre, M.L. (2019) Silk fibroin nanoparticles for celecoxib and curcumin delivery: ROS-scavenging and anti-inflammatory activities in an in vitro model of osteoarthritis. *Eur. J. Pharm. Biopharm.*, **137**, pp. 37–45.

122. El-Naggar, M.E., Al-Joufi, F., Anwar, M., Attia, M.F., and El-Bana, M.A. (2019) Curcumin-loaded PLA-PEG copolymer nanoparticles for treatment of liver inflammation in streptozotocin-induced diabetic rats. *Colloid Surf. B-Biointerfaces.*,**177**, pp. 389–398.

123. Gou, M.L., Men, K., Shi, H.S., Xiang, M.L., Zhang, J.A., Song, J., Long, J.L., Wan, Y., Luo, F., Zhao, X., and Qian, Z.Y. (2011) Curcumin-loaded biodegradable polymeric micelles for colon cancer therapy in vitro and in vivo. *Nanoscale*, **3**, pp. 1558–1567.

124. Huang, X.X., Huang, X.L., Gong, Y.S., Xiao, H., McClements, D.J., and Hu. K. (2016) Enhancement of curcumin water dispersibility and antioxidant activity using coreshell protein-polysaccharide nanoparticles. *Food Res. Int.*, **87**, pp. 1–9.

125. Song, Z.Y., Wu, Y., Wang, H.J., and Han, H.Y. (2019) Synergistic antibacterial effects of curcumin modified silver nanoparticles through ROS-mediated pathways. *Mater. Sci. Eng. C-Mater. Biol. Appl.*, **99**, pp. 255–263.

126. Wu, L.X., Qiao, Z.R., Cai, W.D., Qiu, W.Y., and Yan, J.K. (2019) Quaternized curdlan/pectin polyelectrolyte complexes as biocompatible nanovehicles for curcumin. *Food Chem.*, **291**, pp. 180–186.

127. Abuçafy, M.P., Caetano, B.L., Chiari-Andreo, B.G., Fonseca-Santos, B., do Santos, A.M., Chorilli, M., and Chiavacci, L.A. (2018) Supramolecular cyclodextrin-based metal-organic frameworks as efficient carrier for anti-inflammatory drugs. *Eur. J. Pharm. Biopharm.*, **127**, pp. 112–119.

128. Golmohamadpour, A., Bahramian, B., Shafiee, A., and Ma'mani, L. (2018) Slow released delivery of alendronate using cyclodextrine modified Fe–MOF encapsulated porous hydroxyapatite. *J. Inorg. Organomet. Polym. Mater.*, **28**, pp. 1991–2000.

129. Meng, X., Gui, B., Yuan, D., Zeller, M., and Wang, C. (2016) Mechanized azobenzene-functionalized zirconium metal-organic framework for on-command cargo release. *Sci. Adv.*, **2**.

130. Lajevardi, A., Sadr, M.H., Yaraki, M.T., Badieie, A., and Armaghana, M. (2018) A pH-responsive and magnetic Fe_3O_4@silica@MIL-100 (Fe)/b-CD nanocomposite as a drug nanocarrier: Loading and release study of cephalexin. *New J. Chem.*, **42**, pp. 9690–9701.

131. Zhang, Y.M., Xu, Q.Y., and Liu, Y. (2019) Molecular recognition and biological application of modified cyclodextrins. *Sci. Chin. Chem.*, **62**, pp. 549–560.

132. Ding, M., Flaig, R.W., Jiang, H.L., and Yaghi, O.M. (2019) Carbon capture and conversion using metal–organic frameworks and MOF-based materials. *Chem. Soc. Rev.*, **48**, pp. 2783–2828.

133. Lee, D.T., Zhao, J., Peterson, G.W., and Parsons, G.N. (2017) Catalytic "MOF-Cloth" formed via directed supramolecular assembly of UiO-66-NH2 crystals on atomic layer deposition-coated textiles for rapid degradation of chemical warfare agent simulants. *Chem. Mater.*, **29**, pp. 4894–4903.

134. Sun, D., Adiyala, P. R., Yim, S.-J., and Kim, D.-P. (2019) Pore surface engineering by decorating metal-oxo nodes with phenylsilane for versatile super-hydrophobic metal-organic frameworks (MOFs). *Angew. Chem. Int. Ed.,* **58 (22)**, pp. 7405–7409.

135. Sahoo, P., Roy, I., Wang, Z., Mi, F., Yu, L., Balasubramani. P., Khan, L., and Stoddart, J.F. (2020) MultiCon: A Semi-supervised approach for predicting drug function from chemical structure analysis. *J. Chem. Inf. Model,* **60**, pp. 5995–6006.

Chapter 3

Block Copolymer-Protein/Peptide Nanostructures for Biomedical Applications

Angeliki Chroni, Martha Kafetzi, and Stergios Pispas

Theoretical and Physical Chemistry Institute,
National Hellenic Research Foundation,
48 Vassileos Constantinou Ave., 11635 Athens, Greece

pispas@eie.gr

Over the last three decades, block copolymers have shown great potential as functional blocks for the construction of a variety of nanoparticles and nanostructures with variable morphologies both in solutions and bulk or interfaces. On the other hand, proteins and peptides have emerged as valuable therapeutic agents, nanomaterials building blocks, structure and chemical/biological functionality determinants, and biomimicry examples. The merge of the two worlds has already started to reveal outstanding possibilities for the formation of nanostructures and complex biomaterials toward a gamut of emerging and future applications in the fields of nanomedicine, bioimaging and therapy, biotechnology and enzymatic catalysis, tissue engineering, as well as in (bio)sensor design and technology or even light harvesting approaches. This chapter aims to discuss

Functional Materials in Biomedical Applications
Edited by Costas Demetzos, Natassa Pippa, and Nikolaos Naziris

ISBN 978-981-4968-65-2 (Hardcover), 978-1-003-41146-8 (eBook)
www.jennystanford.com

all these new research aspects, concepts, and possibilities both from the viewpoint of basic understanding and in terms of current and potential applications of hybrid block copolymer/ protein-based nanosystems.

3.1 Introduction

The striking discovery of block copolymers some decades ago reflects the development of abundant nanoparticulates/ nanostructures with remarkable stability, chemical diversity, and processability [1]. The advent of controlled radical polymerizations has led to the renaissance of well-controlled synthesis of amphiphilic [2], double-hydrophilic [3], polyelectrolyte-containing block copolymers [4], etc. being able to create variable self-assembled morphologies in solutions and interfaces and also capable of protein encapsulation and conjugation [5].

Proteins and peptides are the dominant components of organisms possessing a variety of genetically encoded structures, valuable properties, and functions, including gene expression, signal transduction, catalysis of reactions, transportation, and immunity-related functions [6, 7]. Proteins and peptides are also participating in numerous pathological conditions such as diabetes, hypertension, and cancer [8]. In addition, proteins generate strong materials and have the ability to act as biomimicry examples [9] and convert light energy into chemicals [10]. Peptides, on the other hand, have shorter amino acid sequences and smaller sizes than protein drugs. However, protein/peptide pharmaceuticals meet formidable challenges regarding their delivery to specific tissues or cells, such as instability during blood circulation, short half-life, immunogenicity, degradation by enzymes, and inefficacy to cross cell membranes [11].

The ever-growing nanotechnology has created a rich landscape of biosafe and biocompatible protein/peptide/block copolymer nanostructures (PBBCs) by combining the fundamental properties of bare block copolymers and proteins and hence crossing the chasm between two worlds. To this end, the era of PBBCs offers protection from denaturation and degradation of proteins, while in parallel favors the targeted drug delivery, increases the transmembrane efficiency, and regulates the protein release/activity in targeted sites [12–15]. The synthesis of PBBCs devised by researchers is mainly attributed to their intriguing self-assembly process to myriad complex morphologies in aqueous media such as micelles, nanowires, nanotubes, nanoflowers, nanosheets, nanocages, etc. [16, 17]. The physical, chemical, and biological attractive properties of PBBCs have brought continuous vitality to the frontier science of medical imaging, biosensing, biocatalysts, bioelectronics, photovoltaics, tissue engineering, and therapeutic delivery [6, 10, 18].

Hitherto, protein encapsulation into block copolymers stems from physical embedding or chemical bonding strategies [19–22]. The physical embedding method consists of hydrophobic association [23] and electrostatic complexation [24]. Regarding the hydrophobic association, proteins are encapsulated in the micellar hydrophobic core of amphiphilic block copolymers (AmBCs) during micellization. In relation to the electrostatic complexation, positively charged polymers are complexed with negatively charged proteins, leading to the formation of polyion complex (PIC) micelles in aqueous media [25]. On the other hand, the chemical bonding method includes the conjugation of PEG chains on the surface of proteins by chemical linking (PEGylation) to provide long-term blood circulation, enhanced physiological stability, and reduced immunogenicity [26, 27]. Moreover, protein conjugation with block copolymers self-assembled into polymeric micelles results in the formation of prodrugs with significant functionalities, such as stimulus responsiveness and active targeting performance [28].

The present chapter covers the synthesis, structure, self-assembly, properties, and applications of the hybrid PBBCs over the last decade. Specifically, Sections 3.2 and 3.3 refer to the elemental properties of block copolymers and key characteristics of proteins/peptides, respectively. The design of nanoparticulate block copolymer/protein structures using the synthetic strategies of physical embedding and chemical bonding method is described in the subsequent Section 3.4. Moreover, the development of block copolymer/protein thin films and surface structures is reviewed in the following Section 3.5. Lastly, current biomedical and biomaterials applications of PBBCs are discussed in Section 3.6.

3.2 Key Features of Block Copolymers

Block copolymers emerged as the subject of attention of the chemical community more than 40 years ago [29]. Since then they pivotally contributed to the headway of the scientists' propensity in synthesis, characterization, theoretical prediction, and exploitation of this family of materials in the provinces of physics, chemistry, material sciences, pharmaceutics, and medical science [1, 30]. However, the incessant need of developing new materials, due to the ceaseless technological evolution and the without further ado exigent demand to combat life-threatening diseases, still renders block copolymers as the focus of research [31–34]. At this moment, block copolymer application in biomedical devices underwent the experimental stage and is now within reach [32].

Block copolymers consist of a distinct family of copolymers in which the monomeric units of the same chemical nature are connected in a concrete block. The constituent blocks are coupled by covalent bonds and the incompatibility that they exhibit in a common solvent leads to general immiscibility and finally to microphase separation [35]. Block copolymers can be prepared accordingly so as to attain linear, star, graft, and cyclic architectures (Fig. 3.1) [1].

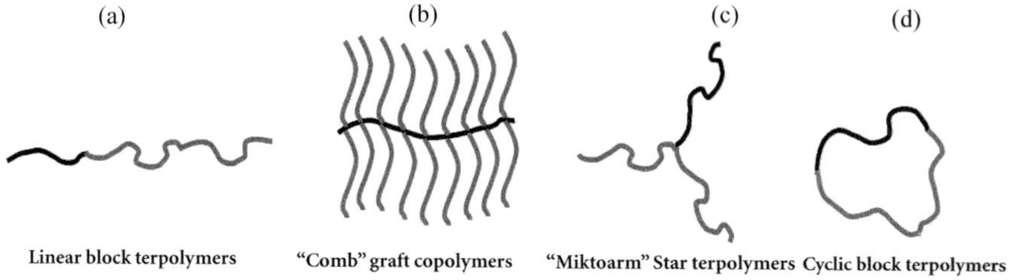

Figure 3.1 Demonstrative examples of (a) linear block terpolymers, (b) "comb" graft copolymers, (c) "miktoarm" star terpolymers, and (d) cyclic block terpolymers. Reproduced from [1].

Block copolymers' competence in forming nanoscale-organized assemblies is the most appealing and researched one over the years, due to their contribution to gene and drug delivery applications, as potential nanocarriers of biomolecules and pharmaceutical substances, respectively, and nanotechnology

[31]. The inconsistency in the chemical nature is at the helm of their self-assembly capability in nanoparticulate nanostructures when inserted in a selective solvent [35]. Factors that affect the self-assembly are the Flory-Huggins interaction parameter, the molecular weight, the degree of polymerization, the volume fraction, the weight fraction of each composite block, and the copolymer's topology. By regulating the above-mentioned parameters in the synthetic process, spherical, cylindrical, lamellar, and other nanoassembly morphologies can be collected [1].

Control over the morphological features of the obtained nanostructures, attributable to the self-organization of block copolymers in a selective media, is achievable by apt design and tailoring of the block copolymers at the molecular level. The synthetic approaches that are able to deliver block copolymers of well-ordered molecular characteristics involve firstly the successive attachment of monomeric segments via "living"/controlled polymerization methodologies and secondly post-polymerization reactions capitalizing on the functional side or end groups of different chain sections. The discussion about the synthetic approaches takes place below.

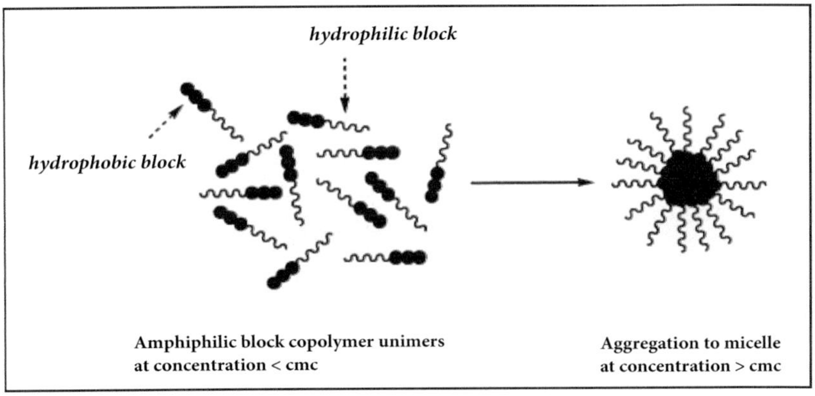

Figure 3.2 Self-assembly of AmBCs in aqueous solutions. Reproduced from [36].

AmBCs consisting of one hydrophobic and one hydrophilic block self-assemble in aqueous solutions (Fig. 3.2) forming micellar-like nanostructures correspondingly to low-molecular-weight surfactants, at a certain concentration, dependable, and characteristic of each macromolecular arrangement that is referred as the critical micelle concentration (CMC) [36]. CMC corresponds to that specific concentration that the first micelles appear. As the concentration of block copolymer rises in the solution, the number of the micelles formed grows and the concentration of non-aggregated chains (unimers) stays stable and equivalent to the CMC. This model status matches a system at its thermodynamic equilibrium [35]. Micellar-like nanoparticulates derived from the self-assembly of AmBCs comprised a core formed by the hydrophobic/insoluble block and a corona/shell forged by the hydrophilic/soluble segments. These types of composite assemblies consisting of at least two components, one in the middle, serving as the core and encircled by the second that acts as the shell, are called core-shell micelles [37]. The corona plays a critical role in the stabilization of the core and contributes as an interface between the aqueous phase and the hydrophobic inner section. Depending on the hydrophobic/hydrophilic compositional balance of the block copolymers, two major structural categories exist. The first one is called "starlike" micelles with a core of smaller dimensions compared to the corona and the second one is called "crew-cut" micelles with a large core and smaller corona [35].

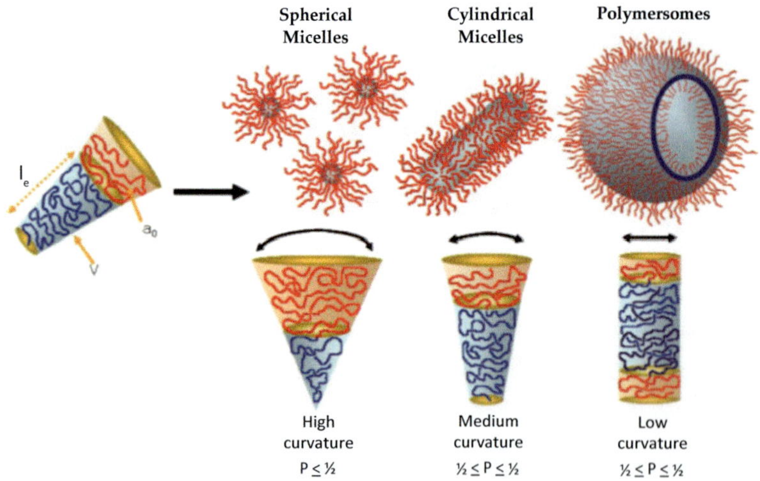

Figure 3.3 Correspondence of the nanostructures derived from the self-assembly of diblock copolymers to the chain packing parameter. Reproduced from [38].

The morphologies of block copolymers are chiefly managed by the packing parameter (Fig. 3.3), $p = v/a_0l_c$, where v stands for the volume of the hydrophobic block, a_0 is the ideal region of the hydrophilic head group, and l_c represents the length of the hydrophobic tale [38]. By regulating the parameters that affect the packing parameter, namely, block copolymer composition and concentration, common solvent, water quantity, and diversity of morphologies have been communicated, including spherical micelles, cylindrical, vesicles, tubules, lamella, etc. [38].

Nanocarriers are synthetic nanostructures that present the ability to encapsulate pharmaceutical substances or form complexes with biomolecules such as DNA/RNA, proteins, liposomes, etc., in order to deliver and release them to target/damaged cells without harming the healthy tissues [39]. Nanocarriers conjoin important physical and chemical properties that upgrade the pharmacokinetics and biodistribution of transferred molecules since they are qualified to distribute the therapeutic components with higher selectivity and specificity [40]. As was already mentioned above, block copolymers are utilized extensively in bioapplications and nanotechnology as nanocarriers and are favored over other types of polymers mostly due to their consequential self-organization ability. Nevertheless, block copolymers in order to be even considered as potential vectors in drug or gene delivery, are required to exhibit specific features. Block copolymers' nanoassemblies triumph over other biomolecular carriers due to their small dimensions, increased solubility in a plethora of solvents, colloidal stability, notable cellular uptake, and elevated cell viability and in vivo biocompatibility. The characteristics stated right above are some of the requirements of a synthetic block copolymer nanovector so as to be included in bioapplications [41].

Those features can be designed, controlled, tailored, and fetched via the synthesis of the block copolymers. Living/controlled radical polymerization techniques represent the most versatile and simple strategy for block copolymers production, mostly due to their compatibility with a plethora of monomers, adequate tolerance of functional groups, and facile experimental process. Three main controlled radical polymerization approaches have been reported and publicized concerning the synthesis of block copolymers, including atom transfer radical polymerization (ATRP), reversible addition-fragmentation chain transfer (RAFT), radical polymerization, and nitroxide-mediated polymerization (NMP) [42].

RAFT polymerization has attained colossal attention in the synthesis of well-defined block copolymers as it is a versatile method, compatible with a diversity of functional monomers and polymerization conditions. Furthermore, the RAFT approach provides control over the molecular weight and composition by regulating appropriately the polymerization conditions. The multiplicity of molecular architectures, mild polymerization conditions, absence of catalysts, potential conduct of the polymerization process in aqueous media, and great accuracy over the final products, with well-defined side-groups and post-polymerization prospects, are only a few beneficial features that RAFT polymerization provides [5, 42–44].

Among the stimuli-responsive (intelligent) block copolymers, polyelectrolyte block copolymers [4, 45] comprise an intriguing class of macromolecules, as they incorporate the structural characteristics of AmBCs, polyelectrolytes, and surfactants [46]. Polyelectrolytes bear weak acidic or basic units that either accept or donate protons, in response to a variation in the environmental pH values. Subsequently, they endure alterations in chain conformation, solubility, aggregation, and surface tension. They have been used widely in gene/protein/peptide delivery, as they are able to form complexes with the biomolecules via developing electrostatic interactions and subsequently distributing the biomolecules at the target cells with success [47, 48].

3.3 Structural Characteristics and Properties of Proteins and Peptides

Proteins and peptides are ubiquitous and essential molecules in a life composed of amino acids connected by peptide bonds, contributing almost to all biochemical processes in the human body. Proteins are formed from one or more polypeptides joined together and are classified into five common roles in a functional perspective, including targeting proteins (antibodies/antigens), fluorescent probes (green fluorescent protein [GFP]/monomeric red fluorescent protein [mCherry]), carriers (blood plasma proteins), and enzymes (glucose oxidase, GOx, or GOD), for biosensing, bioimaging, and drug delivery applications [17].

The major building blocks of proteins are alpha amino acids, the basic structure of which is illustrated in Fig. 3.4. Alpha amino acids are small molecules that contain carboxylic acid and an amino functional group. The alpha designation is used to indicate the separation of the two functional groups by one carbon, which is attached to hydrogen and an additional R group, varied in size/length. Non-polar or hydrophobic R-groups contain carbon and hydrogen, whereas different polar uncharged functional R-groups include alcohols, amides, and thiols. Basic or acidic fully-charged amino acids are capable of forming ionic interactions [49].

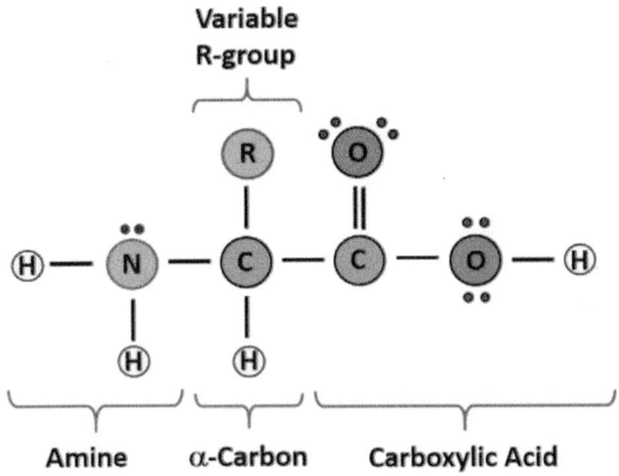

Figure 3.4 General structure of an alpha amino acid. Reproduced from https://wou.edu/chemistry/courses/online-chemistry-textbooks/ch450-and-ch451-biochemistry-defining-life-at-the-molecular-level/chapter-2-protein-structure/.

Protein folding into a characteristic and functional three-dimensional (3D) conformation depends on the number and sequence of amino acid units. The protein's structure is categorized into four structural forms, namely, the primary, secondary, tertiary, and quaternary (Fig. 3.5). The sequence of the 20 amino acids in the protein structure (the common types of which are depicted in Fig. 3.6) is related to the primary structure, according to which a linear polymer with a string of amino acids is linked by peptide bonds. Particularly, more complex protein structures emerge from the interaction/folding of the amino acid chains regarding the secondary, tertiary, and quaternary forms. Secondary structures of proteins such as "Alpha Helices" and "Beta Pleated Sheets" are mainly stabilized by the presence of hydrogen bonds. Likewise, the tertiary structure of a protein denotes a 3D structure stabilized by hydrophobic amino acid entities and disulfide bonds formed among two cysteine amino acids. Interestingly, the tertiary peptide structure contains fewer disulfide bonds developing weak and rigid structures, which are bendable and rupture-resistant, like in hair and wood. On the contrary, the structures that contain more disulfide bonds generate stronger and stiffer structures. In addition, the association of several protein chains into a closely packed arrangement is alluded to as a protein quaternary structure. The ultimate shape of a protein quaternary structure is maintained by a series of bonding interactions such as salt bridges, hydrogen bonds, and disulfide bonds. Notably, fibrous and globular proteins are the major representative categories of protein quaternary structure. Fibrous proteins, such as keratins and collagen, are elongated strand-like structures (e.g., forming rods or wires), while globular proteins like insulin, hemoglobin, and most enzymes are highly compact or coiled structures [17].

Peptides are distinguished from proteins by their size, structure, and even their functions. Peptides are smaller than proteins and are divided into oligopeptides and polypeptides, where the oligopeptides are composed of few amino acids (e.g., 2–20), and the polypeptides are composed of many amino acids. Commonly, peptides consist of 2–50 amino acids, whereas proteins are formed by 50 or more amino acids. Unlike proteins, peptides often lack a well-defined higher-order structure.

Protein therapeutics exhibit several advantages over traditional small-molecule drugs, thanks to a series of highly specific and complex functions possessed that cannot be mimicked by other chemical compounds. Consequently, the high specificity of protein drugs leads to reduced adverse effects. Secondly, protein therapeutics are considered to reduce the risk of an immune response, a fundamental property that renders them highly promising in the treatment of severe diseases [50–52]. Additionally, protein therapeutics may provide effective replacement treatment without needing gene therapy, when a gene is mutated or deleted. Lastly, protein therapeutics have some privileges from a financial perspective, compared to small-molecule drugs. For instance, the clinical development and the FDA approval time of protein therapeutics are usually faster and companies obtain extending patent protection for protein therapeutics compared to small-molecule drugs [50].

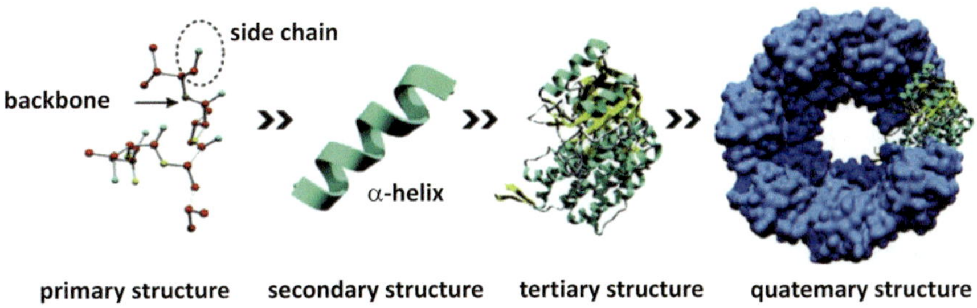

Figure 3.5 The hierarchical structure of proteins. Reproduced from [7].

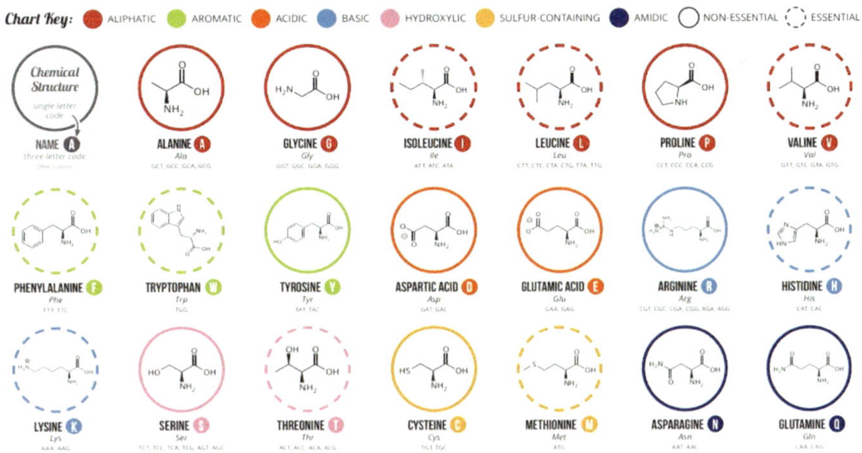

Figure 3.6 Structures of the 20 common amino acids that are found in proteins and peptides. Reproduced from https://www.compoundchem.com/2014/09/16/aminoacids/.

However, the high molecular weight of proteins and peptides along with protein surface charge and fragile tertiary structure, contribute to the limitations of their clinical trials. Specifically, proteins and peptides are unable to cross cellular membranes, disallowing oral administration. Furthermore, the relatively highly hydrophilic proteins and peptides carrying charged groups, further reduce their ability to cross the intestinal membrane [53]. Moreover, the charged groups are highly susceptible to interactions with the surrounding water molecules, enhancing their limitation in clinical applications. The peptide bonds of a few proteins and peptides therapeutics are prone to enzymatic hydrolysis by proteolytic enzymes and become physically hydrolyzed in the gastric environment, making oral administration further risky [54]. Today, transdermal delivery seems to be applicable only for small molecules while protein/peptide delivery via the parenteral route is the most commonly employed method [55]. Significantly, the ideal therapeutic outcome is achieved through regular injections due to their rapid elimination via renal filtration [56]. Yet, the presence of a protective polymeric layer highly benefits most proteins to increase circulation time in the bloodstream [25].

3.4 Nanoparticulate Block Copolymer/Protein Structures

3.4.1 Block Copolymer/Protein Complexes by Electrostatic Interactions

The formation of block copolymer/protein complexes via the electrostatic self-assembly of a polyelectrolyte block copolymer with a protein comprises a facile and effective pathway toward the distribution of proteins for cellular therapy [57]. The development of electrostatic interactions between polyelectrolytes prompts protein encapsulation, immobilization, purification, and separation. At the same time, its study contributes valuable insight into the interactions between biomacromolecules bearing charges that occur in several biological systems [33]. Electrostatic interaction between polyelectrolyte block copolymers and proteins results in the formation of protein-containing nanoassemblies of diverse structures and properties, appropriate for medical applications, and nanobiotechnological implementations such as protein/peptide drug delivery.

Over the last years, numerous publications have been reported discussing the formation of copolymer/protein complexes because of the development of electrostatic interactions between the two counterparts and their prospect in bioapplications. In 2019, Korpi et al. reported on the preparation of multi-sensitive systems established on electrostatic interactions of the synthetic linear diblock copolymer cationized poly[2-(dimethylamino)ethyl methacrylate]-b-poly[di(ethylene glycol) methyl ether methacrylate] (PDMAEMA-b-PDEGMA) and the triblock copolymer cationized poly[2-(dimethylamino)ethyl methacrylate]-b-poly[di(ethylene glycol) methyl ether methacrylate-b-poly[2-(dimethylamino)ethyl methacrylate]-] (PDMAEMA-b-PDEGMA-b-PDMAEMA) with apoferritin [58]. Both linear diblock and triblock copolymers are cationic and respond to temperature changes. Based on their investigations, the protein was capable to self-organize into supramolecular structures in aqueous solutions when the temperature of the solution was changing. The electrostatic interactions between the two components were modulated due to the sensitivity that the mixed system displays to the electrolyte concentration. Moreover, the authors reach the conclusion that whatever the amount of small molecular weight salt in the solutions, the diblock and triblock behave similarly. The mixed systems are self-organized into complexes of micrometer dimensions and reversibly disorganized back to apoferritin's original form when the ideal electrolyte concentration is applied and the temperature solution is regulated.

Another equally interesting case was reported by Lam and his co-workers in 2016. They used a super-folder GFP of a total lattice charge of −8 as the protein standard and solvent-approachable amino acids were used to prepare GFP alternatives of a total lattice charge of −21 [57]. For this purpose, two poly(N-isopropylacrylamide) (PNIPAM) homopolymers of molecular weights of 21.6 and 30.7 kg/mol, respectively, were conjugated to the three GFP alternatives to finally get a group of protein-polymer block copolymers, where the protein electrostatic interactions, as the result of the self-assembly of the two counterparts, would not bring changes in the tertiary structure of the protein. The formation of long-organized nanoassemblies in the supercharged GFP alternative was subdued compared to the conjugates GFP(0) and GFP(−8). GFP(−21) displayed stronger repulsive interactions and subsequently led to the formation of more disordered nanoparticles than those shaped by GFP(0) and GFP(−8). Finally, ameliorated nanostructure formation was noticed in the case of GFP(0) conjugates due to its lattice neutral charge order and self-supplementarily of its Janus-type electrostatic surface charge.

Another important contribution toward synthetic block copolymer/protein complexes was made by Tao and his team (2019). This group reported on the preparation of pH-sensitive micellar nanostructures derived from the self-assembly capability of the novel poly(ethylene glycol)-b-poly(l-Lysine carboxydimethylmaleic anhydride) (PEG-p(Lys-CDM)) block copolymer targeting on protein encapsulation via polyionic complexation and pH-sensitive amide crosslinking [59]. Myoglobin was used as the protein model. The micellar nanostructures appeared to be stable at pH 7.4, while they quickly disassembled at pH 6.5 in a diluted state. The myoglobin-loaded micellar nanostructures exhibited ameliorated in vivo circulation compared to the unbound myoglobin and the micelles resulted only from the PIC formation. Finally, myoglobin was released from the micellar nanoparticles at pH equal to 6.5 and still displayed full oxygenation-deoxygenation ability, showing that the micelles are able to maintain the protein activity.

Recently, clearly defined concavo-convex micelles of increased bioactivity and stability have been reported as a result of the self-assembly of poly(methyl methacrylate)-b-poly (sodium p-styrene sulfonate) (PMMA-b-PSS), shellac enzyme bioconjugates [60]. Chen and his colleagues (2018) stated that the unloaded micelles exhibited bioactivity of 208%, while the stability rate was recorded on 622%, related to the original shellac enzyme. However, the bioactivity and stability of the concavo-convex complexes were further enhanced to reach the high rate of 300% and 760%, respectively. This notable behavior of the complexes is attributed to the improved contact possibility within the substrate and shellac enzyme. That particular set of polymer-shellac enzyme complexes is capable of decomposing catechol with increased degradation efficacy compared to the original enzyme. Finally, the above-mentioned progress in the formation of concavo-convex nanoassemblies will prompt their application in fields like environmental preservation and catalytic enrichment.

A very thorough study concerning the discovery of another possible route toward the enhancement of pharmacokinetics and pharmacodynamics in the field of protein therapeutics includes the non-covalent polymer-protein coupling conducted by Nieto-Orellana and his group (2017) [61]. They studied the influence of the polymer topology of a specific structural group on polymer/protein complexation. They compared the ability of the synthesized in-house PEG-polyanion poly(ethylene glycol)-b-poly(glutamic acid) linear A-B (mPEG-lin-(polyGA)) copolymers and the miktoarm A-B_3 (mPEG-mik-$(polyGA)_3$) analogs to form complexes with the egg white lysozyme that acted as the protein standard. The focus of this research comprised the recognition and understanding of how the structural characteristics of the linear/mikroarm–protein complexes would affect their functionality. The group concluded that the length of protein-binding polyGA chains and their macromolecular architecture played an important role in the complexation efficacy, while for copolymers, comprised the same amount of monomers, the linear copolymers were complexed with lysozyme more efficiently than their miktoarm counterparts. Furthermore, no denaturation and changes in the structural configuration of the protein upon complexation were detected. However, the enzymatic functionality of the lysozyme was reduced, attributed to the inadequate permit of the substrate to the enzyme active part. The macromolecular architecture of the copolymer is considered to be responsible for the latter observation.

In a similar way, Banerjee et al. in their work published in 2013, report firstly on the synthesis of cationic-based 3-(methacrylamidopropyl)-trimethylammonium chloride (MAPTAC) homopolymers and block copolymers derived from MAPTAC and poly(ethylene glycol) methyl ether acrylate (PEGMA) by employing RAFT polymerization strategy and afterward on the investigations of their interactions with human serum albumin (HSA) [62]. In order to monitor the nature and scale of these interactions, they deployed several biophysical characterization techniques. Observations on quenching of intrinsic fluorescence of HSA due to the complexation with the cationic PMAPTAC homopolymers and block copolymers disclosed a rather strong binding of the protein with the PMAPTAC corresponding to electrostatic interactions built between the cationic side-groups of PMAPTAC and the negative charges existent on the surface of the protein. On the other hand, the protein/polymer complexation enervated in sight of the PEG blocks in the two-block copolymer portions. Further fluorescent studies employing ANS as the probe revealed that the cationic polymers do not complex with the hydrophobic segments of the protein molecule, as no alterations were monitored in the emission spectra of ANS-bound HSA in the presence or absence of PEG chains. Circular dichroism (CD) showed a significant loss in the negative ellipticity of the original protein in the presence of both PMAPTAC-based homo and block copolymers. Even though some loss in the secondary structure of HSA occurred, PMAPTAC was proven fruitful in providing stability to HAS against denaturation, which was not influenced by the PEG content in the case of block copolymers.

Along the same lines, the successful loading/delivery of insulin using the pH-sensitive poly(ethylene glycol) monomethylether-b-poly (2-(methacryloyloxy) ethyl trimethylmmonium chloride) (mPEG-b–PMETAC) block copolymer as the vector was reported by Li and his group (2015) [63]. The reversible pH-responsive encapsulation of insulin was accomplished via electrostatic interactions developed between the negatively charged protein and the cationic PMETAC segments. Reversible secondary and tertiary structural alterations in insulin were monitored through the pH-activated formation and disorganization of the self-assembly with mPEG-b-PMETAC. Furthermore, the stability against enzymatic degradation caused by trypsin and chymotrypsin was considerably improved. The group concluded that this particular pH-sensitive assembled polymer system holds great potential in drug delivery applications of proteins and peptides.

3.4.2 Protein Encapsulation into Block Copolymer Nanoparticles

Physical encapsulation of proteins and peptides into block copolymer micelles/nanoparticles is widely applied as a method for the development of an array of biocompatible and biodegradable protein-based polymeric carriers. Encapsulation of proteins in block copolymers/nanoparticles can greatly improve their bioavailability, controlled delivery, and bioactivity. Likewise, encapsulated proteins enable their transportation in the optimum dosage for a long period of time, thus increasing their efficiency. In this respect, a majority of proteins can be utilized (e.g., insulin, L-asparaginase, β-lactamase, lysozyme, immunoglobulin, etc.) even highly toxic, relatively unstable, and poorly soluble proteins [64]. Specifically, the hydrophobic association between proteins and block copolymers is achieved by the physical entrapment of proteins/peptides into the polymeric matrix of synthetic polymers. To date, several encapsulation methods have been developed, such as organic solvent evaporation, dialysis, nanoprecipitation, salting-out, emulsion evaporation, etc. [64].

Over the last three decades, a multitude of studies has successfully utilized physical encapsulation as a method to entrap various enzymes into synthetic polymers and to exert the efficient and prolonged functionality of loaded enzymes in harsh environments. For example, Xiuhua Li et al. described the synthesis of glycose-responsive nanomicelles using a well-defined block copolymer, namely, the poly(ethylene glycol)-b-poly(2-diisopropyl methacrylate) (PEG-b-PDPA), encapsulating insulin and GOD for potential diabetes mellitus (DM) therapy [65]. The PEG-b-PDPA block copolymer was synthesized by ATRP while the glycose-responsive micelles were prepared using the dialysis method. The hydrophilicity of PEG provided nanomicelles with excellent biocompatibility for in vivo biomedical applications. Thanks to the enzymatic catalytic reaction of GOD, the gluconic acid reduced the micro-environmental pH of the nanomicelles. Hence, the synthesized glycose-responsive micelles gradually released insulin due to the partially protonated PDPA block, which was transformed from hydrophobic to hydrophilic, resulting in the core expansion and disassembling of the micelles to individual double-hydrophilic block copolymers (DHBCs). Size, morphology, drug loading efficiency, controlled insulin release behavior, glucose sensitivity, and cytotoxicity characteristics of the resulting glucose-responsive nanomicelles, promote their utilization as insulin-delivery carriers for DM therapy.

Amphiphilic diblock and triblock copolymers of poly(ε-caprolactone)–poly(ethylene glycol) (PCL-PEG) were developed by Payyappilly et al. by coordination-insertion ring-opening polymerization of CL onto mPEG prepolymer for insulin controlled delivery [66]. Insulin-loaded nanoparticles were prepared using amphiphilic diblock and triblock copolymers of PEG and PCL based on the heat-chill method. The high molecular weight of block copolymers led to great colloidal stability, good encapsulation efficiency, and improved insulin release characteristics. Furthermore, CD measurements indicated that insulin retained its secondary structure after micellization. Lastly, in vitro cytotoxicity test revealed that the resulted micelles possessed good biocompatibility.

Recently, Qianqian Guo et al. reported the development of amphiphilic phenylboronic acid-based glycopolymers with block and random sequences by RAFT polymerization [67]. A series of amphiphilic blocks and random glycopolymers were obtained by controlling the feed molar ratio of 3-acryl aminophenylboronic acid (AAPBA) and 2-(acrylamido) glucopyranose (AGA) monomers to the chain transfer agent. The amphiphilic glycopolymers self-assembled into spherical nanoparticles in aqueous media with narrow size distribution. The resulted block copolymer nanoparticles presented a more typical transmittance change as glucose concentration increased, compared to random copolymer nanoparticles. The latter highlighted greater alterations in size and a faster increase in light scattering intensity with respect to control values of nanoparticles without the treatment with glucose (I/I_0 values) in different glucose media. In vitro cytotoxicity assays of p(AAPBA-b-AGA) and p(AAPBA-r-AGA) on NIH3T3 cells, resulted in cell viability above 80%, implying that both block and random copolymers exhibited great cytocompatibility. In addition, insulin was successfully encapsulated into both nanoparticles using the dialysis method. Notably, insulin was released more rapidly in the case of random glycopolymers than block copolymers, induced by the different chain conformations between the block and random glycopolymers within the self-assembled nanoaggregates.

Very recently, Minh-Quan Le et al. introduced the synthesis of lysozyme-loaded microspheres with new poly(lactic-co-glycolic acid) (PLGA)-based pentablock (PB) copolymers for a linear sustained lysozyme release [68]. Two types of PLGA-poloxamer (P188)-PLGA PB copolymers were developed with different molecular weights of PLGA block (20 kDa or 40 kDa). Both lysozyme-loaded microspheres (50P20-MS and 50P40-MS) were prepared using the solid-in-oil-in-water solvent extraction/evaporation (S/O/W) process, the sizes of which were about 40 μm. The encapsulation efficiency values of lysozyme-loaded microspheres ranged from 52% to 61% regardless of the copolymers used. Lysozyme was released from 50P40-MS in accordance with a bi-phasic profile with a moderate burst release of 11% after 24 h, followed by a more sustained and linear release until day 56, where the released cumulative amount reached 54%. Due to the highly porous surface and porous internal structure, the 50P20-MS exhibited a biphasic protein release with also a moderate burst release of 15% after 24 h, followed by a gradual and complete release until day 56, where the cumulative release rate reached 94%. The protein release profile from 50P20-MS and 50P40-MS was successfully modulated using a mixture strategy. The 1:1 microsphere mixture, induced a bi-phasic protein release profile with a moderate initial release followed by a nearly complete linear protein release over 8 weeks, successfully adjusting protein levels.

The formulation of PIC vesicles (PICsomes) loaded with L-asparaginase (ASNase@PICsomes) was described by Sueyoshi et al., for the development of therapeutically relevant in vivo nanoreactors [69]. The resulting ASNase@PICsomes are self-assembled into monodispersed vesicular structures of 100 nm in size. Furthermore, fluorescence cross-correlation spectroscopy corroborated the quantitative formation of therapeutic nanoreactors, as no trace of empty PICsome fraction could be discovered in the product. Fluorescence anisotropy measurements revealed that ASNase@PICsomes were segregated from the external environment and were observed in the inner aqueous phase of PICsomes. In conclusion, ASNase@PICsomes presented long-term enzymatic catalysis after systemic injection into mice, confirming their functionality as in vivo nanoreactors functioning in harsh environments under the blood circulation.

Based on the seminal work by C. Nardin et al., novel nanoreactors based on ABA-triblock copolymer/membrane protein vesicles were synthesized to create stable protein/polymer hybrid membranes [70]. The triblock copolymer shells of the vesicles served as a matrix for membrane-spanning proteins, which can be viewed as membrane mimetic systems. Remarkably, after polymerization of the reactive triblock copolymers, the proteins still remained functional regardless of the increased membrane thickness. The triblock copolymer vesicles had been successfully functionalized by modifying a channel-forming protein from the outer cell wall of Gram-negative bacteria. The outer membrane porin F (OmpF) protein was used as a size-selective filter to allow the passage of molecules with a molecular weight of 400 g mol^{-1} and to reversibly activate/deactivate the resulting nanoreactors. On the other hand, the β-lactamase enzyme was used to demonstrate that substrates may still approach enzymes encapsulated in such protein/polymer hybrid nanocontainers.

Kembaren et al. conducted a recent study on the stability and encapsulation efficiency of spore coat protein A (CotA) laccase-containing complex coacervate core micelles (C3Ms) [71]. The encapsulation of the multicopper oxidase, CotA into C3Ms was accomplished using a strong cationic-neutral diblock copolymer, poly(N-methyl-2-vinyl-pyridinium iodide)-block-poly(ethylene oxide) ($PM2VP_{128}$-b-PEO_{477}) and a negatively charged homopolymer, poly(4-styrenesulfonate) (PSS_{215}). According to DLS data, the three-component C3M system presented better stability against the addition of salt compared to the two-component system. Fluorescence correlation spectroscopy measurements indicated that the release of CotA from the three-component C3M system took place at a lower salt concentration within a narrower concentration range than the dissociation of C3Ms. However, the homopolymer acted as a competitor of the enzyme encapsulation, excluding CotA from the C3Ms at lower ionic strengths.

A broad range of approaches has been applied for the incorporation of membrane proteins into proteopolymersomes, which drastically surpassed the use of proteoliposomes. For instance, various studies were concentrated on the inclusion of membrane-spanning proteins, such as membrane-bound ion channels (ATPases) and bacteriorhodopsin incorporation into polymethyloxazoline-polydimethylsiloxane-polymethyloxazoline (PMOXA-PDMS-PMOXA) triblock copolymer bilayers occurring in planar or vesicular forms [72–74]. Likewise, numerous research teams conducted the incorporation of aquaporins (AQPs) in polymersomes [75]. Specifically, Kumar et al. integrated bacterial AqpZ from *E. coli* in PMOXA-PDMS-PMOXA polymersomes and then confirmed their overall functionality within the stopped-flow light scattering apparatus [76].

Honda et al. introduced the development of protein delivery systems using sequential self-assembly of GFP, tannic acid (TA), and phenylboronic acids-conjugated PEG-poly(L-lysine) (PLL) block copolymers in aqueous solution [26]. The resulting ternary complex of GFP/TA/polymer included a core composed of GFP and TA surrounded by a PEG corona. The ternary complex showed a hydrodynamic diameter of ~10–20 nm and prevented TA interaction with blood components. In addition, the GFP/TA/polymer ternary complex exhibited prolonged blood circulation and enhanced tumor accumulation in a subcutaneous tumor model compared to GFP alone and the GFP/TA complex.

The efficient encapsulation of antibodies/antigens within synthetic polymer nanostructures and their controlled delivery within cells, lead to a powerful research strategy for the development of innovative therapeutics. Patel and his co-workers produced novel polyglycolic acid-polycaprolactone-polyethylene glycol-polycaprolactone-polyglycolic acid (PGA-PCL-PEG-PCL-PGA) and polylactic acid-polycaprolactone-polyethyleneglycol-polycaprolactone-polylactic acid (PLA-PCL-PEG-PCL-PLA) PB copolymers encapsulating human immunoglobulin G (IgG) for the development of protein-loaded sustained release formulation [77]. In vitro cytotoxicity, cell viability, and biocompatibility tests indicated that PB copolymers formed great biomaterials. Likewise, Massignani et al. created a non-cytotoxic delivery system based on a pH-sensitive diblock copolymer, namely, the poly(2-(methacryloyloxy)ethyl phosphorylcholine)-block-(2-(diisopropylamino)ethyl methacrylate) (PMPC-PDPA) for the efficient encapsulation and delivery of AlexaFluor546-labelled IgG antibodies into live cells [78]. The AlexaFluor546-labelled IgG antibodies could target their antigenic determinant by immune-labeling of the cytoskeleton, Golgi, and transcription factor proteins in live cells. The efficacious antibody delivery mechanism could be used as well to control specific subcellular events, modify cell activity, and pro-inflammatory process.

3.4.3 Block Copolymer-Protein Conjugates

Polymer-protein conjugates are hybrid biomacromolecules, tailored to present a multiplicity of functionalities and structural abilities attributed to their dual synthetic and biological nature that can be individually regulated to induce desirable structural characteristics and properties. Polymer-protein conjugates have been mostly developed to address the limitations of protein application imposed by protein enzymatic degradation, the decreased stability under non-physiological conditions, to enhance the stability, biodistribution, solubility, and improve circulation half-life and reduce the antigenicity of that type of proteins [79]. Furthermore, the vast plethora of polymers offers the prospect to impart improved characteristics to natural macromolecules. To extend the enormous application prospect of polymer/protein conjugates, a polymer containing hydrophobic segments has been embodied to further generate self-assembly to the consequentially amphiphilic conjugates [80]. Several works conducting investigations on the preparation of polymer/protein conjugates and the final delivery/distribution of proteins have been reported. Below, significant works discussing polymer/protein interactions via chemical conjugations are discussed.

Recently, Theodorou et al. reported on the development of a phototriggered polymerization grafting protocol that excludes the requirement of deoxygenation and delivers a ubiquitous strategy for the preparation of protein/polymer bioconjugates, utilizing protein macroinitiators. They designed a methodology that evades harm to the secondary structure of the protein and is congruent with proteins such as bovine serum albumin (BSA),

HAS, and GOx, and monomer families including styrene-based, acrylates, methacrylates, etc. By implementing this particular polymerization protocol, such as optimization of the reaction conditions, including catalyst and monomer concentration, they synthesized successfully via the ATRP approach styrene-grafted copolymers containing amphiphilic, hydrophilic, and responsive polymers, namely, acrylamide (Am), acrylate (OEOA), and methacrylate ones, respectively. The resulting grafted copolymers were utilized toward the formation of protein/polymer bioconjugates with HSA, β-gal, and GOx. All the bioconjugates withhold part of the catalytic functionality of the native protein. Nevertheless, bioconjugates resulting from the grafting of styrene from GOx led to higher catalytic functionality.

Fuchs et al. worked on a solid-phase-based methodology to prepare protease cleavable polystyrene-peptide-polystyrene triblock copolymers that subsequently were formulated into nanostructural systems [81]. Two different peptides were used. The central block of the triblock was composed of two different peptide successions. In the first case, a trypsin-based (GFF) sequence was used; while in the second case, a hepsin-based (RQLRVVGG) sequence was used. The synthetic process was conducted in a microwave-equipped solid phase peptide synthesizer. During the conjugation process, no difficulty arose due to the difference in the solubility of hydrophobic polymer (PS) and the peptide. In addition, in order to follow the enzymatic fractionalization, a fluorophore compound was introduced to the enzymatic succession. The finally obtained nanoparticulates presented dimensions between 100 nm and 350 nm, regulated by the peptide sgroup of the copolymer.

Suthiwangcharoen et al. described a facile strategy toward conjugation of the BSA with poly(ethyne oxide)-b-poly(propylene oxide)-b-poly(ethylene oxide) (PEO-b-PPO-b-PEO) pluronic block copolymers [82]. They achieved the formulation of nanoparticles with protein activity as a result of the self-assembly ability of the pluronic copolymer. They determined the molecular weight of the conjugates, the degree of conjugation, the degree of retention of the protein's secondary structure, the biological functionality of the protein in its conjugated condition, and the size and surface charge of the nanoparticulates. They reached the conclusion that the one block copolymer regulates the size of the micellar nanostructure and the protein's density number on the surface by co-assembling with a second one as a hybrid nanoparticle.

Another equally interesting investigation has been reported by Chang et al. about how the polymer block influences both the arrangement transitions and the nature of nanostructures that are formulated throughout the bioconjugate self-assembly process [83]. The self-association of globular protein/polymer conjugates composed of the red fluorescent protein mCherry, and the thermos-sensitive polymers poly(hydroxypropyl acrylate) (PHPA) and poly(oligoethyleneglycol acrylate) (POEGA) synthesized by the RAFT methodology revealed that modifying polymer/protein interactions by altering polymer chemistry affects greatly the kind of the formed self-assembled nanostructures, the phase transitions, and the macrophase separation at elevated temperatures. Similar characteristics of the self-assembly of all three conjugates were also reported. All three bioconjugates present a microphase separation within 40–70 wt% compositions of the components with lamellar or cylindrical phases, which are usually detected in conventional coil-coil diblock copolymers. Finally, the group stated that no matter the coil fraction, bioconjugates form on every occasion, oriented phases in lamellar, perforated lamellar or cubic, and hexagonal order as concentration or temperature are increased.

In a similar way, the self-assembly of four types of mCherry–polymer bioconjugates of different topologies, aka BA, BA_2, ABA, and ABC type, was examined in concentrated solutions [84]. In order to produce ABA and ABC type block copolymers, two different reaction locations were placed on mCherry. The first one is the cysteine for thiol-ene conjugation with maleimide-contained polymers and the second one is a C-terminal LPETG order for sortase A ligation with a triglycine-containing polymer. The bioconjugation reaction was a two-step process toward the successful preparation of PNIPAM–mCherry–PNIPAM and PDMAPS–mCherry–PNIPAM, which belong to the ABA and ABC type block copolymers. This method permits the targeting of a broad range of asymmetric ABC copolymers in order to incorporate functions dependable on polymer structure.

3.4.4 Protein-Based Block Copolymers Formed by Chemical Bonding and Ligand-Like Binding

Surface PEGylation and ligand-functionalization of block copolymers are widely used as strategies in nanotherapy development to enhance protein/peptide encapsulation efficiencies. Specifically, covalent PEGylation is commonly used for the improvement of the pharmacokinetic and pharmacological properties of proteins/peptides. To date, 12 types of PEGylated proteins are commercially available for several diseases, including severe combined immunodeficiency disease, acute lymphoblastic leukemia, and refractory chronic gout [85]. Recent studies, however, have reported non-covalent PEGylation, a promising method for the stabilization of therapeutic proteins [86, 87].

The investigation of the protein–polyelectrolyte interactions between a cationic PEG-b-poly(N,N-dimethylaminoethyl) (PEG-b-PAMA) diblock copolymer and an anionic α-amylase enzyme was conducted by Kurinomaru et al. through enzyme kinetic experiments and molecular dynamics (MD) simulations [88]. The PEG-b-PAMA diblock inhibited the activity of α-amylase due to the binding of PAMA chains. According to MD simulations, the PEG-b-PAMA diblock was located at six different placements, revealing that the copolymer was non-specifically bound to the α-amylase surface. Interestingly, the PEGylated polyelectrolyte did not compromise the enzymatic activity of α-amylase when the ionic strength increased, maybe due to the presence of random electrostatic interactions between protein and polyelectrolyte.

The concept of PEG-functionalized poly(glycidyl methacrylate) (PGMA) nanoparticles conjugated with a fluorescent dye, rhodamine B (RhB) was proposed by Naidu et al. [89]. A qualitative and quantitative comparison between the protein corona consisting of PEGylated-PMGA nanoparticles and non-PEGylated PGMA nanoparticles was carried out. Furthermore, the PEGylated PGMA nanoparticles were preferentially enriched with a range of serum proteins over non-PEGylated PGMA nanoparticles.

The nitrilotriacetic acid (NTA)-functionalization of block copolymers allows the development of amphiphilic PBBCs with enhanced protein-loading efficiency and controlled protein release without disturbing their bioactivity. Chang Li et al.

introduced the synthesis of a novel insulin-loaded glucose-responsive polymeric complex micelle formed by the self-assembly of a PBA-modified diblock and an NTA-functionalized glycopolymer for diabetes treatment [90]. The synthesized PEG-b-poly-(aspartic acid-co-aspartamidophenylboronic acid) (PEG-b-P(Asp-co-AspPBA)) diblock and poly-(aspartic acid-co-aspartglucosamine-co-aspartnitrilotriacetic acid) P(Asp-co-AspGA-co-AspNTA) glycopolymer formed complex micelles with a PEG shell and a cross-linked hydrophilic P(Asp-co-AspPBA)/P(Aspco-AspGA-co-AspNTA) core. Moreover, insulin was successfully encapsulated into complex micelles due to the chelation of zinc ions by NTA groups, thus enhancing its loading efficacy. The resulting complex micelles proved highly stable under physiological conditions and triggered a controlled and gentle release of insulin.

Lu et al. managed to fabricate drug-loaded core-shell micelles using a pyridine grafted poly(caprolactone-graft-pyridine)-block-poly(caprolactone) [P(CL-g-Py)-b-PCL] diblock copolymer, transferrin (Tf), and doxorubicin (DOX) [91]. The resulting DOX-loaded core-shell micelles presented a narrower range of sizes along with improved stability and greater loading efficiency for DOX, compared to Tf/poly(4-vinylpyridine) (P4VP) core-shell micelles. Also, the DOX-loaded Tf/P(CL-g-Py)-b-PCL micelles effectively targeted MCF7 cancer cells through the binding of Tf to transferrin receptors (TfR).

A new class of functional amphiphilic polymeric micelles based on NTA-functionalized poly(styrene)-b-poly(styrene-alt-maleic anhydride) (PS-b-PSMA) was also reported by Lu et al. to immobilize cellulases for enhanced catalytic activity in hydrolyzing cellulose [92]. The RAFT-synthesized and self-assembled copolymer was mixed with $NiSO_4$ solution and formed Ni-NTA-functionalized micelles, which efficiently captured His_6-tagged cellulases on the micelle surfaces and led to enhanced synergistic catalysis. Particularly, fluorescence measurements of PS-b-PSMANi-NTA–mCherry–eGFP particles compared to PS-b-PSMANi-NTA–eGFP, exhibited significant higher intensity at the red (acceptor) channel and lower signal intensity at the green (donor) channel, indicating a strong fluorescence resonance energy transfer (FRET) effect between conjugated eGFP and mCherry proteins. A greater than the 2-fold catalytic activity of the assembled cellulases was achieved after their functionalization with Ni-NTA complexed micelles.

3.5 Block Copolymer/Protein Thin Films and Surface Structures

Block copolymer assemblies in the form of membranes or thin films/layers in combination with active biomolecules (proteins, enzymes, nucleic acids, etc.) provide exciting opportunities in drug delivery, diagnosis, biosensing, catalysis, tissue engineering, food, and environmental sciences. Particularly, polymer membranes serve as ideal matrices for the attachment of biomolecules, obtaining functional/active surfaces and conferring increased mechanical stability, tunable membrane fluidity and thickness, and stimuli-responsiveness by mimicking the architecture of phospholipid biomembranes [93]. Mono-, bi-, and multilayer membranes obtained from amphiphilic di- and triblock copolymers, form thin polymer films that can be employed to immobilize proteins on a solid surface [94]. Block copolymer thin films are of special interest for protein patterning due to their ability to obtain two-dimensional templates with very high regularity. Protein attachment to the polymeric thin films can be achieved either by physical adsorption and chemical binding or by encapsulation into block copolymer assemblies [95].

In 2018, Camelia Draghici and her co-workers developed solid-supported mono and bilayer films of an asymmetric PEG-b-poly(γ-methyl-ε-caprolactone)-b-poly[(2-dimethylamino) ethyl methacrylate] (PEG-b-PMCL-b-PDMAEMA) triblock copolymer using a combination of laccase and tyrosinase [96]. According to the findings of the study, both enzymes maintained their activity after their immobilization on the polymeric substrates. Specifically, bilayer films revealed the most preferable conditions in accordance with overall stability and enzymatic activity.

The synthesis of dual stimuli-responsive thin nanostructured films based on a poly(acrylic acid)-b-poly(N-isopropylacrylamide) (PAA-b-PNIPAM) block copolymer and the examination of its co-assembly with ovalbumin was reported by Osypova and her group [97]. Stimuli-responsive thin films were prepared by layer-by-layer (LbL) sequential assembly of PAA-b-PNIPAM and PAH. Protein adsorption studies revealed that the adsorption behavior of proteins on (PAA-b-PNIPAM/PAH)n surfaces could be tuned by changing the temperature and the pH of the medium. Furthermore, block copolymer-based films presented enhanced performance compared to PAA/PAH films at pH = 5.7, allowing adsorption of a vast amount of ovalbumin at 50 °C.

Kim et al. described a new method for templating protein self-assembly in block copolymer thin films using PNIPAM-b-2-(dimethylamino)-ethyl acrylate) (PNIPAM-b-PDMAEA) [98]. In particular, ionic interactions between the surface charges of the cationic nature of PDMAEA and mCherry fluorescent protein led to the formation of nanopatterned protein films. The resulting coacervate micelles appeared greater in size at pH < 6, according to DLS/ELS measurements, compared to pH > 7.9, where lower-sized micelles were formed. Moreover, UV-Vis data confirmed the successful complex formation by shifts in the absorption spectrum of mCherry. The release rates of mCherry were at least 10 times faster than pH 6.4, due to the deprotonation of PDMAEA. Finally, due to the ionic environment in which the fluorescent protein was confined, a great percentage of the protein (80%) remained active after having been dehydrated in a vacuum and confined in the films.

The utilization of two hydrophobic blocks of a diblock copolymer in a protein patterning template was reported for the first time in the scientific work of Liu et al. [99]. Specifically, the self-assembled poly(styrene-b-isoprene) (PS-b-PI) diblock copolymer was used as a template for the nanopatterning of BSA, forming ultrathin films. After 1 h incubation of diblock templates with BSA, a striped/dense, ringlike BSA structure, similar to polymer templates, emerged. According to the results, BSA molecules were selectively adsorbed on the hard PS segments instead of the soft PI domains. Notably, fewer BSA molecules were adsorbed when more PI blocks were localized at the free surface. Secondary ion mass spectroscopy (SIMS) analysis corroborated the preferential adsorption of BSA on the PS domains.

Protein adsorption on material surfaces is of paramount importance in the field of biomaterials, since plasma protein adsorption on blood-contacting medical devices could result in blood clotting. Phase-separated surfaces composed of AmBCs have the ability to control protein distribution and cell adhesion, as well. The study of Masuda et al. was focused on developing phase-separated surfaces with variable hydrophobic domain sizes using ABA-type block copolymers with different segment lengths [100]. Particularly, the hydrophilic poly(2-methacryloyloxyethyl phosphorylcholine) (PMPC) and hydrophobic poly(3-methacryloyloxy propyltris(trimethylsilyloxy) silane) (PMPTSSi) segments were used to investigate the adsorption behavior of fibronectin, fibrinogen, and lysozyme. Proteins with sizes larger than the nanoscale hydrophobic domains, like fibronectin and fibrinogen, did not adsorb on the phase-separated surfaces, whereas smaller in size lysozyme protein was successfully absorbed on them.

Nagase and his team modified silica beads utilizing a poly(3-acrylamidopropyl trimethylammonium chloride)-b-poly(N-isopropylacrylamide) (PAPTAC-b-PIPAAm) block copolymer [101]. Milk serum protein adsorption and desorption were observed utilizing silica beads as chromatographic matrices. Specifically, milk serum proteins demonstrated that a-lactalbumin and b-lactoglobulin proteins efficiently adsorbed on the copolymer brush layer at elevated temperatures, while they desorbed at lower temperatures. Moreover, the analysis of adenosine nucleotides showed that the ionic properties of the copolymer brush layer could be tuned by the length of the PAPTAC segment.

A study by Schmidt et al. introduced the reversible binding of Annexin-A5 (Anx5) proteins onto polystyrene-b-poly(2-phosphatethyl methacrylate-co-2-hydroxyethyl methacrylate) (PS-b-P(PEMA-co-HEMA)) block copolymer micelles in the presence of Ca^{2+} ions [102]. The results of quartz crystal microbalance with dissipation monitoring (QCM-D) measurements corroborated the reversible binding process and manifested its dependence on the properties of the macromolecular assemblies. Polyacrylamide gel electrophoresis (PAGE) studies successfully quantified the amount of Anx5 binding and confirmed that the binding process was mediated by Ca^{2+} ions. Lastly, based on transmission electron microscopy (TEM) data, Anx5/block copolymer micelle complexes efficiently stabilized and transported hydrophobically modified magnetic nanoparticles.

Membrane protein folding plays a determinant role in the proper cellular function and design of technologies such as vesicle-based biosensors and artificial cells. The study of Jacobs et al. demonstrated the unexplored role of available membrane surface area and membrane area expansion moduli in membrane protein folding [103]. The systematic alteration of the membrane composition of vesicles through the incorporation of a poly(ethylene oxide)-b-poly(butadiene) (PEO-b-PBD) diblock copolymer, contributed to the improvement of membrane protein folding and production. Results showed that the folding and yield of a membrane protein were significantly influenced by the membrane surface area and the membrane expansion modulus.

3.6 Biomedical and Biomaterials Related Applications

Nanotechnology-based delivery systems (nanocarriers) are designed and tailored to accommodate biomolecules, namely, proteins, antibodies, peptides, enzymes, deoxyribonucleic acid (DNA), and ribonucleic acid (RNA), to transfer and finally release them by the implementation of a trigger to the target cells [104]. When these nanomaterials meet certain biological requirements, the term biomaterials describe them entirely. A significant group of them display enhanced longevity in blood circulation and bioactivity, adequate tissue penetrability, response to internal and external stimuli, biocompatibility, and controllable toxicity [104, 105]. Such biomaterials are applied in cancer therapy, treatment of diabetes, and Alzheimer [105–107]. The crucial growth in need for organ and tissue transplants prompted the construction of biomaterials for tissue and organ regeneration. As a result, polymer/ protein nanodevices also find applications in tissue engineering. In addition, polymer-based nanocarriers transferring biomolecules able to diagnose and treat simultaneously are widely utilized in the field of theranostics [108]. Enzymes have been used in a multitude of industrial and medical applications as catalysts and sensors [109]. Recent groundbreaking studies in the field of biomaterials and biomedical applications are discussed below.

An important contribution to the field was the study of Xie et al. in 2020, where micelles for the treatment of neurological diseases were reported [105]. The group formulated a nanocarrier system, which is able to deliver biofunctional antigen-binding fragment antibodies (Fabs) against Aβ specifically into the brain at desirable levels and able to induce treatment with minor antibody uptake into adjacent tissues. The system is composed of a double pH/redox-sensitive nanoscale polymeric micelle composed of cationic disulfide cross-linked poly(ethylene glycol) (PEG)-b-poly(L-lysine) block copolymers complexed with anionic-modified Fabs qualified to reestablish their charge and biofunctionality at acidic pH values. Targeting the brain cells was accomplished by embellishing the micellar surface with glucose molecules to induce interaction with recovering glucose transporter (Glut)-1 proteins. Therefore, 41-fold ameliorated 3D6-Fab accretion in the brain was effectuated by utilizing the polymer micellar system related to unbound 3D6-Fab. Finally, the team declared that therapeutic advantages were acquired by successfully obstructing the $A\beta_{1-42}$ association in Alzheimer's infected mice thoroughly treated with 3D6-Fab-containing glucosylated polymeric micelle.

Hu and coworkers published an equally important work demonstrating a drug delivery system for glioma treatment [106]. For anti-glioma drug delivery purposes, a nanostructural drug delivery approach was designed by embellishing the PEGylated-polyester nanoassemblies with F3 peptide and co-managing the nanostructures containing a tumor hosting and penetrating peptide, tLyp-1 peptide, to induce sufficient tumor targeting along with improved cellular incorporation and in-depth vascular secretion. The F3-nanoparticle exhibited uniform spherical morphology with a particle size of 125±11.12 nm. The obtained information proposed that the above-described drug delivery approach would notably enhance the anti-glioma treatment.

Yu et al. described a novel drug delivery approach including nanostructures conjugated with K237-(HTMYYHHYQHHL) peptides loaded with paclitaxel to target tumor neovasculature [110]. Paclitaxel is a chemotherapeutic factor of potential antiangiogenic functionality that was used as a model drug in this investigation, while the K237 peptide acted as the targeting ligand. The authors prepared and used aldehyde poly(ethylene glycol)–poly(lactide) (aldehyde-PEG–PLA) block copolymer by the ring-opening polymerization technique. Sequentially, nanostructures obtained as a result of the self-assembly of the block copolymer were conjugated on their surface with K237 peptide by applying the N-terminal PEGylation process. Physicochemical studies showed the existence of one population of the final mixed K237-paclitaxel-BC nanostructures, arranged in a spherical shape. Their size was detected at 150 nm (diameter), while the surface charge value was measured at +20 mV. The K237-KDR ensured identification and internalization and notably eased the uptake of K237 conjugated nanoassemblies by endothelial cells. Finally, the longevity of the blood circulation along with the K237 ligand of mixed K237-paclitaxel-BC nanostructures assured quick, extended, and to the point, in vivo tumor neovasculature targeting, and subsequently the considerable apoptosis of tumor neovasculature endothelial cells.

Recently, Sureka et al. have reported advancements in the field of biomaterials by proposing catalytically functionalized protein/polymer hybrid thin films [109]. In order to produce the hybrid thin films, the enzyme alkaline phosphatase was accommodated into accumulated core micelles (C3Ms) formulated as a result of the interactions with the poly[(oligo(ethylene glycol) methacrylate)-r-(benzophenone methacrylate)]-b-(methyl-quaternized 4-vinylpyridine)] ((POEGMA-r-BP)-b-qP4VP) neutral-cationic block copolymer. Afterward, the solution containing the hybrid self-assembled micelles was coated on a solid substrate to generate a biocatalytic film. The installation of both photosensitive and cross-linked segments permits the film to be cross-linked under UV light, turning it insoluble. The morphology of the film proved to be dependable mostly on the protein amount in the film. Subsequently, their potentiality as specific sensors for Zn^{2+} in solution, among other metals, was tested via a prototypical reaction for heavy metal biosensing applicable in environmental detections. The films exhibited adequate functionality and response in sensing for one month after aging under ambient conditions and at 40 °C and 50% relative humidity. The group reached the conclusion that the proposed C3M immobilization method can be applied to a multitude of proteins with minor chemical alteration and can be utilized for the immobilization of macromolecules bearing to generate a plethora of thin-film-based set-ups and devices.

3.7 Conclusions

A large variety of hybrid and functional nanostructures based on block copolymers and proteins/peptides have been reported so far and many more will continue to emerge in the future. This is mainly attributed to perpetual advances made in polymer design and synthesis, nanoscale manipulation of macromolecules and their interactions, and physicochemical characterization techniques, as well as in biology and medicine by constantly unveiling biochemical/biophysical pathways and therapy schemes. The advanced manipulation and fine-tuning of structure and properties of such hybrid nanostructures will allow for the creation of very advanced functionalities and smart nanodevice development in the future, in fields that include mostly nanomedicine (therapy and bioimaging), enzymatic catalysis, (bio)sensing, and tissue engineering, producing beneficial and unprecedented outcomes for human well-being and economic development.

References

1. Feng, H., Lu X., Wang, W., Kang, N.J, and Mays, J.W. (2017). Block copolymers: Synthesis, self-assembly, and applications, *Polymers* (Basel), 9(10), pp. 494.
2. Perin, F., Motta, A., and Maniglio, D. (2021). Amphiphilic copolymers in biomedical applications: Synthesis routes and property control, *Mater. Sci. Eng. C*, pp. 111952.
3. El Jundi, A., Buwalda, S.J, Bakkour, Y., Garric, X., and Nottelet, B. (2020). Double hydrophilic block copolymers self-assemblies in biomedical applications, *Adv. Colloid and Interface Sci.*, 283, pp. 102213.
4. Stuart, M.A.C., Hofs, B., Voets, I.K., and Keizer, A.D. (2005). Assembly of polyelectrolyte-containing block copolymers in aqueous media, *Curr. Opin. Colloid Interface Sci.*, 10(1–2), pp. 30–36.

5. Boyer, C., Stenzel, M.H., and Davis T.P. (2011). Building nanostructures using RAFT polymerization, *J. Polym. Sci. A Polym. Chem.*, 49(3), pp. 551–595.

6. Gagner, J.E., Kim, W., and Chaikof, E.L. (2014). Designing protein-based biomaterials for medical applications, *Acta biomater.*, 10(4), pp. 1542–1557.

7. Heim, M., Roemer, L., and Scheibel, T. (2010). Hierarchical structures made of proteins: The complex architecture of spider webs and their constituent silk proteins, *Chem. Soc. Rev.*, 39(1), pp. 156–164.

8. Voet, D. and Voet, J.G (2011). *Biochemistry,* 4th Ed., NewYork: John Wiley & SonsInc, pp. 492.

9. Czyzewski, A.M. and Barron, A.E. (2008). Protein and peptide biomimicry: Gold-mining inspiration from nature's ingenuity, *AIChE J.*, 54(1), pp. 2–8.

10. Obermeyer, A.C. and Olsen, B.D. (2015). Synthesis and application of protein-containing block copolymers, *ACS Macro. Let.*, 4(1), pp. 101–110.

11. Postupalenko, V., Desplancq, D., Orlov, I., Arntz, Y., Spehner, D., Mely, V., Klaholz, B.P, Schultz, P., Weiss, E, and Zuber, G. (2015). Protein delivery system containing a nickel-immobilized polymer for multimerization of affinity-purified his-tagged proteins enhances cytosolic transfer, *Angew. Chem., Int. Ed.*, 54(36), pp. 10583–10586.

12. Liu, X., Wu, F., Ji, Y., and Yin, L. (2018). Recent advances in anti-cancer protein/peptide delivery, *Bioconjug. Chem.*, 30(2), pp. 305–324.

13. Zuris, J.A., Thompson, D.B., Shu, Y., Guilinger, J.P, Besse, J.L., Hu, J.H, Maeder, M.L, Joung, J.K., Chen, Z.Y., and Liu, D.R. (2015). Cationic lipid-mediated delivery of proteins enables efficient protein-based genome editing in vitro and in vivo, *Nat. Biotechnol.*, 33(1), pp. 73–80.

14. Nischan, N., Herce., H.D., Natele, F., Bohlke, N., Budisa, N., Cardoso, M.C, Hackenberger, C.P.R. (2015). Covalent attachment of cyclic TAT peptides to GFP results in protein delivery into live cells with immediate bioavailability, *Angew. Chem. Int. Ed.*, 54(6), pp. 1950–1953.

15. Brodin, J.D., Sorangers, A.J., McMicllan, J.R., and Mirkin, C.A. (2015). DNA-mediated cellular delivery of functional enzymes, *J. Am. Chem. Soc.*, 137(47), pp. 14838–14841.

16. Rabotyagova, O.S., Cebe, P., and Kaplan D.L. (2011). Protein-based block copolymer, *Biomacromolecules*, 12(2), pp. 269–289.

17. Ding, S., Zhang, N., Lyu, Z., Zhu, W., Chang, Y.C., Hu, X., Du, D., and Lin, Y. (2020). Protein-based nanomaterials and nanosystems for biomedical applications: A review, *Mater. Today*, 43, pp.166–184.

18. Wang, Y., Xia, K., Wu, M., Sang, X., Wan, K., Zhang, X., Liu, X., and Wei, G. (2021). Peptide-engineered fluorescent nanomaterials: Structure design, function tailoring, and biomedical applications, *Small*, 17(5), pp. 2005578.

19. Oliveira, S.F., Bisker, G., Bakh, N.A., Gibbs, S.L., Ladry, M.P., and Strano, N.S. (2015). Protein functionalized carbon nanomaterials for biomedical applications, *Carbon*, 95, pp. 767–779.

20. Kowalczuk, A., Trzcinska, R., Trzebicka, B., Müller, A.H.E., Dworak, A., and Tsvetanov., C.B. (2014). Loading of polymer nanocarriers: Factors, mechanisms and applications, *Prog. Polymer Sci.*, 39(1), pp. 43–86.

21. García-Díaz, M., Foged, C., and Nielsen, H.M. (2015). Improved insulin loading in poly (lactic-co-glycolic) acid (PLGA) nanoparticles upon self-assembly with lipids, *Int. J. Pharm.*, 482(1–2), pp. 84–91.

22. Li, C., Wu, G., Ma, R., Liu, Y., Liu, Y., Lv, J., An, Y., and Shi., L. (2017). Nitrilotriacetic acid (NTA) and phenylboronic acid (PBA) functionalized nanogels for efficient encapsulation and controlled release of insulin, *ACS Biomater. Sci. Eng.*, 4(6), pp. 2007–2017.

23. Wang, B., Ma, R., Liu, G., Li, Y., Liu, X., An, Y., and Shi, L. (2009). Glucose-responsive micelles from self-assembly of poly (ethylene glycol)-b-poly (acrylic acid-co-acrylamidophenylboronic acid) and the controlled release of insulin, *Langmuir*, 25(21), pp. 12522–12528.

24. Park, W., Kim, D., Kang, H.C., Bae, Y.H., and Na, K. (2012). Multi-arm histidine copolymer for controlled release of insulin from poly (lactide-co-glycolide) microsphere, *Biomaterials*, 33(34), pp. 8848–8857.

25. Chen, F. and Stenzel, M.H. (2018). Polyion complex micelles for protein delivery, *Aust. J. Chem.*, 71(10), pp. 768–780.

26. Honda, Y., Nomoto, T., Matsui, M., Takemoto, H., Kaihara, Y., Miura, Y., and Nishiyama N. (2020). Sequential self-assembly using tannic acid and phenylboronic acid-modified copolymers for potential protein delivery, *Biomacromolecules*, 21(9), pp. 3826–3835.

27. Minimol, P., Paul, W., and Sharma, C.P. (2013). PEGylated starch acetate nanoparticles and its potential use for oral insulin delivery, *Carbohydr. Polym.*, 95(1), pp. 1–8.

28. Mao, S., Germershaus, O., Fischer, D., Linn T., Schnepf, R., and Kissel, T. (2005). Uptake and transport of PEG-graft-trimethyl-chitosan copolymer–insulin nanocomplexes by epithelial cells, *Phar. Res.,* 22(12), pp. 2058–2068.

29. Bates, C.M. and Bates, F.S. (2017). 50th anniversary perspective: Block polymers—Pure potential, *Macromolecules,* 50(1), pp. 3–22.

30. Batrakova, E., Bronich, T.K., Vetro, J.A., and Kabanov, A.V. (2006). *Polymer Micelles as Drug Carriers,* Torchilin, V.P. (ed.), Chapter 5 "Nanoparticulates as Drug Carriers," Imperial College Press, pp. 57–93.

31. Ramanathan, M., Shrestha, L.K., Mori, T., Ji, Q., Hill, J.P., and Ariga, K. (2013). Amphiphile nanoarchitectonics: From basic physical chemistry to advanced applications, *Phys. Chem. Chem. Physics,* 15, pp. 10580–10611.

32. Cabral, H., Miyata, K., Osada, K., and Kataoka, K. (2018). Block copolymer micelles in nanomedicine applications, *Chem. Rev.,* 118(14), pp. 6844–6892.

33. Harada, A. and Kataoka, K. (2006). Supramolecular assemblies of block copolymers in aqueous media as nanocontainers relevant to biological applications, *Prog. Polym. Sci.,* 31, pp. 949–982.

34. Kataoka, K., Harada, A., and Nagasaki, Y. (2001). Block copolymer micelles for drug delivery: Design, characterization and biological significance, *Adv. Drug Deliv. Rev.,* 47(1), pp. 113–131.

35. Gohy, J.F. (2005). *Block Copolymer Micelles* 190, Abetz, V. (ed.), "Advances in Polymer Science," Springer, pp. 65–136.

36. Dwańlsa, J.P.L., Rouxlet, L., Préat, V., Brewster, M.E., and Ariën, A. (2007). Prediction of drug solubility in amphiphilic di-block copolymer micelles: The role of polymer-drug compatibility, *Pharmazie,* 62(7), pp. 499–504.

37. Ramli, R., Laftah, W., and Hashim, S. (2013). Core-shell polymers: A review, *RSC Adv.,* 3(36), pp. 15543.

38. Blanazs, A., Armes. S.P., and Ryan, A.J. (2009). *S*elf-assembled block copolymer aggregates: From micelles to vesicles and their biological applications, *Macromol. Rapid Commun.,* 30(4–5), pp. 267–277.

39. Lombardo, D., Kiselev, M., and Caccamo, M.T. (2019). Smart nanoparticles for drug delivery application: Development of versatile nanocarrier platforms in biotechnology and nanomedicine, *J. Nanomater.,* pp. 1–26.

40. Alai, M.S., Lin, W.J., and Pingale, S.S. (2015). Application of polymeric nanoparticles and micelles in insulin oral delivery, *J. Food Drug Anal.*, 23(3), pp. 351–358.

41. Kim, K.T., Meeuwissen, S.A., Nolte, R.M.R., and van Hest, J.C.M. (2010). Smart nanocontainers and nanoreactors, *Nanoscale*, 2(6), pp. 844–858.

42. Perrier, S. (2017). 50th anniversary perspective: RAFT polymerization—A user guide, *Macromolecules*, 50(19), pp. 7433–7447.

43. Moad, G., Rizzardo, E., and Thang, S. (2006). Living radical polymerization by the RAFT process—A first update, *Aust. J. Chem.*, 59, pp. 669–692.

44. Moad, G. (2017). RAFT polymerization to form stimuli-responsive polymers, *Polym. Chem.*, 8(1), pp. 177–219.

45. Förster, S. and Schimdt, M. (1995). *Polyelectrolytes in Solution. In: Physical Properties of Polymers* 120, Chapter 2 "Advances in Polymer Science," Springer, pp. 51–133.

46. Alarcon, C.d.l.H., Pennadam, S., and Alexander, C. (2005). Stimuli responsive polymers for biomedical applications, *Chem. Soc. Rev.*, 34, pp. 276–85.

47. Bawa, P., Pilay, V., Choonara, Y.E, and du Troit L.C. (2009). Stimuli-responsive polymers and their applications in drug delivery, *Biomed. Mater.*, 4(2), pp. 022001.

48. Kayitmazer, A.B., Seeman, D., Minsky, B.B, Bubin, P.L, and Xu, Y. (2013). Protein–polyelectrolyte interactions, *Soft Matter*, 9(9), pp. 2553–2583.

49. Deb, P.K., Al-Attraqchi, O., Chandrasekaran, B., Paradkar, A., and Tekade, R.K. (2019). *Protein/Peptide Drug Delivery Systems: Practical Considerations in Pharmaceutical Product Development*, Chapter 16 "Basic Fundamentals of Drug Delivery", Elsevier, pp. 651–684.

50. Leader, B., Baca, Q.J., and Golan, D.E. (2008). Protein therapeutics: A summary and pharmacological classification, *Nat. Rev. Drug Discov.*, 7(1), pp. 21–39.

51. Lagassé, H.D., Alexaki, K., Simhandri, V.L., Katagiri, N.H., Jankowski, W., Sauna, Z.E., and Kimchi-Sarfaty, C. (2017). Recent advances in (therapeutic protein) drug development, *F1000*, 6 (113).

52. Fosgerau, K. and Hoffmann T. (2015). Peptide therapeutics: Current status and future directions, *Drug Discov. Today*, 20(1), pp. 122–128.

53. Goldberg, M. and Gomez-Orellana, I. (2003). Challenges for the oral delivery of macromolecules, *Nat. Rev. Drug Discov.*, 2(4), pp. 289–295.

54. Yoshioka, S. and Stella, V.J. (2002). *Stability of Peptide and Protein Pharmaceuticals, Stability of Drugs and Dosage Forms*, Springer, pp. 187–203.

55. Bos, J.D. and Meinardi, M.M. (2000). The 500 Dalton rule for the skin penetration of chemical compounds and drugs, *Exp. Dermatol.*, 9(3), pp. 165–169.

56. Torchilin, V.P. and Lukyanov, A.N. (2003). Peptide and protein drug delivery to and into tumors: Challenges and solutions, *Drug Discov. Today*, 8(6), pp. 259–266.

57. Lam, C.N., Yao, H., and Olsen, B.D. (2016). The effect of protein electrostatic interactions on globular protein–polymer block copolymer self-assembly, *Biomacromolecules*, 17(9), pp. 2820–2829.

58. Korpi, A., Skumial, P., and Kostiainen, M. (2019). Thermally induced reversible self-assembly of apoferritin–block copolymer complexes, *Macromol. Rapid Commun.*, 40(18).

59. Tao, A., Huang, G., Igarashi, K., Hing, T., Liao, S., Stellaci, F., Matsumato, Y., Yamaosba, T., Kataoka, K., and Cabral, H. (2019). Polymeric micelles loading proteins through concurrent ion complexation and pH-cleavable covalent bonding for in vivo delivery, *Macromol. Biosci.*, 20, pp. 1900161.

60. Chen, T., Xu, Y., Yang, W., Li, A., Wang, Y., Sun, J., and Liu, J. (2018). Design of enzyme micelles with controllable concavo-convex micromorphologies for highly enhanced stability and catalytical activity, *Macromol. Biosci.*, 18(3), pp. 1700312.

61. Nieto-Orellana, A., Di Antonio, M., Conte, C., Falcone, F.H., Bosquillon, C., Mantovani, G., and Stolnik., S. (2017). Effect of polymer topology on non-covalent polymer-protein complexation: Miktoarm versus linear mPEG-poly(glutamic acid) copolymers, *Polym. Chem.*, 8, pp. 2210–2220.

62. Banerjee, R., Gupta, S., Dey, D., Maiti, S., and Dhara, D. (2013). Synthesis of PEG containing cationic block copolymers and their interaction with human serum albumin, *React. Funct. Polym.*, 74(1).

63. Li, Z., Zhang, Y., Lu, D., and Liu, Z. (2015). Uniform mPEG-b-PMETAC enables pH-responsive delivery of insulin, *J. Appl. Polym. Sci.*, 132(39).

64. Ye, C. and Chi H. (2018). A review of recent progress in drug and protein encapsulation: Approaches, applications and challenges, *Mater. Sci. Eng. C*, 83, pp. 233–246.

65. Li, X., Shang, H., Wu, W., Li, S., Li, Z., Duan, J., Xu, L., and Li, J. (2016). Glucose-responsive micelles for controlled insulin release based on transformation from amphiphilic to double hydrophilic, *J. Nanosci. Nanotechnol.,* 16(6), pp. 5457–5463.

66. Payyappilly, S.S., Panja, S., Mandal, P., Dhara, S., and Chattopadhyay, S. (2015). Organic solvent-free low temperature method of preparation for self assembled amphiphilic poly(ϵ-caprolactone)-poly (ethylene glycol) block copolymer based nanocarriers for protein delivery, *Colloids Surf. B Biointerfaces,* 135, pp. 510–517.

67. Guo, Q., Zhang, T., An, J., Wu, Z., Zhao, Y., Dai, X., Zhang, X., and Li, C. (2015). Block versus random amphiphilic glycopolymer nanopaticles as glucose-responsive vehicles, *Biomacromolecules,* 16(10), pp. 3345–3356.

68. Le, M.Q., Gimel, J-C., Garric, X., Nguyen-Pham, T-Q., paniagua, C., Riou, J., and Venier-Julienne, M. (2020). Modulation of protein release from penta-block copolymer microspher, *Eur. J. Pharm. Biopharm.,* 152, pp. 175–182.

69. Sueyoshi, D., Anraku, Y., Komatsu, T., Urano. Y., and Kataoka, K. (2017). Enzyme-loaded polyion complex vesicles as in vivo nanoreactors working sustainably under the blood circulation: Characterization and functional evaluation, *Biomacromolecules,* 18(4), pp. 1189–1196.

70. Nardin, C., Widmer, J., Winterhalter, M., and Meier, W. (2001). Amphiphilic block copolymer nanocontainers as bioreactors, *Eur. Phys. J. E.,* 4(4), pp. 403–410.

71. Kembaren, R., Fokkink, R., Westphal, A.H., Kamperman, M., Kleijn, J.M., and Willer, J. (2020). Balancing enzyme encapsulation efficiency and stability in complex coacervate core micelles, *Langmuir,* 36(29), pp. 8494–8502.

72. Tanner, P., Baumann, P., Enea, R., Onaca, O., Palivan, C., and Meier, W. (2011). Polymeric vesicles: From drug carriers to nanoreactors and artificial organelles, *Acc. Chemical Res.,* 44(10), pp. 1039–1049.

73. Choi, H.-J. and Montemagno, C.D. (2005). Artificial organelle: ATP synthesis from cellular mimetic polymersomes, *Nano Lett.,* 5(12), pp. 2538–2542.

74. Vriezema, D.M., Garcia, P.M.L, Oltra, N.S., Hatzakis, N.S, Kuiper, S.M., Nolte, R.J.M., Rowan, A.E., and van Hest, J.C.M. (2007). Positional assembly of enzymes in polymersome nanoreactors for cascade reactions, *Angew. Chem. Int.,* 119(39), pp. 7522–7526.

75. Stoenescu, R., Graff, A., and Meier, W. (2004). Asymmetric ABC-triblock copolymer membranes induce a directed insertion of membrane proteins, *Macromol. Biosci.*, 4(10), pp. 930–935.

76. Kumar, M., Grzelakowski, M., Zilles, J., Clark, M., and Meier, W. (2007). Highly permeable polymeric membranes based on the incorporation of the functional water channel protein Aquaporin Z, *Proc. Nati. Acad. Sci.*, 104(52), pp. 20719–20724.

77. Patel, S.P., Vaishya, R., Pal, D., and Mitra, A.K. (2015). Novel pentablock copolymer-based nanoparticulate systems for sustained protein delivery, *Aaps PharmSciTech.*, 16(2), pp. 327–343.

78. Massignani, M., Cantón, I., Patokarnmonthon, N., Warren, N.J., Armes, S.P., Lewis, A.L., and Pattaglia, G. (2010). Cellular delivery of antibodies: Effective targeted subcellular imaging and new therapeutic tool, *Nat. Preced.*, pp. 1–17.

79. Pelegri-O'Day, E.M., Lin, E.-W., and Maynard, H.D. (2014). Therapeutic protein–polymer conjugates: Advancing beyond PEGylation, *J. Am. Chem. Soc.*, 136(41), pp. 14323–14332.

80. Theodorou, A., Liarou, E., Haddleton, D.M, Stavrakaki, I.G, Skordalidis, P., Whitfield, R., Anastasaki, A., and Velonia, K. (2020). Protein-polymer bioconjugates via a versatile oxygen tolerant photoinduced controlled radical polymerization approach, *Nat. Comm.*, 11(1), pp. 1486.

81. Fuchs, A., Kotman, N., Mailänder,V., Weiss, C. K., and Landfester, K. (2013). Enzyme cleavable nanoparticles from peptide based triblock copolymers, *Nanoscale*, 5, pp. 4829–4839.

82. Suthiwangcharoen, N. and Nagarajan, R. (2017). Nanoarmoring of proteins by conjugation to block copolymer micelles, *Meth. Enzymol.*, 590, pp. 277–304.

83. Chang, D., Lam, C.N., Tang, S., and Olsen B.D. (2014). Effect of polymer chemistry on globular protein–polymer block copolymer self-assembly, *Polym. Chem.*, 5, pp. 4884–4895.

84. Suguri, T. and Olsen, B. (2019). Topology effects on protein–polymer block copolymer self-assembly, *Polym. Chem.*, 10, pp. 1751–1761.

85. Alconcel, S.N., Baas, A.S., and Maynard, H.D. (2011). FDA-approved poly (ethylene glycol)–protein conjugate drugs, *Polym. Chem.*, 2(7), pp. 1442–1448.

86. Kurinomaru, T. and Shiraki, K. (2015). Noncovalent PEGylation of L-asparaginase using PEGylated polyelectrolyte, *J. Pharm. Sci.*, 104(2), pp. 587–592.

87. Reichert, C. and Borchard, G. (2016). Noncovalent PEGylation, an innovative subchapter in the field of protein modification, *J. Pharm. Sci.,* 105(2), pp. 386–390.

88. Kurinomaru, T., Kuwada, K., Tomita, S., Kameda, T., and Shiraki, K. (2017). Noncovalent PEGylation through protein–polyelectrolyte interaction: Kinetic experiment and molecular dynamics simulation, *J. Phys. Chem. B,* 121(28), pp. 6785–6791.

89. Naidu, P.S., Norret, M., Smith, N.M, Dunlop, S.A., Taylor, N.L, Fitzerald, M., and Iyer, K.S. (2017). The protein corona of PEGylated PGMA-based nanoparticles is preferentially enriched with specific serum proteins of varied biological function, *Langmuir,* 33(45), pp. 12926–12933.

90. Li, C., Huang, F., Liu, Y., Wu, G., Liu, Y., Ma, Y., An, Y., and Shi, L. (2018). Nitrilotriacetic acid-functionalized glucose-responsive complex micelles for the efficient encapsulation and self-regulated release of insulin, *Langmuir,* 34(40), pp. 12116–12125.

91. Lu, L., Yuan, L., Yan, C., Tang, C, and Wabg, Q. (2016). Development of core–shell nanostructures by in situ assembly of pyridine-grafted diblock copolymer and transferrin for drug delivery applications, *Biomacromolecules,* 17(7), pp. 2321–2328.

92. Lu, L., Zhang, L., Yuan, L., Zhu, T., Chen, W., Wang, G., and Wang, Q. (2019). Artificial cellulosome complex from the self-assembly of Ni-NTA-functionalized polymeric micelles and cellulases, *ChemBioChem,* 20(11), pp. 1394–1399.

93. Gunkel-Grabole, G., Sigg, S., Lomora, M., Lörcher, S., Palivan, C.G., and Meier, W.P. (2015). Polymeric 3D nano-architectures for transport and delivery of therapeutically relevant biomacromolecules, *Biomater. Sci.,* 3(1), pp. 25–40.

94. Garni, M., Thamboo, S., Schoenerberger, C.A., and Palivan, G.G. (2017). Biopores/membrane proteins in synthetic polymer membranes, *Biochim. Biophys. Acta (BBA)-Biomembranes,* 1859(4), pp. 619–638.

95. Hartmann, M. and Jung, D. (2010). Biocatalysis with enzymes immobilized on mesoporous hosts: The status quo and future trends, *J. Mater. Chem.,* 20(5), pp. 844–857.

96. Draghici, C., Mikhalevich, V., Gunkel-Grabole, G., Kowal, J., Meier, W., and Palivan, C.G. (2018). Biomimetic planar polymer membranes decorated with enzymes as functional surfaces, *Langmuir,* 34(30), pp. 9015–9024.

97. Osypova, A., Magnin, D., Sibret, P., Aquil, A., Jérôme, C., Dupont-Gillain, C., Pradier, C.-M., Demoustier-Champagne, S., and Landoulsi, J. (2015).

Dual stimuli-responsive coating designed through layer-by-layer assembly of PAA-b-PNIPAM block copolymers for the control of protein adsorption, *Soft matter,* 11(41), pp. 8154–8164.

98. Kim, B., Lam, C.N., and Olsen, B.D. (2012). Nanopatterned protein films directed by ionic complexation with water-soluble diblock copolymers, *Macromolecules,* 45(11), pp. 4572–4580.
99. Liu, D., Wang, T., and Keddie, J.L. (2009). Protein nanopatterning on self-organized poly (styrene-b-isoprene) thin film templates, *Langmuir,* 25(8), pp. 4526–4534.
100. Masuda, T., Hiraguchi, Y., Hiraguchi, Y., Kushiro, K., Araki, Y., Wada, T., Takai, M. (2020). Protein adsorption behavior in nanoscale phase-separated polymer coatings prepared using poly (2-methacrylolyoxyethyl phosphorylcholine)-containing amphiphilic block copolymers, *Eur. Polym. J.,* 135, pp. 109885.
101. Nagase, K., Koboyashi, J., Kikuchi, A., Akiyama, Y., Kanazawa, H., and Okana, T. (2016). Protein separations via thermally responsive ionic block copolymer brush layers, *RSC Adv.,* 6(31), pp. 26254–26263.
102. Schmidt, V., Giacomelli, C., Gounou, C., Lai-Kee-Him, J., Brisson, A.R., and Borsali, R. (2008). Formation of annexin-a5 protein/block copolymer micelle complexes: QCM-D and PAGE experiments, *Langmuir,* 24(21), pp. 12189–12195.
103. Jacobs, M.L., Boyd, M.A., and Kamat, N.P. (2019). Diblock copolymers enhance folding of a mechanosensitive membrane protein during cell-free expression, *Proceed. Nat. Acad. Sci.,* 116(10), pp. 4031–4036.
104. Magana, R., Sproncken, C., and Voets, I. (2020). On complex coacervate core micelles: Structure-function perspectives, *Polymers,* 12(9), pp. 1953.
105. Xie, J., Gonzalez-Carter, D., Tockary, T.A, Nakamura, N., Xue, Y., Nakakido, M., Akiba, H., Dirisala, A., Liu, X., Toh, K., Yang, T., Wang, Z., Fukushima, S., Li, J., Quader, S., Tsumoto, K., Yokota, T., Anraku, Y., and Kataoka, K. (2020). Dual-sensitive nanomicelles enhancing systemic delivery of therapeutically active antibodies specifically into the brain, *ACS Nano,* 14(6), pp. 6729–6742.
106. Hu, Q., Gu, G., Liu, Z., Jiang, M., Kang, T., Miao, D., Tu, Y., Pang, Z., Song, Q., Yao, L., Xia, H., Chen, H., Jiang, X., Gao, X., and Chen, J. (2012). F3 peptide-functionalized PEG-PLA nanoparticles co-administrated with tLyp-1 peptide for anti-glioma drug delivery, *Biomaterials,* 34(4), pp. 1135–1145.

107. Xie, J., Li, A., and Li, J. (2017). Advances in pH-sensitive polymers for smart insulin delivery, *Macromol. Rap. Commun.,* 38(23), pp. 1700413.

108. Gholami, A., Hashemi, S.A., Yousefi, K., Mousavi, S.M., Chiang, W.H., Ramakrishma, S., Mazraedoost, S., Alizadeh, A., Omidifar, N., Behbudi, G., and Babapoor, A. (2020). 3D nanostructures for tissue engineering, cancer therapy, and gene delivery, *J. Nanomater.,* 2020.

109. Sureka, H., Obermeyer, A.C., Flores, J.R., and Olsen, B.D. (2019). Catalytic biosensors from complex coacervate core micelle (C3M) thin films, *ACS Appl. Mater. Interfaces,* 11(35), pp. 32354–32365.

110. Yu, D.H., Lu, Q., Xie, J., Fang, C., and Chen, H.Z. (2010). Peptide-conjugated biodegradable nanoparticles as a carrier to target paclitaxel to tumor neovasculature, *Biomaterials,* 31(8), pp. 2278–2292.

Chapter 4

Polymeric Stimuli Responsive Theranostic Agents

Maria Psarrou and Maria Vamvakaki

Department of Materials Science and Technology, University of Crete,
Vasilika Vouton 700 13 Heraklion, Crete, Greece and
Institute of Electronic Structure and Laser,
Foundation of Research and Technology-Hellas,
Vasilika Vouton 700 13 Heraklion, Crete, Greece
vamvakak@materials.uoc.gr

The term "theranostic" was first introduced in 2002 by Funkhouser to describe any nanoscale material that combined the therapeutic and diagnostic or imaging modalities. Since then, theranostics has evolved into a new scientific and technological subfield of nanomedicine, and include all image-guided therapies as well as therapeutic agents that can be simultaneously employed for imaging of the diseased site or tissue. Theranostic nanomaterials can be divided into three main classes depending on the material employed, namely, polymer theranostics, hybrid material theranostics, and small organic molecule theranostic systems. In this chapter, we will focus on polymer-based theranostics, which comprise a polymer combined with either photosensitizers (PSs) or inorganic nanoparticles as the imaging probes. A detailed analysis of the mode of action of different polymer-based theranostic nanomaterials reported in the literature,

Functional Materials in Biomedical Applications
Edited by Costas Demetzos, Natassa Pippa, and Nikolaos Naziris

ISBN 978-981-4968-65-2 (Hardcover), 978-1-003-41146-8 (eBook)
www.jennystanford.com

and their therapeutic and diagnostic/imaging capabilities, will be presented. Special emphasis will be given to stimuli-activatable theranostic nanomaterials triggered by external or internal triggers, such as temperature, pH, and light irradiation. Finally, the future research and clinical perspectives of the field will be discussed.

4.1 Introduction

During the last decades, outstanding progress has been witnessed in the field of nanomedicine, which has revolutionized both the research and clinical phases of the technological development process [1–3]. New materials and structures have been developed aiming at the prognosis, diagnosis, and treatment of a wide range of diseases, including cancer, Alzheimer's disease, Parkinson disease, and many other genetic and neurological disorders or autoimmune diseases. The first generation of nanomedicine focused on solving the major problem in conventional chemotherapy, which is related to the low solubility of the most commonly used hydrophobic anticancer drugs, and their poor tissue selectivity, accompanied by a fast clearance from the body through the reticuloendothelial system. This was achieved by passively targeting specific tissues (mainly cancerous) via the enhanced permeation and retention (EPR) effect. In 1964, the first nanotherapeutic system, based on a liposomal structure, was introduced [4]. Since then, great advances in the design, development, and clinical trial of numerous nanotherapeutic drug delivery systems (DDSs), comprising a plethora of materials and chemistries, have been achieved. The existing DDSs can be divided into three different classes depending on the main material used for their development: (a) organic systems, such as polymeric nanocarriers (e.g., nanoparticles, micelles, nanogels), (b) inorganic nanosystems (e.g., mesoporous silica, iron oxide nanoparticles), and (c) a combination of organic with inorganic materials for the development of promising hybrid DDSs.

The early diagnosis of a particular disease is equally important to its treatment. Hence, the development of nanotherapeutics with dual, diagnostic (imaging), and therapeutic actions is very important. This combined modality was first introduced by Funkhouser in 2002 [5]. He used the term "theranostic" to describe the integrated capabilities of the new nanotherapeutics, which opened new paths in the field of nanomedicine. The use of theranostic agents offers multiple advantages, such as non-invasive monitoring of the disease progression and the therapeutic efficacy, analysis of the drug distribution and its triggered release at the tissues of interest, and synergistic modes of therapy (e.g., chemotherapy and photodynamic therapy). In the first part of this chapter, a detailed description of the main therapeutic action of novel theranostic agents, including chemotherapy, photodynamic therapy (PDT), photothermal therapy (PTT), and sonodynamic therapy (SDT), and their diagnostic/imaging modalities, such as optical, fluorescence, magnetic resonance, and ultrasound imaging, will be presented. In the second part, we will summarize the latest developments in the field of theranostic agents comprising either polymeric or hybrid (polymer-inorganic) nanomaterials.

4.2 Therapeutic Action of Theranostic Agents

4.2.1 Chemotherapy

Cancer is a heterogeneous disease with many different subtypes leading to increased death rates, worldwide [6]. Tremendous effort has been devoted by numerous research groups worldwide to the development of more efficient drugs, materials, and methods for cancer treatment [7]. Among the most commonly used approaches for cancer treatment, chemotherapy has dominated both the early-stage and late-stage remedies. In conventional chemotherapy, one or more anti-cancer drugs are used to kill the fast-growing cancer cells in the body by their direct administration into the bloodstream. However, this method of drug administration has major drawbacks, such as the non-specific action of the drug and its uncontrolled biodistribution. Another limitation of conventional chemotherapy is the tumor drug resistance. Many chemotherapeutic compounds act with preferential cytotoxicity on cancer cells, as a result of their rapid proliferation compared to normal cells. However, even in these cases, the cytotoxicity is not restricted only to the cancer cells, the drug can also affect the healthy tissues, the neural system, and the heart and the gastrointestinal tract. This non-specific action results in side effects that limit the maximum tolerated drug dose and eventually hinder the efficacy of the drug. Unfortunately, besides cancer, many other genetic diseases suffer from similar limitations leading to ineffective therapies.

The remarkable progress in the field of nanomedicine has fueled the development of more effective treatment methods, employing the so-called drug delivery vehicles (modern chemotherapy), which possess certain advantages in disease therapy (Table 4.1) [2, 8]. These vehicles usually comprise a nanostructured material (nanocarrier), which can be loaded with the therapeutic compounds and delivered to the diseased sites of interest via passive or active targeting (Fig. 4.1) [9–11]. Passive targeting relies on the EPR effect, which is a unique characteristic of tumor tissues, being anatomically and pathophysiologically different from healthy tissues. Extensive angiogenesis and hypervasculature, lack of the smooth-muscle layer (pericytes), defective vascular architecture (fenestrations), non-constant blood flow, and inefficient lymphatic drainage are some of the major characteristics of the tumor tissues. The passive targeting of tumors is based on these tissue abnormalities, enabling macromolecular structures, such as nanocarriers in the size range of 20–200 nm, to extravagate and accumulate in the tumors. The nanocarriers that enter the tumor sites cannot be removed effectively, due to inefficient lymphatic drainage, and are thus retained in the tumor, where they release the chemotherapeutic drugs (Fig. 4.1a). On the other hand, in active tumor targeting, a ligand is covalently attached to the surface of the nanocarrier, and specifically recognizes and binds to appropriate receptors present in the target tissues but are absent in the normal ones (Fig. 4.1b).

The binding affinity of the ligand to the receptor is an important parameter, which determines the penetration of the nanocarrier into the tumor site, because of the "binding-site barrier". The ligand is usually an antibody or a peptide, which can target either the cancer cells or the tumor endothelium. As mentioned above, theranostic agents possess a dual, therapeutic and diagnostic, modality. In the case of chemotherapy, the theranostic nanoparticles bearing the imaging moieties are loaded with an anticancer drug/compound, which is released from the nanocarriers either passively or on demand, upon application of an external or internal stimulus, such as the pH, temperature, enzymes, light or ultrasound irradiation, magnetic field, and others (Fig. 4.1c).

Table 4.1 Advantages of DDSs in modern chemotherapy

1	Drug accumulation at the diseased sites and low drug concentration in healthy tissues
2	Limited side effects and toxicities
3	Improved drug solubility
4	Higher drug stability and reduced degradation of the drug during circulation
5	Patient compliance by reducing the number of dosages
6	Co-delivery of multiple drugs to specific sites leads to an improved therapeutic efficacy

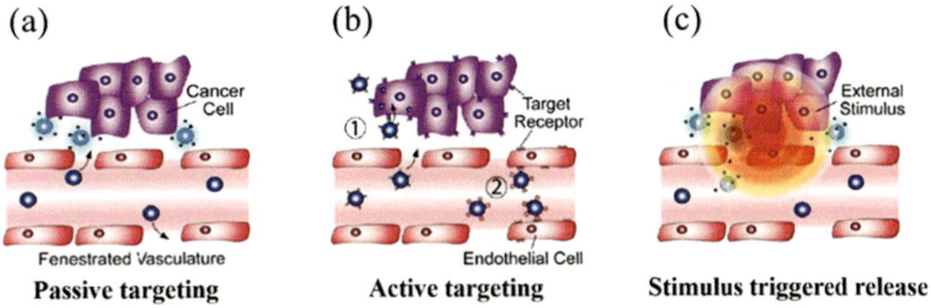

Figure 4.1 Types of tumors targeted by the DDSs [12]. Reproduced with permission from A. Wicki, D. Witzigmann, V. Balasubramanian, and J. Huwyler, "Nanomedicine in cancer therapy: Challenges, opportunities, and clinical applications," *J. Control. Release*, vol. 200, pp. 138–157, 2015, Copyright (2015), Elsevier.

4.2.2 Photodynamic Therapy

The therapeutic effect of light, in combination with an absorber molecule, was first reported at the end of the 19th century [13, 14]. Since then, numerous studies have employed different absorber molecules and light irradiation sources to treat certain diseases [15]. Nowadays, it has been formally established that the absorber molecules are the so-called PSs, and the activation process of a PS upon light irradiation, which results in the damage of the desired tissues, is known as PDT. Among the most widely used PSs for PDT are the cyanine or iodinated cyanine dyes, phthalocyanine and phenazine derivatives, boron dipyrromethene molecules, porphines, and chlorins [16–20].

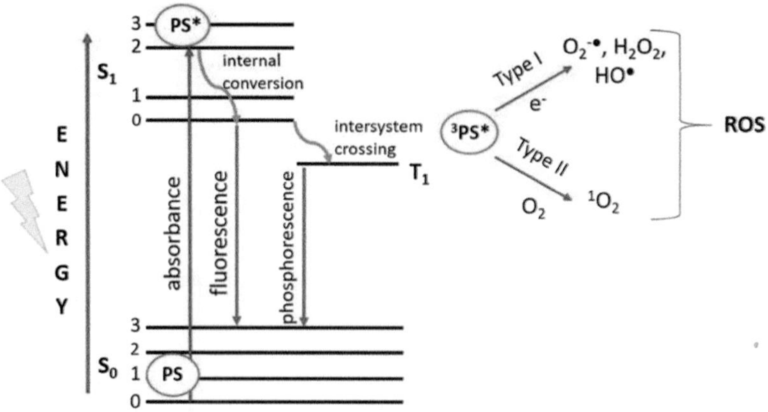

Figure 4.2 Schematic illustration of the Jablonski diagram showing the photochemical pathways in PDT [21]. Reproduced with permission from A. Bekmukhametova, H. Ruprai, J. M. Hook, D. Mawad, J. Houang, and A. Lauto, "Photodynamic therapy with nanoparticles to combat microbial infection and resistance," *Nanoscale*, vol. 12, no. 41, pp. 21034–21059, 2020, Copyright (2020), Royal Society of Chemistry.

In PDT, a non-toxic PS absorbs light of a particular wavelength and produces singlet oxygen ($^1O_2$) or other reactive oxygen species (ROS) ($HO^•$, H_2O_2, $O_2^•$), which are cytotoxic (Fig. 4.2). According to the Jablonski diagram, the PS is excited from the ground state to its singlet state upon light irradiation. Next, the excited electron can either jump back to the ground state, through internal conversion (fluorescence) or can undergo intersystem crossing to form the triplet state (T_1). From the T_1 state, either radical species are formed via a Type I reaction or, more likely, the energy is transferred to the surrounding molecular oxygen ($^3O_2$), which forms $^1O_2$ via a Type II reaction [14, 15, 21, 22]. As already mentioned above, $^1O_2$ is cytotoxic and has been extensively used for the treatment of cancerous tissues [23–26].

On the other hand, PDT has been also applied for the treatment of other diseases, such as atherosclerotic plaque and age-related macular degeneration, as well as against microbial infections [21, 27–29].

4.2.3 Photothermal Therapy

PTT is a treatment approach, in which the temperature of the tissue is artificially increased resulting in the destruction of the targeted cell population (mainly cancer cells) [30, 31]. The main principle of PTT is the light-to-heat conversion through the photo-absorption of light by photothermal agents (PTAs). Ideally, PTAs shall only increase the temperature at the laser irradiation spot, thus reducing the damage to the surrounding healthy tissues. To achieve this effect, the absorption of the PTAs is adjusted to particular wavelengths that can penetrate deep into the tissues, the tissue-transparent window, which ranges from 750 nm to 1350 nm and include the first (750–1000 nm) (NIR I) and the second (1000–1350 nm) (NIR II) NIR windows [32, 33]. Similar to PDT, upon near-infrared (NIR) light irradiation of an organic PTA, an electron is excited from the highest occupied molecular orbital (HOMO) (ground state) to the lower unoccupied molecular orbital (LUMO) (singlet state [S1]). Next, the excited electron can either decay back to the HOMO energy level by emitting a photon (fluorescence) or it can undergo intersystem crossing through non-radiative relaxation processes (Fig. 4.3a) [33]. The latter is responsible for the photothermal effects and the produced local hyperthermia. Compared to the PSs used in PDT, organic PTAs should fulfill the following specific requirements: (a) photo-absorption in the NIR region, with minimum fluorescence quantum yields and singlet oxygen production, so as to maximize the conversion of the photo-absorbed photons to heat, (b) non-toxicity in their nonirradiated form, (c) fast degradation after their use to increase safety, and (d) facile preparation and modification. To date, PTAs that have been found to satisfy the majority of the above requirements and which have been extensively used for PTT studies, are cyanine-based dyes, diketopyrrolo-pyrrole derivatives, croconaine dyes, porphyrin-based molecules, and polyanilines [33, 34].

Another interesting class of PTAs is the plasmonic nanomaterials, such as gold nanoparticles, Cu-based semiconductors, and carbon dots [35, 36]. In this case, the photothermal effect results from the photoexcitation of the localized surface plasmons (LSP) of the nanomaterial following the steps of (a) plasmon excitation, (b) Landau damping, (c) carrier relaxation, and (d) thermal dissipation (Fig. 4.3b) [36, 37].

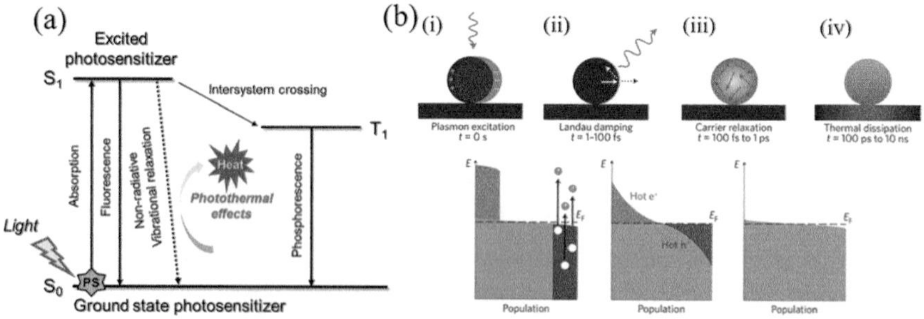

Figure 4.3 (a) Schematic illustration of the Jablonski diagram showing the photochemical processes in PTT and (b) photoexcitation and relaxation processes of LSP in plasmonic nanomaterials [33, 36]. Reproduced with permission from H. S. Jung, P. Verwilst, A. Sharma, J. Shin, J. L. Sessler, and J. S. Kim, "Organic molecule-based photothermal agents: An expanding photothermal therapy universe," *Chem. Soc. Rev.*, vol. 47, no. 7, pp. 2280–2297, 2018, Copyright (2018), Royal Society of Chemistry; and M. Kim, J. H. Lee, and J. M. Nam, "Plasmonic photothermal nanoparticles for biomedical applications," *Adv. Sci.*, vol. 6, no. 17, 2019, Copyright (2019), John Wiley & Sons Inc.

4.2.4 Sonodynamic Therapy

Ultrasound is a mechanical wave that transports energy through a medium. This mechanically produced energy can have a therapeutic effect in many different ways. For example, ultrasound irradiation has been employed for the enhancement of the action of chemotherapeutic substances by opening pores in the cell membrane, a process known as sonoporation, to increase the uptake of the drugs by the cells [38]. In another approach, ultrasound has been used to increase the permeability of poorly vascularized tissues, such as solid tumors, or to temporally disrupt the blood-brain-barrier (BBB), the major factor that leads to the failure of the treatments in brain-related disorders (e.g., Parkinson's disease, Alzheimer), and thus enhance the penetration of the drug molecules in such tissues [38–40]. During the last two decades, ultrasound has been also used in the clinic as a non-surgical method for direct tumor ablation as a result of the thermal effects of cavitation [41].

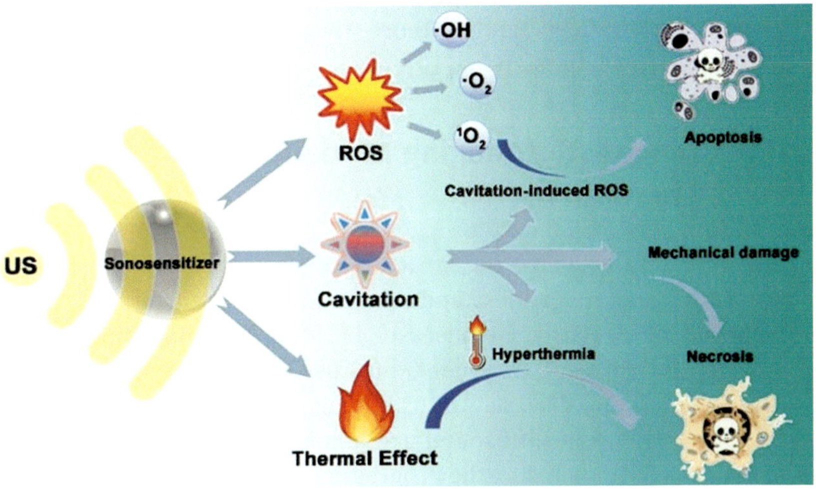

Figure 4.4 Schematic illustration of the proposed SDT mechanism [43]. Reproduced with permission from X. Lin, J. Song, X. Chen, and H. Yang, "Ultrasound-activated sensitizers and applications," *Angew. Chemie–Int. Ed.*, vol. 59, no. 34, pp. 14212– 14233, 2020, Copyright (2020), John Wiley & Sons Inc.

SDT is a novel low-intensity ultrasound-based modality, which is related to many different events, such as cavitation, microbubbles, thermal (hyperthermia), and mechanical effects, as well as the activation of sonosensitizers to produce ROS in a process similar to PDT [42]. The precise mechanism of action of SDT remains unclear, due to the complexity of the process, whereas a widely accepted process is illustrated in Fig. 4.4 [42, 43]. Upon ultrasound exposure, a sonosensitizer is activated to produce ROS, which are cytotoxic, resulting in cell apoptosis. Alternatively, the ultrasound-induced cavitation effect has been also considered to play an important role in SDT. In cavitation, tiny gas bubbles are generated, grew, and collapsed during sonication. The collapse of the gas bubbles is accompanied by thermal (local hot spots) and mechanical (shear stress and elongation forces) effects, both of which cause irreversible damage to the targeted tissue [44].

In contrast to PDT and PTT, which employ light irradiation for the activation of the PSs, SDT uses medical ultrasound as the sole external stimulus, which is non-invasive and non-ionizing, and causes less damage to the healthy tissues, while allowing greater penetration depths (more than 10 cm), rendering it ideal for deep-seated tumors [40].

4.3 Diagnostic/Imaging Modalities in Theranostics

The ability to visualize the structure, morphology, and anatomy of tissue and to understand the complexity, diversity, and behavior of a particular disease, is of great importance not only at the stage of treatment, but also for the prognosis and diagnosis of the disease. Optical imaging, magnetic resonance imaging (MRI), and ultrasound are among the most widely used techniques for monitoring the progression of a disease (Fig. 4.5).

4.3.1 Optical Imaging

Optical imaging is one of the most extensively used visualization methods in the biomedical field and in particular in translation medicine [46]. Optical imaging, in the form of fluorescence or bioluminescence imaging, offers several advantages compared to the other imaging techniques, i.e., low cost, availability of a large number of commercial fluorescent probes, high accuracy and sensitivity, and applicability from the macroscopic down to the molecular level.

Optical imaging relies on the use of fluorescent probes, such as small organic fluorescent dyes, fluorescent proteins, and inorganic nanoparticles (quantum dots [QDs]) [47] to dye the tissues. Numerous small, organic, fluorescent dyes have been designed for in vitro imaging by fluorescence microscopy. However, most of them are not suitable for in vivo imaging, since the latter

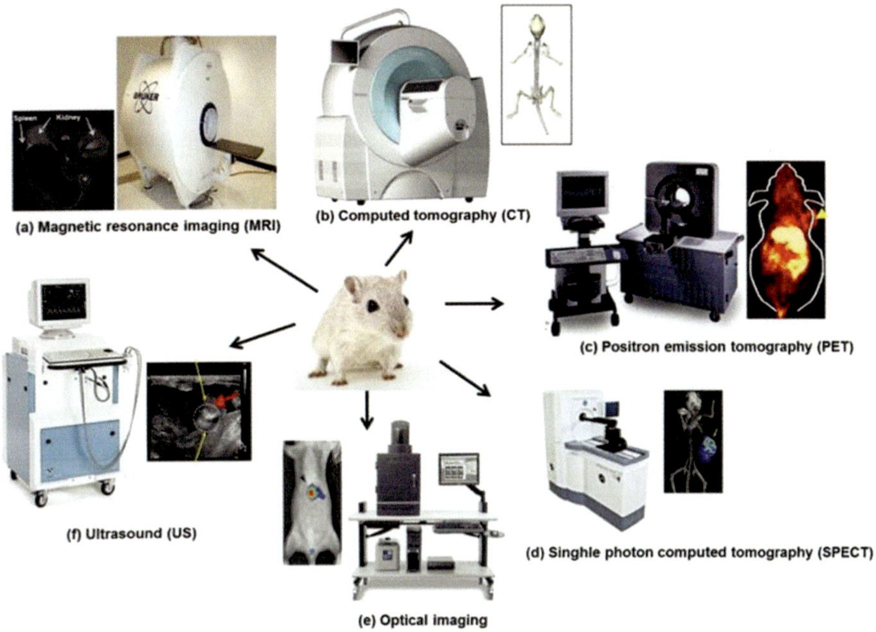

Figure 4.5 Different imaging modalities [45]. Reproduced with permission from R. K. Singh, K. D. Patel, K. W. Leong, and H. W. Kim, "Progress in nanotheranostics based on mesoporous silica nanomaterial platforms," *ACS Appl. Mater. Interfaces*, vol. 9, no. 12, pp. 10309–10337, 2017, Copyright (2017), American Chemical Society.

should satisfy the following important requirements: (a) long wavelength emission to ensure deep tissue penetration, (b) low toxicity, and (c) good stability in the in vivo microenvironment. Among the numerous fluorescent dyes that have been studied for in vivo imaging, the preferred candidates are rhodamine, oxazine dyes, fluorescein [47, 48], and cyanine-based probes that absorb and emit light in the NIR range (650–900 nm), thus allowing a good penetration depth (Fig. 4.6a) [34]. Fluorescent proteins, and in particular the green fluorescent protein (GFP) family, or Luciferaces, have been extensively used for bioimaging and bioluminescence, respectively [49, 50]; nevertheless, none of their mutants have long wavelength emission, and hence their use in vivo is limited. Fluorescence QDs have emerged as a very promising class of materials for use in tissue imaging [51, 52]. QDs comprise inorganic, semiconductor materials with unique optical properties, including high quantum yields, large molar extinction coefficients, high photostability, and size-tunable emission wavelengths. Moreover, their large surface area allows their functionalization with antibodies, proteins, and other bioactive molecules for targeted therapies (Fig. 4.6b) [51, 53].

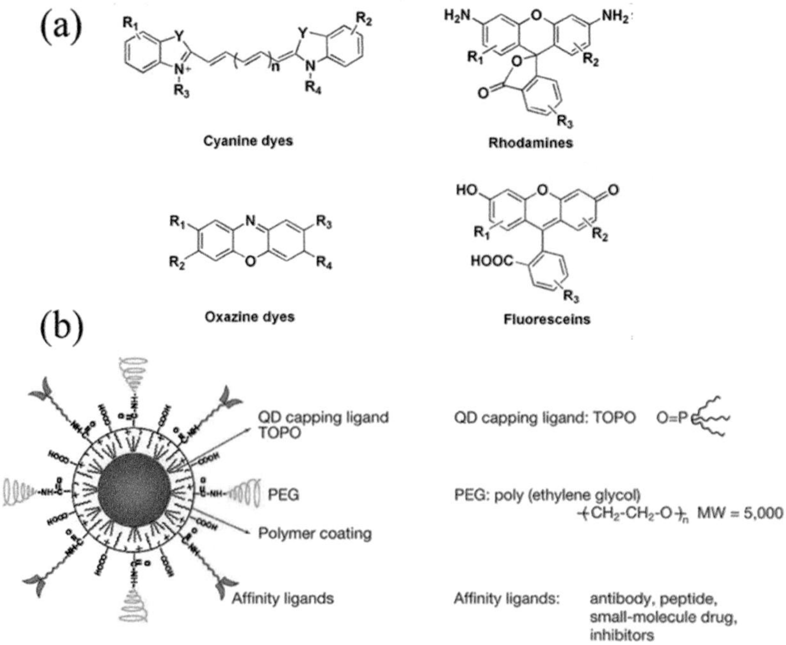

Figure 4.6 (a) Main classes of organic fluorescence probes and (b) schematic illustration of a surface functionalized QD for in vivo tumor targeting and imaging [47, 53]. Reproduced with permission from H. S. Jung, P. Verwilst, A. Sharma, J. Shin, J. L. Sessler, and J. S. Kim, "Organic molecule-based photothermal agents: An expanding photothermal therapy universe," *Chem. Soc. Rev.*, vol. 47, no. 7, pp. 2280–2297, 2018, Copyright (2018), Royal Society of Chemistry; and M. Kim, J. H. Lee, and J. M. Nam, "Plasmonic photothermal nanoparticles for biomedical applications," *Adv. Sci.*, vol. 6, no. 17, 2019, Copyright (2019), John Wiley & Sons Inc.

4.3.2 Magnetic Resonance Imaging

MRI is a widely used imaging technique that produces a detailed 3D image of the diseased area. MRI is non-invasive and provides simultaneously high spatial resolution and sensitivity. In MRI, radiation in the radiofrequency (RF) range is applied in the presence of a strong magnetic field. The hydrogen atoms of the water and fat molecules of the body initially align with the external magnetic field, whereas RF excites the hydrogen atoms causing them to spin out of equilibrium. The technique measures the energy released by the hydrogen atoms as they relax back and realign with the external magnetic field when the RF field ceases. The images obtained in MRI are based on the longitudinal (T_1) and transverse (T_2) relaxation rates. Metal ions, such as Gd^{3+}, $Fe^{2+/3+}$, and $Mn^{2+/3+}$ are normally used as contrast agents to increase the resolution of the captured image [54, 55].

4.3.3 Ultrasound

In ultrasound imaging (sonography), high-frequency ultrasound (20–55 MHz) is used to capture the anatomy inside the body as a result of the reflection of the ultrasound waves from the internal body structures [56]. As already mentioned, ultrasound is a non-invasive, non-ionizing, real-time imaging technique. The contrast of the obtained images can be enhanced by using liquids, microbubbles, or polymer capsules, which increase the reflection. Perfluorocarbons have been extensively used as contrast agents for ultrasound imaging [57].

4.4 Polymeric Stimuli-Activatable Nanotheranostics

Polymer-based theranostic agents have lately revolutionized the development of effective and safe personalized treatments against various diseases, including cancer, leading to significant progress and achievements in the field of nanomedicine. Compared to other theranostic systems, polymer-based theranostics offer important advantages, namely, biocompatibility, (bio)degradability, enhanced water compatibility, surface functionalities, and others.

A polymer-based theranostic system consists of two main parts: the polymeric component and the imaging agent. The polymer can be either synthetic or natural and its macromolecular architecture can vary being a linear polymer chain (e.g., homopolymer, block copolymer), and hyperbranched, dendritic, or cross-linked polymer. The polymer architecture defines the final structure of the theranostic carrier, which can be in the form of polymer micelles, vesicles, solid nanoparticles, or nanogels. On the other hand, imaging agents, such as small, organic fluorescent dyes, or inorganic nanoparticles have been employed in polymer theranostics. In the following, the recent advances in polymer and hybrid stimuli-activatable nanotheranostics will be discussed.

4.4.1 Polymer Nanotheranostics

Stimuli-responsive polymer nanotheranostics is a special class of polymer theranostic systems that has gained great interest recently. Polymer theranostic agents that respond to either internal (pH, enzyme, reducing agents) or external (light, temperature) stimuli have been reported.

For instance, Lee et al. developed a thermo-responsive theranostic system based on a temperature-sensitive diblock copolymer comprising a poly(isopropylacrylamide) block and a poly(ε-caprolactone) block (PNiPAm-*b*-PCL) [58]. Carboplatin, a model anticancer drug, was encapsulated within the PNiPAm-*b*-PCL thermo-responsive micelles to provide the chemotherapeutic modality of the theranostic system, while a NIR fluorescent dye (DiR) was used for optical imaging.

Particular attention has been paid to the development of pH-responsive theranostic systems. In an intriguing study, Pearce et al. developed an interesting pH-responsive hyper-branched polymer theranostic system against prostate cancer, by targeting a prostate-specific membrane antigen (PSMA) [59]. The hyperbranched polymer was synthesized by the reversible addition-fragmentation chain transfer (RAFT) polymerization of poly(ethylene glycol) monomethyl methacrylate using ethylene glycol dimethacrylate as the cross-linker. The RAFT agent was functionalized to bear the targeting ligand, while hydrazide moieties were incorporated along the polymer chains, which allowed the conjugation of a model anticancer drug, fluorene-2-carboxaldehyde, via pH-degradable hydrazone bonds. The optical imaging modality was installed by the copolymerization of a fluorescent dye-modified methacrylate comonomer. The in vitro release studies, showed 90% drug release after 4 h in acidic conditions (pH 5.5), whereas at physiological pH (7.4) a release below 5% was found indicating a very low passive release in the body. In addition, preliminary in vivo experiments showed that the hyperbranched polymer bearing the targeting ligand exhibited four times higher uptake by the tumor cells that overexpressed the PSMA, compared to the normal cells that did not express the protein. A few years later, the same group used this hyperbranched polymer and doxorubicin (DOX) as a model anticancer drug in an in vivo study in mice and showed a 90% reduction of the tumor volume in 28 days, following five intravenous injections of the hyperbranched polymer-DOX conjugate, compared to 30% shrinkage of the tumor when using the free drug [60].

In another study, Guo et al. developed a theranostic system based on a brush-shaped amphiphilic diblock copolymer comprising a poly(2-hydroxyethyl methacrylate) (PHEMA) backbone with poly(L-lactide)-*b*-poly(ethylene glycol) (PLLA-*b*-PEG) grafted chains. The copolymer was prepared by sequential atom transfer radical polymerization (ATRP) and ring-opening polymerization, followed by the grafting of the carboxy-terminated PEG chains onto the hydroxy end-groups of PLLA [61]. Next, the monoclonal antibody TRC105, which targets endoglin (CD105) a widely accepted marker for tumor angiogenesis, was conjugated onto the polymer chains, and 1,4,7-triazacyclononane-N,N', N-triacetic acid, a macrocyclic chelator for ^{64}Cu was also bound to afford the imaging modality. This amphiphilic, brush-shaped copolymer self-assembled into unimolecular micelles in water, and encapsulated the model drug DOX within the hydrophobic cores of the micelles. Drug release studies showed a pH-depended release profile with ~60% release of DOX, after 80 h incubation at pH 5.3, compared to ~10% drug released under physiological conditions. Additionally, the TRC105-conjugated micelles presented a higher accumulation at the tumor site, compared to the antibody-free micelles.

An unconventional pH-responsive polysaccharide/drug conjugate for pH-activatable PDT was reported by Park and coworkers [62]. In their system, a glycol chitosan backbone was grafted with pH-responsive 3-diethylaminopropyl isothiocyanate (DEAP) moieties, a chlorin e6 derivative, to serve as the phototoxic drug and imaging agent, and PEG chains to provide stealth properties (Fig. 4.7a). The grafted chitosan polymer chains self-assembled into supramolecular structures in water at neutral pH, at which the Ce6 PS was in a self-quenched state, whereas under slightly acidic conditions (pH 6.8), the structures disassembled, due to the protonation of the DEAP units at their pK_b value of 6.8 (Fig. 4.7b) to form single polymer chains. The disassembly was accompanied by the generation of singlet oxygen and by a strong fluorescence signal, due to the release of Ce6, specifically at the tumor site, facilitating an effective therapeutic and imaging action.

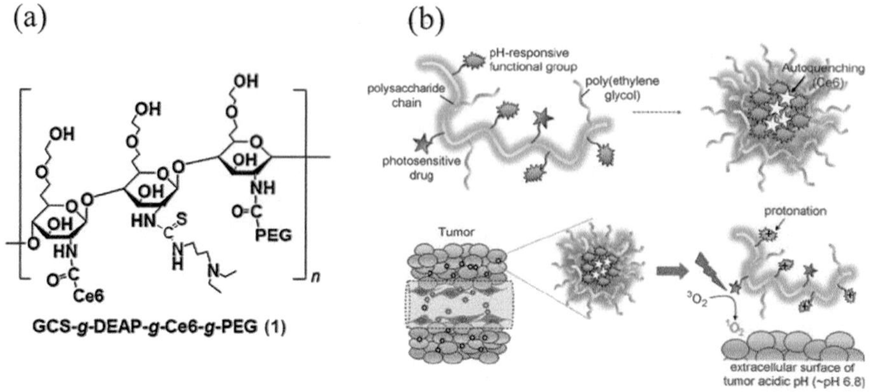

Figure 4.7 (a) Chemical structure of the grafted polysaccharide and (b) schematic illustration of the self-assembly process and the action mode of the polysaccharide-drug conjugate theranostic system [62]. Reproduced with permission from S. Y. Park, H. J. Baik, Y. T. Oh, K. T. Oh, Y. S. Youn, and E. S. Lee, "A smart polysaccharide/drug conjugate for photodynamic therapy," *Angew. Chemie – Int. Ed.*, vol. 50, no. 7, pp. 1644–1647, 2011, Copyright (2011), John Wiley & Sons Inc.

In a later study, Li et al. reported a dual, pH and redox, responsive theranostic nanoplatform based on a PEGylated dendritic supramolecular structure for the delivery of a platinum antitumor drug combined with NIR fluorescence tumor imaging [63]. The dendrons were synthesized via the divergent approach, using lipoic acid, which served as the hydrophobic part of the final self-assembled superstructure. The redox sensitivity was afforded by disulfide moieties used to bind chemically the dendritic parts to form the supramolecular structure, while a PEGylated platinum derivative was synthesized and coordinated onto the peripheral carboxylic acid groups of the dendritic system to act as the pH-responsive antitumor drug source. In vivo experiments showed a very effective anticancer activity of the dendritic theranostic nanosystem in A549 xenograft tumor-bearing mice with good pharmacokinetics, NIR tumor imaging, and platinum distribution.

An interesting enzyme activatable theranostic probe was presented by Zhen and coworkers, which consisted of a D-galactose-caged NIR hemicyanine dye conjugated onto a PEG chain via an azide-alkyne cycloaddition [64]. The caging group could be cleaved in the presence of β-galactosidase, an overexpressed enzyme in ovarian cancer, leading to the activation of NIR fluorescence, photoacoustic, and photothermal effects by the cyanine dye, for imaging-guided therapy.

Hydrogels are particularly attractive as platforms for the development of stimuli-sensitive theranostic systems. An intriguing example of such materials are gels that are sensitive to remote stimuli, i.e., light irradiation. In a recent paper, Xu et al. reported a NIR-triggered, ROS-degradable hydrogel based on hyaluronic acid (HA). The polymer possessed hydrazide functional groups, which could rapidly react with an aldehyde bisfunctionalized thioketal linker via hydrazone bonds to form the hydrogel (Fig. 4.8a) [65]. Protoporphyrin IX (PpIX), as a PS, and DOX, as a model anticancer drug, were also conjugated onto the HA chains. Upon NIR illumination, the PS produced ROS, which on the one hand, cleaved the thioketal linkers, leading to the degradation of the hydrogel, and the release of the DOX molecules (chemotherapy) and on the other hand, induced an effective PDT (Fig. 4.8b). It was also shown that PpIX conjugated hydrogel exhibited an enhanced fluorescence intensity in vivo compared to the free PpIX, which produced only a very weak signal due to self-quenching in the aqueous medium, facilitating the efficacious optical tumor imaging.

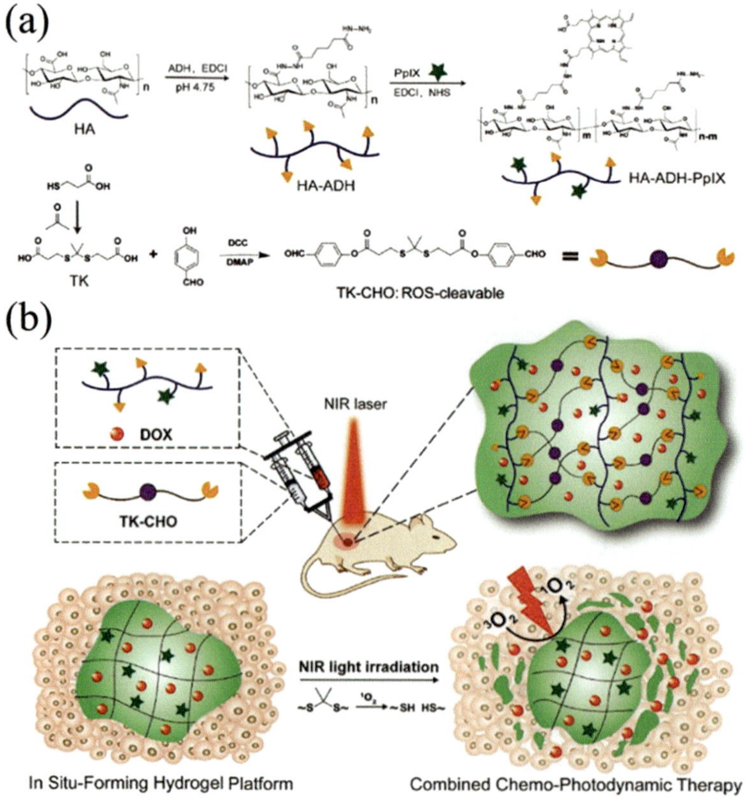

Figure 4.8 (a) Synthesis of an HA-ADH-PpIX conjugate bearing ROS-degradable linkages and (b) in-situ formation of the degradable hydrogel for synergistic chemo-PDT and optical imaging upon NIR light irradiation [65]. Reproduced with permission from X. Xu et al., "Near-infrared light-triggered degradable hyaluronic acid hydrogel for on-demand drug release and combined chemo-photodynamic therapy," *Carbohydr. Polym.*, vol. 229, no. July 2019, p. 115394, 2020, Copyright (2020), Elsevier.

In another study, Biglione et al. prepared a thermo-responsive nanogel based on oligo(ethylene glycol) methacrylate and 2-hydroxyethyl methacrylate using tetra(ethylene glycol) dimethacrylate (TEGDMA) as the cross-linker [66]. A few years later, they combined the thermo-responsive nanogels with a NIR dye from the cyanine family (IR806) to develop a theranostic nanoplatform for simultaneous PDT, PTT, and optical imaging of the nanogel incubated cells [67].

4.4.2 Hybrid (Organic-Inorganic) Nanotheranostic Agents

Inorganic materials (metals, metal oxides, and QDs) have been combined with polymers, to develop hybrid theranostic nanoplatforms for therapy and imaging. Despite the numerous studies on hybrid theranostic materials, stimuli-sensitive polymer-based hybrid nanotheranostic agents are still limited. The recent advances in hybrid theranostic nanoparticles based on thermo-, pH-, and photo-sensitive polymers are discussed below.

Thermo-responsive polymers have been extensively employed in the development of hybrid theranostic nanoformulations. Purusthotham et al. presented a thermo-responsive theranostic system comprising superparamagnetic iron oxide nanoparticles (SPIONs) coated with the temperature-sensitive polymer PNiPAm [68]. In this system, the SPIONs played a dual role, as MRI contrast agents allowing the targeting and imaging of the tumor sites, as well as therapeutic agents by inducing hyperthermia and the release of the chemotherapeutic drug DOX, which was entrapped within the thermo-responsive polymeric shell. A few years later, Wadajkar and coworkers presented another temperature-responsive, hybrid core-shell theranostic system based on poly(N-isopropylacrylamide-acrylamide-allylamine)-coated SPIONs decorated with a polyarginine peptide (R11) for active tumor targeting [69]. In vivo biodistribution experiments verified the higher accumulation of the R11-SPIONs in the tumor tissues, where they were visualized by MRI, compared to the non-targeted SPIONs. Although the authors did not investigate the therapeutic action of their theranostic system, they proposed its use as a prostate cancer-specific drug delivery vehicle for hyperthermia and temperature-stimulated drug release. In an interesting study, Talelli et al. prepared an amphiphilic, poly(ethylene glycol)-*b*-poly[N-(2-hydroxypropyl)methacrylamide dilactate] diblock copolymer exhibiting thermo-responsive and biodegradable properties [70]. The copolymer was self-assembled into core-shell micelles in water-bearing SPIONs encapsulated within the micellar cores, which served both as contrast agents for MRI as well as therapeutic agents for hyperthermia and temperature-controlled chemotherapy treatment. The unique advantages of

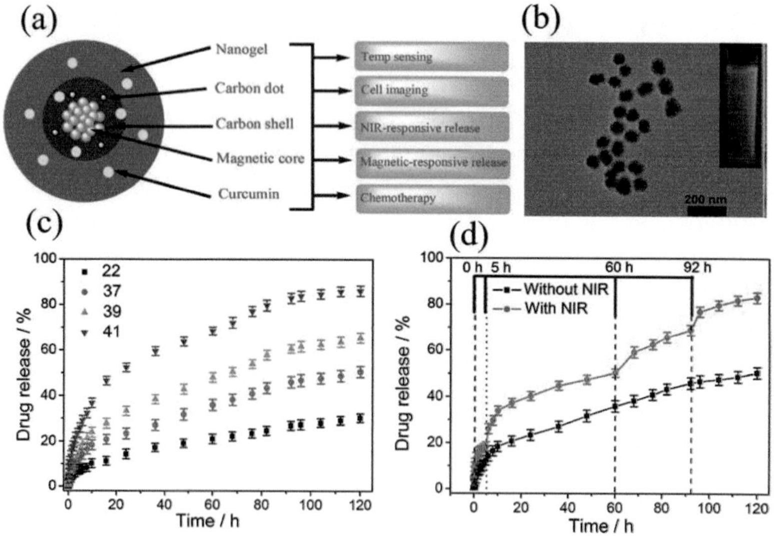

Figure 4.9 (a) Schematic representation of thermo-responsive, magnetic nanogels, (b) TEM image of the core-shell-corona nanogels, (c) release profile of curcumin at different temperatures, and (d) release profile of curcumin with and without NIR light irradiation [71]. Reproduced with permission from H. Wang, J. Yi, S. Mukherjee, P. Banerjee, and S. Zhou, "Magnetic/NIR-thermally responsive hybrid nanogels for optical temperature sensing, tumor cell imaging and triggered drug release," *Nanoscale*, vol. 6, no. 21, pp. 13001–13011, 2014, Copyright (2014), Royal Society of Chemistry.

their system, which combined biodegradability, serum stability, high iron oxide loading, and enhanced MRI contrast, render it promising for application in image-guided drug delivery. An intriguing approach to the development of temperature-sensitive theranostic agents was proposed by Wang et al. They described the synthesis of multifunctional, temperature-responsive core-shell-corona nanogels bearing clustered SPIONs in the core, a porous carbon shell with encapsulated fluorescent carbon dots, and a thermo-responsive poly(N-isopropylacrylamide-*co*-acrylamide) (poly(NiPAm-AAm)) cross-linked corona (Fig. 4.9a,b) [71]. The complex nanoparticles allowed the encapsulation and temperature-controlled release of the anticancer drug curcumin, from the poly(NiPAm-AAm) hydrogel corona as a function of the temperature of the local environmental media or via external stimuli, including NIR light irradiation or an alternating magnetic field (Fig. 4.9c,d). Moreover, the excellent colloidal stability, photoluminescent, and superparamagnetic properties, and the non-toxicity of the hybrid nanogels, in combination with their ability to overcome cellular barriers and enter into the intracellular region, render them highly promising candidates for tunable optical imaging as a function of the environmental temperature variation.

An alternative type of hybrid nanotheranostics, which have also attracted great interest due to the local change of the pH at the tumor site, is the pH-responsive system. Lee and coworkers described a fascinating theranostic platform based on polymer caged nanobins (PCNs) for simultaneous MRI imaging and pH-controlled release of therapeutic molecules [72]. The PCNs comprised a liposomal structure modified with cholesterol and terminated with cross-linked poly(acrylic acid) bearing functional alkyne groups. Gadolinium (III) (Gd^{III}) was used as the MRI contrast agent, which was conjugated onto the alkyne-functionalized surface of the PCNs via copper(I)-catalyzed click ligation, whereas gemcitabine, a well-known anticancer drug, was loaded within the liposomal structure (Fig. 4.10). Biocompatibility results showed minimum toxicity of the gemcitabine-free Gd^{III}-PCNs, high PCN cellular uptake, and significantly enhanced contrast in the MR images of NIH/3T3 mouse cells. The acid-triggered drug release was also demonstrated and attributed to the pH-responsive polymer shells of the PCNs. Another intriguing multifunctional, pH-responsive hybrid theranostic platform was reported by Yang et al. [73]. The theranostic nanocarrier comprised SPION nanoparticles functionalized with hydrophilic maleimide-terminated PEG chains and DOX conjugated onto the SPIONs via pH-sensitive hydrazone linkages. The cRGD peptide, used to increase tumor targeting, and 1,4,7-triazacyclononane-N,N',N-triacetic acid, a macrocyclic chelating agent for ^{64}Cu, employed for positron emission tomography (PET), were both conjugated at the maleimide PEG chain ends, affording a theranostic agent with targeting properties.

A dual, temperature- and pH-responsive theranostic nanoplatform based on core-shell nanoparticles, comprising SPIONs as the inorganic core and a PNiPAm-*b*-PAA diblock copolymer as the responsive polymer shell, was reported by

Sahoo and coworkers [74]. Folic acid was tethered to the surface of the particles as the tumor-targeting ligand, and rhodamine B isothiocyanate was conjugated as a fluorescent imaging agent. The anticancer drug DOX, entrapped within the polymeric shell, was released upon appropriately tuning the solution pH and temperature at lysosomal-relevant values. Therefore, a faster release was found at pH 5.0 and 37 °C compared to the release rate at pH 5.0 and 25 °C, and was attributed to the collapse of the PNiPAm in the shell. Finally, biological studies verified the higher cellular uptake of the nanoparticles by HeLa cancer cells, compared to normal fibroblast cells, due to the EPR effect and the significant cell death caused by the DOX-loaded nanoparticles.

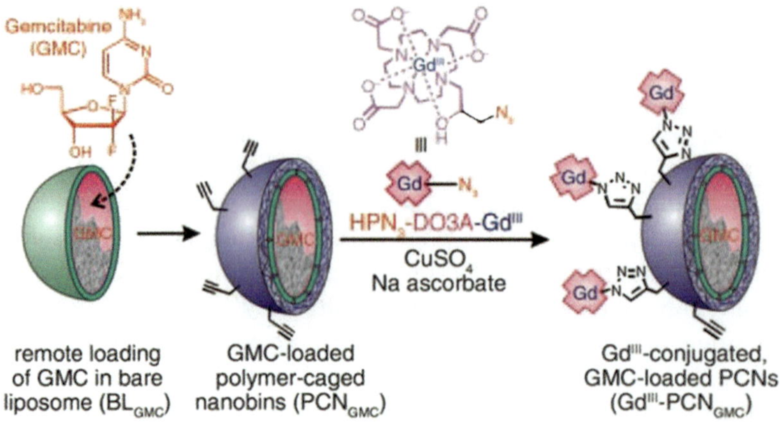

Figure 4.10 Schematic representation of the synthetic approach to prepare gemcitabine-loaded polymer-caged nanobins conjugated with Gd^{III} contrast agents [72]. Reproduced with permission from S. M. Lee et al., "Modular polymer-caged nanobins as a theranostic platform with enhanced magnetic resonance relaxivity and pH-responsive drug release," *Angew. Chemie - Int. Ed.*, vol. 49, no. 51, pp. 9960–9964, 2010, Copyright (2010), John Wiley & Sons Inc.

While temperature and pH have been extensively explored as stimuli in drug release, light has lately emerged as a powerful, spatiotemporally controlled external stimulus, and therefore, photo-sensitive nanocarriers have attracted particular attention. To the best of our knowledge, despite the extensively reported photo-responsive drug release systems, hybrid photo-responsive theranostic nanoparticles are still limited in the literature.

Jalani and coworkers reported for the first time a novel NIR-triggered theranostic system based on lanthanide-doped upconverting nanoparticles (UCNPs) individually coated with a photodegradable hydrogel comprising chitosan cross-linked with a photolabile cross-linker [75]. The therapeutic modality was confirmed for the controlled delivery of large biomolecules by encapsulating a fluorescent protein, FITC-BSA, within the cross-linked polymer matrix and releasing it upon NIR irradiation of the UCNPs at λ = 980 nm, which caused the cleavage of the photo-degradable hydrogel linkages. The imaging modality was conferred by the upconverted NIR light, which allows for the tracking of the particles under the tissue and renders this theranostic system advantageous for deep tissue bioimaging.

4.5 Conclusions and Future Perspectives

Theranostic agents used simultaneously for therapy and imaging of the diseased site or tissue have attracted particular attention during the last two decades. Among them, polymer and hybrid (organic-inorganic) nanotheranostics have been extensively studied as personalized treatment platforms in nanomedicine, because they combine unique advantages, such as higher stability, prolonged circulation time in the body, and non-toxicity. Polymeric activatable or stimuli-responsive theranostic agent is a special class of polymer nanotheranostics that can further enable stimuli-controlled, targeted drug release, and thus minimizing the damage to healthy tissues.

While most examples described in the literature are related to systems that respond to the effect of temperature and pH, nanotheranostic agents being sensitive to other remote, physical stimuli such as light irradiation or a magnetic field, have lately been reported. However, despite the progress in designing and synthesizing such "smart" systems, the field remains highly unexplored and possesses tremendous challenges. The ability to combine diagnostic or imaging modalities that are non-toxic and operate in a cooperative manner requires a fundamental understanding of the materials' properties and their dynamic behavior. To date, there are only very few examples of photoactivatable polymer theranostic agents, which use light irradiation to simultaneously induce drug release and cell imaging, but lack to demonstrate additional responsive properties, such as polymer degradation, which would facilitate its excretion from the body. Moreover, the use of other biologically relevant stimuli, such as magnetic field and ultrasound, have not been reported yet. A challenge in this direction will be the synthesis of polymeric and hybrid materials that respond to these stimuli, while undergoing dynamic changes in their properties and function in a spatiotemporally controlled manner. To address the above challenges, future developments in the field should focus on combining novel materials and nanoparticles' engineering strategies to access intelligent systems that will operate in a complex environment such as biological systems.

References

1. Feng, L., Wang, H., and Xue, X. (2020) Recent progress of nanomedicine in the treatment of central nervous system diseases. *Adv. Ther.*, **1900159**, pp. 1900159.
2. Shi, J., Kantoff, P.W., Wooster, R., and Farokhzad, O.C. (2017) Cancer nanomedicine: Progress, challenges and opportunities. *Nat. Rev. Cancer*, **17**, pp. 20–37.
3. Yuan, F., Thiele, G.M., and Wang, D. (2011) Nanomedicine development for autoimmune diseases. *Drug Dev. Res.*, **72**, pp. 703–716.
4. Press, D. (2012) Clinical development of liposome-based drugs: Formulation, characterization, and therapeutic efficacy. pp. 49–60.
5. Idée, J.-M., Louguet, S., Ballet, S., and Corot, C. (2013) Theranostics and contrast-agents for medical imaging: A pharmaceutical company viewpoint. *Quant. Imaging Med. Surg.*, **3**, pp. 292–297.
6. Siegel, R.L., Miller, K.D., and Jemal, A. (2018) Cancer statistics, 2018. *CA. Cancer J. Clin.*, **68**, pp. 7–30.
7. MacEwan, S.R. and Chilkoti, A. (2017) From composition to cure: A systems engineering approach to anticancer drug carriers. *Angew. Chemie – Int. Ed.*, **56**, pp. 6712–6733.
8. Tran, S., DeGiovanni, P.-J., Piel, B., and Rai, P. (2017) Cancer nanomedicine: A review of recent success in drug delivery. *Clin. Transl. Med.*, **6**, pp. 44.

9. Danhier, F., Feron, O., and Préat, V. (2010) To exploit the tumor microenvironment: Passive and active tumor targeting of nanocarriers for anti-cancer drug delivery. *J. Control. Release*, **148**, pp. 135–146.

10. Kumar Khanna, V. (2012) Targeted delivery of nanomedicines. *ISRN Pharmacol.*, **2012**, pp. 1–9.

11. Fang, J., Nakamura, H., and Maeda, H. (2011) The EPR effect: Unique features of tumor blood vessels for drug delivery, factors involved, and limitations and augmentation of the effect. *Adv. Drug Deliv. Rev.*, **63**, pp. 136–151.

12. Wicki, A., Witzigmann, D., Balasubramanian, V., and Huwyler, J. (2015) Nanomedicine in cancer therapy: Challenges, opportunities, and clinical applications. *J. Control. Release*, **200**, pp. 138–157.

13. Spikes, J.D. (1991) The origin and meaning of the term "photodynamic" (as used in "photodynamic therapy", for example). *J. Photochem. Photobiol. B Biol.*, **9**, pp. 369–371.

14. Bergh, H. van den and J.-P. Ballini (2004) Principles of photodynamic therapy. *Mitochondrion*, pp. 1–27.

15. Macdonald, I.A.N.J. and Dougherty, T.J. (2008) MacDonald2007. *J. Porphyr. Phthalocyanines*, **5**, pp. 1–18.

16. Ormond, A.B. and Freeman, H.S. (2013) Dye sensitizers for photodynamic therapy. *Materials (Basel)*, **6,** pp. 817–840.

17. Chinna Ayya Swamy, P., Sivaraman, G., Priyanka, R.N., Raja, S.O., Ponnuvel, K., Shanmugpriya, J., and Gulyani, A. (2020) Near infrared (NIR) absorbing dyes as promising photosensitizer for photo dynamic therapy. *Coord. Chem. Rev.*, **411**, pp. 213233.

18. Imato, K., Ohira, K., Yamaguchi, M., Enoki, T., and Ooyama, Y. (2020) Phenazine-based photosensitizers for singlet oxygen generation. *Mater. Chem. Front.*, **4,** pp. 589–596.

19. Allison, R.R., Downie, G.H., Cuenca, R., Hu, X.H., Childs, C.J.H., and Sibata, C.H. (2004) Photosensitizers in clinical PDT. *Photodiagnosis Photodyn. Ther.*, **1**, pp. 27–42.

20. Li, L., Chen, Y., Chen, W., Tan, Y., Chen, H., and Yin, J. (2019) Photodynamic therapy based on organic small molecular fluorescent dyes. *Chinese Chem. Lett.*, **30**, pp. 1689–1703.

21. Bekmukhametova, A., Ruprai, H., Hook, J.M., Mawad, D., Houang, J., and Lauto, A. (2020) Photodynamic therapy with nanoparticles to combat microbial infection and resistance. *Nanoscale*, **12**, pp. 21034–21059.

22. Giuliano, E.A., Ota, J., and Tucker, S.A. (2007) Photodynamic therapy: Basic principles and potential uses for the veterinary ophthalmologist. *Vet. Ophthalmol.*, **10**, pp. 337–343.

23. Agostinis, P., Berg, K., Cengel, K.A., Foster, T.H., Girotti, A.W., Gollnick, S.O., Hahn, S.M., Hamblin, M.R., Juzeniene, A., Kessel, D., Korbelik, M., Moan, J., Mroz, P., Nowis, D., Piette, J., Wilson, B.C., and Golab, J. (2011) Photodynamic therapy of cancer: An update. *CA. Cancer J. Clin.*, **61**, pp. 250– 281.

24. Li, X., Kim, J., Yoon, J., and Chen, X. (2017) Cancer-associated, stimuli-driven, turn on theranostics for multimodality imaging and therapy. *Adv. Mater.*, **29**, pp. 1–24.

25. Jo, S.D., Ku, S.H., Won, Y.Y., Kim, S.H., and Kwon, I.C. (2016) Targeted nanotheranostics for future personalized medicine: Recent progress in cancer therapy. *Theranostics*, **6**, pp. 1362–1377.

26. Kormeili, T., Yamauchi, P.S., and Lowe, N.J. (2004) Topical photodynamic therapy in clinical dermatology. *Br. J. Dermatol.*, **150**, pp. 1061–1069.

27. Jain, M., Zellweger, M., Wagnières, G., van den Bergh, H., Cook, S., and Giraud, M.N. (2017) Photodynamic therapy for the treatment of atherosclerotic plaque: Lost in translation? *Cardiovasc. Ther.*, **35** (2).

28. Miller, J., Schmidt-Erfurth, U., and Sickenberg, M. (2000) Photodynamic therapy with verteporfin for choroidal neovascularization caused by age-related macular degeneration. *Evidence-Based Eye Care*, **1**, pp. 94–95.

29. Mahmoudi, H., Bahador, A., Pourhajibagher, M., and Alikhani, M.Y. (2018) Antimicrobial photodynamic therapy: An effective alternative approach to control bacterial infections. *J. Lasers Med. Sci.*, **9**, pp. 154–160.

30. Akimov, A.B., Seregin, V.E., Rusanov, K. V., Tyurina, E.G., Glushko, T.A., Nevzorov, V.P., Nevzorova, O.F., and Akimova, E. V. (1998) Nd:YAG interstitial laser thermotherapy in the treatment of breast cancer. *Lasers Surg. Med.*, **22**, pp. 257–267.

31. Gellci, K. and Mehrmohammadi, M. (2014) Photothermal therapy. *Encycl. Cancer*, pp. 1–5.

32. Golovynskyi, S., Golovynska, I., Stepanova, L.I., Datsenko, O.I., Liu, L., Qu, J., and Ohulchanskyy, T.Y. (2018) Optical windows for head tissues in near-infrared and short-wave infrared regions: Approaching transcranial light applications. *J. Biophotonics*, **11** (12).

33. Jung, H.S., Verwilst, P., Sharma, A., Shin, J., Sessler, J.L., and Kim, J.S. (2018) Organic molecule-based photothermal agents: An expanding photothermal therapy universe. *Chem. Soc. Rev.*, **47**, pp. 2280–2297.

34. Bhattarai, P. and Dai, Z. (2017) Cyanine based nanoprobes for cancer theranostics. *Adv. Healthc. Mater.*, **6**, pp. 1–23.

35. Liu, C., Liu, B., Zhao, J., Di, Z., Chen, D., Gu, Z., Li, L., and Zhao, Y. (2020) Nd^{3+}-Sensitized upconversion metal–organic frameworks for mitochondria-targeted amplified photodynamic therapy. *Angew. Chemie - Int. Ed.*

36. Kim, M., Lee, J.H., and Nam, J.M. (2019) Plasmonic photothermal nanoparticles for biomedical applications. *Adv. Sci.*, **6** (17).

37. Brongersma, M.L., Halas, N.J., and Nordlander, P. (2015) Plasmon-induced hot carrier science and technology. *Nat. Nanotechnol.*, **10**, pp. 25–34.

38. McHale, A.P., Callan, J.F., Nomikou, N., Fowley, C., and Callan, B. (2016) Sonodynamic therapy: Concept, mechanism and application to cancer treatment. *Adv. Exp. Med. Biol.*, **880**, pp. 429–450.

39. Fan, C.H., Lin, C.Y., Liu, H.L., and Yeh, C.K. (2017) Ultrasound targeted CNS gene delivery for Parkinson's disease treatment. *J. Control. Release*, **261**, pp. 246–262.

40. Dogra, V.S., Zhang, M., and Bhatt, S. (2009) High-intensity focused ultrasound (HIFU) therapy applications. *Ultrasound Clin.*, **4**, pp. 307–321.

41. Manthe, R.L., Foy, S.P., Krishnamurthy, N., Sharma, B., and Labhasetwar, V. (2010) Reviews tumor ablation and nanotechnology. *Mol. Pharm.*, pp. 1034– 1044.

42. Wang, X., Zhong, X., Gong, F., Chao, Y., and Cheng, L. (2020) Newly developed strategies for improving sonodynamic therapy. *Mater. Horizons*, **7**, pp. 2028–2046.

43. Lin, X., Song, J., Chen, X., and Yang, H. (2020) Ultrasound-activated sensitizers and applications. *Angew. Chemie - Int. Ed.*, **59**, pp. 14212–14233.

44. Li, D., Yang, Y., Li, D., Pan, J., Chu, C., and Liu, G. (2021) Organic sonosensitizers for sonodynamic therapy: From small molecules and nanoparticles toward clinical development. *Small*, **17**, pp. 1–20.

45. Singh, R.K., Patel, K.D., Leong, K.W., and Kim, H.W. (2017) Progress in nanotheranostics based on mesoporous silica nanomaterial platforms. *ACS Appl. Mater. Interfaces*, **9**, pp. 10309–10337.

46. Weissleder, R. and Pittet, M.J. (2008) Imaging in the era of molecular oncology. *Nature*, **452**, pp. 580–589.

47. Liu, Y., Yu, G., Tian, M., and Zhang, H. (2011) Optical probes and the applications in multimodality imaging. *Contrast Media Mol. Imaging*, **6**, pp. 169–177.

48. Martelli, C., Lo Dico, A., Diceglie, C., Lucignani, G., and Ottobrini, L. (2016) Optical imaging probes in oncology. *Oncotarget*, **7**, pp. 48753–48787.

49. Mezzanotte, L., Blankevoort, V., Löwik, C.W.G.M., and Kaijzel, E.L. (2014) A novel luciferase fusion protein for highly sensitive optical imaging: From single-cell analysis to in vivo whole-body bioluminescence imaging. *Anal. Bioanal. Chem.*, **406**, pp. 5727–5734.

50. Imamura, T., Saitou, T., and Kawakami, R. (2018) In vivo optical imaging of cancer cell function and tumor microenvironment. *Cancer Sci.*, **109**, pp. 912– 918.

51. Bentolila, L.A., Ebenstein, Y., and Weiss, S. (2009) Quantum dots for in vivo small-animal imaging. *J. Nucl. Med.*, **50**, pp. 493–496.

52. So, M.K., Xu, C., Loening, A.M., Gambhir, S.S., and Rao, J. (2006) Self-illuminating quantum dot conjugates for in vivo imaging. *Nat. Biotechnol.*, **24**, pp. 339–343.

53. Gao, X., Cui, Y., Levenson, R.M., Chung, L.W.K., and Nie, S. (2004) In vivo cancer targeting and imaging with semiconductor quantum dots. *Nat. Biotechnol.*, **22**, pp. 969–976.

54. Sedgwick, A.C., Brewster, J.T., Harvey, P., Iovan, D.A., Smith, G., He, X.P., Tian, H., Sessler, J.L., and James, T.D. (2020) Metal-based imaging agents: Progress towards interrogating neurodegenerative disease. *Chem. Soc. Rev.*, **49**, pp. 2886–2915.

55. Kalash, R.S., Lakshmanan, V.K., Cho, C.-S., and Park, I.-K. (2016) In: Ebara, M., ed. *Biomaterials Nanoarchitectonics*, William Andrew Publishing, pp. 197–215.

56. Moran, C.M. and Thomson, A.J.W. (2020) Preclinical ultrasound imaging—A review of techniques and imaging applications. *Front. Phys.*, **8**.

57. Matsunaga, T.O., Sheeran, P.S., Luois, S., Streeter, J.E., Mullin, L.B., Banerjee, B., and Dayton, P.A. (2012) Phase-change nanoparticles using highly volatile perfluorocarbons: Toward a platform for extravascular ultrasound imaging. *Theranostics*, **2**, pp. 1185–1198.

58. Lee, R.S., Lin, C.H., Aljuffali, I.A., Hu, K.Y., and Fang, J.Y. (2015) Passive targeting of thermosensitive diblock copolymer micelles to the lungs:

Synthesis and characterization of poly(N-isopropylacrylamide)-block-poly(ε-caprolactone). *J. Nanobiotechnology*, **13**, pp. 1–12.

59. Pearce, A.K., Rolfe, B.E., Russell, P.J., Tse, B.W.C., Whittaker, A.K., Fuchs, A. V., and Thurecht, K.J. (2014) Development of a polymer theranostic for prostate cancer. *Polym. Chem.*, **5**, pp. 6932–6942.
60. Pearce, A.K., Simpson, J.D., Fletcher, N.L., Houston, Z.H., Fuchs, A. V., Russell, P.J., Whittaker, A.K., and Thurecht, K.J. (2017) Localised delivery of doxorubicin to prostate cancer cells through a PSMA-targeted hyperbranched polymer theranostic. *Biomaterials*, **141**, pp. 330–339.
61. Guo, J., Hong, H., Chen, G., Shi, S., Nayak, T.R., Theuer, C.P., Barnhart, T.E., Cai, W., and Gong, S. (2014) Theranostic unimolecular micelles based on brush-shaped amphiphilic block copolymers for tumor-targeted drug delivery and positron emission tomography imaging. *ACS Appl. Mater. Interfaces*, **6**, pp. 21769–21779.
62. Park, S.Y., Baik, H.J., Oh, Y.T., Oh, K.T., Youn, Y.S., and Lee, E.S. (2011) A smart polysaccharide/drug conjugate for photodynamic therapy. *Angew. Chemie - Int. Ed.*, **50**, pp. 1644–1647.
63. Li, Y., Li, Y., Zhang, X., Xu, X., Zhang, Z., Hu, C., He, Y., and Gu, Z. (2016) Supramolecular PEGylated dendritic systems as pH/redox dual-responsive theranostic nanoplatforms for platinum drug delivery and NIR imaging. *Theranostics*, **6**, pp. 1293–1305.
64. Zhen, X., Zhang, J., Huang, J., Xie, C., Miao, Q., and Pu, K. (2018) Macrotheranostic probe with disease-activated near-infrared fluorescence, photoacoustic, and photothermal signals for imaging-guided therapy. *Angew. Chemie - Int. Ed.*, **57**, pp. 7804–7808.
65. Xu, X., Zeng, Z., Huang, Z., Sun, Y., Huang, Y., Chen, J., Ye, J., Yang, H., Yang, C., and Zhao, C. (2020) Near-infrared light-triggered degradable hyaluronic acid hydrogel for on-demand drug release and combined chemo-photodynamic therapy. *Carbohydr. Polym.*, **229**, pp. 115394.
66. Biglione, C., Sousa-Herves, A., Menger, M., Wedepohl, S., Calderón, M., and Strumia, M.C. (2015) Facile ultrasonication approach for the efficient synthesis of ethylene glycol-based thermoresponsive nanogels. *RSC Adv.*, **5**, pp. 15407– 15413.
67. Asadian-Birjand, M., Bergueiro, J., Wedepohl, S., and Calderón, M. (2016) Near infrared dye conjugated nanogels for combined photodynamic and photothermal therapies. *Macromol. Biosci.*, pp. 1432–1441.

68. Purushotham, S., Chang, P.E.J., Rumpel, H., Kee, I.H.C., Ng, R.T.H., Chow, P.K.H., Tan, C.K., and Ramanujan, R. V. (2009) Thermoresponsive core-shell magnetic nanoparticles for combined modalities of cancer therapy. *Nanotechnology*, **20** (30).

69. Wadajkar, A.S., Menon, J.U., Tsai, Y.S., Gore, C., Dobin, T., Gandee, L., Kangasniemi, K., Takahashi, M., Manandhar, B., Ahn, J.M., Hsieh, J.T., and Nguyen, K.T. (2013) Prostate cancer-specific thermo-responsive polymer-coated iron oxide nanoparticles. *Biomaterials*, **34**, pp. 3618–3625.

70. Talelli, M., Rijcken, C.J.F., Lammers, T., Seevinck, P.R., Storm, G., Van Nostrum, C.F., and Hennink, W.E. (2009) Superparamagnetic iron oxide nanoparticles encapsulated in biodegradable thermosensitive polymeric micelles: Toward a targeted nanomedicine suitable for image-guided drug delivery. *Langmuir*, **25**, pp. 2060–2067.

71. Wang, H., Yi, J., Mukherjee, S., Banerjee, P., and Zhou, S. (2014) Magnetic/NIR-thermally responsive hybrid nanogels for optical temperature sensing, tumor cell imaging and triggered drug release. *Nanoscale*, **6**, pp. 13001–13011.

72. Lee, S.M., Song, Y., Hong, B.J., MacRenaris, K.W., Mastarone, D.J., O'Halloran, T. V., Meade, T.J., and Nguyen, S.T. (2010) Modular polymer-caged nanobins as a theranostic platform with enhanced magnetic resonance relaxivity and pH-responsive drug release. *Angew. Chemie - Int. Ed.*, **49**, pp. 9960–9964.

73. Yang, X., Hong, H., Grailer, J.J., Rowland, I.J., Javadi, A., Hurley, S.A., Xiao, Y., Yang, Y., Zhang, Y., Nickles, R.J., Cai, W., Steeber, D.A., and Gong, S. (2011) CRGD-functionalized, DOX-conjugated, and ^{64}Cu-labeled superparamagnetic iron oxide nanoparticles for targeted anticancer drug delivery and PET/MR imaging. *Biomaterials*, **32**, pp. 4151–4160.

74. Sahoo, B., Devi, K.S.P., Banerjee, R., Maiti, T.K., Pramanik, P., and Dhara, D. (2013) Thermal and pH responsive polymer-tethered multifunctional magnetic nanoparticles for targeted delivery of anticancer drug. *ACS Appl. Mater. Interfaces*, **5**, pp. 3884–3893.

75. Jalani, G., Naccache, R., Rosenzweig, D.H., Haglund, L., Vetrone, F., and Cerruti, M. (2016) Photocleavable hydrogel-coated upconverting nanoparticles: A multifunctional theranostic platform for NIR imaging and on-demand macromolecular delivery. *J. Am. Chem. Soc.*, **138**, pp. 1078– 1083.

Chapter 5

Protein- and Peptide-Inorganic Nanoparticles as Theranostic Vehicles

Chrysoula Kokotidou,[a,b,*] Sara H. Mejías,[c,*] and Evangelos Georgilis[d,e]

[a]*Department of Materials Science and Technology, University of Crete, Voutes Campus, Heraklion, 70013 Crete, Greece*
[b]*Institute for Electronic Structure and Laser, FORTH, N. Plastira 100, Heraklion, 70013 Crete, Greece*
[c]*Department of Chemistry, Ångström Laboratory (Uppsala University), Lägerhyddsvägen, 1, Uppsala 752 37, Sweden*
[d]*CIC nanoGUNE (BRTA), Tolosa Hiribidea 76, Donostia-San Sebastián 20018, Spain*
[e]*Current address: BBD BioPhenix SLU Mikeletegi Pasealekua, 56, 20009 Donostia-San Sebastián, Spain*

evangelosmgeorgilis@gmail.com

Inorganic nanoparticles (NPs) have gained interest in the field of theranostics, primarily due to their unique magnetic and optical properties as well as their capability to deliver drugs and other bioactive molecules. However, they still represent only a small part of the nanomedicine market. The difficulty regarding the clinical translation of inorganic NPs is mostly related to safety issues and undesired interactions with the biological media (e.g.,

*Equally contributing authors.

Functional Materials in Biomedical Applications
Edited by Costas Demetzos, Natassa Pippa, and Nikolaos Naziris

ISBN 978-981-4968-65-2 (Hardcover), 978-1-003-41146-8 (eBook)
www.jennystanford.com

blood and gastrointestinal fluids). In this regard, functionalization with proteins or peptides is being employed to develop hybrids with enhanced biocompatibility and pharmacokinetics. In this chapter, we describe how proteins of natural origin, short peptides, or engineered amino acid sequences are combined with inorganic NPs to produce safe and efficient theranostic nanoformulations. Emphasis will also be given to their use in different biomedical applications, descriptions of their functionality, biomolecule-nanoparticle interactions, and the offered advantages.

5.1 Introduction

5.1.1 Inorganic Particles

5.1.1.1 Definition

Nano-scaled materials that are based on ceramics, metals and their alloys, and carbon are defined as inorganic NPs [1, 2]. The size of these particles ranges between 1 nm and 100 nm, while they can be produced in a variety of shapes.

The interaction of inorganic NPs with biological systems was known since antiquity, when ancient Egyptians, Greeks, and Romans would dye their hair using a lead nanoparticle recipe [3]. Of course, the lethal effect of this dye was not known back in the time because of the short life expectancy. Thousands of years later, with the emergence of nanotechnology in the mid-80s, the variety of nanoscale materials expanded substantially with the synthesis of fullerene, nanocrystals, mesoporous silica, and quantum dots (QDs). These nanomaterials exhibit unique optical, acoustic, and magnetic properties [4]. To our date, these properties are exploited in order to heal the human body rather than to intoxicate it for the sake of beauty. The development of inorganic-based nanomedicines starts with NP synthesis, while further derivatization of the NP surface is often a prerequisite to addressing the challenges associated with in vivo administration.

5.1.1.2 Synthesis

The fabrication of inorganic NPs can be achieved using a variety of physical and chemical approaches. We will hereby list the ones that are commonly used by the particle category:

Metals and metal oxides

The reduction of metal salts is one of the oldest methods employed to produce metal NPs and is frequently used to date. This method was developed by Turkevich et al. in 1951 and refined by Frens et al. in 1973 for the fabrication of gold nanoparticles (AuNPs) [5]. However, the same synthetic route can be applied to create NPs of other metals (e.g., Ag, Pt, Cu), while it can also be applied stepwise to make core-shell NPs with different metals [2]. The reaction can take place in aqueous or organic solvents. The most common reducing agents used are usually sodium citrate, sodium borohydrate, or phosphorous [2]. The reduction of metal ions into atoms leads to the nucleation and growth of the colloids. At the growth step, stabilizing agents (e.g., organic ligands, polymers) are required to prevent the precipitation of agglomerates [6]. The choice of reduction agent, pH, and stabilizing agent play a crucial role in the final shape and size of the NP [7]. The reduction in surfactant-based colloidal assemblies (e.g., micelles, vesicles) provides additional control over the shape and size of the metal colloids [8].

Especially in the case of iron oxide nanoparticles (IONPs), a process that is often performed is coprecipitation [7, 9]. The method involves preparing an aqueous solution of ferric (Fe^{3+}) and ferrous (Fe^{2+}) salts in a 1:2 molar ratio to which base is added under a non-oxidizing atmosphere. Crystallization of the NPs occurs at this step, provided that the salt concentration is above the nucleation threshold. The parameters that affect the size and shape of the NPs depend on experimental conditions such as the type and ratio of the ferric/ferrous salts, the temperature, the pH, and the ionic strength of the solution.

Another method includes the thermal decomposition of metal salts in a solid or liquid state under an inert atmosphere [10, 11]. This process can be coupled with the precipitation of particles after chemical reduction. Even though thermolytic approaches are known to yield well-defined monodisperse particles, they are less commonly used due to the energy consumption and space occupation of the furnace.

Quantum dots

The methods applied for the synthesis of QDs are largely based on the ones applied for metal NP fabrication [12]. Core-shell QDs can be obtained by heating organometallic salts, chemical reduction of metal salts, electrochemical methods, and ion-exchange reactions. The chemical synthesis is usually conducted in organic solvents, so a "greener" alternative in aqueous media is being investigated [13]. For aqueous synthesis, the use of surfactants and polymers may be required to ensure particle stability.

Silica

The aforementioned NP synthesis in surfactant assemblies is also largely applied to obtain silica NPs. Silica precursors (such as tetraethylorthosilicate-TEOS) condensate in the surfactant template (mostly spherical/rod-like micelles or vesicles), yielding different shapes of particles, either compact or porous [14]. The template is then removed by thermal treatment.

Carbon NPs

Carbon-based particle synthesis usually requires a bulk carbon material source. The bulk material is decomposed into the NPs (dots, nanotubes) by laser ablation, electrochemical, or thermal decomposition [15, 16]. Decomposition of small organic molecules is also an alternative to obtain these nanostructures.

The synthesis methods above are continuously being optimized, mainly in order to minimize the adverse environmental impact and increase large-scale production with high batch-to-batch reproducibility. To this end, microfluidics and biomineralization on biological templates are also investigated [17].

5.1.1.3 Applications

Inorganic NPs have already been established in technology for applications in energy storage, catalysis, and electronics [18].

However, their unique properties allow us to expand their use in biomedicine. Starting with the IONPs, the principal reason for their use in the human body is their magnetic properties. IONPs present excellent contrast ultrasound imaging and magnetic resonance imaging (MRI) [19]. They also can be targeted by the use of a magnetic field in order to deliver therapeutics in a targeted manner, and also generate heat under the effect of the field or via absorption of near-infrared (NIR) light, damaging cancer tissue [20]. Silica NPs can also be used as contrast agents in MRI and ultrasound imaging and their porosity allows for a high payload of therapeutics [14, 21].

Noble metal NPs are amenable to chemical modifications and present surface plasmon resonance properties [22], which render them excellent as diagnostic probes. However, these particles are also important for therapeutic applications. AuNPs have been widely used in photothermal therapy (PTT). Due to their unique surface plasmon resonance, they can convert light energy (NIR) into heat. When optical radiation in the NIR wavelength range (700–2000 nm) is applied to the AuNPs, heat is accumulated and that leads to cancer cell death. Being able to target AuNPs to the tumor area offers the advantage of minimizing damage to nearby healthy tissues. Cell-penetrating peptides (CPPs) and tissue targeting peptides conjugates increase the target efficacy of the PTT and chemotherapeutic drugs by binding to cancer cell surface receptors [23]. On the other hand, silver nanoparticles (AgNPs) are known for their antimicrobial and anticancer properties, promoting cell apoptosis via ROS generation and DNA damage [24].

QDs have great fluorescence properties, which make them excellent for cell labeling [25]. However, they can also generate ROS with the application of electromagnetic stimuli, which can be a powerful therapeutic tool against drug-resistant microorganisms [26].

Carbon-based particles present good electrical and optical properties for the development of biosensors [16]. In vivo investigation is currently limited, but there are potential applications of carbon nanoparticles as delivery vehicles, tissue imaging, or regeneration (especially for neuron regeneration because carbon nanotubes [CNTs] are electrically conductive) [15].

Even though we see this broad spectrum of applications, inorganic NPs represent a small part of the nanomedicine industry. The FDA-approved products mainly include IONP-based formulations for the treatment of iron deficiency [27–29]. The contrast agents used in the clinic consist of barium sulfate, organic compounds of iodine, and chelated gadolinium (mostly diethylenetriaminepentaacetic acid-gadolinium, DTPA-Gd), while therapeutic nanoformulations are mostly polymer-based. This is due to various challenges associated with the limited translation of inorganic NPs from the bench to the bedside.

5.1.1.4 Challenges

Nanomedicines are required to be stable, perform their specific therapeutic goal in a well-defined time frame, and once this is achieved, be eliminated from the body without side effects. When administered to the human body, non-functionalized inorganic NPs encounter a water-based environment and various biological entities with which they have the potential to interact [6]. Therefore, hydrophobic NPs lose their colloidal stability and charged NPs present altered properties due to the interaction with ions. Moreover, the large specific surface area and high surface energy of the NPs lead to the adsorption of biomolecules onto their surface. The biomolecules forming the particle corona include opsonins, the proteins that promote NP clearance [30]. Opsonized NPs are phagocytosed by macrophages in the spleen and liver, which may be undesirable if the therapeutic effect is not destined for these organs. The size of inorganic NPs is also important for their fate in vivo: too small particles are rapidly cleared by the renal system, while too large particles may be phagocytosed by cells of the reticuloendothelial system [6]. To avoid these effects, the size of the NPs should be 10–100 nm, which may be restrictive for their properties (e.g., QD fluorescence) [31]. Also, the NPs may consist of metal atoms that are toxic, so it is important to prevent their leakage into the human body [26, 31]. Given the above, it is important to ensure the integrity and colloidal stability of the NPs during their action, which can be primarily achieved using an organic coating.

5.1.1.5 Protein and peptide inorganic hybrids

An important advantage of inorganic NPs is the ease of functionalization on their surface. A well-known example is the functionalization of AuNPs with thiols [32], while other types of NPs can be further derivatized to present desired functional groups [33]. To this end, an additional step of silanization or ligand exchange on the surface may be applied after synthesis [34]. This allows for the conjugation of various polymers and biomolecules on their surface.

Many synthetic polymer coatings are used in nanomedicine formulations, with the most common being polyethylene glycol [9]. The hydrophilicity and biodegradability of this polymer enhance the colloidal stability and minimize opsonization, rendering inorganic NPs as stealth. However, polymer coatings are usually employed in passive targeting formulations, i.e., the NP passively circulates around the body until uptaken by cells or until reaching the damaged tissue through abnormalities, e.g., extravasation via the enhanced permeability and retention (EPR) effect [35].

Biomolecules, on the other hand, are compatible with the human body and can be obtained in abundance from various natural resources, and significantly enhance the bioavailability of inorganic NPs [36, 37]. Furthermore, proteins and peptides are able to produce various biological effects, the most important being their interaction with cellular receptors, so an NP coating based on these materials can introduce a bioactive targeting property [38]. Amino acid sequences are also amenable to chemical modifications, so their properties can be further tuned or supplemented by applying changes to their side groups [39]. In this chapter, we will see how proteins and peptides can be combined with inorganic NPs in order to develop bioactive nanoformulations and we will also review their respective applications.

5.2 Hybrids with Natural Proteins

An important consideration for protein coatings is the minimization of risks associated with immune response. In this regard, proteins of natural origin are highly desired in terms of safety. These proteins are found in abundance in the human body, animals, or plants and can also be harvested from food or insects. For certain proteins, heterologous production is a good alternative to minimize the content of allergens and promote animal welfare. In this part, we will focus on natural proteins, which are generally regarded as safe (GRAS), and we will see how their hybrids with inorganic NPs are prepared in a straightforward manner for theranostic applications in vivo (Table 5.1).

5.2.1 Proteins of Human Origin

5.2.1.1 Albumin

Albumin is a protein found in abundance in the egg white (ovalbumin) and bovine serum (BSA), but the one derived from the human serum (HSA) is frequently used in nanoformulations to avoid immunogenic reactions.

The development of Abraxane (albumin NP-bound Paclitaxel) has been a major source of inspiration for protein-based nanomedicines [40]. The use of albumin significantly decreased the side effects associated with the excipients of liposomal formulations based on polyethoxylated castor oil-ethanol solvent. Due to its structure, albumin can facilitate the loading of hydrophobic drugs in two sites, while the diversity of amino acids in its sequence enables the application of different orthogonal modifications. The active targeting of albumin is still a matter of dispute; however, its interactions with glycoproteins and secreted protein acidic rich in cysteine (SPARC) are often proposed as mechanisms for the therapeutic effect of albumin-based drugs in inflamed tumors and tissues. Therefore, albumin is frequently used for protein coatings of inorganic NPs.

The most common methods for coating inorganic NPs with albumin are passive or active absorption, desolvation, emulsification, and thermal gelation. These methods are often coupled with the synthesis of the inorganic NPs, resulting in coated NPs that serve different theranostic approaches [41]:

Contrast agents

As previously stated, gadolinium is a commonly used contrast agent. Albumin can enhance the contrast properties of gadolinium and its oxide by increasing its in vivo half-life and reducing toxic ion leakage [42,43]. For example, Chen et al. conjugated DTPA on albumin molecules in order to chelate $^{64}Gd^{3+}$, which they further loaded with a NIR dye, IR825 [44]. The dye introduced an additional fluorescence property to the particle for imaging and also enabled PTT. After intratumoral administration in mice, the group found out that the nanosystem would migrate in the sentinel lymph nodes and inhibit cancer cell metastases after photothermal ablation. Conjugates of BSA with DTPA-Gd were also used by Zhang et al. as a template for the growth of Ag_2S QDs [45]. The composite formulation exhibited better MRI contrast compared to the commercial product Magnevist®, while the QD component enabled detection via fluorescence imaging. Albumin hybrids with IONPs can also serve as theranostic agents, combining MRI detection with drug delivery. Quan et al. embedded dopamine-coated IONPs in HSA loaded with doxorubicin (DOX), which were tested for the treatment of 4T1 tumors in mice [46]. The hybrid particle exhibited enhanced biodistribution compared to the commercial drug Doxil®, while the therapeutic effect was similar between the two formulas. The targeting of the IONP hybrid particles can be further enhanced with the application of an external magnetic field, as was shown in the work of Misak et al. [47].

Photodynamic therapy

For photodynamic therapy (PD) applications, albumin is usually employed as a biocompatible coating or template for AuNPs. Liu et al. used desolvation and crosslinking to prepare Au nanorod-HSA particles loaded with sorafenib [48], a potent antiangiogenic drug against renal carcinoma [49]. The formulation was tested in a human metastatic renal cell carcinoma mouse model and showed that the combination of photothermal ablation and drug release achieved 100% tumor necrosis. NIR irradiation of the coated nanorods without the drug yielded a ~63% necrosis, showing that the drug release significantly complemented the therapeutic effect. Further functionalization of the albumin coating is also applied for the presentation of targeting moieties on the surface of the NP. To that end, folic acid is widely used to target the folate receptor, which is overexpressed in many types of cancer cells. Huang et al. developed framboidal AuNPs by metal templating on BSA [50]. The protein was further functionalized at its primary amines with folic acid and doxorubicin for targeted delivery to a gastric cancer model. Computed tomography (CT) imaging showed enhanced accumulation at the tumor site for the hybrid particles bearing folic acid. Furthermore, the pH-sensitive release of doxorubicin in the tumor microenvironment enhanced the tumor regression effect compared to the free drug. The presentation of targeting moieties is also a useful strategy to cross biological barriers, which do not allow the passive diffusion of therapeutics, such as the blood-brain barrier (BBB). Albumin-inorganic hybrids presenting folic acid have been reported to cross this barrier, while the use of transferrin is another biomimetic way to achieve BBB penetration [51].

Combinatorial strategies

In some cases, inorganic NPs may exhibit different properties, which can be combined to achieve a theranostic effect. In this category, we can find IONPs, which are paramagnetic but also photosensitive. Zhang et al. prepared BSA-coated IONPs doped with manganese to enhance MRI contrast and effectively eliminated 4T1 tumors in mice by NIR light-induced hyperthermia [52]. An alternative method to fulfill a combinatorial strategy is by combining elements with different properties into a single hybrid. For example, the diagnostic function of gadolinium may be complemented using photosensitive probes or other inorganic NPs, with albumin playing a key role in the assembly [53, 54]. You et al. prepared a system of hollow Au nanoshells conjugated with Gd-BSA complexes [55]. These hybrid nanostructures exhibited CT and photoacoustic (PA) activity as well as MRI contrast. The hybrids were further loaded with indocyanine green, a molecule that provided photodynamic/photothermal properties and near-infrared fluorescence (NIRF)/PA imaging capabilities. Thus, the group developed a theranostic agent for

NIRF/PA/CT/MR quadmodal imaging, which achieved tumor inhibition via phototherapy in vivo.

Cell therapies

Certain cell lines are attractive as carriers of therapeutics because they home into tumors or damaged tissue via chemotaxis [56]. Xie et al. showed that the encapsulation of dopamine-coated IONPs in HSA reduced the toxicity of the particles and enhanced their uptake by various cell types, outperforming the commercial product Feridex® in MRI detection of tumors and cerebral ischemia in mice [57]. In another study, Chiu et al. used macrophages bearing BSA-coated Au rods loaded with doxorubicin [58]. In a prostate cancer model, they showed that the cells loaded with the nanoformulation could migrate to the tumor site and enhanced the distribution of the nanohybrid compared to passively-diffused pristine particles. The use of the macrophage "Trojan horses" also improved the life quality of the animals, because NIR irradiation at the tumor site with pristine NPs caused unhealable wounds.

5.2.1.2 Lipoprotein

Lipoproteins are natural lipid-protein NPs whose function is the delivery and transportation of cholesterol and other lipids through the bloodstream to other tissues [36, 59]. They are composed of an outer layer of apolipoproteins (Apo), cholesterol, and phospholipids, while their hydrophobic core contains cholesterol esters and triglycerides. Low-density lipoproteins (LDL, aka the "bad" cholesterol) and high-density lipoproteins (HDL, aka the "good" cholesterol) are the major classes of lipoproteins employed in nanomedicine [60]. In terms of production, LDL and HDL can be obtained from the human plasma or reconstituted using recombinant apolipoproteins. The small size and hydrophobic core of LDL and HDL render them potent delivery vehicles of hydrophobic drugs for the treatment of cardiovascular diseases and cancer.

Lipoprotein-inorganic hybrids can be fabricated by conjugation of metal chelators or by encapsulation of NPs in the core. Pérez-Medina et al. labeled HDL NPs with ^{89}Zr by attaching their chelator on either phospholipid or ApoA-I for imaging of atherosclerotic plaques via PET imaging combined with CT or MRI [61]. The particles effectively accumulated in atherosclerotic lesions of mice, rabbits, and pigs. In the work of Alberti et al., they used a synthetic lipid bearing chelated ^{157}Gd and a ^{10}B ortho-carborene group to enable MRI diagnosis and neutron capture therapy (NCT) [62]. The NPs targeted cancer cells overexpressing the LDL receptor. MRI results showed accumulation of the particles and growth suppression of lung tumor metastases in mice after NCT treatment. Cormode et al. encapsulated AuNPs, IONPs, and QDs in HDL NPs to develop contrast agents for MRI and CT [63]. The NPs were associated with macrophages in aortic plaques in mice, with the Au-HDL hybrids yielding the best contrast. Au-HDL hybrids were also employed in the work of Yang et al. to target and reduce the growth of scavenger receptor type B-1 (SR-B1) positive tumors in mice [64]. The hybrid NPs managed to reduce tumor growth by binding to the SR-B1 and restricting cholesterol delivery leading to apoptosis.

5.2.2 Proteins from Food

Food-derived proteins are often safe materials that can be found in high abundance, which is very important for the biocompatibility and sustainable production of nanovectors. In this part, we will focus on food proteins, which are approved by the FDA as GRAS and have found various uses in nanomedical formulations. Thus, we will describe hybrid systems with proteins, which are derived from animal collagen (gelatin), milk (casein), and corn (zein).

Gelatin is a product of acid (gelatin type A) or alkaline (gelatin type B) hydrolysis of collagen. Gelatin type A is usually employed in nanomedical formulations, unless complexation with nucleic acids is required. Because it lacks targeting properties, it is usually modified with functional moieties [65]. Between these moieties, we often find peptides, on which we will focus later in this chapter [66–69]. Tran et al. prepared iron oxide/silica core-shell magnetic nanoparticles (MNPs) functionalized with oleic acid and coated with gelatin [65]. The oleic acid layer served for paclitaxel loading, while gelatin enhanced the biocompatibility of the particle. The nanosystem showed MRI contrast in vitro, while in vivo results showed better biodistribution in rats and increased breast and colon tumor suppression in mice compared with Taxol®. Many nanoformulations based on gelatin rely on the degradation of the protein by matrix metalloproteinases (especially MMP-2 and MMP-9). Wong et al. embedded QDs in a gelatin matrix, ensuring a prolonged circulation of the 100 nm particle until it reached the tumor site (mouse model) through its leaky vasculature [70]. Once located in the tumor, gelatin was degraded by the overexpressed MMP-2, allowing the QDs to penetrate deeper into the tumor tissue. Using a similar strategy, Xu et al. functionalized mesoporous silica NPs with gelatin to deliver doxorubicin (Fig. 5.1) [71]. Their experiments in mice showed that the particles reach the tumor through their leaky vasculature and release doxorubicin after gelatin degradation by MMPs, achieving better growth inhibition than the free drug. Additional targeting properties may be introduced to gelatin hybrids by increasing the complexity of the particle, e.g., by using inorganic shells and antibodies [72].

An important component of milk, casein, is an attractive system in nanomedicine because of its innate propensity to form large micelles. Taking advantage of this property, Cowger et al. prepared casein-coated Fe_5C_2 NPs with remarkable MRI contrast in mice [73]. In another work, Huang et al. coated IONPs with casein and glucose, enabling MRI imaging in mice [74]. The casein component could be further modified with anti-EGFR single-chain fragment variable (scFv) to target EGFR-overexpressing cancer cells in vitro. Later on, the same group tested the oral administration of layer-by-layer coated IONPs with an inner polymer shell and an outer casein shell, which ensured the effective delivery of doxorubicin to the small intestine of mice by oral administration, while it also enabled MRI imaging [75]. That system may show promising results in the oral administration of drugs absorbed by the lower gastrointestinal (GI) tract.

Zein is a major protein of corn that finds use in nanomedicine because of its amphiphilic properties. The applications of zein-inorganic hybrids remain at an early stage and a few of them have been tested in vivo. Briefly, zein-QD hybrids have been tested for transdermal delivery after application on nude mice skin, while a more complex system of zein, polydopamine, and AuNPs was used for MRI and delivery of hydroxycamptothecin [76, 77].

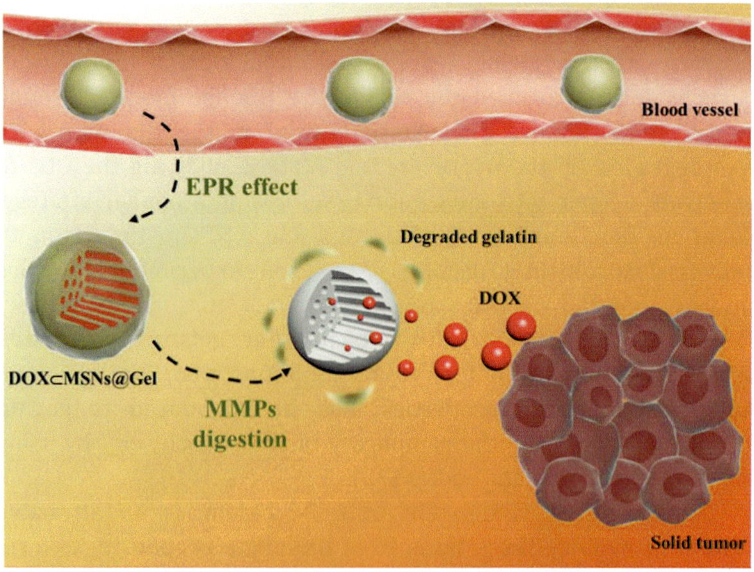

Figure 5.1 Schematic representation of the function of gelatin-functionalized mesoporous silica NPs loaded with doxorubicin (DOX⊂MSNs@Gel). The NPs access the tumor site via the EPR effect and release the drug upon degradation of gelatin by MMPs. Adapted with permission from Xu et al. (2013) [71], Microporous and Mesoporous Materials, Elsevier. https://marketplace.copyright.com/.

5.2.3 Other Natural Resources

5.2.3.1 Silk

The use of silk as a biocompatible material was known since ancient times, when people would use spider webs on their wounds to stop bleeding. Nowadays, the silk fibroin of *Bombyx mori* finds numerous uses in tissue engineering, while nanomedical applications are at an early stage. Tian et al. did an important in vivo study using IONPs embedded in silk fibroin and loaded with doxorubicin [78]. The particles accumulated in multidrug-resistant MCF-7 tumors in mice under a magnetic field. The inhibition of tumor growth was enhanced with the

Table 5.1 Theranostic nanoformulations based on natural protein-inorganic hybrids described in this part*

Albumin based						
Albumin type	*Inorganic NP*	*Drug*	*Hybrid shape*	*Size (nm)*	*In vivo application*	*Ref.*
HSA	Gadolinium (chelated)	IR825	Spherical	8	PTT and MRI of lymph node metastases combined with surgery	[44]
BSA	Gadolinium (chelated)/ Ag_2S QDs	–	Spherical	6	MRI and fluorescence imaging of tumors <2 mm	[45]
HSA	IONP	Doxorubicin	Spherical	50	MRI & chemotherapy of 4T1 (breast cancer) tumors	[46]
HSA	Au nanorods	Sorafenib	Spherical	165	Treatment of renal cell carcinoma via PTT & chemotherapy	[48]
BSA (funct. folate)	Au NPs	Doxorubicin	Framboidal	49	CT imaging and chemotherapy of gastric cancer model	[50]
BSA	Manganese-IONPs	–	Spherical	34	PTT & MRI of 4T1 tumors	[52]
BSA	Gadolinium/Au nanoshells	Indocyanine green	Spherical	151	Multimodal imaging & PTT/PD treatment of breast cancer model	[55]
HSA	IONP	–	Spherical	30	Iron-laden cells for MRI of tumor and cerebral ischemia model	[57]
BSA	Au nanorods	Doxorubicin	Rod	56 (length) 12 (width)	Delivery by macrophages to prostate cancer	[58]

Table 5.1 (*Continued*)

Lipoprotein based						
Lipoprotein	*Inorganic NP*	*Drug*	*Hybrid shape*	*Size (nm)*	*In vivo application*	*Ref.*
HDL	Zirconium isotope	–	Discoidal	8–9	PET/CT PET/MRI imaging of atherosclerosis in mice, rabbits, pigs	[61]
LDL	Gadolinium/ Boron isotopes	–	Spherical	24	MRI/NCT of lung cancer metastases	[62]
HDL	Gold Iron oxide Cd-based QDs	–	Spherical	10–13	MRI, CT imaging of atherosclerosis	[63]
HDL	Gold	–	Spherical	13	Treatment of lymphoma model	[64]
Food protein based						
Food protein	*Inorganic NP*	*Drug*	*Hybrid shape*	*Size (nm)*	*In vivo application*	*Ref.*
Gelatin	Silica (shell) Iron oxide (core)	Paclitaxel	Spherical	84	Suppression of EMT-6 and CT26 tumors	[65]
Gelatin	Qdot 565 ITK amino (PEG)	–	Spherical	100	Imaging of HT-1080 tumor	[70]
Gelatin	Silica	Doxorubicin	Spherical	102	Inhibition of HT-29 tumor growth	[71]
Casein	Iron carbide	–	Spherical	45	MRI imaging	[73]
Casein	Iron oxide	–	Spherical	31	MRI imaging	[74]
Other resources						
Protein	*Inorganic NP*	*Drug*	*Hybrid shape*	*Size (nm)*	*In vivo Application*	*Ref.*
Silk	Iron oxide	Doxorubicin	Spherical	130	MRI and MCF-7 tumor growth inhibition	[78]

*For spherical shapes, the size refers to the diameter of the particle. Applications refer to mouse models unless otherwise indicated.

application of the magnetic field. In the study of Chen et al., silk fibroin-IONPs were used to evaluate the penetration in guinea pig skin ex vivo [79]. Maximal penetration into the skin was achieved by using an alternating magnetic field. Other promising silk-inorganic formulations include silk-nanodiamond and silk-AuNPs, but remain in the in vitro stage [80, 81].

Natural protein-inorganic NP formulations show great potential as theranostic tools. Revising Table 5.1, one can observe their numerous applications, which range from MRI to heat treatment of tumors. Albumin hybrids represent most of the examples, so HSA may be the most promising coating for the transition of inorganic NPs from lab to clinic; HSA is human derived so it minimizes the risk of immune reactions, while its amino acid variety allows for modifications with different bioactive moieties. However, certain alternatives may be needed in order to avoid the use of toxic crosslinkers (e.g., glutaraldehyde) when coating inorganic NPs with HSA. Regarding the inorganic compartment, IONPs are quite promising because of their versatility; IONPs can be visualized, directed, and generate heat under the application of an external magnetic field. It is quite encouraging to see that some of these formulations have outperformed commercial products (e.g., Taxol® or Doxil® in chemotherapy; Feridex® or Magnevist® in MRI).

One would expect antibodies to be included in the list with proteins of human origin. However, because engineered antibodies are often employed for biomedical purposes, their applications will be analyzed in Section 5.4.2.3.

5.3 Hybrids with Peptides

5.3.1 Peptides and Inorganic Material Hybrids

5.3.1.1 Overview of peptides and their source of inspiration

Peptides, either natural or synthetic, have been exploited over the years for their favorable properties that combine both the proteins' functionalities and a high degree of modularity in molecular design. New bioactive peptide sequences can be discovered by isolating sequences from natural proteins based on their structural properties with a method termed the top-down approach. On the contrary, with the bottom-up approach, new peptides are being constructed by screening peptide libraries with sequences composed of random amino acids within a certain macromolecular topology. In both cases, the developed peptide sequences can be used as drugs, to target specific molecules effectively or act as vectors for therapeutic or diagnostic agents [82].

Small therapeutic molecule drugs usually suffer from instability issues, loss of bio-distribution target, and subsequent difficulties in reaching the desired site-of-action in vivo. That may lead to severe side effects and often the efficacy observed in the in vitro trials may be completely different when translated into several in vivo experiments [83]. Peptide-inorganic-drug nanoparticle conjugates are a powerful solution to this problem since they can enhance the drug's stability, activity, and targeting efficiency. Peptide sequences to be conjugated with NPs can be selected mainly in two ways: (a) derived from natural proteins and (b) chemically synthesized by structure-based rational engineering and screening of peptide libraries.

5.3.1.2 Natural peptides

Some of the most commonly used peptides derived from natural sources, for developing peptide-inorganic hybrid structures, are analyzed below.

Cell-penetrating peptides

The discovery of short peptides that can internalize into cell membranes and transfer genetic material or biologically active molecules inside the cells has attracted attention in the field of gene and drug delivery. These CPPs also known as membrane-translocating peptides or Trojan peptides are small 5–30 amino acid peptides and are characterized by a rich content of positively charged residues such as arginine (R) and Lysine (K) that renders them with an overall positive charge. They have various internalization mechanisms with the most dominant being the interaction of their positively charged residues side chains with the negatively charged phospholipids of the cell membrane, a mechanism that facilitates the peptide internalization and endosomal uptake via endocytic pathways [84]. Since they can penetrate cellular membranes, with the insertion of proper functionalization sites they could also carry therapeutic molecules along with inorganic NPs. Figure 5.2 demonstrates how the CPPs can bind to therapeutic cargo and further with NPs for efficient transfer into the cells.

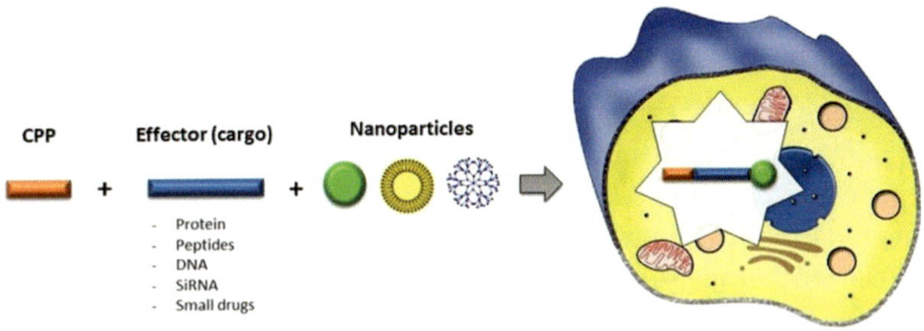

Figure 5.2 Schematic representation of the dual conjugation of CPP with a therapeutic or diagnostic cargo and an NP. The binding enables cell internalization, therapeutic effectiveness and enhancement of the stability of the hybrid. Adapted from Silva et al. (2019) [85], *Biomolecules, MDPI.*

Tat peptide

The first CPP was discovered by Frankel et al. [86] and it is part of the HIV-Tat protein, which is known to be taken up by the cells and is also responsible for the virus replication. Later, the domain that mediated the rapid penetration was discovered by Vives et al. [87] and comprises the residues GRKKRRQRRRR. Since then, it is widely used in a variety of applications as a cell-penetrating and translocating sequence, with alternating combinations of conjugated drugs, genes, and inorganic NPs [85, 88].

Fusogenic peptide HA2

However, even if the Tat peptide can mediate endocytosis and guide the drug or gene vectors into the endosome, there is a high possibility that if the vectors do not escape on time, they are eventually being degraded in the lysosome. Thus, efficient delivery of the drug or gene into the cytosol or nucleus is inefficient and the disruption of this barrier is required. The *N*-terminal domain of the influenza virus hemaglutinin-2 (HA2) could play this role. The fusogenic HA2 peptide can induce lysis of the endosomal membranes at low pH and subsequently mediate the lyso-endosome escape of the loaded vectors [89]. The fusogenic peptide HA2 has been used synergistically as an endosomal escape factor with the Tat peptide for the enhancement of cellular internalization and gene transfer of gelatin-silica (GS) NPs. The in vitro and in vivo studies conducted in HeLa tumor-bearing mice demonstrated that the Tat/HA2-modified GSNP promotes the effective cellular internalization, endosomal escape, and targeting of the carrying gene to the nucleus, which led to a significant increase in gene expression. These hybrid conjugates can form stable aggregates with DNA and protect it from enzymatic degradation. Thus, it can be considered as an attractive alternative to cancer therapy [69].

RGD peptide and cyclic RGD

The arginine-glycine-aspartic acid (RGD) tripeptide sequence has been identified in extracellular matrix proteins, such as vitronectin and laminin [90, 91]. It is a cell targeting and binding motif with applications in the fields of oncology, wound healing, and tissue engineering. It can mediate the cell interactions through the integrins $\alpha v\beta 3$, $\alpha 5\beta 1$, and $\alpha IIb\beta 3$. The integrin $\alpha v\beta 3$ overexpression is encountered in tumor neovasculature and some tumor cells and is correlated with tumor progression and invasiveness of melanoma, glioma, ovarian, and breast cancers. In epithelial cells and mature endothelial cells, it is expressed at low levels whereas the overexpression of this integrin takes place in activated endothelial cells of tumors. This integrin is also a receptor for proteins with the exposed RGD motif, thus they can mediate the transfer of anticancer drugs or diagnostic molecules and NPs that are conjugated with the RGD motif. In the study of Ruan and Gao [92], gelatin-gold fabricated NPs containing the peptide of RGD and octarginine exhibited improved penetration ability and diagnosis of glioma tumors in vivo. Additionally, Chen et al. [93] showed that the incorporation of RGD peptides onto mesoporous silica NPs facilitates the in vitro targeting of cancer cells. Moreover, the cyclic RGD also finds applications conjugated with inorganic NPs as tumor-targeted radiosensitizers and imaging agents [94, 95]. Cyclic RGD exhibits enhanced rigidity and enables the use of a variety of chemical modifications for conjugation with the inorganic NPs.

Angiopep-2

Angiopep-2 (ANG) consists of 19 amino acids (TFFYGGSRGKRNNFKTEEY) and is derived from the human Kunitz domain [96]. It can trigger transcytosis and can penetrate the BBB via receptor-mediated transport by specifically targeting low-density lipoprotein-related protein 1 (LRP1). Angiopep-2 has further been used to modify inorganic and organic NPs entrapping chemotherapy drugs. The group of Ji used angiopep-2 as a dual-targeting drug carrier in vivo in the brain and also in the glioma sites in fusion with anti-VEGF single chain Fab [97]. Additionally, angiopep-2 was conjugated with PEG-b-PCL NPs for the treatment of primary central nervous system lymphoma [98] or with iron oxide NPs in an ex vivo BBB model as a diagnostic agent [99].

5.3.1.3 Synthetic peptides

Artificial peptides are being designed and discovered by screening through libraries or by the phage display method. Phage display is a technology that enables the de novo discovery of peptides against any target of interest by exploring DNA-encoded peptide libraries. This method is a valuable tool for high-throughput screening of protein and peptide interactions and is an effective technique for identifying peptides that can interact and bind target molecules and also regulate their function. It was invented by George Smith in 1985, when he demonstrated that peptides with a few amino acids could be displayed onto phage coat proteins by fusion [100]. It works by using recombinant DNA technology in order to create bacteriophages exposing the desired peptide on their surface. Interactions of potential agonists and antagonists of the target peptide can be identified leading to the development of potential new drugs or tissue targeting sequences [101].

Due to the phenotype-genotype link, these peptide libraries can be used for selecting target-specific binders. This strategy simulates the natural selection approach with the only main difference of being performed in a tube. This method has the advantages of simplicity and cost-effectiveness. Targeting NPs conjugated with various peptides derived from phage display are being developed and evaluated for guided imaging and therapy.

Some examples that lead to the development of peptide-inorganic particles used in biomedicine include the study of Kumar et al., where they conjugated the 16-mer peptide ANTPCGPYTHDCPVKR, known also as G3-C12, with ^{111}In, and used it as a radiopeptide in a human MDA-MB-435 breast tumor-bearing model for breast cancer diagnosis [102]. Also, another group selected the 7-mer peptides HYIDFRW and TVNFKLY from a phage display random peptide library by having the ferromagnetic nanoparticles (Fe_3O_4 NPs) as a target. These peptides exhibit a strong binding affinity to Fe_3O_4 NPs and in combination with the ovarian tumor cell A2780 specific binding peptide (QQTNWSL), enabled the successful binding to these cancer cells with potential applications for magnetic hyperthermia or tumor-targeted drug delivery [103].

Furthermore, peptide discovery is also facilitated through library screening via rational design. The main methods include the de novo method in order to fabricate novel peptides or improve existing ones, and template design. This method is based on identifying useful patterns or crucial residue positions with the goal of creating new amino acid patterns for enhanced interacting, targeting, and transferring abilities [104]. With this method, the rationally designed peptide can obtain controlled morphologies and can be combined with inorganic nanomaterials mimicking biomineralization [105].

5.3.2 Synthesis, Interaction, and Analytical Techniques for the Evaluation of Peptide-Nanoparticle Hybrids

Understanding how biomolecules such as proteins and peptides interact with inorganic materials is of utmost importance for the development of novel and functional hybrid conjugates for use in nanomedicine. Additionally, it will enable the design of robust and stable surfaces and the development of therapeutic and diagnostic strategies for use even in complex in vivo environments.

Peptides, just like proteins, have the tendency of accumulating on surfaces. Usually, the accumulation leads to the adsorption of NPs in a non-reversible manner. The accumulation density of the peptide and the mode of adsorption are determined by both the characteristics of the peptide and the surface of the inorganic NP [106]. Properties of the peptides that affect the adsorption behavior are their amino acid sequence, charge, stability of the folded domains, and their size [107]. Characteristics of the NPs' surface that influence the interaction with biomolecules are their chemical composition and their geometry. The geometry traits include their size, shape, roughness, curvature, and crystallinity. Additionally, some independent factors also influence the binding ability, such as the pH of the solution, ionic strength, and the presence of other molecules and ions.

There are numerous methods and strategies for creating peptide-inorganic NP hybrids. Peptides can be immobilized directly onto the NP surface by physisorption or chemisorption or indirectly via a linker molecule already immobilized on the surface. Physisorption is mainly driven by electrostatic, van der Waals, and hydrophobic interactions. Also, non-covalent interactions like biotin-avidin and 6xHis-tag tails that bind with nickel-nitrilotriacetic acid (Ni-NTA) are used for non-covalent binding. Coating with a polymeric shell that enables further functionalization and attachment of the peptides as well as the deposition of a thin metal or oxide film (core-shell particle) are also employed. Peptides that include cysteine residues can form disulfide bonds with gold NPs since thiols and disulfides form a strong slightly non-polar bond with gold surfaces.

Generally, there are three main strategies for fabricating peptide conjugated NPs: (a) ligand exchange, (b) chemical conjugation, and (c) chemical reduction [108].

(a) *The ligand exchange method:* The ligand exchange method is the simplest strategy and involves the replacement of an already present ligand on the NPs' surface with a peptide ligand or a mixture of peptide/ligand. This method takes place under mild conditions and generates peptide-functionalized NPs, which exhibit high colloidal stability and diverse functionality. Cysteine (Cys) containing peptides conjugated with AuNPs are synthesized by this method through their thiol group (–HS) of cysteine [109]. Also, Levy and colleagues showed that the CALNN peptide can coat citrate-capped AuNPs and enhance their stability and solubility to water. The CALNN peptide can be further functionalized with other biomolecules such as biotin or DNA [110]. Furthermore, robust metal-phosphate coordination bonds can be formed between metallic NPs (Gd^{3+}, Fe^{3+}, Zn^{2+}) and peptides containing phosphorylated amino acids [111].

(b) *The chemical conjugation:* This method involves a two-step strategy of attaching desired peptides to the NP's surface. Initially, the NPs are capped by stabilizers like polyethyleneglycol (PEG) or its derivatives through physical interactions (electrostatic or hydrogen bonds) or through ligand exchange. Usually, these coatings contain active groups where peptides can be further conjugated on the stabilizers. This method is ideal for the immobilization of positively charged or neutral peptides on AuNPs and/or subsequently the transfer of hydrophobic NPs into an aqueous solution. Such an example is the use of the EDC/sulfo-NHS coupling method developed by Bartczak et al. [112], where the KPQPRPLS positively charged peptide was conjugated to carboxy-terminated oligoethyleneglycol stabilized AuNPs.

(c) *The chemical reduction method:* This method is simple and requires mild conditions. It involves the direct synthesis of peptide-functionalized NPs. The main steps are (i) mixing of the peptide with the metal-ion precursor in the reaction solution, (ii) optional addition of a reducing agent, and (iii) purifying the peptide conjugated NPs. The advantage of this method is that the morphologies of the NPs can be controlled by changing reaction conditions. Notably, the peptide stabilizes the NPs and is also responsible for the metal ion reduction to metal, usually through electron transfer between its residues (Tyr, Pro, Trp) [113].

Characterization of peptide-inorganic hybrids

There are several methods for evaluating the hybrid's shape, size, charge, and conjugation ability. The main techniques are: (a) transmission electron microscopy (TEM) and scanning electron microscopy (SEM); for defining the final confirmation of the hybrid, (b) zeta-potential; for measuring the overall charge, (c) dynamic light scattering (DLS); for the size distribution, and (d) circular dichroism (CD) and infrared radiation (IR); for detecting the binding efficiency of the peptide with the inorganic material.

5.3.3 Peptide Properties and Advantages Compared to Proteins

While a broad variety of small molecules has been developed for various diseases, the off-targeting issue remains. Off-target describes the effect that can occur when a designed drug cannot find the correct target to bind protein, peptide, receptor, or other molecules in the body, or can bind to targets other than those for which the drug was originally aimed. Protein- and peptide-based pharmaceuticals have been developed to address this issue since they can have an inherent ability of specific targeting or they can be designed to do so.

Peptides seem to have an advantage in contrast to proteins in this regard and could be successfully used as an interesting alternative to protein molecules for NPs functionalization. Common issues with proteins are usually their demanding and time-consuming methods of preparation, their low thermal stability, and their susceptibility. Peptide sequences can be produced in a straight-forward manner via solid-phase peptide synthesis, in contrast to protein cost-worthy production systems through organisms like *E. coli*. Handling of the peptide assemblies does not pose a problem and there are limited structure instability concerns as opposed to the usually very defined and delicate protein structures. Peptides allow for a very flexible assay design, thus it is possible to overcome many difficulties associated with larger proteins, such as finding generic strategies for functionalizing NPs without disrupting protein functionality or leading to aggregation.

Another very favorable advantage of peptides is their ease of modulation. Changing amino acid residues and also incorporating non-natural amino acids in the peptide sequence can change the assembly properties, stability, ability to interact with other molecules, and its subsequent functionality. When conjugated with an inorganic particle or in combination with a therapeutic molecule, it may enhance the charge, polarity, hydrophobicity/hydrophilicity, and overall functionality of the hybrid nanoconjugate. Moreover, compared to full-size protein targeting molecules, peptides have the capability of forming compact NP conjugates attributed to their small size, which limits the disruption of the NP's hydrodynamic diameter. Also, due to their small size resulting from their short sequences, they demonstrate reduced unspecific binding to other biomolecules when compared to full-length proteins Finally, even if peptides are generally characterized by reduced immunogenicity, there have been cases where in conjugation with inorganic NPs, they exhibited toxic side effects and disruption of intracellular vesicles. However, this effect can be mitigated by modulating the hybrid NP size, content, or coating [114].

5.3.4 Applications of Peptide-Nanoparticle Hybrids: Diagnosis and Therapy

The synergistic effect of the properties of the two classes of materials, the organic/peptide and the inorganic material, allows enhanced control over their biological behavior and helps in overcoming the intrinsic limitations of each individual material. There is an increasing number of peptide-NP conjugates being developed over the past decades and their uses are focused, but are not limited to, the areas of targeted drug delivery, molecular imaging as radiotracers, gene delivery vectors, stability enhancement, and applications as protein interaction inhibitor for pathological diseases, antimicrobials, and tissue engineering.

Below are mentioned such representative examples of peptide-inorganic hybrids with their corresponding applications.

5.3.4.1 Drug delivery

Drug delivery refers to the method of administering pharmaceutical compounds (chemical compounds, proteins, peptides) to the desired body site in order to achieve a therapeutic effect in humans or animals. This process comprises the transport, release, and absorption of the active ingredients through the biological membranes to the specific site of action for effective results. Common hurdles in the delivery are decreased therapeutic efficacy, toxicity, lack of specificity, and lack of biological action. Various strategies, administration methods, and vectors have been employed for this aim including physical methods like electroporation and biochemical methods like the use of viral vectors [115, 116]. However, some of them have been characterized by severe side effects including cell toxicity resulting in decreased viability of healthy cells. Recent studies have focused on the development of alternative strategies that use short peptide sequences, which have the ability to translocate across cellular membranes without compromising their integrity. CPPs, which have been previously described in this chapter (Section 5.3.1.2), offer the advantages of selective targeting, high cellular permeability rates in a wide spectrum of cell types, effective translocation while carrying cargo, and non-cytotoxicity in addition to the absence of immunological responses. The combination of CPPs with inorganic NPs creating peptide/inorganic NP hybrids has been extensively used in biomedicine for targeted drug and gene delivery.

Cell-penetrating inorganic NP hybrids in cancer treatment

Conventional chemotherapy treatment involves drugs that often lack specificity, which arises toxic side effects for the patients since it also affects healthy tissue. Additionally, these methods are characterized by poor water solubility and rapid blood clearance. The CPP/NP hybrid cargo delivery has been exploited as a potential and advantageous method for targeted cancer treatment and tumor eradication without affecting healthy tissues. A wide range of studies has been conducted exhibiting the benefits of using a peptide-inorganic NP system. Some characteristic examples of CPP/inorganic NPs are further described.

In the study of Kalimuthu et al., they coupled the cell internalizing peptide P4 with the anticancer drugs chlorambucil (Chlor), melphalan (Melph), or bendamustine (Bend) and they found that the targeting efficiency of the drugs in A20 cell line was greatly increased. Additionally, the peptide-AuNPs have a longer plasma half-life, and the hybrid stability could be further enhanced in combination with the PEG molecule. All the three combinations of the P4 peptide-AuNPs and anticancer drugs exhibited longer half-life and enhanced cytotoxic effect against cancerous cells [117].

The results of another study where they conjugated the CPP Tat with an AuNP platform carrying doxorubicin, showed improved cytotoxic effects against two brain metastatic breast cancer cell lines. With the administration of peptide-drug-Au NP, the cancer cell population was decreased to 50% (IC_{50}) of its population at least 80% more compared to that of the free doxorubicin drug. Moreover, in vivo experiments demonstrated increased viability in the mice treated with the Tat-Au-DOX conjugate [118].

In another interesting study by Li et al., they designed a multifunctional anti-tumor drug nanocarrier that targeted the anticancer drug doxorubicin toward the cell nucleus of a variety of tumoral cell lines. An enzyme activatable CPP (CRRRQRRKKR-PGFK-EEEEE) was conjugated with mesoporous silica-coated QDs NPs (QDs@mSiO_2). The doxorubicin drug was also loaded. Upon entering the tumor cell environment and being exposed to proteases, the peptide sequence was enzymatically cleaved and triggered the oligocationic Tat residues on the NP's surface to transfer doxorubicin into the cell nucleus of tumor cell line A549 [119].

Another strategy that was developed for cancer treatment, was the use of the RW CCPs (various sequence combinations of Arginine (R) and Tryptophane (W)) incorporated with AgNPs. Results demonstrated that the hybrid of the RW-AgNPs showed significant enhancement in the growth reduction of the cancerous MCF-7 cells. RW greatly enhanced AgNPs internalization and anti-tumor effect showing a 10-fold increase in activity [120].

A notable system with a bi-functional role is the gold nanocluster-bovine serum albumin (AuNCs-BSA) system that was modified with the incorporation of the cRGD, cyclic (arginine-glycine-aspartate) peptide and loaded with doxorubicin. This DOX/RGD-BSA@AuNC system inhibited the growth of cancer cell lines and enabled the detection of the tumor site through in vivo-imaging and thus was employed in the tumor size deduction via laser irradiation [95].

5.3.4.2 Gene therapy

Gene therapy comprises the experimental techniques that are the transfer or the modification of endogenous genes to prevent or cure diseases. The most common mechanisms used are by either delivering and replacing a faulty gene with a healthy copy or by inactivating a disease-causing gene that is not functioning properly. There are three types of therapeutic agents: (a) delivery of a gene copy with a plasmid that is directed to the cell nucleus and then expressed by the cell into a protein, (b) small interfering RNA or silencing RNA (siRNA), which is a double-stranded RNA that interferes and prevents translation, and (c) splicing correcting oligonucleotides (SCOs), which are short, synthetic modified nucleic acids that base-pair with a pre-mRNA and disrupt the normal splicing leading to the correction of the mRNA to be translated. However, the usefulness of these methodologies is hindered by the lack of efficient delivery since oligonucleotides alone show poor permeability of the cell membranes and a relatively rapid degradation [121, 122]. Viral vectors exhibit very high transfection efficiency but their use is often hindered by immune responses. The group of Dowaidar et al. conjugated MNPs (Fe_3O_4) with complexes of cell-penetrating peptides with oligonucleotides (CPPs-ON). They found that this conjugation greatly increases the transfection efficiency in the investigated cells. Six different CPPs (PF220, PF221, PF222, PF223, PF224, and PF14) were combined with three types of gene therapeutic agents: plasmid (luciferase encoding-pGL3), SCOs, and siRNA. The complexes were further bound with MNPs. The peptides facilitated the effective internalization into the cells, whereas the MNPs also provided targeted delivery, protection of the nucleic agents against nuclease degradation, and improved their stability. The combinations studied demonstrated encouraging results, high activity, and transfection rates [123]. The route of MNPs conjugating with oligonucleotides for gene transfer is depicted in Figure 5.3.

The results of another interesting study demonstrated, in vitro and in vivo, the synergistic effect of two peptides in gene transduction of the pGL3 plasmid expressing the luciferase protein. The incorporated Tat CPP mediated endocytosis and the fusogenic peptide HA2 enabled the escape of the plasmid from the endosomes before being degraded by nucleases. The grafting of the peptides-plasmid complex onto GS nanohybrids leads to the controlled aggregation and formation of stable NPs with condensed DNA and high transfection rates [69].

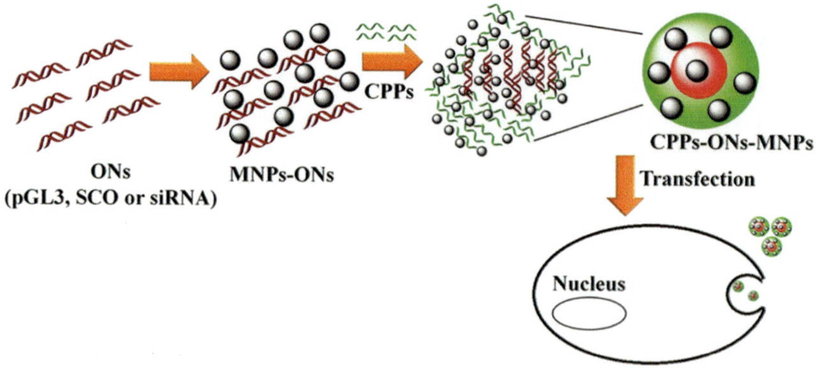

Figure 5.3 Schematic representation of the conjugation of therapeutic oligonucleotides (ONs) such as a plasmid (pGL3), siRNA, and SCO with MNPs. MNPs assist in the self-assembly of CPPs-ONs complexes to further increase the transfection efficiency into the cells for gene delivery applications. Adapted from Dowaidar et al. [123], *Scientific Reports*, Nature Publications. http://creativecommons.org/licenses/by/4.0/.

The Tat peptide was also utilized for the decoration, via a disulfide bond, of gelatin-siloxane nanoparticles carrying the calcitonin gene-related peptide (CGRP) gene for the treatment of cerebral vasospasm. Cerebral vasospasm is described by the delayed narrowing of large capacitance arteries at the base of the brain following subarachnoid hemorrhage. CGRP is an efficient arterial and venous vasodilator, which exhibits favorable results against vasospasm. The use of the Tat-GS-CGRP as a transfection vehicle demonstrated high levels of CGRP overexpression, attenuated vasospasm, and improved neurological results in an experimental rat model of subarachnoid hemorrhage [124].

5.3.4.3 Radiotracers

Molecular imaging focuses on the visualization of biological systems and processes at high resolution by observing molecules of medical interest. It is a non-invasive technique that involves the administration of specific probes (biomarkers or radiolabeled molecules) in order to monitor and quantify clinical or non-clinical molecular or cellular processes and furthermore detect pathological cells or tissue. There is a high demand for radiopharmaceuticals for use in accurate and early diagnosis of diseased states and cardiac function. Positron emission tomography (PET), CT, NIR fluorescence imaging, and MRI are common imaging techniques used in radiology that require imaging probes such as AuNPs, ^{67}Ga, ^{64}Cu, ^{18}F, ^{99m}Tc, near IR fluorescent dyes, and IONPs [125]. Recent advances led to the upgrade and development of novel radiotracers by conjugating a peptide sequence, which subsequently increased the target specificity of the probes. Conjugated peptides have the advantages of tissue targeting specificity, long-term stability, and rapid clearance from the bloodstream. By fabricating peptide-NP conjugates, the challenges of the weak binding affinity and metabolic instability associated with the peptides are further overcome.

In the study of Cheng et al., they conjugated Au tripods with the cyclic Arg-Gly-Asp-D-Phe-Cys (RGDfC). The hybrids were intravenously administrated to U87MG tumor-bearing mice and exhibited 3-fold higher in vivo photoacoustic imaging (PAI) contrasts when measured with the PET method. Au has excellent optical properties due to its high nuclear electron density and is widely used as a contrast agent. Au-tripods offer enhanced optical properties due to the fact that anisotropic colloidal hybrid structures demonstrate superior optical and physical properties in comparison to their counterparts with regular architectures [126]. Moreover, the modification of the Au-tripod surface with the cyclic RGD peptide improved the targeting of the $\alpha v\beta 3$ integrins, which are highly expressed in cancerous cells. The in vivo biodistribution was confirmed by ^{64}Cu radiolabeling of the RGD-Au-tripods and their localization was imaged over time using PET.

In another study, the conjugation of a thrombin-activatable fluorescent peptide (TAP) on silica-coated gold nanoparticles ($TAP\text{-}SiO_2@AuNPs$) was used as an imaging probe for thrombosis detection by using dual NIRF and micro-computed tomography (micro-CT) imaging. The $TAP\text{-}SiO_2@AuNPs$ were effectively accumulated in the thrombus after being administrated in the in situ thrombotic mouse model. In normal blood vessels, the fluorescence was quenched. However, in a thrombosis lesion environment and after exposure to thrombin and its specific cleavage of quenched TAP molecules on the NP surface, the strong NIRF signal of TAP-SiO_2@AuNPs was rapidly recovered. The thrombosis site could be efficiently detected by both NIRF and micro-CT imaging [127].

Furthermore, in vivo detection and quantification of inflammation were achieved by the covalent binding of the hydrophobic peptide on the surface of ^{68}Ga core-doped NPs. cFLFLF, a formyl peptide receptor-1 antagonist shows high selectivity for neutrophils and exhibits high binding affinity. Neutrophil is a type of white blood cell that shows healing activity for damaged tissues and infections. Increased levels in the blood indicate a response to infections and other types of stress. Thus, targeting these molecules with the cFLFLF peptide enables the non-invasive detection of the acute inflammation area with PET/CT imaging. The hydrophobic nature of the peptide that resulted in poor signals and very low in vivo labeling was resolved by conjugating it on the surface of the very hydrophilic gadolinium nano-radiotracers (^{68}Ga-NRT) [128].

5.3.5 Emerging Technologies

Many excellent platforms have been developed based on peptide-inorganic hybrids but only a few of them have been used in clinical trials. These biomaterials have the potential of broad applications in the biomedicine area, due to their good biodistribution, pharmacokinetics, stability, long blood circulation half-life, and specified targeted abilities. Emphasis is given to large-scale and cost-effective production of the hybrids as nanomedicines.

An attractive application that is gaining interest in the last years is the peptide-based gelators that template the in situ formation of metal nanostructures. A short peptide usually containing the Fluorenylmethyloxycarbonyl (Fmoc) or tert-Butyloxycarbonyl (Boc) protecting group in its sequence is the hydrogelator that enables the formation of dynamic supramolecular environments.

Usually, the gel is formed by a network of nanofibers with excellent mechanical properties. Inorganic NPs can be templated directly in the resulting gels without using further reductants or chemical reagents. This can be achieved either through the interaction of the metal ions with the side chains of the peptides' residues and triggering of the gelation or simply by entrapment of the formed NPs into the gel during the course of its formation [129]. For instance, the deposition of silver NPs onto the nanofibers yielded hydrogels with antibacterial properties. The wide use of peptide-inorganic hydrogels opens new horizons toward using these hybrids for biomedicine applications.

Furthermore, the advancements in the use of computational methods have remarkably enhanced the rate of development of novel and functional peptides. These methods are being used for the design of "on-demand" peptide sequences for the desired application [130, 131]. The theoretical design and incorporation of new or modified amino acids in peptide sequences or mimicking parts of a natural protein's sequence, enable the prediction of the assembly, functionality, and interactions with other molecules such as inorganic NPs. Therefore, the outcome can be validated and improved appropriately until reaching a peptide sequence with the finest properties. The peptide sequences can then be synthesized with traditional methods. The computational methods are gradually replacing the time-consuming rational designs based on the experimentalists' intuition that usually yield low success rates.

Although the development of these peptide-inorganic NPs will face constant challenges, they hold great promise for use as theranostics and diagnostics.

5.4 Hybrids with Engineered Proteins

5.4.1 Protein Engineering for Theranostics: Design, Production, and Functionalization

5.4.1.1 Design

Proteins have structural and chemical diversity that makes them a relevant scaffold in cell structure, catalysis, and regulation in nature. Their sophistication renders them great candidates for biotechnological and nanotechnological applications [132–135]. Protein amino acid sequences encode protein folding and functionality; thus, manipulating the protein structure requires controlling the sequence-structure-function relationship. In the last decade, new protein structures have been generated based on computational methods that predict protein folding [136–139]. These designed proteins have provided a powerful toolkit for using proteins for different applications. In engineered proteins, secondary and tertiary structures are usually determined by a few amino acids and the rest of the amino acids can be modified without disrupting the protein structure [140, 141].

5.4.1.2 Production

Nowadays, synthetic proteins are generated in the laboratory as recombinant proteins. Protein-coding gene sequences are cloned into a bacterial expression vector (*E. coli*), and the appropriately tagged proteins are purified with protocols optimized in our laboratory [142]. In molecular biology, protein purification is performed using affinity tags or genetically engineered fusion partners. Some known tags are 6xHis-tag and strep tag, for example. Modifications to protein-encoding genes are carried out by site-directed mutagenesis [143].

5.4.1.3 Functionalization

Bioconjugation is the creation of a complex composed of two or more molecules linked together, usually through a covalent bond [144]. Reaction conditions and reagents control the bioconjugation, and depending on the application, different bioconjugates are generated using different methods and components [145]. Bioconjugates have properties that combine the characteristics of each molecule in the complex and these characteristics are usually not found among naturally occurring substances. For example, a combination of a fluorescence label with an antibody creates a complex that binds to a specific biomolecule through antigen binding sites on the antibody that can be detected due to the fluorescence tag, making the tracking easier compared with the unlabeled antibody [146]. In general, the design of a functional bioconjugate is organized by choosing the desired features that are desired in the final complex and the components necessary to create it. Figure 5.4 illustrates some bioconjugate types that can be made by linking two or more molecules together.

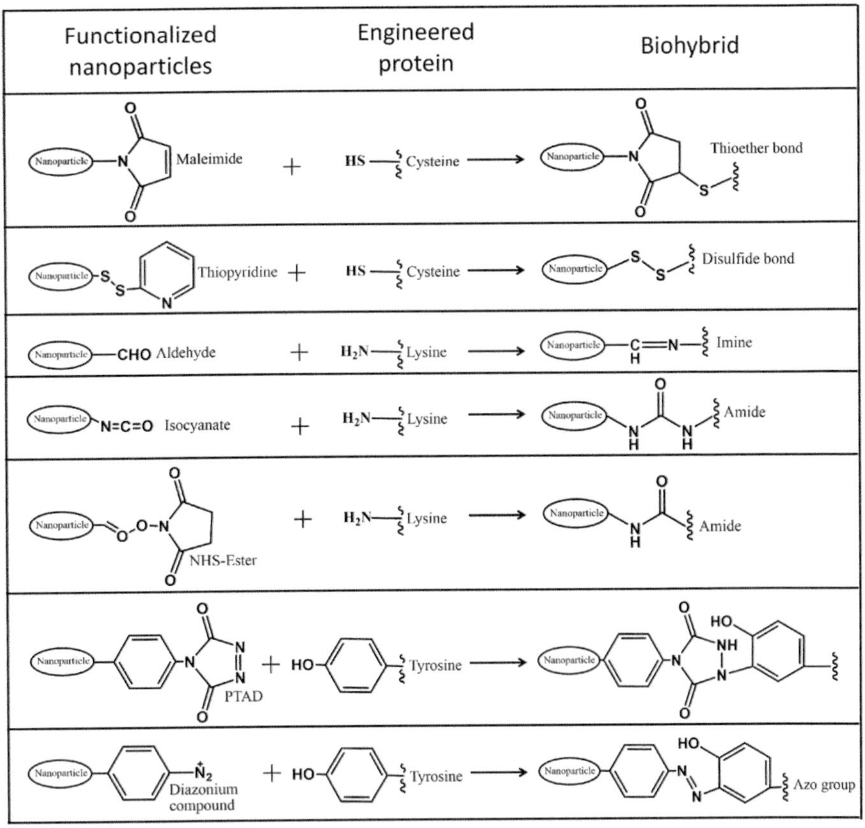

Figure 5.4 Bioconjugation strategies. Functional groups in the NP (left) and in the protein (right) and the resulting biohybrid are indicated in the figure for each reaction.

5.4.2 Multifunctional Bio-Hybrids Based on Engineered Proteins for Diagnosis and Treatment

Bio-hybrid generation has benefited from the emergence of synthetic libraries, evolution technologies, and other protein engineering techniques. Advantages of bio-hybrids are (a) small size for easy handing and reduced non-specific interactions; (b) high chemical, thermal, and proteolytic stability; and (c) the absence of aggregation, which increases the sensitivity. Moreover, pharmacokinetic properties (e.g., lifetime, clearance of imaging probes) can be easily controlled in the designed scaffolds and multiple binding sites can be encoded in a single scaffold to increase the avidity of the designed sensors, among others.

5.4.2.1 Synthesis and characterization of engineered bio-hybrids

Favorable properties in nanomaterials require their surface modification and functionalization. In this sense, NPs show unique properties based on their shape and size, making them versatile for applications [147]. Proteins can be attached to the NP surface, providing them with novel properties, but efficient protein linking to the NP surface requires the modification of the protein and NP [148, 149]. In that sense, protein engineering is essential for generating very effective hybrid compounds with novel properties [150]. The functionalization compounds include small molecules like carboxylic acids, amino groups, biotin, or thiols.

Synthesis of engineered bio-hybrids

Hybrid materials can be designed at the molecular level using molecular recognition strategies and specific protein recognition properties. For example, proteins can be functionalized with chemical groups that recognize inorganic surfaces at the molecular level. Moreover, proteins can be oriented in a controlled manner. Control in the orientation of the proteins in the NP surface improves the functionality of the protein-NP bio-hybrids. For example, it has been shown that the orientation of the antibody in the NPs increases antigen binding [150].

AuNP-protein nanocomplexes

Nowadays, they are many strategies to functionalize AuNPs by different ligands, polymers, or biomolecules based on the application of the bio-hybrid [151]. For example, proteins can be attached to the NP surface by linker molecules. A few examples are listed below:

(a) Antibody glycans coupling to the AuNP surface by amines or hydrazines reactive groups [152, 153].

(b) Chymotrypsin linking by alkanethiol self-assembled monolayers generated on the gold spherical surface. The spacer can be hydrophobic (e.g., ethylene oxide) or polar-like (e.g., hydroxyl, carboxyl head group). The length of the spacer is relevant to maintaining the structure and function of the protein in the AuNP surface [154].

(c) Self-assembled membrane β-barrel proteins from *E. coli* on planar gold surfaces. In the proteins, a single cysteine is added to drive an upright orientation lining the protein in a thiol-alkyl PEG molecule functionalized in the AuNP surface [150].

Characterization of engineered bio-hybrids

Combining different techniques, it is possible to characterize the bio-hybrid NP shape, surface chemistry, functionalization efficiency, etc. Some of these techniques are listed below:

(a) *Time-of-flight secondary ion mass spectrometry (TOF-SIMs):* TOF-SIMs use a pulsed ion beam to ionize molecules from the sample surface. The ionized particles are accelerated into a "flight tube" and the mass is determined by measuring the time they reach the detector. This technique is used to measure the mass of the generated bio-hybrids, which allows obtaining the stoichiometry of the functionalization.

(b) *X-ray photoelectron spectroscopy (XPS):* XPS is based on the photoelectric effect. XPS can quantitatively identify the elements in a material, their chemical state, and their overall electronic structure. This technique gives information on the elements in the materials and to which other elements are bounded too. Thus, this technique allows quantifying the functionalization of the NPs in each step and the bonds formed in the functionalization process, making XPS a powerful technique to characterize the bio-hybrid's structure.

(c) *Transmission Electron Microscopy:* TEM is a technique to image the bio-hybrids by a beam of high-energy electrons through a solid sample. This technique is used to check the size distribution of the NPs and their shape, among others.

5.4.2.2 Sensors for clinical diagnosis using engineered bio-hybrids

Combining designed proteins with NPs or other inorganic materials to develop engineered bio-hybrids has been used to develop more reliable sensors, which show higher sensitivity and selectivity toward a target than traditional methods. A few relevant examples in clinics are listed below:

(a) *Choline detection:* Choline is a metabolite that is involved in cell signaling. Liver problems, infertility, and high blood pressure are related to the lack of this metabolite and, thus, methods to detect the level of this molecule are clinically relevant. Choline oxidase enzyme reacts with choline metabolite producing H_2O_2 and thiocholine in the presence of oxygen. Produced products (e.g., H_2O_2 and thiocholine) from this reaction are used to quantify the choline in the sample. Bio-hybrid systems combining choline oxidase enzyme with AuNPs, QDs, or CNTs have been developed to increase the sensitivity and technical issues found in traditional methods to detect choline. For example, the modulation of the aggregation state of AuNPs in the presence of H_2O_2 produced color changes that can be detected to quantify the H_2O_2 production and, thus, choline amount. Generally, in these hybrid systems, choline oxidase is used in a solution, making it difficult to detect choline in vivo because the electroactive species in the biological sample interfere with the results. To overcome the challenge, strategies for enzyme immobilization in the particles have been employed. For example, glutaraldehyde crosslinker has been used to immobilize choline oxidase enzyme in NPs using amino groups in the protein and NP coatings to generate a covalently linked bio-hybrid. Despite the advances, we still lack a simple, reliable, sensitive, and selective bio-hybrid for choline detection. Recently, the generation of nanoenzymes in which only the active part of the choline oxidase is engineered has been proposed. These novel strategies to design bio-hybrids will increase the performance of the sensors for choline detection [155, 156].

(b) *Glucose detection:* The clinical relevance of disease as diabetes has increased the interest in having sensors to detect glucose with high sensitivity and selectivity. For this purpose, phosphate binding protein (PBP), ribose binding protein (RBP), maltose binding protein (MBP), and glucose/galactose binding protein (GGBP) are combined with fluorophores to detect different sugar types by fluorescence assays. Upon substrate binding, these proteins perform conformational modifications. Depending on the protein, there are three categories of site-directed modifications: endosteric, peristeric, and allosteric. The degree of signal change between free and bound form and the response time are used as sensors for the target. Depending on the protein response, different mutations can be introduced, generating modified proteins with improved properties. In order to engineer the mutants, it is crucial to know the conformational change performed by each class of proteins. This information is obtained from the protein structure in the open (ligand unbound) and the close (ligand-bound) conformation. Protein modifications are made in the binding site, in the periphery, or some distance outside the ligand binding site for endosteric, peristeric, or allosteric changes, respectively. These modifications are used to improve the affinity and/or the selectivity of the protein for the ligand compared to the wild type. For example, the native affinity of GGBP for glucose is 0.2 μM, which is not enough to be used as a sensor of the glucose in human blood. However, a single modification in GGBP protein (e.g., A213R) makes the protein useful to detect glucose in vivo. Modifications are also done to increase the selectivity for the ligand. For example, GGBP protein selectivity can increase by modifying the aspartic acid in position 14 with glutamic acid, allowing the protein to recognize glucose but not galactose.

The conformational changes in sugar-binding proteins are detected by changes in the fluorescence signal of chromophores. For example, proteins are labeled with Förster resonance energy transfer (FRET) dye pairs and conformational changes are detected by changes in FRET rates. FRET is a process where an excited chromophore donor transfers its energy to an acceptor chromophore through non-radiative dipole coupling. The FRET rate depends on chromophores' distance and, thus, FRET is used to monitor and quantify conformational changes in proteins using suitable dye pairs labeled in different protein regions. A single fluorophore label can also be employed as recognition. In this case, conformational change upon ligand binding alters the fluorophore's solvent exposure and polarity of its environment, modifying its emission. For the latest, environment-sensitive fluorophores are selected as pyrene, rhodamine, or coumarins, for example. These fluorophores are attached to specific places in the protein using orthogonal reactivities. In this sense, cysteine residue for functionalization with sulfhydryl-reactive probes is the most used reactivity, due to its high selectivity and conjugation yield [157].

5.4.2.3 Targeted therapies and tissue imaging using bio-hybrids based on engineered antibodies

Radiolabeled antibodies for tumor imaging

PET imaging is a non-invasive technique that allows in vivo visualization of the whole body [158]. In that sense, PET imaging should be a technique that predicts and monitors responses and it is used mainly for diagnosis. PET radioligands are radioactive biochemical substances that interact with receptors in the body. Some PET radioligands are, for example, antibody-derived fragments or small proteins, which are stabilized and optimized for their use. The control of the molecular recognition between the imaging agent and the desired target is key to increasing the sensitivity and specificity of the imaging.

In various advanced cancers, immune checkpoint receptors (ICs) express immune checkpoint proteins as cytotoxic T lymphocyte-associated protein-4 (CTLA-4), programmed cell death protein (PD-1), or programmed cell death ligand-1 (PDL-1) [159]. Spatiotemporal distribution can be quantitatively assessed using non-invasive PET imaging using modified antibodies or small engineered proteins labeled with radioisotopes. As such, PET imaging using ICs biomarkers complements the existing immunohistochemical techniques obtaining a more accurate prediction of the ICs response in the body.

PET imaging of IC proteins with monoclonal antibodies (mAbs)

In vivo visualization of the IC, biodistribution is done using IC-targeted radiolabeled mAbs (immunoPET) [159]. The therapeutic efficacy of the immunoPET has prompted its use in clinical studies. The most used radioisotopes are copper-64 or zirconium with a half-lifetime of 12–15 hours. Specifically, radiolabeled immunoglobins G (IgG) mAbs have been used for PET imaging exploiting their high specific and binding affinity toward their target [160]. IgGs are heterodimeric proteins (150 kDa) composed of two identical heavy and two identical light chains linked by disulfide bonds. Using IgG mAbs, immunoPET changes in tumor expression induced by various therapies, including chemotherapy, are detected without the need for repeated invasive treatments [160].

PET imaging of IC proteins with antibody fragments and small proteins

Nowadays, antibody fragments or small-engineered proteins are in use in clinical trials, as they have many advantages compared to radiolabeled mAbs.

Types of antibody fragments and small proteins are listed below:

(a) The antigen-binding fragment (Fab) is a fragment of IgG antibody, which contains one complete light chain and the variable and one heavy chain.
(b) Single domain antibodies or nanobodies are monovalent antigen-binding fragments from camelid single variable domains.

Some of these advantages of using antibody fragments and small proteins are listed below:

(a) The unbound radioligands are rapidly cleared from the circulation by kidney filtration and urinary excretion. This characteristic comes from their low-molecular weight, which makes their half-life shorter (minutes to hours) than the half-life of the mAbs.

(b) The fast clearance from the body makes the absolute uptake lower than when using full mAbs (generally between 2% and 5% ID/g). However, the body uptake is also faster making it possible to obtain high-contrast images at earlier time points than when using mAbs (e.g., 1–2 h). This fast uptake makes it possible to do the radioligand administration and PET imaging on the same day, making the initiation of the appropriate therapy faster. Moreover, fast PET imaging makes it possible to image the disease on subsequent days to obtain more information on the patient´s disease and its evolution.

(c) The fast body uptake and imaging make it possible to use short-lived PET isotopes like fluorine-18, which reduces the global radiation to the patient, in contrast with when using mAbs long-lived radioisotopes.

(d) Their fast diffusion and improved penetration make possible better intra-tumoral distribution obtaining a better sense of the tumor size and shape even at sites distal from the vasculature.

Bio-hybrids based on antibodies for targeted therapies

The binding of an antibody with a specific antigen is of the most inspiring methods of targeted therapy [161]. Antibody formulations such as Trastuzumab and Bevacizumab are currently used for the inhibition of tumor growth, each one using a different mechanism of action [38, 49]. Trastuzumab binds to human epidermal growth factor receptor-2 (HER-2) overexpressed on the surface of cancer cells and inhibits their proliferation. On the other hand, Bevacizumab binds to the vascular endothelial growth factor (VEGF) expressed by cancer cells under hypoxic conditions, and thus endothelial cells do not get the signal to create tumor vasculature. Targeted therapies with antibodies are coupled with chemotherapy for cancer treatment. Nanomedicine experts focus on the use of antibody-drug conjugates for targeted delivery of chemotherapy, whereas they combine antibodies with inorganic NPs to enhance loading or add diagnostic/therapeutic properties.

In this kind of hybrid vector, it is important to ensure the integrity of the antibody structure after its immobilization. This is why labile polymer linkers are usually employed to conjugate the antibody on a coated particle. Han et al. used norbornene-tetrazine chemistry to conjugate antibodies on QDs with different emission wavelengths, enabling targeted intravital multiphoton imaging of cells in blood vessels and the bone marrow of mice [162]. In another work, monoclonal antibodies against the VEGF were immobilized onto BSA-coated IONPs through an NH_2-PEG-maleimide linker for the MRI visualization of a glioma model in rats, a formulation that was proved more effective than Feridex® [163]. Popovtzer et al. conjugated Cetuximab, a conjugated via an HS-PEG-COOH linker onto PEG-coated AuNPs for the treatment of head and neck tumors in mice [164]. They achieved to target the tumor tissue, while X-ray irradiation effectively inhibited tumor growth thanks to the radio-sensitizing inorganic component. Another group immobilized monoclonal antibodies against the prostate stem cell antigen (PSCA) onto the surface of multi-walled carbon nanotubes (MWCNTs) using a PEI linker [165]. PEI was also functionalized with fluorescein isothiocyanate (FITC) in order to visualize the NPs internalized by PC-3 cells in vitro. Furthermore, the MWCNT component provided ultrasound contrast and enabled the loading of doxorubicin to visualize and suppress the growth of PC-3 tumors in mice.

In antibody formulations, either the whole sequence of the antibody or the fragments responsible for binding may be employed. Ding et al. functionalized IONPs with the anti-HER-2 scFv [166]. These particles exhibited enhanced MRI contrast of HER-2 positive, SUIT-2 tumors in mice compared to PEGylated IONPs.

5.4.2.4 Emerging technologies of bio-hybrids based on engineered proteins

Labeling tumors for imaging or treatment requires strategies to target the bio-markets specifically. For example, engineered proteins can be encoded to recognize the bio-markers while carrying fluorophores for imaging or drugs for treatments. Thus, bio-hybrids based on engineered proteins have the potential to generate complex systems to develop targeted theranostics. However, harnessing their potential requires control over their structure and functionality, which is not trivial. This problem is mitigated when using de novo proteins as scaffolds. Their simple architecture makes them ideal "molecular-Lego" for protein engineering. Simple protein structures usually involve a repeated 20–60 amino acids motif and exhibit a distinctive, regular contact pattern between residues adjacent to the primary sequence. In these simplified proteins, secondary and tertiary structures are usually determined by a few amino acids and the rest of the amino acids can be modified without disrupting the protein structure. Recently, designed consensus tetratricopeptide repeat proteins (CTPR) have been used to stabilize fluorescent metal nanoclusters (NCs) [167, 168]. CTPRs are composed of tandem arrays of 3–20 modular repeats to form superhelical structures of different lengths. Their repeat module is a 34-amino acid helix-turn-helix structure, and eight repeats comprise one complete superhelical turn. The modular structural and functional properties of CTPRs make them suited candidates as templates for the stabilization of NCs. NCs have attracted attention to be contrast agents for imaging, due to their strong fluorescence, photostability, and biocompatibility. Moreover, their size and composition-dependent electronic transitions make them interesting to generate different colors, which are ideal for imaging different cell parts. Prof. Cortajarena and co-workers generated fluorescence NCs using CTPR proteins and metals (e.g., Au, Ag, and Cu). Their work showed that the color of the NCs depends on the amino acids in the proteins and the metal itself. They also showed that engineered bio-hybrids based on the CTPRs enter into living cells without any permeabilization treatment, damage the cells, or affect their fluorescent properties. Overall, the simple and versatile approach shown by Prof. Cortajarena probes the potential of engineered bio-hybrids in the field of cellular imaging or labeling. This work is an example of the increasing interest in emerging technologies based on engineered proteins that will revolutionize treatments and diagnosis in the coming years.

5.5 Conclusions

Inorganic NPs show great potential as diagnostic probes and drug delivery vehicles. However, the functionalization of their surface with macromolecules may be necessary to ensure their stability and add targeting properties. These goals may be fulfilled using natural proteins, isolated or synthetic peptides, and engineered protein sequences. The biocompatibility and biological activity of these molecules may allow for the transition of inorganic NPs to the clinic and also replace coatings of petroleum-based polymers.

Many natural proteins are GRAS and are found in relative abundance in nature. This gives them an important advantage in the production of hybrid nanoformulations. In this protein category, albumin stands out as a promising candidate for applications in cancer theranostics. Albumin coatings can increase the drug loading capacity and enhance the cellular uptake of hybrid nanosystems. The lack of targeting properties in albumin may be compromised with the anchoring of biofunctional ligands, since the variety of amino acids in its sequence allows for different types of chemical modifications. For the diagnosis and treatment of cardiovascular diseases, lipoproteins represent a very effective system. This is mainly due to their innate propensity to accumulate in atherosclerotic plaques, while their protein-lipid composition allows for the loading of hydrophobic drugs. Last, the oral delivery of hybrid NPs may require more robust proteins on the surface, such as casein.

The progress in the design and manufacture of CPPs during the last 20 years has yielded favorable in vivo results. The dual delivery systems that were developed by conjugating the inorganic NPs with cell-penetrating and tissue targeting peptides further improved the stability, administration, and effectiveness of the carried molecules through targeting and accumulating to specific tissues, therefore, reducing side effects and lowering the necessary dose. The small size, ease of sequence manipulation, and ability to independently penetrate the cell membranes are convenient advantages of these conjugates for use in nanomedicine. Additionally, combining various peptide sequences (CPPs, tumor homing peptides) on the NPs' surface enables its use as a promising multi-functional delivery nanoplatform. Many of the applications described in this chapter indicate that CPPs might become a valuable tool for cancer, neurogenerative disorders, and inflammation treatment and diagnosis that can be applied in the near future for addressing the so far unmet medical needs.

Advances in recombinant DNA technology have opened the doors to the use of engineered proteins to generate biohybrids with desired properties, including improved thermostability or pH sensitivity. Furthermore, the use of engineered proteins in therapy also allows for better conjugation efficiencies, which improve the recognition and make the treatments more efficient. Moreover, the new probes based on engineered proteins increase the diagnosis sensitivity, making it possible to monitor the diseases in real-time. Nowadays, the use of engineered proteins in theragnosis is an increasing trend with the potential to obtain personalized treatments for each disease and patient.

Overall, we expect that the different approaches suggested above may lead to the development of protein- or peptide-inorganic clinical tools, which are suitable to combat various diseases. A major consideration in this regard is the adaptation of the systems from the animal models to the human body.

Acknowledgments

E.G. recognizes support from the Maria de Maeztu "Units of Excellence" program MDM-2016-0618.

S.H.M thanks Carl Tryggers Foundation (Sweden) for the support through a postdoc stipend.

References

1. Ghosn, Y., Kamareddine, M.H., Tawk, A., Elia, C., El Mahmoud, A., Terro, K. et al. (2019) Inorganic nanoparticles as drug delivery systems and their potential role in the treatment of chronic myelogenous leukaemia. *Technol. Cancer Res. Treat. (NLM (Medline))*.
2. Bayda, S., Hadla, M., Palazzolo, S., Riello, P., Corona, G., Toffoli, G. et al. (2018) Inorganic nanoparticles for cancer therapy: A transition from lab to clinic. *Curr. Med. Chem.*, **25**, pp. 4269–4303.
3. Walter, P., Welcomme, E., Hallégot, P., Zaluzec, N.J., Deeb, C., Castaing, J. et al. (2006) Early use of PbS nanotechnology for an ancient hair dyeing formula. *Nano Lett.*, **6**, pp. 2215–2219.
4. Smith, B.R. and Gambhir, S.S. (2017) Nanomaterials for in vivo imaging. *Chem. Rev.*, **117**, pp. 901–986.
5. Dong, J., Carpinone, P.L., Pyrgiotakis, G., Demokritou, P., and Moudgil, B.M. (2020) Synthesis of precision gold nanoparticles using turkevich method. *KONA Powder Part. J.*, **37**, pp. 224–232.

6. Jiao, M., Zhang, P., Meng, J., Li, Y., Liu, C., Luo, X. et al. (2018) Recent advancements in biocompatible inorganic nanoparticles towards biomedical applications. *Biomater. Sci.*, Royal Society of Chemistry, pp. 726–745.
7. Ajinkya, N., Yu, X., Kaithal, P., Luo, H., Somani, P., and Ramakrishna, S. (2020) Magnetic iron oxide nanoparticle (IONP) synthesis to applications: Present and future. *Materials (Basel)*, **13**, pp. 1–35.
8. Lisiecki, I. (2005) Size, shape, and structural control of metallic nanocrystals. *J. Phys. Chem. B*, **109**, pp. 12231–12244.
9. Dadfar, S.M., Roemhild, K., Drude, N.I., von Stillfried, S., Knüchel, R., Kiessling, F. et al. (2019) Iron oxide nanoparticles: Diagnostic, therapeutic and theranostic applications. *Adv. Drug Deliv. Rev.*, Elsevier B.V., **138**, pp. 302–325.
10. Odularu, A.T. (2018) Metal nanoparticles: Thermal decomposition, biomedicinal applications to cancer treatment, and future perspectives. *Bioinorg. Chem. Appl.*, **2018**, pp. 1–6.
11. Majerič, P. and Rudolf, R. (2020) Advances in ultrasonic spray pyrolysis processing of noble metal nanoparticles—Review. *Materials (Basel)*, **13**, pp. 3485.
12. Kovalenko, M.V, Manna, L., Cabot, A., Hens, Z., Talapin, D.V, Kagan, C.R. et al. (2015) Prospects of nanoscience with nanocrystals. *ACS Nano*, **9**, pp. 1012–1057.
13. Pu, Y., Cai, F., Wang, D., Wang, J.-X., and Chen, J.-F. (2018) Colloidal synthesis of semiconductor quantum dots toward large-scale production: A review. *Ind. Eng. Chem. Res.*, **57**, pp. 1790–1802.
14. Liberman, A., Mendez, N., Trogler, W.C., and Kummel, A.C. (2014) Synthesis and surface functionalization of silica nanoparticles for nanomedicine. *Surf. Sci. Rep.*, Elsevier, **69**, pp. 132–158.
15. Sajid, M.I., Jamshaid, U., Jamshaid, T., Zafar, N., Fessi, H., and Elaissari, A. (2016) Carbon nanotubes from synthesis to in vivo biomedical applications. *Int. J. Pharm.*, Elsevier B.V., **501**, pp. 278–299.
16. Sharma, A. and Das, J. (2019) Small molecules derived carbon dots: Synthesis and applications in sensing, catalysis, imaging, and biomedicine. *J. Nanobiotechnology*, BioMed Central, **17**, pp. 92.
17. Shen, J., Shafiq, M., Ma, M., and Chen, H. (2020) Synthesis and surface engineering of inorganic nanomaterials based on microfluidic technology. *Nanomaterials*, **10**, pp. 1177.
18. Zou, Y., Zhou, X., Ma, J., Yang, X., and Deng, Y. (2020) Recent advances in amphiphilic block copolymer templated mesoporous metal-based

materials: Assembly engineering and applications. *Chem. Soc. Rev.*, Royal Society of Chemistry, **49**, pp. 1173–1208.

19. Rosenberger, I., Strauss, A., Dobiasch, S., Weis, C., Szanyi, S., Gil-Iceta, L. et al. (2015) Targeted diagnostic magnetic nanoparticles for medical imaging of pancreatic cancer. *J. Control. Release*, Elsevier B.V., **214**, pp. 76–84.
20. Amatya, R., Hwang, S., Park, T., Min, K.A., and Shin, M.C. (2021) In vitro and in vivo evaluation of pegylated starch-coated iron oxide nanoparticles for enhanced photothermal cancer therapy. *Pharmaceutics*, **13**, pp. 871.
21. Tang, F., Li, L., and Chen, D. (2012) Mesoporous silica nanoparticles: Synthesis, biocompatibility and drug delivery. *Adv. Mater.*, **24**, pp. 1504–1534.
22. Leopold, N. and Lendl, B. (2003) A new method for fast preparation of highly surface-enhanced Raman scattering (SERS) active silver colloids at room temperature by reduction of silver nitrate with hydroxylamine hydrochloride. *J. Phys. Chem. B*, **107**, pp. 5723–5727.
23. Lopes, T.S., Alves, G.G., Pereira, M.R., Granjeiro, J.M., and Leite, P.E.C. (2019) Advances and potential application of gold nanoparticles in nanomedicine. *J. Cell. Biochem.*, **120**, pp. 16370–16378.
24. Xu, L., Wang, Y.-Y., Huang, J., Chen, C.-Y., Wang, Z.-X., and Xie, H. (2020) Silver nanoparticles: Synthesis, medical applications and biosafety. *Theranostics*, **10**, pp. 8996–9031.
25. Yukawa, H. and Baba, Y. (2018) In vivo imaging technology of transplanted stem cells using quantum dots for regenerative medicine. *Anal. Sci.*, **34**, pp. 525–532.
26. Levy, M., Chowdhury, P.P., and Nagpal, P. (2019) Quantum dot therapeutics: A new class of radical therapies. *J. Biol. Eng.*, **13**, pp. 48.
27. Bobo, D., Robinson, K.J., Islam, J., Thurecht, K.J., and Corrie, S.R. (2016) Nanoparticle-based medicines: A review of FDA-approved materials and clinical trials to date. *Pharm. Res.*, **33**, pp. 2373–2387.
28. Montané, X., Bajek, A., Roszkowski, K., Montornés, J.M., Giamberini, M., Roszkowski, S. et al. (2020) Encapsulation for cancer therapy. *Molecules*, MDPI AG, **25**, pp. 1605.
29. Anselmo, A.C. and Mitragotri, S. (2019) Nanoparticles in the clinic: An update. *Bioeng. Transl. Med.*, **4**, pp. 1–16.
30. Barbero, F., Russo, L., Vitali, M., Piella, J., Salvo, I., Borrajo, M.L. et al. (2017) Formation of the protein corona: The interface between

nanoparticles and the immune system. *Semin. Immunol.*, Academic Press, **34**, pp. 52–60.

31. Owen, J. and Brus, L. (2017) Chemical synthesis and luminescence applications of colloidal semiconductor quantum dots. *J. Am. Chem. Soc.*, **139**, pp. 10939–10943.
32. Mei, B.C., Susumu, K., Medintz, I.L., and Mattoussi, H. (2009) Polyethylene glycol-based bidentate ligands to enhance quantum dot and gold nanoparticle stability in biological media. *Nat. Protoc.*, **4**, pp. 412–423.
33. Sperling, R.A. and Parak, W.J. (2010) Surface modification, functionalization and bioconjugation of colloidal inorganic nanoparticles. *Philos. Trans. R. Soc. A Math. Phys. Eng. Sci.*, **368**, pp. 1333–1383.
34. McCarthy, S.A., Davies, G.-L., and Gun'ko, Y.K. (2012) Preparation of multifunctional nanoparticles and their assemblies. *Nat. Protoc.*, **7**, pp. 1677–1693.
35. Zhu, L. and Torchilin, V.P. (2013) Stimulus-responsive nano-preparations for tumor targeting. *Integr. Biol.*, Royal Society of Chemistry, **5**, pp. 96–107.
36. Georgilis, E., Abdelghani, M., Pille, J., Aydinlioglu, E., van Hest, J.C.M., Lecommandoux, S. et al. (2020) Nanoparticles based on natural, engineered or synthetic proteins and polypeptides for drug delivery applications. *Int. J. Pharm.*, **586**.
37. Vakhrusheva, T. V., Gusev, A.A., Gusev, S.A., and Vlasova, I.I. (2013) Albumin reduces thrombogenic potential of single-walled carbon nanotubes. *Toxicol. Lett.*, Elsevier Ireland Ltd., **221**, pp. 137–145.
38. Elzoghby, A.O., Hemasa, A.L., and Freag, M.S. (2016) Hybrid protein-inorganic nanoparticles: From tumor-targeted drug delivery to cancer imaging. *J. Control. Release*, Elsevier B.V., **243**, pp. 303–322.
39. Taylor, M.T., Nelson, J.E., Suero, M.G., and Gaunt, M.J. (2018) A protein functionalization platform based on selective reactions at methionine residues. *Nature*, Springer US, **562**, pp. 563–568.
40. Fu, Q., Sun, J., Zhang, W., Sui, X., Yan, Z., and He, Z. (2009) Nanoparticle albumin-bound (NAB) technology is a promising method for anti-cancer drug delivery. *Recent Pat. Anticancer. Drug Discov.*, **4**, pp. 262–272.
41. Bolaños, K., Kogan, M.J., and Araya, E. (2019) Capping gold nanoparticles with albumin to improve their biomedical properties. *Int. J. Nanomedicine*, Dove Medical Press Ltd., **14**, pp. 6387–6406.

42. Watcharin, W., Schmithals, C., Pleli, T., Köberle, V., Korkusuz, H., Huebner, F. et al. (2014) Biodegradable human serum albumin nanoparticles as contrast agents for the detection of hepatocellular carcinoma by magnetic resonance imaging. *Eur. J. Pharm. Biopharm.*, Elsevier B.V., **87**, pp. 132–141.

43. Ahmad, M.W., Kim, C.R., Baeck, J.S., Chang, Y., Kim, T.J., Bae, J.E. et al. (2014) Bovine serum albumin (BSA) and cleaved-BSA conjugated ultrasmall Gd_2O_3 nanoparticles: Synthesis, characterization, and application to MRI contrast agents. *Colloids Surfaces A Physicochem. Eng. Asp.*, Elsevier B.V., **450**, pp. 67–75.

44. Chen, Q., Liang, C., Wang, X., He, J., Li, Y., and Liu, Z. (2014) An albumin-based theranostic nano-agent for dual-modal imaging guided photothermal therapy to inhibit lymphatic metastasis of cancer post surgery. *Biomaterials*, Elsevier Ltd., **35**, pp. 9355–9362.

45. Zhang, J., Hao, G., Yao, C., Yu, J., Wang, J., Yang, W. et al. (2016) Albumin-mediated biomineralization of paramagnetic NIR Ag_2S QDs for tiny tumor bimodal targeted imaging in vivo. *ACS Appl. Mater. Interfaces*, **8**, pp. 16612–16621.

46. Quan, Q., Xie, J., Gao, H., Yang, M., Zhang, F., Liu, G. et al. (2011) HSA coated iron oxide nanoparticles as drug delivery vehicles for cancer therapy. *Mol. Pharm.*, **8**, pp. 1669–1676.

47. Misak, H., Zacharias, N., Song, Z., Hwang, S., Man, K.P., Asmatulu, R. et al. (2013) Skin cancer treatment by albumin/5-Fu loaded magnetic nanocomposite spheres in a mouse model. *J. Biotechnol.*, Elsevier B.V., **164**, pp. 130–136.

48. Liu, J., Abshire, C., Carry, C., Sholl, A.B., Mandava, S.H., Datta, A. et al. (2017) Nanotechnology combined therapy: Tyrosine kinase-bound gold nanorod and laser thermal ablation produce a synergistic higher treatment response of renal cell carcinoma in a murine model. *BJU Int.*, **119**, pp. 342–348.

49. Rassy, E., Flippot, R., and Albiges, L. (2020) Tyrosine kinase inhibitors and immunotherapy combinations in renal cell carcinoma. *Ther. Adv. Med. Oncol.*, **12**, pp. 175883592090750.

50. Huang, H., Yang, D.-P., Liu, M., Wang, X., Zhang, Z., Zhou, G. et al. (2017) pH-sensitive Au-BSA-DOX-FA nanocomposites for combined CT imaging and targeted drug delivery. *Int. J. Nanomedicine*, **12**, pp. 2829–2843.

51. Chopra, A. (2004) Transferrin-coated gadolinium-labeled human serum albumin nanoparticles [Internet]. *Mol. Imaging Contrast Agent Database*.

52. Zhang, M., Cao, Y., Wang, L., Ma, Y., Tu, X., and Zhang, Z. (2015) Manganese doped iron oxide theranostic nanoparticles for combined T1 magnetic resonance imaging and photothermal therapy. *ACS Appl. Mater. Interfaces*, **7**, pp. 4650–4658.

53. Wang, Y., Yang, T., Ke, H., Zhu, A., Wang, Y., Wang, J. et al. (2015) Smart albumin-biomineralized nanocomposites for multimodal imaging and photothermal tumor ablation. *Adv. Mater.*, **27**, pp. 3874–3882.

54. Wang, Q., Lv, L., Ling, Z., Wang, Y., Liu, Y., Li, L. et al. (2015) Long-circulating iodinated albumin-gadolinium nanoparticles as enhanced magnetic resonance and computed tomography imaging probes for osteosarcoma visualization. *Anal. Chem.*, **87**, pp. 4299–4304.

55. You, Q., Sun, Q., Yu, M., Wang, J., Wang, S., Liu, L. et al. (2017) BSA-bioinspired gadolinium hybrid-functionalized hollow gold nanoshells for NIRF/PA/CT/MR quadmodal diagnostic imaging-guided photothermal/photodynamic cancer therapy. *ACS Appl. Mater. Interfaces*.

56. Qi, Y., Yan, X., Xia, T., and Liu, S. (2021) Use of macrophage as a Trojan horse for cancer nanotheranostics. *Mater. Des.*, **198**.

57. Xie, J., Wang, J., Niu, G., Huang, J., Chen, K., Li, X. et al. (2010) Human serum albumin coated iron oxide nanoparticles for efficient cell labeling. *Chem. Commun.*, **46**, pp. 433–435.

58. Chiu, H.T., Su, C.K., Sun, Y.C., Chiang, C.S., and Huang, Y.F. (2017) Albumin-gold nanorod nanoplatform for cell-mediated tumoritropic delivery with homogenous chemodrug distribution and enhanced retention ability. *Theranostics*, **7**, pp. 3034–3052.

59. Mahmoudian, M., Salatin, S., and Khosroushahi, A.Y. (2018) Natural low- and high-density lipoproteins as mighty bio-nanocarriers for anticancer drug delivery. *Cancer Chemother. Pharmacol.*, Springer Berlin Heidelberg, **82**, pp. 371–382.

60. Di, L. and Maiseyeu, A. (2021) Low-density lipoprotein nano-medicines: Mechanisms of targeting, biology, and theranostic potential. *Drug Deliv.*, Taylor & Francis, **28**, pp. 408–421.

61. Pérez-Medina, C., Binderup, T., Lobatto, M.E., Tang, J., Calcagno, C., Giesen, L. et al. (2016) In vivo PET imaging of high-density lipoprotein in multiple atherosclerosis models. *JACC Cardiovasc Imaging*, **9**, pp. 950–961.

62. Alberti, D., Protti, N., Toppino, A., Deagostino, A., Lanzardo, S., Bortolussi, S. et al. (2015) A theranostic approach based on the use of a dual boron/Gd agent to improve the efficacy of boron neutron

capture therapy in the lung cancer treatment. *Nanomedicine Nanotechnology, Biol. Med.*, Elsevier B.V., **11**, pp. 741–750.

63. Cormode, D.P., Skajaa, T., van Schooneveld, M.M., Koole, R., Jarzyna, P., Lobatto, M.E. et al. (2008) Nanocrystal core high-density lipoproteins: A multimodal molecular imaging contrast agent platform. *Nano Lett.*, **8**, pp. 3715–3723.

64. Yang, S., Damiano, M.G., Zhang, H., Tripathy, S., Luthi, A.J., Rink, J.S. et al. (2013) Biomimetic, synthetic HDL nanostructures for lymphoma. *Proc. Natl. Acad. Sci.*, **110**, pp. 2511–2516.

65. Tran, T.T.D., Tran, P.H.L., Amin, H.H., and Lee, B.J. (2017) Biodistribution and in vivo performance of fattigation-platform theranostic nanoparticles. *Mater. Sci. Eng. C*, Elsevier B.V., **79**, pp. 671–678.

66. Hu, G., Chun, X., Wang, Y., He, Q., and Gao, H. (2015) Peptide mediated active targeting and intelligent particle size reduction-mediated enhanced penetrating of fabricated nanoparticles for triple-negative breast cancer treatment. *Oncotarget*, **6**, pp. 41258–41274.

67. Ruan, S., He, Q., and Gao, H. (2015) Matrix metalloproteinase triggered size-shrinkable gelatin-gold fabricated nanoparticles for tumor microenvironment sensitive penetration and diagnosis of glioma. *Nanoscale*, Royal Society of Chemistry, **7**, pp. 9487–9496.

68. Tian, X.H., Wang, Z.G., Meng, H., Wang, Y.H., Feng, W., Wei, F. et al. (2013) Tat peptide-decorated gelatin-siloxane nanoparticles for delivery of CGRP transgene in treatment of cerebral vasospasm. *Int. J. Nanomedicine*, **8**, pp. 865–876.

69. Ye, S., Tian, M., Wang, T., Ren, L., Wang, D., Shen, L. et al. (2012) Synergistic effects of cell-penetrating peptide Tat and fusogenic peptide HA2-enhanced cellular internalization and gene transduction of organosilica nanoparticles. *Nanomedicine*, United States, **8**, pp. 833–841.

70. Wong, C., Stylianopoulos, T., Cui, J., Martin, J., Chauhan, V.P., Jiang, W. et al. (2011) Multistage nanoparticle delivery system for deep penetration into tumor tissue. *Proc. Natl. Acad. Sci.*, **108**, pp. 2426–2431.

71. Xu, J.H., Gao, F.P., Li, L.L., Ma, H.L., Fan, Y.S., Liu, W. et al. (2013) Gelatin-mesoporous silica nanoparticles as matrix metalloproteinases-degradable drug delivery systems in vivo. *Microporous Mesoporous Mater.*, **182**, pp. 165–172.

72. Li, W.M., Chiang, C.S., Huang, W.C., Su, C.W., Chiang, M.Y., Chen, J.Y. et al. (2015) Amifostine-conjugated pH-sensitive calcium phosphate-covered magnetic-amphiphilic gelatin nanoparticles for controlled

intracellular dual drug release for dual-targeting in HER-2-overexpressing breast cancer. *J. Control. Release*, Elsevier B.V., **220**, pp. 107–118.

73. Cowger, T.A., Tang, W., Zhen, Z., Hu, K., Rink, D.E., Todd, T.J. et al. (2015) Casein-coated Fe_5C_2 nanoparticles with superior r2 relaxivity for liver-specific magnetic resonance imaging. *Theranostics*, **5**, pp. 1225–1232.

74. Huang, J., Wang, L., Lin, R., Wang, A.Y., Yang, L., Kuang, M. et al. (2013) Casein-coated iron oxide nanoparticles for high MRI contrast enhancement and efficient cell targeting. *ACS Appl. Mater. Interfaces*, **5**, pp. 4632–4639.

75. Huang, J., Shu, Q., Wang, L., Wu, H., Wang, A.Y., and Mao, H. (2015) Layer-by-layer assembled milk protein coated magnetic nanoparticle enabled oral drug delivery with high stability in stomach and enzyme-responsive release in small intestine. *Biomaterials*, **39**, pp. 105–113.

76. Wang, L., Qin, G., Geng, S., Dai, Y., and Wang, J.Y. (2013) Preparation of zein conjugated quantum dots and their in vivo transdermal delivery capacity through nude mouse skin. *J. Biomed. Nanotechnol.*, **9**, pp. 367–376.

77. Wang, H., Zhu, W., Huang, Y., Li, Z., Jiang, Y., and Xie, Q. (2017) Facile encapsulation of hydroxycamptothecin nanocrystals into zein-based nanocomplexes for active targeting in drug delivery and cell imaging. *Acta Biomater.*, **61**, pp. 88–100.

78. Tian, Y., Jiang, X., Chen, X., Shao, Z., and Yang, W. (2014) Doxorubicin-loaded magnetic silk fibroin nanoparticles for targeted therapy of multidrug-resistant cancer. *Adv. Mater.*, **26**, pp. 7393–7398.

79. Chen, A.Z., Chen, L.Q., Wang, S. Bin, Wang, Y.Q., and Zha, J.Z. (2015) Study of magnetic silk fibroin nanoparticles for massage-like transdermal drug delivery. *Int. J. Nanomedicine*, **10**, pp. 4639–4651.

80. Khalid, A., Mitropoulos, A.N., Marelli, B., Tomljenovic-Hanic, S., and Omenetto, F.G. (2016) Doxorubicin loaded nanodiamond-silk spheres for fluorescence tracking and controlled drug release. *Biomed. Opt. Express*, **7**, pp. 132.

81. Jia, L., Guo, L., Zhu, J., and Ma, Y. (2014) Stability and cytocompatibility of silk fibroin-capped gold nanoparticles. *Mater. Sci. Eng. C*, Elsevier B.V., **43**, pp. 231–236.

82. Jeong, W. jin, Bu, J., Kubiatowicz, L.J., Chen, S.S., Kim, Y.S., and Hong, S. (2018) Peptide–nanoparticle conjugates: A next generation

of diagnostic and therapeutic platforms? *Nano Converg.*, Springer Singapore, **5**, pp. 1–18.

83. Spicer, C.D., Jumeaux, C., Gupta, B., and Stevens, M.M. (2018) Peptide and protein nanoparticle conjugates: Versatile platforms for biomedical applications. *Chem. Soc. Rev.*, **47**, pp. 3574–3620.

84. Wang, F., Wang, Y., Zhang, X., Zhang, W., Guo, S., and Jin, F. (2014) Recent progress of cell-penetrating peptides as new carriers for intracellular cargo delivery. *J. Control. Release*, Netherlands, **174**, pp. 126–136.

85. Silva, S., Almeida, A.J., and Vale, N. (2019) Combination of cell-penetrating peptides with nanoparticles for therapeutic application: A review. *Biomolecules*, **9**.

86. Frankel, A.D. and Pabo, C.O. (1988) Cellular uptake of the Tat protein from human immunodeficiency virus. *Cell*, United States, **55**, pp. 1189–1193.

87. Vivès, E., Brodin, P., and Lebleu, B. (1997) A Truncated HIV-1 Tat protein basic domain rapidly translocates through the plasma membrane and accumulates in the cell nucleus. *J. Biol. Chem.*, **272**, pp. 16010–16017.

88. Xie, J., Bi, Y., Zhang, H., Dong, S., Teng, L., Lee, R.J. et al. (2020) Cell-penetrating peptides in diagnosis and treatment of human diseases: From preclinical research to clinical application. *Front. Pharmacol.*, **11**, pp. 697.

89. Esbjörner, E.K., Oglęcka, K., Lincoln, P., Gräslund, A., and Nordén, B. (2007) Membrane binding of pH-sensitive influenza fusion peptides: Positioning, configuration, and induced leakage in a lipid vesicle model. *Biochemistry*, American Chemical Society, **46**, pp. 13490–13504.

90. Felding-Habermann, B. and Cheresh, D.A. (1993) Vitronectin and its receptors. *Curr. Opin. Cell Biol.*, England, **5**, pp. 864–868.

91. Ruoslahti, E. (1988) Fibronectin and its receptors. *Annu. Rev. Biochem.*, Annual Reviews, **57**, pp. 375–413.

92. Ruan, S., He, Q., and Gao, H. (2015) Matrix metalloproteinase triggered size-shrinkable gelatin-gold fabricated nanoparticles for tumor microenvironment sensitive penetration and diagnosis of glioma. *Nanoscale*, The Royal Society of Chemistry, **7**, pp. 9487–9496.

93. Chen, G., Xie, Y., Peltier, R., Lei, H., Wang, P., Chen, J. et al. (2016) Peptide-decorated gold nanoparticles as functional nano-capping agent of mesoporous silica container for targeting drug delivery.

ACS Appl. Mater. Interfaces, American Chemical Society, **8**, pp. 11204–11209.

94. Su, N., Dang, Y., Liang, G., and Liu, G. (2015) Iodine-125-labeled cRGD-gold nanoparticles as tumor-targeted radiosensitizer and imaging agent. *Nanoscale Res. Lett.*, **10**, pp. 160.

95. Ding, C., Xu, Y., Zhao, Y., Zhong, H., and Luo, X. (2018) Fabrication of BSA@AuNC-based nanostructures for cell fluoresce imaging and target drug delivery. *ACS Appl. Mater. Interfaces*, United States, **10**, pp. 8947–8954.

96. Wei, X., Zhan, C., Chen, X., Hou, J., Xie, C., and Lu, W. (2014) Retro-inverso isomer of Angiopep-2: A stable d-peptide ligand inspires brain-targeted drug delivery. *Mol. Pharm.*, United States, **11**, pp. 3261–3268.

97. Ji, X., Wang, H., Chen, Y., Zhou, J., and Liu, Y. (2019) Recombinant expressing angiopep-2 fused anti-VEGF single chain Fab (scFab) could cross blood-brain barrier and target glioma. *AMB Express*, **9**, pp. 165.

98. Shi, X.-X., Miao, W.-M., Pang, D.-W., Wu, J.-S., Tong, Q.-S., Li, J.-X. et al. (2020) Angiopep-2 conjugated nanoparticles loaded with doxorubicin for the treatment of primary central nervous system lymphoma. *Biomater. Sci.*, The Royal Society of Chemistry, **8**, pp. 1290–1297.

99. Chen, G.-J., Su, Y.-Z., Hsu, C., Lo, Y.-L., Huang, S.-J., Ke, J.-H. et al. (2014) Angiopep-pluronic F127-conjugated superparamagnetic iron oxide nanoparticles as nanotheranostic agents for BBB targeting. *J. Mater. Chem. B*, The Royal Society of Chemistry, **2**, pp. 5666–5675.

100. Smith, G.P. (1985) Filamentous fusion phage: Novel expression vectors that display cloned antigens on the virion surface. *Science*, United States, **228**, pp. 1315–1317.

101. Cutler, C.S., Chanda, N., Shukla, R., Sisay, N., Cantorias, M., Zambre, A. et al. (2013) Nanoparticles and phage display selected peptides for imaging and therapy of cancer. *Recent Results Cancer Res. Fortschritte Der Krebsforsch. Prog. Dans Les Rech. Sur Le Cancer*, Germany, **194**, pp. 133–147.

102. Kumar, S.R. and Deutscher, S.L. (2008) ^{111}In-labeled galectin-3-targeting peptide as a SPECT agent for imaging breast tumors. *J. Nucl. Med.*, United States, **49**, pp. 796–803.

103. You, F., Yin, G., Pu, X., Li, Y., Hu, Y., Huang, Z. et al. (2016) Biopanning and characterization of peptides with Fe_3O_4 nanoparticles-binding

capability via phage display random peptide library technique. *Colloids Surf. B. Biointerfaces*, Netherlands, **141**, pp. 537–545.

104. Vilas Boas, L.C.P., Campos, M.L., Berlanda, R.L.A., de Carvalho Neves, N., and Franco, O.L. (2019) Antiviral peptides as promising therapeutic drugs. *Cell. Mol. Life Sci.*, **76**, pp. 3525–3542.

105. Liu, C., Jiang, Z., Tong, Z., Li, Y., and Yang, D. (2014) Biomimetic synthesis of inorganic nanocomposites by a de novo designed peptide. *RSC Adv.*, The Royal Society of Chemistry, **4**, pp. 434–441.

106. Aili, D. and Stevens, M.M. (2010) Bioresponsive peptide–inorganic hybrid nanomaterials. *Chem. Soc. Rev.*, The Royal Society of Chemistry, **39**, pp. 3358–3370.

107. Nakanishi, K., Sakiyama, T., and Imamura, K. (2001) On the adsorption of proteins on solid surfaces, a common but very complicated phenomenon. *J. Biosci. Bioeng.*, Japan, **91**, pp. 233–244.

108. Li, X., Jian, M., Sun, Y., Zhu, Q., and Wang, Z. (2021) The peptide functionalized inorganic nanoparticles for cancer-related bioanalytical and biomedical applications. *Molecules*, **26**.

109. Natarajan, P., Sukthankar, P., Changstrom, J., Holland, C.S., Barry, S., Hunter, W.B. et al. (2018) Synthesis and characterization of multifunctional branched amphiphilic peptide bilayer conjugated gold nanoparticles. *ACS Omega*, American Chemical Society, **3**, pp. 11071–11083.

110. Lévy, R., Thanh, N.T.K., Doty, R.C., Hussain, I., Nichols, R.J., Schiffrin, D.J. et al. (2004) Rational and combinatorial design of peptide capping ligands for gold nanoparticles. *J. Am. Chem. Soc.*, United States, **126**, pp. 10076–10084.

111. Chen, H., Li, X., Liu, F., Zhang, H., and Wang, Z. (2017) Renal clearable peptide functionalized NaGdF(4) nanodots for high-efficiency tracking orthotopic colorectal tumor in mouse. *Mol. Pharm.*, United States, **14**, pp. 3134–3141.

112. Bartczak, D. and Kanaras, A.G. (2011) Preparation of peptide-functionalized gold nanoparticles using one pot EDC/Sulfo-NHS coupling. *Langmuir*, American Chemical Society, **27**, pp. 10119–10123.

113. Upert, G., Bouillère, F., and Wennemers, H. (2012) Oligoprolines as scaffolds for the formation of silver nanoparticles in defined sizes: Correlating molecular and nanoscopic dimensions. *Angew. Chem. Int. Ed. Engl.*, Germany, **51**, pp. 4231–4234.

114. Field, L.D., Delehanty, J.B., Chen, Y., and Medintz, I.L. (2015) Peptides for specifically targeting nanoparticles to cellular organelles: Quo vadis? *Acc. Chem. Res.*, United States, **48**, pp. 1380–1390.

115. Zorko, M. and Langel, U. (2005) Cell-penetrating peptides: Mechanism and kinetics of cargo delivery. *Adv. Drug Deliv. Rev.*, Netherlands, **57**, pp. 529–545.

116. Temsamani, J. and Vidal, P. (2004) The use of cell-penetrating peptides for drug delivery. *Drug Discov. Today*, England, **9**, pp. 1012–1019.

117. Kalimuthu, K., Lubin, B.-C., Bazylevich, A., Gellerman, G., Shpilberg, O., Luboshits, G. et al. (2018) Gold nanoparticles stabilize peptide-drug-conjugates for sustained targeted drug delivery to cancer cells. *J. Nanobiotechnology*, **16**, pp. 34.

118. Morshed, R.A., Muroski, M.E., Dai, Q., Wegscheid, M.L., Auffinger, B., Yu, D. et al. (2016) Cell-penetrating peptide-modified gold nanoparticles for the delivery of doxorubicin to brain metastatic breast Cancer. *Mol. Pharm.*, United States, **13**, pp. 1843–1854.

119. Li, J., Liu, F., Shao, Q., Min, Y., Costa, M., Yeow, E.K.L. et al. (2014) Enzyme-responsive cell-penetrating peptide conjugated mesoporous silica quantum dot nanocarriers for controlled release of nucleus-targeted drug molecules and real-time intracellular fluorescence imaging of tumor cells. *Adv. Healthc. Mater.*, Germany, **3**, pp. 1230–1239.

120. Mussa Farkhani, S., Asoudeh Fard, A., Zakeri-Milani, P., Shahbazi Mojarrad, J., and Valizadeh, H. (2017) Enhancing antitumor activity of silver nanoparticles by modification with cell-penetrating peptides. *Artif. Cells, Nanomedicine, Biotechnol.*, England, **45**, pp. 1029–1035.

121. Boisguérin, P., Deshayes, S., Gait, M.J., O'Donovan, L., Godfrey, C., Betts, C.A. et al. (2015) Delivery of therapeutic oligonucleotides with cell penetrating peptides. *Adv. Drug Deliv. Rev.*, **87**, pp. 52–67.

122. Juliano, R.L., Ming, X., Carver, K., and Laing, B. (2014) Cellular uptake and intracellular trafficking of oligonucleotides: Implications for oligonucleotide pharmacology. *Nucleic Acid Ther.*, **24**, pp. 101–113.

123. Dowaidar, M., Abdelhamid, H.N., Hällbrink, M., Freimann, K., Kurrikoff, K., Zou, X. et al. (2017) Magnetic nanoparticle assisted self-assembly of cell penetrating peptides-oligonucleotides complexes for gene delivery. *Sci. Rep.*, **7**, pp. 9159.

124. Tian, X.-H., Wang, Z.-G., Meng, H., Wang, Y.-H., Feng, W., Wei, F. et al. (2013) Tat peptide-decorated gelatin-siloxane nanoparticles for delivery of CGRP transgene in treatment of cerebral vasospasm. *Int. J. Nanomedicine*, **8**, pp. 865–876.

125. Chen, K. and Chen, X. (2010) Design and development of molecular imaging probes. *Curr. Top. Med. Chem.*, **10**, pp. 1227–1236.

126. Cheng, K., Kothapalli, S.-R., Liu, H., Koh, A.L., Jokerst, J. V, Jiang, H. et al. (2014) Construction and validation of nano gold tripods for molecular imaging of living subjects. *J. Am. Chem. Soc.*, American Chemical Society, **136**, pp. 3560–3571.

127. Kwon, S.-P., Jeon, S., Lee, S.-H., Yoon, H.Y., Ryu, J.H., Choi, D. et al. (2018) Thrombin-activatable fluorescent peptide incorporated gold nanoparticles for dual optical/computed tomography thrombus imaging. *Biomaterials*, Netherlands, **150**, pp. 125–136.

128. Pellico, J., Lechuga-Vieco, A. V, Almarza, E., Hidalgo, A., Mesa-Nuñez, C., Fernández-Barahona, I. et al. (2017) In vivo imaging of lung inflammation with neutrophil-specific 68Ga nano-radiotracer. *Sci. Rep.*, **7**, pp. 13242.

129. Bellotto, O., Cringoli, M.C., Perathoner, S., Fornasiero, P., and Marchesan, S. (2021) Peptide gelators to template inorganic nanoparticle formation. *Gels*, Basel, Switzerland, **7**.

130. Jonnalagadda, S.V.R., Kokotidou, C., Orr, A.A., Fotopoulou, E., Henderson, K.J., Choi, C.-H. et al. (2018) Computational design of functional amyloid materials with cesium binding, deposition, and capture properties. *J. Phys. Chem. B*, **122**, pp. 7555–7568.

131. Kokotidou, C., Jonnalagadda, S.V.R., Orr, A.A., Vrentzos, G., Kretsovali, A., Tamamis, P. et al. (2020) Designer amyloid cell-penetrating peptides for potential use as gene transfer vehicles. *Biomolecules*, **10**, pp. 1–31.

132. Dimonte, A., Frache, S., Erokhin, V., Piccinini, G., Demarchi, D., Milano, F. et al. (2012) Nanosized optoelectronic devices based on photoactivated proteins. *Biomacromolecules*, United States, **13**, pp. 3503–3509.

133. Mejias, S.H., Couleaud, P., Casado, S., Granados, D., Garcia, M.A., Abad, J.M. et al. (2016) Assembly of designed protein scaffolds into monolayers for nanoparticle patterning. *Colloids Surfaces B Biointerfaces*, **141**, pp. 93–101.

134. Forstater, J.H., Kleinhammes, A., and Wu, Y. (2013) Self-assembly of protein-based biomaterials initiated by titania nanotubes. *Langmuir*, United States, **29**, pp. 15013–15021.

135. Gagner, J.E., Kim, W., and Chaikof, E.L. (2014) Designing protein-based biomaterials for medical applications. *Acta Biomater.*, **10**, pp. 1542–1557.

136. Vorobieva, A.A., White, P., Liang, B., Horne, J.E., Bera, A.K., Chow, C.M. et al. (2021) De novo design of transmembrane β barrels. *Science (80-).*, American Association for the Advancement of Science, **371**.

137. Hiranuma, N., Park, H., Baek, M., Anishchenko, I., Dauparas, J., and Baker, D. (2021) Improved protein structure refinement guided by deep learning-based accuracy estimation. *Nat. Commun.*, **12**, pp. 1340.

138. Norn, C., Wicky, B.I.M., Juergens, D., Liu, S., Kim, D., Tischer, D. et al. (2021) Protein sequence design by conformational landscape optimization. Coral A, Bubar AJ, Boykov A, Valle Pérez AU, MacMillan A, Lubow A, et al. (eds.). *Proc. Natl. Acad. Sci.*, National Academy of Sciences, **118**.

139. Dawson, W.M., Rhys, G.G., and Woolfson, D.N. (2019) Towards functional de novo designed proteins. *Curr. Opin. Chem. Biol.*, England, **52**, pp. 102–111.

140. Clarke, J. and Regan, L. (2010) Protein engineering and design: From first principles to new technologies. *Curr. Opin. Struct. Biol.*

141. Cortajarena, A.L. and Regan, L. (2011) Calorimetric study of a series of designed repeat proteins: Modular structure and modular folding. *Protein Sci.*

142. Kajander, T., Cortajarena, A.L., and Regan, L. (2006) Consensus design as a tool for engineering repeat proteins. *Methods Mol. Biol.*

143. Liu, H. and Naismith, J.H. (2008) An efficient one-step site-directed deletion, insertion, single and multiple-site plasmid mutagenesis protocol. *BMC Biotechnol.*, **8**, pp. 91.

144. Hermanson, G.T. (2013) Chapter 1: Introduction to bioconjugation. In: Hermanson GTBT-BT, Third E (ed.), Academic Press, Boston, pp. 1–125.

145. Hermanson, G.T. (2013) Chapter 3: The reactions of bioconjugation. In: Hermanson GTBT-BT, Third E (ed.), Academic Press, Boston, pp. 229–258.

146. Hermanson, G.T. (2013) Chapter 10: Fluorescent probes. In: Hermanson GTBT-BT, Third E (ed.), Academic Press, Boston, pp. 395–463.

147. Carneiro, L. (2018) Nanoparticles-based hybrid systems: Nanotechnology and protein engineering. *Biochem. Mol. Biol. J.*, **4**.

148. Spampinato, V., Parracino, M.A., La Spina, R., Rossi, F., and Ceccone, G. (2016) Surface analysis of gold nanoparticles functionalized with thiol-modified glucose SAMs for biosensor applications. *Front. Chem.*, **4**, pp. 8.

149. Cheung-Lau, J.C., Liu, D., Pulsipher, K.W., Liu, W., and Dmochowski, I.J. (2014) Engineering a well-ordered, functional protein-gold nanoparticle assembly. *J. Inorg. Biochem.*, United States, **130**, pp. 59–68.

150. Robson, T., Shah, D.S.H., Solovyova, A.S., and Lakey, J.H. (2018) Modular protein engineering approach to the functionalization of gold nanoparticles for use in clinical diagnostics. *ACS Appl. Nano Mater.*, American Chemical Society, **1**, pp. 3590–3599.

151. Tiwari, P.M., Vig, K., Dennis, V.A., and Singh, S.R. (2011) Functionalized gold nanoparticles and their biomedical applications. *Nanomater.*, Basel, Switzerland, **1**, pp. 31–63.

152. Van Vught, R., Pieters, R.J., and Breukink, E. (2014) Site-specific functionalization of proteins and their applications to therapeutic antibodies. *Comput. Struct. Biotechnol. J.*, **9**, pp. e201402001.

153. O'Neil, C.L., Stine, K.J., and Demchenko, A.V. (2018) Immobilization of glycans on solid surfaces for application in glycomics. *J. Carbohydr. Chem.*, **37**, pp. 225–249.

154. Vericat, C., Vela, M.E., Benitez, G., Carro, P., and Salvarezza, R.C. (2010) Self-assembled monolayers of thiols and dithiols on gold: New challenges for a well-known system. *Chem. Soc. Rev.*, The Royal Society of Chemistry, **39**, pp. 1805–1834.

155. Xia, N., Wang, Q., and Liu, L. (2015) Nanomaterials-based optical techniques for the detection of acetylcholinesterase and pesticides. *Sensors*, **15**, pp. 499–514.

156. Rahimi, P. and Joseph, Y. (2018) Enzyme-based biosensors for choline analysis: A review. *TrAC Trends Anal. Chem.*, **110**.

157. Edwards, K.A. (2021) Periplasmic-binding protein-based biosensors and bioanalytical assay platforms: Advances, considerations, and strategies for optimal utility. *Talanta Open*, **3**, pp. 100038.

158. Vaquero, J.J. and Kinahan, P. (2015) Positron emission tomography: Current challenges and opportunities for technological advances in clinical and preclinical imaging systems. *Annu. Rev. Biomed. Eng.*, **17**, pp. 385–414.

159. Bouleau, A., Lebon, V., and Truillet, C. (2021) PET imaging of immune checkpoint proteins in oncology. *Pharmacol. Ther.*, England, **222**, pp. 107786.

160. Dammes, N. and Peer, D. (2020) Monoclonal antibody-based molecular imaging strategies and theranostic opportunities. *Theranostics*, Ivyspring International Publisher, **10**, pp. 938–955.

161. Farahavar, G., Abolmaali, S.S., Gholijani, N., and Nejatollahi, F. (2019) Antibody-guided nanomedicines as novel breakthrough therapeutic, diagnostic and theranostic tools. *Biomater. Sci.*, **7**, pp. 4000–4016.

162. Han, H.-S., Niemeyer, E., Huang, Y., Kamoun, W.S., Martin, J.D., Bhaumik, J. et al. (2015) Quantum dot/antibody conjugates for in vivo cytometric imaging in mice. *Proc. Natl. Acad. Sci.*, **112**, pp. 1350–1355.

163. Abakumov, M.A., Nukolova, N. V., Sokolsky-Papkov, M., Shein, S.A., Sandalova, T.O., Vishwasrao, H.M. et al. (2015) VEGF-targeted magnetic nanoparticles for MRI visualization of brain tumor. *Nanomedicine Nanotechnology, Biol. Med.*, Elsevier B.V., **11**, pp. 825–833.

164. Popovtzer, A., Mizrachi, A., Motiei, M., Bragilovski, D., Lubimov, L., Levi, M. et al. (2016) Actively targeted gold nanoparticles as novel radiosensitizer agents: An in vivo head and neck cancer model. *Nanoscale*, Royal Society of Chemistry, **8**, pp. 2678–2685.

165. Wu, H., Shi, H., Zhang, H., Wang, X., Yang, Y., Yu, C. et al. (2014) Prostate stem cell antigen antibody-conjugated multiwalled carbon nanotubes for targeted ultrasound imaging and drug delivery. *Biomaterials*, **35**, pp. 5369–5380.

166. Ding, N., Sano, K., Kanazaki, K., Ohashi, M., Deguchi, J., Kanada, Y. et al. (2016) In vivo HER2-targeted magnetic resonance tumor imaging using iron oxide nanoparticles conjugated with anti-HER2 fragment antibody. *Mol. Imaging Biol.*, **18**, pp. 870–876.

167. Couleaud, P., Adan-Bermudez, S., Aires, A., Mejías, S.H., Sot, B., Somoza, A. et al. (2015) Designed modular proteins as scaffolds to stabilize fluorescent nanoclusters. *Biomacromolecules*, **16**, pp. 3836–3844.

168. Aires, A., Llarena, I., Moller, M., Castro-Smirnov, J., Cabanillas-Gonzalez, J., and Cortajarena, A.L. (2019) A simple approach to design proteins for the sustainable synthesis of metal nanoclusters. *Angew. Chem. Int. Ed.*, **58**, pp. 6214–6219.

Chapter 6

Conjugated Polymer Nanoparticles as Emerging Nanomaterials for Cancer Theranostic Applications

Christos L. Chochos,[a] Panagiota Koralli,[a] Maria Goulielmaki,[a] Andriana Schiza,[a] Antonia Dimitrakopoulou-Strauss,[b] Alkmenis D. Nega,[b] and Vasilis G. Gregoriou[c]

[a]*Institute of Chemical Biology, National Hellenic Research Foundation, 48 Vassileos Constantinou Avenue, Athens 11635, Greece*
[b]*Clinical Cooperation Unit Nuclear Medicine, German Cancer Research Center, 69120 Heidelberg, Germany*
[c]*National Hellenic Research Foundation, 48 Vassileos Constantinou Avenue, Athens, 11635, Greece*

chochos@eie.gr

In this chapter, the conjugated polymer nanoparticles (CPNs) will be presented as an emerged new class of cancer theranostic nanomaterials, due to their dual roles in bioimaging and therapy of different cancer types. As contrast agents in optical bioimaging, CPNs have been utilized in fluorescence imaging, photoacoustic imaging (PAI), Raman imaging, multimodal molecular, and cell imaging applications, as well as in small animal imaging, due to their desirable optical features, such as high absorption coefficient and photoluminescence quantum yields, spanning from the ultraviolet to the NIR-I/NIR-II biological window,

Functional Materials in Biomedical Applications
Edited by Costas Demetzos, Natassa Pippa, and Nikolaos Naziris

ISBN 978-981-4968-65-2 (Hardcover), 978-1-003-41146-8 (eBook)
www.jennystanford.com

good photostability, and low cytotoxicity providing simultaneously target detection and intrinsic molecular information of biomolecules. Apart from diagnosis and disease monitoring, CPNs are also exploited for therapeutic applications in minimally invasive settings, namely, photodynamic therapy (PDT) and photothermal therapy (PTT). PDT is based on the use of photosensitizers that transfer energy from light to oxygen molecules, leading to the generation of reactive oxygen species (ROS), which, in turn, will kill the target cells. Alternatively, PTT employs light-absorbing agents that transform light into thermal energy for tumor ablation. More recently, conjugation of pharmacological agents (antibodies, drugs, etc.) with CPNs has emerged as a novel strategy for enhancing therapeutic efficacy and specific tissue targeting.

6.1 Introduction

In developed countries, worldwide, cancer is the second most common cause of death after cardiovascular diseases, since one out of three individuals is predicted to develop some form of cancer during their lifetime, while one in four will die. According to data published by Cancer Research UK, the worldwide incidence of cancer in 2018 was around 17 million, while the number of new cases is estimated to reach 27.5 million by 2040. Cancer deaths worldwide in 2018 reached 9.6 million and were mainly attributed to lung, liver, intestine, and stomach tumors [1]. Since it is widely accepted that malignant cancer cells can be treated more successfully at the early stages of the disease [2], the necessity for reliable and trustworthy tumor recognition and monitoring is mandatory for diagnosis, image-guided surgery leading to a more accurate assessment of tumor margins to maximize cancer excision and minimize resection of normal tissues, as well as evaluation of cancer therapeutics [3, 4]. Nowadays, different non-invasive bioimaging techniques have been developed, which can provide pieces of information regarding the pathology and physiology of bioorganisms as well as monitoring biological processes [5, 6].

Multi-modal imaging uses one modality's physical properties to confirm the results of another to provide rigorous in vivo validation. Fluorescence imaging techniques have become indispensable for biomedical imaging providing vital information since they offer high contrast, temporal resolution, and high sensitivity, but their main drawbacks are limited tissue penetration and low spatial resolution [7–9]. PAI is an emerging non-invasive imaging modality that combines the advantages of deep ultrasound penetration with high temporal and spatial resolution and high optical contrast to increase imaging depth on the centimeter scale. In PAI, contrast agents are used to improving the contrast and specificity of the image or an image of a particular molecular mechanism such as cell-surface protein, etc. [10].

Besides the aforementioned optical imaging techniques, in the last decade, Raman imaging has emerged as a label-free, high-contrast, non-invasive, and non-destructive imaging technique for bioimaging [11]. Unique molecular fingerprint information can be extracted through the visualization of specific vibrations [12, 13], whilst differences in the composition of lipids, proteins, carbohydrates, and nucleic acids in normal/cancer cells can be identified through the evaluation of Raman spectra profile contributing to the assessment, characterization, and discrimination of cancer stages [14–16]. Nevertheless, there is a high demand for synthesizing more efficient Raman-active materials that will exhibit a large cross-section of Raman scattering and strong signal in the so-called "silent region" of cells, between 1800 and 2800 cm^{-1}, for the application of Raman imaging in a living system.

CPNs have emerged as a new promising class of nanomaterials for fluorescence imaging, taking advantage of its superior properties such as easy modification, highly efficient light-harvesting, high brightness, photostability, and high quantum yield, generated through fine-tuning of the backbone or side-chain structures, in combination with small particle size, low cytotoxicity, and biocompatibility [9, 17–19]. Researchers currently show increasing attention to evolving CPNs for fluorescence imaging, multimodal molecular, cell imaging, and drug/gene delivery [20–23].

From the view of therapy, traditional cancer therapeutics, like chemotherapy, radiotherapy, immunotherapy, and their combinations, fail to prove adequately efficient against primary and/or advanced tumors. Toward the discovery of novel and highly effective treatment approaches, cancer theranostics is a novel field of cancer treatment strategies, aiming for early diagnosis and precise treatment of the patients, followed by real-time monitoring of treatment efficacy. However, the first attempts for developing appropriate agents did not meet great success since these small or macromolecular compounds and moieties have shown non-negligible flaws, including insufficient delivery and/or activity, rapid clearance, inappropriate targeting, and even undesirable toxicity.

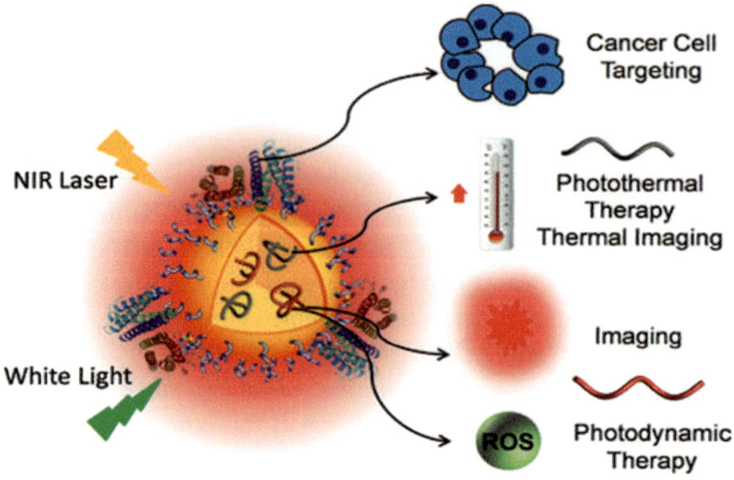

Figure 6.1 Schematic of utilizing conjugated polymer nanomaterials for theranostics [24].

Nanotechnology, defined as the use of nanoscale materials of different nature for various scientific purposes, is currently being exploited for, among others, medical applications in an effort to overcome the issues mentioned above. In the field of cancer therapeutics, such non-invasive systems are being developed for specifically targeting a given tumor for subsequent imaging and/or therapeutic purposes. The use of polymeric nanomaterials, especially conjugated polymer nanostructures, has shown high efficiency for the delivery of diagnostic and therapeutic agents to target tissues while additionally giving the possibility to incorporate a variety of multi-functional moieties within specific compartments of the nanoparticles and subsequently monitor their distribution within the body and to the target sites (Fig. 6.1).

6.2 Conjugated Polymer Nanoparticles

The discovery of highly conductive polyacetylene by MacDiarmid, Heeger, and Shirakawa in 1977 demolished our perception of polymers as the perfect example of insulators, and the Nobel Prize in Chemistry 2000 was awarded to these three pioneers. Despite the inferior charge carrier mobility and conductivity (compared to inorganic semiconductors and metals), conjugated polymers (CPs) possess distinct advantages of structural and functional versatility by molecular design, solution processability, lightweight, and low processing cost. Furthermore, the bottom-up synthetic process of CPs is considered more environmentally friendly than the mining process for inorganic semiconductors and metals.

CPs are made up of unsaturated building blocks, such as arenes, olefins, or acetylenes, which are connected by single bonds that have some π-bond character to create large domains of delocalized, polarizable π-electrons. Classical prototypes of CPs are (1) polyacetylene, (2) poly(*p*-phenylene), (3) poly(*p*-phenylene vinylene), (4) poly(*p*-phenylene ethynylene), and (5) polyfluorene, as shown in Fig. 6.2. It is easy to envisage the large variety of different CPs that can be synthesized by changing the aromatic repeat unit (i.e., substituting larger polycyclic aromatic hydrocarbons for the benzene ring) [25] or by changing the bond linkage (i.e., poly(*m*-phenylene) and poly(*o*-phenylene)) [26]. Furthermore, even more complicated CPs have become possible upon incorporating heteroatoms into the aromatic ring, such as polythiophene, polypyrrole, and polycarbazole, or as a separate part of the chain as in polyaniline.

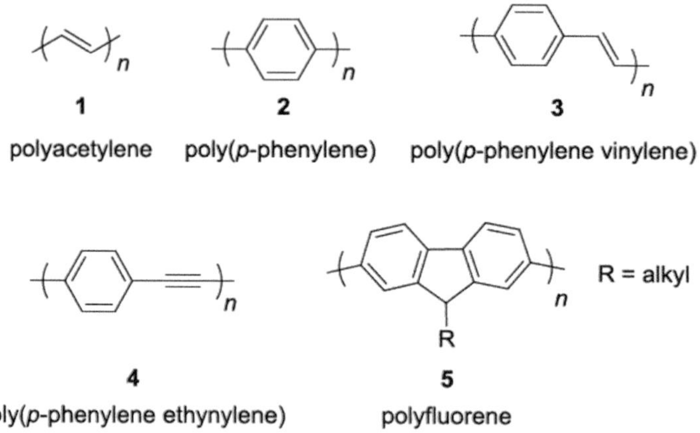

Figure 6.2 Chemical structures of the most classical prototypes of CPs [27].

Their mobile π-electrons allow macromolecules to serve as chromophores and electrophores, hence they can interact with light to take up, transport, or store electrical charges. In turn, this qualifies them as bright light emitters for sensors or as active components in (opto)electronic devices and in batteries [28–31]. Thus, their electronic band gap determines the wavelength of light absorption and/or emission, as well as the energies of valence and conduction bands that dictate the ability to accommodate charges. Regarding charge-carrier transport, CPs can become electrical conductors and exhibit metallic or semiconducting behavior. Once again, this stands in contrast to most conventional polymers, which are typically characterized as insulators.

While CPs have been employed extensively in many optoelectronic fields, their utilization in biological and health applications is limited mostly due to their hydrophobic nature, and thus requires significant improvement of their water solubility to be applied for in vitro and in vivo applications. Several strategies to impart colloidal stability in water have been developed. These include nanoprecipitation, encapsulation, or functionalization with hydrophilic groups preparing the so-called CPNs. CPNs with smaller representatives below 20 nm in diameter are sometimes also termed CP dots.

In post-polymerization approaches, previously synthesized CPs are formed into particles. This can be done via micro-

and mini-emulsification of a CP solution in a non-solvent. Alternatively, the CP solution can be injected into a non-solvent for the CP (which is miscible with the solvent of the CP). Here, CP particles nanoprecipitate. Finally, specific CP geometries such as amphiphilic block copolymers or conjugated polyelectrolytes (CPEs) can be self-assembled into CPNs. Figure 6.3 shows a positively charged CP, which is precipitated by the addition of a negatively charged (flocculation agent) polymer.

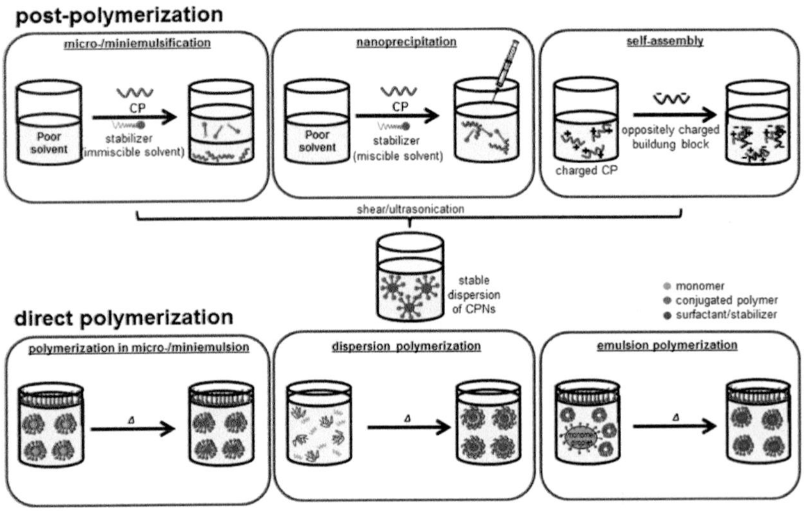

Figure 6.3 Synthetic strategies for the preparation of CPNs [32].

By contrast, in direct polymerization approaches, we start from the conjugated monomers and form the CPNs in situ. The monomers can be emulsified in a micro- or mini-emulsion, where the polymerization is performed in the stabilized droplets and delivers polydisperse particles. Alternatively, the polymerization is performed in a solvent, which is good for the monomers but poor for the CP, leading to precipitation during polymerization. Added stabilizers prevent aggregation and maintain the particles in dispersed form. Finally, when the monomers are liquid, emulsion polymerization can be performed, where particle growth is started in micelles.

Upon light illumination of CPNs, electrons are excited from the ground state to the excited state. The CPNs are subsequently placed in the lowest vibrational level of the excited state through internal relaxation. Further relaxation of the molecule could then lead to three different results: (a) the emission of a photon with a Stokes shift in wavelength; (b) the transfer of energy to its surrounding environment as heat; or (c) the intersystem crossing from the singlet to the triplet state, followed by photon emission, or generation of free radicals (type I reaction), or singlet oxygen $^1O_2$ (type II reaction) (Fig. 6.4). All the three pathways are very useful for biological applications. The photon emission is widely used in fluorescence imaging, the thermal relaxation is for PTT, while the generation of free radicals or singlet oxygen leads to the development of PDT.

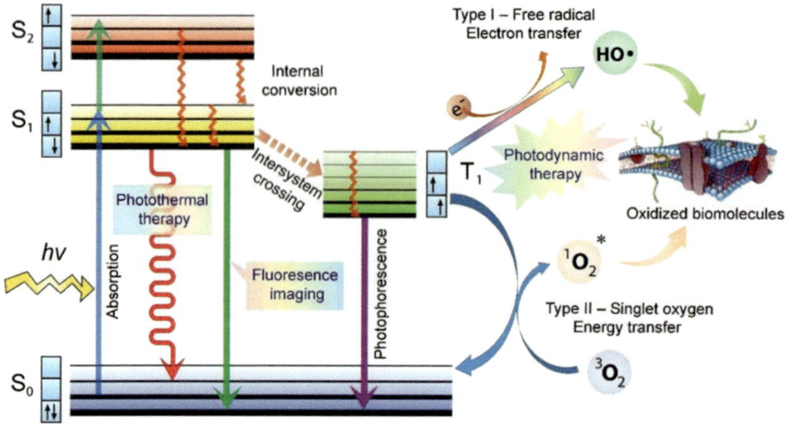

Figure 6.4 Indicative photophysical mechanisms of CPNs upon light illumination [33].

6.3 Relationship among Enhanced Permeability, Retention Effect, and Nanoparticles' Size

The enhanced permeability and retention (EPR) effect is a transport phenomenon characterized primarily by the presence of fenestrations in tumor vasculature that enables passive accumulation of nanoparticles in tumors (Fig. 6.5). Normal vasculature typically possesses tight inter endothelial junctions that prevent the extravasation of particles into tissues. The imbalance of several factors influences the size of fenestrations in tumor vasculature (Fig. 6.5a,ii). As an example, VEGF and nitric oxide have been shown to increase the size of gaps in the endothelial (Fig. 6.5b,i). Tumors oftentimes possess a dense extracellular matrix that prevents adequate penetration of nanoparticles into the tumor (Fig. 6.5b,ii).

The size of a nanoparticle, which can now be engineered to precise dimensions and high monodispersity, is a crucial design parameter that can be tailored for the purpose of directing particle distribution in vivo. The NP size and surface area play an important role, largely determining the unique mechanism of NP interaction with living systems. Size drives several biological phenomena with discrete cut-off size ranges that include circulation half-lives, extravasation through leaky vasculature, and macrophage uptake. Generally, the acceptable size for long-lasting circulation and spherical nanoparticles is an average size up to 200 nm [34]. The sizes of nanoparticles (from 1 to 100 nm) are comparable with the size of protein globules (2–10 nm), the diameter of DNA helix (2 nm), and the thickness of cell membranes (10 nm), which allows them to easily enter cells and cell organelles [35].

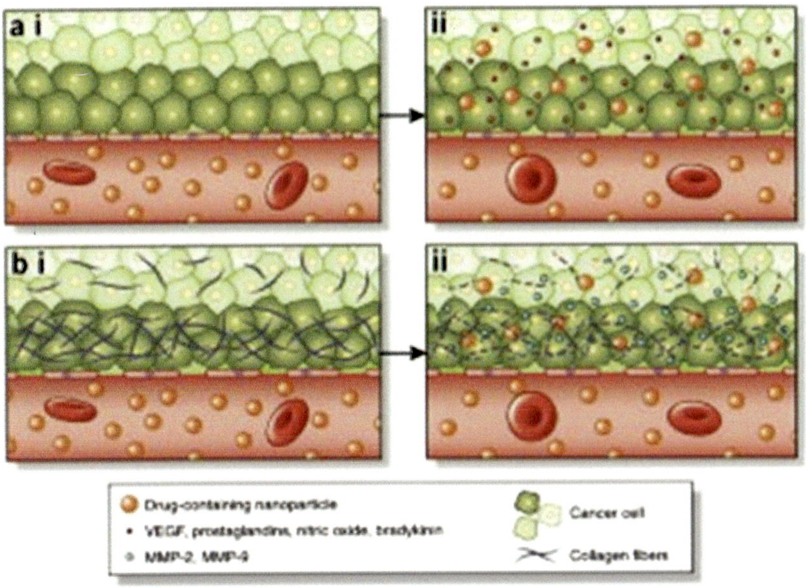

Figure 6.5 EPR effect in normal and tumor vasculature [35].

6.4 Near-Infrared Light Interactions with Biological Tissue

Several phenomena occur as the light propagates into biological tissue, including reflection, absorption, auto-florescence, and scattering, as shown in Fig. 6.6a. Especially, scattering and absorption are the most essential factors in deciding the imaging depth of PAI. Deep PAI is usually simple to obtain if an illumined laser beam could penetrate without any energy loss due to scattering or absorption. The absorption coefficients of blood and lipids are mostly between 200 and 600 nm, with some peaks at about 980 nm. These absorption peaks are useful for imaging blood vessels and plaques, but they obstruct deep tissue imaging. The disadvantage is that absorption coefficients rapidly decrease in the near-infrared (NIR) region (700–1600 nm). Many PAI studies focused on deep tissue imaging have used contrast agents such as organic materials (e.g., ICG [36] or methylene blue [37]) and inorganic materials (e.g., carbon-based nanoparticles [38]) in the NIR-I window (i.e., 700–1000 nm), due to the relatively low absorption by whole blood. However, due to its scattering factor, the NIR-I window is not an ideal spectrum for deep tissue PAI. While most human tissues' scattering coefficients decrease exponentially beyond 700 nm, they still have a low degree of scattering beyond 1000 nm. Furthermore, when considering the NIR-II window (i.e., 1000–1700 nm), water has significant absorption above 1400 nm; the absorption coefficient of water increases continuously from 500 nm and becomes greater than that of biological tissues above 1200 nm. The deep imaging window should be in the 1000–1200 nm range to account for biological absorption or scattering as well as water absorption (Fig. 6.6b).

PAI can determine functional factors, such as vascular networks and cellular structure, as well as structural factors, such as hemoglobin, lipids, water, and melanin of biological tissue based on their ability to absorb light.

6.5 Fluorescence Imaging

Fluorescence imaging is a valuable method to study the location or concentration of molecules, as it is comparatively non-invasive and can be performed with high sensitivity, and can offer good specificity. Fluorescence occurs when light absorbed by a molecule is emitted after a concise period (approximately 10^{-8} s) following light absorption. The emitted light is always produced at a longer wavelength than that absorbed (the Stokes shift); this results from a small dissipation of energy during the excited state. This shift is crucial for detecting fluorescence as it makes it possible to discriminate between the excitation and the emission signal. The fluorescence process is cyclical unless the fluorochrome, a molecule that fluoresces, is destroyed during the excited state, a phenomenon known as photobleaching. The complex polyatomic nature of fluorescent molecules produces a broad spectral band over which they absorb and emit light. This is referred to as the excitation and emission spectra. These spectra are of particular importance when attempting to detect signals from more than a single fluorochrome simultaneously. Fluorescence from living cells can be detected with spectroscopic or microscopic techniques. Specific microscopy approaches are considered below [40].

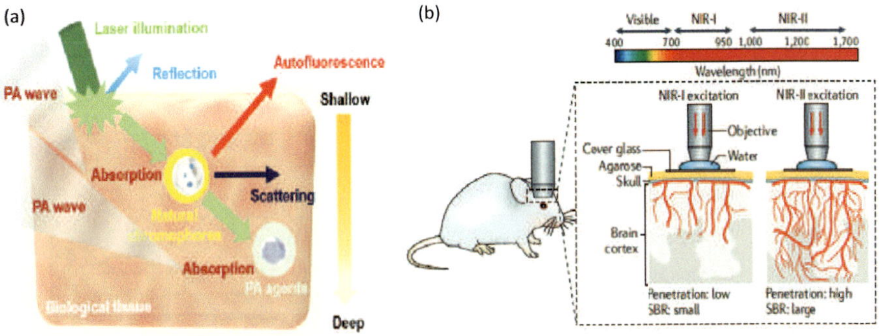

Figure 6.6 (a) Interactions between light and tissue in a different spectrum, and (b) penetration depth of NIR-I and NIR-II [39].

6.5.1 Fluorescence Contrast Agents in NIR-I (700–950 nm) Biological Window

Water-soluble CPs have been extensively studied as new fluorescent platforms for sensitive biosensors due to their signal amplification abilities. These assays are easy, fast, and sensitive, and they do not require any special equipment. Through electrostatic interactions, the CPs can form complexes with oppositely charged biomacromolecules, eliminating the need to mark the biomacromolecules covalently.

Recently, CPNs have been synthesized via the encapsulation method in phospholipid micelles. Four different CPs were used, yielding aqueous dispersions of nanoparticles that emit across the visible spectrum. In vitro imaging experiments were performed in SH-SY5Y neuroblastoma and live HeLa cells where the MEH-PPV was successfully inserted, as confocal measurements have shown [41] (Table 6.1).

Table 6.1 Summary of photophysical properties on NIR-I fluorescent semiconducting polymer nanoparticles

CPN		Absorption maximum (nm)	Emission maximum (nm)	Quantum yield	Diameter (nm)	Refs.
MEH-PPV		600	593	1.3	93.43	[41]
PFBTDBT1036		465	698	0.27	80	[42]
BTTPF		400,580	690	–	180±28.9	[43]
SPN1-M		545	630	7.7	18	[44]
SPN2-M		540	640	4.25	19	
SPN3-M		615	670	2.06	18	
SPN4-M		660	735	2.28	19	
PF-TC6FQ-BODIPY		362,495	732	33	26	[45]
T2fQf	Nanoprecipitation	518	692	18	75.03	[46]
	Encapsulation	515	662	17	52.26	
T2fQ2f	Nanoprecipitation	474	647	18	33.34	
	Encapsulation	471	650	16	58.3	

Another group has synthesized an FR/NIR fluorescent CP, PFBTDBT10, as a contrast agent for in vivo applications. The PFBTDBT10 possesses highly emissive FR/NIR fluorescence, and the resulting nanoparticles, CPDP-FA, had a spherical uniform morphology with an average hydrodynamic diameter of ~80 nm. More importantly, the CPDP-FA nanoparticles show efficient FR/NIR fluorescence with a quantum yield of 0.27 in an aqueous solution. Via confocal laser scanning microscopy (CLSM), fluorescence signals in MCF-7 breast cancer cells were observed [42].

pH-responsive nanoparticles are of great importance since the cancer environment is basically acidic. Drug delivery systems have exploited this fact by synthesizing nanoparticles with bonds that can break in an acidic environment and thus realize the drug contents. A drug fluorescent nanocarrier for the antibiotic doxorubicin (DOX) pyrazine-based SP (BTTPF) was formed via the emulsion method [43]. The nanoparticles were spherical with a low size distribution and a maximum fluorescent peak at 690 nm. Its biocompatibility is due to the dimethylamino propyl side groups and as in vivo imaging probes seem to have significantly low background signals from tissue autofluorescence (Fig. 6.7).

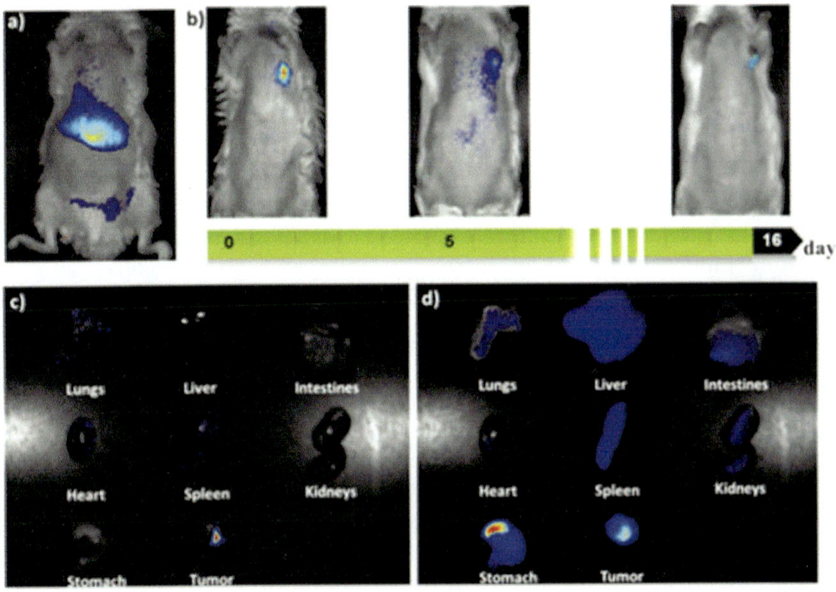

Figure 6.7 (a) NIR image of the mouse after intravenous injection with the nanoparticles. (b) NIR images of subcutaneous the tumor-bearing mouse following subcutaneous injection with the nanoparticles (ex = 455 nm). Ex vivo NIR fluorescence imaging on tumor tissue (c) at 455 nm and (d) 595 nm excitation source [43].

An extended series of NIR-fluorescent CPNs with multilayered architecture were also synthesized for in vivo imaging. They combine four different CPs to formulate different CPNs with each one. By comparing them in terms of their optical and biochemical properties, the middle silica layer of CPNs-M plays a crucial role in enhancing the NIR fluorescence by up to 100-fold depending on CP's structure and the polyethylene glycol (PEG) coating effectively reduces non-specific cellular uptake and reticuloendothelial system (RES) uptake. The CPNs-M were tested in vitro and in vivo, and they note that the enhanced NIR fluorescence and their good biodistribution allow the in vivo lymph node tracking with SNR ~85 and ~8-fold higher intensity ratio of in vivo imaging of tumor (liver) than those CPNs where containing silica [44].

The bulky structures of the π-bridges in the donor-acceptor system could effectively increase the quantum yields of the resulting nanoparticles. Ke et al. have successfully synthesized a series of NIR fluorescent Pdots with narrow-band emissions and large Stokes shifts based on donor–bridge–acceptor systems. By comparing them with Qdot 705 NIR-fluorescence probe, they notable found that the Pdots can be 3–4 times brighter. Notable is the fact that the PF-TC6FQ-BODIPY Pdot presented a quantum yield of the order of 33%. These specific Pdots were tested for their biocompatibility in vitro (in HeLa and MCF-7 cells) and in vivo (in zebrafish) after their functionalization with the carboxyl group presenting multiplex bioimaging applications and in cancer diagnostics [45].

Recently, a promising group of CPs (TQs) was synthesized with up to four fluorine atoms in the different positions of the polymer backbone, consisting of thiophene and quinoxaline building blocks (Fig. 6.8). The nanoparticles were formed via nanoprecipitation and encapsulation method, and then fluorescence measurements took place in order to investigate their potential use as fluorescent probes for bioimaging. The far-red emitting TQ-based polymer nanoparticles with three and four fluorine atoms on the repeat unit of the polymers demonstrate higher quantum yield values regardless of the preparation method as compared to the NIR emitting TQ-based polymer nanoparticles with none, one, and two fluorine atoms on the repeat unit [46].

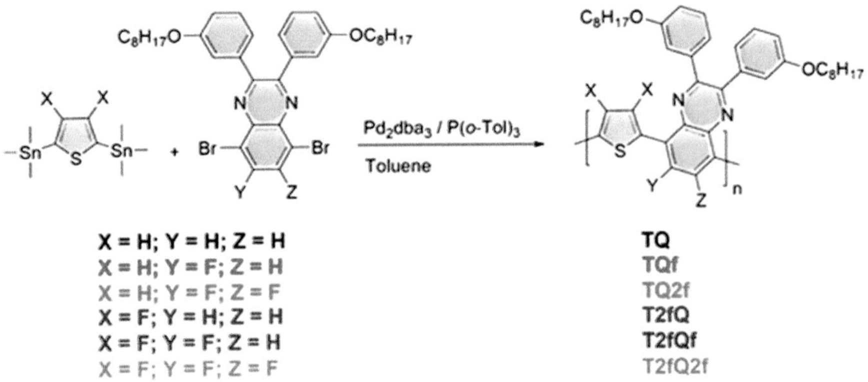

Figure 6.8 Far-red emitting TQs-based CPs [46].

6.5.2 Fluorescence Contrast Agents in NIR-II (1000–1700 nm) Biological Window

Due to its deep tissue penetration depth and high spatial resolution, the second near-infrared window (NIR-II) imaging is a promising method for in vivo imaging. Thus, Dai's group synthesized a NIR-II fluorescence CP through a donor-acceptor approach (Fig. 9A). To increase the water solubility and biocompatibility, they mixed the amphiphilic polymer with polydopamine (PDA) and then, via the nanoprecipitation method, they formed the nanoparticles (Figs. 9B,C). Its optical and physical characteristics are shown in Table 6.2. Figure 9D,E presents the imaging from the in vivo mouse arterial blood flow. It seems that the nanoparticles achieve deeper penetration depth and enabled imaging with great spatiotemporal resolution confirming that they are suitable for clinical applications [47].

Recently, a diketopyrrolopyrrole (DPP)-based CPN (PDFT1032) was also developed as a NIR-II fluorescent probe. It showed high photostability, a favorable absorption peak at 809 nm, outstanding biocompatibility, and minimal in vivo toxicity. The novel DPP-based CP (PDFT) with a low bandgap was prepared through donor-acceptor alternating copolymerization. This probe is able to achieve several meaningful biomedical real-time imaging applications, including tumor diagnosis. More importantly,

NIR-II imaging using PDFT1032 can aid us in accomplishing accurate image-guided tumor surgery, vascular embolization therapy, and image-guided sentinel lymph node biopsy (SLNB) with high spatial and temporal resolution [48].

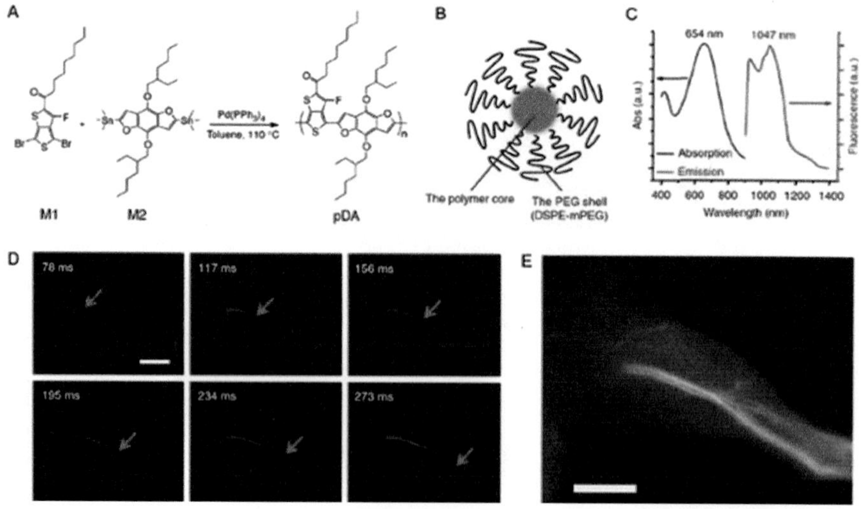

Figure 6.9 (A) Synthetic route of the CP PDA. (B) The nanoparticle (PDA-PEG) with improved hydrophilicity. (C) Absorption and emission spectra of PDA-PEG. (D) Ultrafast second near-infrared (NIR-II) imaging of arterial blood flow at different time points. (E) The NIR-II fluorescence image of the same mouse hindlimb after full perfusion of PDA-PEG [47].

Table 6.2 Summary of optical and physical properties of NIR-II fluorescent CPNs

CPN	Absorption maximum (nm)	Emission maximum (nm)	Quantum yield (%)	Diameter (nm)	Reference
PDFT1032	809	1032	–	68	[47]
PDA	654	1047	1.7	17	[48]

6.6 Photoacoustic Imaging

During the last few decades, photoacoustic (PA) technology has emerged as an exciting imaging technique that has drawn growing interest in biomedical applications [49–52]. The PA effect, first observed in 1880 by Alexander G. Bell [53, 54], explains acoustic waves' development when light pulses are absorbed. PAI was applied to biomedical applications more than a century after the PA effect was discovered. Non-invasive PAI has been thoroughly investigated as a technology for biomedical imaging and diagnostics [55, 56] since the groundbreaking work by Wang et al. in 2003 [57] that realized in vivo PAI in a rat brain. PAI's function is dependent on energy conversion between light, heat, and sound (Fig. 6.10).

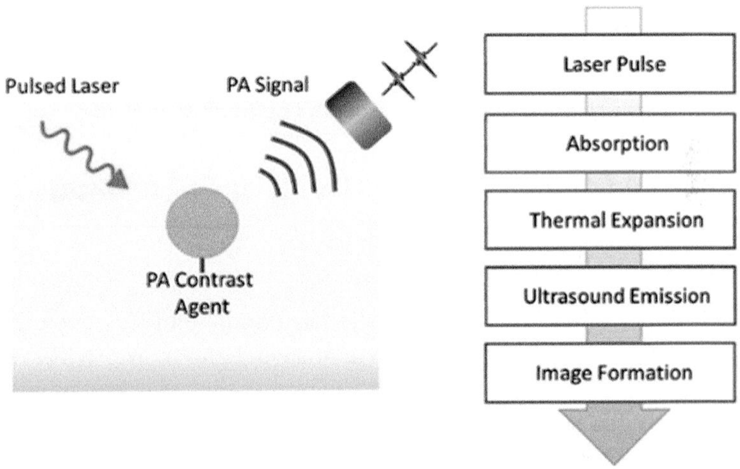

Figure 6.10 Schematic description of the generation of a PA signal.

When a nanosecond pulsed laser illuminates a sample containing absorbing chromophores, the light energy is absorbed, and heat is produced. More specifically, the PA effect occurs when the temperature of the tissue rises due to heat. Tissue heating caused by the absorption of short laser pulses by endogenous chromophores or exogenous contrast agents generates megahertz-frequency broadband acoustic waves causing thermal elastic expansion and the generation of acoustic waves. PAI enables the mapping of the absorber's position in biological tissue by detecting these propagating acoustic waves using traditional ultrasonic transducers [58, 59]. Since the scattering and the speed of ultrasound are less than those of light, PAI can achieve deep tissue imaging in the order of several centimeters by overcoming the bottleneck of the typical penetration depth, which is theoretically ~1 mm [60].

Moreover, through the endogenous contrast agents (oxy- and deoxy-hemoglobin, fat, melanin, etc.), PA can visualize anatomical details such as vasculature networks, distributions of fat and melanin, and cellular structure, as well as physiological details such as concentrations of hemoglobin, blood velocity, and saturated oxygen levels. Furthermore, with the contribution of exogenous contrast agents, such as inorganic agents (e.g., gold nanoparticles) [61], carbon-based agents (e.g., carbon nanotubes) [62], organic agents (e.g., polypyrrole) [63], CPs [64], and in particular, targeted ones, it is possible to achieve visualization of colorless organs with low absorption coefficients [60, 65].

6.6.1 PA Contrast Agents in NIR-I (700–950 nm) Biological Window

The modification of chemical structures in CPs backbones, in particular, results in a major shift in the bandgap of CPs, resulting in narrow bandgap polymers that absorb light in the NIR. The absorbance in the NIR region increases as the conjugation length increases. Additionally, biocompatible polymer components may be used to encapsulate core polymers or directly tethered onto the backbone of polymers as a pendant group, reducing cytotoxicity and improving solubility, or dispersibility under biological conditions.

Lui et al. synthesized a CP, poly[9,9-bis(4-(2-ethylhexyl)phenyl) fluorene-alt-co-6,7-bis(4-(hexyloxy)phenyl)-4,9-di(thiophen-2-yl)-thiadiazoloquinoxaline] (PFTTQ) by Suzuki polymerization, which shows strong absorption in the NIR-I biological window. Using the amphiphilic polymer DSPE-PEG2000, they formed nanoparticles dispersed into water (PFTTQ nanoparticles) [66]. Pu et al. [67] notably demonstrated a new series of low-band-gap CPNs using DPP-based CPs as PA contrast agents (Fig. 6.11). The CPNs exhibited a uniform morphology, and the diameters were measured on an average of 46 nm. The absorption and mass extinction coefficients maxima are shown in Table 6.3. The nanoparticle SPN4 exhibited the highest PA signal (3.3-times brighter) in comparison to the other three, which is justified because of its molecular structure. By intravenous injection of the SPN4 into mice, the PA signal from the tumor area can be enhanced by 5.3-fold, and in combination with the low cytotoxicity, it is greatly promising for in vivo tumor imaging.

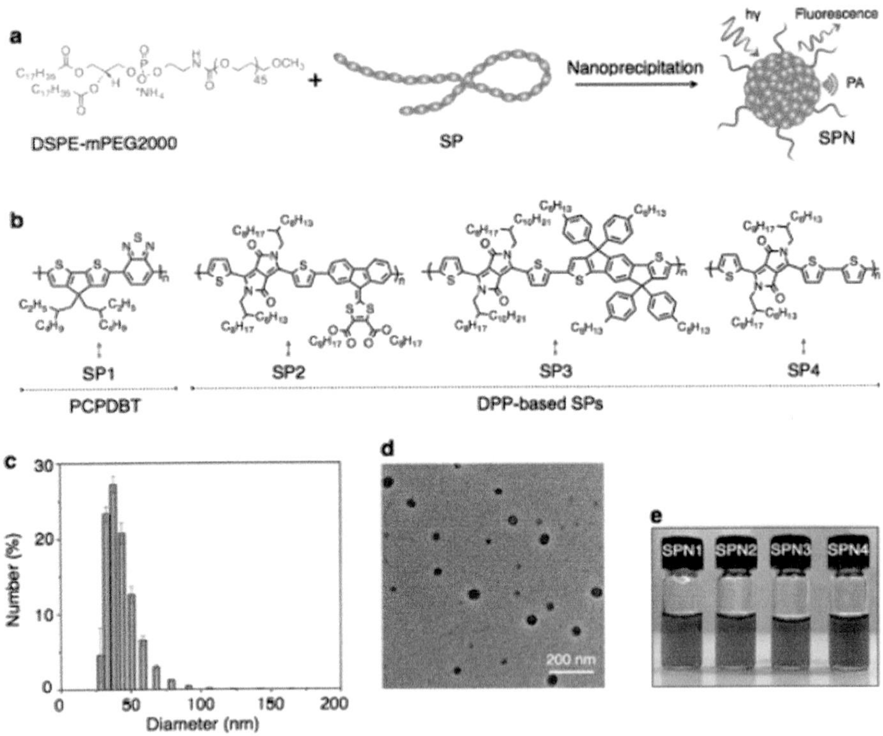

Figure 6.11 CPNs synthesis and characterization. (a) Scheme illustration of the preparation of CPNs via nanoprecipitation and (b) chemical structures of SP1 and DPP-based SPs (SP2–4). Representative (c) DLS and (d) TEM of SPN4. (e) Photograph of CPNs in aqueous solutions (20 μg mL^{-1}). The error bars represent standard deviations of three separate measurements [67].

A series of CPNs based on DPPT-DT with absorption in NIR was synthesized in three different average molecular weights per weight (Mw) by varying the polymerization time and fully characterized. The CP with the larger Mw (DPP-DT-H) presented higher absorption (Table 6.3) compared to the other two with lower molecular weights, indicating that the larger the polymer's molecular weight, the higher the absorption. Moreover, it seems that the optical properties are size-dependent. The in vivo experiments in an H22 (and/or 4T1) tumor model DPP-DT-H nanoparticle displayed a linear relationship between PA signal and the concentration [68].

Two other CP derivatives with strong absorption in the NIR region (Fig. 6.12) have been also reported [64]. The PA amplitudes of both CPNs at 700 nm were determined at different concentrations in an agar phantom, displaying a linear relationship between PA signal and concentration for SPN1 and SPN2. After a single low-dose (50 mg) intravenous administration, their favorable size (40 nm) allowed effective PAI in living mice. The mice were imaged with both PA and fluorescence modalities 24 h after injection (Fig. 6.12a,b).

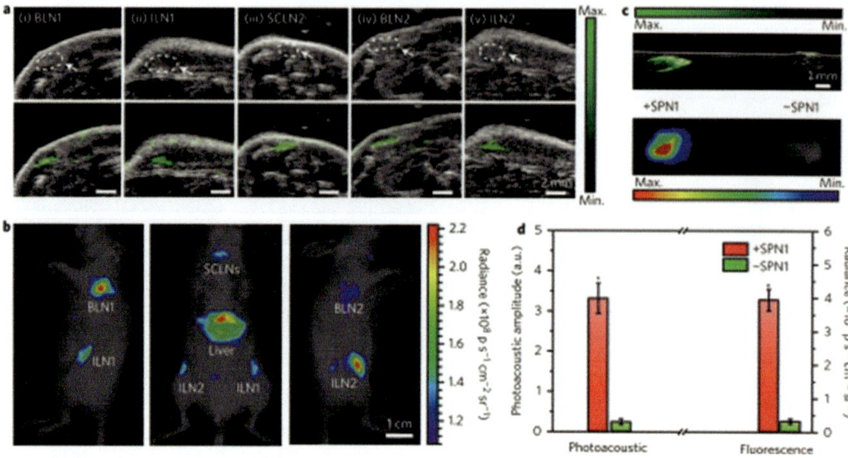

Figure 6.12 (a) Ultrasound (upper) and PA/ultrasound co-registered (lower) images of mouse lymph nodes injected with SPN1 (50 mg/mouse). BLN is a brachial lymph node, ILN is an inguinal lymph node, and SCLN is a superficial cervical lymph node. (b) Fluorescence/bright-field images of the mouse. (c) Ex vivo PA/ultrasound co-registered (top) and fluorescent/bright-field (bottom) images of resected lymph nodes from the mouse in a (left) or a control mouse without SPN1 injection (right) in an agar phantom. (d) Ex vivo quantification of PA and fluorescence signals of the lymph nodes from SPN1-administrated mice (n'O4) and control mice (n'O4) [64].

Powerful PA and fluorescence signals were observed in the lymphatic networks of living mice, including aggregation in the brachial lymph nodes (BLNs), inguinal lymph nodes (ILNs), and superficial cervical lymph nodes (SCLNs), which had previously been undetectable. After necropsy, the high accumulation of SPN1 in the LNs was reported, revealing that the LNs had the second-highest nanoparticle accumulation, with a fluorescence strength that was 63% that of the liver ex vivo LN imaging revealed a 13.3-fold increase in PA signal following SPN administration compared to saline-treated LNs (Fig. 6.12 c,d), which was close to the observed fluorescence signal enhancement (12.3-fold). SPN1 can be used for LN mapping for both PA and fluorescence imaging, as shown by this result.

A self-quenched molecular approach has been suggested to increase the PA brightness of CPNs. They used PDPPF (SP0) as the control CP and by inserting benzothiadiazole (BT) as the electron-deficient unit in different compositions, yielding the BT-containing CPs (SPN5&SPN10) with no apparent differences in size (~40 nm). These CPNs in incorporation with the PDPPF induced fluorescence quenching. The conjugation of cyclic-RGD to the surface of SPN10 proved capable of targeting the 4T1 tumors in living mice, and the SPN10-RGD delineated the tumor more clearly than non-targeted nanoparticles with a PA intensity that was 1.8-fold greater [69].

Figure 6.13 depicts a series of CPs for use as exogenous contrast agents for PAI in vivo. The nanoparticles formed via nanoprecipitation for the PCPDTBT, resulting in SPN1, and the mini-emulsion method for the rest three (INDT-T, INDT-S, and INDT-BT) since the last was not fully soluble in THF. The optical properties and the diameter of the resulting nanoparticles are presented in Table 6.3. Cytotoxicity assay was performed for all the nanoparticles in the 293T human embryonic kidney cell line with no significant effect on cell viability, indicating that nanoparticles are biocompatible in vitro. The most promising nanoparticle, SPN4, in terms of extinction coefficient (253 cm^{-1} L g^{-1}) was chosen for in vivo application. The in vivo PA images were shouted before and after the subcutaneous injection of SPN4, indicating the presence of nanoparticles after injection [70].

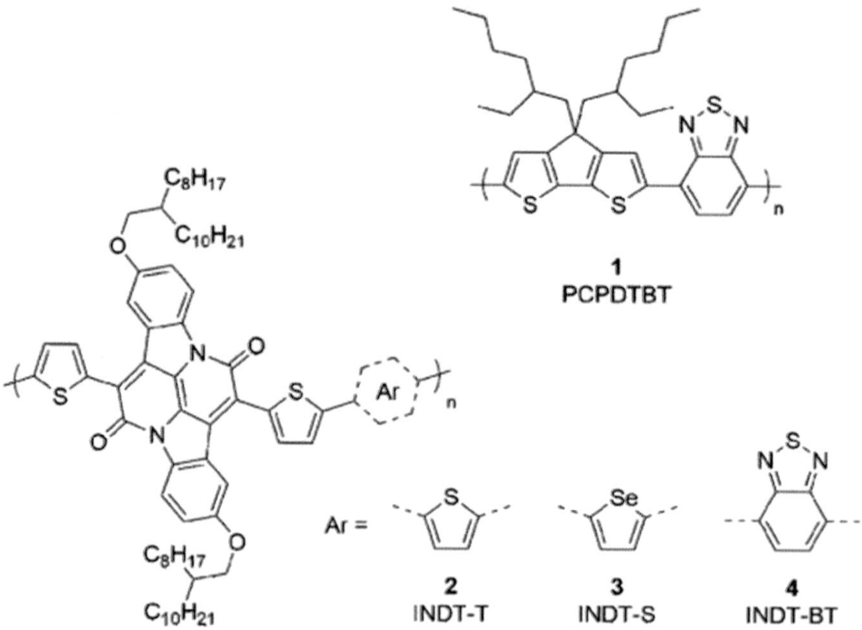

Figure 6.13 CPs as exogenous contrast agents for PAI [70].

The clearance of exogenous agents is crucial after completing its purpose since its accumulation in the organs for a long time can be toxic. Lyu et al. synthesized and characterized two biodegradable CPs, and they formed nanoparticles by using the amphiphilic polymer PLGA-PEG (SPNV and SPNT). Both CPNs presented broad absorption in the NIR region, ranging with no significant effect on absorption (Table 6.3) by vinyl group presence on the SPNV backbone. The PA signals of SPVN at 810 nm were higher than SPNT, and a linear correlation between PA signals and SPNs' concentration was observed in both nanoparticles. The biodegradability of both SPNs was studied in the enzyme myeloperoxidase (MPO), where after 48 h of incubation, the absorption peak of SPVN at 819 nm disappeared, due to the presence of vinyl group among the backbone chain. The SPNV was further studied to verify the first results in macrophage RAW264.7 cells. The incubation of the cell was performed in presence of lipopolysaccharides (LPS) and SPNV; the results confirmed the biodegradability of SPNV [71].

Table 6.3 Summary of photophysical properties on NIR-I semiconducting polymer nanoparticles

CPN	Absorption coefficient ε_{max} (L g^{-1} cm^{-1})	Absorption maximum (nm)	Diameter (nm)	Refs.
PFTTQ	3.6	805	46	[66]
SP1	93	660	40	[64]
SP2	20	700	40	
SPN1	90	660	46	[67]
SPN2	50	635	46	
SPN3	60	712	46	
SPN4	76	748	46	
SPN0/SPN5/SPN10	-	–	–	[69]
PCPDTBT-1	83	700	145	[70]
INDT-T-2	79	780	159	
INDT-S-3	139	790	120	
INDT-BT-4	253	800	160	
SPNV	40	819	32	[71]
SPNT	30	828	32	
DPP-DT-H	81.7	727, 789	78	[68]
		795	122	
		808	220	
		811	25	

6.6.2 PA Contrast Agents in NIR-II (1000–1700 nm) Biological Window

The second NIR biological window (1000–1700 nm) has recently attracted scientists' attention since it presents some not negligible at all advantages compared to NIR-I in vivo imaging, such as deeper penetration depth, higher sensitivity, and better resolution. A typical example is the work of Pu et al. [72]. They synthesized PA contrast agents SPNs (Fig. 6.14) with broadband absorption in both NIR-I and NIR-II windows. The SPN-I structure is a typical D-A-type approach consisting of pyrrolo[3,4-c]pyrrole-1,4(2H,5H)-dione and thiophene with absorption in the NIR-I window. The SPN-II is a D-A_1-D-A_2-type structure of pyrrolo[3,4-c] pyrrole-1,4(2H,5H)-dione and thiadiazoloquinoxaline (TDQ) as electron acceptors building blocks A_1 and A_2, respectively, and thiophene as the electron donor one (D). This order is further lowered down the bandgap due to the strong electron-withdrawing ability of TDQ, leading to the absorption in the NIR-II window. The two SPNs were formed via the encapsulation method by using the amphiphilic polymer PEG-b-PPG-b-PEG and were compared in terms of the PA ability. The measurements took place at the same concentration, and they found that the PA signals of SPN-II at 70 nm were 1.2-fold higher as compared with that of SPN-I. When comparing at the imaging depth of 3 cm, the signal-to-noise ratio (SNR) of SPN-II resulted in PA images at 1064 nm can be 1.4-times higher than that at 750 nm due to weaker background PA signals from biological tissues in the NIR-II window. In vivo imaging of brain vasculature in living rats demonstrated the proof-of-concept application of NIR-II PAI, which showed 1.5 times higher SNR than NIR-I PAI.

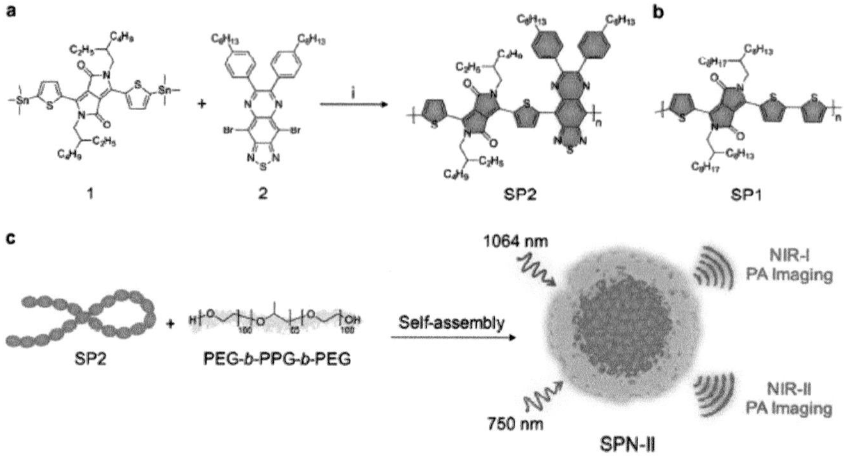

Figure 6.14 (a) The "acceptor" monomers used. (b) The resulting polymers, SP1 and SP2. (c) Schematic illustration from the SPN formation [72].

NIR-II CPs were also synthesized from another group (Fig. 6.15). They extensively studied the physical and PA properties of P1 nanoparticles in vitro and in vivo (Table 6.4). The nanoparticles demonstrated good biocompatibility, excellent PA stability, and PAI ability from NIR-I to NIR-II region. Using a 1064 nm laser, the NIR-II CPNs demonstrated more effective brain skull penetration and a much higher signal/background ratio than current contrast agents for PAI [73].

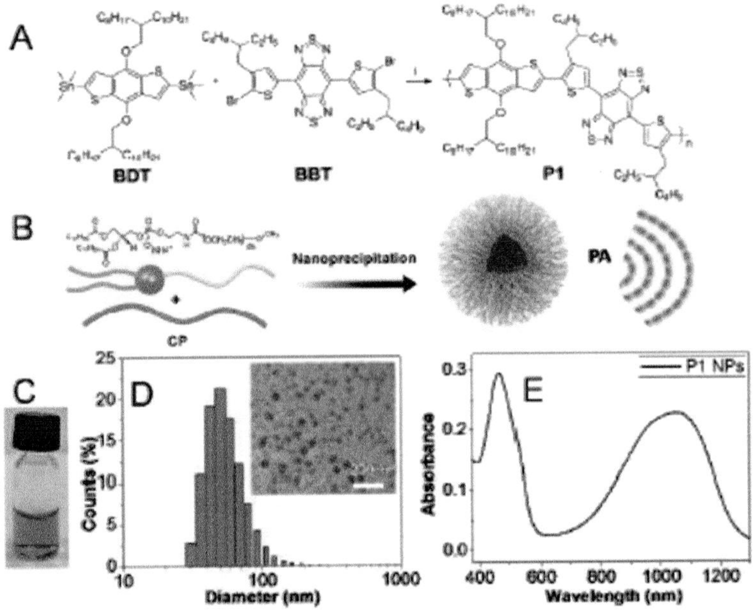

Figure 6.15 (A) Synthetic route of D-A CP (P1). (B) Nanoparticles formulation by using an amphiphilic polymer and the nanoprecipitation method. (C) Photograph from the aqueous solution. (D) Dynamic light scattering spectrum and the transmission electron microscopy image. (E) UV-Vis absorption spectrum [74].

Table 6.4 Summary of photophysical properties of NIR-II CPNs

CPN	Absorption coefficient ε_{max} (L g^{-1} cm^{-1})	Absorption maximum (nm)	Diameter (nm)	Refs
SPN-I	27.5	744	11	[72]
SPN-II	30	1253	54	
P1	22.6	1064	50	[73]
OSPNs	10	916/1025	113.2	[74]
TBDOPV-DT	39.5	1100	171.6	[75]
PDPPTBZ	43	1064	30	[76]
SPN-PT	3	1079	30	[77]

Throughout the different approaches for targeting contrast agents, Yin et al. formulated positively charged organic CPNs ($OSPNs^+$) for stem cell PAI in the NIR-II window. The $OSPNs^+$ were formulated via a "layer-by-layer modification" approach. First, the OSPNs were encapsulated into amphiphilic poly(styrene maleic anhydrite) (PSMA) to form $OSPNs^-$ followed by electrostatic interaction with the use of poly(L-lysing) (PLL) to form the cationic nanoparticles ($OSPNs^+$), which are preferable for enhancing the cellular uptake. Since the aqueous solution of $OSPNs^+$ has a broadband absorption profile into the NIR-I and NIR-II regions, they also exhibit strong NIR-I and NIR-II PA signals. Moreover, the PA signal increased linearly with increasing concentration. The in vitro experiments showed that the PA signal intensity of OSPNs+ in stem cells was high, proving the interaction between the nanoparticles and the negatively charged cell membrane. In vivo investigations show that this probe creates PA contrast enhancements of 21.7 and 40.6-fold compared with unlabeled cells when present in the brain and subcutaneous human mesenchymal stem cells (hMSCs), respectively [74].

A novel NIR-II contrast agent based on a narrow bandgap D-A-type CP (TBDOPV-DT nanoparticles) has been developed recently. A higher PA signal was detected with increasing concentrations of the nanoparticles, and the PA signals of TBDOPV-DT nanoparticles are linearly strengthened with concentrations. Its optical and physical characteristics are shown in Table 6.4. The nanoparticles were further used on HeLa tumor-bearing nude mice. Notably, the PA signal reached maximum accumulation after intravenous injection of TBDOPV-DT nanoparticles for 12 h (Fig. 6.16) [75].

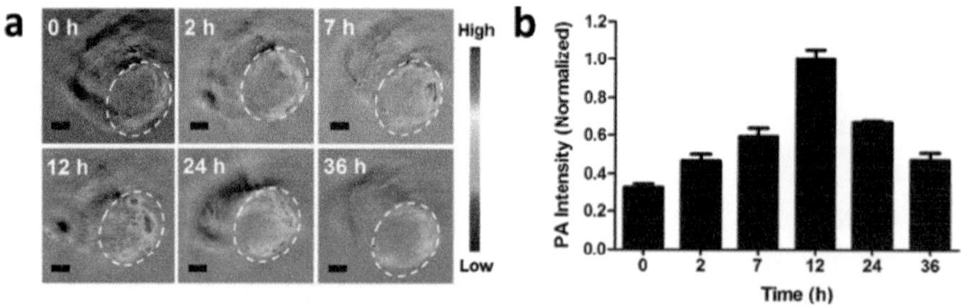

Figure 6.16 (a) PA images from HeLa tumor in a mouse. (b) PA signal intensities of tumor at different time points of TBDOPV-nanoparticles [75].

PDPPTBZ nanoparticles are based on pyrrole and thiadiazole building blocks. The formation of the nanoparticles was created through the encapsulation method with DSPE-PEG amphiphilic polymer as an outer shell (Fig. 6.17). The resulting nanoparticles exhibited excellent colloidal stability and spherical shape with an average diameter of 30 nm. The optical and physical characteristics are presented in Table 6.4. The studies of those nanoparticles as contrast agents for PAI showed that PDPPTBZ could be used for brain tumor imaging since its high mass extinction coefficient at 1064 nm leads to deeper in vivo glioma imaging (3.8 mm) [76].

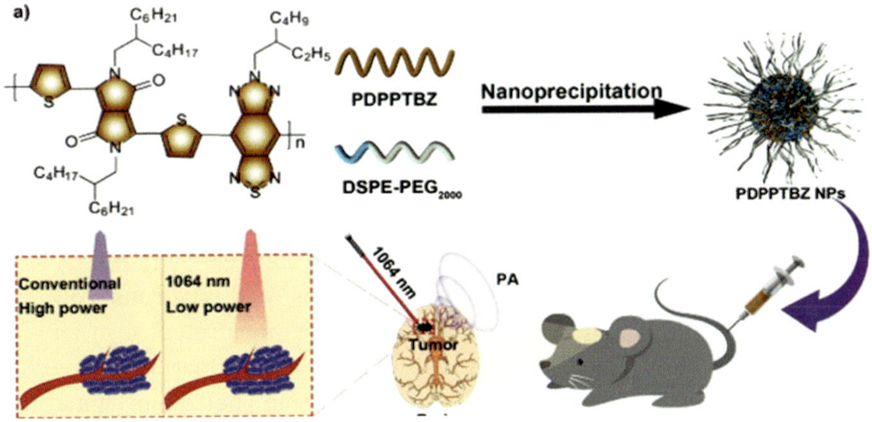

Figure 6.17 Nanoparticles formation of PDPPTBZ for PAI using 1064 nm laser [76].

As mentioned before, the contrast agents' biodegradation after being injected into a living organism is an essential factor to consider. Jiang et al. synthesized three CPs with strong absorption in the NIR-II window: PBBT-OT, PBBT-PT, and PBBT-DT. For the formation of the nanoparticles, the FDA-approved biodegradable amphiphilic copolymer PLGA-PEG was selected, resulting in the SPNs SPN-OT, SPN-PT, and SPN-DT. All three CPNs were incubated with macrophages to investigate their degradation ability. The fluorescence intensities of macrophages cultured with SPN-PT, SNP-DT, and SPN-OT were 2.9, 2.0, and 3.7-folds higher than that of control cells, respectively. Due to their small hydrodynamic size, which is highly required for the clearance system, all CPNs could be effectively cleared from living mice through renal and hepatobiliary excretions within 15 days after the injection. The SPN-PT, which was used as the representative CP, presented an excellent NIR-II PA signal, achieving a high signal-to-background ratio (SBRs) for tumor and brain vasculature in living mice [77].

6.7 Raman Spectroscopy

Raman spectroscopy has become a widely used tool in biomedical engineering and life sciences for its diagnostic potential, making significant progress in the field of clinical evaluation. Since it is a free-label, non-invasive, non-destructive, and non-contact imaging technique, it is used in medical research for studying the biochemical environment of single cells or monitoring the reaction of cells to drugs, and the pharmaceutical industry for process and quality control in the manufacturing of drugs (Fig. 6.18) [78].

Moreover, in recent years Raman scattering-based vibrational microscopy has emerged as an auspicious and vigorous cell imaging tool, due to intriguing features it demonstrates, such as visualization of specific vibrations providing information about molecular structure, quantitative relationship between signal intensity and substance concentration, and narrow-band enabled multi-color imaging [11–13, 79–81]. The spectrum for a specific molecule can be used as a fingerprint for the identification of the molecule with high specificity and sensitivity; thus, differences in the composition of biological molecules, such as lipids, proteins, carbohydrates, and nucleic acids in normal/cancer cells, can be identified and classified through the evaluation of Raman spectra profile contributing to the assessment, characterization, and discrimination of cancer stages [14–16].

For biological samples, which comprise different molecules in a cell, the spectra regions between 400 and 1800 cm^{-1} and 2800 and 3100 cm^{-1} are of interest. Proteins, lipids, and nucleic acids display intense Raman signals in the cellular fingerprint and high wavenumber regions (Fig. 6.19), enabling label-free imaging of those molecules by targeting endogenous chemical bonds including O–H, C–H, C=C, C=O, S=O, O–P–O, amide, and several ring-breathing modes [82].

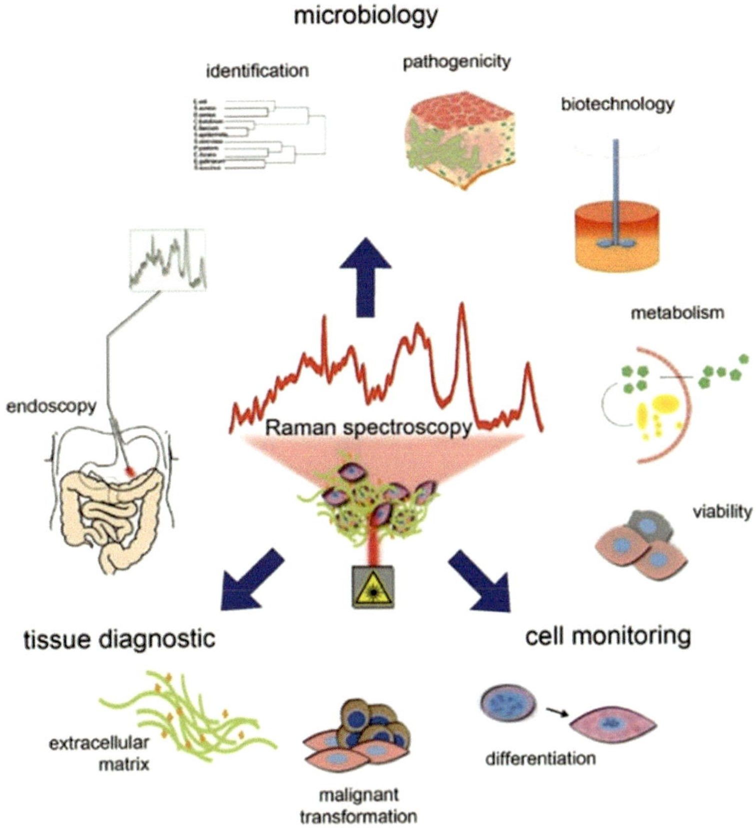

Figure 6.18 Applications of Raman spectroscopy in biomedicine [78].

However, Raman scattering is a weak process. The cross-section of conventional spontaneous Raman scattering is intrinsically extremely small compared to fluorescence, while there is interference derived from the endogenous cellular background. This has led to various techniques being developed to amplify the Raman signal or Raman probes, such as stimulated Raman scattering (SRS) [84–87], surface enhanced Raman scattering (SERS) [88–91], and coherent anti-Stokes Raman scattering (CARS) [12, 92, 93]. Under this strategy, the development of probe materials possessing a strong Raman signal in the cell-silent vibration region of the spectra (1800–2800 cm^{-1}) is extremely desired to achieve improved detection specificity and sensitivity. Bioorthogonal Raman probes, including isotopes (C-N) and triple-bond (C≡C and C≡N)-based tags that exhibit distinctive signals in the cell-silent vibrational region have been used for labeled Raman imaging. During the last decade, several reports demonstrate that alkyne-containing molecules are promising for live-cell imaging since they display strong Raman scattering at 2100–2200 cm^{-1} in combination with their low toxicity and easy accessibility [94–97].

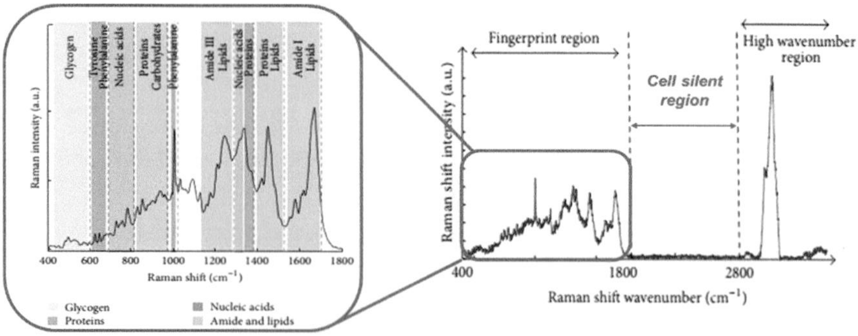

Figure 6.19 Raman spectrum of cervical cancer CaSki cell line, where the fingerprint and the high wavenumber (HW) regions of the spectrum are indicated by the arrows. The major assignments related to glycogen, proteins, lipids, and nucleic acids are highlighted in the Raman spectrum's fingerprint region [83].

Recently, CPs have been investigated as new promising materials for Raman imaging applications in living cells. Li et al. reported the development of water-soluble cationic poly(phenylene ethynylene) (PPE) derivatives for use as alkyne-state-dependent Raman probes for living cell imaging due to the synergetic enhancement effect of alkyne vibrations in Raman-silent region compared to alkyne-containing small molecules [98]. Upon excitation of 785 nm laser, PPE cationic CPs exhibit a strong, sharp, and narrow Raman peak located at the cell-silent region around 2200 cm^{-1}, which corresponds to the C≡C stretching bond. Six PEE derivatives with different types of pendants were synthesized in order to explore their Raman shift/intensity relationship. As shown in Fig. 6.20a, P5 and P6 exhibit the stronger Raman peak at the Raman-silent region of cells compared to the other four PPE derivatives, revealing that alkyne unit conjugated into the middle of two aromatic rings can effectively enhance the Raman intensity of alkyne vibrations.

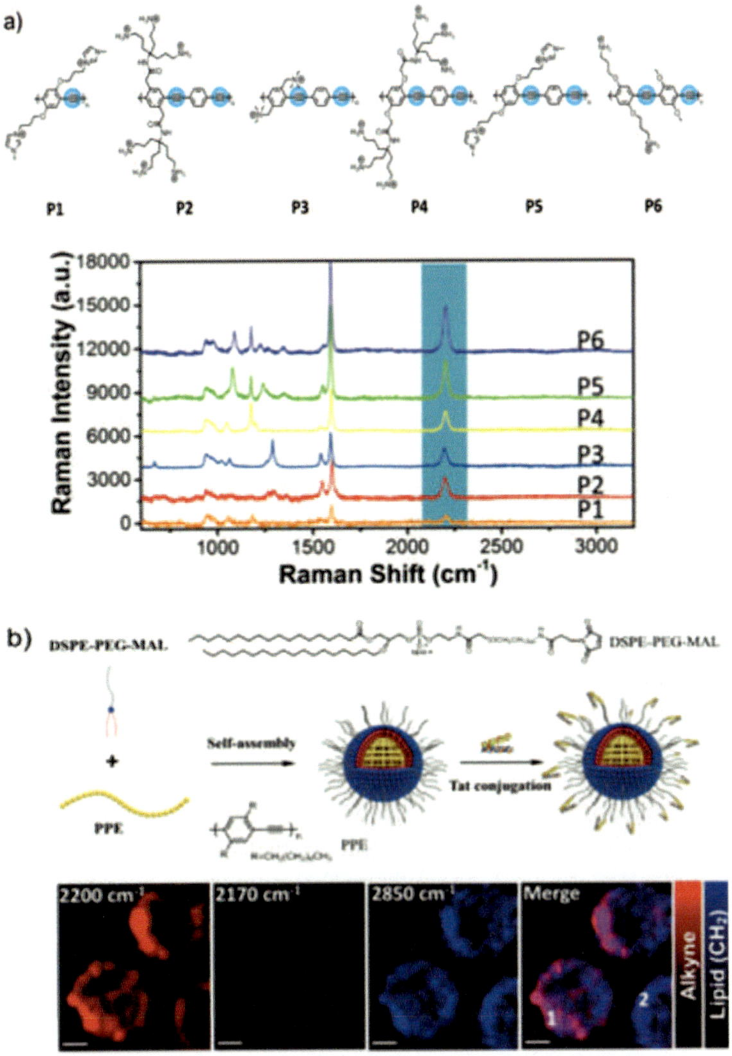

Figure 6.20 (a) Chemical structures of PPE derivatives and their corresponding spontaneous Raman spectra. (b) Schematic illustration for preparation of Tat-PPE nanoparticles and living cell Raman images of HeLa cells treated with Tat-PPE nanoparticles (10 mg mL^{-1}) or 6 h. Scale bars: 5 mm [98].

Further testing of P5 and P6 derivatives as vibrational probes for living cell imaging under Raman microscopy was employed. Dual-color Raman imaging of HeLa cells was acquired with the employment of 2200 cm^{-1} for alkyne and 2850 cm^{-1} for lipid (CH_2), showing that P5 and P6 were widely distributed in the cytoplasm of HeLa cells. Finally, PPE-based CPNs were formatted and functionalized with cell-penetrating peptides Tat for enhanced living cell imaging (Fig. 6.20b). Dual-color Raman imaging of HeLa cells after treatment with Tat-PPE nanoparticles for 6 h, presents a strong signal of the alkyne in the cytoplasm, disclosing the intracellular distribution of Tat-PPE nanoparticles.

Nevertheless, the synthesis of a triple bond onto an arbitrary position of a molecule does not offer always satisfying signal intensity in the cell-silent region, affecting the detection sensitivity [97, 99]. Another class of CPs has been proposed as potential Raman probes. Polydiacetylenes, owing to the large π-conjugation and the polarizability of all-planar polymer backbones, can produce strong Raman signals. Although this class of CPs generally suffers from poor solubility in common solvents, limiting their processibility and functionality in biological applications applying Raman imaging. However, Tian and co-workers successfully synthesized biocompatible, water-soluble, and functionalized polydiacetylene poly(deca-4,6-diynedioic acid) (PDDA) using a host-guest topochemical polymerization strategy [94]. PDDA possesses an up to ~10^4-fold increase of alkyne vibration compared to conventional alkyne Raman probes. In this study, the authors achieved to prepare three PDDA derivatives via modifications with different functional groups for subcellular organelle targeting in living cells, as shown in Fig. 6.21 (left).

More specifically, they used a tertiary amine for lysosome targeting (P2), and two peptides for mitochondria (P3) and nucleus (P4) targeting. SRS was applied for imaging of HeLa cells labeled with P2, P3, and P4 PDDA-based vibrational tags, respectively, in order to investigate the distribution of the polymer tags in the cells using 2120 cm^{-1} for the C≡C stretching bond. SRS imaging of HeLa cells treated with P2 displays alkyne signals in the cells' lysosomes, while SRS imaging of HeLa cells treated with P3 shows clearly accumulation of the tag in the cytoplasm of the cell where mitochondria are distributed. Finally, HeLa cells treated with P4 demonstrate a strong alkyne signal in cell nuclei (Fig. 6.21, right).

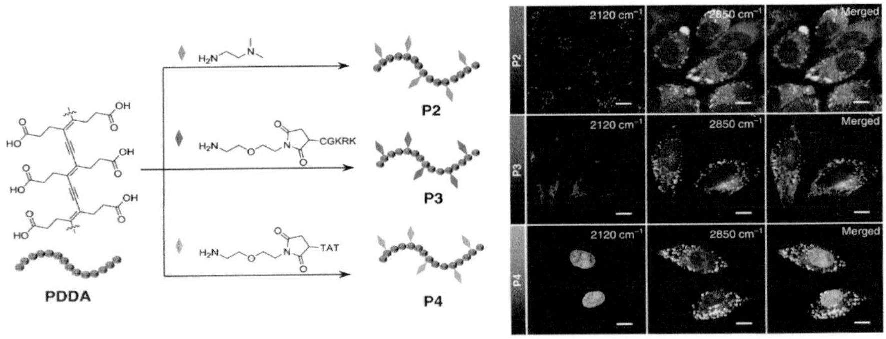

Figure 6.21 Side chain modification of PDDA with different functional groups to derivatives P2, P3, and P4 that can be targeted to specific subcellular organelles (left). SRS images of HeLa cells treated with 50 μM of P2, P3, and P4, respectively (right). Images shown from left to right are the alkyne (2120 cm^{-1}), lipids (2850 cm^{-1}), and merged images. Scale bar: 10 μm [94].

Under another strategy for the enhancement of the Raman signal, Demirel et al. reported the development of a nanostructured film of the small organic semiconductor molecule DFP-4T, consisting of a fully π-conjugated diperfluorophenyl-substituted quaterthiophene structure, prepared via thermal evaporation deposition technique (Fig. 6.22a) [100]. DFP-4T exhibits a very large Raman enhancement factor (>10^5) and a low limit of detection (10^{-9} M) for the methylene blue (MB) probe molecule, whose results are comparable to those reported for the best inorganic semiconductor and even intrinsic plasmonic metal-based SERS platforms.

As shown in Fig. 6.22b, several prominent bands originating from MB molecules are detected at 450 cm^{-1}, 1186 cm^{-1}, 1459 cm^{-1}, and 1621 cm^{-1}, which correspond to (C–N–C) skeletal stretching, (C–N) stretching, (C–N) asymmetric stretching, and (C–C) ring stretching, respectively. The significant Raman intensity enhancement for the peak at 1621 cm^{-1} suggests that the MB molecules adopt very favorable molecular orientations on the nanostructured DFP-4T film encouraging substrate–molecule electronic interactions and charge-transfer processes. The molecular detection ability of the DFP-4T film was also explored by collecting SERS spectra at different MB probe concentrations from 10^{-3} to 10^{-9} M (Fig. 6.22c), where we can easily ascertain that even at the lowest concentration of 10^{-9} M there is an obvious Raman signal at 1621 cm^{-1}.

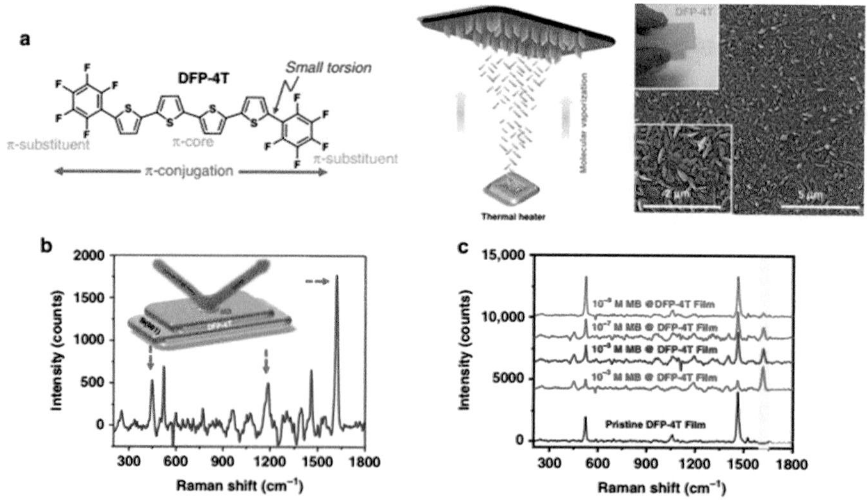

Figure 6.22 (a) Fabrication and characterization of DFP-4T. Chemical structure of the DFP-4T CP (left) and SEM image of the produced DFP-4T film on Si (001) substrate through thermal evaporation process (right). (b) The SERS spectrum of MB probe (10^{-3} M) on nanostructured DFP-4T film, where characteristic Raman peaks are indicated. (c) SERS spectra of MB on nanostructured DFP-4T film at different concentrations [100].

6.8 Innovative CPN-Based Phototherapeutic Strategies for Cancer Treatment

Light-induced phototherapies exhibit certain advantages. To begin with, the use of NIR light enables deep tissue penetration [101], providing the possibility of exploiting such phototherapeutic applications for the treatment and imaging of tumors that are localized in deeper tissues or inner organs. In vivo administration and direction of selected nanomaterials pose minimal risk for the patient, since they are inactive in the dark and can only be triggered via the light application. In turn, their activation can induce targeted cytotoxicity against malignant cells in different ways: either through the selective homing properties of these "smart" nanoagents, or through the strict orientation of the light beam only toward tumor lesions, leaving the surrounding healthy tissue unaffected [102].

Multiple nanosystems have been designed and are currently evaluated for light-induced phototherapies, including Au nanoparticles [103], carbon nanocomposites [104], Pd nanosheets [105], magnetic nanoparticles [106], fullerenes [107], etc. Recently, the use of CPs has emerged as a novel strategy, showing remarkable efficiency in both diagnostic and therapeutic biomedical applications due to their unique structure and optical and electronic properties [108, 109]. All these features can be suitably deployed to yield different functions, such as bright fluorescence, ROS production, or heat generation, which can, in turn, be harnessed for bio-imaging, photodynamic, or photothermal therapies, respectively [110, 111]. Of most importance, CPs can be readily formulated to form CPNs with further advantages, including nanoscale sizes, water solubility, and marked biocompatibility [112, 113], while the surface of these CPNs can be selectively amended for the elimination of undesirable cellular interaction (e.g., with normal cells) and internalization [113]. Moreover, conjugation of target-specific antibodies to CPNs can navigate them with high accuracy to the desired site, thus enhancing imaging and therapeutic efficacy [24].

Apart from diagnosis and disease monitoring, CPNs are also exploited in therapeutic procedures comprising minimal or non-invasive techniques, namely PDT and PTT. PDT is based on the use of photosensitizing CPNs to achieve energy transfer from light to oxygen molecules, and to mediate the generation of ROS, which, in turn, will kill the target cells. Alternatively, PTT employs light-absorbing agents to transform light energy into thermal (vibrational) energy for cancer cell elimination. CPNs are basically inactive upon entering the body and become activated by local application or irradiation (Fig. 6.23). More recently, conjugation of pharmacological agents (antibodies, drugs, etc.) with CPNs has emerged as a novel strategy for the enhancement of therapeutic efficacy and specific tissue targeting.

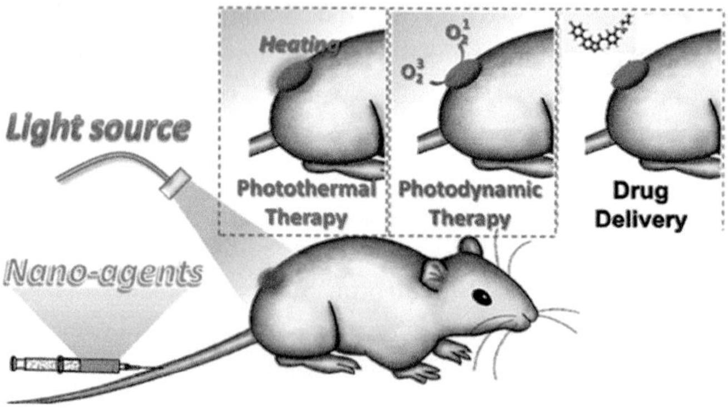

Figure 6.23 Methodologies for the in vivo delivery and activation of nanoagents of therapeutic interest for cancer treatment. The selected nanomaterials are injected by the desired administration route and selectively delivered to the target site. In turn, the agents are activated either photothermally or photodynamically, or they are triggered to release encapsulated pharmacological agents [102].

6.8.1 CPN-Based PTT

Hyperthermia (HT), meaning the increase in body temperature, has been thoroughly investigated as an alternative to conventional cancer treatment approaches, where cancer cells undergo thermal stress, resulting in clearance through apoptotic cell death [114]. Even if thermal treatments are considered highly effective, their main drawback is that cell death activation is not only taking place in cancer cells but also in healthy ones. It is widely assumed that the efficacy of thermal treatment is given by two main factors [115]: the magnitude of the temperature increment and the duration of the treatment. Depending on the magnitude of the induced temperature increment, thermal treatments and related effects on cancerous tumors can be classified as in Fig. 6.24.

Diathermia treatments: These are based on heating processes up to 41 °C and have beneficial health effects that are associated with the increase of blood flow and ion diffusion rate across cellular membranes. The temperature does not provoke relevant modifications at the cellular level.

Hyperthermia treatments: These consist of setting the tumor temperature within the range of 41–48 °C. These thermal treatments are usually combined with other cancer treatments, such as chemotherapy or radiotherapy, whose efficacy is increased after hyperthermia. The cellular temperature at 41 °C causes cell inactivation for several hours and temperature between 43 °C and 45 °C causes long-term cell inactivation, during which we observe the increase of the intracellular density of ROS that can cause damage to proteins, lipids, and nucleic acids. Further temperature increment (45–48 °C) produces rapid necrotic cell death in cancer cells that are resistant to standard hyperthermia.

Irreversible injury treatments: These are carried out by increasing the tumor temperature above 48 °C for a few minutes. In this case, a drastic activation of cell death is achieved as a consequence of coagulative necrosis processes. At temperatures above 60 °C, protein denaturation is caused, and at even higher temperatures (above 80 °C), tissue ablation is taking place due to water vaporization [116, 117].

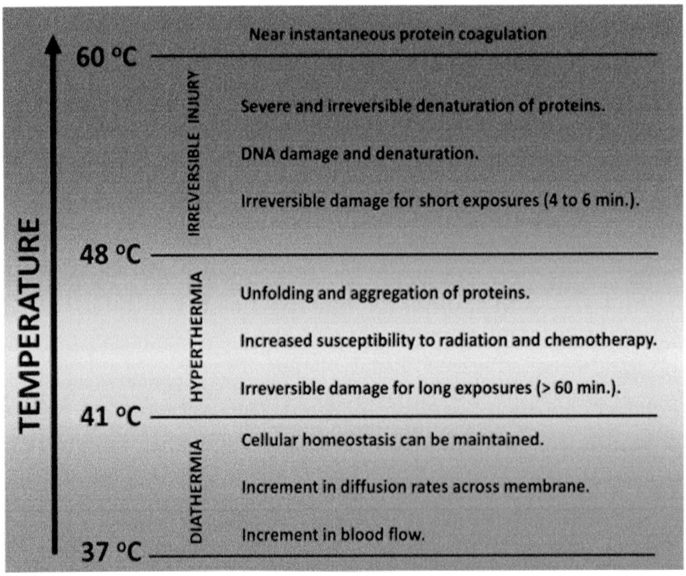

Figure 6.24 Schematic diagram of the variety of effects caused by the different thermal treatments as classified by the corresponding operating temperature [115].

PTT has emerged as an appealing novel approach for cancer treatment due to its non-invasive nature. This method's principle is based on the utilization of CPNs that absorbs light to generate heat (Fig. 6.4), which subsequently attenuate cancer cell proliferation and induce cell death. Appropriate candidates for PTT should hold specific properties: high absorbance in the NIR spectrum, where bioassays are applicable without harmful effects on biological tissues, and subsequent efficient conversion of this absorbed optical energy into heat. Additionally, they should be well-tolerated by normal cells and tissues and, at the same time, highly specific and cytotoxic against tumor cells.

6.8.1.1 Main CPN cores used as photothermal agents

There is a great variety of PTT agents. Their main drawback, though, is that these are mainly inorganic materials with certain disadvantages, including high toxicity due to decomposition resistance [118]. During the last decade, CPNs have emerged as promising phototherapeutic tools (Table 6.5), due to their unique properties that are in accordance with those required for phototherapeutic applications.

Among the first CPN materials shown to act as promising photothermal agents against epithelial cancer types was polyaniline. The optical-absorbance peak of polyaniline can be red-shifted toward the NIR region through its transition from the emeraldine base (EB) to the emeraldine salt (ES), which occurs in the presence of acidic/oxidative conditions that predominate within cells (Fig. 6.25). In an early study by Yang and his colleagues, NIR-stimulated polyaniline ES nanoparticles exhibited a highly efficient ablation of A-431 epidermal cancer cells both in vitro and in vivo [119].

Further studies have highlighted the anti-cancer efficiency of polyaniline nanoparticles against different cancer types. Functional nanoparticles with F-127 surfactant capping were able to induce NIR-mediated photothermal elimination of HCT-116 colon cancer cells and tumor xenografts, through activation of apoptosis [120] (Fig. 6.26). More recently, Wang and his colleagues performed chemical oxidation to cap polyaniline onto UiO-66. The synthesized nanoparticles showed strong NIR absorbance and elicited cancer cell death and tumor growth inhibition, upon laser irradiation [121].

Table 6.5 A summary of CPs used for PTT of cancer

Core material	Stabilizer/ modification	Tumor target (cell lines)	Refs
Polyaniline	Poly(ethylene glycol) stearate	Skin cancer (A-431)	[119]
	F-127	Colon cancer (HCT-116)	[120]
	UiO-66	Colon cancer (HCT-116, CT26)	[121]
Polypyrrole	Poly(vinyl alcohol)	Murine mammary tumor (4T1)	[122]
	Polyvinyl-pyrrolidone	Murine mammary tumor (4T1)	[123]
	Poly(vinyl alcohol)	Cervical cancer (HeLa)	[124]
PDA	Melanin	Murine mammary tumor (4T1)	[125]
Poly(3,4-ethylenedioxythiophene): poly(4-styrenesulfonate)	Coating: charged polymers; conjugated with branched PEG	Murine mammary tumor (4T1)	[126]
Poly(N-phenylglycine)	Hyaluronic acid (HA) and PEG-diamine	Murine melanoma (B16)	[127]
	Sulfonation and engraftment onto the surface of supercharged green fluorescent protein (ScGFP)	Cervical cancer (HeLa), Murine mammary tumor (4T1), Murine melanoma (B16)	[128]
Polythiophene	Ammonium persulfate as the oxidative agent	Murine colorectal cancer (CT-26)	[129]
	PEGylated DPP-dithiophene	Murine hepatocellular carcinoma (H22)	[68]

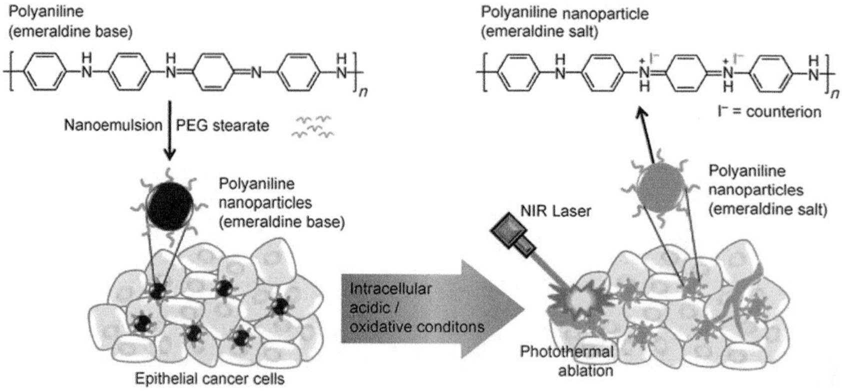

Figure 6.25 Polyaniline nanoparticles for photothermal cancer treatment. Polyaniline nanoparticles are introduced into the cancer cells at their native EB state (visible absorbance) and are converted into the ES state (NIR absorbance) due to intracellular acidic or oxidative conditions. Subsequent application of NIR irradiation leads to photothermal ablation of cancer cells [119].

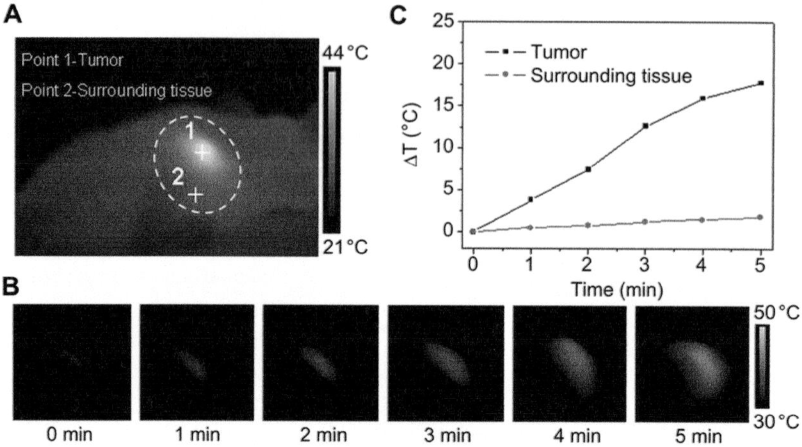

Figure 6.26 Polyaniline-based nanoparticles for PTT [120]. (A) Temperature elevation in the tumor (1+) and surrounding tissue (2+) of a mouse after intratumoral injection of F127-capped polyaniline nanoparticles (1 mg/mL) with an 808 nm laser (0.5 W*cm^{-2}, 3 min). (B) Photothermal images of the tumor were acquired at 0–5 minutes. The temperature distinction between 30 °C and 50 °C is indicated with the scale bars. (C) Graph showing the changes in temperature within the tumor and the surrounding tissue through time.

Polypyrrole is another widely used material in CPN synthesis for PTT due to its high conductivity, great stability, and good biocompatibility. In an early study by Yang and his colleagues in 2012, poly(vinyl alcohol)-coated polypyrrole nanoparticles were able to completely eradicate 4T1 murine mammary tumors, without any profound side effect in normal tissues (Fig. 6.27) [122]. In another study, polypyrrole nanoparticles with an average size of ~50 nm were produced, with $FeCl_3$ as an oxidation agent and capped with polyvinylpyrrolidone. The synthesized nanoparticles were highly biocompatible, with no cytotoxic effects on QSG-7701 human hepatocytes up to 200 ppm. Treatment of mice bearing 4T1 mammary tumors with the above polypyrrole nanoparticles led to complete eradication of the tumors and an over 60-day survival [123].

Other groups have utilized a variety of core materials for the development of photothermal nanoagents, including PDA [125], poly(3,4-ethylenedioxythiophene):poly(4-styrenesulfonate) (PEDOT:PSS) [126], poly(n-phenylglycine) [127, 128], polythiophene [129], etc. (Table 6.5). The resulting nanoparticles showed good biodegradability, low toxicity, and selective elimination of cancer cells and/ or tumors in all cases.

Finally, CPs with a donor-acceptor (D-A) structure, which are widely used in organic photovoltaics [130], are being further exploited as nanomedicinal agents. In Levi-Polyachenko and colleagues' work, low-band-gap D-A nanoparticles (nano-PCPDTBT) were synthesized through copolymerization of 2-ethylhexyl cyclopentadithiophene and 2,1,3-benzothiadiazole and showed minimal cytotoxicity in concentrations below 1 mg/mL, in the absence of light activation. However, administration of the nanoparticles and subsequent irradiation with an 808 nm NIR laser (0.6 W/cm^2), raised the temperature above 50 °C and successfully killed human colon cancer cells [131]. To improve the photothermal nanoagents' conversion efficiency, researchers aim to synthesize nanoparticles with improved absorbance in the NIR spectrum. Toward this end, Liu and colleagues developed an optimized porphyrin-containing CP (Por CP) nanocomposite with strong anti-cancer efficiency against U87 human glioma cells and tumors, as shown by their low IC_{50} [132]. Many researcher groups have recently focused on the D-A structure for the development of polymer-based nanoparticles for photothermal cancer therapy, including, BODIPY-DPP CPs [133] and BODIPY-based polymer dots [134].

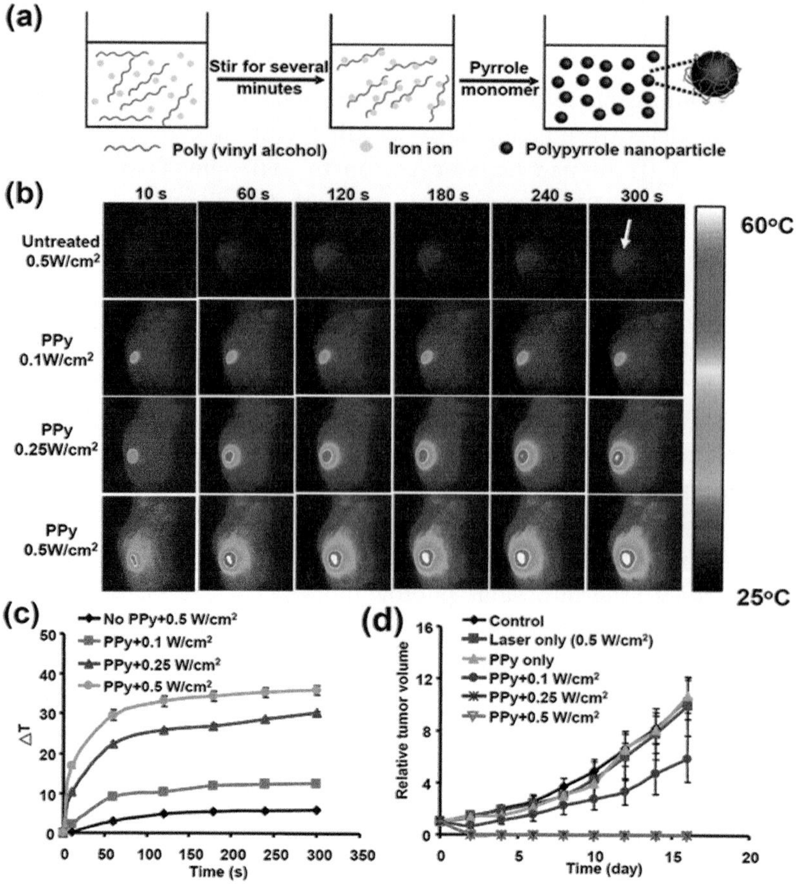

Figure 6.27 Polypyrrole organic nanoparticles for in vitro PTT. (a) Schematic representation of the synthesis of poly(vinyl alcohol)-coated polypyrrole nanoparticles. (b) IR thermal images of 4T1 tumor-bearing mice that were intratumorally injected with polypyrrole nanoparticles and irradicated with an 808 nm laser at different power densities. (c) Change in the temperature of the tumors after treatment. (d) Tumor growth in different groups of mice after the indicated treatments [122].

6.8.1.2 Mechanisms of photothermal anti-cancer activity

Regarding the general principle for photothermal cancer therapy, a threshold temperature between 70 °C and 80 °C is required for the complete elimination of cancer cells in vitro [135], while for tumor ablation in vivo, temperatures between 55 °C and 95 °C have been reported successful [136]. For this reason, the selected nanoagents should hold great NIR absorption capacity and heat conversion efficiency.

PTT, unlike PDT, mainly exerts its anti-tumorigenic effects by increasing the temperature within the tumor and its microenvironment; therefore, the presence of oxygen is not required in order to exert its therapeutic actions. The anti-cancer activity of elevated temperature relies on distinct outcomes, including a regional increase in blood flow, accompanied by increased perfusion rates inside the tumors, and in the normal tissues [137]. These effects facilitate drug delivery and are extremely useful when CPNs act as carriers of anti-cancer compounds. Moreover, hyperthermia has been shown to increase oxygen delivery to the tumor, thus enhancing the therapeutic efficiency of photo- and radiotherapy combination. In this way, tumor cells cannot repair the damage caused by radiation, even after the therapeutic regime's end [138].

The differential response between transformed and normal tissues to heat lies in the fact that tumor cells are already stressed due to low oxygen conditions and nutrient unavailability; consequently, they are unable to respond efficiently to the additional stress induced by the application of heat, as compared to normal tissues (Fig. 6.28). In general, PTT may have different effects on cancer cells, depending on the performed temperature range. Extremely high temperatures (up to 90 °C) are used to completely eliminate tumors; however, lower temperatures might also have favorable effects, while lowering the risk of adverse effects on normal tissues mild hyperthermia (up to 40 °C temperature) triggers the host immune response to attack the tumor. Moderate hyperthermia (40–42 °C) acts multimodally: it can damage cancer cells directly; it renders them more sensitive to radiotherapy; it facilitates the delivery of chemotherapeutic and immunotherapeutic agents of high molecular weights; and it increases the cellular uptake of small molecule inhibitors [139].

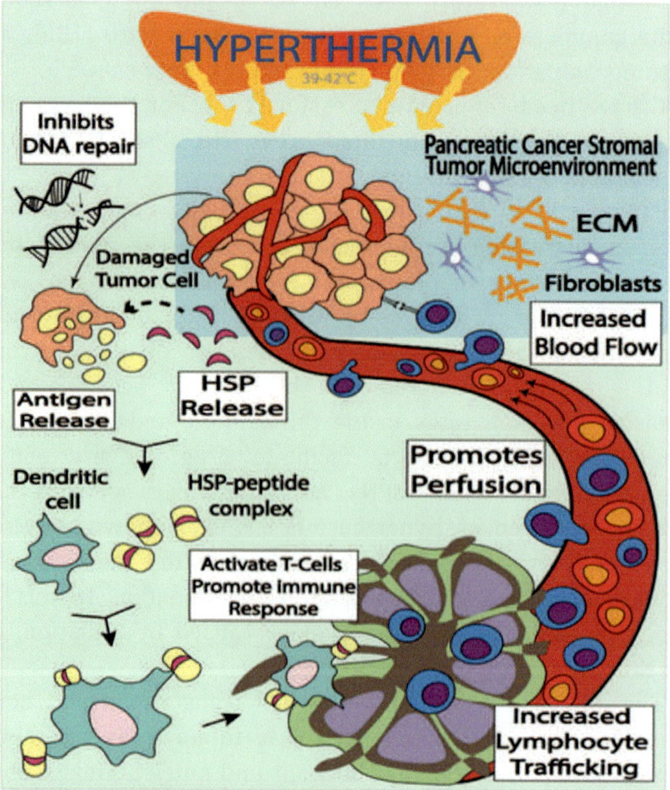

Figure 6.28 Effects of mild to moderate PTT on cancer cells [140]. ECM: Extracellular matrix; HSP: Heat shock protein.

The application of nanoparticle-guided hyperthermia can lead to synergistic effects against cancer cells and tumors. Nanoparticles enter the cells mainly through endocytosis; they get trapped within the plasma membrane to form endocytic vesicles, which detach and eventually give rise to endolysosomes. Internalized nanoparticles can interrupt crucial cellular processes and induce stress, leading to hampered proliferation rates, induction of oxidative stress, cytoskeleton disruption, hindered differentiation, and DNA damage. Autophagy and lysosomal dysfunctions may also be triggered, eventually resulting in cell death [114]. Interestingly, regarding the type of cell death, which is induced by nanoparticle-driven hyperthermia, Perez-Hernandez and colleagues demonstrated that PTT induces programmed cell death through activation of the intrinsic pathway, rather than necrotic cell death, thus avoiding the generation of inflammatory responses, which may usually compromise the antitumor activity [141].

Regarding nanoparticle clearance from the body, it has been shown that nanoparticles with reduced sizes (below 5.5 nm) are more easily subjected to renal clearance and avoid reticuloendothelial capture [114].

6.8.2 Application of CPNs for PDT of Cancer

The term "photodynamic" action was first recorded at the beginning of the 20th century, with the topical application of eosin and white light for the treatment of skin tumors [142]; since then, the expansion of research on the combination of light and chemical agents for therapeutic applications gave rise to PDT. The PDT relies on the combinatorial exploitation of three main factors: a photosensitive molecule used for the desirable targeting of cells/tissues, called a photosensitizer; the light of a specific wavelength for the activation of the photosensitizer; and the presence of oxygen, which is also a prerequisite [143]. The net effect of these elements' combination is the triggering of oxygen-dependent cytotoxic effects on the targeted tissue (Fig. 6.29).

Regarding the mechanism that orchestrates the cytotoxic effects of PDT, it is described in Fig. 6.4 [143, 144]. Focusing on PDT applications, the resulting intersystem crossing from singlet to triplet state leads to the generation of free radicals (type I reaction), or singlet oxygen $^1O_2$ (type II reaction) (Fig. 6.4). In type I reaction, the photosensitizer reacts directly with a cell component or structure, such as the cell membrane or a cellular protein, by transferring a proton or an electron to form a radical anion or cation, respectively, which, in turn, may react with oxygen and produce ROS. On the other hand, in the type II reaction, singlet oxygen interaction with distinct cellular components results in functional impairment and/or cell death. For example, the reaction with membrane lipids can induce lipid peroxidation with subsequent disruption of cellular membranes; the reaction with amino acids might dysregulate vital proteins; and the reaction with nucleic acids would generate toxic and mutagenic effects. The cellular and molecular mechanisms involved in PDT are presented in Fig. 6.4.

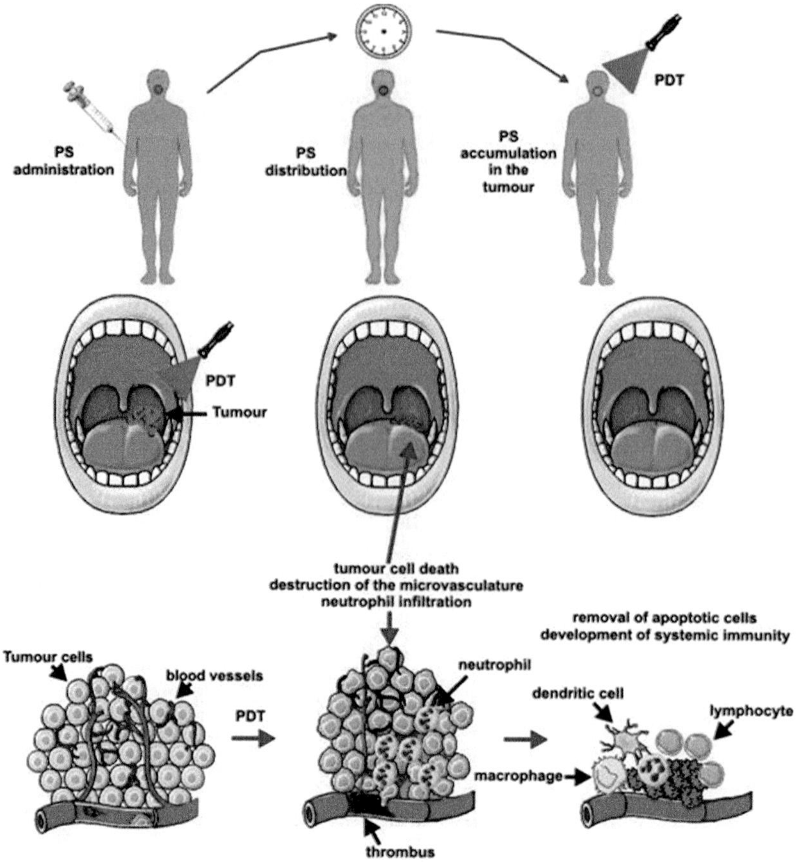

Figure 6.29 A course of PDT application and end effects on tumor [144]. After the administration of the photosensitizer and its subsequent systemic distribution, it finally accumulates in the tumor, where it gets activated via light illumination in presence of oxygen. The produced ROS induces irreversible damage to cellular components, leading to cell death via multiple pathways. In parallel, local inflammation aids in the removal of necrotic cells, restoration of healthy tissue homeostasis, and potentially in the development of systemic immunity.

6.8.2.1 CP-based nanostructures used in PDT of cancer

Like PTT, there is a great variety of molecules and nanoagents, both organic and inorganic, that have been employed in the PDT of cancer. Nevertheless, CP-based nanoparticles hold great potential for this type of therapy due to their unique native photophysical properties [145]. Among these are: (a) high extinction coefficients ($\varepsilon > 10^7$ L $mol^{-1} \cdot cm^{-1}$), (b) strong triplet formation, (c) intrinsic capability of ROS formation, (d) negligible cytotoxicity in vitro in absence of light activation, (e) buffer dispersibility and stability, (f) intrinsic fluorescence, useful for tracking of delivery, and (g) tuning possibility for targeted delivery.

Among the first CPN-based PDT approaches was the development of phosphorescent CPNs containing Ir(III) complexes and conjugated polyfluorene for optical oxygen sensing and photodynamic cancer therapy [146]. In this system, the acceptor phosphorescent Ir(III) complex was introduced into the blue-emitting polyfluorene backbone as an optical oxygen sensor and a photosensitizing agent for effective cancer cell elimination through ROS generation. Interestingly, the developed nanodots caused a dramatic reduction in HeLa cell proliferation, with over 50% increase in apoptotic cell numbers, upon light irradiation. In specific, polyfluorene-based CPNs have been extensively exploited for PDT of cancer. Poly[(9,9-dioctylfluorenyl-2,7-diyl)-alt-co-(1,4-benzo-{2,1′,3}-thiadiazole)] (PFBT)-based CPNs, with tetraphenylporphyrin (TPP) as the photosensitizer, have shown great potential as phototherapeutic agents against both breast and gastric cancer in vivo (Fig. 6.30) [147, 148].

Multiple other formulations have also been employed (Table 6.6). Metalated porphyrin-doped CPNs were shown effective against colorectal cancer and brain cancer, one of the most aggressive and challenging formulations to treat cancer types [149]. While Pdots consisting of the CPs (MEH-PPV and CN-PPV-DPD) and meso-tetrahydroxyphenylchlorin (mTHPC) as the photosensitizer, mediated strong cell death signals against breast cancer cells, upon implementation of Forster resonance energy transfer (FRET) [150].

Table 6.6 Selected CPNs used for PDT of cancer

Backbone	Photosensitizer	Targeting ligand	CPN average size (nm)	Irradiation wavelength (nm)/power	Tumor target/type of experiments	Refs
Polyfluorene	Ir(III) complex	NA	10	488/4.5 J/cm^2	Cervical (HeLa)/in vitro	[146]
Poly(9,9-dioctylfluorene-altbenzothiadiazole) (F8BT)	Platinum octaethyl-porphyrin (PtOEP)	NA	28	420/ 5–10 J/cm^2	Brain (T98G) colorectal (SW480)/in vitro	[149]
Poly[2-methoxy-5(2-ethylhexyloxy)-1,4-phenylene-vinylene] (MEH-PPV)	mTHPC	NA	15–30	473	Breast (MCF-7)/in vitro	[150]
Poly[2-methoxy-5(2-ethylhexyloxy)-1,4-(1-cyanovinylenephenylene)-co-{2,5-bis(N,N′-diphenylamino)-1,4-phenylene}] (CN-PPV-DPD)						
Poly[(9,9-dioctylfluorenyl-2,7-diyl)-alt-co-(1,4-benzo-{2,1′,3}-thiadiazole)] (PFBT)	TPP	NA	20	100 mW/cm^2	Breast (MCF-7)/ in vitro, in vivo	[147]
		NA	25	90 J/cm^2	Gastric adenocarcinoma (SGC-7901)/ in vitro, in vivo	[148]
5,15-bis(pentafluorophenyl)-10, 20-bis(4-bromophenyl)	Pt(II) porphyrin	NA	10	532	Hepatocellular (HepG2)/in vitro	[151]
Poly(cyclopentadithiophene-altbenzothiadiazole) (PCPDTBT) (+ cerium oxide)		NA	53	808/440 mW/cm^2	Murine mammary (4T1)/in vitro, in vivo	[152]

Backbone	Photosensitizer	Targeting ligand	CPN average size (nm)	Irradiation wavelength (nm)/power	Tumor target/type of experiments	Refs
Poly[(9,9-diocetilfluorenil-2,7-diyl)-co-(1,4-benzo-{2,1′,3}-tiadiazol)] (F8BT)	Pt(II) octaethylporphyrin (PtOEP)	NA	19–28	460/20–40 J/cm^2	Glioioblastoma (U-87 MG, M059K, T98G)/in vitro	[153]
Poly[9,9-dioctyl-9H fluorene-co-4,7-di(thiophen2-yl)benzo(c)(1,2,5)thiadiazole-co-4,7-di-tert-butyldithieno (3,2-c:2′,3′-i) (1,10) phenanthroline]		Folic acid	110	600/6.3 J/cm^2	Cervical (HeLa)/in vitro	[154]
Poly[2-methoxy-5-(2-ethylhexyl-oxy)-p-phenylenevinylene] (MEH-PPV)	Phenyl-C61-butyric acid methyl ester (PCBM)		20–100	60–180 J/cm^2	Ovarian (OVCAR3)/in vitro	[155]
Poly[1,4-bis(4-phenyl-phenylaminostyryl)-benzene-alt-2,7-dioctylfluorene] (PPBF)	TPP		40–50	750/910 mW/cm^2	Oral (KB)/in vitro	[156]
Poly[9,9-bis(2-(2-(2-methoxyethoxy) ethoxy)-ethyl) fluorenyldivinylene]-alt-4,7-(2,1,3-benzothiadiazole) (PFVBT)		Anti-HER2 affibody	30	White light (3 mW/cm^2), followed by 808 nm (500 mW/cm^2)	Murine mammary (SKBR-3)/in vitro, in vivo	[24]
Di-tert-butyl ((2,7-bis(4,4,5,5- tetramethyl-1,3,2-dioxaborolan-2-yl)-9H-fluorene-9,9-diyl)bis(hexane-6,1-diyl))dicarbamate		Anti-EpCAM antibody, Tat protein	30	White light/ 10 mW/cm^2	Breast (MCF-7)/in vitro	[23]
Poly[2,1,3-benzothiadiazole- 4,7- diyl [4,4-bis (2-ethylhexyl)-4H-cyclopenta [2,1-b:3,4-b′] dithiophene-2,6-diyl]] (PCPDTBT)		Endothelin-3 (EDN3) polypeptide	62	No light activation	Melanoma (A375, malme-3M)/in vitro	[157]

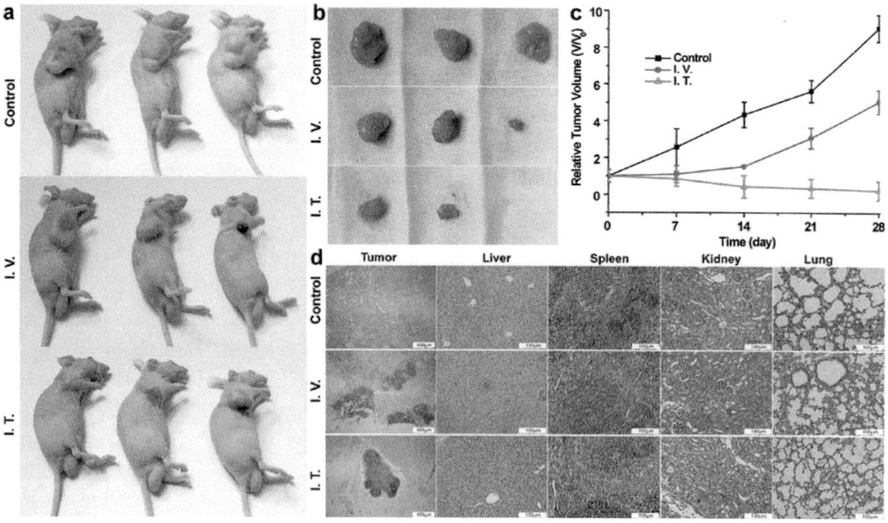

Figure 6.30 Polyfluorene-based CPNs are highly effective as PDT agents against human gastric cancer in vivo [148]. (a) Representative photographs of mice bearing SGC-7901 tumors, on the 28th day after various treatments. Mice were divided into three groups: the first group of control mice was only light irradiated; the second group of mice was treated with I.V. injection of the PFBT-TPP CPNs and were subjected to light irradiation; and the third group of mice were treated with I.T. injection of the PFBT-TPP CPNs and were subjected to light irradiation. (b) Representative photographs of the tumors were collected from distinct groups of mice after various treatments. (c) Tumor growth curves in the tumor-bearing mice after different treatments. Tumor volumes were normalized to their initial sizes. Error bars represent the standard deviations of eight mice per group. (d) Histological H&E staining of various organs from the mice of the control group, I.V. group, and I.T. group.

An approach worth mentioning is that of Pu and his colleagues, who developed a hybrid CPN system with a selective photodynamic effect against tumor cells [152]. In this approach, CPNs were developed using two components. PCPDTBT was used as both the polymeric backbone and the photosensitizer, while cerium oxide (nanoceria) possesses a unique property, such as it can switch oxidation states between III and IV within a specific pH range due to the high density of surface oxygen vacancies. Notably, this property renders nanoceria capable of behaving as a ROS scavenging agent and a ROS converter at neutral and acidic pH, respectively. These hybrid nanoparticles showed strong anti-cancer activity against murine mammary cancer upon light activation, both in vitro and in vivo, with limited off-target toxicity.

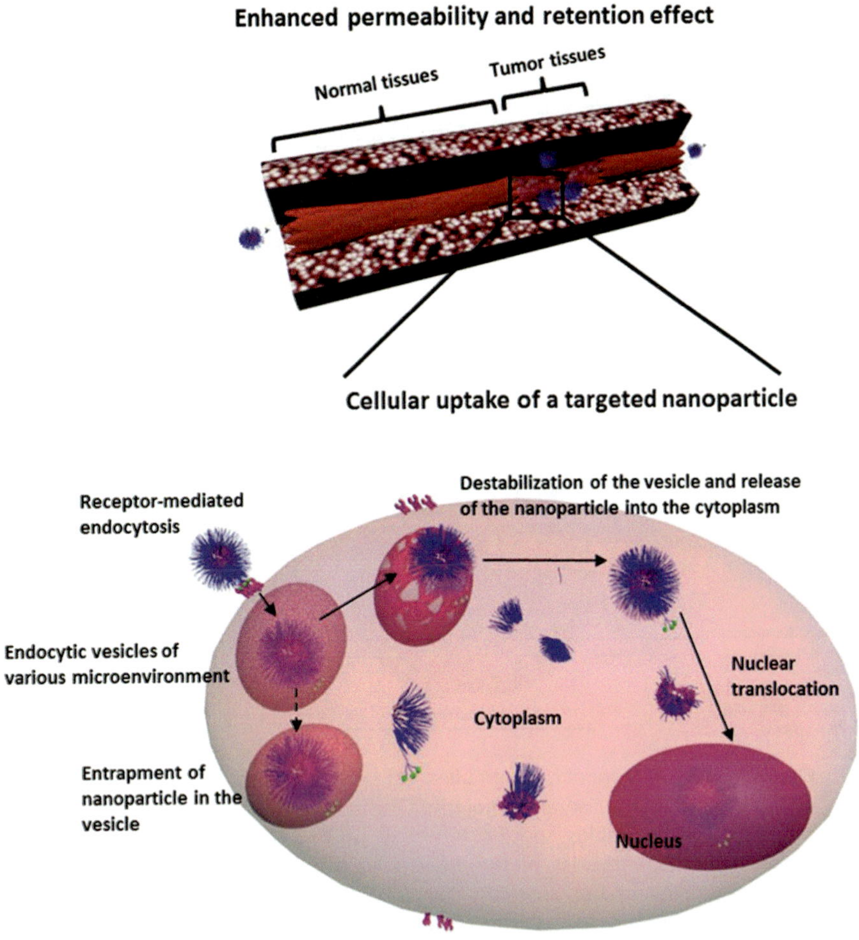

Figure 6.31 Non-specific and targeted cellular uptake of CPNs [158]. In non-specific trafficking, the nanoparticles are passively directed toward pathological sites with leaky vasculature (e.g., tumors) due to the EPR effect. In targeted delivery, the conjugated ligands on the surface of the nanoparticles achieve cellular uptake by binding to specific receptors that are overexpressed on the target cells. Targeting may also take place through escaping from endosomes/lysosomes and/or enhancing nuclear translocation.

Although bare CPNs have proved effective against cancer cells and tumors, the formulated nanoparticles can be further processed in order to specifically target cancer cells in both in vitro and in vivo settings (Fig. 6.31). This approach can further diminish the chances of potential off-target toxicity. Folic acid is frequently chosen as the targeting agent, since it is well-established that a number of cancer cells express folate receptors on their plasma membrane. Indeed, several studies have proposed that folate-modified CPNs can accurately target cancer cells of the cervix [154], ovary [155], and oral cavity [156], and subsequently eliminate them through photodynamic activation.

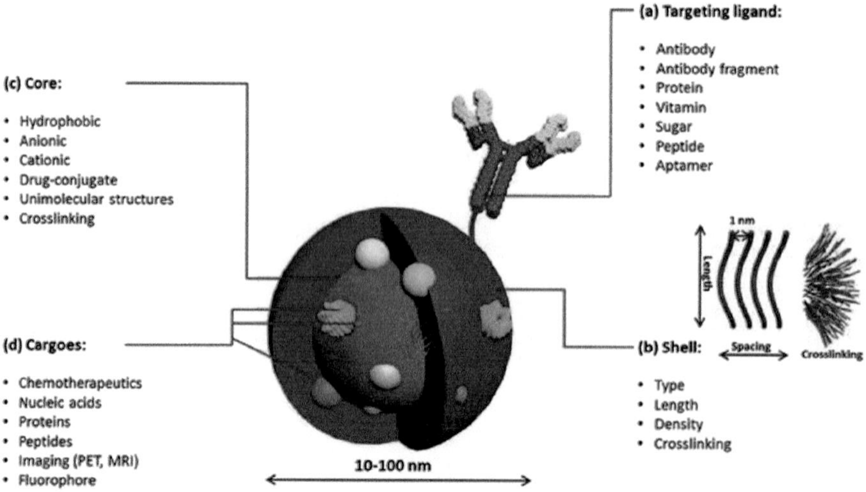

Figure 6.32 Multimodal assemblies of nanoparticles for theranostic applications [158]. (a) Targeting moieties: The incorporation of the appropriate targeting ligand enables specific targeting of cancer cells. (b) Shell: The nature and characteristics of the shell polymers may determine the half-life and stability of the nanoparticles. (c) Core: The features of the core polymers determine the physicochemical characteristics of the resulting nanoparticles, as well as the type of drug that can be incorporated. (d) Cargo: Depending on the desired applications, a variety of molecules and agents can be incorporated within the synthesized nanoparticle, including macromolecular drugs and small-molecule inhibitors.

Among the most popular strategies that are employed is the conjugation of monoclonal antibodies or antibody fragments on the outer shell of the CPNs. Alternatively, antibody mimetics, namely, affibodies, are also a ligand of choice, since they retain the desirable properties of monoclonal antibodies, but are characterized by much smaller sizes. All these molecules target specific surface antigens that are expressed only on the surface of cancer cells, leaving normal cells unaffected. Depending on the tumor type that will be targeted, different antibodies are selected. CPNs carrying anti-Her2 affibody have proven successful in targeting cancer cells in in vitro and in vivo PDT of murine mammary carcinoma [24]. Moreover, polyfluorene-thiazole CPNs were bio-functionalized through simultaneous incorporation of mAb against EpCAM for the recognition of breast tumor cells and a transcriptional activator protein (Tat) for targeted localization in the cell cytoplasm [23]. Apart from antibodies and vitamins, other molecules are also used for specific targeting of tumor cells, such as peptides, sugars, and aptamers (Fig. 6.32).

6.8.2.2 Mechanisms of anti-cancer effects triggered by PDT

The basis of PDT lies in the generation of radical oxygen species in cancer cells or within the tumor microenvironment, which, in turn, produces extensive redox imbalance and finally leads to cancer cell ablation. The main targets of PDT can be resumed in the following cellular processes: cell survival, cell cycle, vascularization, and immune response (Fig. 6.33).

The enhanced production of singlet oxygen and free radicals triggers intracellular signals that will ultimately eradicate malignant cells, through activation of cell death pathways. Regarding this point, cells can die through three distinct pathways, namely, apoptosis, necrosis, or autophagy. The type and extent of PDT-induced cell death depend on a variety of factors, including the type of photosensitizer, its subcellular localization and uptake concentration, and its physicochemical properties. Moreover, the wavelength and intensity of the applied irradiation can also play a role [159]. Notably, the localization of the photosensitizer plays a major role that predisposes cells to certain death pathways, since singlet oxygen can diffuse to an extremely restricted proximity in cells. Thus, photodynamic damage will occur very close to the intracellular location of the photosensitizer [160]. For example, photofrin, a mixture of porphyrin ethers, is mainly localized on lipid membranes. Chlorin NPe6 targets lysosomes, benzoporphyrin, mTHPC, and phthalocyanine Pc4 can all be found mostly in the mitochondria [161].

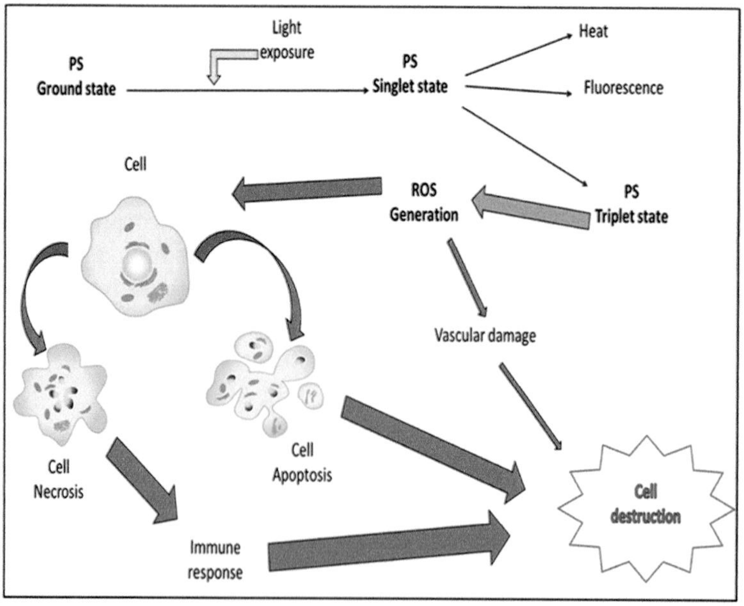

Figure 6.33 Cellular mechanisms of photodynamic anti-cancer treatment. Upon administration, CPNs localize in tumor cells and then the photosensitizer is converted from its ground to singlet state form through light activation and in turn into the triplet state form. Triplet state photosensitizers mediate ROS generation within cells. ROS induces cytotoxic effects that render tumor cells prone to irreversible destruction [162].

Apoptosis is the most preferred way for a cell to die, since inflammation and other crucial functional alterations are avoided through activation of a programmed, highly-regulated death signal. In order for apoptosis to be triggered, the caspase-mediated apoptotic pathway must be activated. This can result from cytochrome leakage to cell cytoplasm due to mitochondrial damage caused by photodynamically generated ROS [163]. In more detail, evoked damage to Bcl-2 on the mitochondrial membrane can trigger the membrane's permeabilization and subsequent release of caspase activators, such as cytochrome c and Smac/DIABLO, or other pro-apoptotic molecules [164]. Alternatively, PDT can activate death receptor-mediated apoptosis. Although many research groups have shown apoptosis triggered by different types of CPNs, the involved activating mechanisms and pathways have not been adequately characterized. However, it has been shown that apoptosis induced by radicals, such as H_2O_2, is associated with increased levels of pro-apoptotic proteins, including p53, Puma, Noxa, and Bax, and increased p53 phosphorylation at Ser15 and Ser46, in several cancer cell types [165].

Under excessive PDT-dosage conditions, the apoptotic pathway can be bypassed, and then cells might die via necrosis. Although cellular destruction is achieved, this is not a preferable type of death since inflammatory stimuli and undesirable alterations to the surrounding tissue are generated. The necrotic pathway is usually activated when CPNs are integrated into the plasma membrane or into the lysosomes [166]. In this case, photosensitization can rapidly switch the balance toward necrotic cell death due to corruption of plasma membrane integrity and rapid depletion of cellular ATP. Furthermore, high doses of PDT could photochemically inactivate the apoptotic cascade's principal components; perylenequinones that were activated by high dose irradiation inhibited apoptosis by interfering with lamins [167].

Autophagy has also been reported as a cell death mechanism that can alternatively be activated in response to PDT. It is well established that ROS can interfere with the interaction between Beclin and Bcl-2 or induce 5′ adenosine monophosphate-activated protein kinase (AMPK) and initiate autophagy [168]. Many proteins involved in the autophagic process are negatively affected by ROS. Apart from Bcl-2, IP-3, another regulator of the autophagic process associated with the endoplasmic reticulum is affected by phthalocyanine [169]. The photosensitizer AlPcS damages the mammalian target of rapamycin, mTOR, which can play a central role in the autophagic process. Nevertheless, the majority of the proteins involved in the autophagosome formation are not affected by PDT [168]. PDT can also affect autophagy by directly damaging the major organelles that are involved in autophagy, namely lysosomes and endosomes.

The close relationship with cell death activation is PDT-induced cell cycle arrest. Many studies have shown that CPN-mediated PDT induces cell cycle arrest, mainly G0/G1, along with the activation of apoptosis [170]. However, other studies report a G2/M arrest with concomitant activation of apoptosis. Generally, it is widely accepted that phase arrest is dependent on multiple factors, such as the examined cancer cell type and the photosensitizer.

Tumor vasculature is a vital component of the tumor microenvironment, since it provides the growing tumor with necessary elements, such as nutrients and gases. It is also a major target of the photodynamic process. As a result of PDT-induced irradiation, the vascular endothelium and the sub-endothelial cells are destroyed, cell junctions become widened, activated platelets, and vascular intima exposure leads to platelet aggregation, thrombosis, and vascular obstruction. These events finally contribute to blood flow stasis, tissue hypoxia, and nutrient deprivation [171]. The destruction of the developed vasculature or blockade of neovascularization can deteriorate tumor growth. Moreover, the induced damage can facilitate nanoparticle extravasation at the tumor site.

Finally, regarding the in vivo effects of PDT, where there are more complex interrelationships between the host's components and systems, the immune system has been shown to participate in the tumor suppressive effects of PDT. CPN-mediated phototherapies can attract immune cells at the tumor sites, including lymphocytes, leukocytes, and macrophages, and thus, evoke a strong immune/inflammatory response [172]. The induction of cell death pathways can stimulate the activation of dendritic cells, capable of identifying surface antigens on tumor cells, and subsequently the maturation of cytotoxic T-lymphocytes, which will ultimately generate distinct cellular immune responses against tumor cells [173].

6.9 Combinatorial Use of CPNs as Multimodal Imaging Probes, Phototherapeutic Agents, and Drug Delivery Systems: Future Perspectives

Several researcher groups have made great efforts to combine different optical modalities into one organic imaging agent using CPs. Similar to this approach, although CPN-based PDT and

PTT monotherapies have shown high anti-cancer efficacy, their combinations with other treatment modalities could potentiate the therapeutic outcomes. Toward this direction, the development of CPNs that can serve as phototherapeutic agents and, at the same time, as drug delivery vehicles is gaining ground.

Miao et al. developed and synthesized new multimodal CPs recently (Fig. 6.34). The FI properties in the NIR-II area, as well as the PA properties, were investigated. These studies show that CPNs can be used in advanced molecular imaging applications as dual-mode imaging agents. In addition, photothermal experiments in vitro revealed that the multifunctional CPNs had a high photothermal conversion efficiency. The concentration of nanoparticle solution exceeds 44.5 °C when laser irradiated at 660 nm, indicating that multifunctional nanoparticles can be used to make PTs. It proposes a new approach to developing multifunctional organic polymer materials for diagnosis and treatment [174].

Phototheranostic nanoagents hold promise for cancer early detection and precision therapy. However, due to the existence of distribution barriers in the tumor microenvironment, their imaging capacity and therapeutic efficacy are frequently reduced. Pu's group has developed organic multimodal phototheranostic nanoagents that can biomimetically target cancer-associated fibroblasts in the tumor microenvironment for improved multimodal imaging-guided cancer therapy. A NIR absorbing CPN coated with the cell membranes of activated fibroblasts is used in biomimetic nanostealth (AF-SPN). AF-SPN preferentially targeted cancer-associate fibroblasts through the targeting binding mechanism, resulting in higher accumulation in tumor tissues than both the uncoated (uSPN) and cancer cell membrane coated counterparts (CC-SPN). As a result, AF-SPN served as the best phototheranostic nanoagents for tumor imaging and cancer treatment, providing amplified NIR fluorescence and PA signals and improved phototherapeutic performance. This study shows how a cell membrane-coated biomimetic organic phototheranostic nanoagent targets a component in the tumor microenvironment, which aids in the development of therapeutic strategies to overcome tumor delivery barriers. Other pharmaceutical and imaging agents may also be loaded into biomimetic nanocamouflages, allowing multimodal theranostic systems to be used in addition to optical imaging and phototherapy [175].

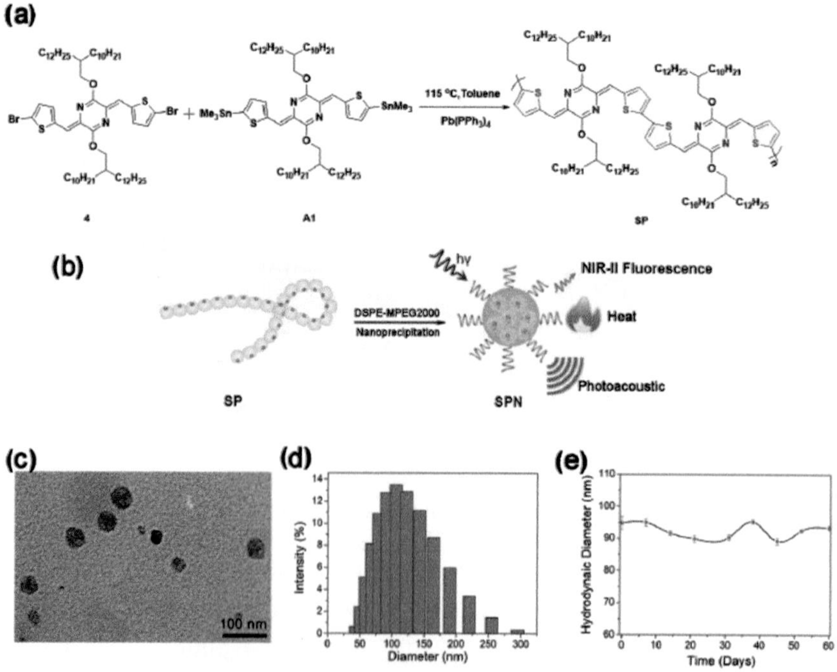

Figure 6.34 (a) Synthetic route of SP, (b) preparation of nanoparticles via nanoprecipitation, (c) TEM images of the nanoparticles, (d) DLS measurements for the nanoparticles' size, and (e) study of change of the hydrodynamic diameter of the nanoparticles during 60 days [174].

Since NIR SERS is considered a promising molecular imaging technology, Liu et al. successfully fabricate dye-free NIR SERS nanoprobes as Raman reporters for tumor detection and imaging, both in vitro and in vivo. In this design, two different biocompatible CPs (PANI and polypyrrole) were coated onto the surface of gold nanorods (GNRs) via facile oxidative polymerization, taking advantage of the enhancement of CP molecule's Raman signal by the metal nanostructure under NIR laser excitation. The reported GNR-CPs exhibit good biocompatibility, structural stability, and improved NIR photothermal energy conversion efficiency, compared with the bare GNRs, promoting their potential application in PTT strategies. The theranostic potential of those

NIR SERS nanoprobes could contribute to elevate image-guided cancer therapy [176].

It is well known that among the imaging signals of SPNs, PA amplitude and fluorescence occur due to electron transition processes, where radiative electron transition pathways lead to fluorescence or photoluminescence, and non-radiative ones lead to PA amplitude. Owing to the competing relationship among radiative and non-radiative pathways, there is difficulty in synthesizing CPNs that exhibit fluorescence and increased PA amplitude, simultaneously [67, 177]. Nevertheless, Raman scattering arises from the vibration and rotation of molecular structures, whilst CPNs demonstrate strong Raman scattering due to their large conjugated backbone. Thus, during the last decade, several studies combined Raman imaging with fluorescence and PAI in cancer.

Liu et al. presented a dual-imaging platform based on complexes of CPEs and carboxylated multi-walled carbon nanotubes (cMWNTs) [178]. Taking advantage of the unique CPEs optical properties and the characteristic Raman vibration modes of MWNTs, they prepared CPE-cMWNT nanocomposites (TBtPFN/cMWNTs and BtPFS/TBtPFN/ cMWNTs) based on layer-by-layer electrostatic absorption between oppositely charged cMWNTs and CPEs (Fig. 6.35). The fabricated biocompatible nanocomposites combine fluorescence and Raman imaging, and this design enables the tracking of cellular uptake and location of MWNTs.

Another approach by Lin et al. reported the development of a dual-modal contrast agent based on CPs under a bandgap engineering strategy to combine the deep penetration depth of PAI with the high spatial resolution of Raman imaging [179]. A polypyrrole-polydopamine (PPy-PDA) hybrid was coated onto a silica nanoparticle through a one-pot reaction creating a Raman-PA active probe (SiO_2–CS@PPy–PDA) that was able to enhance Raman scattering by 3.2 times and PA amplitude by 2.4 times. The feasibility for cellular imaging was investigated by incubating HeLa cells with SiO_2–CS@PPy–PDA nanoparticles, whilst they were also investigated in vivo through intratumoral injection of A549-tumor-bearing mice (Fig. 6.36).

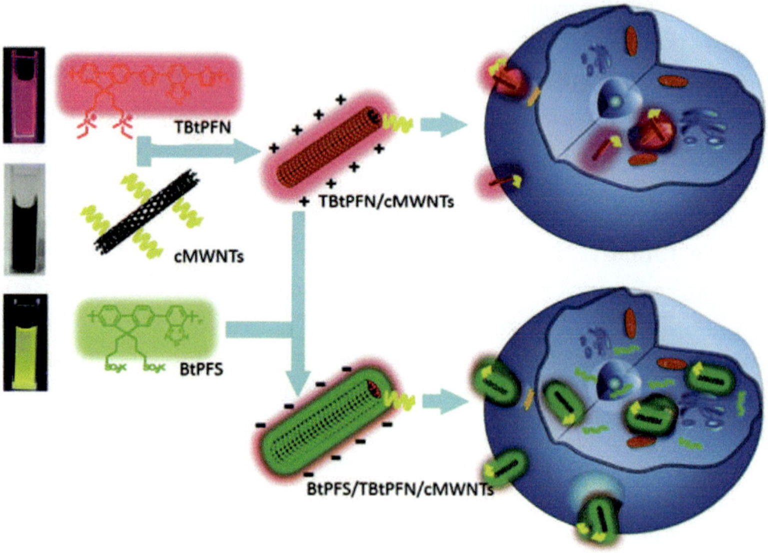

Figure 6.35 Fabrication of the positively charged TBtPFN/cMWNTs and negatively charged BtPFS/TBtPFN/cMWNTs, and their typical uptake pathways and intracellular distributions [178].

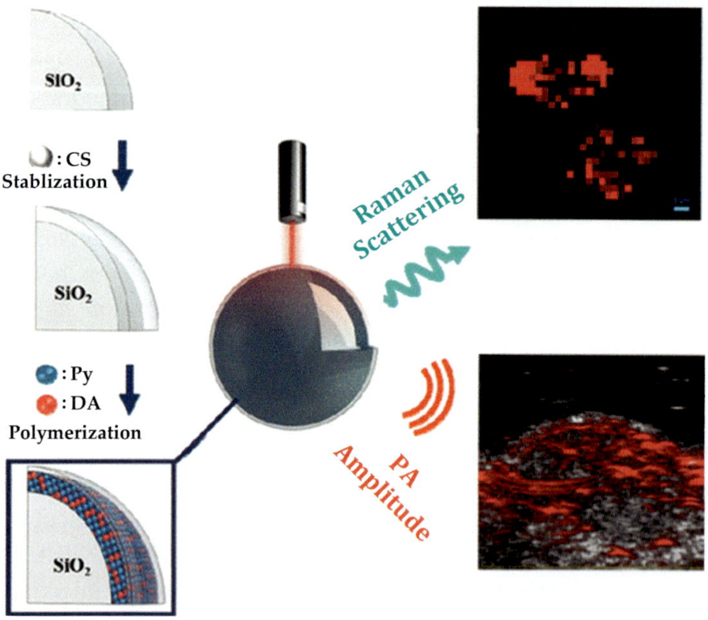

Figure 6.36 Schematic of the preparation and energy transfer of PPy–PDA hybrid nanoshells [179].

Up to now, organic agents that exhibit more than two imaging modalities simultaneously have been scarcely reported. Recently, Qi and co-workers presented the development of one organic fluorophore with CP at the backbone, which demonstrates concurrent fluorescence, PA, and Raman imaging capabilities that are strongly affected by the molecular structure and the intramolecular motions [180]. Under this strategy, the design and synthesis of a series of OTPA-TQ1-3 were performed comprising NIR-absorbing organic fluorophores with different substituted units (phenyl, phenyl-alkyne, and phenyl-alkyne-phenyl). The researchers conclude that the OTPA-TQ3 compound with the larger substituted unit exhibited high fluorescence, PA, and Raman signal in the cell-silent region at 2215 cm^{-1}. This triple-modality organic agent's formation into nanoparticles was successfully tested for image-guided cancer surgery, since NIR fluorescence and PAI could provide vital information for the tumor preoperatively, whilst intraoperative fluorescence and Raman imaging can locate possibly tumor's residuals (Fig. 6.37), improving cancer surgery outcomes.

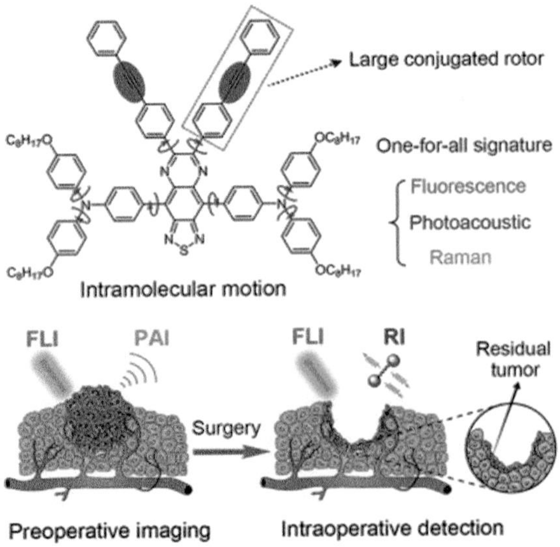

Figure 6.37 Schematic illustration of a multi-modality organic imaging agent for image-guided surgery. OTPA-TQ3-based nanoagent can be used for comprehensive preoperative fluorescence and PAI of tumors, and intraoperative fluorescence and Raman imaging of tiny residual tumors to boost cancer surgery outcomes [180].

A way to enhance the therapeutic efficacy of PDT is to use CPNs that combine the presence of a photosensitizer for ROS generation, and a chemotherapeutic drug for induction of more specific anti-cancer responses. Such a CPN-based system was manufactured by Liu and his colleagues (Fig. 6.38) [181]. In this experimental setting, a PEGylated CPE poly[9,9-bis(N-but-3′-ynyl-N,N-dimethylaminohexyl)-fluorenyldivinylene-alt-4,7-(2′,1′,3′,-benzothiadiazole) dibromide] (PFVBT, P45) with carboxyl groups on side chains was first synthesized. The produced nanoparticles were then bimodally functionalized, for encapsulation of paclitaxel (PTX), a hydrophobic anti-cancer agent, and for surface carriage of a tripeptide with cyclic arginine-glycine-aspartate motif (cRGD), which could target cancer cells that specifically overexpress $\alpha v\beta 3$ integrin. This combination therapy was significantly more effective against brain cancer cells, as compared to PDT or chemotherapy alone.

Further studies by the same group led to the development of another theranostic nanoplatform for targeted and image-guided on-demand combinatorial anti-cancer therapy [182]. Using the same technique as before, the researchers encapsulated another chemotherapeutic drug, DOX, into PFVBT nanoparticles and again recorded higher therapeutic efficacies than the corresponding monotherapies. An effective synergistic effect of chemotherapy and PDT was also reported against breast cancer cells by encapsulation of DOX into poly(fluorene-co-vinylene) (PFV) and temperature-responsive poly(N-isopropylacrylamide) (PNIPAM) CPNs [183].

The combination of chemotherapeutics and PTT can also enhance the therapeutic effects of the last. In this case, a light-responsive drug release system that will be activated by a NIR laser is needed, since inefficient or slow drug release during PTT could decrease its bioavailability, and thus, its therapeutic potential. Toward this direction, Liu and his group synthesized nanoparticles composed of four distinct parts: (a) the two-photon-responsive polymer PLL-g-PEG/DNQ, (b) the chemotherapeutic DOX, (c) the photothermal CP poly[9,9-bis(4-(2-ethylhexyl)phenyl) fluorene-alt-co-6,7-bis(4-(hexyloxy)phenyl)-4,9-di(thiophen-2-yl)-thiadiazolo-quinoxaline] (PFTTQ), and (d) cRGD on the surface, as the targeting agent. These CPNs were well-dispersed and stable and were able to accumulate selectively in cancer cells that overexpressed αvβ3, while they could also release DOX fast via transformation of DNQ to a hydrophilic structure under laser irradiation. This approach resulted in remarkable anti-cancer activity, which was significantly stronger than PTT or chemotherapy alone [184].

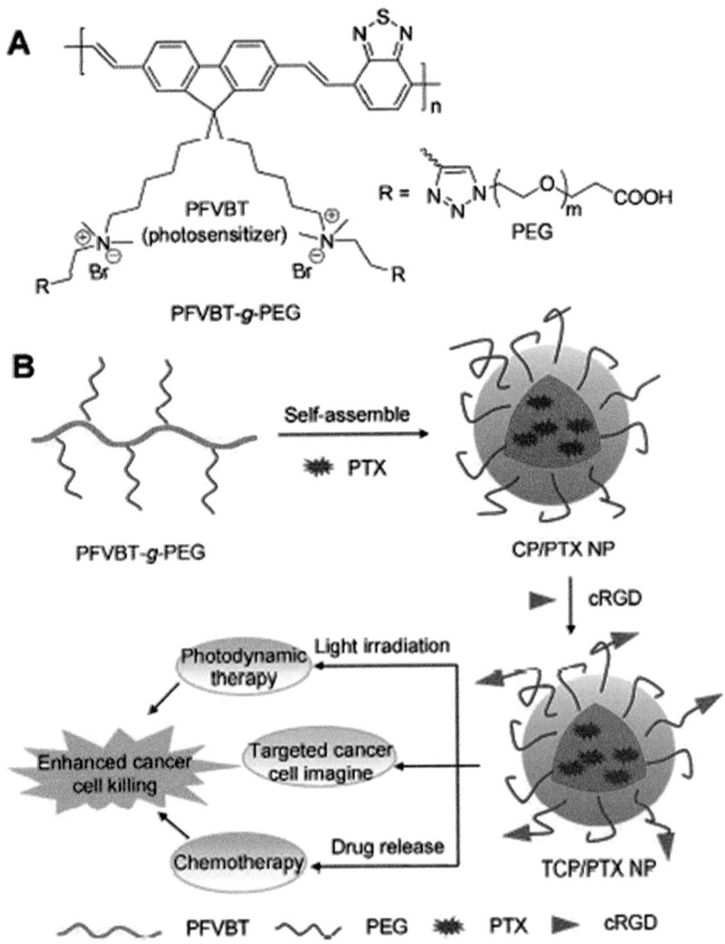

Figure 6.38 CPNs as carriers of chemotherapeutics for combinatorial image-guided PDT and chemotherapy [172]. (a) Chemical structure and (b) assembly of PFVBT-g-PEG nanoparticles, carrying paclitaxel as the anti-cancer agent.

In another experimental setting, CPNs were developed via a combination of poly(diketopyrrolopyrole) derivative and dipalmitoyl phosphatidylethanolamine-polyethylene glycol-maleimide, and were conjugated with calmodulin antibody (CaM). Upon NIR laser irradiation, apoptotic cell death was activated through the nanoparticles' interference with the PI3K/Akt pathway (Fig. 6.39) [185].

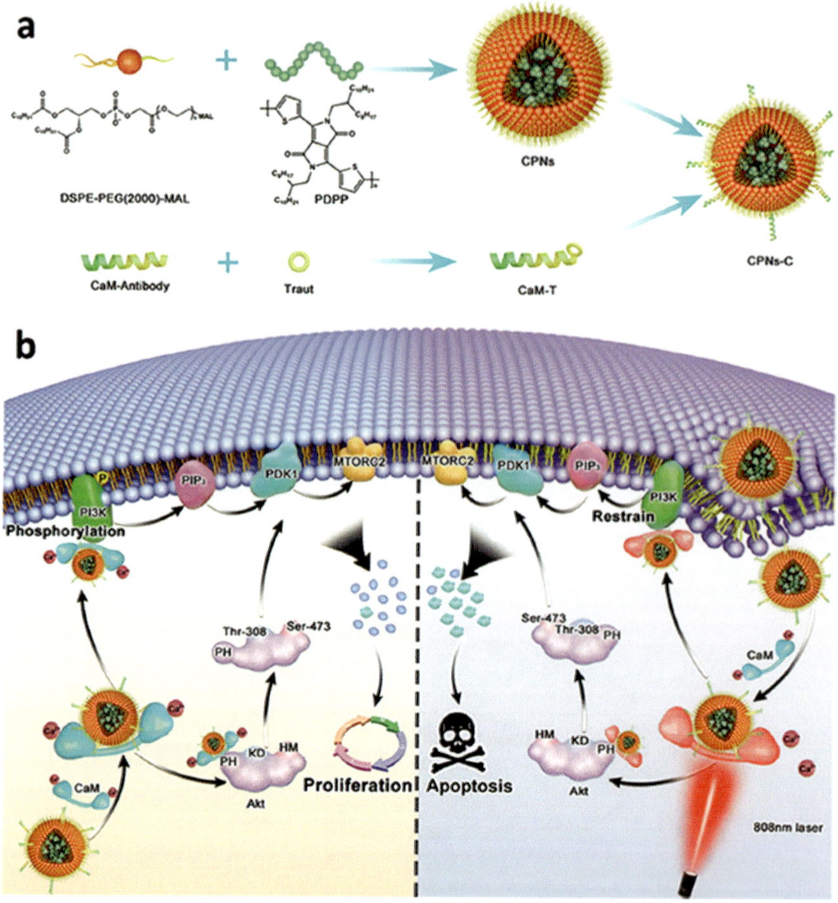

Figure 6.39 Calmodulin-conjugated CPNs for PI3K/Akt signaling pathway targeting in cancer cells [185]. (a) Synthesis and assembly of polypyrrole dione and dipalmitoyl phosphatidylethanolamine-polyethylene glycol-maleimide CPNs and (b) mechanism of interfering with the PI3K/Akt pathway in cancer cells.

Due to their unique structure and optical and electronic properties, along with their enhanced biocompatibility, CPNs are paving the way for more efficient outcomes in both diagnostic and therapeutic everyday practice. Regarding practical applications, until now more than 150 clinical studies assessing that potential of PDT for cancer treatment have been completed and more than 150 are in different phases of production in the U.S. [186]. Hyperthermia is also exploited in clinical practice, with more than 800 completed studies on a wide range of tumors. Nevertheless, PTT for cancer needs further investigation since only five studies have been announced in the U.S., with only two of them being completed. More interestingly, only a few clinical studies are assessing the efficacy and safety of CPNs in cancer patients. CRLX101 is a nanoparticle conjugate that consists of a cyclodextrin-based polymer (CDP) that serves as the delivery vehicle, and an anti-cancer compound (camptothecin). CRLX101 has already been studied in clinical trials, either alone or in combination mainly with chemotherapeutics, with encouraging results [186]. However, since CPN-based PTT and PDT have produced worth-studying results both in vitro and in vivo, and taking into account the lack of ideal cancer therapeutics, the exploitation of these nanoagents in clinical studies could fill the gap toward efficient treatment of cancer patients.

Acknowledgments

The authors would like to thank the Helmholtz European partnering program for the cooperation between German Cancer Research Center (DKFZ) and National Hellenic Research Foundation (NHRF) to build the Athens Comprehensive Cancer Center (ACCC). Panagiota Koralli thanks for the financial support from the Operational Programme, Human Resources Development, and Education and Lifelong Learning, in the context of the project "Reinforcement of Postdoctoral Researchers: 2nd Cycle" (MIS-5033021), implemented by the State Scholarships Foundation (IKY) co-financed by Greece and the European Union (European Social Fund).

References

1. UK CR. Accessed on Dec 2019 [Available from: https://www.cancerresearchuk.org/health-professional/cancer-statistics/worldwide-cancer].
2. Jenkins, R.; Burdette, M.K.; Foulger, S.H. Mini-review: Fluorescence imaging in cancer cells using dye-doped nanoparticles. *RSC Adv.* **2016**, *6*, 65459–65474, doi:10.1039/C6RA10473H.
3. Shi, J.; Kantoff, P.W.; Wooster, R.; Farokhzad, O.C. Cancer nanomedicine: Progress, challenges and opportunities. *Nat. Rev. Cancer* **2017**, *17*, 20–37, doi:10.1038/nrc.2016.108.
4. Ma, H.; Hu, D.; Zhao, J.; Tian, M.; Yuan, J.; Wei, Y. Ultrastable near-infrared aggregation-induced emission nanoparticles as a fluorescent probe: Long-term tumor monitoring and lipid droplet tracking. *CCS Chem.* **2020**, 1569–1606, doi:10.31635/ccschem.020.202000383.
5. Cheng, Y.; Sun, C.; Ou, X.; Liu, B.; Lou, X.; Xia, F. Dual-targeted peptide-conjugated multifunctional fluorescent probe with AIEgen for efficient nucleus-specific imaging and long-term tracing of cancer cells. *Chem. Sci.* **2017**, *8*, 4571–4578, doi:10.1039/c7sc00402h.
6. Guan, Y.; Sun, T.; Ding, J.; Xie, Z. Robust organic nanoparticles for noninvasive long-term fluorescence imaging. *J. Mater. Chem. B* **2019**, *7*, 6879–6889, doi:10.1039/c9tb01905g.
7. Janib, S.M.; Moses, A.S.; MacKay, J.A. Imaging and drug delivery using theranostic nanoparticles. *Adv. Drug Deliv. Rev.* **2010**, *62*, 1052–1063, doi:10.1016/j.addr.2010.08.004.
8. Kim, S.; Lim, C.K.; Na, J.; Lee, Y.D.; Kim, K.; Choi, K.; Leary, J.F.; Kwon, I.C. Conjugated polymer nanoparticles for biomedical in vivo imaging. *Chem. Commun.* **2010**, *46*, 1617–1619, doi:10.1039/b923309a.
9. Qian, C.G.; Chen, Y.L.; Feng, P.J.; Xiao, X.Z.; Dong, M.; Yu, J.C.; Hu, Q.Y.; Shen, Q.D.; Gu, Z. Conjugated polymer nanomaterials for theranostics. *Acta Pharmacol. Sin.* **2017**, *38*, 764–781, doi:10.1038/aps.2017.42.
10. Chen, J.; Gao, Z.; Li, G.; Wang, T.D. Dual-modal in vivo fluorescence and photoacoustic imaging using a heterodimeric peptide. *Chem. Commun.* **2018**, *54*, 13196–13199, doi:10.1039/C8CC06774K.
11. Elumalai, S.; Managó, S.; De Luca, A.C. Raman microscopy: Progress in research on cancer cell sensing. *Sensors (Switzerland)* **2020**, *20*, 1–19, doi:10.3390/s20195525.

12. Krafft, C.; Schie, I.W.; Meyer, T.; Schmitt, M.; Popp, J. Developments in spontaneous and coherent Raman scattering microscopic imaging for biomedical applications. *Chem. Soc. Rev.* **2016**, *45*, 1819–1849, doi:10.1039/c5cs00564g.

13. Pence, I.; Mahadevan-Jansen, A. Clinical instrumentation and applications of Raman spectroscopy. *Chem. Soc. Rev.* **2016**, *45*, 1958–1979, doi:10.1039/c5cs00581g.

14. Managò, S.; Valente, C.; Mirabelli, P.; Circolo, D.; Basile, F.; Corda, D.; De Luca, A.C. A reliable Raman-spectroscopy-based approach for diagnosis, classification and follow-up of B-cell acute lymphoblastic leukemia. *Sci. Rep.* **2016**, *6*, 1–13, doi:10.1038/srep24821.

15. Kuhar, N.; Sil, S.; Verma, T.; Umapathy, S. Challenges in application of Raman spectroscopy to biology and materials. *RSC Adv.* **2018**, *8*, 25888–25908, doi:10.1039/c8ra04491k.

16. Chaturvedi, D.; Balaji, S.A.; Bn, V.K.; Ariese, F.; Umapathy, S.; Rangarajan, A. Different phases of breast cancer cells: Raman study of immortalized, transformed, and invasive cells. *Biosensors* **2016**, *6*, doi:10.3390/bios6040057.

17. Feng, G.; Liu, J.; Geng, J.; Liu, B. Conjugated polymer microparticles for selective cancer cell image-guided photothermal therapy. *J. Mater. Chem. B* **2015**, *3*, 1135–1141, doi:10.1039/c4tb01590h.

18. Li, K.; Liu, B. Polymer encapsulated conjugated polymer nanoparticles for fluorescence bioimaging. *J. Mater. Chem.* **2012**, *22*, 1257–1264, doi:10.1039/c1jm14397b.

19. Gao, D.; Hu, D.; Liu, X.; Zhang, X.; Yuan, Z.; Sheng, Z.; Zheng, H. Recent advances in conjugated polymer nanoparticles for NIR-II imaging and therapy. *ACS Appl. Polym. Mater.* **2020**, *2*, 4241–4257, doi:10.1021/acsapm.0c00679.

20. Sun, M.; Sun, B.; Liu, Y.; Shen, Q.D.; Jiang, S. Dual-color fluorescence imaging of magnetic nanoparticles in live cancer cells using conjugated polymer probes. *Sci. Rep.* **2016**, *6*, 1–12, doi:10.1038/srep22368.

21. Choi, J.; Kim, H.; Choi, Y. Theranostic nanoparticles for enzyme-activatable fluorescence imaging and photodynamic/chemo dual therapy of triple-negative breast cancer. *Quant. Imaging Med. Surg.* **2015**, *5*, 656–65664, doi:10.3978/j.issn.2223-4292.2015.08.09.

22. Wu, W.; Feng, G.; Xu, S.; Liu, B. A photostable far-red/near-infrared conjugated polymer photosensitizer with aggregation-induced

emission for image-guided cancer cell ablation. *Macromolecules* **2016**, *49*, 5017–5025, doi:10.1021/acs.macromol.6b00958.

23. Feng, L.; Zhu, J.; Wang, Z. Biological functionalization of conjugated polymer nanoparticles for targeted imaging and photodynamic killing of tumor cells. *ACS Appl. Mater. Interfaces* **2016**, *8*, 19364–19370, doi:10.1021/acsami.6b06642.
24. Feng, G.; Fang, Y.; Liu, J.; Geng, J.; Ding, D.; Liu, B. Multifunctional conjugated polymer nanoparticles for image-guided photodynamic and photothermal therapy. *Small* **2017**, *13*, 1–12, doi:10.1002/smll.201602807.
25. Lafleur-Lambert, A.; Giguère, J.B.; Morin, J.F. Anthanthrene as a large PAH building block for the synthesis of conjugated polymers. *Polym. Chem.* **2015**, *6*, 4859–4863, doi:10.1039/c5py00603a.
26. Mizukoshi, Y.; Mikami, K.; Uchiyama, M. Aryne polymerization enabling straightforward synthesis of elusive poly(ortho-arylene)s. *J. Am. Chem. Soc.* **2015**, *137*, 74–77, doi:10.1021/ja5112207.
27. Qiu, Z.; Hammer, B.A.G.; Müllen, K. Conjugated polymers: Problems and promises. *Prog. Polym. Sci.* **2020**, *100*, doi:10.1016/j.progpolymsci.2019.101179.
28. Wu, W.; Bazan, G.C.; Liu, B. Conjugated-polymer-amplified sensing, imaging, and therapy. *Chem* **2017**, *2*, 760–790, doi:10.1016/j.chempr.2017.05.002.
29. McGehee, M.D.; Heeger, A.J. Semiconducting (conjugated) polymers as materials for solid-state lasers. *Adv. Mater.* **2000**, *12*, 1655–1668, doi:10.1002/1521-4095(200011)12:22<1655::aid-adma1655>3.3.co;2-u.
30. Grimsdale, A.C.; Chan, K.L.; Martin, R.E.; Jokisz, P.G.; Holmes, A.B. Synthesis of light-emitting conjugated polymers for applications in electroluminescent devices. *Chem. Rev.* **2009**, *109*, 897–1091, doi:10.1021/cr000013v.
31. Cheng, Y.J.; Yang, S.H.; Hsu, C.S. Synthesis of conjugated polymers for organic solar cell applications. *Chem. Rev.* **2009**, *109*, 5868–5923, doi:10.1021/cr900182s.
32. Kuehne, A.J.C. Conjugated polymer nanoparticles toward in vivo theranostics: Focus on targeting, imaging, therapy, and the importance of clearance. *Adv. Biosyst.* **2017**, *1*, doi:10.1002/adbi.201700100.
33. Meng, Z.; Hou, W.; Zhou, H.; Zhou, L.; Chen, H.; Wu, C. Therapeutic considerations and conjugated polymer-based photosensitizers

for photodynamic therapy. *Macromol. Rapid Commun.* **2018**, *39*, doi:10.1002/marc.201700614.

34. Blanco, E.; Shen, H.; Ferrari, M. Principles of nanoparticle design for overcoming biological barriers to drug delivery. *Nat. Biotechnol.* **2015**, *33*, 941–951, doi:10.1038/nbt.3330.

35. Sukhanova, A.; Bozrova, S.; Sokolov, P.; Berestovoy, M.; Karaulov, A.; Nabiev, I. Dependence of nanoparticle toxicity on their physical and chemical properties. *Nanoscale Res. Lett.* **2018**, *13*, doi:10.1186/s11671-018-2457-x.

36. Xiao, Q.; Chen, T.; Chen, S. Fluorescent contrast agents for tumor surgery (review). *Exp. Ther. Med.* **2018**, *16*, 1577–1585, doi:10.3892/etm.2018.6401.

37. Palma, J.A.; Kim, W.; Serafino, M.; Kim, S.; Jo, J.A.; Charoenphol, P.; Applegate, B.E. PLGA encapsulated methylene blue as a contrast agent for optical coherence tomography. *2019 IEEE Photonics Conf. IPC 2019–Proc.* **2019**, 19–20, doi:10.1109/IPCon.2019.8908365.

38. Zhang, Y.; Wu, M.; Wu, M.; Zhu, J.; Zhang, X. Multifunctional carbon-based nanomaterials: Applications in biomolecular imaging and therapy. *ACS Omega* **2018**, *3*, 9126–9145, doi:10.1021/acsomega.8b01071.

39. MacFarlane, L.R.; Shaikh, H.; Garcia-Hernandez, J.D.; Vespa, M.; Fukui, T.; Manners, I. Functional nanoparticles through p-conjugated polymer self-assembly. *Nat. Rev. Mater.* **2021**, *6*, 7–26, doi:10.1038/s41578-020-00233-4.

40. Emptage, N.J. Fluorescent imaging in living systems. *Curr. Opin. Pharmacol.* **2001**, *1*, 521–525, doi:10.1016/S1471-4892(01)00090-X.

41. Howes, P.; Greenff, M.; Levitt, J.; Suhling, K.; Hughes, M. Phospholipid encapsulated semiconducting polymer nanoparticles: Their use in cell imaging and protein attachment. *J. Am. Chem. Soc.* **2010**, *132*, 3989–3996, doi:10.1021/ja1002179.

42. Ding, D.; Liu, J.; Feng, G.; Li, K.; Hu, Y.; Liu, B. Bright far-red/near-infrared conjugated polymer nanoparticles for in vivo bioimaging. *Small* **2013**, *9*, 3093–3102, doi:10.1002/smll.201300171.

43. Yu, J.C.; Chen, Y.L.; Zhang, Y.Q.; Yao, X.K.; Qian, C.G.; Huang, J.; Zhu, S.; Jiang, X.Q.; Shen, Q.D.; Gu, Z. PH-Responsive and near-infrared-emissive polymer nanoparticles for simultaneous delivery, release, and fluorescence tracking of doxorubicin in vivo. *Chem. Commun.* **2014**, *50*, 4699–4702, doi:10.1039/c3cc49870k.

44. Zhu, H.; Fang, Y.; Zhen, X.; Wei, N.; Gao, Y.; Luo, K.Q.; Xu, C.; Duan, H.; Ding, D.; Chen, P.; et al. Multilayered semiconducting polymer

nanoparticles with enhanced NIR fluorescence for molecular imaging in cells, zebrafish and mice. *Chem. Sci.* **2016**, *7*, 5118–5125, doi:10.1039/c6sc01251e.

45. Ke, C.S.; Fang, C.C.; Yan, J.Y.; Tseng, P.J.; Pyle, J.R.; Chen, C.P.; Lin, S.Y.; Chen, J.; Zhang, X.; Chan, Y.H. Molecular engineering and design of semiconducting polymer dots with narrow-band, near-infrared emission for in vivo biological imaging. *ACS Nano* **2017**, *11*, 3166–3177, doi:10.1021/acsnano.7b00215.
46. Koralli, P.; Nega, A.D.; Vagiaki, L.E.; Pavlou, A.; Siskos, M.G.; Dimitrakopoulou-Strauss, A.; Gregoriou, V.G.; Chochos, C.L. New conjugated polymer nanoparticles with high photoluminescence quantum yields for far-red and near-infrared fluorescence bioimaging. *Mater. Chem. Front.* **2020**, *4*, 2357–2369, doi:10.1039/d0qm00195c.
47. Hong, G.; Zou, Y.; Antaris, A.L.; Diao, S.; Wu, D.; Cheng, K.; Zhang, X.; Chen, C.; Liu, B.; He, Y.; et al. Ultrafast fluorescence imaging in vivo with conjugated polymer fluorophores in the second near-infrared window. *Nat. Commun.* **2014**, *5*, 1–9, doi:10.1038/ncomms5206.
48. Shou, K.; Tang, Y.; Chen, H.; Chen, S.; Zhang, L.; Zhang, A.; Fan, Q.; Yu, A.; Cheng, Z. Diketopyrrolopyrrole-based semiconducting polymer nanoparticles for in vivo second near-infrared window imaging and image-guided tumor surgery. *Chem. Sci.* **2018**, *9*, 3105–3110, doi:10.1039/c8sc00206a.
49. Wang, L. V. Prospects of photoacoustic tomography. *Med. Phys.* **2008**, *35*, 5758–5767, doi:10.1118/1.3013698.
50. Ntziachristos, V.; Ripoll, J.; Wang, L. V.; Weissleder, R. Looking and listening to light: The evolution of whole-body photonic imaging. *Nat. Biotechnol.* **2005**, *23*, 313–320, doi:10.1038/nbt1074.
51. Wang, L. V.; Hu, S. Photoacoustic tomography: In vivo imaging from organelles to organs. *Science (80-.)* **2012**, *335*, 1458–1462, doi:10.1126/science.1216210.
52. Taruttis, A.; Ntziachristos, V. Advances in real-time multispectral optoacoustic imaging and its applications. *Nat. Photonics* **2015**, *9*, 219–227, doi:10.1038/nphoton.2015.29.
53. Bell, A.G. The production of sound by radiant energy. *Am. Assoc. Adv. Sci.* **1881**, *2*, 242–253.
54. Bell, A.G. The photophone. *Science (80-.)* **1881**, 130–134.
55. Mallidi, S.; Luke, G.P.; Emelianov, S. Photoacoustic imaging in cancer detection, diagnosis, and treatment guidance. *Trends Biotechnol.* **2011**, *29*, 213–221, doi:10.1016/j.tibtech.2011.01.006.

56. Beard, P. Biomedical photoacoustic imaging. *Interface Focus* **2011**, *1*, 602–631, doi:10.1098/rsfs.2011.0028.

57. Wang, X.; Pang, Y.; Ku, G.; Xie, X.; Stoica, G.; Wang, L. V. Noninvasive laser-induced photoacoustic tomography for structural and functional in vivo imaging of the brain. *Nat. Biotechnol.* **2003**, *21*, 803–806, doi:10.1038/nbt839.

58. Jung, D.; Park, S.; Lee, C.; Kim, H. Recent progress on near-infrared photoacoustic imaging: Imaging modality and organic semiconducting agents. *Polymers (Basel)* **2019**, *11*, doi:10.3390/polym11101693.

59. Weber, J.; Beard, P.C.; Bohndiek, S.E. Contrast agents for molecular photoacoustic imaging. *Nat. Methods* **2016**, *13*, 639–650, doi:10.1038/nmeth.3929.

60. Yoo, S.W.; Jung, D.; Min, J.J.; Kim, H.; Lee, C. Biodegradable contrast agents for photoacoustic imaging. *Appl. Sci.* **2018**, *8*, doi:10.3390/app8091567.

61. Chen, J.; Yang, M.; Zhang, Q.; Cho, E.C.; Cobley, C.M.; Kim, C.; Glaus, C.; Wang, L. V.; Welch, M.J.; Xia, Y. Gold nanocages: A novel class of multifunctional nanomaterials for theranostic applications. *Adv. Funct. Mater.* **2010**, *20*, 3684–3694, doi:10.1002/adfm.201001329.

62. De La Zerda, A.; Zavaleta, C.; Keren, S.; Vaithilingam, S.; Bodapati, S.; Liu, Z.; Levi, J.; Smith, B.R.; Ma, T.J.; Oralkan, O.; et al. Carbon nanotubes as photoacoustic molecular imaging agents in living mice. *Nat. Nanotechnol.* **2008**, *3*, 557–562, doi:10.1038/nnano.2008.231.

63. Zha, Z.; Deng, Z.; Li, Y.; Li, C.; Wang, J.; Wang, S.; Qu, E.; Dai, Z. Biocompatible polypyrrole nanoparticles as a novel organic photoacoustic contrast agent for deep tissue imaging. *Nanoscale* **2013**, *5*, 4462–4467, doi:10.1039/c3nr00627a.

64. Pu, K.; Shuhendler, A.J.; Jokerst, J. V.; Mei, J.; Gambhir, S.S.; Bao, Z.; Rao, J. Semiconducting polymer nanoparticles as photoacoustic molecular imaging probes in living mice. *Nat. Nanotechnol.* **2014**, *9*, 233–239, doi:10.1038/nnano.2013.302.

65. Roy, I.; Shetty, D.; Hota, R.; Baek, K.; Kim, J.; Kim, C.; Kappert, S.; Kim, K. A multifunctional subphthalocyanine nanosphere for targeting, labeling, and killing of antibiotic-resistant bacteria. *Angew. Chemie – Int. Ed.* **2015**, *54*, 15152–15155, doi:10.1002/anie.201507140.

66. Liu, J.; Geng, J.; Liao, L. De; Thakor, N.; Gao, X.; Liu, B. Conjugated polymer nanoparticles for photoacoustic vascular imaging. *Polym. Chem.* **2014**, *5*, 2854–2862, doi:10.1039/c3py01587d.

67. Pu, K.; Mei, J.; Jokerst, J. V.; Hong, G.; Antaris, A.L.; Chattopadhyay, N.; Shuhendler, A.J.; Kurosawa, T.; Zhou, Y.; Gambhir, S.S.; et al. Diketopyrrolopyrrole-based semiconducting polymer nanoparticles for in vivo photoacoustic imaging. *Adv. Mater.* **2015**, *27*, 5184–5190, doi:10.1002/adma.201502285.

68. Chen, H.; Zhang, J.; Chang, K.; Men, X.; Fang, X.; Zhou, L.; Li, D.; Gao, D.; Yin, S.; Zhang, X.; et al. Highly absorbing multispectral near-infrared polymer nanoparticles from one conjugated backbone for photoacoustic imaging and photothermal therapy. *Biomaterials* **2017**, *144*, 42–52, doi:10.1016/j.biomaterials.2017.08.007.

69. Xie, C.; Upputuri, P.K.; Zhen, X.; Pramanik, M.; Pu, K. Self-quenched semiconducting polymer nanoparticles for amplified in vivo photoacoustic imaging. *Biomaterials* **2017**, *119*, 1–8, doi:10.1016/j.biomaterials.2016.12.004.

70. Stahl, T.; Bofinger, R.; Lam, I.; Fallon, K.J.; Johnson, P.; Ogunlade, O.; Vassileva, V.; Pedley, R.B.; Beard, P.C.; Hailes, H.C.; et al. Tunable semiconducting polymer nanoparticles with INDT-based conjugated polymers for photoacoustic molecular imaging. *Bioconjug. Chem.* **2017**, *28*, 1734–1740, doi:10.1021/acs.bioconjchem.7b00185.

71. Lyu, Y.; Zeng, J.; Jiang, Y.; Zhen, X.; Wang, T.; Qiu, S.; Lou, X.; Gao, M.; Pu, K. Enhancing both biodegradability and efficacy of semiconducting polymer nanoparticles for photoacoustic imaging and photothermal therapy. *ACS Nano* **2018**, *12*, 1801–1810, doi:10.1021/acsnano.7b08616.

72. Jiang, Y.; Upputuri, P.K.; Xie, C.; Lyu, Y.; Zhang, L.; Xiong, Q.; Pramanik, M.; Pu, K. Broadband absorbing semiconducting polymer nanoparticles for photoacoustic imaging in second near-infrared window. *Nano Lett.* **2017**, *17*, 4964–4969, doi:10.1021/acs.nanolett.7b02106.

73. Guo, B.; Sheng, Z.; Kenry; Hu, D.; Lin, X.; Xu, S.; Liu, C.; Zheng, H.; Liu, B. Biocompatible conjugated polymer nanoparticles for highly efficient photoacoustic imaging of orthotopic brain tumors in the second near-infrared window. *Mater. Horizons* **2017**, *4*, 1151–1156, doi:10.1039/c7mh00672a.

74. Yin, C.; Wen, G.; Liu, C.; Yang, B.; Lin, S.; Huang, J.; Zhao, P.; Wong, S.H.D.; Zhang, K.; Chen, X.; et al. Organic semiconducting polymer nanoparticles for photoacoustic labeling and tracking of stem cells in the second near-infrared window. *ACS Nano* **2018**, *12*, 12201–12211, doi:10.1021/acsnano.8b05906.

75. Sun, T.; Dou, J.H.; Liu, S.; Wang, X.; Zheng, X.; Wang, Y.; Pei, J.; Xie, Z. Second near-infrared conjugated polymer nanoparticles for photoacoustic imaging and photothermal therapy. *ACS Appl. Mater. Interfaces* **2018**, *10*, 7919–7926, doi:10.1021/acsami.8b01458.

76. Yang, Y.; Chen, J.; Yang, Y.; Xie, Z.; Song, L.; Zhang, P.; Liu, C.; Liu, J. A 1064 nm excitable semiconducting polymer nanoparticle for photoacoustic imaging of gliomas. *Nanoscale* **2019**, *11*, 7754–7760, doi:10.1039/c9nr00552h.

77. Jiang, Y.; Upputuri, P.K.; Xie, C.; Zeng, Z.; Sharma, A.; Zhen, X.; Li, J.; Huang, J.; Pramanik, M.; Pu, K. Metabolizable semiconducting polymer nanoparticles for second near-infrared photoacoustic imaging. *Adv. Mater.* **2019**, *31*, 1–9, doi:10.1002/adma.201808166.

78. Brauchle, E.; Schenke-Layland, K. Raman spectroscopy in biomedicine: Non-invasive in vitro analysis of cells and extracellular matrix components in tissues. *Biotechnol. J.* **2013**, *8*, 288–297, doi:10.1002/biot.201200163.

79. Lane, L.A.; Qian, X.; Nie, S. SERS nanoparticles in medicine: From label-free detection to spectroscopic tagging. *Chem. Rev.* **2015**, *115*, 10489–10529, doi:10.1021/acs.chemrev.5b00265.

80. Brown, P.O.; Botstein, D.; Lapidot, M.; Pilpel, Y.; Mazo, A.; Hodgson, J.W.; Petruk, S.; Sedkov, Y.; Brock, H.W.; Timmons, J. A.; et al. Label-free biomedical imaging with. *Science (80-.)* **2008**, *1857*, 1857–1861.

81. Fu, D.; Lu, F.K.; Zhang, X.; Freudiger, C.; Pernik, D.R.; Holtom, G.; Xie, X.S. Quantitative chemical imaging with multiplex stimulated Raman scattering microscopy. *J. Am. Chem. Soc.* **2012**, *134*, 3623–3626, doi:10.1021/ja210081h.

82. Cheng, J.X.; Xie, X.S. Vibrational spectroscopic imaging of living systems: An emerging platform for biology and medicine. *Science (80-.)* **2015**, *350*, doi:10.1126/science.aaa8870.

83. Ramos, I.R.M.; Malkin, A.; Lyng, F.M. Current advances in the application of Raman spectroscopy for molecular diagnosis of cervical cancer. *Biomed Res. Int.* **2015**, *2015*, doi:10.1155/2015/561242.

84. Fu, D.; Yang, W.; Xie, X.S. Label-free imaging of neurotransmitter acetylcholine at neuromuscular junctions with stimulated Raman scattering. *J. Am. Chem. Soc.* **2017**, *139*, 583–586, doi:10.1021/jacs.6b10727.

85. Wei, L.; Hu, F.; Chen, Z.; Shen, Y.; Zhang, L.; Min, W. Live-cell bioorthogonal chemical imaging: Stimulated raman scattering microscopy of vibrational probes. *Acc. Chem. Res.* **2016**, *49*, 1494–1502, doi:10.1021/acs.accounts.6b00210.

86. Saar, B.G.; Freudiger, C.W.; Reichman, J.; Stanley, C.M.; Holtom, G.R.; Xie, X.S. Video-rate molecular imaging in vivo with stimulated Raman scattering. *Science (80-.)* **2010**, *330*, 1368–1370, doi:10.1126/science.1197236.

87. Hu, F.; Zeng, C.; Long, R.; Miao, Y.; Wei, L.; Xu, Q.; Min, W. Supermultiplexed optical imaging and barcoding with engineered polyynes. *Nat. Methods* **2018**, *15*, 194–200, doi:10.1038/nmeth.4578.

88. Kim, N.H.; Hwang, W.; Baek, K.; Rohman, M.R.; Kim, J.; Kim, H.W.; Mun, J.; Lee, S.Y.; Yun, G.; Murray, J.; et al. Smart SERS hot spots: Single molecules can be positioned in a plasmonic nanojunction using host-guest chemistry. *J. Am. Chem. Soc.* **2018**, *140*, 4705–4711, doi:10.1021/jacs.8b01501.

89. Qian, X.M.; Nie, S.M. Single-molecule and single-nanoparticle SERS: From fundamental mechanisms to biomedical applications. *Chem. Soc. Rev.* **2008**, *37*, 912–920, doi:10.1039/b708839f.

90. Kang, J.W.; So, P.T.C.; Dasari, R.R.; Lim, D.K. High resolution live cell Raman imaging using subcellular organelle-targeting SERS-sensitive gold nanoparticles with highly narrow intra-nanogap. *Nano Lett.* **2015**, *15*, 1766–1772, doi:10.1021/nl504444w.

91. Nam, J.M.; Oh, J.W.; Lee, H.; Suh, Y.D. Plasmonic nanogap-enhanced raman scattering with nanoparticles. *Acc. Chem. Res.* **2016**, *49*, 2746–2755, doi:10.1021/acs.accounts.6b00409.

92. Arzumanyan, G.M.; Doroshkevich, N. V.; Mamatkulov, K.Z.; Shashkov, S.N.; Zinovev, E. V.; Vlasov, A. V.; Round, E.S.; Gordeliy, V.I. Highly sensitive coherent anti-stokes raman scattering imaging of protein crystals. *J. Am. Chem. Soc.* **2016**, *138*, 13457–13460, doi:10.1021/jacs.6b04464.

93. Biochemistry, T.F.O.R. Xie2006. **2005**, *515*.

94. Tian, S.; Li, H.; Li, Z.; Tang, H.; Yin, M.; Chen, Y.; Wang, S.; Gao, Y.; Yang, X.; Meng, F.; et al. Polydiacetylene-based ultrastrong bioorthogonal Raman probes for targeted live-cell Raman imaging. *Nat. Commun.* **2020**, *11*, 1–9, doi:10.1038/s41467-019-13784-0.

95. Hong, S.; Chen, T.; Zhu, Y.; Li, A.; Huang, Y.; Chen, X. Live-cell stimulated raman scattering imaging of alkyne-tagged biomolecules. *Angew. Chemie* **2014**, *126*, 5937–5941, doi:10.1002/ange.201400328.

96. Ando, J.; Asanuma, M.; Dodo, K.; Yamakoshi, H.; Kawata, S.; Fujita, K.; Sodeoka, M. Alkyne-Tag SERS screening and identification of small-molecule-binding sites in protein. *J. Am. Chem. Soc.* **2016**, *138*, 13901–13910, doi:10.1021/jacs.6b06003.

97. Wei, L.; Hu, F.; Shen, Y.; Chen, Z.; Yu, Y.; Lin, C.C.; Wang, M.C.; Min, W. Live-cell imaging of alkyne-tagged small biomolecules by stimulated Raman scattering. *Nat. Methods* **2014**, *11*, 410–412, doi:10.1038/nmeth.2878.

98. Li, S.; Chen, T.; Wang, Y.; Liu, L.; Lv, F.; Li, Z.; Huang, Y.; Schanze, K.S.; Wang, S. Conjugated polymer with intrinsic alkyne units for synergistically enhanced raman imaging in living cells. *Angew. Chemie–Int. Ed.* **2017**, *56*, 13455–13458, doi:10.1002/anie.201707042.

99. Wei, L.; Chen, Z.; Shi, L.; Long, R.; Anzalone, A. V.; Zhang, L.; Hu, F.; Yuste, R.; Cornish, V.W.; Min, W. Super-multiplex vibrational imaging. *Nature* **2017**, *544*, 465–470, doi:10.1038/nature22051.

100. Demirel, G.; Gieseking, R.L.M.; Ozdemir, R.; Kahmann, S.; Loi, M.A.; Schatz, G.C.; Facchetti, A.; Usta, H. Molecular engineering of organic semiconductors enables noble metal-comparable SERS enhancement and sensitivity. *Nat. Commun.* **2019**, *10*, 1–9, doi:10.1038/s41467-019-13505-7.

101. Yu, N.; Huang, L.; Zhou, Y.; Xue, T.; Chen, Z.; Han, G. Near-infrared-light activatable nanoparticles for deep-tissue-penetrating wireless optogenetics. *Adv. Healthc. Mater.* **2019**, *8*, e1801132, doi:10.1002/adhm.201801132.

102. Cheng, L.; Wang, C.; Feng, L.; Yang, K.; Liu, Z. Functional nanomaterials for phototherapies of cancer. *Chem. Rev.* **2014**, *114*, 10869–10939, doi:10.1021/cr400532z.

103. Liu, C.-P.; Lin, F.-S.; Chien, C.-T.; Tseng, S.-Y.; Luo, C.-W.; Chen, C.-H.; Chen, J.-K.; Tseng, F.-G.; Hwu, Y.; Lo, L.-W.; et al. In-situ formation and assembly of gold nanoparticles by gum arabic as efficient photothermal agent for killing cancer cells. *Macromol. Biosci.* **2013**, *13*, 1314–1320, doi:10.1002/mabi.201300162.

104. Shi, X.; Gong, H.; Li, Y.; Wang, C.; Cheng, L.; Liu, Z. Graphene-based magnetic plasmonic nanocomposite for dual bioimaging and photothermal therapy. *Biomaterials* **2013**, *34*, 4786–4793, doi:10.1016/j.biomaterials.2013.03.023.

105. Liu, Y.; Li, J.; Chen, M.; Chen, X.; Zheng, N. Palladium-based nanomaterials for cancer imaging and therapy. *Theranostics* **2020**, *10*, 10057–10074, doi:10.7150/thno.45990.

106. Li, Z.; Wang, C.; Cheng, L.; Gong, H.; Yin, S.; Gong, Q.; Li, Y.; Liu, Z. PEG-functionalized iron oxide nanoclusters loaded with chlorin e6 for targeted, NIR light induced, photodynamic therapy. *Biomaterials* **2013**, *34*, 9160–9170, doi:10.1016/j.biomaterials.2013.08.041.

107. Chen, Z.; Ma, L.; Liu, Y.; Chen, C. Applications of functionalized fullerenes in tumor theranostics. *Theranostics* **2012**, *2*, 238–250, doi:10.7150/thno.3509.

108. Zhu, C.; Liu, L.; Yang, Q.; Lv, F.; Wang, S. Water-soluble conjugated polymers for imaging, diagnosis, and therapy. *Chem. Rev.* **2012**, *112*, 4687–4735, doi:10.1021/cr200263w.

109. Duarte, A.; Pu, K.-Y.; Liu, B.; Bazan, G.C. Recent advances in conjugated polyelectrolytes for emerging optoelectronic applications. *Chem. Mater.* **2011**, *23*, 501–515, doi:10.1021/cm102196t.

110. Ding, D.; Liu, J.; Feng, G.; Li, K.; Hu, Y.; Liu, B. Bright far-red/near-infrared conjugated polymer nanoparticles for in vivo bioimaging. *Small* **2013**, *9*, 3093–3102, doi:10.1002/smll.201300171.

111. Song, X.; Liang, C.; Gong, H.; Chen, Q.; Wang, C.; Liu, Z. Photosensitizer-conjugated albumin-polypyrrole nanoparticles for imaging-guided in vivo photodynamic/photothermal therapy. *Small* **2015**, *11*, 3932–3941, doi:10.1002/smll.201500550.

112. Li, K.; Pan, J.; Feng, S.-S.; Wu, A.W.; Pu, K.-Y.; Liu, Y.; Liu, B. Generic strategy of preparing fluorescent conjugated-polymer-loaded poly (dl-lactide-co-glycolide) nanoparticles for targeted cell imaging. *Adv. Funct. Mater.* **2009**, *19*, 3535–3542, doi:https://doi.org/10.1002/adfm.200901098.

113. Li, K.; Liu, B. Polymer-encapsulated organic nanoparticles for fluorescence and photoacoustic imaging. *Chem. Soc. Rev.* **2014**, *43*, 6570–6597, doi:10.1039/C4CS00014E.

114. Kaur, P.; Aliru, M.L.; Chadha, A.S.; Asea, A.; Krishnan, S. Hyperthermia using nanoparticles: Promises and pitfalls. *Int. J. Hyperth. Off. J. Eur. Soc. Hyperthermic Oncol. North Am. Hyperth. Gr.* **2016**, *32*, 76–88, doi:10.3109/02656736.2015.1120889.

115. Jaque, D.; Martínez Maestro, L.; Del Rosal, B.; Haro-Gonzalez, P. Benayas, A.; Plaza, J.L.; Martín Rodríguez, E.; García Solé, J. Nanoparticles for photothermal therapies. *Nanoscale* **2014**, *6*, 9494–9530, doi:10.1039/c4nr00708e.

116. Ritter, C.; Makler, S.S.; Latge, A. A theoretical study. *Phys. Rev. B* **2008**, *77*, 195443–195445.

117. Welch, J. Review article laser thermal ablation. **1991**, *53*, 815–823.

118. Gong, H.; Dong, Z.; Liu, Y.; Yin, S.; Cheng, L.; Xi, W.; Xiang, J.; Liu, K.; Li, Y.; Liu, Z. Engineering of multifunctional nano-micelles for combined photothermal and photodynamic therapy under the guidance of multimodal imaging. *Adv. Funct. Mater.* **2014**, *24*, 6492–6502, doi:https://doi.org/10.1002/adfm.201401451.

119. Yang, J.; Choi, J.; Bang, D.; Kim, E.; Lim, E.-K.; Park, H.; Suh, J.-S.; Lee, K.; Yoo, K.-H.; Kim, E.-K.; et al. Convertible organic nanoparticles for near-infrared photothermal ablation of cancer cells. *Angew. Chem. Int. Ed. Engl.* **2011**, *50*, 441–444, doi:10.1002/anie.201005075.

120. Zhou, J.; Lu, Z.; Zhu, X.; Wang, X.; Liao, Y.; Ma, Z.; Li, F. NIR photothermal therapy using polyaniline nanoparticles. *Biomaterials* **2013**, *34*, 9584–9592, doi:10.1016/j.biomaterials.2013.08.075.

121. Wang, W.; Wang, L.; Li, Y.; Liu, S.; Xie, Z.; Jing, X. Nanoscale polymer metal–organic framework hybrids for effective photothermal therapy of colon cancers. *Adv. Mater.* **2016**, *28*, 9320–9325, doi:https://doi.org/10.1002/adma.201602997.

122. Yang, K.; Xu, H.; Cheng, L.; Sun, C.; Wang, J.; Liu, Z. In vitro and in vivo near-infrared photothermal therapy of cancer using polypyrrole organic nanoparticles. *Adv. Mater.* **2012**, *24*, 5586–5592, doi:https://doi.org/10.1002/adma.201202625.

123. Chen, M.; Fang, X.; Tang, S.; Zheng, N. Polypyrrole nanoparticles for high-performance in vivo near-infrared photothermal cancer therapy. *Chem. Commun. (Camb)* **2012**, *48*, 8934–8936, doi:10.1039/c2cc34463g.

124. Zha, Z.; Yue, X.; Ren, Q.; Dai, Z. Uniform polypyrrole nanoparticles with high photothermal conversion efficiency for photothermal ablation of cancer cells. *Adv. Mater.* **2013**, *25*, 777–782, doi:https://doi.org/10.1002/adma.201202211.

125. Liu, Y.; Ai, K.; Liu, J.; Deng, M.; He, Y.; Lu, L. Dopamine-melanin colloidal nanospheres: An efficient near-infrared photothermal therapeutic agent for in vivo cancer therapy. *Adv. Mater.* **2013**, *25*, 1353–1359, doi:10.1002/adma.201204683.

126. Cheng, L.; Yang, K.; Chen, Q.; Liu, Z. Organic stealth nanoparticles for highly effective in vivo near-infrared photothermal therapy of cancer. *ACS Nano* **2012**, *6*, 5605–5613, doi:10.1021/nn301539m.

127. Jiang, B.-P.; Zhang, L.; Guo, X.-L.; Shen, X.-C.; Wang, Y.; Zhu, Y.; Liang, H. Poly(N-phenylglycine)-based nanoparticles as highly effective and targeted near-infrared photothermal therapy/photodynamic therapeutic agents for malignant melanoma. *Small* **2017**, *13*, doi:10.1002/smll.201602496.

128. Chen, H.; Liang, W.; Zhu, Y.; Guo, Z.; Jian, J.; Jiang, B.-P.; Liang, H.; Shen, X.-C. Supercharged fluorescent protein functionalized water-soluble poly(N-phenylglycine) nanoparticles for highly effective imaging-guided photothermal therapy. *Chem. Commun.* **2018**, *54*, 10292–10295, doi:10.1039/C8CC05278F.

129. Bhattarai, D.P.; Kim, B.S. NIR-triggered hyperthermal effect of polythiophene nanoparticles synthesized by surfactant-free oxidative polymerization method on colorectal carcinoma cells. *Cells* **2020**, *9*, doi:10.3390/cells9092122.

130. Cheng, P.; Wang, J.; Zhang, Q.; Huang, W.; Zhu, J.; Wang, R.; Chang, S.-Y.; Sun, P.; Meng, L.; Zhao, H.; et al. Unique energy alignments of a ternary material system toward high-performance organic photovoltaics. *Adv. Mater.* **2018**, *30*, 1801501, doi:https://doi.org/10.1002/adma.201801501.

131. MacNeill, C.M.; Coffin, R.C.; Carroll, D.L.; Levi-Polyachenko, N.H. Low band gap donor-acceptor conjugated polymer nanoparticles and their NIR-mediated thermal ablation of cancer cells. *Macromol. Biosci.* **2013**, *13*, 28–34, doi:https://doi.org/10.1002/mabi.201200241.

132. Guo, B.; Sheng, Z.; Hu, D.; Li, A.; Xu, S.; Manghnani, P.N.; Liu, C.; Guo, L.; Zheng, H.; Liu, B. Molecular engineering of conjugated polymers for biocompatible organic nanoparticles with highly efficient photoacoustic and photothermal performance in cancer theranostics. *ACS Nano* **2017**, *11*, 10124–10134, doi:10.1021/acsnano.7b04685.

133. Zhang, W.; Lin, W.; Li, C.; Liu, S.; Hu, X.; Xie, Z. Rational design of BODIPY-diketopyrrolopyrrole conjugated polymers for photothermal tumor ablation. *ACS Appl. Mater. Interfaces* **2019**, *11*, 32720–32728, doi:10.1021/acsami.9b10713.

134. Chen, L.; Chen, D.; Jiang, Y.; Zhang, J.; Yu, J.; DuFort, C.C.; Hingorani, S.R.; Zhang, X.; Wu, C.; Chiu, D.T. A BODIPY-based donor/donor–acceptor system: Towards highly efficient long-wavelength-excitable near-IR polymer dots with narrow and strong absorption features. *Angew. Chemie Int. Ed.* **2019**, *58*, 7008–7012, doi:https://doi.org/10.1002/anie.201902077.

135. Huang, X.; El-Sayed, I.H.; Qian, W.; El-Sayed, M.A. Cancer cell imaging and photothermal therapy in the near-infrared region by using gold nanorods. *J. Am. Chem. Soc.* **2006**, *128*, 2115–2120, doi:10.1021/ja057254a.

136. Thomsen, S. Pathologic analysis of photothermal and photomechanical effects of laser-tissue interactions. *Photochem. Photobiol.* **1991**, *53*, 825–835, doi:10.1111/j.1751-1097.1991.tb09897.x.

137. Hildebrandt, B.; Wust, P.; Ahlers, O.; Dieing, A.; Sreenivasa, G.; Kerner, T.; Felix, R.; Riess, H. The cellular and molecular basis of hyperthermia. *Crit. Rev. Oncol. Hematol.* **2002**, *43*, 33–56, doi:10.1016/s1040-8428(01)00179-2.

138. Hegyi, G.; Szigeti, G.P.; Szász, A. Hyperthermia versus oncothermia: Cellular effects in complementary cancer therapy. *Evid. Based. Complement. Alternat. Med.* **2013**, *2013*, 672873, doi:10.1155/2013/672873.

139. Sheng, W.; He, S.; Seare, W.J.; Almutairi, A. Review of the progress toward achieving heat confinement-the holy grail of photothermal therapy. *J. Biomed. Opt.* **2017**, *22*, 80901, doi:10.1117/1.JBO.22.8.080901.

140. Mahmood, J.; Shukla, H.D.; Soman, S.; Samanta, S.; Singh, P.; Kamlapurkar, S.; Saeed, A.; Amin, N.P.; Vujaskovic, Z. Immunotherapy, radiotherapy, and hyperthermia: A combined therapeutic approach in pancreatic cancer treatment. *Cancers* **2018**, *10*.

141. Pérez-Hernández, M.; Del Pino, P.; Mitchell, S.G.; Moros, M.; Stepien, G.; Pelaz, B.; Parak, W.J.; Gálvez, E.M.; Pardo, J.; de la Fuente, J.M. Dissecting the molecular mechanism of apoptosis during photothermal therapy using gold nanoprisms. *ACS Nano* **2015**, *9*, 52–61, doi:10.1021/nn505468v.

142. Von Tappeiner, H., Jodlbauer, A. Die sensibilisierende wirkung fluorescierender substanzen: Gesammelte untersuchungen über die photodynamische erscheinung. *Voger, F.C., Leipzig* **1907**.

143. Dolmans, D.E.J.G.J.; Fukumura, D.; Jain, R.K. Photodynamic therapy for cancer. *Nat. Rev. Cancer* **2003**, *3*, 380–387, doi:10.1038/nrc1071.

144. Agostinis, P.; Berg, K.; Cengel, K.A.; Foster, T.H.; Girotti, A.W.; Gollnick, S.O.; Hahn, S.M.; Hamblin, M.R.; Juzeniene, A.; Kessel, D.; et al. Photodynamic therapy of cancer: An update. *CA. Cancer J. Clin.* **2011**, *61*, 250–281, doi:10.3322/caac.20114.

145. Gesquiere, A. Photodynamic therapy with conjugated polymer nanoparticles: Recent advances and therapeutic considerations. *J. Cancer Treat. Diagnosis* **2018**, *2*, 1–6, doi:10.29245/2578-2967/2018/3.1134.

146. Shi, H.; Ma, X.; Zhao, Q.; Liu, B.; Qu, Q.; An, Z.; Zhao, Y.; Huang, W. Ultrasmall phosphorescent polymer dots for ratiometric oxygen sensing and photodynamic cancer therapy. *Adv. Funct. Mater.* **2014**, *24*, 4823–4830, doi:https://doi.org/10.1002/adfm.201400647.

147. Chang, K.; Tang, Y.; Fang, X.; Yin, S.; Xu, H.; Wu, C. Incorporation of porphyrin to π-conjugated backbone for polymer-dot-sensitized photodynamic therapy. *Biomacromolecules* **2016**, *17*, 2128–2136, doi:10.1021/acs.biomac.6b00356.

148. Li, S.; Chang, K.; Sun, K.; Tang, Y.; Cui, N.; Wang, Y.; Qin, W.; Xu, H.; Wu, C. Amplified singlet oxygen generation in semiconductor polymer

dots for photodynamic cancer therapy. *ACS Appl. Mater. Interfaces* **2016**, *8*, 3624–3634, doi:10.1021/acsami.5b07995.

149. Ibarra, L.E.; Porcal, G.V.; Macor, L.P.; Ponzio, R.A.; Spada, R.M.; Lorente, C.; Chesta, C.A.; Rivarola, V.A.; Palacios, R.E. Metallated porphyrin-doped conjugated polymer nanoparticles for efficient photodynamic therapy of brain and colorectal tumor cells. *Nanomedicine* **2018**, *13*, 605–624, doi:10.2217/nnm-2017-0292.

150. Haupt, S.; Lazar, I.; Weitman, H.; Shav-Tal, Y.; Ehrenberg, B. FRET energy transfer via Pdots improves the efficiency of photodynamic therapy and leads to rapid cell death. *J. Photochem. Photobiol. B Biol.* **2016**, *164*, 123–131, doi:https://doi.org/10.1016/j.jphotobiol.2016.09.019.

151. Zhou, X.; Liang, H.; Jiang, P.; Zhang, K.Y.; Liu, S.; Yang, T.; Zhao, Q.; Yang, L.; Lv, W.; Yu, Q.; et al. Multifunctional phosphorescent conjugated polymer dots for hypoxia imaging and photodynamic therapy of cancer cells. *Adv. Sci. (Weinheim, Baden-Wurttemberg, Ger.)* **2016**, *3*, 1500155, doi:10.1002/advs.201500155.

152. Zhu, H.; Fang, Y.; Miao, Q.; Qi, X.; Ding, D.; Chen, P.; Pu, K. Regulating near-infrared photodynamic properties of semiconducting polymer nanotheranostics for optimized cancer therapy. *ACS Nano* **2017**, *11*, 8998–9009, doi:10.1021/acsnano.7b03507.

153. Caverzán, M.D.; Beaugé, L.; Chesta, C.A.; Palacios, R.E.; Ibarra, L.E. Photodynamic therapy of Glioblastoma cells using doped conjugated polymer nanoparticles: An in vitro comparative study based on redox status. *J. Photochem. Photobiol. B Biol.* **2020**, *212*, 112045, doi:https://doi.org/10.1016/j.jphotobiol.2020.112045.

154. Peng, F.; Qiu, L.; Chai, R.; Meng, F.; Yan, C.; Chen, Y.; Qi, J.; Zhan, Y.; Xing, C. Conjugated polymer-based nanoparticles for cancer cell-targeted and image-guided photodynamic therapy. *Macromol. Chem. Phys.* **2018**, *219*, 1700440, doi:https://doi.org/10.1002/macp.201700440.

155. Gesquiere, A.; Jasim, K.; Topps, M.; Shroff, S.; Ortiz Ortiz, A.M.; George, O.; Abdellatif, Y. Conjugated polymer nanotherapeutics for next generation photodynamic therapy. *Med. Res. Arch.* **2018**, *6(2)*, doi:10.18103/mra.v6i2.1673.

156. Duan, X.; Jiang, X.-F.; Hu, D.; Liu, P.; Li, S.; Huang, F.; Ma, Y.; Xu, Q.-H.; Cao, Y. Red emitting conjugated polymer based nanophotosensitizers for selectively targeted two-photon excitation imaging guided photodynamic therapy. *Nanoscale* **2019**, *11*, 185–192, doi:10.1039/C8NR06957C.

157. Khalaf, J. Tumor-targeted conjugated polymer nanoparticles with encapsulated iron and its biomedical application for in vitro killing of melanoma cell lines through ferroptosis assisted chemodynamic therapy, 2019.

158. Elsabahy, M.; Heo, G.S.; Lim, S.-M.; Sun, G.; Wooley, K.L. Polymeric nanostructures for imaging and therapy. *Chem. Rev.* **2015**, *115*, 10967–11011, doi:10.1021/acs.chemrev.5b00135.

159. Conte, C.; Maiolino, S.; Pellosi, D.S.; Miro, A.; Ungaro, F.; Quaglia, F. Polymeric nanoparticles for cancer photodynamic therapy. *Top. Curr. Chem.* **2016**, *370*, 61–112, doi:10.1007/978-3-319-22942-3_3.

160. Moan, J.; Berg, K.; Kvam, E.; Western, A.; Malik, Z.; Rück, A.; Schneckenburger, H. Intracellular localization of photosensitizers. *Ciba Found. Symp.* **1989**, *146*, 11–95, doi:10.1002/9780470513842.ch7.

161. Allison, R.R.; Sibata, C.H. Oncologic photodynamic therapy photosensitizers: A clinical review. *Photodiagnosis Photodyn. Ther.* **2010**, *7*, 61–75, doi:10.1016/j.pdpdt.2010.02.001.

162. Mfouo-Tynga, I.; Abrahamse, H. Cell death pathways and phthalocyanine as an efficient agent for photodynamic cancer therapy. *Int. J. Mol. Sci.* **2015**, *16*.

163. Saneesh Babu, P.S.; Manu, P.M.; Dhanya, T.J.; Tapas, P.; Meera, R.N.; Surendran, A.; Aneesh, K.A.; Vadakkancheril, S.J.; Ramaiah, D.; Nair, S.A.; et al. Bis(3,5-diiodo-2,4,6-trihydroxyphenyl)squaraine photodynamic therapy disrupts redox homeostasis and induce mitochondria-mediated apoptosis in human breast cancer cells. *Sci. Rep.* **2017**, *7*, 42126, doi:10.1038/srep42126.

164. Kessel, D.; Castelli, M. Evidence that Bcl-2 is the target of three photosensitizers that induce a rapid apoptotic response. *Photochem. Photobiol.* **2001**, *74*, 318–322, doi:10.1562/0031-8655(2001)074<0318:etbitt>2.0.co;2.

165. Chandra, J.; Samali, A.; Orrenius, S. Triggering and modulation of apoptosis by oxidative stress. *Free Radic. Biol. Med.* **2000**, *29*, 323–333, doi:10.1016/s0891-5849(00)00302-6.

166. Mroz, P.; Yaroslavsky, A.; Kharkwal, G.B.; Hamblin, M.R. Cell death pathways in photodynamic therapy of cancer. *Cancers (Basel)* **2011**, *3*, 2516–2539, doi:10.3390/cancers3022516.

167. Lavie, G.; Kaplinsky, C.; Toren, A.; Aizman, I.; Meruelo, D.; Mazur, Y.; Mandel, M. A photodynamic pathway to apoptosis and necrosis induced by dimethyl tetrahydroxyhelianthrone and hypericin in

leukaemic cells: Possible relevance to photodynamic therapy. *Br. J. Cancer* **1999**, *79*, 423–432, doi:10.1038/sj.bjc.6690066.

168. Kessel, D.; Oleinick, N.L.B.T.-M. in E. Chapter 1 Initiation of autophagy by photodynamic therapy. In *Autophagy in Disease and Clinical Applications, Part C*; Academic Press, **2009**, *453*, 1–16, ISBN 0076-6879.
169. Xue, L.; Chiu, S.; Azizuddin, K.; Joseph, S.; Oleinick, N.L. The death of human cancer cells following photodynamic therapy: Apoptosis competence is necessary for Bcl-2 protection but not for induction of autophagy. *Photochem. Photobiol.* **2007**, *83*, 1016–1023, doi:https://doi.org/10.1111/j.1751-1097.2007.00159.x.
170. Haywood-Small, S.L.; Vernon, D.I.; Griffiths, J.; Schofield, J.; Brown, S.B. Phthalocyanine-mediated photodynamic therapy induces cell death and a G0/G1 cell cycle arrest in cervical cancer cells. *Biochem. Biophys. Res. Commun.* **2006**, *339*, 569–576, doi:https://doi.org/10.1016/j.bbrc.2005.11.046.
171. Middelburg, T.A.; de Vijlder, H.C.; de Bruijn, H.S.; van der Ploeg-van den Heuvel, A.; Neumann, H.A.M.; de Haas, E.R.M.; Robinson, D.J. Topical photodynamic therapy using different porphyrin precursors leads to differences in vascular photosensitization and vascular damage in normal mouse skin. *Photochem. Photobiol.* **2014**, *90*, 896–902, doi:https://doi.org/10.1111/php.12271.
172. Castano, A.P.; Mroz, P.; Hamblin, M.R. Photodynamic therapy and anti-tumour immunity. *Nat. Rev. Cancer* **2006**, *6*, 535–545, doi:10.1038/nrc1894.
173. Korbelik, M.; Sun, J. Photodynamic therapy-generated vaccine for cancer therapy. *Cancer Immunol. Immunother.* **2006**, *55*, 900–909, doi:10.1007/s00262-005-0088-4.
174. Miao, Y.; Gu, C.; Yu, B.; Zhu, Y.; Zou, W.; Shen, Y.; Cong, H. Conjugated-polymer-based nanoparticles with efficient NIR-II fluorescent, photoacoustic and photothermal performance. *ChemBioChem* **2019**, *20*, 2793–2799, doi:10.1002/cbic.201900309.
175. Li, J.; Zhen, X.; Lyu, Y.; Jiang, Y.; Huang, J.; Pu, K. Cell membrane coated semiconducting polymer nanoparticles for enhanced multimodal cancer phototheranostics. *ACS Nano* **2018**, *12*, 8520–8530, doi:10.1021/acsnano.8b04066.
176. Liu, Z.; Ye, B.; Jin, M.; Chen, H.; Zhong, H.; Wang, X.; Guo, Z. Dye-free near-infrared surface-enhanced Raman scattering nanoprobes for bioimaging and high-performance photothermal cancer therapy. *Nanoscale* **2015**, *7*, 6754–6761, doi:10.1039/c5nr01055a.

177. Geng, J.; Sun, C.; Liu, J.; Liao, L. De; Yuan, Y.; Thakor, N.; Wang, J.; Liu, B. Biocompatible conjugated polymer nanoparticles for efficient photothermal tumor therapy. *Small* **2015**, *11*, 1603–1610, doi:10.1002/smll.201402092.

178. Liu, Y.; Huang, J.; Sun, M.J.; Yu, J.C.; Chen, Y.L.; Zhang, Y.Q.; Jiang, S.J.; Shen, Q.D. A fluorescence-Raman dual-imaging platform based on complexes of conjugated polymers and carbon nanotubes. *Nanoscale* **2014**, *6*, 1480–1489, doi:10.1039/c3nr04430k.

179. Lin, Q.; Yang, Y.; Ma, Y.; Zhang, R.; Wang, J.; Chen, X.; Shao, Z. Bandgap engineered polypyrrole-polydopamine hybrid with intrinsic raman and photoacoustic imaging contrasts. *Nano Lett.* **2018**, *18*, 7485–7493, doi:10.1021/acs.nanolett.8b02901.

180. Qi, J.; Li, J.; Liu, R.; Li, Q.; Zhang, H.; Lam, J.W.Y.; Kwok, R.T.K.; Liu, D.; Ding, D.; Tang, B.Z. Boosting fluorescence-photoacoustic-raman properties in one fluorophore for precise cancer surgery. *Chem* **2019**, *5*, 2657–2677, doi:10.1016/j.chempr.2019.07.015.

181. Yuan, Y.; Liu, B. Self-assembled nanoparticles based on pegylated conjugated polyelectrolyte and drug molecules for image-guided drug delivery and photodynamic therapy. *ACS Appl. Mater. Interfaces* **2014**, *6*, 14903–14910, doi:10.1021/am5020925.

182. Yuan, Y.; Liu, J.; Liu, B. Conjugated-polyelectrolyte-based polyprodrug: Targeted and image-guided photodynamic and chemotherapy with on-demand drug release upon irradiation with a single light source. *Angew. Chem. Int. Ed. Engl.* **2014**, *53*, 7163–7168, doi:10.1002/anie.201402189.

183. Lu, Z.; Zhang, Z.; Tang, Y. Conjugated polymers-based thermal-responsive nanoparticles for controlled drug delivery, tracking, and synergistic photodynamic therapy/chemotherapy. *ACS Appl. Bio Mater.* **2019**, *2*, 4485–4492, doi:10.1021/acsabm.9b00640.

184. Yuan, Y.; Wang, Z.; Cai, P.; Liu, J.; Liao, L.-D.; Hong, M.; Chen, X.; Thakor, N.; Liu, B. Conjugated polymer and drug co-encapsulated nanoparticles for chemo- and photo-thermal combination therapy with two-photon regulated fast drug release. *Nanoscale* **2015**, *7*, 3067–3076, doi:10.1039/C4NR06420H.

185. Bao, B.; Gao, D.; Li, N.; Wu, M.; Xing, C. Near-infrared light regulation of tumor PI3K/Akt signaling pathway for enhancing cancer cell apoptosis through conjugated polymer nanoparticles. *ACS Appl. Bio Mater.* **2020**, *3*, 2428–2437, doi:10.1021/acsabm.0c00161.

186. U.S. National Library of Medicine: ClinicalTrials.gov, https://clinicaltrials.gov, Accessed March 31, 2021.

Chapter 7

Chemically Functionalized Carbon Nanohorns for Drug Delivery Applications

Christina Stangel and Nikos Tagmatarchis

Theoretical and Physical Chemistry Institute,
National Hellenic Research Foundation,
48 Vassileos Constantinou Avenue, 11635 Athens, Greece

stangel@eie.gr

Carbon nanohorns (CNHs) have been widely researched for drug delivery, due to their large surface area, abundance of conical interstice sites, stability, and negligible toxicity in animal testing. In the last decade, a variety of methodologies have been developed for the chemical functionalization of CNHs resulting not only in the incorporation of functional groups onto their skeleton but also in increased biocompatibility and hydrophilicity. Herein, we review the recent progress of chemically functionalized CNHs via covalent and non-covalent approaches enroute to the development of smart drug carriers for in vitro and/or in vivo transport of anticancer drugs or other biologically active compounds.

Functional Materials in Biomedical Applications
Edited by Costas Demetzos, Natassa Pippa, and Nikolaos Naziris

ISBN 978-981-4968-65-2 (Hardcover), 978-1-003-41146-8 (eBook)
www.jennystanford.com

7.1 Introduction

CNHs were discovered by Iijima et al. in 1999 and produced by CO_2 laser ablation of carbon, in large quantities and high purity, without a metal catalyst, at room temperature [1]. CNHs consist of graphene closed tubules with sharp conical closed tips of sp^2 hybridized carbon atoms, which are 2–5 nm in diameter and around 40–50 nm in length. About 2000 of CNHs assemble to form spherical aggregates, resembling dahlia flowers, with a diameter of around 100 nm (Fig. 7.1) [2]. CNHs are accounted as a good alternative to carbon nanotubes (CNTs) [3, 4], due to their high yield production, large specific surface area, low toxicity, high chemical stability, great catalytic properties, and superior porosity. Due to all these properties, CNHs find applicability in diverse fields, including sensing [5, 6], biosensing [7, 8], electrocatalysis [9, 10], gas storage devices [11, 12], energy conversion [13–19], photothermal and photodynamic cancer therapy [20–28], as well as in drug delivery systems (DDSs) [29–35].

As mentioned above, CNHs have an extensive surface area and multitudes of conical interstices that can accommodate large amounts of adsorbed biomolecules. Furthermore, the surface area can be expanded by oxidization, leading to the formation of nanowindows at the CNHs sidewalls, through which diverse small biomolecules can enter the inner space, permitting the slow release of those biomolecules [36, 37]. Oxidized carbon nanohorns (oxCNHs) also contain holes at the tips, allowing the entrance of various materials, such as drugs, which can be stored inside the nanostructure and then released [38]. Furthermore, chemical oxidization introduces carboxylic groups that can be used for further functionalization of CNHs with the appropriate drugs [39] biomolecules, or liposomes [40]. For example, CNHs can be treated with a soft oxidant, such as hydrogen peroxide, under light irradiation, generating a plethora of carboxyl groups at the edges of the holes, as well as causing rapid hole openings in the graphene walls of CNHs [41]. Furthermore, the number of carboxylic and other oxygenated groups upon hydrogen peroxide oxidation was larger than when oxidized with oxygen gas. In addition, the oxidation of CNHs has been revealed to improve biocompatibility and excretion in a sufficient way [41].

The ability of oxCNHs to store and release drugs, including cisplatin [30, 37, 39], doxorubicin (DXR) [38], and dexamethasone (DEX) [42], has been established, and no acute toxicity has been shown for CNHs in animal tests [43–45], emphasizing their usefulness for biological applications. The absence of metal impurities in CNHs compared to other carbon-based materials, like CNTs, was found to be a key factor in avoiding potential carcinogenic risk in cells [46]. Hence, their biodistribution and toxicity can be examined without considering the effects of metals. In addition, CNH biodistribution is significantly influenced by chemical functionalization [32, 47, 48]. Although CNTs and CNHs present low toxicity, it has been shown that these materials are trapped by the liver, spleen, or lung after administration to animals, especially in mononuclear phagocytic system cells, such as macrophages. Nevertheless, due to their chemical modification, diameter, and length, they are excreted from the body. In a recent study, CNHs were incorporated within the macrophages by endocytosis and degraded by reactive oxygen species (ROSs) [49]. However, this process occurs without governing any inflammatory response, because of their weak interaction with glycoprotein non-metastatic melanoma protein B (GPNMB). GPNMB is found to initiate nanotoxicity. In addition, it was confirmed by several approaches that CNHs are more biocompatible and safer than CNTs [49]. In another study, the size-dependent biodistribution of CNHs was examined. Small and large CNHs were dispersed with lipid polyethylene glycol (PEG) and administered to mice, in order to study biodistribution and accumulation characteristics. No accumulation of small CNHs in lung, skin, or kidney, slower accumulation in liver and spleen, and no obvious hematologic or immunologic toxicity was detected [50].

Since CNHs, belonging to the larger carbon allotrope family, are mainly hydrophobic, their solubility to various organic solvents and water relies on their chemical functionalization [51]. To this end, various strategies like the covalent addition of organic species onto the outer skeleton of CNHs [52–64], along with π–π stacking interactions [16, 65] with planar aromatic molecules and/or non-covalent interactions through electrostatic association [15, 66, 67] have been reported. In this chapter, recent case studies are divided in accordance with the chemical functionalization of CNHs, via covalent and non-covalent approaches, for the development of smart drug carriers for in vitro and/or in vivo transport of anticancer drugs or other biologically active compounds. The synthetic methods, loading efficiency, biocompatibility, and drug-loading capacity of these functionalized CNH nanomaterials have been systematically studied and are shown herein.

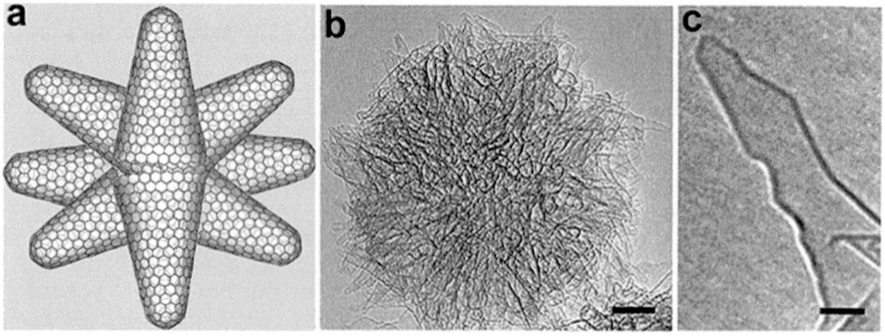

Figure 7.1 (a) Schematic illustration. (b) HRTEM image of a CNH "dahlia" aggregate (scale bar 10 nm). (c) HRTEM image of an individual CNH (scale bar 2 nm). Reproduced from Ref. [9].

7.2 Covalently Functionalized CNHs as Drug Carriers

A plethora of anticancer drugs or biomolecules has been grafted covalently onto CNHs for the creation of efficient DDS. In this context, amidation reactions on oxCNHs are a common strategy to connect bioactive units. As previously mentioned, light-assisted oxidation with H_2O_2 (LAOx) is forceful in creating rich oxygenated groups, such as carboxylic acid groups, at hole edges. Following this route, protein bovine serum albumin (BSA) was covalently attached to the oxygenated groups of oxCNHs via a diimide-activated amidation reaction [41, 44]. oxCNHs are referred to as 2h-LAOx because CNHs were irradiated for 2h under light and H_2O_2. The sufficient attachment of BSA caused hybrid material (2h-LAOx-NH-BSA) to disperse homogeneously into phosphate buffer saline (PBS) for a long period of time. The dispersion enabled the internalization inside mammalian cells, via an endocytosis mechanism [41]. Moreover, the 2h-LAOx-NH-BSA hybrid did not show high toxicity, as confirmed by the normal gross appearance and normal weight gain of the mice. Despite the fact that oxCNH–BSA hybrids were highly hydrophilic, owing to the BSA moieties, they were mostly trapped by the macrophages, and accumulated in the lungs [44].

Furthermore, using water dispersible oxCNH–BSA hybrids, a unique gene expression system was developed [68]. Notably, heat shock promoter-mediated gene expression systems by laser light are appealing targets for controlling cellular functions. Biological systems are transparent to light within the diagnostic window, i.e., within 650–1100 nm [69]. CNHs possess remarkable photothermal energy conversion efficiency and high absorption cross-sections, in a wavelength range for transmission within the diagnostic window [70, 71]. The current system is using the photothermal properties of BSA–CNH complexes, and utilized to convert light energy to the necessary thermal energy for heat shock promoter-mediated gene expression. The complexes enable remote in vitro gene expression in various cells and transgenic medaka (Oryzias latipes) by external laser irradiation. Also, the gene expression was controlled remotely in mice using a low-power laser that can penetrate living tissue [68]. This study could find applications in various biological fields, such as the investigation of genetic mechanisms, analysis of cell signaling within organisms, and cell therapies.

CNHs attract attention as a promising material for multimodal therapies for delivery of heat and chemotherapy to produce a synergistic effect, thus the therapeutic efficacy of the transported drug could be enhanced. In this context, BSA–CNH complexes and zinc phthalocyanine (ZnPc) were combined to create a unique system for double photodynamic therapy (PDT) and photohyperthermia (PHT), a cancer phototherapy system that uses a single laser [72]. Briefly, ZnPc was loaded onto oxCNHs by immersing the oxCNHs in a ZnPc solution and BSA was attached via a condensation reaction. In this system, where BSA enhanced biocompatibility, ZnPc was the PDT agent and oxCNHs was the

PHT agent, while the double phototherapy effect was confirmed both in vitro and in vivo. ZnPc is a promising drug for PDT, generating ROSs by light absorption [73]. In in vivo tests, ZnPc–oxCNHs–BSA hybrid was locally injected into tumors and subcutaneously transplanted in mice. After 10 days of laser irradiation for 15 min/day upon 670 nm laser irradiation, the tumors almost disappeared. In contrast, the tumors continued to grow when only ZnPc or oxCNHs–BSA was injected, indicating that the enhanced efficiency is due to the double phototherapy [73].

Therapies using mild hyperthermia (41–43 °C) and a wide range of chemotherapeutic drugs, such as cisplatin (cis-diamine dichloroplatinum-(II)) (CDDP), have been utilized as potential urinary cancer treatments. In this frame, the CDDP nanocarrier was covalently attached to the surface of oxCNH, and the capability of heat to enhance the efficacy of the corresponding CDDP–CNH conjugate was studied [74]. In more detail, a carbodiimide chemical reaction was employed to attach CDDP to the exterior surface of CNHs and nitric acid to incorporate CDDP in the interior volume. Rat bladder transitional carcinoma cells were exposed to free CDDP or CDDP–CNH hybrid in vitro at 37 °C and 42 °C with the half maximal inhibitory concentration (IC_{50}) for each treatment. Unlike free CDDP, no thermal enhancement of the efficacy of the drug in the CDDP–CNH conjugates around the IC_{50} of the drug in vitro was observed. It was concluded that the disparity in thermal enhancement efficacy observed for free drugs compared to the drug–CNH conjugates is most probably due to their intrinsic size differences and, therefore, their mode of cellular uptake, namely, diffusion or endocytosis [74].

To further examine this issue, the efficiency of the CDDP–CNH hybrid was compared with a conjugate synthesized by inserting the drug in the inner cavity of CNHs, and functionalized with CdSe/ZnS quantum dots (QDs) for imaging transport of the corresponding hybrid CNH-QD to tumor cells (Fig. 7.2) [75]. In particular, CNHs were oxidized using HNO_3 and then reacted with the thiol-based ligand through a carbodiimide reaction. CDDP was loaded through capillary action into cone interiors through defects created by the oxidation process. In particular,

QDs were used as the fluorescent probe for real-time imaging. Drug release profiles and 50% inhibitory concentration determination displayed that QDs do not hinder the therapeutic ability of CNHs. It was indicated that the functionalization procedure to attach QDs to CNH surfaces did not significantly affect their ability to release cisplatin. Furthermore, the hybrids were trackable over the course of a 3-day period, which indicates that internalized CNHs can continue to deliver therapy after removal of the nanoagents from the cell culture, and the significant cell death was confirmed. Thus, this CNH-QD hybrid can be used not only as an imaging agent to study nanoparticle transport but also can deliver therapeutics for the treatment of bladder cancer [75].

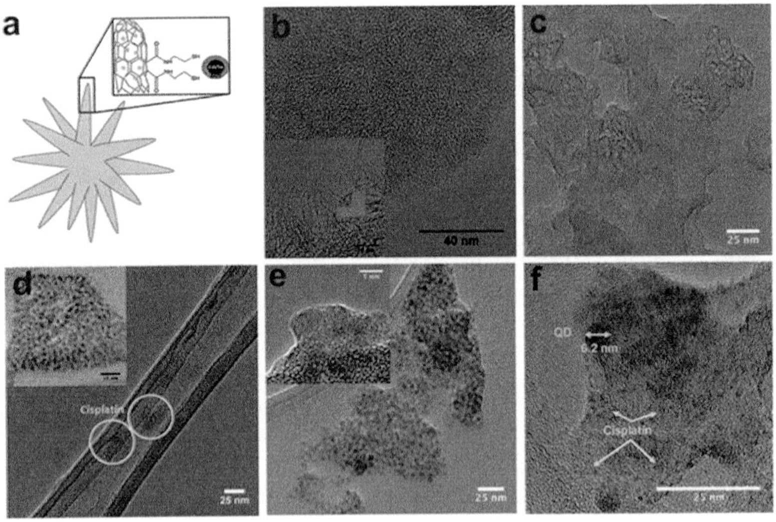

Figure 7.2 (a) Schematic structure of the complex CNH-QD/cisplatin. TEM images of (b) pristine CNHs showing individual conical structures protruding from the ends of the aggregate, (c) functionalized CNHs, (d) cisplatin particles, (e) QDs, and (f) CNH-QD/cisplatin particles. The arrow indicating QD shows a highly ordered lattice structure from the CdSe crystal while the dark small spots indicate cisplatin. Reprinted with permission from [75]. Copyright (2015) Elsevier.

Another approach is based on oxCNHs and polyethyleneimine (PEI) and magnetite (MAG) nanoparticles, for the development of novel cancer treatment [76]. In this study, three different approaches were combined. Firstly, oxCNHs were double-functionalized using PEI and MAG nanoparticles furnishing PEI–MAG–CNHox nanohybrids, and were exploited for fluorescent bioimaging, direct vectorization of nanocomplexes into cells, and effective cancer elimination. Secondly, human cervical cancer cells (HeLa) were incubated with PEI–MAG–CNHox alone or in the presence of a magnet, and the cellular uptake of the nanocomplexes and their cytotoxicity were examined. Thirdly, it was studied if PEI–MAG–CNHox is able to deliver and generate heat for cancer cell elimination. oxCNHs were synthesized under an O_2 flow at 500 °C and then treated with iron (II) acetate, which can be converted into ferromagnetic Fe_3O_4 at temperatures above 300 °C. The CNH-based hybrids were then coupled to an Alexa fluorophore to investigate the intracellular distribution of the nanocomplexes. Magnetic metal nanoparticles could be directed to a tumor for bioimaging and to generate magnetic hyperthermia using an external magnetic field. Chemical functionalization of the MAG–CNH conjugates with PEI improved their water dispersibility. It was shown that the application of an external magnet enhanced the cellular uptake of the hybrids. Finally, laser irradiation of the cells showed a significant enhancement in the photothermal effects of CNHs, leading to cell death and confirming that the photothermal properties and ferromagnetic characteristics of CNH hybrids showed efficient cell elimination [76].

The same research group moved a step forward in their PEI–MAG–CNHox hybrid system by using folic acid (FA) as a targeting unit, namely, FA–PEI–MAG–CNHox conjugate for the treatment of human epidermal carcinoma [77]. The synthesized FA–PEI–MAG–CNHox hybrid targets the epidermal carcinoma cells with high specificity, as the FA moiety on the molecules specifically interacts with FA receptors on the surface of cancer cells (Fig. 7.3). Furthermore, a stronger interaction between the nanoconjugates and the cancer cells was observed in the presence of a magnet due to the ferromagnetic properties of the conjugated MAG nanoparticles.

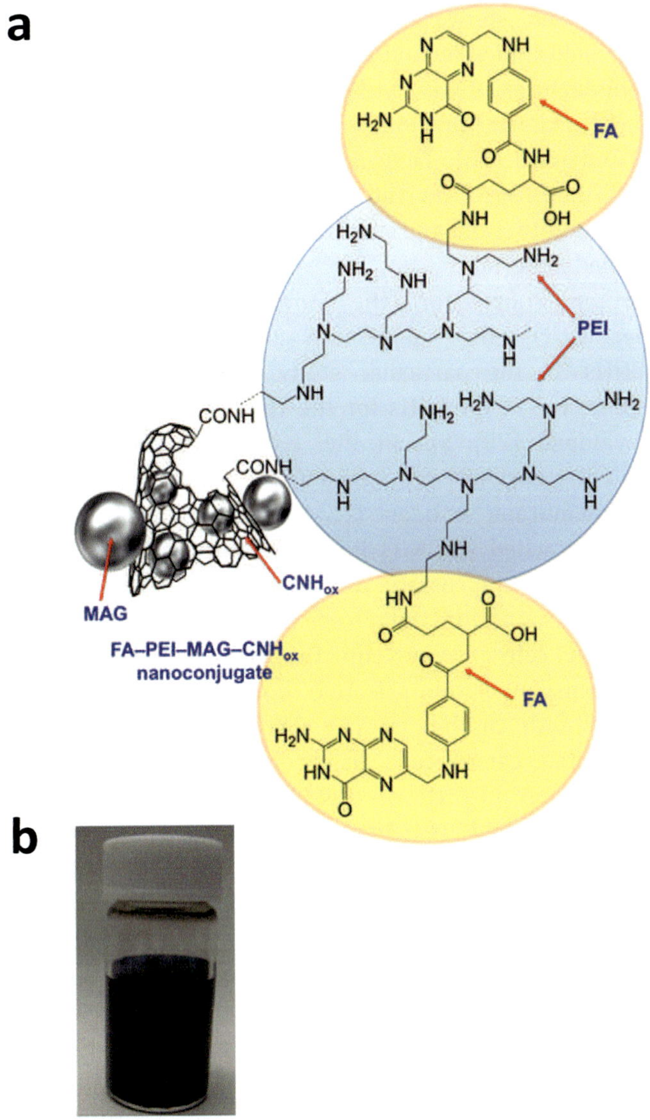

Figure 7.3 Chemical structure and water-dispersibility of FA–PEI–MAG–CNHox conjugates. (a) A schematic illustration of the chemical structure of FA–PEI–MAG–CNHox. (b) FA–PEI–MAG–CNHox in an aqueous solution. The FA–PEI–MAG–CNHox was dispersed in HEPES buffer (100 mM, pH 7.4) at a concentration of 300 μg/mL. Reproduced with permission from [77]. Copyright (2015) Elsevier.

In another study, the same research group developed magnetic field and laser-induced nanorobots, based on magnetic iron nanoparticles, CNHs, and liposomes, for the spatiotemporal control of cellular functions in human cervical cancer cells (HeLa) and mice [78]. They demonstrated controlled enzymatic reactions that relied on the application of a strong magnetic field, and photothermal and substrate-controlled-release properties of combined materials.

Another route for the covalent functionalization of biomolecules is the application of cycloaddition reactions onto CNHs. In the particular study, a selective antibody-drug nanosystem based on CNHs for the treatment of prostate cancer was developed [79]. Specifically, cisplatin CDDP in a prodrug form and the antibody (Ab) D2B (*f*-D2B) selective for prostate-specific membrane antigen ($PSMA^+$) cancer cells, have been covalently attached to CNHs inspired by the current application of this antigen in prostate cancer therapy. Hybrids Ab–CNHs, cisplatin–CNHs, and functionalized-CNHs have also been prepared to be used as reference systems. Different biological experiments have demonstrated the selective binding and uptake of the conjugates with antibodies (Ab–CNH and Ab–Drug–CNH) on $PSMA^+$ prostate cancer cells. In conclusion, the selectivity of the derivative Ab–Drug–CNH on $PSMA^+$ prostate cancer cells has made possible their selective killing against $PSMA^-$ prostate cancer cells.

Cycloaddition reactions were also utilized to covalent attach polyamidoamine dendrimers (PAMAM) onto CNHs in order to create conjugates that act as siRNA graspers [80]. Biocompatibility of CNHs can be modified through the anchoring of PAMAM dendrimers, namely, G4-NH_2 and G6-NH_2 dendrimers (Fig. 7.4). The system is able to release interfering genetic material decreasing the levels of a house-keeping protein and a protein directly involved in prostate cancer development. PAMAM dendrimers can bind Au nanoparticles and this ability was used to determine the localization of the dendrimers on the CNH surface. Furthermore, the CNH hybrid that was synthesized using the fourth-generation PAMAM dendrimers (G4-NH_2), does not display any cytotoxicity up to 25 μg/mL. Finally, this CNH hybrid was able to bind siRNA and release it in the presence of an excess of the polyanion heparin [81].

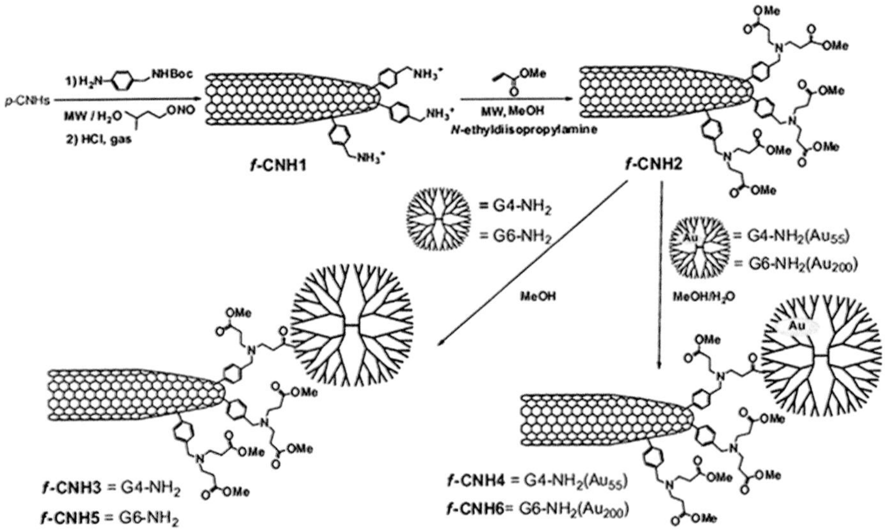

Figure 7.4 Synthesis of the dendrimer-functionalized CNHs. The symbol illustrated for the dendrimer represents fourth- and sixth-generation PAMAM dendrimers in the presence and the absence of gold nanoparticles. Reproduced with permission from [80]. Copyright (2015) Elsevier.

7.3 Non-Covalent Interactions between CNHs and Biologically Active Compounds

The filling of the inner cavity of CNHs with biomolecules or drugs as well as the immobilization of bioactive molecules onto the side walls of CNHs is a common non-covalent strategy for the development of effective delivery nanocarriers. As the drug is inside the CNH, for instance, via adsorption or encapsulation, it is protected from degradation during transportation, while later can be released under certain conditions. Drug incorporation inside oxCNHs and then subsequent in vitro release was first achieved with DEX, an anti-inflammatory drug, via adsorption [42]. Adsorption analyses were used to determine the amount of DEX adsorbed by oxCNHs, which was almost six times larger than that obtained for as-grown CNHs. Additionally, DEX–oxCNHs conjugates displayed sustained release of DEX in mammalian cells without important side effects.

One year later, cisplatin (CDDP) was incorporated into oxCNHs using nanoprecipitation [30]. This is an easy and simple method. CNHs were the first treated in flowing O_2 gas at 570–580 °C to form holes on their walls and additionally heated at 1200 °C in H_2 gas to remove the oxygen-containing functional groups attached to the hole edges. Then, CDDP was dissolved in N,N-dimethylformamide (DMF), and in the same solution, the prepared oxCNHs were dispersed, followed by evaporation of DMF under dry air. The CDDP-incorporated oxCNHs (CDDP/oxCNHs) hybrid contained almost 50% CDDP. The incorporation of cisplatin inside oxCNHs was confirmed by high-resolution transmission electron microscopy (HRTEM), Z-contrast imaging with a scanning TEM (STEM), and thermogravimetric analysis (TGA). The efficiency against the growth of human lung cancer cells of CDDP/oxCNHs has been studied in vitro and in vivo and found to be higher than that of CDDP itself in both cases. This anticancer efficiency was a result of slow CDDP release from oxCNHs and an affinity of oxCNHs to attach to the cell surface in vitro. This slow release was observed in phosphate-buffered saline and cell culture when 40% of the CDDP was not released from the oxCNHs even after 48 h. In fact, 20% of the CDDP was not released even after 14 days.

With the same nanoprecipitation method, using water instead, vancomycin hydrochloride (VCM), an important antibiotic against bacteria, was incorporated into oxCNHs in a high loading yield [82].

In addition, phospholipid–PEG was used to improve the hydrophobic part of oxCNHs in order to enhance its dispersion in aqueous media. A stable and slow release of VCM for an extended period of time was observed. The slow release was proposed due to the stacking of aromatic rings of VCM molecules on the graphitic walls of oxCNHs [82].

In another study, the in vitro release of prednisolone (PSL) immobilized on oxCNHs was tested [35]. PSL is an anti-inflammatory glucocorticoid drug commonly used to treat inflammatory diseases, such as rheumatoid arthritis, lupus erythematosus, or ulcerative colitis, but it exhibits many side effects. In this case, the corresponding PSL–oxCNH hybrid was synthesized by the adsorption of PSL on both the outside and the inside of oxCNHs. This experimental method is called nanoextraction. PSL was dissolved in ethanol/water (1:2) and oxCNHs were added to this solution. The resultant mixture was filtered, and the resulted black powder (PSL–oxCNH) was dried under N_2. Then, the anti-inflammatory effect of the obtained PSL–oxCNH complexes has been studied in vivo by administering the hybrid to rats with collagen-induced arthritis (CIA), a rat type of rheumatoid arthritis. It was found that drug loading was 3.2 times higher on oxCNHs than on pristine CNHs. The PSL release was fast in cell culture media and slow in PBS, approaching about 40% and 9%, respectively. Histological analysis of ankle joints, using an anti-CD68 antibody, a marker of osteoclasts, showed lower arthritis scores in the PSL–oxCNH treated rats compared to both control groups. In a conclusion, oxCNHs can act as a potential PSL vesicle for controlled drug release inside CD68-positive cells [35].

In addition to the successful non-covalent interaction of cisplatin with CNHs, other chemotherapeutics drugs have been also incorporated outside and inside CNHs through π–π stacking interactions, hydrophobic interactions, and physical adsorption. These are DXR [38, 83–85], vincristine [29], and methotrexate [86]. An advantage of using CNHs as carriers for chemotherapeutics drugs is that the drugs can be released more slowly in the problematic tissue, as these nanomaterials' size would not be rapidly cleared from the blood by the liver and spleen and would exert an enhanced permeability and retention (EPR) effect in tumors [87, 88]. That means they tend to be accumulated in tumor tissues due to this effect. The EPR effect enables CNHs to transport therapeutic biomolecules preferentially to tumor sites and makes the delivery of antitumor drugs more effective. This could lower the administered dose of the chemotherapeutics drug.

In more detail, doxorubicin-loaded CNHs (DXR-CNHs) are prepared and further modified by amphiphilic deoxycholic acid-modified-hydropropyl chitosan (DCA-HPCHS) to improve their biocompatibility, yielding to the DOX-CNH/DCA-HPCHS DDS [84]. DOX-CNH/DCA-HPCHS was prepared with a vacuum-assisted solvent evaporation method. DXR was loaded onto CNHs through π–π stacking interactions. The DCA-HPCHS served as an amphiphilic surfactant in CNH/DCA-HPCHS, with its hydrophobic moiety anchoring onto CNHs and the hydrophilic hydropropyl group maintaining the stability in an aqueous environment. Cell viabilities of 4T1 cells incubated with either DOX-CNH/DCA-HPCHS or CNH/DCA-HPCHS with or without 808-nm laser treatments were determined by CCK-8 assays, respectively. Then, mice bearing 4T1 tumors in the laser-treated groups were irradiated with the laser for 20 min, to produce mild photothermal heating to 43 °C and simultaneously imaged by an IR thermal camera. The hybrid DDS combines the photothermal properties from CNHs and chemotherapeutic properties from DOX. The chemotherapy curative effect of DXR is remarkably enhanced by mild photothermal heating through the 808-nm laser irradiation both in vitro and in vivo [84].

In another recent study, a dual chemodrug-loaded theranostic system based on CNHs is developed for targeting both primary breast tumors and their lung metastases [85]. Creating a combination therapy system able to target both primary tumors and their metastases at distant sites with synergistic therapy is beneficial for the complete eradication of tumors. For this purpose, CNHs were modified with poly(maleic anhydride-alt-1-octadecene) and methoxypolyethylene glycol-b-poly(d,l-lactide), via hydrophobic–hydrophobic interactions and π–π stacking. Then, different drugs, namely, cisplatin and DXR were loaded with high efficiency for combined chemo-photothermic therapy (Fig. 7.5). The in vivo behavior and tumor accumulation of the drug-loaded CNHs were studied by photoacoustic imaging. For chemo-photothermal therapy of tumors, 4T1 tumor-bearing mice were intravenously injected with the hybrid material and tumors were illuminated by an 808 nm laser. The drugs have been released in a pH-responsive, tandem, and sustainable manner. Then, tumor cells were completely ablated by chemo-photothermal therapy using relatively mild conditions. For solid tumor treatment, this dual drug-loaded CNH hybrid exhibited prolonged blood circulation and could efficiently target both the primary tumors and their lung metastases [85].

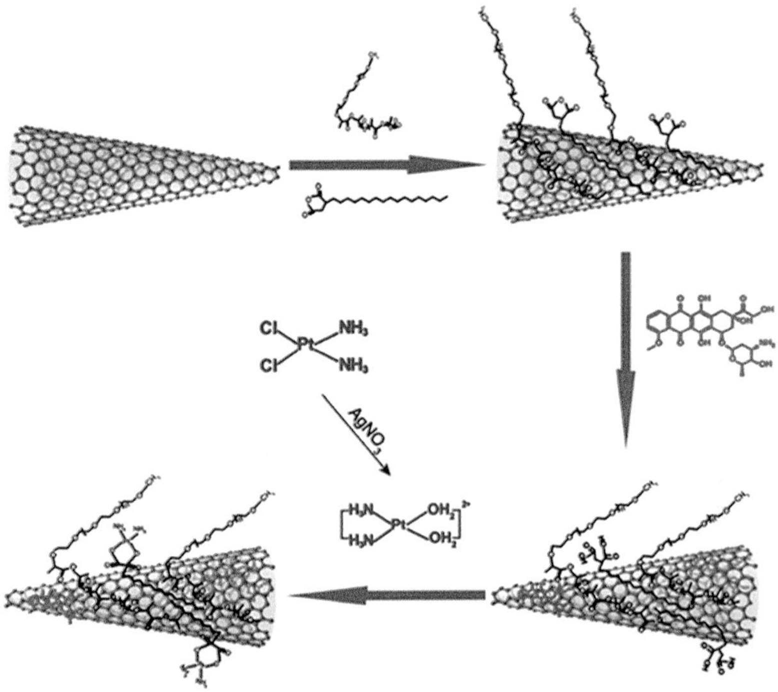

Figure 7.5 Schematic illustration of the preparation of dual drug-loaded CNHs. Reproduced from [85].

As previously mentioned, CNHs have high optical absorption in the NIR region and can efficiently convert NIR light into heat, resulting in hyperthermia of harmful cells and tissues. Thus, CNHs have emerged as novel photothermic agents for photothermal therapy (PTT). However, their poor water dispersibility and unavoidable surface interactions with plasma proteins to form protein corona due to their large surface area are disadvantages. Thus, their chemical modification is crucial. In addition, CNHs have been used for the transfer of photosensitizing agents through non-covalent interactions, for their application in PDT. As previously discussed here to some extent, in PDT, a photosensitizer is employed and is irradiated with a specific wavelength of light energy, usually from a laser. Then, the photosensitizer is in its excited state and can interact with molecular triplet oxygen and produce radicals and ROSs that elicit cancer cell death where the laser is irradiating.

In a recent study, a functionalized CNH hybrid (PC/CNHs) was developed, where phycocyanin (PC) is used to achieve the preformation of a protein corona around CNHs through non-covalent interface interactions [25] (Fig. 7.6). PC is a blue natural protein with maximum absorption at around 618 nm and has been used as a PDT agent [89]. CNHs were sonicated in an aqueous solution of PC for 2 h and then the aggregates of CNHs were eliminated by centrifugation. In the PC/CNHs, the preformed PC corona effectively improves the water dispersibility of the CNHs and protects them from plasma protein adsorption. Also, the great photodynamic activity of PC overcomes the inability of CNHs to generate ROSs. In addition, CNHs give the hybrid a PTT function and increase the photostability of the PC. The PC/CNH hybrid was applied in vitro and in vivo experiments, where synergistic PDT/PTT is achieved.

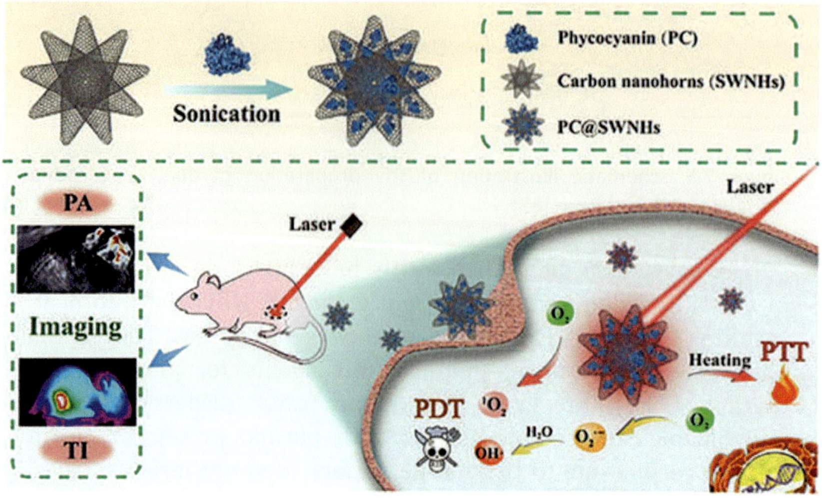

Figure 7.6 Schematic diagram of the route for the synthesis of PC/CNHs and the use of PC/CNHs for NIR light-mediated PTT/PDT of tumors under the guidance of dual-modality TI/PA imaging. Reproduced with permission from [25]. Copyright (2018) Elsevier.

In the same manner, copper phthalocyanine (CuPc) [26], and more recently indocyanine green (ICG) [24] and hypericin (Hyp) have interacted non-covalently with CNHs, developing efficient DDS, and effective PTT and PDT protocols. Specifically, the hydrophilic CuPc (tetrasulfonic acid tetrasodium salt CuPc) is coated outside of CNHs via noncovalent π–π interaction using the sonication method (Fig. 7.7) [26]. In the resulting water-soluble CNHs–CuPc nanohybrid, CNHs act as a photosensitizer vehicle and PTT agent, while CuPc acts as a hydrophilic and PDT agent. It has been shown that the nanohybrid generates ROSs, not only from the photoinduced electron transfer process from CuPc to CNHs, but also from CNHs without exciting CuPc. In addition, the photothermal test confirmed that CNHs contribute to the PTT effect but CuPc may also contribute to that effect when exposed to a 650-nm laser. In vitro studies, using human cervical cancer cells (HeLa), the cell viability test revealed that the combination of PTT and PDT shows much better cell killing efficacy.

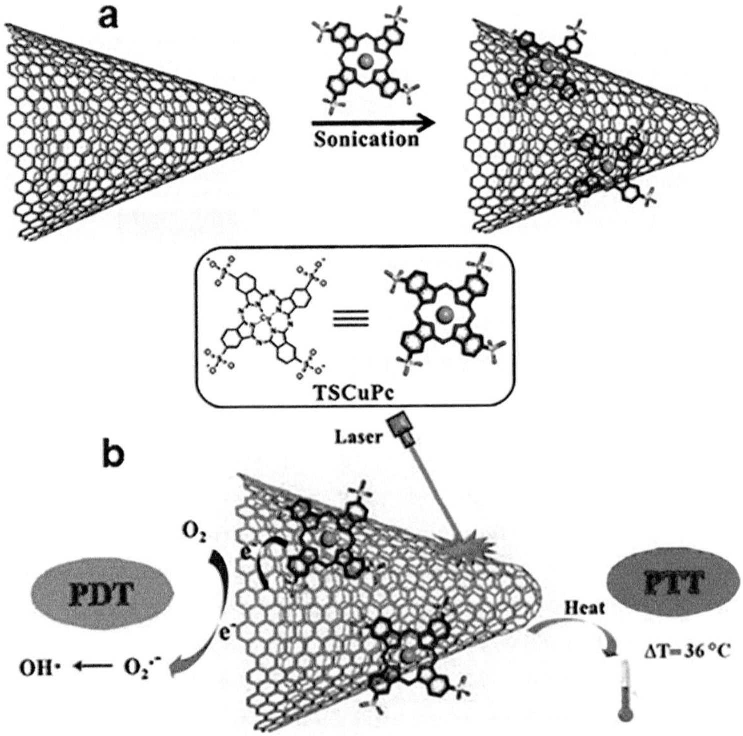

Figure 7.7 (a) Schematic Illustration of the preparation of the CNHs–TSCuPc nanohybrid. (b) Schematic illustration of PTT/PDT therapy. Reproduced with permission from [26]. Copyright (2014) American Chemical Society.

As it is mentioned above, ICG interacted non-covalently, in particular, via π–π interactions with CNHs [24]. ICG is an amphiphilic tricarbocyanine dye that has been utilized for PDT-producing ROSs to destroy cancer cells. However, this dye tends to aggregate and degrade rapidly in water, thus its applications are limited. In the current study, a nanoplatform was developed by coating ICG on the surface of CNHs obtaining CNH/ICGs hybrids with high solubility and stability in physiological conditions. The hybrid can produce satisfactory hyperthermia and ROSs under NIR laser irradiation. Furthermore, CNH/ICGs improved the photostability of ICG in water but also protected it from light degradation. Combined PTT and PDT effectively destroy triple-negative breast cancer 4T1 cells, revealing a noticeably improved and synergistic therapeutic effect compared to PTT or PDT alone. Furthermore, in vivo important tumor cell death and also tumor growth inhibition have been shown following PTT/PDT at 808-nm laser irradiation, confirming the synergistic effect of CNH–ICGs [24].

Regarding Hyp, CNH/Hyp nanohybrids were synthesized for combined photodynamic and PTT in vivo (Fig. 7.8) [90]. Hyp is a natural product and photosensitizing pigment, owing to a planar π-conjugate aromatic structure. Although Hyp has been shown to display a strong photosensitizing effect for PDT, as it could produce a large number of $^1O_2$, it tends to self-aggregate and its solubility in water is not satisfying [91]. In this study, CNH–Hyp nanohybrids were first synthesized by loading Hyp on the outer surface of CNHs via π–π interactions and thus, displayed high solubility and stability in aqueous media. CNHs not only improved water solubility and photostability, but also protected Hyp from light degradation. In vitro cytotoxicity and in vivo antitumor experiments proved that CNH–Hyp hybrids not only clearly destroyed 4T1 cells with laser irradiation upon 590 and 808 nm but also in a notable way suppressed the growth of 4T1 tumors following synergistic PDT and PTT. In addition, the results suggested that CNH–Hyp hybrid exhibited great biocompatibility and low toxicity in mice [90]. In conclusion, therapeutic nanoplatforms based on CNHs and PDT photosensitizers make CNHs very promising in cancer therapy. It has been shown that the biomedical applications of CNHs, particularly integrating PTT and PDT into a single system, have tremendous potential in cancer treatment.

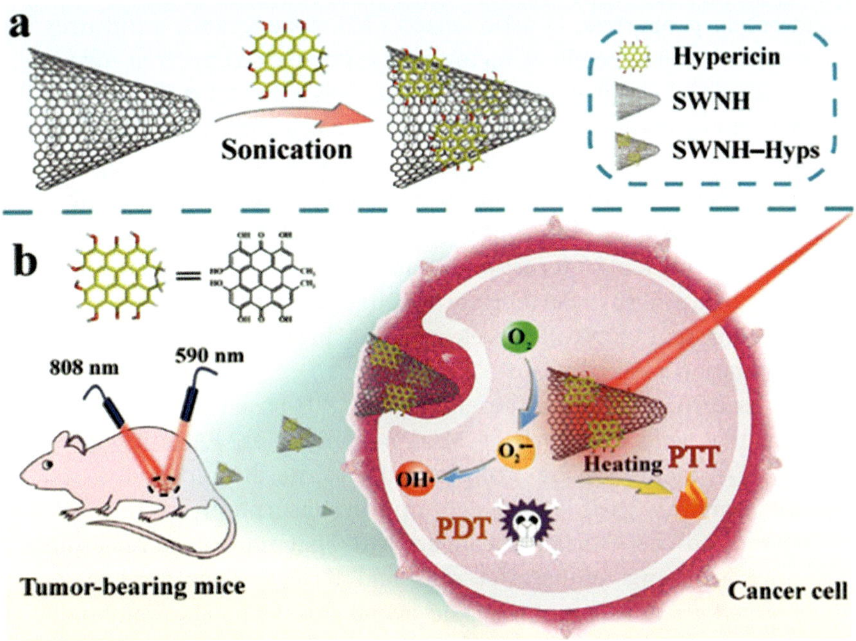

Figure 7.8 Schematic exhibition of the process for fabricating CNH–Hyp and schematic of PTT and PDT elimination of a tumor. Reproduced with permission from [90]. Copyright (2019) American Chemical Society.

7.4 Conclusion

In this chapter, we summarized the recent development of functionalized CNHs as intelligent drug carriers for the delivery of anticancer drugs and other biologically active compounds in vitro and in vivo. Our main focus is on the different methods of preparation of drug-loaded CNHs, including their modification, via covalent or non-covalent approach, and their applications as drug delivery carriers. CNHs are characterized by their easy and simple synthesis on a large scale, high purity, and low toxicity, rendering them remarkable candidates for DDSs. In contrast to CNTs, CNHs do not contain metal impurities because they are produced by CO_2 laser ablation of carbon without a metal catalyst. Therefore, their toxicity and biodistribution can be examined without considering the effects of metals. Moreover, they can be simply functionalized to improve their biocompatibility or targeting properties. Functionalized CNHs loaded with anticancer drugs showed excellent cytotoxicity compared to free drugs at the same dose incubation with cancer cells. The first characteristic that makes them attractive for drug delivery carriers, is the EPR effect that enables the CNHs to transport therapeutic agents preferentially to tumor sites. Second, they exhibit a remarkable ability for drug loading onto the surface through both covalent and non-covalent interactions, due to their high aspect ratios and surface areas. Furthermore, CNH-drug carriers allow drug targeting and controlled release and protect the drug from degradation as they encapsulate it.

To further increase the efficacy of CNH-based DDSs, various targeting molecules such as MAG nanoparticles, FA, antibodies, and PDT agents can be incorporated into the drug-loaded CNHs. Furthermore, CNHs have high optical absorption in the NIR region and can efficiently convert NIR light into heat, resulting in hyperthermia of harmful cells and tissues. Thus, they have emerged as novel photothermic agents for PTT. The combined photothermal/PDT using CNHs is achievable and specifically interesting as a potential anticancer therapy.

It should be mentioned that despite the very encouraging results obtained from in vitro models, the lack of adequate studies using appropriate in vivo models strongly limits the current understanding of how these nanomaterials act in biological systems. For example, oxCNHs accumulated rapidly in the spleen and kidney after intravenous administration to mice, but did not cause any abnormalities at least for two weeks. In addition, at the cellular level, CNHs are mostly captured by macrophages. Current toxicity studies in vitro and in vivo are not comparable, something which would be valuable in developing trustworthy cancer therapies for application in clinical trials. Nevertheless, CNHs have undoubtedly shown great potential as DDS for chemotherapeutic drugs and other therapeutic drugs such as antibiotics or anti-inflammatories. Future studies should shed light on their long-term effects and metabolism in the body.

References

1. Iijima, S., Yudasaka, M., Yamada, R., Bandow, S., Suenaga, K., Kokai, F., and Takahashi, K. (1999). Nanoaggregates of single-walled graphitic carbon nanohorns, *Chem. Phys. Lett.*, **309**, pp. 165–170.
2. Karousis, N., Martinez, I. S., Ewels, C. P., and Tagmatarchis, N. (2016). Structure, properties, functionalization, and applications of carbon nanohorns, *Chem. Rev.*, **116**, pp. 4850–4883.
3. Park, T.-J., Banerjee, S., Hemraj-Benny, T., and Wong, S. S. (2006). Purification strategies and purity visualization techniques for single-walled carbon nanotubes, *J. Mater. Chem.*, **16**, pp. 141–154.
4. Kostarelos, K. (2008). The long and short of carbon nanotube toxicity, *Nat. Biotechnol.*, **26**, pp. 774–776.
5. Bracamonte, M. V., Melchionna, M., Giuliani, A., Nasi, L., Tavagnacco, C., Prato, M., and Fornasiero, P. (2017). H_2O_2 Sensing enhancement by mutual integration of single walled carbon nanohorns with metal oxide catalysts: The CeO_2 case, *Sens. Actuators B-Chem*, **239**, pp. 923–932.
6. Liu, X., Ying, Y., and Ping, J. (2020). Structure, synthesis, and sensing applications of single-walled carbon nanohorns, *BiosensBioelectron*, **167**, pp. 112495.
7. Liu, X., Shi, L., Niu, W., Li, H., and Xu, G. (2008). Amperometric glucose biosensor based on single walled carbon nanohorns, *BiosensBioelectron*, **23**, pp. 1887–1890.
8. Yang, F., Han, J., Zhuo, Y., Yang, Z., Chai, Y., and Yuan, R. (2014). Highly sensitive impedimetric immunosensor based on single-walled carbon nanohorns as labels and bienzyme biocatalyzed precipitation as enhancer for cancer biomarkerdetection, *BiosensBioelectron*, **55**, pp. 360–365.
9. Kagkoura, A. and Tagmatarchis, N. (2020). Carbon nanohorn-based electrocatalysts for energy conversion, *Nanomaterials*, **10**, pp. 1407.
10. Kagkoura, A., Arenal, R., and Tagmatarchis, N. (2020). Sulfur-doped carbon nanohorn bifunctional electrocatalyst for water splitting, *Nanomaterials*, **10**, pp. 2416.
11. Sano, N., Taniguchi, K., and Tamon, H. (2014). Hydrogen storage in porous single-walled carbon nanohorns dispersed with Pd–Ni alloy nanoparticles, *J. Phys. Chem. C*, **118**, pp. 3402–3408.
12. Bekyarova, E., Murata, K., Yudasaka, M., Kasuya, D., Iijima, S., Tanaka, H., Kahoh, H., and Kaneko, K. (2003). Single-wall nanostructured carbon for methane storage, *J. Phys. Chem. B*, **107**, pp. 4681–4684.

13. Pagona, G., Sandanayaka, A. S. D., Hasobe, T., Charalambidis, G., Coutsolelos, A. G., Yudasaka, M., Iijima, S., and Tagmatarchis N. (2008). Characterization and photoelectrochemical properties of nanostructured thin film composed of carbon nanohorns covalently functionalized porphyrins, *J. Phys. Chem. C*, **112**, pp. 15735–15741.

14. Rotas, G., Sandanayaka, A.S.D., Tagmatarchis, N., Ichihashi T., Yudasaka M., Iijima, S., and Ito, O. (2008). (Terpyridine) copper(II)–carbon nanohorns: Metallo-nanocomplexes for photoinduced charge separation, *J. Am. Chem. Soc.*, **130**, pp. 4725–4731.

15. Vizuete, M.,. Gomez-Escalonilla, M. J, Fierro, J. L. G., Sandanayaka, A. S. D., Hasobe, T., Yudasaka, M., Iijima, S., Ito, O., and Fernando, L. (2010). A carbon nanohorn porphyrin supramolecular assembly for photoinduced electron-transfer processes, *Chem. Eur. J.*, **16**, pp. 10752–10763.

16. Pagona, G., Sandanayaka, A. S. D., Araki, Y., Fan, J., Tagmatarchis, N., Yudasaka, M., Iijima S., and Ito, O. (2006). Electronic interplay on illuminated aqueous carbon nanohorn–porphyrin ensembles, *J. Phys. Chem. B*, **110**, pp. 20729–20732.

17. Pagona, G., Fan, J., Maigne, A., Yudasaka, M. Iijima S., and Tagmatarchis N. (2007). Aqueous carbon nanohorn–pyrene–porphyrin nanoensembles: Controlling charge-transfer interactions, *Diam. Relat. Mater.*, **16**, pp. 1150–1153.

18. Pagona, G., Sandanayaka, A. S. D., Araki, Y., Fan, J., Tagmatarchis N., Charalambidis G., Coutsolelos A. G., Boitrel, B., Yudasaka, M., Iijima S., and Ito, O. (2007). Covalent functionalization of carbon nanohorns with porphyrins: Nanohybrid formation and photoinduced electron and energy transfer, *Adv. Funct. Mater.*, **17**, pp. 1705–1711.

19. Vizuete, M., Gomez-Escalonilla, M. J., Fierro, J. L. G., Ohkubo, K., Fukuzumi, S., Yudasaka, M., Yudasaka, M., Iijima, S., Nierengarten, J.-F., and Langa, F. (2014). Photoinduced electron transfer in a carbon nanohorn–C_{60} conjugate, *Chem. Sci.*, **5**, pp. 2072–2080.

20. Yang, J., Su, H., Sun, W., Cai, J., Liu, S. Chai, Y., and Zhang, C. (2018). Dual chemodrug-loaded single-walled carbon nanohorns for multimodal imaging-guided chemo-photothermal therapy of tumors and lung metastases, *Theranostics*, **8**, pp. 1966–1984.

21. Whitney, J. R., Sarkar, S., Zhang, J., Do, T., Young, T., Manson, M. K., Campbell, T. A., Puretzky, A. A., Rouleau, C.M., More, K. L., Geohegan, D. B., Rylander, C. G., Dorn, H. C., and Rylander, M. N. (2011). Single walled carbon nanohorns as photothermal cancer agents, *Lasers Surg. Med.*, **43**, pp. 43–51.

22. Fang, D., Zhang, S., Dai, H., and Lin, Y. (2019). An ultrasensitive ratiometric electrochemiluminescence immunosensor combining photothermal amplification for ovarian cancer marker detection, *Biosens. Bioelectron.*, **146**, pp. 1–7.

23. Wang, J., Wang, R., Zhang, F., Yin, Y., Mei, L., Song, F., Tao, M., Yue, W., and Zhong, W. (2016). Overcoming multidrug resistance by a combination of chemotherapy and photothermal therapy mediated by carbon nanohorns, *J. Mater. Chem. B*, **4**, pp. 6043–6051.

24. Gao, C., Dong, P., Lin, Z., Guo, X., Jiang, B. P., Ji, S., Liang, H., and Shen, X. C. (2018). Near-infrared light responsive imaging-guided photothermal and photodynamic synergistic therapy nanoplatform based on carbon nanohorns for efficient cancer treatment, *Chem. A Eur. J.*, **24**, pp. 12827–12837.

25. Lin, Z., Jiang, B. P., Liang, J., Wen, C., and Shen, X. C. (2019). Phycocyanin functionalized single-walled carbon nanohorns hybrid for near-infrared light-mediated cancer phototheranostics, *Carbon*, **143**, pp. 814–827.

26. Jiang, B. P., Hu, L. F., Shen, X. C., Ji, S. C., Shi, Z., Liu, C. J., Zhang, L., and Liang H. (2014). One-step preparation of a water-soluble carbon nanohorn/phthalocyanine hybrid for dual-modality photothermal and photodynamic therapy, *ACS Appl. Mater. Interfaces*, **6**, pp. 18008–18017.

27. Chen, D., Wang, C., Nie, X., Li, S., Li, R., Guan, M., Liu, Z., Chen, C., Wang, C., Shu, C., and Wan, L. (2014). Photoacoustic imaging guided near-infrared photothermal therapy using highly water-dispersible single-walled carbon nanohorns as theranostic agents, *Adv. Funct. Mater.*, **24**, pp. 6621–6628.

28. Whitney, J., Dewitt, M., Whited, B. M., Carswell, W., Simon, A., Rylander, C. G., and Rylander M. N. (2013). 3D viability imaging of tumor phantoms treated with single-walled carbon nanohorns and photothermal therapy, *Nanotechnology*, **24**, pp. 275102.

29. Li, N., Zhao, Q., Shu, C., Ma, X., Li, R., Shen, H., and Zhong, W. (2015). Targeted killing of cancer cells in vivo and in vitro with IGF-IR antibody-directed carbon nanohorns based drug delivery, *Int. J. Pharm.*, **478**, pp. 644–654.

30. Ajima, K., Yudasaka, M., Murakami, T., Maigne, A., Shiba, K., and Iijima S. (2005). Carbon nanohorns as anticancer drug carriers, *Mol. Pharm.* **2**, pp. 475–480.

31. Guerra, J., Herrero, M. A., and Vazquez, E. (2014). Carbon nanohorns as alternative gene delivery vectors, *RSC Adv.*, **4**, pp. 27315–27321.

32. Moreno-Lanceta, A., Medrano-Bosch, M., and Melgar-Lesmes, P. (2020). Single-walled carbon nanohorns as promising nanotube-derived delivery systems to treat cancer, *Pharmaceutics.*, **12**, pp. 850.
33. Curcio, M., Cirillo, G., Saletta, F., Michniewicz, F., Nicoletta, F. P., Vittorio, O., Hampel, S., and Iemma, F. (2021). Carbon nanohorns as effective nanotherapeutics in cancer therapy, *Carbon*, **7**, pp. 3.
34. Kokubun, K., Matsumura, S., Yudasaka, M., Iijima, S., and Shiba, K. (2018). Immobilization of a carbon nanomaterial-based localized drug-release system using a bispecific material-binding peptide, *Int J Nanomedicine, **13***, pp. 1643–1652.
35. Nakamura M., Tahara, Y., Ikehara, Y., Murakami, T., Tsuchida, K., Iijima, S., Waga, I., and Yudasakau, M. (2011). Single-walled carbon nanohorns as drug carriers: Adsorption of prednisolone and anti-inflammatory effects on arthritis, *Nanotechnology.*, **22**, pp. 465102.
36. Isaac, K. M., Sabaraya, I. V., Ghousifam, N., Das, D., Pekkanen, A. M., Romanovicz, D. K., Long, T. E., Saleh, N. B., and Rylander, M. N. (2018). Functionalization of single-walled carbon nanohorns for simultaneous fluorescence imaging and cisplatin delivery in vitro, *Carbon*, **138**, pp. 309–318.
37. Ajima, K., Yudasaka, M., Maigné, A., Miyawaki, J., and Iijima, S. (2006). Effect of functional groups at hole edges on cisplatin release from inside single-wall carbon nanohorns, *J. Phys. Chem. B*, **110**, pp. 5773–5778.
38. Murakami, T., Fan, J., Yudasaka, M., Iijima, S., and Shiba, K. (2006). Solubilization of single-wall carbon nanohorns using a PEG-doxorubicin conjugate, *Mol. Pharm.*, **3**, pp. 407–414.
39. Matsumura, S., Ajima, K., Yudasaka, M., Iijima, S., and Shiba, K. (2007). Dispersion of cisplatin-loaded carbon nanohorns with a conjugate comprised of an artifcial peptide aptamer and polyethylene glycol, *Mol Pharm.*, **4**, pp. 723–729.
40. Pippa, N., Stangel, C., Kastanas, I., Triantafyllopoulou, E., Naziris, N., Stellas, D., Zhange, M., Yudasaka, M., Demetzos, C., and Tagmatarchis, N. (2019). Carbon nanohorn/liposome systems: Preformulation, design and in vitro toxicity studies, *Materials Science & Engineering C*, **105**, pp. 110114.
41. Zhang, M., Yudasaka, M., Ajima, K., Miyawaki, J., and Iijima, S. (2007). Light-assisted oxidation of single-wall carbon nanohorns for abundant creation of oxygenated groups that enable chemical modifications with proteins to enhance biocompatibility, *ACS Nano*, **1**, pp. 265–272.

42. Murakami, T., Ajima, K., Miyawaki, J., Yudasaka, M., Iijima, S., and Shiba, K. (2004). Drug-loaded carbon nanohorns: Adsorption and release of dexamethasone in vitro, *Mol Pharm.*, **1**, pp. 399–405.

43. Miyawaki, J., Yudasaka, M., Azami, T., Kubo, Y., and Iijima, S. (2008). Toxicity of single-walled carbon nanohorns, *ACS Nano.* **2**, pp. 213–226.

44. Tahara, Y., Miyawaki, J., Zhang, M., Yang, M., Waga, I., Iijima, S., Irie, H., and Yudasaka M. (2011). Histological assessments for toxicity and functionalization-dependent biodistribution of carbon nanohorns, *Nanotechnology*, **22**, pp. 265106.

45. Lynch, R. M., Voy, B. H., Glass, D. F., Mahurin, S. M., Zhao, B., Hu, H., Saxton, A. M., Donnell, R. L., and Cheng, M.-D. (2007). Assessing the pulmonary toxicity of single-walled carbon nanohorns, *Nanotoxicology*, **1**, pp. 157–166.

46. Zhu, S. and Xu, G. (2010). Single-walled carbon nanohorns and their applications, *Nanoscale*, **2**, pp. 2538–2549.

47. Zhang, M., Yang, M., Bussy, C., Iijima, S., Kostarelos, K., and Yudasaka, M. (2015). Biodegradation of carbon nanohorns in macrophage cells, *Nanoscale*, **7**, pp. 2834–2840.

48. Zhu, S. and Xu G. (2012). Nanomaterials for the life sciences, 9, *Carbon Nanomaterials*, S. S. Challa and Kumar, R. (eds.), Chapter 4 Carbon nanohorns and their biomedical applications (Wiley-VCH), pp. 87–109.

49. He, B., Shi, Y., Liang, Y., Yang, A., Fan, Z., Yuan, L., Zou, X., Chang, X., Zhang, H., Wang, X., Wenbin, D., Wang, Y., and Zhang, Q. (2018). Single-walled carbonnanohorns improve biocompatibility over nanotubes by triggering less protein-initiated pyroptosis and apoptosis in macrophages, *Nat. Commun.*, **9**, pp. 1–21.

50. Zhang, M., Yamaguchi, T., Iijima, S., and Yudasaka, M. (2013). Size-dependent biodistribution of carbon nanohorns in vivo, *Nanomed. Nanotechnol. Biol. Med.*, **9**, pp. 657–664.

51. Pagona, G., Mountrichas, G., Rotas, G., Karousis, N., Pispas, S., and Tagmatarchis, N. (2009). Properties, applications and functionalization of carbon nanohorns, *Int. J. Nanotechnol.*, **6**, pp. 176.

52. Tagmatarchis, N., Maigne, A., Yudasaka, M., and Iijima, S. (2006). Functionalization of carbon nanohorns with azomethine ylides: Towards solubility enhancement and electrontransfer processes, *Small*, **2**, pp. 490–494.

53. Cioffi, C., Campidelli, S., Brunetti, F. G., Meneghetti, M., and Prato, M. (2006). Functionalisation of carbon nanohorns, *Chem. Commun.,* **10**, pp. 2129–2131.

54. Pagona, G., Karousis, N., and Tagmatarchis, N. (2008). Aryl diazonium functionalization of carbon nanohorns, *Carbon*, **46**, pp. 604–610.

55. Nakamura, E., Koshino, M., Tanaka, T., Niimi Y., Harano K., Nakamura, Y., and Isobe, H. (2008). Imaging of conformational changes of biotinylated triamide molecules covalently bonded to a carbon nanotube surface, *J. Am. Chem. Soc.*, **130**, pp. 7808–7809.

56. Karousis, N., Ichihashi, T., Yudasaka, M., Iijima, S., and Tagmatarchis N. (2011). Microwave-assisted functionalization of carbon nanohorns via [2+1] nitrenes cycloaddition, *Chem. Commun.*, **47**, pp. 1604–1606.

57. Lacotte, S., García, A., Décossas, M., Al-Jamal, W., Li, S., Kostarelos, K., Muller, S., Prato, M., Dumortier, H., and Bianco, A. (2008). Interfacing functionalized carbon nanohorns with primary phagocytic cells, *Advanced Materials*, **20**, pp. 2421–2426.

58. Vizuete, M., Escalonilla, M.J., Fierro, G., Yudasaka, M., Iijima, S., Vartanian, M., Iehl, J., Nierengarten, J.-F., and Langa, F. (2011). A soluble hybrid material combining carbon nanohorns and C_{60}, *ChemCommun*, **47**, pp. 12771–12773.

59. Karousis, N., Sato, Y., Suenaga, K., and Tagmatarchis, N. (2012). Direct evidence for covalent functionalization of carbon nanohorns by high-resolution electron microscopy imaging of C_{60} conjugated onto their skeleton, *Carbon*, **50**, pp. 3909–3914.

60. Pagona, G., Zervaki, G. E., Sandanayaka, A. D., Ito, O., Charalambidis, G., Hasobe, T., Coutsolelos A. G., and. Tagmatarchis, N. (2012). Carbon nanohorn–porphyrin dimer hybrid material for enhancing light-energy conversion, *J. Phys. Chem. C*, **116**, pp. 9439–9449.

61. Chronopoulos, D.D., Liu, Z., Suenaga, K., Yudasaka, M., and Tagmatarchis, N. (2016). [3 + 2] cycloaddition reaction of azomethine ylides generated by thermal ring opening of aziridines onto carbon nanohorns, *RSC Adv.*, **6**, pp. 44782–44787.

62. Economopoulos, S. P., Pagona G., Yudasaka, M., Iijima S., and Tagmatarchis, N. (2009). Solvent-free microwave-assisted bingel reaction in carbon nanohorns, *J. Mater. Chem.*, **19**, pp. 7326–7331.

63. Rotas, G., Sandanayaka, A. S. D., Tagmatarchis N., Ichihashi, T., Yudasaka, M., Iijima, S., and Ito O. (2008). Terpyridine Cu^{II}-carbon nanohorns: Metallo-nanocomplexes for photoinduced charge-separation, *J. Am. Chem. Soc.*, **130**, pp. 4725–4731.

64. Pagona, G., Tagmatarchis, N., Fan, J., Yudasaka, M., and Iijima, S. (2006). Cone-end functionalization of carbon nanohorns, *Chem. Mater.,* **18**, pp. 3918–3920.

65. Pagona, G., Fan, J., Maigne, A., Yudasaka, M., Iijima, S., and Tagmatarchis N. (2007). Aqueous carbon nanohorn–pyrene porphyrinnanoensembles: Controlling charge-transfer interactions, *Diam. Relat. Mater.*, **16**, pp. 1150–1153.

66. Mountrichas, G., Ichihashi, T., Pispas, S., Yudasaka, M., Iijima, S., and Tagmatarchis, N. (2009). Solubilization of carbon nanohorns by block polyelectrolyte wrapping and templated formation of gold nanoparticles, *J. Phys. Chem. C,* **113**, pp. 5444–5449.

67. Pagona, G., Sandanayaka, A. S. D., Maigné A., Fan, G. Papavassiliou, G. C., Petsalakis, I. D., Steele, B. R., Tagmatarchis, N., Yudasaka, M., Iijima, S., and Ito, O. (2007). Electron-transfer on aqueous photoactive carbon nanohorn-pyrene-tetrathiafulvalene hybrids, *Chem. Eur. J.,* **13**, pp. 7600–7607.

68. Miyako, E., Deguchi, T., Nakajima, Y., Yudasaka, M., Hagihara, Y., Horie, M., Shichiri, M., Higuchi, Y., Yamashita, F., Hashida, M., Shigery, Y., and Iijima, S. (2012). Photothermic regulation of gene expression triggered by laser induced carbon nanohorns, *Proc. Natl. Acad. Sci. U.S.A.*, **109**, pp. 7523–7528.

69. König, K. (2000). Multiphoton microscopy in life sciences. *J. Microsc,* 200, pp. 83–104.

70. Miyako, E.,. Nagata, H, Hirano, K., Makita, Y., Nakayama, K.-I., and T. Hirotsu (2007). Near-infrared laser-triggered carbon nanohorns for selective elimination of microbes, *Nanotechnology*, **18**, pp. 475103.

71. Sarkar, S., Gurjarpadhye, A. A., Rylander, C. G., and Nichole Rylander, M. (2011). Optical properties of breast tumor phantoms containing carbon nanotubes and nanohorns, *J. Biomed. Opt.*, **16**, pp. 051304.

72. Zhang, M., Murakami, T., Ajima, K., Tsuchida, K., Sandanayaka, A. S. D., Ito, O., Iijima, S., and Yudasaka, M. (2008). Fabrication of ZnPc/protein nanohorns for double photodynamic and hyperthermic cancer phototherapy, *Proc. Natl. Acad. Sci.*, **105**, pp. 14773–14778.

73. X., Li, Peng, X.-H, Zheng, B.-D., Tang, J., Zhao Y., Zheng, B.-Y., Kea, M.-R., and Huang, J.-D. (2018). New application of phthalocyanine molecules: From photodynamic therapy to photothermal therapy by means of structural regulation rather than formation of aggregates, *Chem. Sci.,* **9**, pp. 2098–2104.

74. DeWitt, M. R., Pekkanen, A. M., Robertson, J., Rylander, C. G., and Rylander, M. N. (2014). Influence of hyperthermia on efficacy and uptake of carbon nanohorn-cisplatin conjugates, *J. Biomech. Eng.*, **136**, pp. 021003.

75. Isaac, K. M., Sabaraya, I. V., Ghousifam, N., Das, D., Pekkanen, A. M., Romanovicz, D. K., Long, T. E., Saleh, N. B., and Rylander, M. N. (2018). Functionalization of single-walled carbon nanohorns for simultaneous fluorescence imaging and cisplatin delivery in vitro, *Carbon,* **138**, pp. 309–318.

76. Chechetka, S. A., Pichon, B., Zhang, M., Yudasaka, M., Bégin-Colin, S., Bianco, A., and Miyako, E. (2015). Multifunctional carbon nanohorn complexes for cancer treatment, *Chem. Asian J.*, **10**, pp. 160–165.

77. Chechetka, S. A., Zhang, M., Yudasaka, M., Miyako, E. (2016). Physicochemically functionalized carbon nanohorns for multi-dimensional cancer elimination, *Carbon,* **97**, pp. 45–53.

78. Chechetka, S. A., Yuba, E., Kono, K., Yudasaka, M., Bianco, A., and Miyako, E. (2016). Magnetically and near-infrared light-powered supramolecular nanotransporters for the remote control of enzymatic reactions, *Angew. Chem. Int. Ed.*, **55**, pp. 6476–6481.

79. Lucío, M. I., Opri, R., Pinto, M., Scarsi, A., Fierro, J. L. G., Meneghetti, M., Fracasso, G., Prato, M., Vázquez, E., and Herrero, M. A. (2017). Targeted killing of prostate cancer cells using antibody-drug conjugated carbon nanohorns. *J. Mater. Chem. B,* **5**, pp. 8821–8832.

80. Guerra, J., Herrero, M. A., Carrión, B., Pérez-Martínez, F. C., Lucío, M., Rubio, N., Meneghetti, M., Prato, M., Ceña, V., and Vázquez, E. (2012). Carbon nanohorns functionalized with polyamidoamine dendrimers as efficient biocarrier materials for gene therapy, *Carbon,* **50**, pp. 2832–2844.

81. Pérez-Martínez, F. C., Carrión, B., Lucío, M. I., Rubio, N., Herrero, M. A., Vázquez, E., and Ceña, V. (2012). Enhanced docetaxel-mediated cytotoxicity in human prostate cancer cells through knockdown of cofilin-1 by carbon nanohorn delivered siRNA, *Biomaterials,* **33**, pp. 8152–8159.

82. Xu, J. Yudasaka, M., Kouraba, S., Sekido, M., Yamamoto, Y., and S. Iijima. (2008). Single wall carbon nanohorn as a drug carrier for controlled release, *Chemical Physics Letters,* **461**, pp. 189–192.

83. Zhao, Q., Li, N., Shu, C., Li, R., Ma, X., Li, X., Wang, R., and Zhong, W. (2014). Targeted cancer therapy based on single-wall carbon nanohorns with doxorubicin in vitro and in vivo. *J. Nanopart. Res.,* **16**, pp. 2497.

84. Chen, D., Wang, C., Jiang, F., Liu, Z., Shu, C., and Wan, L. J. (2014). In vitro and in vivo photothermally enhanced chemotherapy by single-walled carbon nanohorns as a drug delivery system, *J. Mater. Chem. B*, **2**, pp. 4726–4732.

85. Yang, J., Su, H., Sun, W. Cai, J., Liu, S., Chai, Y., and Zhang, C. (2018). Dual chemodrug-loaded single-walled carbon nanohorns for multimodal imaging-guided chemo-photothermal therapy of tumors and lung metastases, *Theranostics*, **8**, pp. 1966–1984.

86. Wang, R., Cui, H., Wang, J., Li, N., Zhao, Q., Zhou, Y., Lv, Z., and Zhong, W. (2016). Enhancing the antitumor effect of methotrexate: In intro and in vivo by a novel targeted single-walled carbon nanohorn-based drug delivery system, *RSC Adv.*, **6**, pp. 47272–47280.

87. Maeda, H., Wu, J., Sawa, T., Matsumura, Y., and Hori, K. (2000). Tumor vascular permeability and the EPR effect in macromolecular therapeutics: A review., *J. Control. Release*, **65**, pp. 271–284.

88. Brigger, I., Dubernet, C., and Couvreur, P. (2002). Nanoparticles in cancer therapy and diagnosis, *Adv. Drug Deliv. Rev.*, **54**, pp. 631– 651.

89. Wan, D. H., Zheng, B. Y., Ke, M. R., Duan, J. Y., Zheng, Y. Q., Yeh, C. K., and Huang, J. D. (2017). C-phycocyanin as a tumour-associated macrophage-targeted photosensitiser and a vehicle of phthalocyanine for enhanced photodynamic therapy, *Chem Commun*, **53**, pp. 4112–4115.

90. Gao, C., Jian, J., Lin, Z., Yu, Y. X., Jiang, B. P., Chen, H., and Shen, X. C. (2019). Hypericin-loaded carbon nanohorn hybrid for combined photodynamic and photothermal therapy in vivo, *Langmuir*, **35**, pp. 8228–8237.

91. Kiesslich, T., Krammer, B., and Plaetzer, K. (2006). Cellular mechanisms and prospective applications of hypericin in photodynamic therapy, *Curr. Med. Chem.*, **13**, pp. 2189–2204.

Chapter 8

Nanodispersions: A Tool for Efficient Dermal Drug Delivery

Ioanna Theochari, Ilias Matis, Vassiliki Papadimitriou, and Aristotelis Xenakis

Institute of Chemical Biology, National Hellenic Research Foundation, 48 Vassileos Constantinou Ave., 11635, Athens, Greece

arisx@eie.gr

The skin is one of the most challenging biological targets as it constitutes the body's primary defense against a variety of environmental attacks. As a barrier, it protects against external threats such as infectious agents, chemicals, and allergens. Many research groups have focused on the development of formulations that can be administered topically to protect the skin or even heal serious skin damage, including wound healing, skin irritations, and various types of skin cancer, including melanoma. Dermal drug delivery via nanodispersions, namely, microemulsions, nanoemulsions, and solid-in-oil (S/O) nanodispersions, has been highly investigated especially during the past decade. Such formulations have proven to be efficient for both transdermal and dermal delivery of lipophilic or hydrophilic compounds, as they manage to overcome the skin barrier through an enhanced skin penetration capacity.

Functional Materials in Biomedical Applications
Edited by Costas Demetzos, Natassa Pippa, and Nikolaos Naziris

ISBN 978-981-4968-65-2 (Hardcover), 978-1-003-41146-8 (eBook)
www.jennystanford.com

Microemulsions and nanoemulsions are considered colloidal nanodispersions that can be formulated by mixing water, oil, and surfactants; the ratio of which affects their physicochemical properties, biocompatibility, and their penetration efficacy. In this context, the relation between a nanodispersion's composition and its dermal drug delivery efficacy still remains a great challenge. Thus, it is essential to place emphasis on the formulation and structural characterization of such systems, in order to reveal their potency in dermal drug delivery. Key factors, including biocompatibility and enhanced penetration, play an important role in the rational design of such formulations and are strongly affected by their properties. This chapter is a systemic review of the literature spanning the last five years, focusing on the use of nanodispersions as efficient drug delivery systems in dermal applications, centering on skin cancer.

8.1 Introduction

Nanotechnology is a cutting-edge, multidisciplinary field that brings together the science and technology of nanosized, and nanostructured materials. Its broad applicability has resulted among others in different research and industrial applications in nutrition, cosmetics, nutraceuticals, and nanomedicine. The term "nanomedicine" was firstly mentioned in the literature in the late 1960s. However, only a few research groups dealt with this field, until the early 2000s when an increase in the number of publications was observed, explained by greater access to nanomedicine-related funds, and advancements in the formulation technologies [1].

Nanomaterials are defined as materials with size ranges in the nanoscale, characterized by varying physical, chemical, and biological properties. Such materials have found many applications in medicine, especially in the diagnosis and therapy of a variety of diseases and pathological conditions. Nanomedicine enables the formulation and monitoring of nanoscaled vesicles, which effectively carry and release different kinds of cargo such as drugs/lead compounds, peptides, proteins, nutrients, and antioxidants. Their considerable encapsulation capability and capacity for overcoming biological barriers, make them ideal candidates for the effective delivery of bioactive compounds through various routes of administration, including oral, parenteral, topical, transdermal, nasal, and ocular [2, 3].

Nanocarriers have been extensively studied in the transport and effective release of a variety of drugs and/or bioactive compounds with varying polarity, hydrophilicity, and lipophilicity. Overall, research has shown an increased interest in the delivery of lipophilic compounds, as the majority of drugs and lead compounds present low or no solubility in water. The experimental design of delivery systems and the drugs' distribution profile, pharmacokinetics, and release were always combined with a deep understanding of the related biological background, depending on the target tissue. The formulation of biocompatible and/or biodegradable delivery systems, capable of enhancing the penetration of drugs through biological barriers and, at the same time, increasing the drugs' bioavailability in blood circulation is the greatest challenge that researchers face [4]. Moreover, the formulation of a drug delivery system should take into consideration any potential therapeutic compound toxicities and off-target interactions, minimizing dosages to limit potential side effects. To this effect, the rational design of nanoformulations, in combination with the continued investigation of permeation and release mechanisms, satisfies the current demand for improved drug bioavailability.

In the context of effective delivery systems, several literature reports on different types of nanocarriers have been included in this chapter, with an explicit focus on nanodispersions. These include microemulsions, nanoemulsions, and S/O drug-delivery systems that present interest for medicinal and pharmacological applications in skin delivery (Fig. 8.1). This systemic literature review refers to studies that were published in the past five years, highlighting the significant contribution of such systems in basic and applied research, as carriers of drugs for skin delivery.

The skin is regarded as the largest organ in the body and a challenging obstacle in the delivery of bioactive compounds. Though several physicochemical factors, such as the partition coefficient (logP), molecular mass, water solubility, and dissociation constant (pKa) influence the permeability of a chosen compound, nanocarriers have proven efficient in facilitating or improving dermal drug delivery. As such, nanodispersions are intensively studied as suitable carriers for topical delivery, owing to certain attractive advantages: drug encapsulation in nanodispersions provides enhanced stability and bioavailability and decreased side effects [5], while easy administration and painless application suggest a potential for high patient compliance.

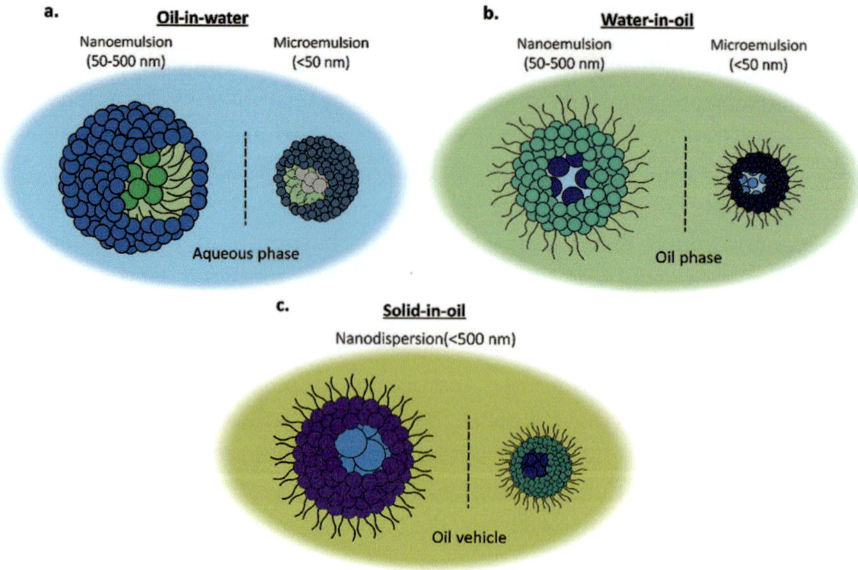

Figure 8.1 Representations of (a) oil-in-water (O/W) and (b) water-in-oil (W/O) nano- and micro-emulsions, and (c) S/O nanodispersions.

There are various mechanisms by which nanocarriers may interact with skin tissue and deliver their cargo: (a) integration with lipids, (b) passage through the spaces between skin cells, (c) penetration by osmotic phenomena, caused by the high water content beneath stratum corneum, (d) transcellular penetration (through the keratinocytes), (e) absorption through stratum corneum by the release of their cargo and diffusion, and (f) passage through hair follicles and sebaceous glands [6].

There are three different routes described in the literature, concerning the delivery of drugs through human skin; epidermal administration is achieved when the applied drug does not penetrate deeper skin layers and is localized on the skin surface. This is the case for cosmetics, nutraceuticals, repellents, and UV-protection creams. Topical administration is achieved when the applied drug is localized in deeper regions of the skin (epidermis, dermis), without being distributed to other organs via blood circulation. Transdermal administration is achieved when the drug penetrates through skin layers and is systemically distributed by the blood circulation to other tissues. Various factors such as skin type, drug properties, and physicochemical properties of nanocarriers affect the permeation of the drug, thus when monitoring the type of administration, it is important to regulate these features [7].

The mechanisms by which the loaded drugs are released through nanodispersions (microemulsions, nanoemulsions, and S/O nanodispersions) in dermal drug delivery, are being studied by several research groups. Furthermore, in the literature, various penetration enhancers that facilitate the delivery of bioactive compounds through the skin, have been evaluated. Surfactants and co-surfactants (such as propylene glycol), have been proposed as penetration enhancers, as they interfere both with lipids present in the stratum corneum and with keratin. There are four types of surfactants, categorized by charge: (a) cationic (positively charged), (b) anionic (negatively charged), (c) non-ionic (neutral), and (d) zwitterionic (possessing both positive and negative charge) [8]. Cationic surfactants were proven more efficient when compared to anionic or non-ionic ones. However, skin irritation has been linked to the effects of cationic surfactants and as a result in the case of the dermal route, non-ionic surfactants are regarded as safer (generally recognized as safe [GRAS]).

Co-surfactants are molecules that reduce the interfacial tension and increase the flexibility of the oil-water interface, in combination with surfactants. Propylene glycol, esters, fatty acids, terpenes, and terpenoids are some of such molecules that may be used to formulate nanodispersions to enhance skin penetration, without using organic solvents such as dimethyl sulfoxide (DMSO), which can cause irritations or display toxicity [7, 9, 10]. Indeed, many research groups have concluded that various symptoms, such as erythema, scaling, feeling of burning, and systemic symptoms, appeared after the application of DMSO as a skin penetration enhancer [11].

8.2 Nanodispersions: Principles and Physicochemical Properties

8.2.1 Microemulsions

As defined by Danielsson and Lindmann, the term "microemulsion" refers to a thermodynamically stable, optically isotropic liquid solution system, which is formed spontaneously by mixing oils, surfactants, and aqueous phase [12]. Microemulsions were first reported in 1943, by Hoar and Schulman who formulated homogeneous, monophasic formulation starting from a milky solution and hexanol [13]. Up to 1960, microemulsion research had furtherly expanded, by studying both the formation of microemulsions and their physicochemical background [14, 15].

Microemulsions consist of an aqueous phase, an oil phase, and surfactants. Water insoluble liquids are defined as "oils" and in terms of formulation suitability, different compounds and mixtures can be used. There are various oils that can be used in microemulsions' formulations and thus, the application of microemulsion is critical for the researcher's decision. In the food, cosmetic, and pharmaceutical industries, the oils that are used must be safe and biocompatible; olive oil (extra virgin or refined), sunflower oil, soybean oil, medium chain triglyceride, isopropyl myristate, isopropyl palmitate, but also essential oils (limonene, thyme, oregano, etc.) are typical examples of oils, reported in the literature [16].

A surfactant molecule is composed of two district regions; a polar head oriented toward the aqueous phase and a non-polar tail oriented toward the oil phase. Due to the presence of surfactants, the O/W interface increases, and thus, the aqueous and oil phase disperse within each other, as the surface tension decreases. Surfactants should also present low cytotoxicity and high biocompatibility, when used for the formulation of microemulsions for food, pharmaceutical, and cosmetics applications. Non-ionic surfactants, such as polysorbates, sugar and sorbitan esters, labrasol, poloxamers, saponins, are preferred for such applications, as indicated by several studies [17, 18]. Zwitterionic surfactants, such as phospholipids, have also been proven safe and efficient [19]. Nevertheless, as mentioned previously, co-surfactants can often be employed as emulsification enhancers.

Microemulsions are classified into three main categories: W/O microemulsions, O/W microemulsions, and bicontinuous structures [20]. W/O microemulsions are systems where water droplets are dispersed in the oil phase (reverse micelles), whereas O/W microemulsions refer to systems where oil droplets are dispersed in the aqueous phase. Bicontinuous structures are formulated using comparable quantities of water and oil, and since the surfactant molecules are less tightly packed their structure can be described as continuous water and oil regions, separated by surfactant monolayers [19, 21, 22]. Microemulsions are suitable systems to encapsulate bioactives of different polarities, including lipophilic, amphiphilic, or hydrophilic compounds. Therefore, microemulsions can contribute to the increase of both the solubilization and bioavailability of water-insoluble or slightly soluble bioactive compounds [23].

8.2.2 Nanoemulsions

Nanoemulsions are defined as colloidal dispersions consisting of two immiscible liquids (water and oil) and surfactants. A nanoemulsion's appearance differs, depending on the diameter of the spherical droplets; it ranges between 50 to 200 nm and thus, nanoemulsions can be clear and become turbid as the size of the nanodroplet increases. In comparison to microemulsions, which exhibit thermodynamic stability, nanoemulsions are described as kinetically stable systems, due to the destabilization phenomena that occur during storage [20]. However, their stability can be adjusted through optimization of their composition, storage conditions, and the emulsification method used to produce them. Nanoemulsions, cannot be formed spontaneously and as a result, energy input is essential for their formulation. They can be formed by using either high-energy methods (high-pressure homogenization, ultrasonication) or low-energy methods (phase inversion temperature [PIT], self-emulsification, emulsion inversion point [EIP]) [24]. These different approaches are described below.

Nanoemulsion components are similar to those used in microemulsion formulations, although nanoemulsions present different properties. The scientific community uses the term "nanoemulsion" when describing emulsions whose droplets are on a sub-micrometer scale. Moreover, microemulsions were studied prior to nanoemulsions and the nomenclature has persisted although the average diameter of nanoemulsions droplets is greater compared to microemulsions. Nanoemulsions find applications in many fields including the food, pharmaceutical, cosmetics, and agrochemical industries [25, 26]. It is important to note that nanoemulsions contain lower quantities of surfactants compared to microemulsions. This fact is advantageous, especially in applications where the quantity of surfactants is restricted by legislation. Table 8.1 presents the most common differences between micro- and nano-emulsions, in terms of formulation, physicochemical properties, and stability.

Table 8.1 Differences between microemulsions, nanoemulsions, and S/O nanodispersions [20]

	Microemulsions	Nanoemulsions	S/O nanodispersions
Composition	Oil, water, surfactants/co-surfactants	Oil, water, surfactants/co-surfactants	Oil, surfactants
Stability	Thermodynamically stable	Kinetically stable	Thermodynamically stable
Appearance	Transparent/clear	Clear, turbid, or milky	Clear, turbid, or milky
Size of droplets	5–50 nm	50–200 nm	<500 nm
Emulsification methods	Spontaneous formulation	High-pressure homogenization, ultrasonication, PIT, self-emulsification, EIP	High-pressure homogenization, ultrasonication, rotor-stator
Destabilization phenomena	Temperature, pH value	Ostwald ripening, sedimentation, coalescence, flocculation, creaming	Ostwald ripening, aggregation

8.2.3 Solid-in-Oil Nanodispersions

S/O nanodispersions consist of nanocarriers for hydrophilic compounds, dispersed in a lipophilic vehicle. While they are lipid-based systems, they do not constitute a separate type of emulsion since they are derived from W/O micro- or nano-emulsions. S/O nanodispersions are produced from such W/O emulsions by removing the aqueous phase, creating a core that consists of a hydrophilic powder, surrounded by a surfactant that facilitates the dispersion in a lipophilic vehicle. Nanocarrier sizes for such W/O emulsions and S/O nanodispersions typically range below 500 nm in diameter. However, the evaporation of the aqueous phase in S/O nanodispersions allows them to maintain a lower surface tension between the hydrophilic core and the oil phase. The lack of water also allows for smaller nanocarrier sizes with higher hydrophilic loads [27]. S/O nanodispersions are also more stable in storage compared to W/O emulsions and are less prone to Ostwald ripening [28, 29]. Their preparation typically consists of generating a W/O emulsion, from which both the aqueous and the organic phases are removed by lyophilization. The lyophilized nanocarriers are then resuspended in the oil vehicle of choice resulting in the final S/O nanodispersion.

S/O nanodispersions have become popular in transdermal drug delivery, especially in cases where the intended cargo consists of proteins or peptides. Most of such biomolecules show limited penetration of the stratum corneum because of their hydrophilic nature, therefore their transdermal delivery stands to benefit from nanocarriers dispersed in an oil vehicle. Isopropyl myristate is a commonly used oil vehicle in transdermal delivery S/O systems since it has been deemed safe for use in several pharmaceutical and cosmetic products. Moreover, it facilitates the permeation of the stratum corneum by interacting with its lipids, causing their partial dissolution [30]. However, the preparation of S/O uses an oil phase like cyclohexane, during the emulsification process that allows surfactant solubilization. The organic solvent is usually required to have a boiling point similar to, or lower than that of water, since it will also be evaporated during the lyophilization process, to allow redispersion of the resulting powder in a suitable oil vehicle. Finally, when the S/O is used to encapsulate a protein, the surfactant can be chosen on the basis of favorable interactions with the protein, such as an ability to form a complex with the protein cargo [31].

8.2.4 Emulsification Methods

Microemulsions and nanoemulsions possess different properties, despite sharing a similar physicochemical background. Despite the fact that both systems can be formulated using oil, water, and surfactant(s) in different ratios, the emulsification process strongly affects the structural characteristics and the stability of each formulation. Microemulsions do not require energy input for their formulation, as they form spontaneously by mixing the aqueous and oil phase with the surfactant at specific ratios. Therefore, microemulsions are considered thermodynamically stable systems and remain transparent and monophasic under specific conditions (given temperature, pH value, etc.).

On the other hand, nanoemulsions require an energy input for their formulation. In particular, nanoemulsions can be formulated by following one of two approaches extensively described in the literature: high- or low-energy formulation. Their primary difference involves the amount of external energy needed to reduce the size of a droplet. As the amount of energy increases, the quantity of surfactant can be reduced [20, 32]. Mechanical stirring is a commonly used method to prepare macroemulsions. In the case of nanoemulsions, a higher amount of energy or a higher quantity of surfactant is essential to obtain droplets on the nanoscale.

High-energy input can be obtained by various techniques such as high shear stirrer, high-pressure homogenizer, microfluidizer, and ultrasonic device. In literature, the size of nanodroplets is often correlated with the type of oil phase, aqueous phase, surfactant, applied pressure or ultrasound, number of cycles (in case of high-pressure homogenization), or the emulsification time [33–35]. It has been reported that the size of nanodroplets depends on the duration of the emulsification process, as the longer the emulsification lasts, the smaller the nanodroplets that can be formulated. Overall, the energy input from the utilized device plays also a crucial role in nanodroplet size [24, 34].

High-pressure homogenization is based on the application of high pressure on a system composed of two immiscible liquids (oil and water), as it is pumped through a valve. The generated shearing stress reduces the diameter of the dispersed nanodroplets and aids the formulation of nanodroplets in the range of 50–200 nm. Prior to emulsification, the components are mixed under mechanical stirring to prepare a macroemulsion or coarse emulsion, which will then pass through the valve. As the pump increases the pressure, the sample flows through the stream and droplets break up [36]. Likewise, a microfluidizer provides a comparable magnitude of pressure generated by a pump. The microfluidizer technique relies on the flow of an emulsion through two-separate streams that collide with each other, causing the reduction of droplet size. The reduction occurs due to high agitation and shear caused by this collision [37]. Moreover, during ultrasonic emulsification, high shear forces are applied by high-power ultrasound. Prior to sonication, the components of the system are mixed under mechanical stirring to prepare a macroemulsion. Then, an interfacial acoustic wave facilitates the dispersion of the droplets of one phase into the other. Droplets further break up as a result of the acoustic waves, resulting in a formulation sized on the nanoscale [38].

A low-energy approach is often adapted to prepare stable nanoemulsions by various methods, namely, PIT, self-emulsification, emulsification by low shearing rate, and EIP [39, 40]. The spontaneous curvature of the surfactant's layer can be affected by different factors such as temperature, pH value, and salinity. The alteration of one or more factors during formulation may lead to the conversion of an O/W emulsion to a W/O emulsion and vice versa [41]. Low-energy methods possess certain advantages compared to high-energy methods due to their low cost in terms of equipment and energy input. However, their use is subjected to restrictions and limitations, such as selecting the proper combination of oils and surfactants to form stable nanoemulsions. The EIP technique describes the formation of nanosized systems, based on the spontaneous formation of nanodroplets. EIP can be applied by altering the composition in an initial mixture of oil, water, and surfactant [42]. The self-emulsification process can be performed by diluting a microemulsion with its continuous phase under constant temperature and results in a nanoemulsion without phase transitions [43]. Nanoemulsions can also be formulated under low-energy conditions by subjecting a conventional emulsion to a low shear rate, which breaks the emulsion droplets into smaller droplets sized in the nanoscale [40, 44].

8.3 Nanodispersions in Dermal and Transdermal Drug Delivery

Both micro- and nano-emulsions have been placed at the epicenter of nanomedicine research, as they affect the pharmacokinetics and the bio-distribution of the encapsulated compounds. As vehicles, micro- and nano-emulsions, facilitate the penetration of their cargo through a biological barrier, while protecting it from a variety of factors (chemical alteration/ enzymatic degradation, oxidation, etc.) [14]. Both transdermal and dermal drug delivery provides a simple and convenient treatment for patients, as the administration is painless and in most cases, the patient can apply the formulation without the guidance of their doctor. The enhancement of skin penetration and the increase in bioavailability of poorly soluble drugs have been extensively researched by various research groups [45].

The skin is not only the largest organ in the human body but also one of its principal biological barriers. The dermal route is restricted to any drugs and compounds that intend to treat skin disorders such as skin inflammation or irritation, acne, psoriasis, and various types of skin cancer, such as melanoma. On the other hand, the transdermal route offers accessibility to blood circulation and thus, nanodispersions are ideal vesicles for drugs that target other tissues. In the literature, many research groups focused on transdermal applications of nanodispersions, in order to encapsulate and deliver drugs and compounds for modulation of blood glucose (e.g., insulin), inflammation (e.g., non-steroid anti-inflammatory drugs [NSAIDs]), and other applications [46, 47].

8.3.1 Skin Cancer

Skin, as a biological system, serves as a model target for nanodispersions, as indicated by intensive research efforts worldwide. It acts as the body's pre-eminent organ against a variety of environmental attacks and at the same time is constantly affected by them. Ultraviolet sunlight (UV-A, UV-B, UV-C), a form of high-energy electromagnetic radiation, is the primary cause of genotoxic effects on all living organisms. In particular, UV-B radiation (280–320 nm) causes damage to biological macromolecules, e.g., DNA, and induces acute inflammatory skin disorders, such as erythema. Chronic exposure to UVB radiation may lead to premature skin aging, immunosuppression, and skin cancer [48]. Research in recent years has focused on the development of topical formulations that can protect the skin from UV radiation or treat serious skin disorders, including cancer.

The most common types of skin cancer, basal cell carcinoma, and squamous cell carcinoma, are potentially curable either surgically or by administering specific chemotherapeutic drugs. Melanoma is an exception as it represents 5–7% of malignant skin diseases and is responsible for 75% of deaths from skin tumors. Melanoma shows resistance to conventional anti-neoplastic treatments and therefore is one of the most demanding and difficult topics in oncology [49]. Additionally, conventional chemotherapy causes significant side effects, as it also affects the proliferation rate of normal, non-cancerous cells. Therefore, it is necessary to develop innovative approaches for targeting cancer tissues that will overcome conventional chemotherapies to address the major clinical problem of tumor chemo-resistance [50]. The development of nanodispersions for the encapsulation of chemotherapeutic drugs, combined with their controlled release toward cancer tissues, reflects this necessity. In literature, the use of nanodispersions against skin cancer is well-documented and established [51–57]. This review intends to highlight the latest advances in the use of nanodispersions in the skin delivery of drugs, especially for cancer treatment.

The majority of chemotherapeutic agents are slightly soluble or insoluble in water. Therefore, the bioavailability of these compounds is limited, unless they are administered through nanocarriers, such as those in nanodispersions. As this review focuses primarily on nanodispersions for the treatment of skin cancer, most of the formulations are created for topical administration. Recently, Wu et al. prepared an O/W microemulsion to encapsulate 3,5,4′-trimethoxy-trans-stilbene (BTM) for transdermal application proposed for melanoma treatment. In vitro and in vivo assessment revealed the high penetration profile of BTM and its significant uptake by melanoma cells. Compared to non-encapsulated BTM, they proved both the efficacy of the microemulsion to deliver BTM and also its low toxicity, underlying the necessity to restrict the potential side effects of chemotherapy [58]. Meanwhile, oral administration of drugs against various skin cancers is limited due to systemic side effects. To overcome these side effects, cutaneous drug delivery has been extensively investigated as an alternative route of treatment. Olesen et al. developed an O/W microemulsion stabilized by polysorbate 80 to encapsulate Vismodegib, a commercially available drug for basal-cell carcinoma treatment. In vivo assessment of pig skin was performed to investigate both safety of the formulation and skin biodistribution of the released drug [59, 60]. Overall, nanodispersions facilitate the drug delivery of chemotherapeutic drugs through the skin, thus, they can increase their bioavailability and biodistribution within the skin tissue and consequently improve drug efficiency.

Another useful feature of nanodispersions is that they can aid in the assessment of lead compounds, designed for the treatment of various types of skin cancers. In particular, Theochari et al. suggested the use of microemulsion composed of PBS buffer, Tween 80, and triacetin to encapsulate both anticancer drugs and lead compounds designed for cancer types related to $BRAF^{V600E}$ mutation. The research group evaluated the microemulsions' cytotoxic activity and cell death mechanism against melanoma in vitro, as well as the release profile of the encapsulated compound through ex vivo experiments, using porcine ear skin [61–63].

Late-stage and metastatic melanoma present a low survival rate due to chemoresistance to most applied drugs and the severe side effects of chemotherapy. Consequently, an alternative combination of anti-melanoma drugs and nanotechnology principles, such as the use of nanoemulsions, is currently under investigation. In this context, Giacone et al. developed nanoemulsions for topical delivery of a cytotoxic compound, known as Piplartine (piperlongumine). In order to enhance the penetration of the encapsulated compound, nanoemulsions were modified by adding chitosan or sodium alginate. The effects of chitosan or sodium alginate in the modified nanoemulsion were evaluated in terms of its physicochemical properties, Piplartine delivery, and formulation efficacy. The formulated nanoemulsion was effective against 2D and 3D skin cancer models [64]. In another study, the enhanced penetration of encapsulated Piplartine was confirmed, as it exhibited 1.5 times greater oral bioavailability in melanoma-induced mice when loaded in nanoemulsion [65].

Dalmolin et al. formulated a cationic nanoemulsion to solubilize zinc phthalocyanine (ZnPc), a promising drug against melanoma. The structural characterization of the formulation was followed by in vitro and in vivo cutaneous and tumor penetration studies. The nanoemulsion solubilized 2.5-fold more phthalocyanine compared to a conventional macroemulsion that was used as a reference. At the same concentration of phthalocyanine, in vitro penetration studies showed that the penetration of the drug, when encapsulated in nanoemulsion, was increased up to 4-fold in the viable layers of the skin, when compared to the macroemulsion, highlighting the potentially significant contribution of such nanosystems in transcutaneous drug delivery [66].

Despite the apparent usefulness of micro- and nano-emulsions in the delivery of mostly lipophilic cancer therapeutics, in recent years, the development of peptide and protein therapeutics against various types of cancers has revealed an increasing need for carriers of such hydrophilic biomolecules. Lipid-based carriers like liposomes have shown promise for the delivery of such therapeutics, however, S/O nanodispersions display certain advantages that suit the requirements of cancer treatment via transcutaneous delivery, since the lipophilic skin barrier prohibits penetration of hydrophilic biomolecules. The S/O nanodispersions' main advantage in transcutaneous delivery is found in the use of an oil vehicle like isopropyl myristate for the dispersion, which can partially dissolve the lipids of the stratum corneum and facilitate the diffusion of the carrier in it [30, 67]. In a recent article by Wakabayashi et al., the authors showed the potential of S/O nanodispersions for use as cancer vaccines against melanoma, by showing that a S/O nanodispersion that carried the TRP-$2_{180-188}$ peptide antigen, could suppress melanoma growth on tumor-bearing mice [68].

In a similar, later study by the same group, the authors tested the ability of the tumor-associated antigen (TAA), ovalbumin, to elicit an immune response against E.G7-OVA tumors in mice, when the antigen was delivered transcutaneously by a S/O nanodispersion that contained the TLR7/8 ligand Resiquimod in the oil vehicle [69]. The TAA and the TLR ligand are capable of producing an immune response and their co-delivery to dendritic cells of the skin, i.e., Langerhans cells, which are part of a strategy to induce a strong immune reaction while avoiding a non-specific activation of the immune system [70, 71]. In this study, the authors showed that both the ovalbumin antigen and Resiquimod were able to transcutaneously reach Langerhans cells in the epidermal layer of the skin, and cause an ensuing antitumor immunization that suppressed E.G7-OVA tumor growth in a specific manner [69]. This study showcased the potential of S/O nanodispersions as a tool that employs the interconnectedness of the immune system, to achieve immunization against more than skin cancers.

8.3.2 Acne and Dermal Inflammation

Microemulsions and nanoemulsions have been assessed for their efficacy toward inflammatory skin pathologies such as acne [72, 73]. Acne vulgaris is a common inflammatory skin condition, which is treated using drugs such as tretinoin. O/W micro- or nano-emulsions are usually preferred for anti-acne systems, due to their low viscosity and low concentration of oil phase, as required in dermatologic preparations [74]. Sabouri et al. developed an O/W nanoemulsion with a particle size of 150 nm. They performed a pilot study, which confirmed the clinical safety of the formulation in humans and also showed significant results against acne vulgaris lesions within six weeks of topical application [75]. In another work by Hosny et al., the authors formulated a self-emulsifying nanoemulsion to deliver isotretinoin in combination with quercetin to assess its efficacy toward acne vulgaris. In vitro and ex vivo permeation studies confirmed the enhanced permeation of the encapsulated compounds, while in vivo studies further enhanced the obtained results [76].

Patel et al. formulated a microemulsion to encapsulate tazarotene as a topical therapy for acne. Microemulsion consisted of 12% isopropyl myristate, 15% Labrasol-Cremophor-RH 40 (1:1), 15% Capmul MCM, and 58% water as a continuous phase. The skin uptake of tazarotene through rat skin was assessed for both free and encapsulated tazarotene. The results indicated that the penetration of encapsulated tazarotene was enhanced compared to its free form. The surface epithelium lining and the granular cellular structure of the skin were not affected by the treatment [77]. Shao et al. suggested microemulsions to encapsulate adapalene in order to support epidermal penetration, dermal retention, and skin bioavailability compared to a commercial formulation. The results obtained from the pharmacodynamics assessment showed that the effect of encapsulated adapalene was more efficient compared to Differin® in the acne model of rabbit auricle [78].

Tretinoin is also one of the most tested bioactive compounds, incorporated in microemulsions and nanoemulsions for the treatment of acne. Wani et al. developed a microemulsion-based spray comprised basil oil, Kolliphor RH40, ethanol, and water for the skin delivery of isotretinoin. Moreover, they prepared a microemulsion-based gel using Carbopol ETD 2020 for comparison. The formulations were evaluated for their physicochemical properties and their antibacterial activity against *Propionibacterium acnes*, *Staphylococcus epidermidis*, and *Staphylococcus aureus*, all responsible for acne vulgaris incidents. The microemulsion-based spray exhibited higher photostability, better patient compliance, antibacterial activity, and higher penetration compared to microemulsion-based gel [79]. Pajic et al. developed biocompatible microemulsions for dermal delivery of adapalene, a retinoid used for acne therapy. In vivo assessment of the formulation presented high safety profiles of placebo microemulsions. Ex vivo experiments provided data on the amount of adapalene that penetrated porcine skin, under an infinite dosage. This data indicated that the quantity of released adapalene from microemulsions was comparable to a chosen commercial product [80].

8.3.3 Psoriasis

Psoriasis is a chronic skin disease affecting 2–4% of the population. Approximately 80% of total cases can be described as moderate and are treatable by topical application of corticosteroids. However, in more severe cases, no single treatment is efficient [81]. A possible alternative therapy is the administration of cyclosporine, an immunosuppressant cyclic peptide that is administered orally in most cases. Benigni et al. developed nine microemulsions (five Tween 80-based and four Tocopheryl Polyethylene Glycol 1000 Succinate [TPGS]-based), possessing low viscosity and encapsulated 6 mg/g cyclosporine to assess the release of the drug through ex vivo experiments [82]. TPGS has been also used by other research groups as a surfactant for the formulation of microemulsions for psoriasis treatment, as it serves as an enhancer of percutaneous delivery [83]. In addition, methotrexate (MTX) is an immunosuppressive drug in the treatment of skin disorders such as psoriasis, however, MTX is hepatotoxic. Recently, a research group developed a potent delivery system for MTX, based on microemulsions composed of a glycol copolymer-based silicone fluid (SFGC) as their oil phase, polyether functional siloxane (PFS) as their surfactant, and a carbomer homopolymer type A (C971) dispersion at 0.5% (w/w) as their aqueous phase [84].

Rajitha et al. composed a chaulmoogra oil-based nanoemulsion, loaded with MTX, and assessed its efficacy through in vitro, ex vivo, and in vivo experiments. Their results indicated superior anti-psoriatic efficacy, accompanied by remarkable skin retention when compared to an orally administered MTX tablet [85]. In another slightly older study by Yang et al., MTX was encapsulated in a S/O nanodispersion using non-ionic surfactants, isopropyl myristate as oil vehicle basic amino acids to enhance the surfactant-MTX complex stability. Their results indicated that the generated S/O nanocarriers were able to better penetrate the stratum corneum compared to other systems such as liposomes [86]. Nanoemulsions have also been studied for the encapsulation of cyclosporine. In vitro release studies have proven the efficacy of nanoemulsions across both rat skin and a synthetic membrane, while in vivo skin analyses have shown increases in skin hydration at the stratum corneum [87, 88].

8.4 Conclusion

An increasing portion of current literature reflects a scientific interest in the development of nanodispersions as a tool for dermal applications. Most studies have focused on the optimization of formulations in terms of stability, increased bioavailability of their cargo, and reduction of side effects upon administration. On the other hand, there is a lack of research at the clinical level despite the many promising pre-clinical results. Due to their unique characteristics, nanodispersions can be designed to overcome biological barriers such as the skin and facilitate the administration of lipophilic and hydrophilic substances.

Both micro- and nano-emulsions have been successfully developed for different aspects of skin drug delivery such as cancer treatment, acne/skin inflammation, and psoriasis; in all cases, formulations have presented encouraging results in dermal drug delivery due to the enhanced drug penetration through the skin barrier. Similarly, S/O nanodispersions show promise as tools against dermal and other types of cancer. They can effectively deliver peptide and protein cargos through the stratum corneum by relying on the lipophilic nature of the utilized vehicle, while protecting the hydrophilic load in a surfactant-encased vehicle.

References

1. Boisseau, P. and Loubaton, B. (2011). Nanomedicine, nanotechnology in medicine. *Comptes Rendus Phys.*, **12**, pp. 620–636.
2. Fanun, M. (2012). Microemulsions as delivery systems. *Curr. Opin. Colloid Interface Sci.*, **17**, pp. 306–313.

3. Prakash, U. and Thiagarajan, P. (2011). Nanoemulsions for drug delivery through different routes. *Res. Biotechnol.*, **2**, pp. 61–69.
4. Vasir, J. K. and Labhasetwar, V. (2007). Biodegradable nanoparticles for cytosolic delivery of therapeutics. *Adv. Drug Deliv. Rev.*, **59**, pp. 718–728.
5. Shakeel, F., Shafiq, S., Haq, N., Alanazi, F. K., and Alsarra, I. A. (2012). Nanoemulsions as potential vehicles for transdermal and dermal delivery of hydrophobic compounds: An overview. *Expert Opin. Drug Deliv.*, **9**, pp. 953–974.
6. Raza, K., Kumar, M., Kumar, P., Malik, R., Sharma, G., Kaur, M., and Katare, O. P. (2014). Topical delivery of aceclofenac: Challenges and promises of novel drug delivery systems. *Biomed Res. Int.*, **2014**, pp. 1–12.
7. Trommer, H. and Neubert, R. H. H. (2006). Overcoming the stratum corneum: The modulation of skin penetration: A review. *Skin Pharmacol. Physiol.*, **19**, pp. 106–121.
8. Rahimpour, A., Madaeni, S. S., and Mansourpanah, Y. (2007). The effect of anionic, non-ionic and cationic surfactants on morphology and performance of polyethersulfone ultrafiltration membranes for milk concentration. *J. Memb. Sci.*, **296**, pp. 110–121.
9. Larrucea, E., Arellano, A., Santoyo, S., and Ygartua, P. (2001). Combined effect of oleic acid and propylene glycol on the percutaneous penetration of tenoxicam and its retention in the skin. *Eur. J. Pharm. Biopharm.*, **52**, pp. 113–119.
10. Cázares-Delgadillo, J., Naik, A., Kalia, Y. N., Quintanar-Guerrero, D., and Ganem-Quintanar, A. (2005). Skin permeation enhancement by sucrose esters: A pH-dependent phenomenon. *Int. J. Pharm.*, **297**, pp. 204–212.
11. Iliev, D., Hinnen, U., and Elsner, P. (1997). Skin roughness is negatively correlated to irritation with DMSO, but not with NaOH and SLS. *Exp. Dermatol.*, **6**, pp. 157–160.
12. Danielsson, I. and Lindman, B. (1981). The definition of microemulsion. *Colloids Surf.*, **3**, pp. 391–392.
13. Hoar, T. P. and Schulman, J. H. (1943). Transparent water-in-oil dispersions: The oleopathic hydro-micelle. *Nature*, **152**, pp. 102–103.
14. Schulman, J. H. and Montagne, J. B. (1961). Formation of microemulsions by amino alkyl alcohols. *Ann. N. Y. Acad. Sci.*, **92**, pp. 366–371.
15. Stoeckenius, W., Schulman, J. H., and Prince, L. M. (1960). The structure of myelin figures and microemulsions as observed with the electron microscope. *Kolloid-Zeitschrift*, **169**, pp. 170–180.

16. Gupta, S. and Moulik, S. P. (2008). Biocompatible microemulsions and their prospective uses in drug delivery. *J. Pharm. Sci.*, **97**, pp. 22–45.

17. Szuts, A. and Szabó-Révész, P. (2012). Sucrose esters as natural surfactants in drug delivery systems: A mini-review. *Int. J. Pharm.*, **433**, pp. 1–9.

18. Lawrence, M. J. and Rees, G. D. (2012). Microemulsion-based media as novel drug delivery systems. *Adv. Drug Deliv. Rev.*, **64**, pp. 175–193.

19. Flanagan, J. and Singh, H. (2006). Microemulsions: A potential delivery system for bioactives in food. *Crit. Rev. Food Sci. Nutr.*, **46**, pp. 221–237.

20. McClements, D. J. (2012). Nanoemulsions versus microemulsions: Terminology, differences, and similarities. *Soft Matter*, **8**, pp. 1719–1729.

21. McClements, D. J. (2011). Edible nanoemulsions: Fabrication, properties, and functional performance. *Soft Matter*, **7**, pp. 2297–2316.

22. Yu, Z. J. and Neuman, R. D. (1995). Reversed micellar solution-to-bicontinuous microemulsion transition in sodium bis(2-ethylhexyl) phosphate/n-heptane/water system. *Langmuir*, **11**, pp. 1081–1086.

23. Fanun, M. (2009). Properties of microemulsions based on mixed nonionic surfactants and mixed oils. *J. Mol. Liq.*, **150**, pp. 25–32.

24. Solans, C., Izquierdo, P., Nolla, J., Azemar, N., and Garcia-Celma, M. J. (2005). Nano-emulsions. *Curr. Opin. Colloid Interface Sci.*, **10**, pp. 102–110.

25. Wang, L., Li, X., Zhang, G., Dong, J., and Eastoe, J. (2007). Oil-in-water nanoemulsions for pesticide formulations. *J. Colloid Interface Sci.*, **314**, pp. 230–235.

26. Singh, Y., Meher, J. G., Raval, K., Khan, F. A., Chaurasia, M., Jain, N. K., and Chourasia, M. K. (2017). Nanoemulsion: Concepts, development and applications in drug delivery. *J. Control. Release*, **252**, pp. 28–49.

27. Kitaoka, M., Wakabayashi, R., Kamiya, N., and Goto, M. (2016). Solid-in-oil nanodispersions for transdermal drug delivery systems. *Biotechnol. J.*, **11**, pp. 1375–1385.

28. Piao, H., Kamiya, N., Cui, F., and Goto, M. (2011). Preparation of a solid-in-oil nanosuspension containing l-ascorbic acid as a novel long-term stable topical formulation. *Int. J. Pharm.*, **420**, pp. 156–160.

29. Martins, M., Azoia, N. G., Ribeiro, A., Shimanovich, U., Silva, C., and Cavaco-Paulo, A. (2013). In vitro and computational studies of transdermal

perfusion of nanoformulations containing a large molecular weight protein. *Colloids Surf. B Biointerfaces*, **108**, pp. 271–278.

30. Arellano, A., Santoyo, S., Martín, C., and Ygartua, P. (1999). Influence of propylene glycol and isopropyl myristate on the in vitro percutaneous penetration of diclofenac sodium from carbopol gels. *Eur. J. Pharm. Sci.*, **7**, pp. 129–135.
31. Tahara, Y., Honda, S., Kamiya, N., Piao, H., Hirata, A., Hayakawa, E., Fujii, T., and Goto, M. (2008). A solid-in-oil nanodispersion for transcutaneous protein delivery. *J. Control. Release*, **131**, pp. 14–18.
32. Tadros, T., Izquierdo, P., Esquena, J., and Solans, C. (2004). Formation and stability of nano-emulsions. *Adv. Colloid Interface Sci.*, **108–109**, pp. 303–318.
33. Henry, J. V. L., Fryer, P. J., Frith, W. J., and Norton, I. T. (2009). Emulsification mechanism and storage instabilities of hydrocarbon-in-water sub-micron emulsions stabilised with tweens (20 and 80), Brij 96v and sucrose monoesters. *J. Colloid Interface Sci.*, **338**, pp. 201–206.
34. Qian, C. and McClements, D. J. (2011). Formation of nanoemulsions stabilized by model food-grade emulsifiers using high-pressure homogenization: Factors affecting particle size. *Food Hydrocoll.*, **25**, pp. 1000–1008.
35. Delmas, T., Piraux, H., Couffin, A. C., Texier, I., Vinet, F., Poulin, P., Cates, M. E., and Bibette, J. (2011). How to prepare and stabilize very small nanoemulsions. *Langmuir*, **27**, pp. 1683–1692.
36. Sanguansri, P. and Augustin, M. A. (2006). Nanoscale materials development: A food industry perspective. *Trends Food Sci. Technol.*, **17**, pp. 547–556.
37. Lee, L. and Norton, I. T. (2013). Comparing droplet breakup for a high-pressure valve homogeniser and a Microfluidizer for the potential production of food-grade nanoemulsions. *J. Food Eng.*, **114**, pp. 158–163.
38. Canselier, J. P., Delmas, H., Wilhelm, A. M., and Abismaïl, B. (2002). Ultrasound emulsification: An overview. *J. Dispers. Sci. Technol.*, **23**, pp. 333–349.
39. Abbas, S., Hayat, K., Karangwa, E., Bashari, M., and Zhang, X. (2013). An overview of ultrasound-assisted food-grade nanoemulsions. *Food Eng. Rev.*, **5**, pp. 139–157.
40. Amadei, D., Chatzidaki, M. D., Devienne, J., Monteil, J., Cansell, M., Xenakis, A., and Leal-Calderon, F. (2014). Low shear-rate process to

obtain transparent W/O fine emulsions as functional foods. *Food Res. Int.*, **62**, pp. 533–540.

41. Fernandez, P., André, V., Rieger, J., and Kühnle, A. (2004). Nano-emulsion formation by emulsion phase inversion. *Colloids Surf. A Physicochem. Eng. Asp.*, **251**, pp. 53–58.
42. Ostertag, F., Weiss, J., and McClements, D. J. (2012). Low-energy formation of edible nanoemulsions: Factors influencing droplet size produced by emulsion phase inversion. *J. Colloid Interface Sci.*, **388**, pp. 95–102.
43. Solans, C. and Solé, I. (2012). Nano-emulsions: Formation by low-energy methods. *Curr. Opin. Colloid Interface Sci.*, **17**, pp. 246–254.
44. Mabille, C., Leal-Calderon, F., Bibette, J., and Schmitt, V. (2003). Monodisperse fragmentation in emulsions: Mechanisms and kinetics. *Europhys. Lett.*, **61**, pp. 708–714.
45. Shukla, T., Upmanyu, N., Agrawal, M., Saraf, S., and Alexander, A. (2018). Biomedical applications of microemulsion through dermal and transdermal route. *Biomed. Pharmacother.*, **108**, pp. 1477–1494.
46. Theochari, I., Mitsou, E., Nikolic, I., Ilic, T., Dobricic, V., Pletsa, V., Savic, S., Xenakis, A., and Papadimitriou, V. (2021). Colloidal nanodispersions for the topical delivery of Ibuprofen: Structure, dynamics and bioperformances. *J. Mol. Liq.*, **334**, pp. 116021.
47. Zhang, Y., Yu, J., Kahkoska, A. R., Wang, J., Buse, J. B., and Gu, Z. (2019). Advances in transdermal insulin delivery. *Adv. Drug Deliv. Rev.*, **139**, pp. 51–70.
48. Zhu, X., Zeng, X., Zhang, X., Cao, W., Wang, Y., Chen, H., Wang, T., Tsai, H. I., Zhang, R., Chang, D., et al. (2016). The effects of quercetin-loaded PLGA-TPGS nanoparticles on ultraviolet B-induced skin damages in vivo. *Nanomedicine*, **12**, pp. 623–632.
49. Paluncic, J., Kovacevic, Z., Jansson, P. J., Kalinowski, D., Merlot, A. M., Huang, M. L. H., Lok, H. C., Sahni, S., Lane, D. J. R., and Richardson, D. R. (2016). Roads to melanoma: Key pathways and emerging players in melanoma progression and oncogenic signaling. *Biochim. Biophys. Acta Mol. Cell Res.*, **1863**, pp. 770–784.
50. Koryllou, A., Patrinou-Georgoula, M., Troungos, C., and Pletsa, V. (2009). Cell death induced by N-methyl-N-nitrosourea, a model SN_1 methylating agent, in two lung cancer cell lines of human origin. *Apoptosis*, **14**, pp. 1121–1133.
51. Theochari, I., Papadimitriou, V., and Xenakis, A. (2019). *Smart nanocontainers: Micro and nano technologies*, Nguyen Tri, P., Do, T.-O.,

and Nguyen, T. A. (eds.), Chapter 19 "Nanocarriers for effective drug delivery," Elsevier, Amsterdam, pp. 315–341.

52. Ezrahi, S., Aserin, A., and Garti, N. (2019). Basic principles of drug delivery systems: The case of paclitaxel. *Adv. Colloid Interface Sci.*, **263**, pp. 95–130.
53. Ravikumar, P. and Tatke, P. (2019). Advances in encapsulated dermal formulations in chemoprevention of melanoma: An overview. *J. Cosmet. Dermatol.*, **18**, pp. 1606–1612.
54. Gupta, V. and Trivedi, P. (2018). *Lipid nanocarriers for drug targeting*, Alexandru Mihai Grumezescu (ed.), Chapter 15 "In vitro and in vivo characterization of pharmaceutical topical nanocarriers containing anticancer drugs for skin cancer treatment," Elsevier, Amsterdam, pp. 563–627.
55. Rai, V. K., Mishra, N., Yadav, K. S., and Yadav, N. P. (2018). Nanoemulsion as pharmaceutical carrier for dermal and transdermal drug delivery: Formulation development, stability issues, basic considerations and applications. *J. Control. Release*, **270**, pp. 203–225.
56. Sánchez-López, E., Guerra, M., Dias-Ferreira, J., Lopez-Machado, A., Ettcheto, M., Cano, A., Espina, M., Camins, A., Garcia, M. L., and Souto, E. B. (2019). Current applications of nanoemulsions in cancer therapeutics. *Nanomaterials*, **9**.
57. Mishra, H., Mishra, P. K., Ekielski, A., Jaggi, M., Iqbal, Z., and Talegaonkar, S. (2018). Melanoma treatment: From conventional to nanotechnology. *J. Cancer Res. Clin. Oncol.*, **144**, pp. 2283–2302.
58. Wu, J. Y., Cai, J. X., Li, Y. J., Hu, X. Bin, Liu, X. Y., Wang, J. M., Tang, T. T., and Xiang, D. X. (2021). 3,5,4′-Trimethoxy-trans-stilbene loaded microemulsion for cutaneous melanoma therapy by transdermal drug delivery. *Drug Deliv. Transl. Res.*, **11**, pp. 169–181.
59. Olesen, U. H., Clergeaud, G., Hendel, K. K., Yeung, K., Lerche, C. M., Andresen, T. L., and Haedersdal, M. (2020). Enhanced and sustained cutaneous delivery of vismodegib by ablative fractional laser and microemulsion formulation. *J. Invest. Dermatol.*, **140**, pp. 2051–2059.
60. Olesen, U. H., Clergeaud, G., Lerche, C. M., Andresen, T. L., and Haedersdal, M. (2019). Topical delivery of vismodegib using ablative fractional laser and micro-emulsion formulation in vitro. *Lasers Surg. Med.* **51**, pp. 79–87.
61. Theochari, I., Goulielmaki, M., Danino, D., Papadimitriou, V., Pintzas, A., and Xenakis, A. (2017). Drug nanocarriers for cancer chemotherapy based on microemulsions: The case of Vemurafenib analog PLX4720. *Colloids Surf. B Biointerfaces*, **154**, pp. 350–356.

62. Theochari, I., Papadimitriou, V., Papahatjis, D., Assimomytis, N., Pappou, E., Pratsinis, H., Xenakis, A., and Pletsa, V. (2018). Oil-in-water microemulsions as hosts for benzothiophene-based cytotoxic compounds: An effective combination. *Biomimetics*, **3**, pp. 13.

63. Theochari, I., Ilic, T., Nicolic, I., Dobricic, V., Tenchiou, A., Papahatjis, D., Savic, S., Xenakis, A., Papadimitriou, V., and Pletsa, V. (2021). Biological evaluation of oil-in-water microemulsions as carriers of benzothiophene analogues for dermal applications. *Biomimetics*, **6**, pp. 1–15.

64. Giacone, D. V., Dartora, V. F. M. C., de Matos, J. K. R., Passos, J. S., Miranda, D. A. G., de Oliveira, E. A., Silveira, E. R., Costa-Lotufo, L. V., Maria-Engler, S. S., and Lopes, L. B. (2020). Effect of nanoemulsion modification with chitosan and sodium alginate on the topical delivery and efficacy of the cytotoxic agent piplartine in 2D and 3D skin cancer models. *Int. J. Biol. Macromol.*, **165**, pp. 1055–1065.

65. Fofaria, N. M., Qhattal, H. S. S., Liu, X., and Srivastava, S. K. (2016). Nanoemulsion formulations for anti-cancer agent piplartine: Characterization, toxicological, pharmacokinetics and efficacy studies. *Int. J. Pharm.*, **498**, pp. 12–22.

66. Dalmolin, L. F. and Lopez, R. F. V. (2018). Nanoemulsion as a platform for iontophoretic delivery of lipophilic drugs in skin tumors. *Pharmaceutics*, **10**, pp. 1–18.

67. Sato, K., Sugibayashi, K., and Morimoto, Y. (1988). Effect and mode of action of aliphatic esters on the in vitro skin permeation of nicorandil. *Int. J. Pharm.*, **43**, pp. 31–40.

68. Wakabayashi, R., Sakuragi, M., Kozaka, S., Tahara, Y., Kamiya, N., and Goto, M. (2018). Solid-in-oil peptide nanocarriers for transcutaneous cancer vaccine delivery against melanoma. *Mol. Pharm.*, **15**, pp. 955–961.

69 Wakabayashi, R., Kono, H., Kozaka, S., Tahara, Y., Kamiya, N., and Goto, M. (2019). Transcutaneous codelivery of tumor antigen and resiquimod in solid-in-oil nanodispersions promotes antitumor immunity. *Biomater. Sci. Eng.*, **5**, pp. 2297–2306.

70. Neek, M., Tucker, J. A., Kim, T. Il, Molino, N. M., Nelson, E. L., and Wang, S. W. (2018). Co-delivery of human cancer-testis antigens with adjuvant in protein nanoparticles induces higher cell-mediated immune responses. *Biomaterials*, **156**, pp. 194–203.

71. Krieg, A. M. and Vollmer, J. (2007). Toll-like receptors 7, 8, and 9: Linking innate immunity to autoimmunity. *Immunol. Rev.*, **220**, pp. 251–269.

72. Patel, R. and Prabhu, P. (2020). Nanocarriers as versatile delivery systems for effective management of acne. *Int. J. Pharm.*, **579**, pp. 119140.

73. Latter, G., Grice, J. E., Mohammed, Y., Roberts, M. S., and Benson, H. A. E. (2019). Targeted topical delivery of retinoids in the management of acne vulgaris: Current formulations and novel delivery systems. *Pharmaceutics*, **11**.

74. Talianu, M. T., Dinu-Pîrvu, C. E., Ghica, M. V., Anuţa, V., Jinga, V., and Popa, L. (2020). Foray into concepts of design and evaluation of microemulsions as a modern approach for topical applications in acne pathology. *Nanomaterials*, **10**, pp. 1–43.

75. Sabouri, M., Samadi, A., Ahmad Nasrollahi, S., Farboud, E. S., Mirrahimi, B., Hassanzadeh, H., Nassiri Kashani, M., Dinarvand, R., and Firooz, A. (2018). Tretinoin loaded nanoemulsion for acne vulgaris: Fabrication, physicochemical and clinical efficacy assessments. *Skin Pharmacol. Physiol.*, **31**, pp. 316–323.

76. Hosny, K. M., Al Nahyah, K. S., and Alhakamy, N. A. (2021). Self-nanoemulsion loaded with a combination of isotretinoin, an anti-acne drug, and quercetin: Preparation, optimization, and in vivo assessment. *Pharmaceutics*, **13**, pp. 1–16.

77. Patel, M. R., Patel, R. B., Parikh, J. R., and Patel, B. G. (2016). Formulation consideration and skin retention study of microemulsion containing tazarotene for targeted therapy of acne. *J. Pharm. Investig.*, **46**, pp. 55–66.

78. Shao, B., Sun, L., Xu, N., Gu, H., Ji, H., and Wu, L. (2021). Development and evaluation of topical delivery of microemulsions containing adapalene (MEs-Ap) for acne. *AAPS PharmSciTech*, **22**, pp. 1–11.

79. Wani, A., Sanghani, C., and Wani, S. (2018). Formulation, characterization, and in vitro evaluation of novel microemulsion-based spray for topical delivery of isotretinoin. *Asian J. Pharm. Clin. Res.*, **11**, pp. 226–232.

80. Bubić Pajić, N., Ilić, T., Nikolić, I., Dobričić, V., Pantelić, I., and Savić, S. (2019). Alkyl polyglucoside-based adapalene-loaded microemulsions for targeted dermal delivery: Structure, stability and comparative biopharmaceutical characterization with a conventional dosage form. *J. Drug Deliv. Sci. Technol.*, **54**, pp. 101245.

81. Fereig, S. A., El-Zaafarany, G. M., Arafa, M. G., and Abdel-Mottaleb, M. M. A. (2020). Tackling the various classes of nano-therapeutics employed in topical therapy of psoriasis. *Drug Deliv.*, **27**, pp. 662–680.

82. Benigni, M., Pescina, S., Grimaudo, M. A., Padula, C., Santi, P., and Nicoli, S. (2018). Development of microemulsions of suitable viscosity for cyclosporine skin delivery. *Int. J. Pharm.*, **545**, pp. 197–205.

83. Wan, T., Pan, J., Long, Y., Yu, K., Wang, Y., Pan, W., Ruan, W., Qin, M., Wu, C., and Xu, Y. (2017). Dual roles of TPGS based microemulsion for tacrolimus: Enhancing the percutaneous delivery and anti-psoriatic efficacy. *Int. J. Pharm.*, **528**, pp. 511–523.

84. Cintra, G. A. de S., Pinto, L. A., Calixto, G. M. F., Soares, C. P., Von Zuben, E. de S., Scarpa, M. V., Gremião, M. P. D., and Chorilli, M. (2016). Bioadhesive surfactant systems for methotrexate skin delivery. *Molecules*, **21**, pp. 1–13.

85. Rajitha, P., Shammika, P., Aiswarya, S., Gopikrishnan, A., Jayakumar, R., and Sabitha, M. (2019). Chaulmoogra oil based methotrexate loaded topical nanoemulsion for the treatment of psoriasis. *J. Drug Deliv. Sci. Technol.*, **49**, pp. 463–476.

86. Yang, F., Kamiya, N., and Goto, M. (2012). Transdermal delivery of the anti-rheumatic agent methotrexate using a solid-in-oil nanocarrier. *Eur. J. Pharm. Biopharm.*, **82**, pp. 158–163.

87. Musa, S. H., Basri, M., Masoumi, H. R. F., Shamsudin, N., and Salim, N. (2017). Enhancement of physicochemical properties of nanocolloidal carrier loaded with cyclosporine for topical treatment of psoriasis: In vitro diffusion and in vivo hydrating action. *Int. J. Nanomedicine*, **12**, pp. 2427–2441.

88. Musa, S. H., Razali, F. N., Shamsudin, N., Salim, N., and Basri, M. (2021). Novel topical nano-colloidal carrier loaded with cyclosporine: Biological evaluation potentially for psoriasis treatment. *J. Drug Deliv. Sci. Technol.*, **63**, pp. 102440.

Chapter 9

Functional Peptides for Skin Disorders

Mellou Fotini,[a] Varvaresou Athanasia,[a,b] and Papageorgiou Spyridon[a,b]

[a]*Division of Aesthetics and Cosmetic Science, Department of Biomedical Sciences, University of West Attica, 12243 Egaleo, Greece*
[b]*Laboratory of Chemistry, Biochemistry and Cosmetic Science, Department of Biomedical Sciences, University of West Attica, 12243 Egaleo, Greece*
fmellou@uniwa.gr

Functional peptides are molecules that affect cellular behavior in a way that could promote the biological functions of the body, thus might eventually improve human health. Numerous properties have been attributed to bioactive peptides, such as antimicrobial, antioxidant, anti-thrombotic, anti-hypertensive, and immunomodulatory activities.

Functional peptides have been shown to modulate various biological processes in the skin, rendering them promising functional candidates as therapies for dermatologic disorders. Recent studies suggest that treatment with various peptides can result in favorable clinical outcomes for the treatment of skin disorders, i.e., aging, hyperpigmentation laxity, or diseases like atopic dermatitis, acne dental disorders, and melanoma. In this study, the roles of functional skin active short sequence peptides with biomedical applications are explored. The advantages and disadvantages of their use and future aspects are also discussed.

Functional Materials in Biomedical Applications
Edited by Costas Demetzos, Natassa Pippa, and Nikolaos Naziris

ISBN 978-981-4968-65-2 (Hardcover), 978-1-003-41146-8 (eBook)
www.jennystanford.com

9.1 The Skin

The skin is the largest organ of the body, representing one-sixth of the total body weight. Its main role is to protect the body against undesired external environmental agents, such as pathogens, ultraviolet (UV) radiation exposure, chemical threats, temperature changes, and dehydration [1–3]. The skin comprises three main layers having different underlying structures: (a) the epidermis, (b) the dermis, and (c) hypodermis or subcutaneous tissue [4]. The epidermis, of ectodermal origin, is located at the surface of the skin and is in continuous contact with the environment. The stratum corneum is the outermost layer of the epidermis, consists of dead cells or corneocytes, and has a thickness between 10 μm and 30 μm. Underneath the stratum corneum, there are living keratinocytes, melanocytes, and Langerhans cells [2, 3, 5]. Keratinocytes are the major cell type in the epidermis producing keratin. Melanocytes form a heterogeneous group of cells in the human body and are present in the epidermis–dermal junction and hair follicles. Melanocytes produce melanin, a fundamental molecule responsible for skin pigmentation and photoprotection. Melanin has various important physiological functions, including the regulatory influence of epidermal homeostasis, free radical scavenging activity to protect against oxidative stress, and also antimicrobial activity [6–12]. Langerhans cells are classified as immune dendritic cells protecting against external substances and microorganisms [13, 14].

The dermis is the connector tissue between the hypodermis and the epidermis. It provides most of the mechanical strength and elasticity to the skin. It includes the vascular, lymphatic, and neuronal systems. It also contains sweat pores and hair follicles. The dermis is mainly composed of complex extracellular matrix (ECM) proteins, especially collagen fibers. ECM proteins can be categorized as either structural (collagen and elastin) or non-structural (glycoproteins), depending on their function. Integrins are essential compounds of the ECM, in addition to a group of matrix metalloproteinases (MMPs) and growth factors (GFs) [15, 16]. Dermal collagen represents the most abundant ECM protein representing 90% dry weight of the skin, being responsible for the skin's tensile strength and mechanical properties [17]. Numerous immune cells and fibroblasts (the major cell type present in this layer), involved in the synthesis of many of the ECM components, are also present in the dermis. The dermis also contains blood vessels, which provide nutrients to the skin and help thermoregulation.

The hypodermis or subcutaneous tissue insulates the body from heat and cold, provides shock absorption cells of the hypodermis, and also stores nutrients and energy. The hypodermis is the thickest in the buttocks, palms of the hands, and soles of the feet. During aging, the hypodermis begins to atrophy, contributing to the thinning of aging skin [18].

9.2 Cosmetics or Skin Care Products or Drugs

The field of skin care products, which merges cosmetics and pharmaceuticals, appears particularly promising. This is a wide market area ranging from pure cosmetics to products with topical dermatological properties, including cosmeceutical products, which lie in a gray area between cosmetics and drugs; and, in spite of their large use, they are not recognized by the Food and Drug Administration so far [19].

The scope of these products has been almost exponentially expanding, with the incorporation, for instance, of alpha-hydroxy acids for exfoliation and skin rejuvenation, vitamin C for topical treatments, peptides, and a variety of antioxidants, among others. The suitability of the term "cosmeceutical" gained more ground as it represents a new class of cosmetic products, which provide effects beyond simple cosmetic enhancement but fell short of qualifying for a drug or pharmaceutical [20].

Recent research advances in the biochemical processes involved in wound healing and skin aging have led to the development of novel skin care products that are based on functional peptides [21, 22].

The development of comprehensive in silico techniques combined with efficient advanced synthetic methods facilitates the production of peptide-based chemical species of almost many applicabilities, and thus, short peptides can be employed in smart therapies [23].

The potential adverse effects of these skin care products should not be ignored. Most of the products thoroughly manufactured have good tolerance and require or even at all minor management approaches for the typically mild and transient undesirable effects like a burning sensation, erythema, irritation, etc. An experienced physician can manage most of these various adverse effects if using mild concentrations, and with early intervention [20].

9.3 Functional Peptides

Peptides are chains formed by amino acids linked by peptide bonds. They have aroused considerable interest since some of them, the bioactive peptides, carry out important biological activities especially as signaling/regulating molecules in a variety of physiological processes, including defense, immunity, stress, growth, homeostasis, and reproduction.

Many properties have been attributed to bioactive peptides, such as antimicrobial [24], antioxidant [25], anti-thrombotic [26], anti-hypertensive [27], and immunomodulatory activities [28, 29].

There are vasodilators, vasoconstrictors, and further substances acting upon cell metabolism. For example, substance P, which is consisted of 11 amino acids, can be found in the epidermis, and acts as a potent vasodilator thus contributing to the balance between cell differentiation and cell renewal. The peptides somatostatin and neuropeptide Y found in the skin (NPY—family of endocrine neurotransmitter peptides) contribute to the vascular tonus of the skin through vasodilation, by accelerating the release of histamine and vasoconstriction, respectively [30, 31]. Adipocytes found in the hypodermis are able to release bioactive peptides, called adipocytokines, such as interleukin-6, leptin, resistin, tumor necrosis factor-α (TNF-α), acylation stimulating protein, and adiponectin [32]. Attention to bioactive peptides has increased in recent years to design and develop effective drugs with minimal adverse effects for the treatment of different diseases like cancer, diabetes, inflammatory, and infectious disorders [29, 33].

These aspects have also been used in the field of dermatology and cosmetic science to produce functional short, stable peptides for the management of pigmentation, innate immunity, and inflammation. The advantages of using peptides in cosmetic products include their involvement in many physiological functions of the skin and their relative selectivity. However, there are disadvantages, such as clinical evidence for efficacy is often weak, dermal absorption may be poor due to low lipophilicity, high molecular weight, and binding to other ingredients, and prices can be quite high. Transdermal delivery of peptides can be made more effective by penetration enhancers, chemical modification, or encapsulation [34].

Biomimetic peptides are biotechnologically originated compounds, which have an identical amino acid sequence to physiological peptides (oligopeptides with a sequence ranging from 10 to 15 amino acids). They imitate GFs action since they interact with their receptors, resulting in clinical effects, such as aging deceleration [35]. Acetyl decapeptide-3 (Rejuline), oligopeptide-24 (CG-EGP3), oligopeptide-34 (CG-TGP2), and oligopeptide-72 (Boostrin) represent some examples of biomimetic peptides. Functional topical peptides may also be synthetic compounds, and they consist of modified amino acid chains, offering improved physiological function, such as increasing skin permeability, stability, solubility, and better interaction with cell receptors [34, 36–38]. Thus, functional peptides are gaining great attention as agents with clinical applications in different skin conditions [37, 38]. The multiple employment of these functional compounds offers treatment alternatives, after incorporation in formulations designed for topical application, preventing, or attenuating the clinical aspects of skin damaged by dysfunctions such as hyperpigmentation, increase of body fat, aging, and wrinkle development [35, 37, 38]. These peptides can promote the synthesis of collagen and elastin [34, 35, 39], improve wound healing [40, 41] and fibroblast proliferation [34, 35, 39], and act as GFs [42] or even as tensioning and tightening agents [34, 35, 39, 43].

Emil Fischer and Hofmeister described the first peptides in the early 19th century, while the first peptide synthesis was published by Fischer and Fourneauin, in 1901 [44]. In the years that followed, new peptides were synthesized, more natural peptides were identified, and more knowledge was gained about their functions. Loren Pickard developed copper glycine-histidine-lysine (Cu-GHK) in 1973, and the first copper peptide incorporated into skin care products was held in the late 1980s. Even then, peptide development carried on gradually until the beginning of 2000, when palmitoyl pentapeptide-4 was established. Thereafter, many short, stable, and synthetic peptides were developed, which are involved in ECM synthesis, pigmentation, innate immunity, and inflammation. These peptides are used for collagen stimulation, wound healing, "Botox-like" wrinkle smoothing, as well as antimicrobial [45], antioxidant, and whitening effects [46].

These peptides should have certain properties in order to be effective. Formerly, it was assumed that the molecular weight of peptides should be less than 500 Da, due to the skin barrier, otherwise the peptide would not be able to pass the barrier. The moderate log of the partition coefficient for octanol/water should be between 1 and 3, the melting point should be below 200 °C, water solubility should be >1 mg/mL, and there should be no or a few polar centers [39]. Recent studies have shown that larger molecules can pass through the skin barrier, especially in the case of dry and aged skin [47, 48]. Synthetic peptides consist of amino acid chains, which can be modified in various ways to obtain better properties regarding skin penetration, special receptor binding, stability in the formulations, and solubility.

9.4 Classification of Functional Peptides Used in Cosmetic Products

Topical bioactive-functional skin peptides can be classified according to their mechanism of action in signal, carrier, neurotransmitter inhibitor, enzyme inhibitor structural protein digestion, and antioxidant peptides.

Table 9.1 classified some peptides used in cosmetic products, according to their mechanism of action.

Table 9.1 Peptides used in cosmetic products

Peptide category	Examples of peptides (names)
Signal	Copper tripeptide, trifluoroacetyl-tripeptide-2, tripeptide-10 citrulline, acetyl tetrapeptide-5, acetyl tetrapeptide-9, acetyl tetrapeptide-11, tetrapeptide PKEK, tetrapeptide-21, hexapeptide, hexapeptide-11, palmitoyl pentapeptide-4, palmitoyl tripeptide-3/5, palmitoyl tetrapeptide-7, palmitoyl hexapeptide-12, palmitoyl oligopeptide, palmitoyl tripeptide-1, pentamide-6, lipospondin (elaidyl-Lys-Phe-Lys-OH)
Carriers	Copper tripeptide, manganese tripeptide-1, pep-1 (cell penetrating peptide), neuropeptide Y, RV24 (amphipathic peptide), glycyl-L-histidyl-L-lysine
Peptide mimetics or neurotransmitter-inhibiting peptides	Acetyl hexapeptide-3 or acetyl hexapeptide-8 (argireline), pentapeptide-18 (leuphasyl), pentapeptide-3, pripeptide-3 syn-ake), acetyl octapeptide-1/-3 (sNAP-8) peptides
Enzyme inhibitors	Soybean and silk fibroin peptides, black rice oligopeptides
Structural protein digestion	Keratinpeptide
Antioxidants	Carnosine, N-acetyl-carnosine

9.5 Signal Peptides

Signal peptides, also called matricin peptides or collagen stimulators, are able to trigger a signaling cascade. They are released from the ECM and they contribute to the increase of the proliferation of collagen, elastin, proteoglycan, glycosaminoglycan, and fibronectin.

Thus, by the regeneration of the skin matrix cells, both pigmentation of photo-damaged skin and fine lines as well wrinkles are reduced, while skin elasticity increases, and it looks smoother and firmer. Synthetic peptides developed on repair signaling sequences have been used to rejuvenate skin. Some of the peptides that are used in cosmetic formulations are summarized below:

9.5.1 Trifluoroacetyl-Tripeptide-2

According to studies performed, trifluoroacetyl-tripeptide-2 (TFA-Val-Try-Val-OH) has progressive effects on wrinkles, firmness, elasticity, and sagging [49].

9.5.2 Tripeptide-10 Citrulline

Tripeptide-10 citrulline (Lys-α-Asp-Ile-Citrulline), a decorin-like tetrapeptide, Decorinyl™ is used to particularly target collagen fiber organization (Fig. 9.1). The peptide showed uniformity in fibril diameter, and increased skin suppleness from better collagen fiber cohesion [50, 51].

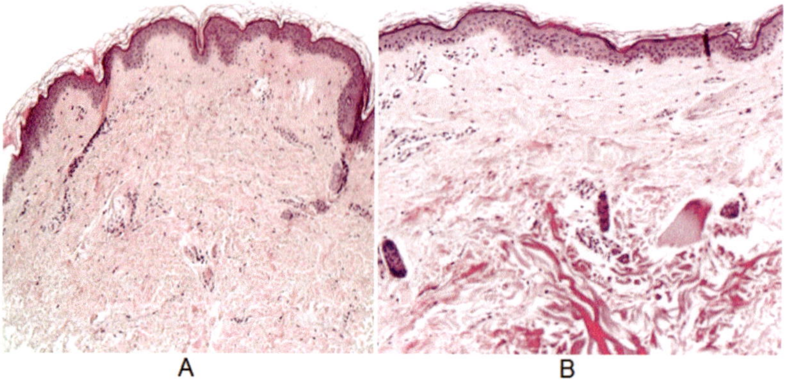

Figure 9.1 Skin specimens stained with hematoxylin and eosin before (A) and after two months of application of a cream containing peptide tripeptide-10 citrulline (B) indicative of collagen fibers increase and better organization. Athanasia Varvaresou, Vassiliki Raikou, Vasileios Pagkalos, Vasiliki Karavana, Vasiliki Gardiki, Kapetanstrataki Melpo, Panderi Irene, "Preliminary skin histological study after the application of acetyl hexapeptide-3 and tripeptide-10 citrulline," *The European Congress on Advanced Treatment and Technologies in Skin and Aesthetics, Skin-Med 2019*, Munich, December 5–6, 2019, Abstracts, p. 5.

9.5.3 Palmitoyl Tripeptide-1

Palmitoyl tripeptide-1, also called pal-GHK (Pal-Gly-His-Lys), is a messenger peptide for collagen rejuvenation. Comparable to retinoic acid with regards to its activity, it does not cause irritation.

It stimulates collagen and glycosaminoglycan synthesis and leads to the decrease of wrinkles. This peptide is suggested to act on TGFβ to stimulate fibrillogenesis and it is incorporated in cosmetic anti-wrinkle skin care and make-up products.

Studies have indicated statistically significant reductions in wrinkle length, depth and skin roughness while a small but statistically significant increase in skin thickness has been observed compared to the vehicle alone [52].

A combination of palmitoyl tetrapeptide-7 (pal-GQPR) and pal-GHK tripeptide is marketed as an anti-wrinkle complex with the trade name Matrixyl™3000. A clinical study carried out confirmed anti-wrinkle efficacy; reduction of wrinkle depth, density, volume, skin roughness and complexity, and area occupied by deep wrinkles; and an increase in skin tone [53].

9.5.4 Palmitoyl Tripeptide-3/5

Palmitoyl tripeptide-3/5 (Pal-Lys-Val-Lys bistrifluoracetae salt) imitates the effects of thrombospondin-1 (TSP-1), a naturally occurring ECM protein that increases TGFβ activity. Subsequently, TGFβ causes a constant rise in the amounts of collagen type I and III produced by dermal fibroblasts. In vitro and in vivo studies have shown that palmitoyl tripeptide-3/5(SYN®-COLL) stimulates collagen production through the TGFβ.

In all study models, a dose-dependent wrinkle reduction was confirmed, measured by PRIMOS surface topography [54].

Additionally, a study regarding anti-wrinkle efficacy and skin roughness was superior compared to the control groups, placebo, and pal-KTTKS-containing cosmetic emulsions [39].

9.5.5 Tetrapeptide PKEK

Tetrapeptide (Pro-Lys-Glu-Lys, PKEK) can display whitening effects. For its production, Lys-Glu-Lys-Lys-Glu-Lys (KEK) was modified with proline in order to stabilize the peptide structure. Study results defined that PKEK reduces interleukin-6, interleukin-8, and TNF-a, as well as cyclooxygenase gene expression in UV light-stressed keratinocytes [55].

Studies involving healthy volunteers confirmed that PKEK is capable of decreasing UVB-induced skin pigmentation, and it may be appropriate as a skin tone-modulating agent in cosmetic products [56].

9.5.6 Palmitoyl Tripeptide-38

Dermo cosmetic products containing palmitoyl tripeptide-38 Pal-Lys-Met(O_2)-Lys-OH) applied on sensitive skin bearing crow's feet wrinkles displayed a considerable increase in dermal density and elasticity and showed anti-wrinkle effects also, while were characterized as well-tolerated [57, 58].

9.5.7 Palmitoyl Tetrapeptide-7

Palmitoyl tetrapeptide-7 (Rigin™) (Pal-Gly-Gln-Pro-Arg or pal-GQPR) reduces interleukin-6 secretion in a basal setting and acts as an anti-inflammatory agent after exposure to UVB-irradiation. A blend of palmitoyl oligopeptide and palmitoyl tetrapeptide-7 enhanced the ECM structure in comparison with placebo as indicated by in vivo reflectance confocal microscopy studies [59].

9.5.8 Palmitoyl Pentapeptide-4

Palmitoyl pentapeptide-4, (Matrixyl®, Pal-Lys-Thr-Thr-Lys-Ser-OH or pal-KTTKS-OH) is a small, highly specific biologically active peptide, which has been stated to stimulate the production of elastin, glucosaminoglycan, fibronectin, and collagens (especially I, III, and IV type), support of the ECM and wound healing. Application of formulations containing pal-KTTKS resulted in a quantitative decrease in fold depth, fold thickness, and skin rigidity [60–62].

9.5.9 Palmitoyl Hexapeptide-12

Palmitoyl hexapeptide-12 (Pal-Val-Gly-Val-Ala-Pro-Gly) stimulates collagen and elastin fibroblasts leading to fibronectin and glycosaminoglycans development. It is believed that it reduces the production of interleukin-6, which promotes inflammation, leading to faster degradation of the skin matrix, and as a result, contributes to the development of wrinkles, loss of firmness, and elasticity of the skin. Studies including female volunteers involving palmitoyl hexapeptide treatment showed improved elasticity, tone, skin fatigue, and firmness [63].

9.5.10 Acetyl Tetrapeptide-9/11

Acetyl tetrapeptide-9 (Dermican™) (N-Acetyl-Gln-Asp-Val-His) and acetyl tetrapeptide-11 (N-Acetyl-Pro-Pro-Tyr-Leu) (Syniorage™) are referred to enhance collagen type I, lumican synthesis, and keratinocyte cell growth, and syndecan-1 synthesis, respectively. It is documented that treatment of female volunteers with acetyl tetrapeptide-9 or acetyl tetrapeptide-11 led to more thick and firmer skin [64].

9.5.11 Tetrapeptide-21

Tetrapeptide-21, or GEKG (Gly-Glu-Lys-Gly), was derived from ECM proteins. In vitro studies confirmed that this peptide increased collagen type I, production on the protein level, and mRNA level, and it stimulated the production of hyaluronic acid synthase 1 and increased fibronectin. In a double-blind, randomized, placebo-controlled study, GEKG significantly decreased skin roughness [55].

9.5.12 Hexapeptide-11

Hexapeptide-11 (Phe-Val-Ala-Pro-Phe-Pro) was firstly isolated from *Saccharomyces* yeast fermentation, but later was synthesized due to purity issues. Hexapeptide-11 can influence the beginning of senescence in both intrinsically and extrinsically aged fibroblasts, and extrinsically aged dermal papillae cells in vitro [65]. Initial skin elasticity and deformation response are improved after treatment of healthy volunteers with Hexapeptide-11 [39].

9.5.13 Hexapeptide-14

Hexapeptide-14 (palmitoyl hexapeptide-14) has been reported to stimulate collagen synthesis, cell migration, fibroblast proliferation, and scaffolding [37]. Study results showed reduced wrinkles and fine lines by palmitoyl hexapeptide-14 [39].

9.6 Carrier Peptides

Carrier peptides can deliver or stabilize trace elements that are necessary for enzymatic progress and wound healing. These peptides are obtained by binding copper with a tripeptide and they contribute to the transport of copper or manganese into skin cells [66].

9.6.1 Manganese Tripeptide-1

A clinical study focusing on manganese tripeptide-1 (GHK-Mn2+) evaluated the effects of a manganese peptide complex in the treatment of various signs of cutaneous facial photo-damage. Results illustrated that skin's photo-damage ranking shifted from moderate to mild. The most significantly improved parameters were related to hyperpigmentation, whereas no significant cutaneous inflammation was mentioned [67].

9.6.2 Copper Tripeptide

Copper tripeptide (Cu-GHK, lamin®) complex (copper Gly-L-His-L-Lys) is one of the most well-examined peptides. It is involved in the ECM and is released in wounds or inflammation to support healing. It acts as a signal and carrier peptide; stimulates cellular regulatory molecules such as collagen, elastin, proteoglycan, and glycosaminoglycan synthesis; and provides anti-inflammatory, wound healing, and antioxidant responses. In cosmetic applications, Cu-GHK is used in anti-aging, anti-wrinkle, after-sun, skin renewal, skin moisturizing, and hair growth stimulating products [68].

Moreover, Cu-GHK can stimulate hair growth by ensuring follicular enlargement and helping cover the follicle with downy hair, an effect comparable with that of Minoxidil [69].

In addition, topical Cu-GHK products stimulate collagen synthesis on the scalp, strengthen existing hair, and promote hair growth [69].

Several studies have confirmed Cu-GHK efficacy in various areas, including skin collagen, increasing keratinocyte proliferation, firmness, elasticity, skin thickness, wrinkles, spotty hyperpigmentation, light damage, and strengthening proteins of the skin protection barrier [69–71].

9.7 Neurotransmitter Inhibitor Peptides

Muscle contraction is an additional approach to reducing ordinary aging signs like wrinkles and fine lines. Muscles are contracted by neurotransmitters released by neurons. A cascade with protein-protein interactions is started by the neurotransmitter that ends in the fusion of neurotransmitter-loaded vesicles with the neuron membrane. It is possible that a local modification in the membrane triggers the entry of calcium ions into the neuron via the terminal end of the neurotransmitter. When the calcium ions enter the pre-synaptic terminal, vesicles containing acetylcholine join other parts of the neuron and acetylcholine are released. This procedure is mediated by a SNAP receptor protein, which includes vesicle-associated membrane protein, membrane-associated protein syntaxin, and synaptosomal-associated protein-25. These proteins control vesicle docking and fusion via the formation of the SNARE complex, which captures vesicles and fuses them with the membrane. After the fusion of these vesicles, acetylcholine is released into the synapse between muscle and nerve. Finally, acetylcholine binds to acetylcholine receptors on the surface of the muscle cells, and this leads to muscle contraction.

Peptides, which imitate the amino acid sequence of the synaptic protein SNAP-25, were found to be specific inhibitors of neurosecretion. These peptides, also called neurotransmitter inhibitor peptides, are supposed to have mediated the penetration of the skin and relaxed muscles, causing the reduction and softening of wrinkles and fine lines [46].

9.7.1 Tripeptide-3

Tripeptide-3 (β-Ala-Pro-Dab-NHBn-2-Acetate), or dipeptide diaminobutyroyl benzylamide diacetate or SYN®-AKE, mimics the waglerin-1 function, a peptide found in the venom of the viper *Tropidolaemuswagleri*. Tripeptide-3 acts at the postsynaptic membrane and is a reversible antagonist of the acetylcholine receptor. Studies using female volunteers demonstrated that a tripeptide-3 formulation treatment provided both immediate and long-term improvements in the appearance of fine and coarse wrinkles [72].

9.7.2 Pentapeptide-3

Pentapeptide-3 (Vialox®) has the sequence Gly-Pro-Arg-Pro-Ala and is derived from snake venom. Experiments conducted on healthy volunteers verified a reduction of wrinkles and slighter skin roughness after treatment [73].

9.7.3 Pentapeptide-18

Pentapeptide-18 (Leuphasyl®) (SeTyr-D-Ala-Gly-Phe-Leu) imitates the natural mechanism of enkephalins, inhibiting neuronal activity and catecholamine release. It has been proven to reduce fine lines and wrinkles, moisturize the skin, and improve firmness and skin tone. Topical treatment demonstrated a potentiated effect for botulinum toxin treatment (Botox-like effects) and extended the anti-wrinkle benefit on the skin [74].

9.7.4 Acetylhexapeptide-3 or Acetylhexapeptide-8

Acetylhexapeptide-3 or Acetylhexapeptide-8 (Acetylhexapeptide-8 is the most recent name), (Argireline®) (Acetyl-Glu-Glu-Met-Gln-Arg-Arg-NH2), is a copy of the synaptosomal-associated protein-25, which competes for a position in the SNARE complex, and destabilizes its formation without breaking any of its constituent parts. This peptide is shown to inhibit the release of neurotransmitters, which is followed by anti-wrinkle and moisturizing effects.

Studies reported that acetylhexapeptide-3-treated skin areas showed a significant improvement in wrinkles in the eye area [75] while all parameters of roughness were decreased and the fold depth was also significantly reduced [76].

9.8 Enzyme Inhibitor Peptides

Enzyme inhibitor peptides inhibit enzymes in a direct or indirect way. Silk fibroin peptides, soy oligopeptides, and rice peptides act on the skin cells by inhibiting enzymes, such as tTAT-superoxide dismutase, and stimulating hyaluronan synthase 2, whereas soy oligopeptides inhibit proteinases. Although these peptides show promising results, only a very few or no in vivo studies have been performed. Hence, their relevance is still unclear [46].

9.8.1 Silk Fibroin Peptides

Silk fibroin peptide is obtained from the silkworm *Bombyx mori*. Results show inhibitory inflammation and enhance the anti-inflammatory activity of tTAT-superoxide dismutase, which was previously reported to effectively penetrate various cells and tissues, and present antioxidant properties in a mouse model of inflammation [16] but no human in vivo data concerning efficacy is available at present.

9.8.2 Soybean Peptides

Soy oligopeptides are derived from soybean proteins, and consist of 3–6 amino acids, with a size of 300–700 kDa. It has been identified that soybean oligopeptides possess various biological activities such as antioxidants, reducing blood pressure, and minimizing blood lipid effects. Topically applied soy oligopeptides significantly increased Bcl-2 protein expression and reduced cyclobutane-pyrimidine dimers-positive cells, apoptotic cells, sunburn cells, p53 protein expression, and Bax protein expressions in the epidermis of UVB-irradiated foreskin. In addition, the topical application seems to protect human skin against UVB-induced photo-damage [46].

9.8.3 Rice Peptides

Low molecular weight peptides (<3000 Da) can be obtained by rice bran protein after special processing. Black rice oligopeptides were measured at about 1300 Da. These oligopeptides acted by inhibiting MMPs activity and stimulated hyaluronan synthase-2 gene expression in human keratinocytes in a dose-dependent way [77]. Formulations including niosomes entrapped with rice bran bioactive compounds exhibit clinical anti-aging properties [78]. Yet, there are no in vivo studies concerning purified black rice oligopeptides available.

9.9 Peptides Derived from Structural Protein Digestion

Keratin-based peptides are shown to have hemostatic, moisturizing, and repair-promoting properties. Results also indicated that a keratin-based peptide cream treatment can prevent some of the damaging effects associated with surfactant exposure [79]. Topical formulations containing Keratin-based peptides improved the integrity and water-holding capacity of the skin barrier. No detailed report about the mechanism of action of these peptides was available [46, 80].

9.10 Antioxidant Peptides

Carnosine(β-Ala-His) is naturally present in high concentrations in muscle and brain tissues and has been proven an aqueous antioxidant with wound healing activity.

Moreover, carnosine is a scavenging reactive oxygen species and also an α-β unsaturated aldehyde formed by the peroxidation of cell membrane fatty acids during oxidative stress. The unmodified water-soluble dipeptide β-Ala-His does not penetrate beyond the first layer of the stratum corneum, whereas the lipophilic peptide palmitoyl β-Ala-His diffuses into the stratum corneum, epidermal, and dermal skin layers. No systemic activity has been observed [81]. Studies have shown that tested products containing carnosine among others ameliorated periorbital wrinkles in women, improving skin smoothness.

Moreover, research concerning a complex containing different active ingredients (SPF 50, photolyase, endonuclease, 8-oxoguanine glycosylase, carnosine, atrazine, and ergothioneine) in available products with DNA repair, antioxidant, and GF ingredients, demonstrated the formulation to be efficient in reducing pyrimidine dimers generated by UV irradiation, protein carbonylation, and 8-oxo-7,8-dihydro-20-deoxyguanosine in human skin biopsies, and also seemed to reinforce the genomic and proteomic integrity of skin cells after continual UV exposure. Consequently, this product could be regarded as potentially lowering the risk of UV-induced cutaneous aging and non-melanoma skin cancer [82].

Treatment with carnosine and N-acetylcarnosine formulations showed that carnosine and N-acetylcarnosine in a water solution reduced erythema compared to the control. Both peptides showed antioxidant ability with a higher significance in conjunction with vehicles improving the substances' skin penetration capabilities. N-acetylcarnosine was indicated as an interesting hydrophilic antioxidant for dermatological purposes [83].

Undoubtedly, the development or topical treatment with synthetic or natural functional cosmetic peptides has been proven very effective. Researchers identified peptide sequences, which allowed the peptides to be targeted to cosmetically important skin layers. The application of peptides in skin personal care products is considerably increasing.

Thus, it is necessary to get analytical information on different molecules and the physiological principles underlying their use. These molecules have high commercial potential, especially for those peptide sequences with cosmetic activities, i.e., anti-aging, antioxidant, and depigmenting.

Selected peptides are not irritant and stable agents. Numerous studies clearly show a wide range of possible topical skin applications of biologically active peptides, for improving the skin and its properties. There is still a lot of work required, and a lot of further research to be done. While many synthetic peptides with confirmed efficacy in skin treatment have been researched to a satisfying extent, only some clinical study results have been obtained by using formulations containing peptides and other active ingredients, or in the presence of a basic moisturizer. Many clinical in vivo trials did not distinguish the function of the peptide used specifically with other active ingredients in the formulation. Consequently, the results received cannot be claimed clearly to be the effect of the used peptide for enhanced skin benefits and improved skin appearance.

Research results seem to be very promising, but for efficacy reasons, these peptides should be tested further. Moreover, there are many interesting peptides whose effects should be more closely investigated as the reported beneficial clinical effects and the mode of action are not thoroughly explained.

There are still some open questions, such as how it may be possible to overcome the barrier to allow permeation of such compounds and thereby enhance the concentrations delivered to the target site in the dermis. New questions will lead to new study designs, hopefully, new answers and solutions, and, finally, new skin-acting peptides [46].

9.11 Applications of Functional Peptides in Skin Disorders

The rising commercial development of peptide drugs led researchers to carry out extensive studies in this field resulting in an increasing number of peptide-based drugs. More than 500 peptide drugs are under study in different clinical trial phases [29, 84].

9.11.1 Skin Hypopigmentation

Bioactive peptides contribute to skin and hair pigmentation and can constitute an effective treatment for conditions like vitiligo, an acquired idiopathic hypomelanotic disorder described by the loss of melanocytes in the skin. The neuropeptide melanin-concentrating hormone (MCH: H-Asp-Thr-Met-Arg-Cys-Met-Val-Gly-Arg-Val-Tyr-Arg-Pro-Cys-Trp-Glu-Val-OH), found primarily in the hypothalamus and in many regions of the brain, causes the aggregation of melanin granules thus regulating skin color in humans [85]. Moreover, $Nle^4DPhe^7\alpha$-MSH is a synthetic analog of alpha-melanocyte stimulating hormone (α-MSH), which has been used as a skin darkener in cosmetics for several years [86].

9.11.2 Skin Hyperpigmentation

Excessive accumulation of melanin may cause skin pigmentation disorders, often followed by noteworthy psychological tension.

Even if the regulation of melanogenesis biochemistry can be achieved by numerous natural and synthetic products that have been developed, the management of unwanted pigmentation of skin remains difficult. The potential hypopigmented effects of peptide sequences that originated from milk proteins like β-lactoglobulin and κ-casein have been investigated. These proteins are identified to inhibit melanogenesis and their hydrolysates are reported as antioxidant peptides. Tetrapeptide fragments of the milk protein hydrolysates were synthesized and the amino acids that were essential for designing peptides with tyrosinase inhibitory and antioxidant activities were also investigated. It was revealed that the peptide methionine-histidine-isoleucine-arginine amide sufficiently inhibits mushroom tyrosinase activity, exhibits strong antioxidant activity, and effectively delays melanogenesis in cultured melanocytes through cooperative biological activities. Consequently, the possible effects of the aforementioned bioactive tetrapeptide from milk proteins as a chemical alternative to hypopigmented agents were demonstrated [87].

9.12 Anti-Inflammatory Treatments

Inflammatory skin diseases, including eczema, dermatitis, psoriasis, and urticaria, are commonly treated with topical agents [85].

Lately, numerous studies are focused to develop alternative and more selective anti-inflammatory treatments, a lot of which involve the use of peptides. Several endogenous peptides identified during inflammatory responses illustrated anti-inflammatory activities by inhibition, reduction, and/or modulation of the expression and activity of mediators. The activities and therapeutic applications of peptides as anti-inflammatory agents in healing different inflammatory diseases are discussed and also the importance of peptide-based therapies is pointed out in the literature [88].

The clinical use of cyclosporin in psoriasis management is well established, while the tetradecapeptide somatostatin is a regulatory peptide that exhibits an inhibitory effect on inflammation and nociception. Cortistatin, another cyclic neuropeptide, has been reported as a potential endogenous anti-inflammatory factor [85].

9.13 Atopic Dermatitis

In order to treat atopic dermatitis with the use of small interfering RNA, a flexible liposome combination with the peptide AT1002 (seq: Phe–Cys–Ile–Gly–Arg–Leu) was tested in a specific concentration of liposomes that opens tight junctions for better delivery by phosphorylating the structural protein ZO-1. It was found that the enhanced intradermal penetration of the material was increased without causing toxicity due to the action of the AT1002 and the flexibility of the liposome [89].

Antimicrobial peptides restore the skin barrier structure and function, decrease itching, and suppress T-helper type 2 cell-mediated inflammation, constituting alternative candidates for barrier repair therapy in dealing with atopic dermatitis [90].

Recent studies have demonstrated that antimicrobial peptides, such as cathelicidin LL-37, human beta-defensin (hBD)-1, hBD-3, and S100A7 protein, increase the levels of TJ-related proteins and promote epidermal barrier function. Their role in atopic dermatitis must be clarified since atopic dermatitis is characterized by less expression of these peptides, which may contribute to the increased susceptibility to skin infections.

The antimicrobial peptides overexpression in human skin appears to go along with increased protection against infection in psoriasis, rosacea, and other inflammatory skin diseases. Data provided indicates that antimicrobial peptides have strong potential as therapeutics [91].

9.14 Skin Protectant Peptides

Photoaging is an adverse effect on the skin attributed to extended UV-B irradiation. The effects of the whey peptides consumption on chronic UV-B radiation-induced skin changes (thickness, flexibility, and wrinkle formation) were investigated in mice models. The peptides inhibited the increase in dermal rigidity, wrinkling, and melanin granule formation, thus improving photoaging. Moreover, the peptides lowered the expression of matrix metalloproteinase (MMP-2 and pro-MMP-9) and vascular endothelial growth factor (VEGF). Also, they prevented an increase in the number of apoptotic, Ki-67-positive, and 8-hydroxy-2′-deoxyguanosine (8-OHdG)-positive cells induced by constant exposure to UV radiations. The peptides prevented type IV collagen degradation, proliferation, angiogenesis, and DNA damage caused by irradiation in male hairless mice. It seems that the probable mechanism is the scavenging of free radicals [92, 93].

9.15 Applications in Skin Diseases

Bioactive peptides demonstrate immense potential for their use as medical and therapeutic interventions. Their multiple potential health benefits in an increasing range of skin disorders have already been demonstrated.

The ease at which peptide analogs might be modified provides the opportunity for effective design and ultimately optimization of therapy. Thus, they represent a novel approach to therapeutic medicine and may revolutionize the treatments and preventions of several skin diseases, among others [94].

9.15.1 Wound Healing

Brevinins are natural antimicrobial peptides (AMPs) and have been found in various species of frogs presenting therapeutic potentials, including wound healing.

Recently, the wound healing properties of frog skin secretions and extractions have been investigated [95]. It is reported that the extract obtained from Rana *ridibunda* frog skin secretions (especially those products under 10 kDa) accelerated the process of wound healing [96]. The efficiency of dermal (FS) and epidermal (RFS) sides of this frog skin were tested as wound dressing [97]. However, these studies do not provide adequate characterizations of special compounds to determine the factor(s) involved in such properties. This function has been attributed to the collagen and lipid content of the frog skin [98, 99]. Additionally, the antimicrobial property of the skin secretion possibly reduces wound infection, inducing the proliferation and migration of endothelial cells to the damaged area. The therapeutic potential of the Brevinin-2GU, isolated from *Hylaranaguentheri* [100], and B2RP-ERa from *Hylaranaerythraea* [101] were examined as wound healing agents for common skin rashes. It was revealed that these peptides displayed a bactericidal effect against *Propionibacterium* acnes as major pathogenesis in acne vulgaris development [100]. For that reason, the action of Brevinins on the wound healing process can be explained by their antimicrobial activities, up to now.

It should be noted that Brevinin peptides show low or no hemolytic activity even at high concentrations. However, the main limitation is the short half-life of Brevinins in circulation, which could significantly restrict their systemic administration and topical application [29].

The effects of active peptides of the mantle of *Pinctada martensii* were observed on wound healing. The effect of active peptides on promoting healing was studied through a whole cortex wound model on the back of mice. Results of in vitro experiments using mice fed with the mentioned peptides lead to a shortened epithelialization time, due to a shortening inflammatory period. Moreover, enhanced collagen synthesis was observed and increased type III collagen content. Therefore, scar formation was inhibited, and wound healing efficiency was improved considerably. These results demonstrate the active peptides of *Pinctada martensii* that promote dermal wound healing in mice and have remarkable potential for the development and utilization in skin wound healing [102].

The research for new pharmacological agents is driven by infectious diseases and the rapid development of pathogens resistant to conventional drugs. In this perspective, cationic peptides without disulfide bridges coming from different species of scorpion venom, possess multifunctional activities, and thus have been the subject of many scientific studies. Stigmurin is a linear peptide composed of 17 amino acid residues (Phe-Phe-Ser-Leu-Ile-Pro-Ser-Leu-Val-Gly-Gly-Leu-Ile-Ser-Ala-Phe-Lys-NH_2), which is found in the venom gland of the scorpion *Tityus stigmurus*. In studies performed, Stigmurin showed hydroxyl radical scavenging and antibiotic action in the skin wound, reducing considerably the number of viable microorganisms. Stigmurin increased the retraction rate of the lesion, with an important reduction of the wound area, indicating its ability to induce tissue repair. This multifunctional activity of Stigmurin makes it an interesting candidate for the development of novel therapeutic agents [103].

9.15.2 Acne Management

The application of antimicrobial peptides for skin infections and related conditions such as acne is an area with great potential for future skin therapeutics. Bioactive peptides propose new treatment alternatives for bacterial infections resistant to customary antibiotics [85].

Recent studies about the important roles of autophagy signaling in sebaceous lipogenesis and epidermal differentiation suggest potential benefits of autophagy activation in acne. Results demonstrated that topical application of the autophagy-activating peptide pentasodiumtetracarboxymethyl heptadecanoyl dipeptide-12 clinically improves acne-prone skin, by downregulating sebaceous lipogenesis and supporting the skin barrier function. Since the activation of autophagy signaling, sebocytes differ in the method of action with the commonly applied anti-acne ingredients, a combination of autophagy-activating peptides with other active components can ameliorate the clinical results of topical formulation or be exempted from adverse effects of topical formulation by using lower concentrations of potentially irritating actives.

Consequently, autophagy activation might represent a new therapeutic option in early forms of acne [104].

9.15.3 Melanoma Treatment

In a study concerning liposome-based melanoma treatment, liposomes with TNF-related apoptosis inducing-ligand, anticancer taxane derivative paclitaxel, and a peptide that binds to $\alpha_v\beta_3$ integrin receptors attached, were tested in female mice and rats. The results showed that animals treated with liposomes had a tumor reduction of 95.3% and 93.8% compared with those treated with saline. Though research is still required on the incorporation of bioactive peptides into liposomes for skin cancer treatment, in order to offer a new perspective avoiding the numerous side effects, cancer therapy produces [89].

Further results provided evidence that the use of bioactive cyclic peptides inhibited the proliferation of melanoma xenografts in nude mice and can act as anti-angiogenesis agents in skin cancer therapy [85].

9.16 Applications in Oral Diseases

The oral cavity in humans accommodates hundreds of species of microorganisms including yeasts, bacteria, protozoa, and viruses. There is an appropriate environment for the development of biofilms, which can accumulate and result in diseases such as caries, gingivitis, and periodontitis. Antibiofilm peptides have been found to be active for possible use in a number of therapeutic applications against dental biofilms. Many studies have identified antibiofilm peptides as potential novel alternatives to traditional antimicrobial therapy in the oral cavity [105, 106].

9.16.1 Periodontitis

Various peptides with antimicrobial activity are secreted by epithelial cells, neutrophils, and salivary glands in the oral cavity, such as the gingival crevicular fluid. In the case of periodontitis disease, their expression is increased. Periodontal disease is an inflammatory disease initiated by the formation of multispecies biofilms on teeth, implants, and gingival tissues. *Porphyromonasgingivalis* is an anaerobic Gram-negative bacterium involved in the pounce of inflammation and tissue deterioration during periodontal disease. When it binds and accumulates on the tooth surface leads to the development of a mixed biofilm. Antibiofilm peptides have unique properties, which contribute to the prevention or elimination of oral biofilms. They coevolve with oral bacteria and do not appear to prevent biofilm formation on their own. Nonetheless, when they are used in higher doses, or their peptide sequence is modified properly, their effectiveness is increased. The antimicrobial decapeptide NH^{3+}-Lys-Lys-Val-Val-Phe-Trp-Val-Lys-Phe-Lys-CONH2 (KSL-W) has studied and demonstrated a range of antibacterial activities [105, 106]. In vitro studies have shown that it directly prevents the development of oral biofilms formed by human salivary bacteria, and inhibits the growth of oral bacterial pathogens associated with periodontitis and oral biofilm development [107–109]. However, its mechanism of action is not yet fully elucidated. Some peptides for oral care were developed by Cragen C. Ltd. and studied their mechanism. Oligopeptide-83 (trade name: CG Bucanol) seems to promote bone remodeling by inducing osteoblast differentiation, restores damaged teeth tissue, and reduces bone loss by inhibiting osteoclast differentiation through the activation of a BMP receptor.

9.17 Nutraceuticals

New strategies are developed by the food and cosmetic industries to establish the relationship between nutrient consumption and skin health. As a result, the incorporation of food ingredients and supplements that claim to reduce the risk of skin disorders or alleviate skin aging is rising. Dietary supplements with vitamins, essential fatty acids, or minerals are proposed to improve skin conditions [110]. Most of the bioactive food compounds responsible for the positive effects on health are mainly of plant origin while a few are derived from animal sources [111]. The term "nutraceutical" derives from the combination of "nutrition" and "pharmaceutical" and was established by Stephen DeFelice, a founder and chairman of the Foundation for Innovation in Medicine (FIM), Cranford, New Jersey, in 1989 [112, 113]. According to DeFelice, a nutraceutical can be defined as "a food (or a part of it) that provides medical or health benefits, including the prevention and/or treatment of a disease". Nutraceuticals may be employed for health improvement, delay the aging process, prevent diseases such as obesity, support the structure or function of the body, or even increase life expectancy. Nutraceuticals are continuously receiving considerable interest due to their nutritional potential, safety, and therapeutic effects.

In fact, nutritional supplements and herbal/natural products are the most rapidly growing segments of the nutraceutical industry. Several market factors such as increasing healthcare, growing popularity of nutrition, and rising demand for nutraceuticals have been related to the significant development of this sector [114]. Nutraceuticals can be categorized by food source, mechanism of action, chemical nature, and specific benefits for health. They may be macronutrients (nutrients salts/chemicals elements required in large amounts, e.g., omega 3 acids, and magnesium), micronutrients (nutrients salts/chemicals elements required in small quantities, e.g., minerals and vitamins), and phytochemicals. Food sources used as nutraceuticals are all natural and can be classified as amino acids and peptides, dietary fiber, prebiotics, probiotics, polyunsaturated fatty acids, minerals, vitamins, carotenoids, phytochemicals, and spices. However, although nutraceuticals have shown positive potential in various issues, their uncontrolled use may not be devoid of undesired effects so they should be strictly regulated as prescription drugs.

The intake of the bioactive collagen peptide VERISOL® showed a statistically significant reduction of eye wrinkle volume (compared to placebo) and a statistically significant higher content of procollagen type I and elastin [115].

Oral intake of Peptan®F, which is a specific mixture of collagen peptides of fish origin, showed a significant increase in skin moisture after treatment. Moreover, the same supplement was shown to reduce collagen fragmentation contributing to an anti-aging effect [116]. Additionally, Peptan®P, a specific mixture of collagen peptides of porcine origin, improved skin moisture and minimized skin micro-relief.

Also, the supplementation of CELERGEN®, a nutraceutical product that contains marine collagen peptides (MCPs) derived from deep sea fish, among other plant-derived antioxidant ingredients, enhanced skin elasticity and sebum production, but there was no alteration in several oxidative stress markers.

It can be assumed that a combination of MCPs with plant-derived antioxidants could comprise an efficient and safe supplement to improve skin properties without the risk of oxidative damage [18, 117].

9.18 Aspects to be Considered

Peptides constitute an interesting group of ingredients with biomedical-cosmetic applications, which meet most of the requirements presented by the industry when composing new formulas. Besides bioactivity, two additional aspects have been recently considered, when dealing with peptides as cosmetic ingredients: bioavailability and stability. At this point, novel methods applied in order to enhance peptides' skin-penetration and stability issues in the skin care products arena are going to be described [118].

9.18.1 Skin Permeability Enhancement

The skin possesses a very effective barrier to the permeability of major ingredients in drugs or cosmetics due to its particular properties, like multilayering, lipophilicity, and the action of numerous active enzymes. Consequently, efficacious permeable molecules should have appropriate physicochemical features, like comparatively low molecular weight (up to 500 Da), average lipophilicity (log P between 1 and 3), and good water solubility (over 1 mg/mL) [119].

Concerning macromolecules, dermal delivery can be improved either by the conjugation of different moieties such as alcohols and fatty acids or by surfactants (chemical enhancers) in their composition. Chemical modification like acylation of the amino-terminal or esterification of the carboxylic acid ends with the appropriate carboxylic acid or alcohol, respectively, which may remarkably enhance dermal permeability. Peptide cyclization is another method to augment peptide stability and permeability, since the cyclic peptides may possess different physicochemical properties as compared to their linear counterparts.

The cyclization usually improves stability and may affect the type and the number of interactions between the peptide and target active site, so possibly lead to increasing bioactivity.

Moreover, chemical penetration enhancer alcohols (e.g., propylene glycol), surfactants (e.g., sodium lauryl sulfate), fatty acids (e.g., palmitic acid, myristic acid), and triterpenoids (e.g., ursolic acid). However, a chemical enhancer can play a critical role in the formulation, thus facilitating the membrane permeation (e.g., alcohol as a solvent enhancing the permeation of low soluble active ingredients).

Delivery systems, such as liposomes, nanoparticles, nanostructured liquids, lyotropic liquid crystals, microemulsions, hydrogels, and polymer-based techniques, are also applicable [120].

The employment of physical enhancers, such as microneedles (classic microneedles, microneedle patches, coated microneedles), low electrical current, and ultrasonic waves could be sometimes beneficial.

Chemical and physical methods were developed to improve the bioavailability of bioactive ingredients and also to pave the way for dermal delivery in general. Their mechanisms of action include one or more of three of the following:

(a) disruption of stratum corneum lipid layer, (b) intercellular protein interfering, or (c) advanced partition of the drug into the stratum corneum, obtained by co-enhancers or solvents [121].

On the other hand, physical penetration enhancers do not involve peptide structure modification. They can be divided into a few classes, depending on the mechanism of transdermal delivery: (a) sonophoresis, (b) iontophoresis, (c) electroporation, (d) microneedles, and (e) radiofrequency [122]. Microneedles, pricking skin external layers, create a pathway for molecule delivery. This technique is particularly interesting to the field of cosmetic acting peptides.

9.18.2 Peptide Stability Challenge in Topical Formulation

The number of bioactive peptides exponentially increased over the last decade and will definitely continue to rise in the coming years.

Now, the development of bioactive peptides is targeted toward the improvement of some specific characteristics such as skin permeability or enhancing metabolic stability, thus the number of these molecules is continually increasing.

Half-life under physiological conditions is one of the key aspects of the use of peptides in general, and to improve it is always a big challenge. In spite of their generally topical application, chemical degradation of peptides is one of the major challenges due to their high susceptibility to the proteases widely abundant all over the skin, resulting in limited bioavailability.

Some of the modifications recently established in the peptides with cosmetic applications for their dermal stability improvement include:

1. **Backbone Modifications**: The development of eptidomimetics can be an advantageous strategy since the disadvantages due to the low bioavailability and short half-life of peptides with sequences derived from proteins are overcome.
2. **Use of Non-Coded Amino Acids**: It is an approach to protect synthetic peptides from proteolytic enzymic activity.
3. **Use of D-Amino Acids**: The use of a modified peptide backbone is widely known both in therapeutics [123] and cosmetics.
4. **Cyclic Peptides**: The cyclization of linear active peptides is one of the most common alterations presented in the literature for the enhancement of peptide stability. There are two classes of cyclic peptides: the homodetic, if the bridge that contributes to the ring is a peptide bond, and the heterodetic, if the cyclization includes other bridges such as disulfide between two cysteine residues, ester (lactone), and thioether bridges. However, to the best of our knowledge, no examples of this modification have been practically applied in the cosmetic field.

5. **Peptide Conjugations**: As mentioned, conjugation of bioactive molecular entities with other molecules is one of the easiest ways to alter the physicochemical properties of organic molecules, e.g., enhanced permeability or stability.
6. **PEGylation**: Polyethylene glycol (PEG) is a polyether molecule commonly used in several different industries, thanks to its low toxicity.

   In the form of PEG hexadecyl ether, PEG is used as a basic component of topical creams, sometimes in combination with glycerin. A currently developed technique to increase peptide stability is N-conjugation with PEG [124]. The modifications were shown to increase half-lives in the presence of skin proteases extracted from rat skin homogenates, suggesting that PEGylation protects against aminopeptidase, proteases specific to free amino termini. Moreover, the conjugates were not cytotoxic at the concentration tested.
7. **Ascorbic Acid Conjugation**: Ascorbic acid (vitamin C) and its derivatives are used in numerous cosmetic products because ascorbic acid is involved in several processes localized in human skin, one of these is collagen biosynthesis. Studies revealed that ascorbyl conjugated peptides showed increased stability against peptidases and also a more stimulating effect on collagen biosynthesis, even in comparison with vitamin C alone [55, 125].
8. **Biotinylation**: Biotin (a part of the B-complex group of vitamins, previously named as H vitamin) is another vitamin used in cosmetic products. There are few biotinylated peptides in cosmetics whose improved physical stability was studied [81, 118, 126].

9.19 Conclusion

Bioactive peptides are biomolecules with different effects on cellular behavior in a way that could promote the biological functions of the skin, thereby might ultimately improve skin disorders [29].

Short peptides have several advantages compared to their larger analogs, such as economical synthesis on a small and large-scale, broad chemical diversity, can easily be modified, highly bio-active, high selectivity and specificity, absorbability, accessibility, tunable functionalization, biocompatibility, high safety, low toxicity (due to their safe metabolites-amino acids and the limited possibility for accumulation in the body), and low immunogenicity [127].

Peptides have diverse bio-functionalities of their components (amino acids) and good biomolecular recognition [128, 129]. Thus, they have a high binding affinity for a wide range of specific targets.

However, short peptides have disadvantages, such as high conformational flexibility that can result for example in the lack of receptor selectivity, or problems in permeability of greater peptides via physiological barriers (due to the strong interactions of peptide backbone with water molecules) [130]. Different ways and methods are followed to overcome peptide restrictions and increase their biomedical applications [131]. Structural modifications can lead to the improvement of physicochemical properties or can result in greater general stability. Further improvement can be achieved by "double-bridged peptides" when peptides are cyclized via two chemical bridges. It reduces peptide backbone flexibility and consequently leads to limited availability for enzymes. Variations in the sequence length and side chains, peptide backbone modification, C-terminal acylation, N-terminal acylation, the addition of stabilizing (sugars, salts), and chelating agents, e.g., ethylenediaminetetraacetic acid (EDTA), conjugations with large biocompatible polymers, such as PEG, or fatty acids can be applied and thus peptides can be stabilized in their bioactive conformation, show increased efficiency, hydrodynamic volume, and also greater membrane permeability and target selectivity [129–133]. Additionally, the conjugation to cell-penetrating peptides enhances cellular membrane crossing and allocates accessing intracellular targets by peptide-drugs or acts as gene delivery vectors revealing great perspective as theragnostics for clinical use leading both to improved drug bioavailability and also therapeutic efficiency [134, 135]. The conjugations of short peptides with non-peptidic parts enhance bioactivities [136] while synthetic short peptides being exact copies of protein parts imitate protein sites [135]. In addition, peptoids, native peptide-based moieties, can lead to improved pharmacokinetic profile [137, 138].

In conclusion, bioactive peptides demonstrate a significant range of biological functions, which may be applied by innovative therapies in almost all medical aspects. These peptides can be employed in biomedical, diagnostic, pharmaceutical, and cosmetic applications. Peptides can act either as drugs or play a supporting role in diagnosis, treatment, cell penetration, targeting, etc. Natural and synthetic short peptides, including peptidomimetics, find numerous applications in nanotechnology [23].

The application of functional peptides to the cosmetics industry holds great promise due to a wide range of actions, chemistries, and indications that can be developed, contributing to skin tone and texture improvement – ECM homeostasis, skin tone and texture improvement – ECM homeostasis, acne management, cell renewal, skin whitening, and oxidative stress management [139].

The cost-benefit ratio is key in this area, and the balance of economics, peptide concentration, and reproducible, stable, and deliverable bioactivity, will be the other drivers for the success of each peptide on an individual basis [36].

References

1. Pullar J.M., Carr A.C., Vissers M.C.M. (2017). The roles of vitamin C in skin health, *Nutrients*, **9**, pp. 866–892.
2. Madison K.C. (2003). Barrier function of the skin: "La raison d'etre" of the epidermis, *J. Investig. Dermatol.*, **121**, pp. 231–241.
3. Shindo Y., Witt E., Han D., Epstein W., Packer L. (1994). Enzymic and non-enzymic antioxidants in epidermis and dermis of human skin, *J. Investig. Dermatol.*, **102**, pp. 122–124.
4. Katiyar S., Elmets C.A., Katiyar S.K. (2007). Green tea and skin cancer: Photoimmunology, angiogenesis and DNA repair, *J. Nutr. Biochem.*, **18**, pp. 287–296.
5. Menon G.K. (2002). New insights into skin structure: Scratching the surface, *Adv. Drug Deliv. Rev.*, **54**, pp. S3–S17.

6. Slominski A., Paus R., Schadendorf D. (1993). Melanocytes as "sensory" and regulatory cells in the epidermis, *J. Theor. Biol.*, **164**, pp. 103–120.

7. Slominski A., Tobin D.J., Shibahara S., Wortsman J. (2004). Melanin pigmentation in mammalian skin and its hormonal regulation, *Physiol. Rev.*, **84**, pp. 1155–1228.

8. Kalka K., Mukhtar H., Turowski-Wanke A., Merk H. (2000). Biomelanin antioxidants in cosmetics: Assessment based on inhibition of lipid peroxidation, *Skin Pharmacol. Appl. Skin Physiol.*, **13**, pp. 143–149.

9. Mackintosh J.A. (2001). The antimicrobial properties of melanocytes, melanosomes and melanin and the evolution of black skin, *J. Theor. Biol.*, **211,** pp. 101–113.

10. Meyskens F.L. Jr., Farmer P., Fruehauf J.P. (2001). Redox regulation in human melanocytes and melanoma, *Pigment Cell Res.*, **14**, pp. 148–154.

11. Double K.L., Ben-Shachar D., Youdim M.B., Zecca L., Riederer P., Gerlach M. (2002). Influence of neuromelanin on oxidative pathways within the human substantia nigra, *Neurotoxicol. Teratol.*, **24,** pp. 621–628.

12. Wang A., Marino A.R., Gasyna Z., Gasyna E., Norris J. Jr. (2008). Photoprotection by porcine eumelanin against singlet oxygen production, *Photochem. Photobiol.*, **84**, pp. 679–682.

13. Natarajan V.T., Ganju P., Ramkumar A., Grover R., Gokhale R.S. (2014). Multifaceted pathways protect human skin from UV radiation, *Nat. Chem. Biol.*, **10**, pp. 542–551.

14. Singh T.P., Zhang H.H., Borek I., Wolf P., Hedrick M.N., Singh S.P., Kelsall B.L., Clausen B.E., Farber J.M. (2016). Monocyte-derived inflammatory langerhans cells and dermal dendritic cells mediate psoriasis-like inflammation, *Nat. Commun.*, **7,** pp. 13581–13598.

15. Labat-Robert J. (2012). Information exchanges between cells and extracellular matrix, influence of ageing, *Biol. Aujourdhui*, **206**, pp. 103–109.

16. Kim D.W., Hwang H.S., Kim D.S., Sheen S.H., Heo D.H., Hwang G. Kang S.H., Kweon H., Jo Y.Y., Kang S.W., Lee K.G., Park K.W., Han K.H., Park J., Eum W.S., Cho Y.J., Choi H.C. (2011). Effect of silk fibroin peptide derived from silkworm Bombyx mori on the anti-inflammatory effect of Tat-SOD in a mice edema model, *BMB Rep.*, **44**, pp. 787–792.

17. Quan T., Fisher G.J. (2015). Role of age-associated alterations of the dermal extracellular matrix microenvironment in human skin ageing: A mini-review, *Gerontology*, **61**, pp. 427–434.

18. Sánchez A.P., Catalán E.B., López M.H., Micol V. (2018). Skin, neutraceuticals, bioactive peptides, nutraceuticals for skin care: A comprehensive review of human clinical studies, *Nutrients*, **10**, pp. 403–424.

19. Errante F., Ledwoǹ P., Latajka R., Rovero P., Papini A.M. (2020). Cosmeceutical peptides in the framework of sustainable wellness economy, *Frontiers in Chemistry*, **8**, pp. 1–8.

20. Pandey A., Jatana G.K., Sonthalia S. (2021). *Cosmeceuticals*, Treasure Island (FL): Statpearls Publishing, Bookshelf ID: NBK430685.

21. Varvaresou A., Papageorgiou S., Protopapa E., Katsarou A. (2011). Efficacy and tolerance study of an oligopeptide with potential anti-aging activity cosmetics, *J.C.D.S.A.*, **1**, pp. 133–140.

22. Varvaresou A., Papageorgiou S., Mellou F., Protopapa E. (2016). Study in anti-wrinkle activity of a night cream containing a combination of antioxidants, phyto-steroids and acetyl-tetrapeptide-9 by biophysical methods and objective evaluation, *Rev. Clin. Pharmacol. Pharmacokinet. Int. Ed.*, **30**, pp. 67–70.

23. Apostolopoulos V., Bojarska J., Chai T.T., Elnagdy S., Kaczmarek K., Matsoukas J., New R., Parang K., Lopez O.P., Parhiz H., Perera C.O., Pickholz M., Remko M., Saviano M., Skwarczynski M., Tang Y., Wolf W.M., Yoshiya T., Zabrocki J., Zielenkiewicz P., AlKhazindar M., Barriga V., Kelaidonis K., Sarasia E.M., Toth I.A. (2021). Global review on short peptides: Frontiers and perspectives, *Molecules*, **26**, pp. 430–474.

24. Li Y., Xiang Q., Zhang Q., Huang Y., Su Z. (2012). Overview on the recent study of antimicrobial peptides: Origins, functions, relative mechanisms and application, *Peptides*, **37**, pp. 207–215.

25. Power O., Jakeman P., FitzGerald R. (2013). Antioxidative peptides: Enzymatic production, in vitro and in vivo antioxidant activity and potential applications of milk-derived antioxidative peptides, *Amino Acids*, **44**, 797–820.

26. Khiari Z., Rico D., Martin-Diana A.B., Barry-Ryan C. (2014). Structure elucidation of ACE-inhibitory and antithrombotic peptides isolated from mackerel skin gelatine hydrolysates, *J. Sci. Food Agric.*, **94**, pp. 1663–1671.

27. Pokora M., Zambrowicz A., Dąbrowska A., Eckert E., Setner B., Szołtysik M., Szewczuk Z., Zabłocka A., Polanowski A., Trziszka T., Chrzanowska J. (2014). An attractive way of egg white protein by product use for producing of novel anti-hypertensive peptides, *Food Chem.*, **151**, pp. 500–505.

28. Haney E.F., Hancock R.E. (2013). Peptide design for antimicrobial and immunomodulatory applications, *Pept. Sci.*, **100**, pp. 572–583.

29. Zohrab F., Askarian S., Jalili A., Oskuee R.K. (2019). Biological properties, current applications and potential therapeutic applications of brevinin peptide superfamily, *Int. J. Pept. Res. Ther.*, **25**, pp. 39–48.

30. Gaspar P.K. (2003). Neuropeptides in the skin, *An. Bras. Dermatol.*, **78**, pp. 483–498.

31. Scholzen T., Armstrong C., Burnett N., Luger T., Olerud J., Ansel J. (1998). Neuropeptides in the skin: Interactions between the neuroendocrine and the skin immune systems, *Exp. Dermatol.*, **7**, pp. 81–96.

32. Guimaraes D.E.D., Sardinha F.L.C., Mizurini D.M., Carmo M.G.T. (2007). Adipocinas: Uma nova visão do tecido adipose, *Rev. Nutr.*, **20**, pp. 549–559.

33. Seo M.D., Won H.S., Kim J.H., Mishig-Ochir T., Lee B.J. (2012). Antimicrobial peptides for therapeutic applications: A review, *Molecules*, **17**, pp.12276–12286.

34. Pai V.V., Bhandari P., Shukla P. (2017). Topical peptides as cosmeceuticals, *Indian J. Dermatol. Venereol. Leprol.*, **83**, pp. 9–18.

35. Gazitaeva Z.I., Drobintsev, A.O., Chung Y., Polyakova V.O., Kvetnoy I.M. (2017). Cosmeceutical product consisting of biomimetic peptides: Antiaging effects in vivo and in vitro, *Clin. Cosmet. Investig. Dermatol.*, **10**, pp. 11–16.

36. Zhang L., Falla T.J. (2009). Cosmeceuticals and peptides, *Clin. Dermatol.*, **27**, pp. 485–494.

37. Fields K., Falla T.J., Rodan K., Bush L. (2009). Bioactive peptides: Signaling the future, *J. Cosmet. Dermatol.*, **8**, pp. 8–13.

38. Lintner K., Mas-Chamberlin C., Mondon P., Peschard O., Lamy L. (2009). Cosmeceuticals and active ingredients, *Clin. Dermatol.*, **27**, pp. 461–468.

39. Gorouhi F., Maibach H. (2009). Role of topical peptides in preventing or treating aged skin, *Int. J. Cosmet. Sci.*, **31**, pp. 327–345.

40. Siméon A., Monier F., Emonard H., Gillery P., Birembaut P., Hornebeck W., Maquart F.X. (1999). Expression and activation of matrix metalloproteinases in wounds: Modulation by the tripeptide-copper complex glycyl-L-histidyl-L-lysine-Cu^{2+}, *J. Investig. Dermatol.*, **112**, pp. 957–964.

41. Netto J.C., Mendonça R.J. (2009). Aspectos celulares da cicatrização, *An. Bras. Dermatol.*, **84**, pp. 257–262.

42. Carpenter G., Cohen S. (1990). Epidermal growth factor, *J. Biol. Chem.*, **265**, pp. 7709–7712.
43. Lima T.N., Moraes C.A.P. (2018). Bioactive peptides: Applications and relevance for cosmeceuticals, *Cosmetics,* **5**, pp. 21–29.
44. Fischer E., Fourneau E. (1901). Ueber einige derivate des glykocolls, *Eur. J. Inorg. Chem.*, **34**, pp. 2868–2877.
45. Rahnamaeian M., Vilcinskas A. (2015). Short antimicrobial peptides as cosmetic ingredients to deter dermatological pathogens, *Appl. Microbiol. Biotechnol.*, **99**, pp. 8847–8855.
46. Schagen S.K. (2017). Topical peptide treatments with effective anti-aging results, *Cosmetics*, **4**, pp. 16–29.
47. Mitragotri S. (2003). Modeling skin permeability to hydrophilic and hydrophobic solutes based on four permeation pathways, *J. Control. Release*, **86**, pp. 69–92.
48. Partidos C.D., Beignon A.S., Brown F., Kramer E., Briand J.P., Muller S. (2002). Applying peptide antigens onto bare skin: Induction of humoral and cellular immune responses and potential for vaccination, *J. Control. Release*, **85**, pp. 27–34.
49. Loing E. Unipex Innovations, Québec, Canada; Thiery Suere, Elisabeth Lamarque, Unipex Innovations, Ramonville St. Agne, France, Trifluoroacetyl-tripeptide-2 to target senescence for anti-aging benefits, Available online: http://www.cosmeticsandtoiletries.com/formulating/category/skincare/premium-Trifluoroacetyl-Tripept, accessed on April 22, 2017.
50. Puig A., Antón J.M., Mangues M. (2008). A new decorin-like tetrapeptide for optimal organization of collagen fibres, *Int. J. Cosmet. Sci.*, **30**, pp. 97–104.
51. Raikou V., Varvaresou A., Panderi I., Papageorgiou E. (2017). The efficacy study of the combination of Acetyl Hexapeptide-3 and Tripeptide-10-citrulline: A prospective, randomized controlled study, *J. Cosmet. Dermatol.*, **16**, pp. 271–278.
52. Scientific Literature Review. (2017). Safety assessment of palmitoyl oligopeptides as used in cosmetics, pp. 1–22.
53. Fournial A., Mondon P. (2017). New cosmetic or dermopharmaceutical topical use of a mixture of a Ghk tripeptide and Gqpr tetrapeptide, Availableonline: www.google.com/patents/WO2012164488A2?cl=en, accessed on April 22, 2017.
54. Imfeld D., Jackson E., Heidl M., Campiche R. (2015). Activation of TGF a gateway to skin rejuvenation small synthetic-peptide mimics

natural protein activity in skin to unlock TGF potential, H&PC today-househ, *Pers. Care Today*, **10**, pp. 6–11.

55. Farwick M., Grether-Beck S., Marini A., Maczkiewitz U., Lange J., Köhler T. Lersch P., Falla T., Felsner I., Brenden H., Jaenicke T., Franke S., Krutmann J. (2011). Bioactive tetrapeptide GEKG boosts extracellular matrix formation: In vitro and in vivo molecular and clinical proof, *Exp. Dermatol.*, **20**, pp. 602–604.
56. Marini A., Farwick M., Grether-Beck S., Brenden H., Felsner I., Jaenicke T., Weber M., Schild J., Maczkiewitz U., Köhler T., Bonfigli A., Pagani V., Krutmann J. (2012). Modulation of skin pigmentation by the tetrapeptide PKEK: In vitro and in vivo evidence for skin whitening effects, *Exp. Dermatol.*, **21**, pp. 140–146.
57. Sanz M.T., Campos C., Milani M., Foyaca M., Lamy A., Kurdian K., Trullas C. (2016). Biorevitalizing effect of a novel facial serum containing apple stem cell extract, pro-collagen lipopeptide, creatine, and urea on skin aging signs, *J. Cosmet. Dermatol.*, **15**, pp. 24–30.
58. Herndon J.H. Jr., Jiang L., Kononov T., Fox T. (2015). An open label clinical trial of a multi-ingredient anti-aging moisturizer designed to improve the appearance of facial skin, *J. Drugs Dermatol.*, **14**, pp. 699–704.
59. Mondon P., Hillion M., Peschard O., Andre N., Marchand T., Doridot E., Feuilloley M.G., Pionneau C., Chardonnet S. (2015). Evaluation of dermal extracellular matrix and epidermal-dermal junction modifications using matrix-assisted laser desorption/ionization mass spectrometric imaging, in vivo reflectance confocal microscopy, echography, and histology: Effect of age and pepti, *J. Cosmet. Dermatol.*, **14**, pp. 152–160.
60. Kaczvinsky J.R., Griffiths C.E., Schnicker M.S., Li J. (2009). Efficacy of anti-aging products for periorbital wrinkles as measured by 3-D imaging, *J. Cosmet. Dermatol.*, **8**, pp. 228–233.
61. Lintner K. (2003). Cosmetic or dermopharmaceutical use of peptides for healing, hydrating and improving skin appearances during natural or induced ageing (Heliodermia, Pollution), US Patent 6,620,419.
62. Robinson L.R., Fitzgerald N.C., Doughty D.G., Dawes N.C., Berge C.A., Bissett D.L. (2005). Topical palmitoyl pentapeptide provides improvement in photoaged human facial skin, *Int. J. Cosmet. Sci.*, **27**, pp. 155–160.
63. Biopeptide EL™, Available online: http://www.webareal.com.ua/fotky27371/BIOPEPTIDE_EL_.pdf, accessed on April 22, 2017.

64. Rodrigues A.L., Benoit I., Clarius T., Pauly G. (2009). Counter acting ageing phenomena by new pure tetrapeptides with targeted efficacy, *Cosmet. Sci. Technol.*, **27**, pp. 63–71.

65. Gruber J.V., Ludwig P., Holtz R. (2013). Modulation of cellular senescence in fibroblasts and dermal papillae cells in vitro, *J. Cosmet. Sci.*, **64**, pp. 79–87.

66. Linder J. (2012). The science behind peptides, *Plast. Surg. Nurs.*, **32**, pp. 71–72.

67. Hussain M., Goldberg, D.J. (2007). Topical manganese peptide in the treatment of photodamaged skin, *J. Cosmet. Laser Ther.*, **9**, pp. 232–236.

68. Pickar L., Schagen S. (2015). New data of the cosmeceutical and tripeptide GHK, *SOFW J.*, **9**, pp. 141–146.

69. Leyden J.J., Stevens T., Finkey M.B., Barkovic S. (2002). Skin care benefits of copper peptide containing facial cream, *In Proceedings of the American Academy of Dermatology 60th Annual Meeting*, New Orleans, LA, USA, February 22–27, pp. 29.

70. Abdulghani A., Sherr A., Shirin S., Solodkina G., Tapia E., Wolf B., Gottlieb A. (1998). Effects of topical creams containing vitamin C, a copper-binding peptide cream and melatonin compared with tretinoin on the ultrastructure of normal skin: A pilot clinical, histologic, and ultrastructural study, *Dis. Manag. Clin. Outcomes*, **1**, pp. 136–141.

71. Finkley M., Appa Y., Bhandarkar S. (2005). *Cosmeceuticals and Active Cosmetics: Drugs vs. Cosmetics,* Elsner P., Maibach H. (eds.), Chapter "Copper Peptide and Skin", Marcel Dekker, New York, USA, pp. 549–563.

72. Trookman N.S., Rizer R.L., Ford R., Ho E., Gotz V. (2009). Immediate and long-term clinical benefits of a topical treatment for facial lines and wrinkles, *J. Clin. Aesthet. Dermatol.*, **2**, pp. 38–43.

73. Zhmak M.N., Utkin Y.N., Andreeva T.V., Kudryavtsev D.S., Kryudova E.V., Tsetlin V.I., Shelukhina I.V.E. (2015). Peptide inhibitors of nicotinic acetylcholine receptor, US Patent, US 20,150,361,137 A1, 17.

74. Rull M., Davi C., Cañadas E., Almiñana N., Delgado R. (2017). Peptide approach to enhance anti-wrinkle efficacy between injections, Available online: http://www.cosmeticsandtoiletries.com/formulating/category/antiaging/Peptide-Approach-to-Enhance-Anti-wrinkle-Efficacy Between-Injections-premium-273052431.html.

75. Blanes-Mira C., Clemente J., Jodas G., Gil A., Fernández-Ballester G., Ponsati B., Gutierrez L., Pérez-Payá E., Ferrer-Montiel A. (2002). A synthetic hexapeptide (Argireline) with antiwrinkle activity, *Int. J. Cosmet. Sci.*, **24**, pp. 303–310.

76. Wang Y., Wang M., Xiao S., Pan P., Li P., Huo J. (2013). The anti-wrinkle efficacy of argireline, a synthetic hexapeptide, in Chinese subjects: A randomized, placebo-controlled study, *Am. J. Clin. Dermatol.*, **14**, pp. 147–153.

77. Sim G.S., Lee D.H., Kim J.H., An S.K., Choe T.B., Kwon T.J., Pyo H.B., Lee B.C. (2007). Black rice (*Oryza sativa* L. var. *japonica*) hydrolyzed peptides induce expression of hyaluronan synthase 2 gene in HaCaT keratinocytes, *J. Microbiol. Biotechnol.*, **17**, pp. 271–279.

78. Manosroi A., Chutoprapat R., Abe M., Manosroi W., Manosroi J. (2012). Anti-aging efficacy of topical formulations containing niosomes entrapped with rice bran bioactive compounds, *Pharm. Biol.*, **50**, pp. 208–224.

79. Barba C., Méndez S., Roddick-Lanzilotta A., Kelly R., Parra J.L., Coderch L. (2007). Wool peptide derivatives for hand care, *J. Cosmet. Sci.*, **58**, pp. 99–107.

80. Barba C., Méndez S., Roddick-Lanzilotta A., Kelly R., Parra J.L., Coderch L. (2008). Cosmetic effectiveness of topically applied hydrolysed keratin peptides and lipids derived from wool, *Skin Res. Technol.*, **14**, pp. 243–248.

81. Lintner K., Peschard O. (2000). Biologically active peptides: From a laboratory bench curiosity to a functional skin care product, *Int. J. Cosmet. Sci.*, **22**, pp. 207–218.

82. Emanuele E., Spencer J.M., Braun M. (2014). An experimental double-blind irradiation study of a novel topical product (TPF 50) compared to other topical products with DNA repair enzymes, antioxidants, and growth factors with sunscreens: Implications for preventing skin aging and cancer, *J. Drugs Dermatol.*, **13**, pp. 309–314.

83. Nino M., Iovine B., Santoianni P. (2011). Carnosine and N-acetylcarnosine induce inhibition of UVB erythema in human skin, *J. Cosmet. Dermatol. Sci. Appl.*, **1**, pp. 177–179.

84. Fosgerau K., Hoffmann T. (2015). Peptide therapeutics: Current status and future directions, *Drug Discov. Today*, **20**, pp. 122–128.

85. Namjoshi S., Benson H.A.E. (2010). Cyclic peptides as potential therapeutic agents for skin disorders, *J. Pept. Sci.*, **94**, pp. 673–680.

86. Carney B.C., McKesey J.P., Rosenthal D.S., Shupp J.W., (2018). Treatment strategies for hypopigmentation in the context of burn hypertrophic scars, *Plastic and Reconstructive Surgery – Global Open*, pp. **6**, 1–9.

87. Kong S., Choi H.R., Kim Y.J., Lee Y.S., Park K.C., Kwak S.Y. (2020). Milk protein-derived antioxidant tetrapeptides as potential hypopigmenting agents, *Antioxidants-Basel*, **9**, pp. 1106–1117.

88. La Manna S., Di Natale C., Florio D., Marasco D. (2018). Peptides as therapeutic agents for inflammatory-related diseases, *Int. J. Mol. Sci.*, **19**, pp. 2714–2731.

89. Castañeda-Reyes E.D., de Jesús Perea-Flores M., Davila-Ortiz G., Lee Y., de Mejia E.G. (2020). Development, characterization and use of liposomes as amphipathic transporters of bioactive compounds for melanoma treatment and reduction of skin inflammation: A review, *Int. J. Nanomedicine*, **8**, pp. 7627–7650.

90. Nguyen H. Le T., Trujillo-Paez J.V., Umehara Y., Yue H., Kiatsurayanon G.P.C., Chieosilapatham P., Song P., Okumura K., Ogawa H., Ikeda S., Niyonsaba F. (2020). Role of antimicrobial peptides in skin barrier repairin individuals with atopic dermatitis, *Int. J. Mol. Sci.*, **21**, pp. 7607–7623.

91. Korting H.C., Schöllmann C., Stauss-Grabo M., Schäfer-Korting M. (2012). Antimicrobial peptides and skin: A paradigm of translational medicine skin, *Pharmacol. Physiol.*, **25**, pp. 323–334.

92. Kimura Y., Sumiyoshi M., Kobayashi T. (2014). Whey peptides prevent chronic ultraviolet B radiation-induced skin aging in melanin possessing male hairless mice, *J. Nutr.*, **144**, pp. 27–32.

93. Patel S. (2015). Emerging trends in nutraceutical applications of whey protein and its derivatives, *J. Food Sci. Technol.*, **52**, pp. 6847–6858.

94. Reddy B.Y., Jow T., Hantash B.M. (2012). Bioactive oligopeptides in dermatology: Part II, *John Wiley & Sons A/S Experimental Dermatology*, **21**, pp. 569–575.

95. Liu H., Mu L., Tang J., Shen C., Gao C., Rong M., Zhang Z., Liu J., Wu X., Lai R. (2014). A potential wound healing-promoting peptide from frog skin, *Int. J. Biochem. Cell. Biol.*, **49**, pp. 32–41.

96. Mashreghi M., Bazaz M.R., Shahri N.M., Asoodeh A., Mashreghi M., Rassouli M.B., Golmohammadzadeh S. (2013). Topical effects of frog "Rana ridibunda" skin secretions on wound healing and reduction of wound microbial load, *J Ethnopharmacol.*, **145**, pp. 793–797.

97. Rezazade Bazaz M., Mashreghi M., Mahdavi Shahri N., Mashreghi M., Asoodeh A., Behnam Rassouli M. (2015). Evaluation of antimicrobial

and healing activities of frog skin on Guinea pigs wounds, *Jundishapur, J. Microbiol.*, **8**, pp. e21218–e21223.

98. Kumar K., Sai K.P., Babu M. (2002). Application of frog (Rana tigerina Daudin) skin collagen as a novel substrate in cell culture, *J. Biomed. Mater. Res. Part A*, **61**, pp. 197–202.

99. Raghavan K.V., Babu M., Rajaram R., Sai K.P. (2010). Efficacy of frog skin lipids in wound healing, *Lipids Health Dis.*, **9**, pp. 74–80.

100. Popovic S., Urban E., Lukic M., Conlon J.M. (2012). Peptides with antimicrobial and anti-inflammatory activities that have therapeutic potential for treatment of acne vulgaris, *Peptides*, **34**, pp. 275–282.

101. Al-Ghaferi N., Kolodziejek J., Nowotny N., Coquet L., Jouenne T., Leprince J., Vaudry H., King J.D., Conlon J.M. (2010). Antimicrobial peptides from the skin secretions of the South-East Asian frog Hylarana erythraea (Ranidae), *Peptides*, **31**, pp. 548–554.

102. Yang F., Qin X., Zhang T., Zhang C., Lin H. (2019). Effect of oral administration of active peptides of pinctada martensii on the repair of skin wounds, *Mar. Drugs*, **17**, pp. 697–710.

103. Silva A.D., Rodrigues S. de C. S., Dos Santos E.C.G., Neto M.F., de Q., Hugo Alexandre de Oliveira Rocha H.A., de O., da Silva-Júnior A.A., Resende J.M., Araújo R.M., Pedrosa M.F. (2021). NMR three-dimensional structure of the cationic peptide Stigmurin from *Tityus stigmurus* scorpion venom: In vitro antioxidant and in vivo antibacterial and healing activity, *Peptides*, **137**, pp. 170478–170486.

104. Lee Y., Shin K., Shin K.O., Yoon S., Jung J., Hwang E., Chung H.J., Hossini A.M., Zouboulis C.C., Baek M.J., Baek J.H., Chi Y.M., Lee S., Jeong S. (2021). Topical application of autophagy-activating peptide improved skin barrier function and reduced acne symptoms in acneprone skin, *J. Cosmet. Dermatol.*, **20**, pp. 1009–1016.

105. Wang Z., Shen Y., Haapasalo M. (2017). Antibiofilm peptides against oral biofilms, *J. Oral Microbiol.*, **9**, pp. 1327308–1327318.

106. Bernegossi J., Calixto G.M.F., Sanches P.R. da S., Fontana C.R., Cilli E.M., Garrido S.S., Chorilli M. (2016). Peptide KSL-W-loaded mucoadhesive liquid crystalline vehicle as an alternative treatment for multispecies oral biofilm, *Molecules*, **21**, pp. 37–50.

107. Darveau R.P., Belton C.M., Reife R.A. (1998). Lamont R.J. Local chemokine paralysis, a novel pathogenic mechanism for porphyromonas gingivalis, *Infect. Immun.*, **66**, pp. 1660–1665, 105/8*.

108. Abusleme L., Dupuy A.K., Dutzan N., Silva N., Burleson J.A., Strausbaugh L.D., Gamonal J., Diaz P.I. (2013). The subgingival microbiome in

health and periodontitis and its relation-ship with community biomass and inflammation. *ISME J.*, **7**, pp. 1016–1041.

109. Hajishengallis G., Liang S., Payne M.A., Hashim A., Jotwani R., Eskan M.A., McIntosh M.L., Alsam A., Kirkwood K.L., Lambris J.D., Darveau R.P., Curtis M.A. (2011). Low-abundance biofilm species orchestrates inflammatory periodontal disease through the commensal microbiota and complement, *Cell Host Microbe.*, **10**, pp. 497–506.

110. Boelsma E., Hendriks H.F., Roza L. (2001). Nutritional skin care: Health effects of micronutrients and fatty acids, *Am. J. Clin. Nutr.*, **73**, pp. 853–864.

111. Kussmann M., Affolter M., Nagy K., Holst B., Fay L.B. (2007). Mass spectrometry in nutrition: Understanding dietary health effects at the molecular level, *Mass Spectrom. Rev.*, **26**, pp. 727–750.

112. Brower V. (1998). Nutraceuticals: Poised for a healthy slice of the healthcare market, *Nat. Biotechnol.*, **16**, pp. 728–731.

113. Kalra E.K. (2003). Nutraceutical–definition and introduction, *AAPS PharmSci.*, **5**, pp. 27–28.

114. Variant Market Research. Available online: https://www.variantmarketresearch.com/report-categories/food-beverages/nutraceuticals-market, accessed on October 3, 2017.

115. Proksch E., Schunck M., Zague V., Segger D., Degwert J., Oesser S. (2014). Oral intake of specific bioactiven collagen peptides reduces skin wrinkles and increases dermal matrix synthesis, *Skin Pharmacol. Physiol.*, **27**, pp. 113–119.

116. Asserin J., Lati E., Shioya T., Prawitt J. (2015). The effect of oral collagen peptide supplementation on skin moisture and the dermal collagen network: Evidence from an ex vivo model and randomized, placebo-controlled clinical trials, *J. Cosmet. Dermatol.*, **14**, pp. 291–301.

117. De Luca C., Mikhal'chik E.V., Suprun M.V., Papacharalambous M., Truhanov A.I., Korkina L.G. (2016). Skin anti-ageing and systemic redox effects of supplementation with marine collagen peptides and plant-derived antioxidants: A single-blind case-control clinical study, *Oxid. Med. Cell. Longev.*, **2016**, pp. 1–14.

118. Ledwoń P., Errante F., Papini A.M., Rovero P., Latajka R. (2021). Peptides as active ingredients: A challenge for cosmeceutical industry, *Chem Biodivers.*, **18**, pp. 1–14.

119. Bos J.D., Meinardi M.M.H.M. (2000). The 500 Dalton rule for the skin penetration of chemical compounds and drugs, *Exp. Dermatol.*, **9**, pp. 165–169.

120. Nasrollahi S.A., Taghibiglou C., Azizi E., Farboud E.S. (2012). Cell penetrating peptides as a novel transdermal drug delivery system, *Chem. Biol. Drug Des.*, **80**, pp. 639–646.

121. Mathur V., Satrawala Y., Rajput M. (2010). Physical and chemical penetration enhancers in transdermal drug delivery system, *Asian J. Pharm.*, **4**, pp. 173–183.

122. Rodriguez-Cruz I. M., Dominguez-Delgado C.L., Escobar-Chavez J.J., Lopez-Cervantes M., Diaz-Torres R. (2016). Current technologies to increase the transdermal delivery of drugs, *Bentham Science Publishers*, **2**, eISBN: 978-1-68108-363-6, pp. 3–34.

123. Chorev M. (2005). The partial retro-inverso modification: A road traveled together, *Biopolymers*, **80**, pp. 67–84.

124. Kim M.S., Park E.J., Na D.H. (2015). Synthesis and characterization of monodisperse poly(ethylene glycol)-conjugated collagen pentapeptides with collagen biosynthesis-stimulating activity, *Bioorg. Med. Chem. Lett.*, **25**, pp. 38–42.

125. Choi H.I., Kim H.J., Park J.I., Shin E.H., Kim D.W., Kim S.-S. (2009). Design and efficient synthesis of novel ascorbyl conjugated peptide with high collagen biosynthesis stimulating effects, *Bioorg. Med. Chem. Lett.*, **19**, pp. 2079–2082.

126. Jeong S., Yoon S., Kim S., Jung J., Kor M., Shin K., Lim C., Han H. S., Lee H., Park K.Y., Kim J., Chung H.J., Kim H.J. (2019). Anti-wrinkle benefits of peptides complex stimulating skin basement membrane proteins expression, *Int. J. Mol. Sci.*, **21**, pp. 73–84.

127. Soudy R., Kimura R., Patel A., Fu W., Kaur K., Westaway D., Yang J., Jhamandas J. (2019). Short amylin receptor antagonist peptides improve memory deficits in Alzheimer's disease mouse model, *Sci. Rep.*, **9**, pp. 10942–10953.

128. Hamley I.W. (2017). Small bioactive peptides for biomaterials design and therapeutics, *Chem. Rev.*, **117**, pp. 14015–14041.

129. Morimoto B.H. (2018). Therapeutic peptides for CNS indications: Progress and challenges, *Bioorganic Med. Chem.*, **26**, pp. 2859–2862.

130. Haggag Y.A., Donia A.A., Osman M.A., El-Gizawy S.A. (2018). Peptides as drug candidates: Limitations and recent development perspectives, *Biomed. J. Sci. Tech. Res.*, **8**, pp. 6659–6663.

131. Lee A.C., Harris J.L., Khanna K.K., Hong J.H. (2019). A comprehensive review on current advances in peptide drug development and design, *Int. J. Mol. Sci.*, **20**, pp. 2383–2404.

132. Henninot A., Collins J.C., Nuss J.M. (2018). The current state of peptide drug discovery: Back to the future?, *J. Med. Chem.*, **61**, pp. 1382–1414.

133. Qian Z., Liu T., Liu Y.Y., Briesewitz R., Barrios A.M., Jhiang S.M. (2013). Efficient delivery of cyclic peptides into mammalian cells with short sequence motifs, *ACS Chem. Biol.*, **8**, pp. 423–431.

134. Taylor R.E., Zahid M. (2020). Cell penetrating peptides, novel vectors for gene therapy, *Pharmaceutics*, **12**, pp. 225–246.

135. Ellert-Miklaszewska A., Poleszak K., Kaminska B. (2017). Short peptides interfering with signaling pathways as new therapeutic tools for cancer treatments, *Future Med. Chem.*, **9**, pp. 199–221.

136. Lenci E., Trabocchi A. (2020). Peptidomimetic toolbox for drug discovery, *Chem. Soc. Rev.*, **49**, pp. 3262–3277.

137. Zhang R., Leeper C.N., Wang X., White T.A., Ulery B.D. (2018). Immunomodulatory vasoactive intestinal peptide amphiphile micelles, *Biomater. Sci.*, **6**, pp. 1717–1722.

138. Kalafatovic D., Giralt E. (2017). Cell-penetrating peptides: Design strategies beyond primary structure and amphipathicity, *Molecules*, **22**, pp. 1929–1966.

139. Silva T.A., Braga M.C., Santana G.O.S., Araujob F.S., Poguea R., Diasa S.C., Francoa O.L., Carvalho J.L. (2018). Breaking the frontiers of cosmetology with antimicrobial peptides, *Biotechnol. Adv.*, **36**, pp. 2019–2031.

Chapter 10

Investigations of Complex Functional Bionanoformulations by Small Angle Neutron Scattering

Aristeidis Papagiannopoulos

Theoretical and Physical Chemistry Institute, National Hellenic Research Foundation, 48 Vassileos Constantinou Avenue, Athens, 11635, Greece

apapagiannopoulos@eie.gr

Small angle scattering (SAS) techniques are established non-invasive methods in the fields of soft matter, biomaterial, and food science. They provide information on the spatial organization at length scales of 1–1000 nm, which are relevant to the function and interaction of biomacromolecules and bioactive substances, averaging over macroscopic sample volumes. Small angle neutron scattering (SANS), in particular, has the advantages of solvent contrast variation and selective deuteration, which allows the extraction of the conformation of individual components in mixed systems. This chapter will present the necessary theoretical background of SANS, provide the relevant experimental details, and describe data analysis procedures so that it is self-contained and sufficient as a guide for new investigations. The possibilities of SANS on nanoformulations related to nanocarriers of substances, such as drugs and proteins, which are based on natural and

Functional Materials in Biomedical Applications
Edited by Costas Demetzos, Natassa Pippa, and Nikolaos Naziris

ISBN 978-981-4968-65-2 (Hardcover), 978-1-003-41146-8 (eBook)
www.jennystanford.com

synthetic polymers, lipids, and proteins, will be illustrated by case studies from the recent literature.

10.1 Introduction

SANS is a powerful technique for the investigation of biological and synthetic soft matter that has been used to probe structure non-invasively in proteins [1], biological matter [2], and polymer science [3]. SANS is able to study the complexity of morphology at length scales between 1 nm and 1 μm and in this way quantify the multi-scale and hierarchical organization in soft materials. At small length scales, it may probe spatial correlations that are relevant to molecular and macromolecular arrangements and interactions (e.g., protein-protein, polymer-polymer, polymer-protein, etc.). At large length scales, SANS probes the overall size and shape of nanoparticles and nano-assemblies. Therefore, investigations of systems that are responsive to external stimuli [4–6], biomaterials [7], food matrices and hydrocolloids [8, 9], and plant materials [10] are possible.

SANS experiments provide significant information with nm-resolution on spatial morphology in a quantitative manner, as the scattered intensities are determined by the spatial concentration distribution in a sample [11, 12]. Probing broad length scales that are averaged over macroscopic sample volumes is often connected to multi-level hierarchical and complex organizations. Therefore, the information that is provided by a SANS experiment is rich in terms of extracted parameters and experimental conditions that can be realized. However, data analysis and interpretation are laborious and complex tasks that demand training and experience. In most cases within current research interest, multi-component systems able to form multi-level structures are investigated. In addition, a successful SANS experiment depends on cautious planning concerning sample preparation and conditions, careful choice of composition, consideration of neutron scattering contrasts, and preliminary characterization.

In this chapter, the fundamental theoretical concepts of SANS and the basic SANS instrument's characteristics will be described.

The preliminary work and arrangements for a successful SANS experiment will be discussed. A detailed account of the scattering functions that are used in SANS, e.g., for dilute and semidilute polymer solutions, self-assembled nanoparticles of well-defined shape, and fractal aggregates. Representative works from recent literature will be used as case studies to illustrate the resolving power of SANS in investigating self-assembled polymeric nanostructures, nanoformulations based on proteins, liposomes with complex membranes, and nanostructured hydrogels. This chapter will be a valuable guide for scientists that are interested to apply SANS to soft materials of their interest.

10.2 Theoretical Background of SANS

The geometry of a SANS experiment is illustrated in Fig. 10.1. Thermal neutrons that are directed toward a sample within a collimated neutron beam interact with the atomic nuclei of the sample's material with a scattering power that is described by the scattering length [13] of each nucleus b_k. The total scattering amplitude from the ensemble of the nuclei [12] in the beam path is provided in Eq. (10.1) and it is based on the scattering amplitude of a single nucleus $A_k = b_k e^{i\vec{q}\vec{r}_k}$. This scattering amplitude [14] depends on the position of the nucleus $\vec{r}_k$ and the neutron momentum transfer, which is provided by the scattering wave vector $\vec{q} = \vec{k}_s - \vec{k}_i$. The vectors $\vec{k}_i$ and $\vec{k}_s$ are the incident and scattered wave vectors (Fig. 10.1), which in elastic scattering have equal magnitudes. In principle, scattered intensity is measured on a 2D detector for many values of scattering wave vector, i.e., values of scattering angle θ and azimuthal angle φ, and possibly for different neutron wavelengths λ. The magnitude of the scattered wave vector is $q = |\vec{q}| = \frac{4\pi}{\lambda}\sin\frac{\theta}{2}$.

$$I(\vec{q}) = |\Sigma_k b_k e^{i\vec{q}\vec{r}_k}|^2. \tag{10.1}$$

Scattered intensity depends on the direction of the scattered wavelength, i.e., $I = I(\vec{q})$, which is related to the angles θ and φ on the 2D detector, i.e., $I = I(\theta, \varphi)$. In many cases, scattered intensity is isotropic, for example, as in dilute solutions of particles that undergo random translational and rotational diffusion. In the scattering experiment, a vast number of particles are irradiated that have random orientations and are also able to sample many different orientations during the measurement. The isotropic scattering pattern on the 2D detector is obtained by an azimuthal average $I(q)=\frac{1}{2\pi}\int_0^{2\pi} d\varphi I(q,\varphi)$. Throughout this chapter, isotropic scattering will be discussed.

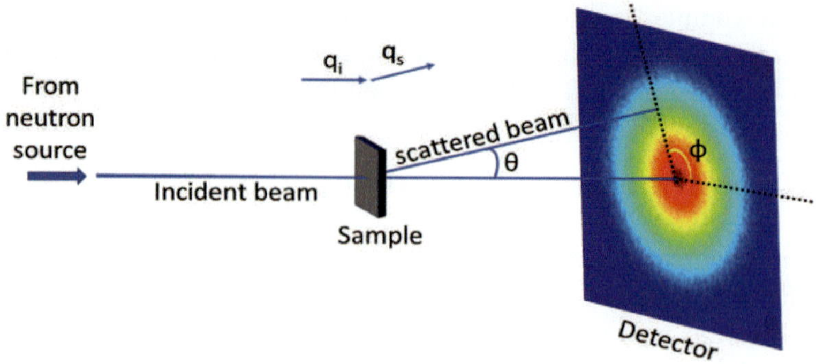

Figure 10.1 Schematic illustration of a SANS experiment.

Optimization of SAS data is very often applied by using theoretical scattering functions for $I(q)$ under predefined models, such as specific particle shapes, certain macromolecular conformations, and specific interaction potentials. In an actual SANS experiment, each scattering wave vector value q is accompanied by a finite uncertainty Δq. The function that describes the uncertainty for the set of experimental q values is called the instrumental resolution function $\Delta q(q)$ and one has to take it into account so that the theoretical and experimental data can be compared with each other. To this end, the theoretically calculated model data $I^{\text{th}}(q)$ is convoluted by the instrumental function as in Eq. (10.2), where a Gaussian distribution of q around its nominal value is assumed. The convoluted (smeared) scattered intensity $I^{\text{conv}}(q)$ is the one to be compared with the experimental data $I^{\text{exp}}(q)$.

$$I^{\text{conv}}(q)=\frac{1}{\sqrt{2\pi}''\,q(q)}\cdot\int_{-\infty}^{+\infty} dQ\cdot\exp\left(-\left(\frac{Q-q}{\sqrt{2}\Delta q(q)}\right)^2\right)\cdot I^{\text{th}}(Q). \quad (10.2)$$

The uncertainty in q originates from the geometrical characteristics of the instrument's set-up and the distribution of wavelengths in the incident neutron beam [15, 16]. Smearing of $I(q)$ results in the weakening and smoothing of characteristic features (fringes and sharp maxima) of the predicted SANS profiles.

The cross-section of the incoming neutron beam defines the flux of neutrons that hit the sample. Therefore, the finite size of the beam cross-section is defined by apertures, which allow a distribution of directions around the central one to be scattered by the sample and reach the detector. Therefore, incident neutrons travel slightly off the vertical direction to the detector plane. This effect is described by a q-independent error the so-called geometrical error Δq_{geo}. There is an additional cause of uncertainty in q which is related to the wavelength spread of the incident beam $\Delta\lambda$. This contribution is q-dependent as $\Delta q_{\lambda} = q\frac{\Delta\lambda}{\lambda}$. The instrument resolution function is written as $\Delta q(q) = \sqrt{\Delta q_{\text{geo}}^2 + \Delta q_{\lambda}^2}$. More details on the sources of uncertainties and the calculation of the instrument resolution function can be found elsewhere [15, 16].

10.3 Experiment Preparation and Data Optimization

A SANS experiment is performed in large-scale facilities through a proposal evaluation procedure. Careful planning is needed for a successful experiment, regarding sample stability and adequate SANS intensity. A minimum amount of hydrogen in the sample is desirable to suppress incoherent scattering. In aqueous solutions, D_2O is a conventional safe choice of solvent. Preliminary results on the planned system are crucial. For solution studies, light scattering measurements provide valuable information on sample stability and size distribution of particles. In addition, an estimation of the SANS intensity can be made based on light scattering data. Imaging by microscopy methods, such as transmission electron microscopy (TEM), cryo-TEM, and atomic force microscopy (AFM), can be used to measure the size, shape, and in many cases, the internal morphology of nano and microparticles. Although the conditions of measurement may not be exactly the ones of SANS due to the interaction with a solid surface (except in cryo-TEM), and the ensemble of particles measured is very small in comparison to SANS, these methods assist in greatly narrowing down the possible models to fit the SANS data.

$$\chi^2(\vec{P}) = \sum_{i=1}^{N} \left(\frac{I^{\text{model}}(q_i;\vec{P}) - I^{\text{exp}}(q_i)}{\delta I^{\text{exp}}(q_i)} \right)^2 . \tag{10.3}$$

In SANS data optimization, structural models are pre-assumed and are compared to the experimental data. A model is defined by a set of parameters $\{P_1, P_2, ..., P_M\}$ that can be grouped within a vector $\vec{P}$. Deviations between the theoretical from the experimental data are expressed by $\chi^2(\vec{P})$ (Eq. (10.3)). The target of the optimization is to minimize χ^2 and this way obtain the value for $\vec{P}$ that best describes the N experimental data $I^{\text{exp}}(q_i)$ (Eq. (10.3)). The differences between the model and experimental values are weighted by the uncertainty in measured intensity $\delta I^{\text{exp}}(q_i)$.

Popular non-linear methods for minimization are the Simplex and Levenberg-Marquardt algorithms [17]. A versatile methodology is the Monte Carlo simulated annealing minimization algorithm [18].

10.4 Scattering Functions of Nanoparticles, Macromolecules, and Complex Hierarchical Systems

10.4.1 Neutron Scattering Length Density and Form Factor

In SANS, the scattered intensity is conveniently presented in scattered intensity per unit sample volume. For an ensemble of non-interacting identical particles diffusing freely in a solution, $I(q)$ is provided by Eq. (10.4). N_p is the number density of particles and the integration is over the particle's volume. $\Delta p(\vec{r})$ is the neutron scattering length density (NSLD) contrast, which in a solution is written as the difference between the NSLD of the particle ρ_p and the NSLD of the solvent ρ_S, i.e., $\Delta\rho(\vec{r}) = \Delta\rho_P(\vec{r})$. Equation (10.5) is equivalent to Eq. (10.4), while it also illustrates the form factor $P(\vec{q})$. The form factor is normalized to unity sothat $P(q \rightarrow 0) = 1$ contains the q-dependence of the scattering from the particles and, therefore, contains the information on the size and shape of the particles. The forward scattering $I(q \rightarrow 0) = N_p V_p^2 \Delta\rho_p^2$ contains the volume V_P and the volume-averaged contrast $\Delta\rho_P$ of the particle.

$$I(q) = N_p \,|\int d\tau \Delta\rho(\vec{r}) e^{i\vec{q}\vec{r}}\,|^2, \tag{10.4}$$

$$I(q) = N_p V_p^2 \Delta\rho_p^2 P(q). \tag{10.5}$$

In neutron scattering techniques, the NSLD difference between isotopic nuclei such as the hydrogen/deuterium pair is exploited to highlight specific parts in a sample [19]. Commonly, a normal hydrogenated polymer is dissolved in a deuterated solvent (D_2O) so that adequate contrast is achieved. In a polymer/protein solution, a mixture of H_2O and D_2O (contrast variation) can be used so that the mixed solvent's NSLD to matches (contrast matching) the NSLD of one of the components, e.g., the protein. This way the conformation of the polymer in the presence of the protein will be measured without the interference of the scattering from the protein.

10.4.2 Scattering in Limits of Low and High *q*

The form factor of a scattering particle is defined by its shape and size as discussed previously. An extended list of form factors for particles of certain shapes and macromolecules in several conformations can be found in Pedersen's articles [20]. $P(q)$ has two limiting behaviors as a function of q. At very low q, Guinier approximation (Eq. (10.6)) holds for all cases independently of the particle's shape. The regime of very low q is defined by the radius of gyration of the particle as $qR_g < 1$. In this regime, large length scales (in comparison to the particle size) are probed and the overall size (radius of gyration R_g) and the forward scattering $I(q \rightarrow 0) = N_p V_p^2 \Delta\rho_p^2$ of the particles are measured.

$$P(q) = e^{-1/3(qR_g)^2}. \tag{10.6}$$

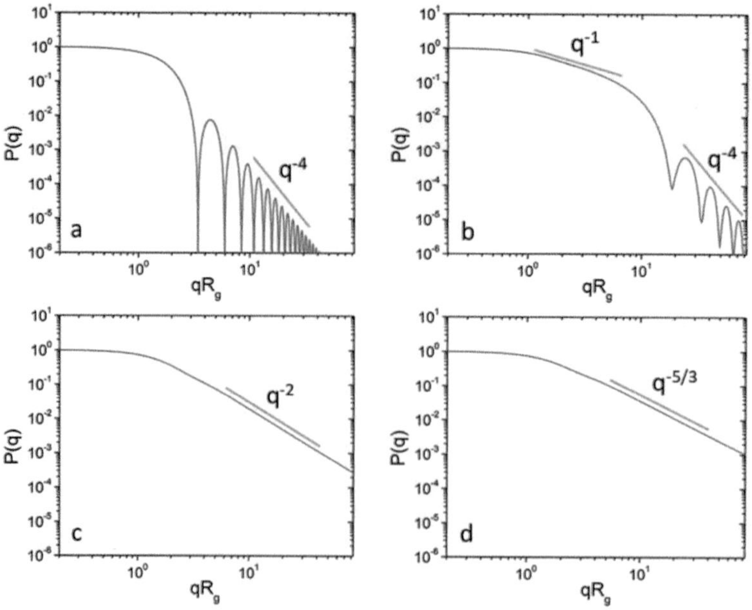

Figure 10.2 Form factors from (a) spheres, (b) cylinders, (c) gaussian coils, and (d) self-avoiding coils.

At $qR_g > 1$, the internal and local structures of the particle are measured. This is the small length-scales regime and has a different SANS signature for different scattering objects. For solid objects, such as spheres and cylinders, $P(q)$ contains oscillations at high q whose "period" in the q-space depends on their radius R (Fig. 10.2). The envelope of the characteristic maxima drops as $P(q) \propto q^{-4}$, which is the Porod's law that characterizes sharp interfaces. In the case of cylinders, there exists an intermediate regime $R_g^{-1} < q < R^{-1}$, where the behavior of rigid rods $P(q) \propto q^{-1}$ is met. For soft objects such as macromolecular chains in a solution, the power law $I(q) \sim q^{-d}$ at $qR_g > 1$ provides the characteristic fractal dimension of the object D_f. The fractal dimension is the inverse of the characteristic exponent $v(D_f = 1/v)$ that connects the number of monomeric units N and size R in polymer chains and generally in mass fractals as $R \sim N^v$. The fractal dimension D_f is readily extracted by SANS experiments and is a tool to identify the nature of the scattering particles (Table 10.1).

10.4.3 SANS from Well-Defined Objects

The scattering amplitude of objects of radius R that are spherically symmetric $(\Delta\rho(\vec{r}) = \Delta\rho(r))$ is generally expressed as in Eq. (10.7). Based on Eq. (10.1), the scattering amplitude is connected to the scattered intensity via $I(q) = |A(q)|^2$.

$$A_{\text{sph,sym}}(q) = \int_0^R 4\pi r^2 \frac{\sin qr}{qr} \Delta\rho(r) dr. \quad (10.7)$$

Equation (10.7) can readily lead to the scattering amplitude of a spherical shell of homogeneous NSLD contrast $\Delta\rho_{\text{sh}}$, internal radius R_{in}, and external radius R_{out} (Eq. (10.8)).

$$A_{\text{shell}}(q) = \frac{4\pi\Delta\rho_{\text{sh}}}{q^3} \cdot ((\sin qR_{\text{out}} - qR_{\text{out}} \cos qR_{\text{out}}) - (\sin qR_{\text{in}} - qR_{\text{in}} \cos qR_{\text{in}})). \quad (10.8)$$

Setting $R_{\text{in}} = 0$ in Eq. (10.8), the scattering amplitude of a sphere of radius R and NSLD contrast $\Delta\rho_{\text{sph}}$ is obtained (Eq. (10.9)).

$$A_{\text{sphere}}(q) = \frac{4\pi\Delta\rho_{\text{sph}}}{q^3} \cdot (\sin qR - qR\cos qR). \quad (10.9)$$

Equation (10.8) can be generalized for the superposition of concentric shells to model multi-shell objects as multi-lamellar vesicles by summing up the scattering amplitudes of N shells, i.e., $A_{\text{multi-shell}}(q) = \sum_{i=1}^{N} \frac{4\pi\Delta\rho_{\text{shi}}}{q^3} \cdot ((\sin qR_{\text{out},i} - qR_{\text{out},i} \cos qR_{\text{out},i}) - (\sin qR_{\text{in},i} - qR_{\text{in},i} \cos qR_{\text{in},i})$.

For spherically symmetric objects that have a non-uniform NSLD, Eq. (10.7) is applied, in general using numerical integration. Core-shell particles with a homogeneous core and a shell where the NSLD gradually passes from the NSLD of the core to the NSLD of the solvent are a common example.

The scattering amplitude from anisotropic particles depends on their relative orientation in comparison to $\vec{q}$. In the case of objects with cylindrical symmetry, the profile of the NSLD contrast leads to the scattering amplitude as in Eq. (10.10). J_i is the Bessel function of order i, R the cylinder's radius, L the cylinder's length, and a the angle between $\vec{q}$ and the cylinder's axis of symmetry. For isotropic scattering, $I(q)$ is calculated by averaging over all orientations (Eq. (10.11)).

$$A_{\text{cyl,sym}}(q,a) = \frac{J_1\left(\frac{qL}{2}\cos a\right)}{\frac{qL}{2}\cos a} \cdot \int_0^R 2\pi r J_0(qR\sin a)\Delta\rho(r)dr. \quad (10.10)$$

$$I_{\text{cyl,sym}}(q) = \int_0^{\pi/2} A^2_{\text{cyl,sym}}(q,a)\sin a\,da. \quad (10.11)$$

Similarly, the scattering from ellipsoids of revolution is calculated by the scattering amplitude of Eq. (10.12) and the average of Eq. (10.13).

$$A_{\text{ell,sym}}(q) = \int_0^{R(a)} 4\pi r^2 \frac{\sin qr}{qr}\Delta\rho(r)dr. \quad (10.12)$$

The ellipsoid is represented by a semi-minor axis R_{minor} and an eccentricity a, whereas $R(a) = R_{\text{minor}}(\sin^2 a + \varepsilon^2\cos^2 a)$.

$$I_{\text{ell,sym}}(q) = \int_0^{\pi/2} A^2_{\text{ell,sym}}(q,a)\sin a\,da \quad (10.13)$$

The polydispersity of scattering particles in size or other parameters affects the SANS profiles by smearing their characteristics and therefore have to be taken into account in the calculation of the form factors (Eq. (10.14)). To this end, a distribution function is used. For example, polydispersity in one of the mentioned radii would be introduced in a distribution function of the form $f(R, \Delta R)$, which is very often a Schulz or a Gaussian function [21].

$$I^{\mathrm{poly}}(q;R) = \int_0^{+\infty} dR' \cdot f(R', \Delta R) \cdot I^{\mathrm{th}}(q;R') \qquad (10.14)$$

10.4.4 Scattering Functions of Fractal and Hierarchical Systems

Soft matter nanostructures may arrange differently at different length scales giving rise to hierarchical structures. Associations with highly fluctuating interiors give rise to SANS patterns with smooth shapes without characteristic oscillations (Fig. 10.2). In addition, self-similarity is observed in the form of characteristic power laws. The scale dependence of the spatial organization is expressed in terms of hierarchy. A large structure may contain sub-structures, which contain sub-units, etc.

Table 10.1 Fractal dimensions for several objects with self-similarity [22,23]

Self-similar structure	Fractal dimension D_f
Rigid rod	1
Self-avoiding coil	5/3
Gaussian coil	2
Mass fractal	2–3
Surface fractal	3–4
Sharp interface	4

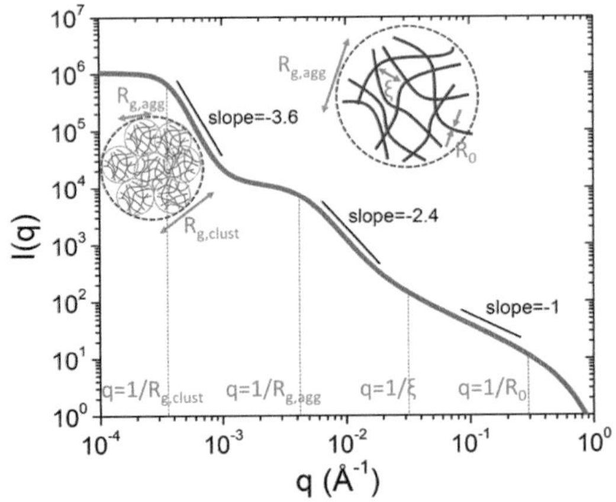

Figure 10.3 SANS from hypothetical hierarchical structure from a solution of a semi-flexible associative polymer.

An illustrative SANS profile is presented in Fig. 10.3, where it is assumed that a semi-flexible polymer with self-assembly properties in solution is investigated. There are three distinctive power law regimes, which are denoted by their corresponding slopes in the log-log plot. These regimes are described by $I \sim q^{D_f}$ where the slope *Df* is the characteristic fractal exponent. A list of the characteristic fractal dimensions for different fractal objects is provided in Table 10.1. The power law regimes are separated by Guinier (quasi-plateau) regimes from each other. The q-value at the transition from a plateau to a power law behavior is defined by the inverse radius of gyration or characteristic length of the relevant scattering object [24].

Looking at the data in Fig. 10.3, one would "interpret" the results as originating from a hierarchical structure. At $q < 10^{-3}$ Å^{-1}, scattering from large objects dominates the signal. These objects could be termed clusters. At $q = 3.5 \cdot 10^{-4}$ Å^{-1}, the Guinier regime gives space to the power law regime. The size of the clusters can be calculated at $R_{g,\mathrm{clust}} \approx 300$ nm. The SANS intensity scales as $I \sim q^{3.6}$ at $3.5 \cdot 10^{-4}$ Å$^{-1} < q < 10^{-3}$ Å^{-1}, which is related to fractally rough interfaces. Increasing q another Guinier regime appears defined by a structural level that can be attributed to aggregates that are contained in the clusters. They would have a radius of gyration $R_{g,\mathrm{agg}} \approx 25$ nm and their internal structure would be related to dense mass fractals as $D_f = 2.4$ (Table 10.1). In a similar way, the aggregates would appear to consist of aggregated polymeric chains. This chain network shows a characteristic length-scale at $q = 3 \cdot 10^{-2}$ Å^{-1}, which is normally termed the correlation length ξ and is the mean distance between chain segments within the aggregates. This is estimated at $\xi \approx 3$ nm from the q-value at the intersection of the mass fractal and the rigid rod regime. Above this q, length scales smaller than the correlation length are probed. The scattering from the conformation of unperturbed polymer chains is observed and therefore, $D_f = 1$, which is the fractal dimension of linear objects. At even smaller length scales $q > 5 \cdot 10^{-1}$ Å^{-1}, the scattering of the building blocks (e.g., monomer) of the polymer chains is observed with characteristic size $R_0 \approx 0.3$ nm. It has to be kept in mind that estimations of characteristic sizes and lengths are very approximate, however, very useful for order-of-magnitude estimations.

$$I_{\text{frac}}(q) = \int 4\pi r^2 \cdot \frac{\sin(qr)}{qr} \cdot g(r) \, . \, dr. \tag{10.15}$$

The fractal internal organization of a particle defines the average relative positions of its components giving rise to a self-similar structure [22, 25]. Equation (10.15) shows the utilization of the density autocorrelation function $g(r)$ in the calculation of a fractal's scattered intensity [26, 27]. A general formula $g(r) = r^{d-D_f} \cdot h(r/L_c)$ may be used, where d is the spatial dimension and the boundary of the fractal object is defined by the characteristic length L_c by the cut-off function $h(r/L_c)$. Depending on the choice of the cut-off function, different expressions are derived. However, they all share the same asymptotic behaviors at low and high q, which are the Guinier and the power law regime, respectively.

The unified Beaucage model captures the asymptotic trends as mentioned above and has been used in many cases as a superposition of contributions from separate hierarchical levels to model complex systems (Eq. (10.16)). A single Beaucage term consists of a Guinier term $G_i \cdot \exp\left(-\frac{1}{3} q^2 R_{g,i}^2\right)$ and a power law term $B_i \cdot q^{-D_i}$. The Guinier term dominates at $q \cdot R_{g,i} < 1$, whereas the power law is dominant at $q \cdot R_{g,i} > 1$ (it is canceled at $q \cdot R_{g,i} << 1$ by the error function). Equation (10.14) captures the radius of gyration $R_{g,i}$ of an object and its characteristic fractal exponent D_i. The pre-factor B_i is used to bridge the two asymptotic terms smoothly [28], i.e., $B_i = \frac{G_i}{R_{g,i}^{D_i}} \cdot \left(\frac{6 \cdot D_i^2}{(2+D_i) \cdot (2+2D_i)}\right)^{\frac{D_i}{2}} \cdot \Gamma\left(\frac{D_i}{2}\right)$. The N-level hierarchical model is employed under the constraint $R_{g,1} > R_{g,2} > \ldots > R_{g,N}$. The exponential cut-off terms [29] ensure that scattering from a structural level i does interfere with the scattering of the next-in-hierarchy level $i + 1$. Therefore, the cut-off length is set equal to the radius of gyration of the next level, i.e., $R_{\text{cut},i} = R_{g,i+1}$.

$$I(q)=\sum_{i=1}^{N} G_i\cdot \exp\left(-\frac{1}{3}q^2R_{g,i}^2\right)+B_i\cdot q^{-D_i}\cdot\left[\operatorname{erf}\left(\frac{q\cdot R_{g,i}}{\sqrt{6}}\right)\right]^{3D_i}\cdot \exp\left(-\frac{1}{3}q^2R_{\mathrm{cut},i}^2\right). \tag{10.16}$$

10.4.5 Scattering Functions of Polymer Chains in Dilute and Semidilute Solutions and Gels

Dilute and semidilute concentration regimes in polymer solutions are distinguished by the critical overlap concentration c^*. At very low concentrations, polymer chains are far apart from each other and their mutual interactions are negligible. Therefore, chains are considered isolated and their conformation and size are unperturbed. Increasing the concentration, polymer chains come closer to each other and begin to overlap when the average inter-chain distance R_{int} is of the order of the size of the unperturbed chain R_{chain} [30, 31]. In a dilute solution, R_{int} and R_{chain} are the main characteristic length scales; whereas, in semidilute solutions, the average distance between chain segments is shorter than R_{int}. This distance is the correlation length ξ and it depends on solution concentration but not on the degree of polymerization of the chains. The correlation length is the main length scale. At length scales larger than ξ, the chain has a random conformation (at least for flexible polymers); while at length scales smaller than ξ, it has the unperturbed conformation of the isolated case.

A SANS profile from a dilute polymer solution would be in general a unified Guinier/power law scattering function. This would describe the radius of gyration and the fractal dimension of the unperturbed conformation. The exact expression of a Gaussian's chain form factor (Eq. (10.17)) and the generalized chain form factor from excluded volume chains (Eq. (10.18)) are good examples [32].

$$P(q)=\frac{2}{q^4R_g^4}\left(\exp(-q^2R_g^2)+q^2R_g^2-1\right), \tag{10.17}$$

$$P(q)=\frac{1}{\nu U^{1/2\nu}}\gamma\left(\frac{1}{2\nu},U\right)-\frac{1}{\nu U^{\frac{1}{\nu}}}\gamma\left(\frac{1}{\nu},U\right). \quad (10.18)$$

Where $\gamma(x,U)=\int_0^U \exp(-t)t^{x-1}dt$ is the incomplete gamma function and $U=\frac{q^2R_g^2}{6}(2\nu+1)(2\nu+2)$ with ν the characteristic exponent of the polymer conformation. Regarding the fractal dimension, it holds $\nu = 1/D_f$.

In a semidilute solution, SANS contains information on the intra- and inter-chain correlations [33]. At $q < \xi^{-1}$, the density autocorrelation function behaves as $g(r) - 1/r$ while at $q > \xi^{-1}$ unperturbed chain correlations dominate and $g(r) \sim r^{-d+1/\nu}$ (Eq. (10.19)).

$$I(q)\sim\begin{cases}\frac{1}{1+q^2\xi^2} \text{ for } q<1/\xi \\ q^{-1/\nu} \text{ for } q>1/\xi\end{cases}. \quad (10.19)$$

Polymer gels can be considered to be in the semidilute concentration regime. Crosslinks create static concentration inhomogeneities in contrast to uncrosslinked polymer solutions where concentration fluctuations relax in time by thermal diffusion [34]. The unique monomer concentration distribution that is to some extent fixed by the cross-linking reaction is accompanied by frozen concentration fluctuations. In an uncrosslinked solution, the time average concentration $\langle c\rangle_t$ is independent of the position and is equal to the nominal solution concentration c (Fig. 10.4). The crosslinked network $\langle c\rangle_t$ is not uniform in space and shows stationary speckle patterns around c. At length scales shorter than the correlation length density fluctuations are expected to be similar to the ones in the semidilute solution without crosslinks.

In crosslinked polymer networks, the scattering functions are described by a superposition of two terms (Eq. (10.20)). The Ornstein-Zernike function $I_{\mathrm{OL}}(q)$ function captures the thermal fluctuations of concentration while the Deby-Bueche function $I_{\mathrm{SL}}(q)$ describes the static inhomogeneities [35, 36]. Two length scales are involved and therefore a hierarchical structure is described. These are the correlation length ξ of the semidilute solution and the characteristic size of the inhomogeneities Ξ. As $\chi < \Xi$ the term $I_{\mathrm{OL}}(q)$ dominates at small length scales, while $I_{\mathrm{SL}}(q)$ dominates at large length scales.

$$I(q) = \frac{I_{\mathrm{OZ}}(0)}{1+q^2\xi^2} + \frac{I_{\mathrm{SL}}(0)}{\left(1+q^2\Xi^2\right)^2}, \tag{10.20}$$

$$I(q) = \frac{I_{\mathrm{OZ}}(0)}{1+q^2\xi^2} + \frac{I_{fr}(0)}{\left(1+\frac{D_f+1}{3}q^2\check{\mathrm{z}}^2\right)^{\frac{1}{2}D_f}}. \tag{10.21}$$

The structural complexity in gels may lead to observed fractal power laws with characteristic exponents $D_f \neq 4$ at $q > 1/\Xi$, which is the exponent that is predicted by the Deby-Bueche function. A generalized Zimm function can be applied (Eq. (10.21)) to model the data in such situations [37].

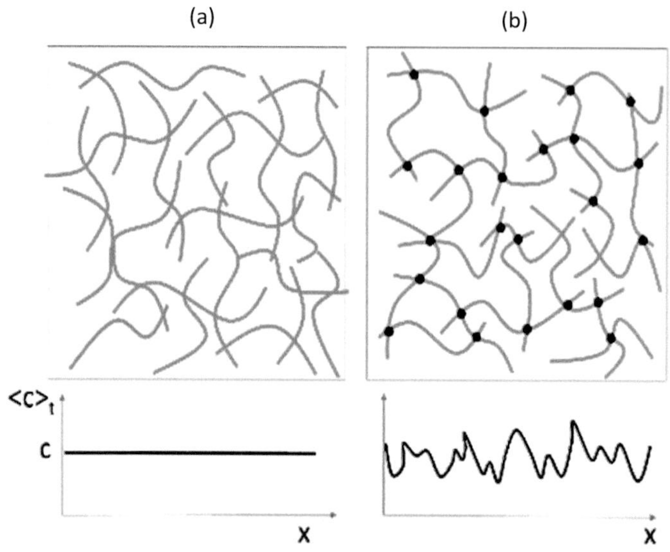

Figure 10.4 Illustration uncrosslinked (a) and crosslinked (b) semidilute polymer solution and time-averaged concentration of monomers.

10.5 Self-Assembled and Stimuli-Responsive Polymeric Nanoparticles

Stimuli-responsive amphiphilic block copolymers of poly(n-butyl acrylate)-b-poly(N-isopropylacrylamide)-carboxylic acid (PnBA-b-PNIPAM-COOH) have been studied by SANS in aqueous solutions [38]. PNIPAM is very commonly used as a thermoresponsive block in temperature-responsive block copolymers because of its lower critical solution behavior (LCST) and its critical transition temperature at 32 °C, which is between room temperature and human body temperature [39–41]. Data were fitted by a superposition of unified Guinier/power law models for low and high q, whereas the intermediate q regime was fitted by a core-shell micelle form factor. Core-shell micelles of core and micellar radius at about 6 nm and 20 nm, respectively, were formed. The response of this system to temperature depended on the length scale. The high-q intra-micellar scattering was temperature independent. Micelles grew in size as temperature increased while their inter-micellar aggregates were enhanced. Interestingly, strong correlations between them appeared at high temperatures, which were modeled by hard-sphere interactions.

A triblock copolymer containing PNIPAM and polystyrene (PS), i.e., the PS-b-PNIPAM-b-PS triblock copolymer was shown to form flower-like micelles in aqueous solutions that were hierarchically organized in aggregates and clusters [42]. The formation of clusters depended on the solution concentration. The aggregates were found to consist of a dense core and a shell of density profile that decreased with the distance from the center of the sphere. Upon temperature rise, the radius of their core slightly increased, whereas their overall radius decreased. At the same time, the cluster mass significantly increases. This was a characteristic case where the hydrophilic-to-hydrophobic transition of the PNIPAM block leads to a combined shrinkage and association effects.

The conjugation of an amphiphilic cyclic peptide [43] with a hydrophobic block of poly(2-(diisopropylamino)ethyl methacrylate) (pDPA) and a hydrophilic block of poly(2-hydroxypropyl methacrylamide) (pHPMA) led to a polymer that could assemble and disassemble reversibly upon changes in pH. An increase in size (from 6–7 nm to 12–14 nm) and mass (from 40–80 kg/mol to 300–600 kg/mol) was observed by dynamic and static light scattering upon pH increase from pH 5 to pH 7.4. SANS showed very clearly a transition from single chains to self-assembled nanoparticles upon pH increase (Fig. 10.5). The data were fitted with a core-corona spherical and cylindrical micelle model at pH 7.4, depending on whether the polymer was peptide-conjugated or not. This system showed a high potential for drug delivery to the acidic environment of cancerous tissues.

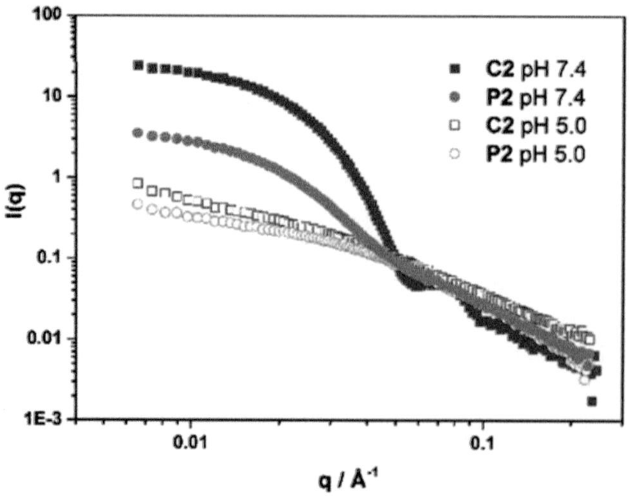

Figure 10.5 SANS from the cyclic peptide-conjugated PDPA-CP(CPAETC)2-PHPMA polymer at pH 5 (open symbols) and pH 7.4 (full symbols). Reprinted with permission from [43]. Copyright 2017 American Chemical Society.

10.6 Protein-Based Nanoformulations

Interactions of proteins with polyelectrolytes, mainly of electrostatic nature, lead to self-organized structures in aqueous media. These structures may be viewed beyond the scope of protein separation and protein delivery applications and used as multi-functional nanostructures in which the proteins are building blocks with unique properties.

Hybrid protein/polyelectrolyte nanoparticles were prepared by the associations between bovine serum albumin (BSA) and the partially hydrolyzed poly(2-phenyl-2-oxazoline) (HPPhOx) in aqueous solutions [44]. With the increasing salt content, well-defined nanoparticles (50–80 nm) are formed by the breakage of BSA-induced bridging between HPPhOx aggregates (~110 nm). This was observed by light scattering experiments where the overall size of the nanostructured aggregates was measured. SANS data was modeled by a superposition of three hierarchical terms, namely, aggregates, internal domains, and scattering from individual chains (Fig. 10.6).

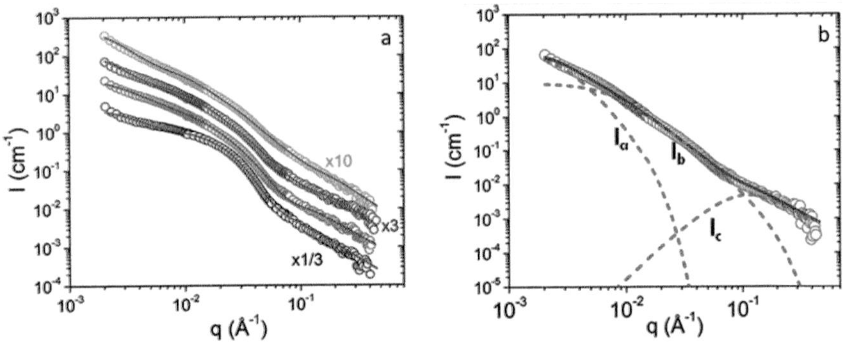

Figure 10.6 (a) SANS from HPPhOx in D_2O at (3.75 mgml^{-1}) combined with BSA at 0 (black), 0.469 mgml^{-1} (red), 0.938 mgml^{-1} (blue), and 1.875 mgml^{-1} (green) at 0.03 M NaCl. Continuous lines are best fits to the experimental data. (b) Fitting SANS profile from HPPhOx 3.75 mgml^{-1} in D_2O in the absence of salt. Separate contributions are shown with dashed lines. Reprinted with permission from [44]. Copyright 2018 American Chemical Society.

In this system, SANS probed mainly internal correlations of the hybrid aggregates. Diffuse open morphology was observed at low salt content, however, at high salt content, compact hydrophobic domains were observed. This was due to the interplay between hydrophobic and electrostatic interactions at the nanometer scale. The incorporation of BSA did not interfere strongly with the interior of the nanoparticles at low salt content. This was due to the interaction and bridging of the protein with the periphery of the aggregates. As salt content increases, the largest hierarchical level is weakened in favor of the intermediate hierarchical level, which shows that BSA gradually enters the nanoparticles. In addition, the characteristic size and fractal dimension increased as a function of salt content, which reveals the formation of denser compact domains of the order 3–6 nm.

Figure 10.7 illustrates the possible interactions within the hybrid BSA/HPPhOx associations. The hydrophobic monomers PhOx of the random copolymer may interact with each other to drive HPPhOx self-assembly while they can also interact with the hydrophobic amino acids on the BSA surface. The positively charged ethyleneimine (EI) units of HPPhOx may interact with the BSA's negatively charged amino acids. Bridging interactions of both hydrophobic and electrostatic nature act between BSA and HPPhOx aggregates.

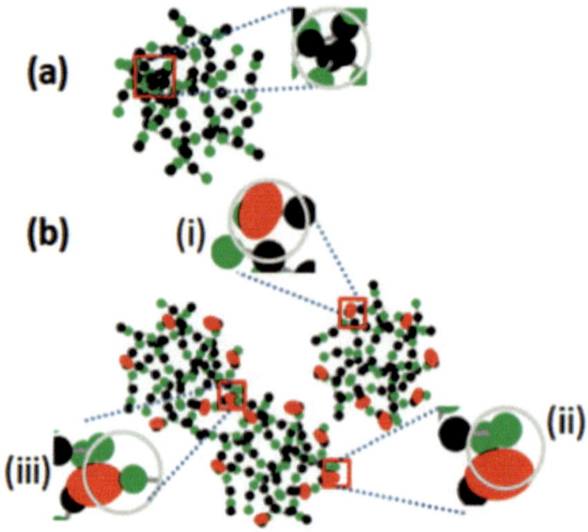

Figure 10.7 Interactions in HPPhOx (a) and BSA/HPPhOx (b). (a) PhOx-PhOx hydrophobic interactions. (b) (i) BSA-PHOx hydrophobic interaction, (ii) BSA-EI electrostatic interaction, and (iii) BSA-HPPhOx aggregate bridging. Separate units are PhOx (black), EI (green), and BSA (red). Reprinted with permission from [44]. Copyright 2018 American Chemical Society.

In water solutions of another hydrophobic polyelectrolyte, the quaternized poly(chloromethyl styrene) (QIm-PCMS) SANS revealed that the internal structure of its aggregates shared many similarities with the morphology of semidilute polyelectrolyte solutions [45]. A characteristic peak was observed at the intermediate *q*-range, which provided the correlation length in the interior of the self-assembled aggregates. Two polymers

QIm-PCMS1 and QIm-PCMS2 were used with degrees of quaternization of 73% and 100%, respectively. No measurable difference in the internal morphology was observed between the two regarding their mesh size and overall SANS profile (Fig. 10.8). On the contrary, their hydrophobic content (which is higher for a lower degree of quaternization) played a critical role in the interactions with BSA. The enhancement of scattering at larger length scales (Fig. 10.8), which signifies BSA-polyelectrolyte associations was more pronounced in the case of QIm-PCMS1.

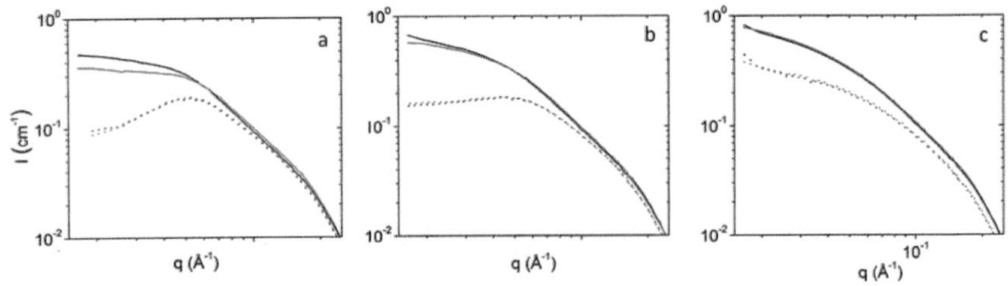

Figure 10.8 SANS from BSA (16 mgml^{-1})/QIm-PCMS (4 mgml^{-1}) complexes at 16:4 concentration ratios for PCMS1 (black) and PCMS2 (red) for 0 M NaCl (a) 0.01 M NaCl (b), and 0.15 M NaCl (c). SANS from the corresponding blank polymer solutions is shown with dotted lines. Reproduced from Ref. [45] with permission from the PCCP Owner Societies.

10.7 Liposomal Nanoassemblies with Multi-Component Membranes

In recent work, hybrid liposomes of the phospholipid 1,2-dipalmitoyl-sn-glycero-3-phosphocholine (DPPC) and the amphiphilic diblock copolymer poly (ethylene oxide)-block-poly(ε-caprolactone) (PEO-b-PCL) were found to consist of stable uni-lamellar vesicles [46]. That was in contrast to liposomes of pure DPPC or its mixtures with poly(2-methyl-2-oxazoline)-grad-poly(2-phenyl-2-oxazoline) (MPOx) where multi-lamellar vesicles were observed in coexistence with unilamellar vesicles [47]. The size distribution of the mixed liposomes, their bilayer characteristics, and the contribution from non-vesicular clusters and aggregates were resolved by SANS modeling. In more detail, the used model was a superposition of a Guinier term for the clusters, a Beaucage function for the aggregates, and a vesicular term, which consisted of a bilamellar membrane (three spherical concentric shells). In addition, SANS could quantify the delicate temperature response of the system.

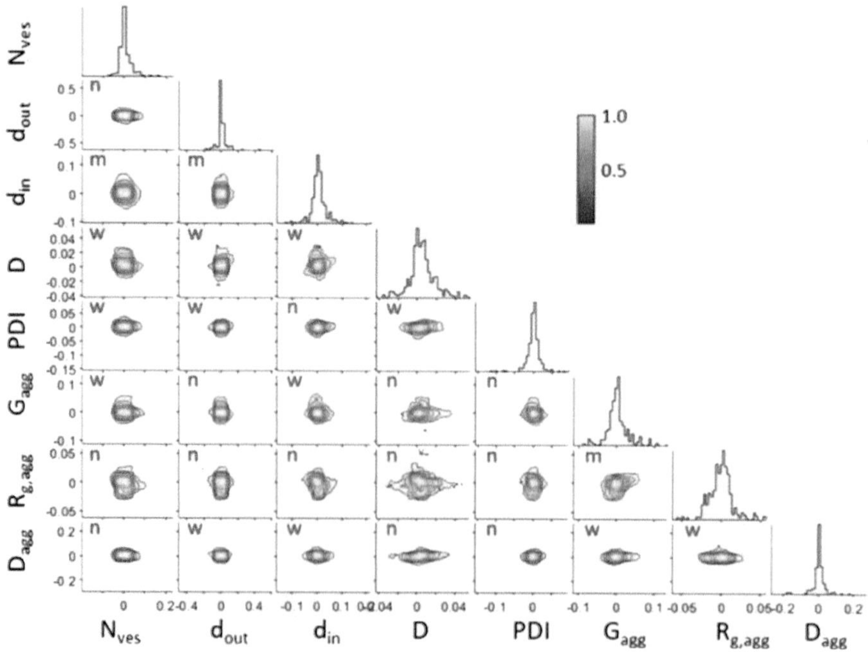

Figure 10.9 Fitted parameters' distributions (corner plots) for DPPC/PEO-b-PCL mixtures. Interdependencies of parameters are denoted as "n" (negligible), "w" (weak) and "m" (moderate). Reprinted from Ref. [46].

In order to make sure that the observed changes in size and their polydispersity were reliable for further interpretations, especially in the case of temperature response, uncertainty analysis of the extracted parameters was performed using the Bayesian inference under a Markov Chain Monte Carlo algorithm (MCMC) [48]. The corner plots of Fig. 10.9 show the probability distributions between all pairs of parameters used to model the SANS data. The degree of correlation could be characterized as negligible, weak, moderate, strong, and very strong, depending on the extracted mutual correlation coefficient. The uncertainties in parameter estimation were extracted from the distributions of individual parameters, which are presented in the diagonal of the plot (Fig. 10.9). Finally, solvent contrast variation was performed to support the uniqueness of the extracted NSLD profiles. SANS profiles from different volume ratios of D_2O/H_2O could be reproduced by only changing the solvent's NSLD while keeping all other parameters fixed. In addition, this reproducibility proved that there is no detectable sign of lateral inhomogeneities on the membranes [49].

Addition of hydrophobically modified chitosan to uni-lamellar vesicles of the mixed cationic surfactant cetyltrimethylammonium tosylate (CTAT) with the anionic surfactant sodium dodecyl benzene sulfonate (SDBS) was found to increase the lamellarity of the vesicles, i.e., resulting to the coexistence of uni-lamellar, bi-lamellar, and tri-lamellar vesicles. This effect was attributed to the ability of chitosan to stabilize two concentric bilayers by bridging. The model function for SANS data could extract the lamellarity distribution in the solution but also the membrane rigidity. As the rigidity increased by the chitosan addition, the vesicles' radius decreased, owing to the increased stability at higher curvature radii [50].

A vesicle-forming copolymer comprising a poly-(dimethylsiloxane) backbone main chain and two poly-(ethylene oxide) pendant blocks in the form of grafted (PDMS-g-$(PEO)_2$) or triblock copolymer (PEO-b-PDMS-b-PEO) was mixed with DPPC to investigate the lateral inhomogeneities on the polymersome membranes [51]. SANS contrast variation was employed and experiments were run in full contrast, polymer contrast (invisible phospholipid), and lipid contrast (invisible polymer). A form factor was introduced to fit the SANS data from the hybrid vesicles. This form factor took into account the non-uniform arrangement of lipids within the polymersome membrane. Lipids were assumed to create disk-like domains on the bilayer membranes. The new model was based on subtracting the scattering of thin disks that represent the missing polymer and adding the scattering amplitude of lipid-containing disks to the scattering amplitude of the polymersomes. With the aid of this form factor and the application of contrast variation, the number of lipid domains, their diameter, and the thickness could be estimated.

10.8 Multifunctional Hydrogels and Nanogels

Recently, we have applied a two-level hierarchical model to fit the SANS data from peroxide-crosslinked PEO-hydrogels [52]. These hydrogels were aimed at controllably releasing globular proteins by sterically hindering their diffusion. The correlation length (7–12 nm) was independently estimated from swelling experiments and it was compatible with the one of SANS. The elastic modulus estimated by swelling experiments was in agreement with rheology measurements. The diffusion coefficient of lysozyme and BSA was controlled, as their size is comparable to the correlation length. Similarly, the two-level hierarchical model was used to fit the data from injectable hydrogels that were physically and chemically crosslinked. These hydrogels were aimed for sustained protein release. The hydrophobic domains of the oligo (lactic acid) units changed the nanostructure of the networks as revealed by SANS and swelling experiments. They additionally increased the uptake of BSA and decreased its release rate [53].

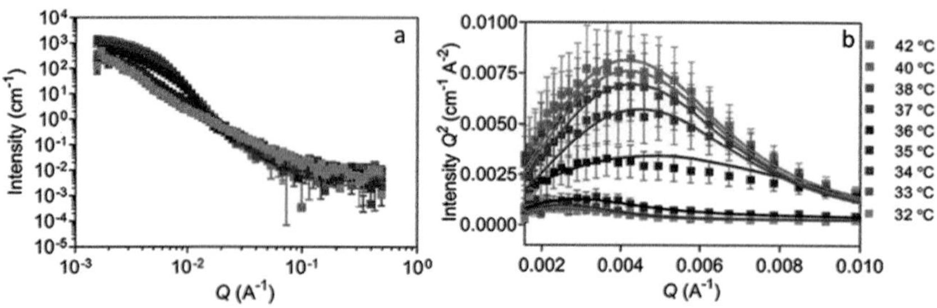

Figure 10.10 SANS intensities (a) and Kratky plots (b) for different temperatures in thermoresponsive crosslinked nanogels. From Ref. [54]. Published by The Royal Society of Chemistry.

Nanogels are nano-networks or in other words, gels with nanoscopic dimensions, and therefore, they can be used to deliver bioactive substances in relevant applications. A diblock copolymer of a hydrophilic and a temperature responsive block, i.e., poly(ethylene glycol)-b-poly(N-isopropylacrylamide-co-N-cyclopropylacrylamide) (PEG-b-(NIPAM-co-NCPAM)) with an intermediate functional group as a crosslinker that could be degraded by enzymes was synthesized [54]. Shrinking of the hydrogel at 37 °C was used to load a model protein drug and keep it trapped within the nanogels at body temperature. The drug could be released in the presence of metalloproteinase (MMP-7) that cleaved the peptide crosslinks. MMP's overexpression is responsible for several diseases, including cardiovascular conditions and cancer. The volume phase transition of the nanogels was confirmed by SANS. Kratky plots $q^2(q)$ vs q (Fig. 10.10) showed the transformation of an open structure to a globular structure upon temperature increase. In the $I(q)$ representation, this is equivalent to a transition from a power law behavior of an open fractal $I(q) \sim q^{-2}$ to a well-defined Guinier behavior.

SANS has been used to resolve the radial concentration distributions in ibuprofen-loaded nanoparticles with a poly-caprolactone (PCL) nanogel core and a PEG (114 ethylene glycol monomers, EG_{114}) shell [55]. The connection of PEG to the nanogel PCL could be direct in nGEL-$(EG_{114})_f$, via one hydrophobic block poly(valerolactone) in nGEL-$(VL_{23}$-$EG_{114})_f$, or via one more poly(4-tert-butylcarprolactone hydrophobic block in nGEL-VL_{11}-$tBuCL_{10}$-$EG_{114})_f$, where *f* is the number of daggling arms.

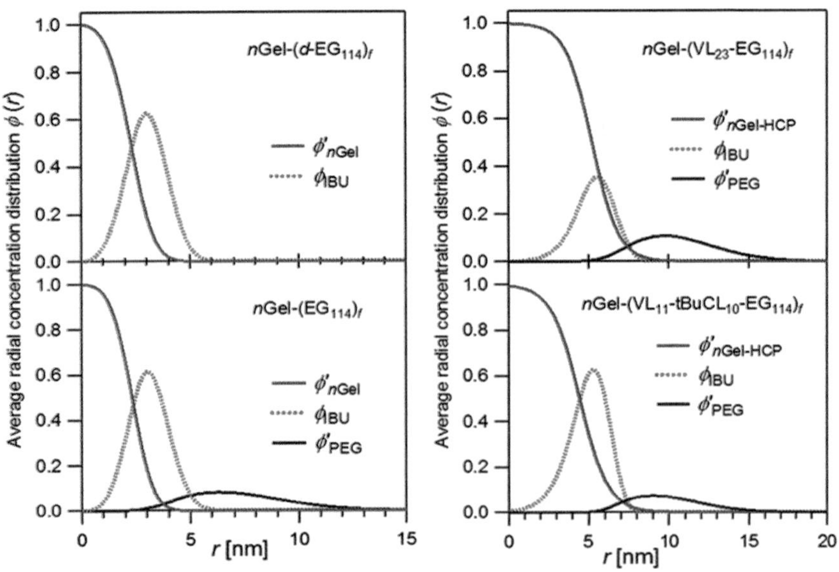

Figure 10.11 Hydrophobic core (black), PEG corona (blue), and ibuprofen (red) radial concentration distributions from nanogel core-PEG corona nanoparticles. Reprinted with permission from [55]. Copyright 2017 American Chemical Society.

The radial concentration profile (Fig. 10.11) was written as a hyperbolic tangent function for the core and a superposition of two cubic splines for the corona chains [56, 57]. The concentration profile of the drug was estimated by the differences of the core concentration profile from the polymeric concentration profile of the core (PCL and hydrophobic copolymer segments) under the restrictions that the PCL nanogel does not swell and the mass of the hydrophobic polymer segments in the core is conserved upon drug incorporation. It was this way supported that the drug adsorbed at the core-corona interface.

10.9 Conclusion and Future Perspective

SANS has been proven a powerful method for the investigation of soft materials and biomaterials. Non-invasivity and nm-scale sensitivity allow it to provide invaluable insights into complex structures of great and growing interest such as drug-loaded nanocarriers and protein nanoformulations. SANS data modeling is able to resolve hierarchical and multi-component structures, shed light on the length-scale dependence of their response to external stimuli, and readily detect self-assembly and fractal morphology transitions. This way SANS provides explanations of the functional properties of bionanomaterials and facilitates the design of new ones for more demanding applications. SANS will definitely accompany cutting-edge research and discoveries in new bionanoformulations for the next decades.

References

1. Mahieu, E. and Gabel, F. (2018). Biological small-angle neutron scattering: Recent results and development, *Acta Crystallogr.,* **D74**, pp. 715–26.
2. Chaudhuri, B. N. (2015). Emerging applications of small angle solution scattering in structural biology, *Protein Sci.,* **24**, pp. 267–76.
3. Hollamby, M. J. (2013). Practical applications of small-angle neutron scattering, *Phys. Chem. Chem. Phys.,* **15**, pp. 10566–79.
4. Karimi, M., Ghasemi, A., Sahandi Zangabad, P., Rahighi, R., Moosavi Basri, S. M., Mirshekari, H., Amiri, M., Shafaei Pishabad, Z., Aslani A.,

Bozorgomid, M., Ghosh D., Beyzavi, A., Vaseghi, A., Aref, A. R., Haghani, L., Bahrami, S., and Hamblin, M. R. (2016). Smart micro/nanoparticles in stimulus-responsive drug/gene delivery systems, *Chem. Soc. Rev.*, **45**, pp. 1457–501.

5. Tang, Q., Yu, B., Gao, L., Cong, H., Song, N., and Lu, C. (2018). Stimuli responsive nanoparticles for controlled anti-cancer drug release, *Curr. Med. Chem.*, **25**, pp. 1837–66.
6. Rao, N. V., Ko, H., Lee, J., and Park, J. H. (2018). Recent progress and advances in stimuli-responsive polymers for cancer therapy. *Front. Bioeng. Biotechnol.*, **6**, pp. 110.
7. Lombardo, D., Calandra, P., and Kiselev, M. A. (2020). Structural characterization of biomaterials by means of small angle X-rays and neutron scattering (SAXS and SANS) and light scattering experiments, *Molecules*, **25**, pp. 5624.
8. Darnay, L., Len, A., Koncz, Á., Friedrich, L., and Rosta, L. (2015). Small angle neutron scattering study of nanostructural changes in microbial transglutaminase-treated low-fat yogurt during fermentation, *Food Sci. Biotechnol.*, **24**, pp. 2125–8.
9. Tian, B., Wang, Z., de Campo, L., Gilbert E. P., Dalgliesh, R. M., Velichko, E., van der Goot, A. J., and Bouwman, W. G. (2020). Small angle neutron scattering quantifies the hierarchical structure in fibrous calcium caseinate, *Food Hydrocoll.*, **106**, pp. 105912.
10. Martínez-Sanz, M., Gidley, M. J., and Gilbert, E. P. (2015). Application of X-ray and neutron small angle scattering techniques to study the hierarchical structure of plant cell walls: A review, *Carbohydr. Polym.*, **125**, pp. 120–34.
11. Krueger, J. K. and Wignall, G. D. (2006) Small-angle neutron scattering from biological molecules, *Neutron Scattering in Biology: Techniques and Applications*, J. Fitter, T. Gutberlet, and J. Katsaras (eds.), Heidelberg: Springer Berlin Heidelberg, pp. 127–60.
12. Pynn, R. (2009). Neutron scattering—A non-destructive microscope for seeing inside matter, *Neutron Applications in Earth, Energy and Environmental Sciences*, Neutron Scattering Applications and Techniques, pp. 15–36.
13. Grillo, I. (2008). Small-angle neutron scattering and applications in soft condensed matter, *Soft-Matter Characterization*, Springer, USA, pp. 723–82.
14. Higgins, J. S. and Benoit, H. C. (1994). *Polymers and Neutron Scattering*, Clarendon Press, Oxford, UK.

15. Barker, J. G. and Pedersen, J. S. (1995). Instrumental smearing effects in radially symmetric small-angle neutron scattering by numerical and analytical methods, *J. Appl. Crystallogr.*, **28**, pp. 105–14.

16. Radulescu, A., Székely, N. K., Polachowski, S., Leyendecker, M., Amann, M., Buitenhuis, J., Drochner, M., Engels, R., Hanslik, R., Kemmerling, G., Lindner, P., Papagiannopoulos, A., Pipich, V., Willner, L., Frielinghaus, H., and Richter, D. (2015). Tuning the instrument resolution using chopper and time of flight at the small-angle neutron scattering diffractometer KWS-2, *J. Appl. Crystallogr.*, **48**, pp. 1849–59.

17. Press, W. H., Teukolsky, S. A., Vetterling, W. T., and Flannery, B. P. (2007). *Numerical Recipes*, 3rd edition, Cambridge University Press, UK.

18. Vanderbilt, D. and Louie, S. G. (1984). A Monte carlo simulated annealing approach to optimization over continuous variables, *J. Comput. Phys.*, **56**, pp. 259–71.

19. Heller, W. T. (2010). Small-angle neutron scattering and contrast variation: A powerful combination for studying biological structures, *Acta Crystallogr. Sect. D*, **66**, pp. 1213–7.

20. Pedersen, J. S. (1997). Analysis of small-angle scattering data from colloids and polymer solutions: modeling and least-squares fitting, *Adv. Colloid Interface Sci.*, **70**, pp. 171–210.

21. Borsali, R. and Pecora, R. (2008). *Soft Matter Characterization*, Springer, USA.

22. Beaucage, G. (1996). Small-angle scattering from polymeric mass fractals of arbitrary mass-fractal dimension, *J. Appl. Crystallogr.*, **29**, pp. 134–46.

23. Schmidt, P. W. (1991). Small-angle scattering studies of disordered, porous and fractal systems, *J. Appl. Crystallogr.*, **24**, pp. 414–35.

24. Roessle, M. and Svergun, D. I. (2013). Small angle X-ray scattering, *Encyclopedia of Biophysics*, G. C. K. Roberts (ed.), Springer Berlin Heidelberg, Germany, pp. 2382–9.

25. Sorensen, C. M. (2001). Light scattering by fractal aggregates: A review, *Aerosol Sci. Technol.*, **35**, pp. 648–87.

26. Glatter, O. (1977). A new method for the evaluation of small-angle scattering data, *J. Appl. Crystallogr.*, **10**, pp. 415–21.

27. Svergun, D. I. and Koch, M. H. J. (2003). Small-angle scattering studies of biological macromolecules in solution, *Rep. Prog. Phys.*, **66**, pp. 1735–82.

28. Hammouda, B. (2010). Analysis of the Beaucage model, *J. Appl. Crystallogr.,* **43**, pp. 1474–8.

29. Beaucage, G., Ulibarri, T. A., Black, E. P., and Schaefer, D. W. (1995). Multiple size scale structures in silica—siloxane composites studied by small-angle scattering, *Hybrid Organic-Inorganic Composites,* ACS Symposium Series, **585** (American Chemical Society), pp. 97–111.

30. Gennes and Pierre-Gilles de. (1979). *Scaling concepts in polymer physics,* Ithaca N.Y.: Cornell University Press.

31. Rubinstein, M. and Colby, R. H. (2003). *Polymer Physics,* Oxford University Press, UK.

32. Hammouda, B. and Kim, M.-H. (2017). The empirical core-chain model, *J. Mol. Liq.,* **247**, pp. 434–40.

33. Daoud, M., Cotton, J. P., Farnoux, B., Jannink, G., Sarma, G., Benoit, H., Duplessix, C., Picot, C., and de Gennes, P. G. (1975). Solutions of flexible polymers: Neutron experiments and interpretation, *Macromolecules,* **8**, pp. 804–18.

34. Panyukov, S. and Rabin, Y. (1996). Polymer gels: Frozen inhomogeneities and density fluctuations, *Macromolecules,* **29**, pp. 7960–75.

35. Horkay, F., McKenna, G. B., Deschamps, P., and Geissler, E. (2000). Neutron scattering properties of randomly cross-linked polyisoprene gels, *Macromolecules,* **33**, pp. 5215–20

36. Shibayama, M. (2011). Small-angle neutron scattering on polymer gels: Phase behavior, inhomogeneities and deformation mechanisms, *Polym. J.,* **43**, pp. 18–34.

37. Shibayama, M., Kurokawa, H., Nomura, S., Muthukumar, M., Stein, R. S., and Roy, S. (1992). Small-angle neutron scattering from poly(vinyl alcohol)-borate gels, *Polymer,* **33,** pp. 2883–90.

38. Papagiannopoulos, A., Meristoudi, A., Pispas, S., and Keiderling, U. (2016). Thermoresponsive behavior of micellar aggregates from end-functionalized PnBA-b-PNIPAM-COOH block copolymers and their complexes with lysozyme, *Soft Matter,* **12**, pp. 6547–56.

39. Hirokawa, Y. and Tanaka, T. (1984). Volume phase transition in a nonionic gel, *J. Chem. Phys.,* **81**, pp. 6379–80.

40. Kim, K. T., Meeuwissen, S. A., Nolte, R. J. M., and van Hest, J. C. M. (2010). Smart nanocontainers and nanoreactors, *Nanoscale,* **2**, pp. 844–58.

41. Ward, M. A. and Georgiou, T. K. (2011). Thermoresponsive polymers for biomedical applications, *Polymers,* **3**, pp. 1215–1242.

42. Papagiannopoulos, A., Zhao, J., Zhang, G., Pispas, S., and Radulescu, A. (2014). Thermoresponsive aggregation of PS–PNIPAM–PS triblock copolymer: A combined study of light scattering and small angle neutron scattering, *Eur. Polym. J.*, **56**, pp. 59–68.
43. Larnaudie, S. C., Brendel, J. C., Jolliffe, K. A., and Perrier, S. (2017). pH-responsive, amphiphilic core–shell supramolecular polymer brushes from cyclic peptide–polymer conjugates, *ACS Macro Lett.*, **6**, pp. 1347–51.
44. Papagiannopoulos, A., Vlassi, E., Pispas, S., and Houston, J. E. (2018). Association and internal morphology of self-assembled HPPhOx/BSA hybrid nanoparticles in aqueous solutions, *J. Phys. Chem. B*, **122**, pp. 7426–35.
45. Papagiannopoulos, A., Vlassi, E., Pispas, S., and Jafta, C. J. (2017). Tuning the solution organization of cationic polymers through interactions with bovine serum albumin, *Phys. Chem. Chem. Phys.*, **19**, pp. 18471–80.
46. Papagiannopoulos, A., Pippa, N., Demetzos, C., Pispas, S., and Radulescu, A. (2021). Formation of uni-lamellar vesicles in mixtures of DPPC with PEO-b-PCL amphiphilic diblock copolymers, *Polymers*, **13**, pp. 4.
47. Papagiannopoulos, A., Pippa, N., Demetzos, C., Pispas, S., and Radulescu, A. (2021). Lamellarity and size distributions in mixed DPPC/amphiphilic poly(2-oxazoline) gradient copolymer vesicles and their temperature response, *Chem. Phys. Lipids*, **234**, pp. 105008.
48. Winslow, S. W., Shcherbakov-Wu, W., Liu, Y., Tisdale, W. A., and Swan, J. W. (2019). Characterization of colloidal nanocrystal surface structure using small angle neutron scattering and efficient Bayesian parameter estimation, *J. Chem. Phys.*, **150**, pp. 244702.
49. Heberle, F. A., Anghel, V. N. P., and Katsaras, J. (2015). Scattering from phase-separated vesicles. I. An analytical form factor for multiple static domains, *J. Appl. Crystallogr.*, **48**, pp. 1391–404.
50. Lee, J.-H., Agarwal, V., Bose, A., Payne, G. F., and Raghavan, S. R. (2006). Transition from unilamellar to bilamellar vesicles induced by an amphiphilic biopolymer, *Phys. Rev. Lett.*, **96**, pp. 048102.
51. Dao, T. P. T., Brûlet, A., Fernandes, F., Er-Rafik, M., Ferji, K., Schweins, R., Chapel, J.-P., Fedorov, A., Schmutz, M., Prieto, M., Sandre, O., and Le Meins, J.-F. (2017). Mixing block copolymers with phospholipids at the nanoscale: From hybrid polymer/lipid wormlike micelles to vesicles presenting lipid nanodomains, *Langmuir*, **33**, pp. 1705–15.

52. Papagiannopoulos, A., Vlassi, E., Pispas, S., Tsitsilianis, C., and Radulescu, A. (2021). Polyethylene oxide hydrogels crosslinked by peroxide for the controlled release of proteins, *Macromol.*, **1**, pp. 37–48.

53. Smeets, N. M. B., Patenaude, M., Kinio, D., Yavitt, F. M., Bakaic, E., Yang, F.-C., Rheinstädter, M., and Hoare, T. (2014). Injectable hydrogels with in situ-forming hydrophobic domains: Oligo(d,l-lactide) modified poly(oligoethylene glycol methacrylate) hydrogels, *Polym. Chem.*, **5**, pp. 6811–23.

54. Massi, L., Najer, A., Chapman, R., Spicer, C. D., Nele, V., Che, J., Booth, M. A., Doutch, J. J., and Stevens, M. M. (2020). Tuneable peptide cross-linked nanogels for enzyme-triggered protein delivery, *J. Mater. Chem. B*, **8**, pp. 8894–907.

55. Wei, G., Prabhu, V. M., Piunova, V. A., Carr, A. C., Swope, W. C., and Miller, R. D. (2017). Spatial distribution of hydrophobic drugs in model nanogel-core star polymers, *Macromolecules*, **50**, pp. 9702–12.

56. Pedersen, J. S., Svaneborg, C., Almdal, K., Hamley, I. W., and Young, R. N. (2003). A small-angle neutron and X-ray contrast variation scattering study of the structure of block copolymer micelles: Corona shape and excluded volume interactions, *Macromolecules*, **36**, pp. 416–33.

57. Pedersen, J. S. and Gerstenberg, M. C. (2003). The structure of P85 Pluronic block copolymer micelles determined by small-angle neutron scattering, *Colloids Surf. Physicochem. Eng. Asp.*, **213**, pp. 175–87.

Index

For Product Safety Concerns and Information please contact our EU representative GPSR@taylorandfrancis.com Taylor & Francis Verlag GmbH, Kaufingerstraße 24, 80331 München, Germany